Garfield

FAT CAT 3-PACK

VOLUME 15

Garfield

FAT CAT 3-PACK

VOLUME 15

BY
JIM DAVIS

BALLANTINE BOOKS · NEW YORK

2011 Ballantine Books Trade Paperback Edition

Based on the Garfield® characters created by Jim Davis.

Published in the United States by Ballantine Books, an imprint of Random House, a division of Penguin Random House LLC, New York.

GARFIELD BLOTS OUT THE SUN and GARFIELD GOES BANANAS were each published separately by Ballantine Books, an imprint of Random House, a division of Penguin Random House LLC, in 2007. GARFIELD LARGE & IN CHARGE was published separately by Ballantine Books, an imprint of Random House, a division of Penguin Random House LLC, in 2008.

ISBN 978-0-345-52585-7

Printed in China

randomhousebooks.com

12

Garfield

BLOTS OUT THE SUN

BY JIM DAVIS

Ballantine Books • New York

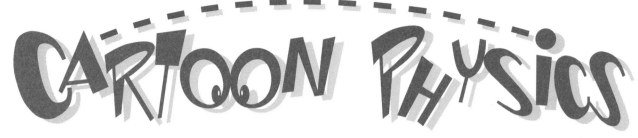

CARTOON PHYSICS

Forget the law of gravity! Cartoons follow the law of laughter. Here's Garfield's goofy guide to this silly science.

Fig. 1

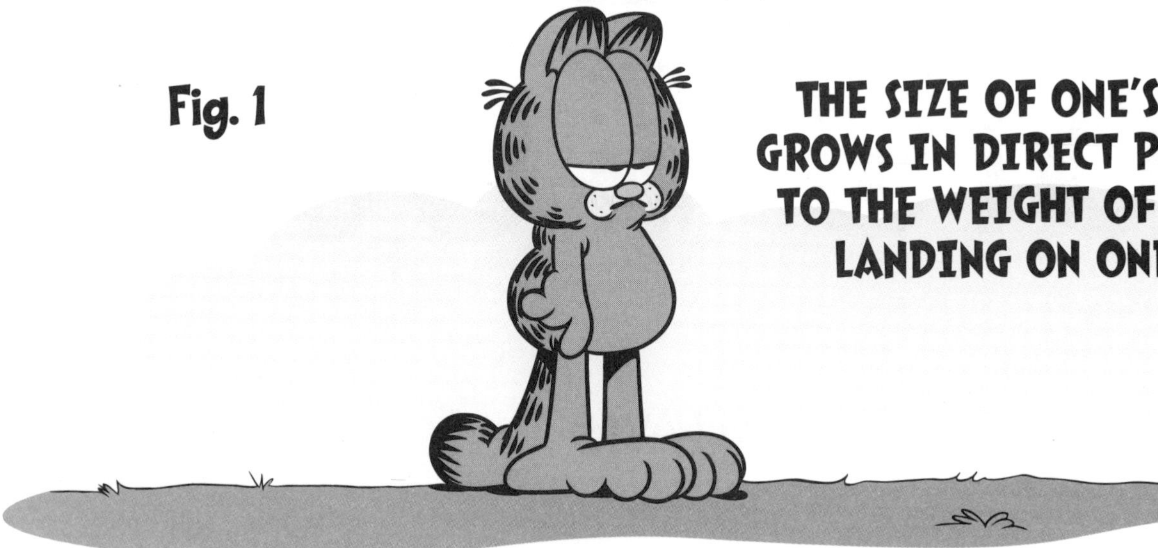

THE SIZE OF ONE'S EYEBALLS GROWS IN DIRECT PROPORTION TO THE WEIGHT OF THE ANVIL LANDING ON ONE'S TAIL.

Fig. 2

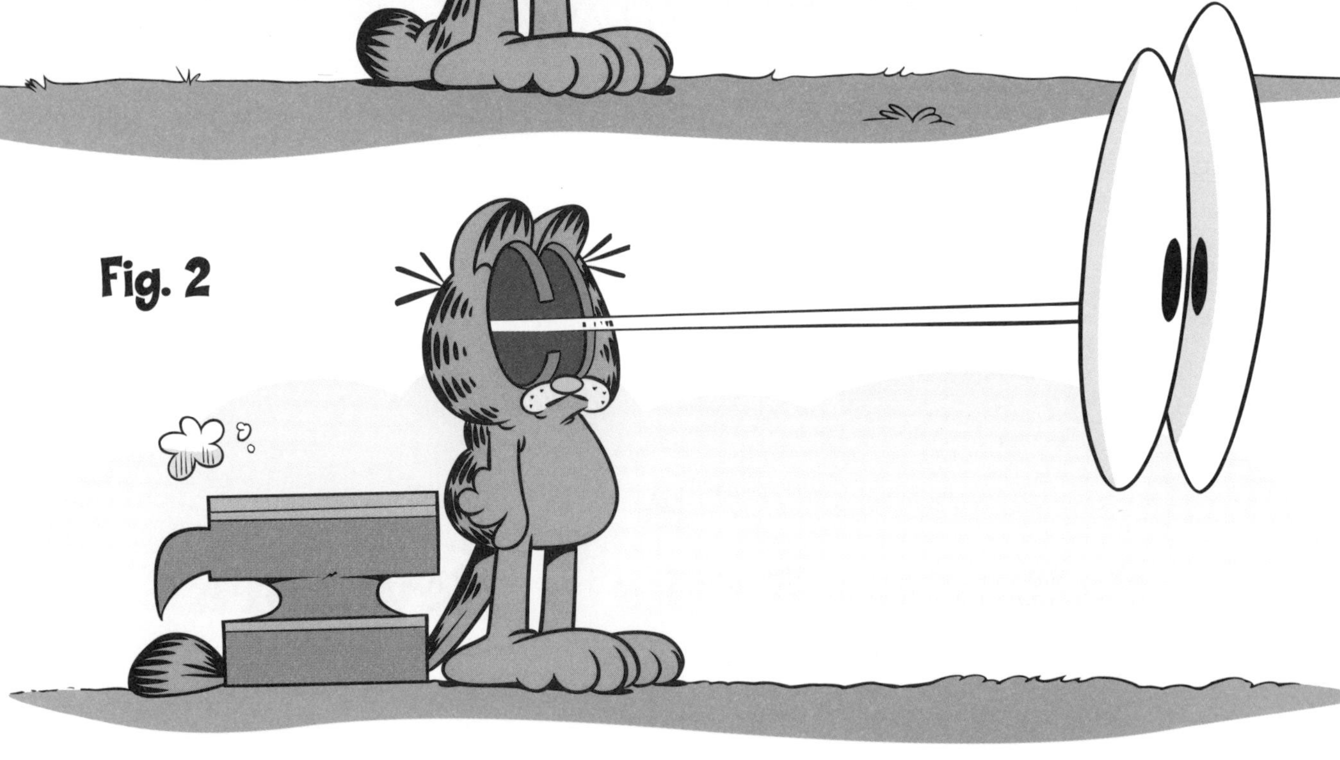

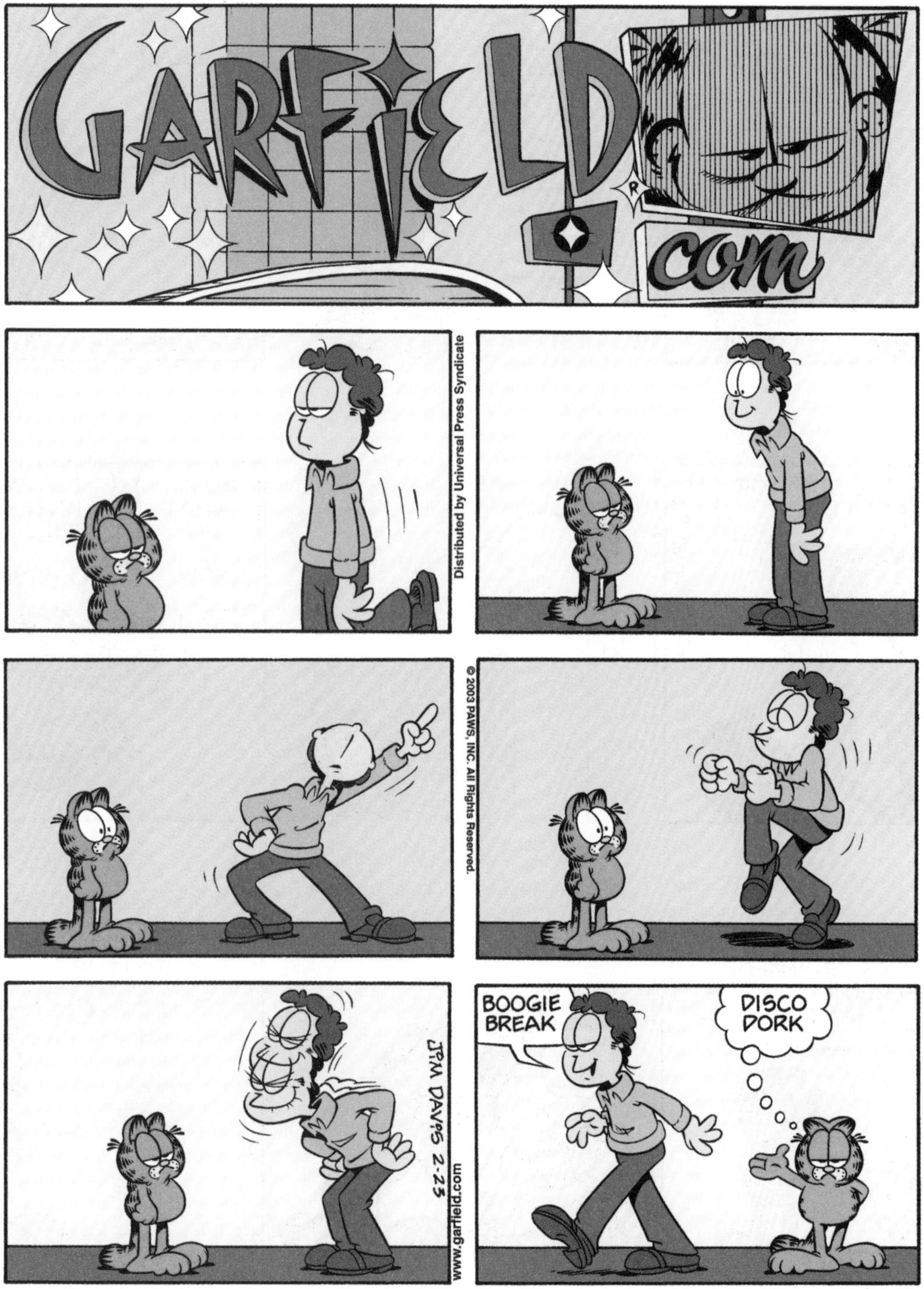
GARFIELD .com
Distributed by Universal Press Syndicate
© 2003 PAWS, INC. All Rights Reserved.
JPM DAVIS 2-23
www.garfield.com
BOOGIE BREAK
DISCO DORK

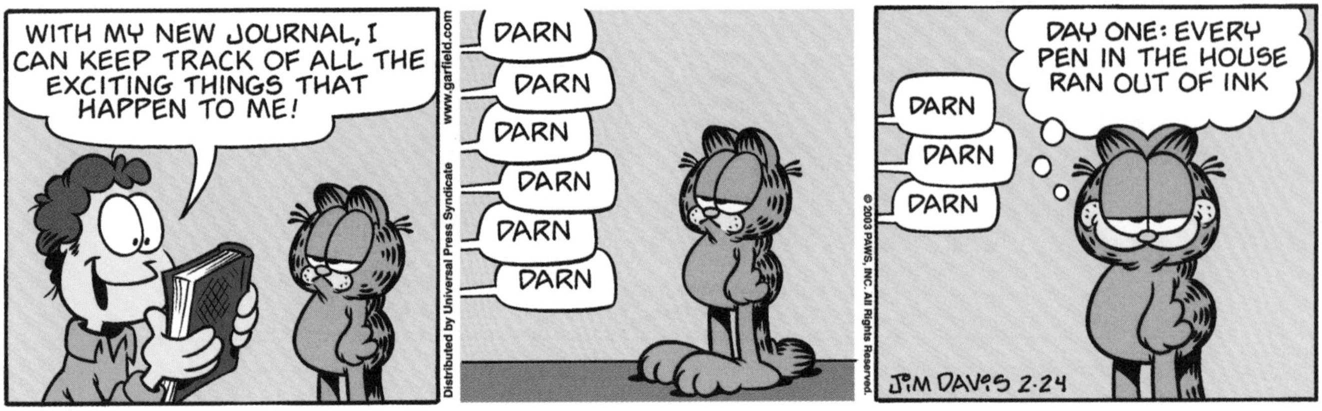
WITH MY NEW JOURNAL, I CAN KEEP TRACK OF ALL THE EXCITING THINGS THAT HAPPEN TO ME!
www.garfield.com
Distributed by Universal Press Syndicate
DARN
DARN
DARN
DARN
DARN
DARN
© 2003 PAWS, INC. All Rights Reserved.
DARN
DARN
DARN
DAY ONE: EVERY PEN IN THE HOUSE RAN OUT OF INK
JIM DAVIS 2-24

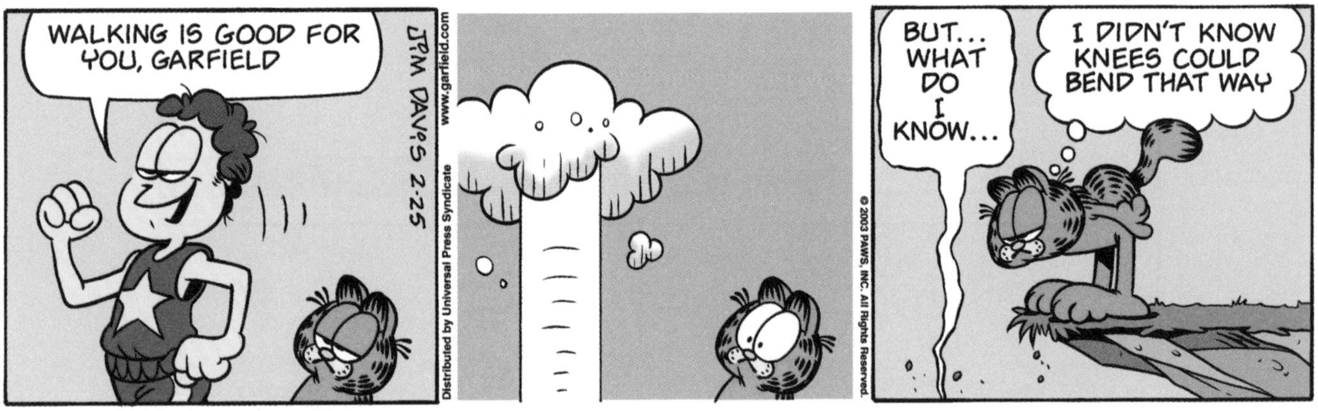
WALKING IS GOOD FOR YOU, GARFIELD
JIM DAVIS 2-25
www.garfield.com
Distributed by Universal Press Syndicate
© 2003 PAWS, INC. All Rights Reserved.
BUT... WHAT DO I KNOW...
I DIDN'T KNOW KNEES COULD BEND THAT WAY

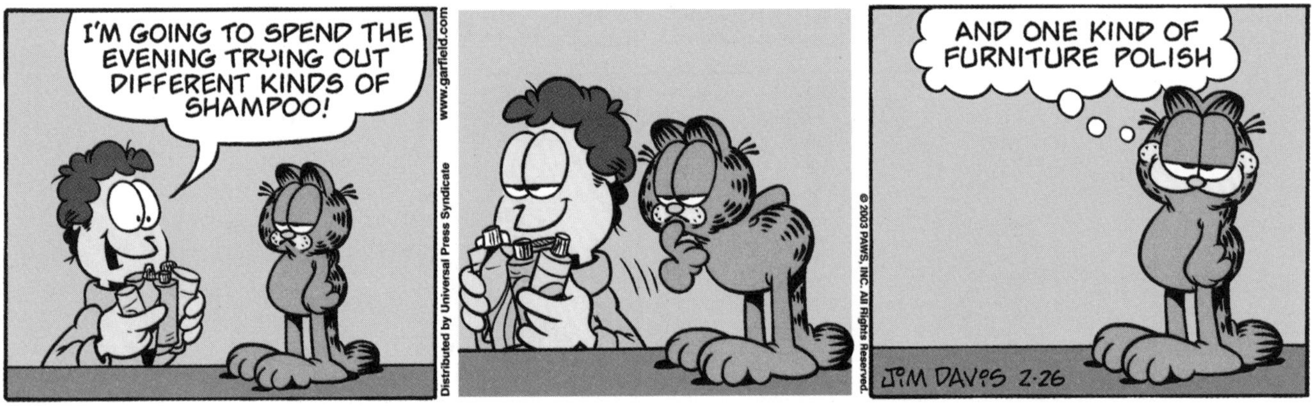
I'M GOING TO SPEND THE EVENING TRYING OUT DIFFERENT KINDS OF SHAMPOO!
www.garfield.com
Distributed by Universal Press Syndicate
© 2003 PAWS, INC. All Rights Reserved.
AND ONE KIND OF FURNITURE POLISH
JIM DAVIS 2-26

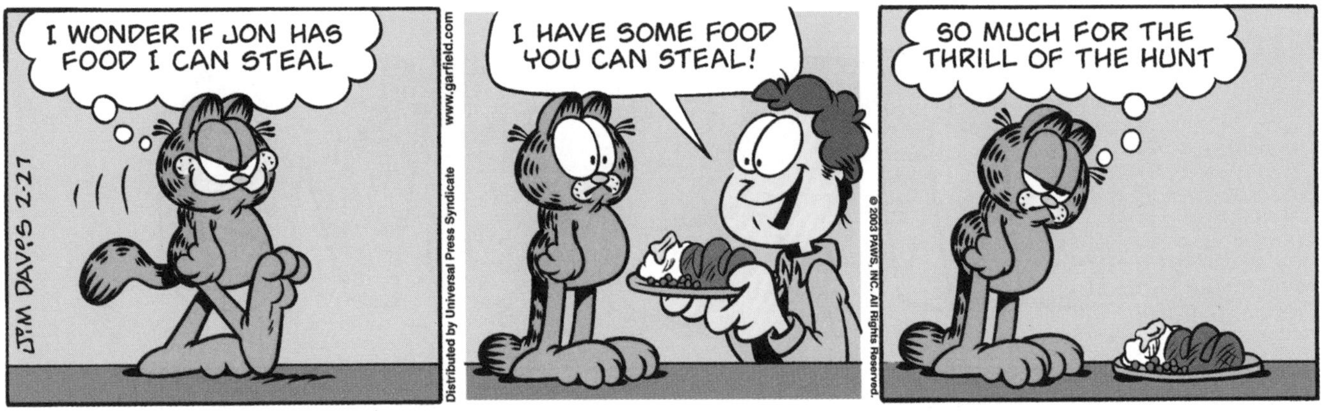
I WONDER IF JON HAS FOOD I CAN STEAL
JIM DAVIS 2-27
www.garfield.com
Distributed by Universal Press Syndicate
I HAVE SOME FOOD YOU CAN STEAL!
© 2003 PAWS, INC. All Rights Reserved.
SO MUCH FOR THE THRILL OF THE HUNT

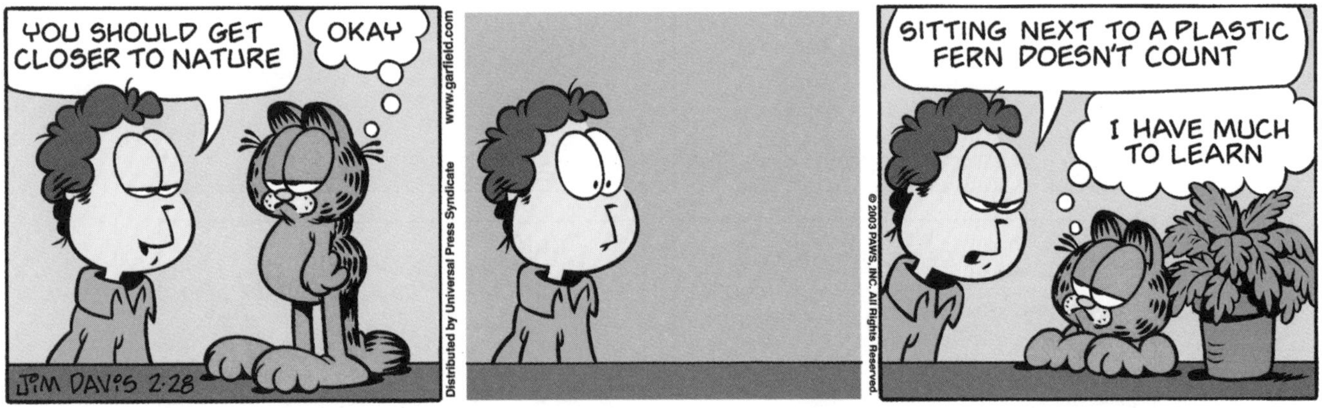
YOU SHOULD GET CLOSER TO NATURE
OKAY
JIM DAVIS 2-28
www.garfield.com
Distributed by Universal Press Syndicate
© 2003 PAWS, INC. All Rights Reserved.
SITTING NEXT TO A PLASTIC FERN DOESN'T COUNT
I HAVE MUCH TO LEARN

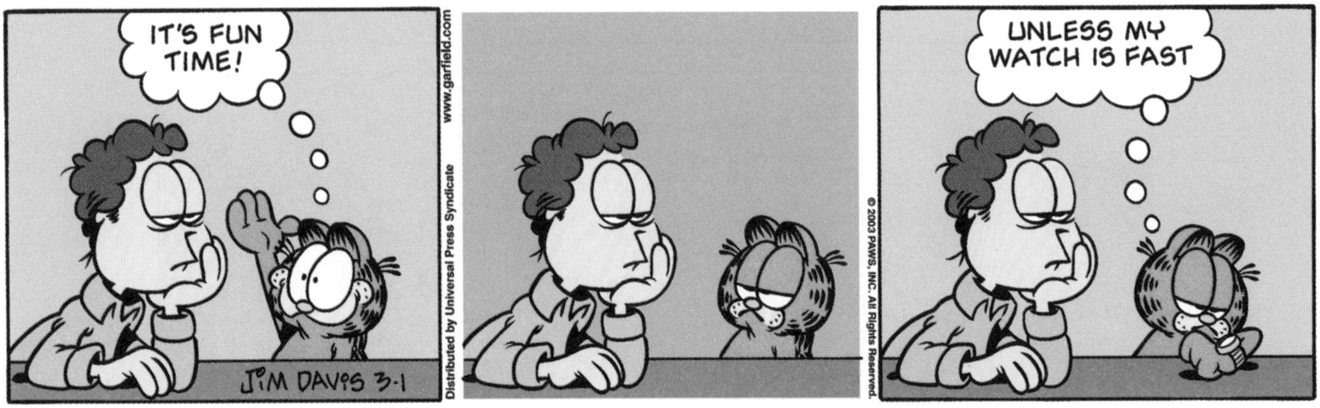
IT'S FUN TIME!
JIM DAVIS 3-1
www.garfield.com
Distributed by Universal Press Syndicate
© 2003 PAWS, INC. All Rights Reserved.
UNLESS MY WATCH IS FAST

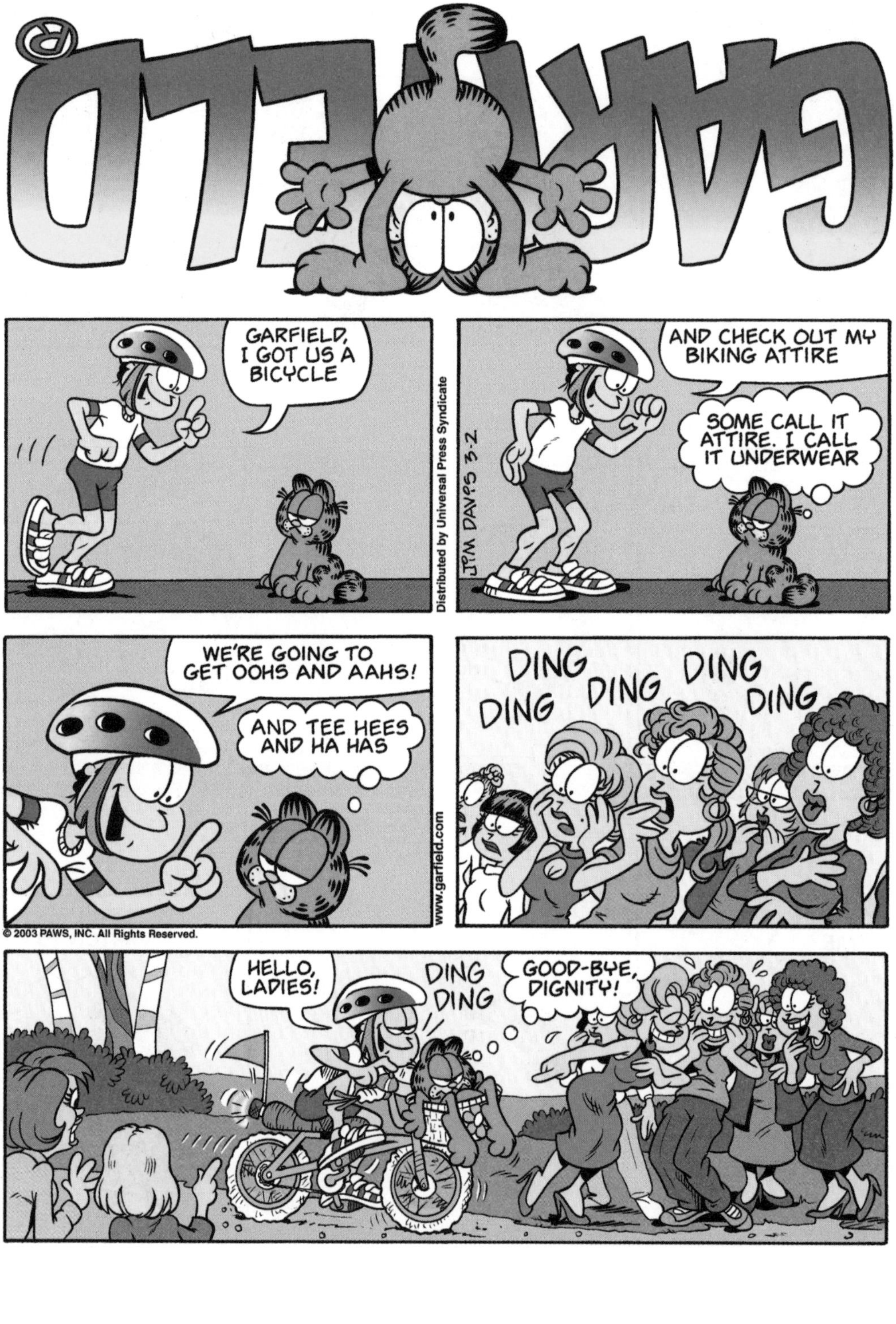
GARFIELD
GARFIELD, I GOT US A BICYCLE
AND CHECK OUT MY BIKING ATTIRE
SOME CALL IT ATTIRE. I CALL IT UNDERWEAR
JPM DAVPS 3-2
Distributed by Universal Press Syndicate
WE'RE GOING TO GET OOHS AND AAHS!
AND TEE HEES AND HA HAS
www.garfield.com
DING DING DING DING DING DING
HELLO, LADIES!
DING DING
GOOD-BYE, DIGNITY!

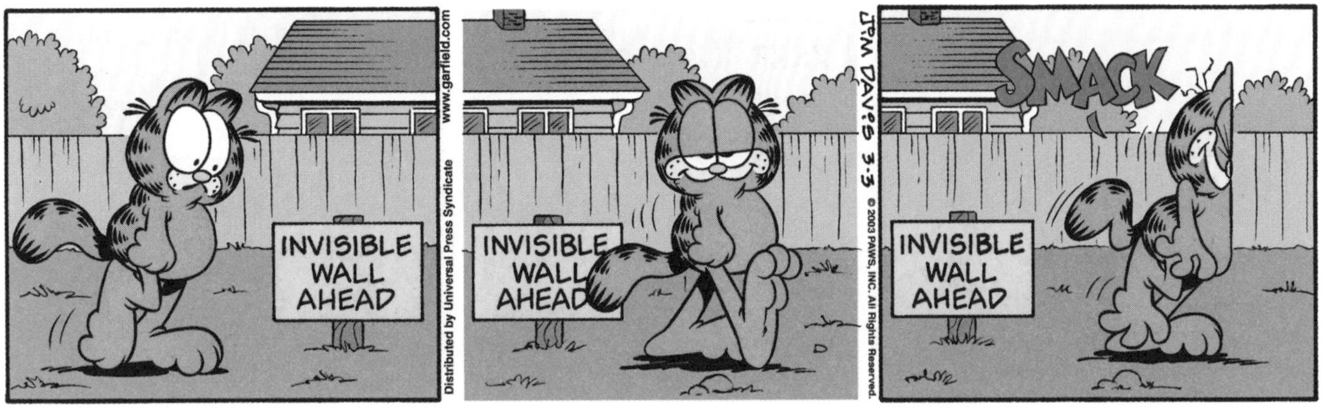
INVISIBLE WALL AHEAD
www.garfield.com
Distributed by Universal Press Syndicate
INVISIBLE WALL AHEAD
JIM DAVIS 3-3
© 2003 PAWS, INC. All Rights Reserved.
SMACK
INVISIBLE WALL AHEAD

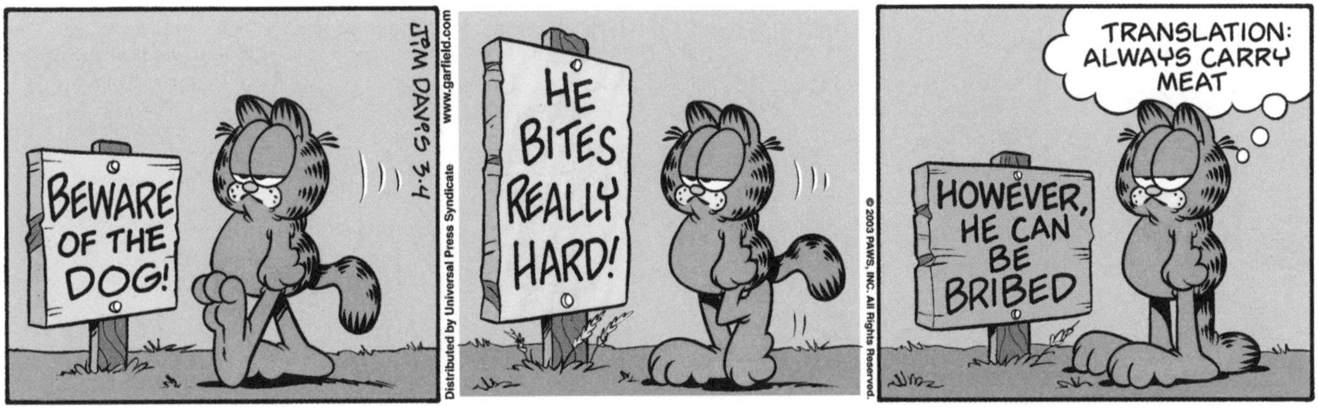
BEWARE OF THE DOG!
JIM DAVIS 3-4
www.garfield.com
Distributed by Universal Press Syndicate
HE BITES REALLY HARD!
© 2003 PAWS, INC. All Rights Reserved.
HOWEVER, HE CAN BE BRIBED
TRANSLATION: ALWAYS CARRY MEAT

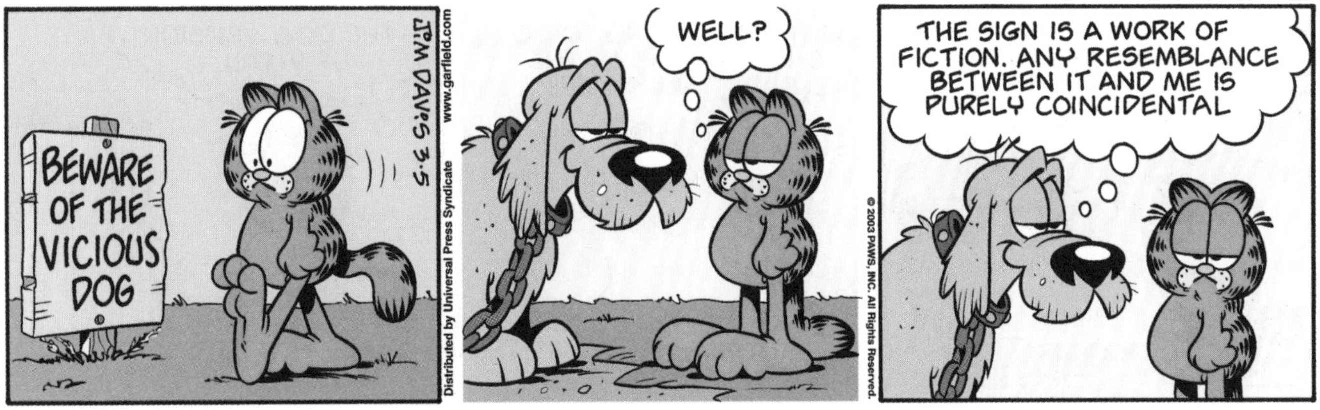
BEWARE OF THE VICIOUS DOG
JIM DAVIS 3-5
www.garfield.com
Distributed by Universal Press Syndicate
WELL?
© 2003 PAWS, INC. All Rights Reserved.
THE SIGN IS A WORK OF FICTION. ANY RESEMBLANCE BETWEEN IT AND ME IS PURELY COINCIDENTAL

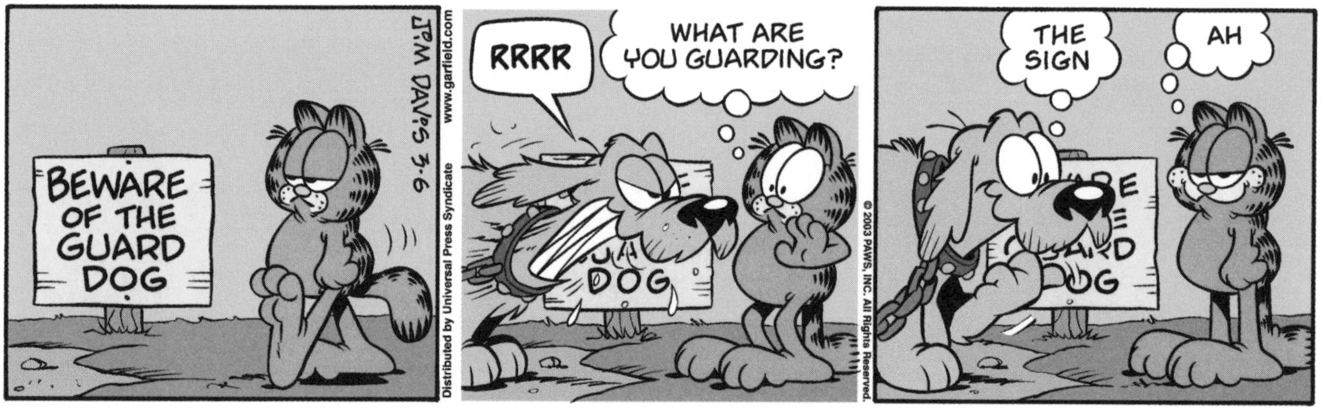
BEWARE OF THE GUARD DOG
JIM DAVIS 3-6
www.garfield.com
Distributed by Universal Press Syndicate
RRRR
WHAT ARE YOU GUARDING?
© 2003 PAWS, INC. All Rights Reserved.
THE SIGN
AH

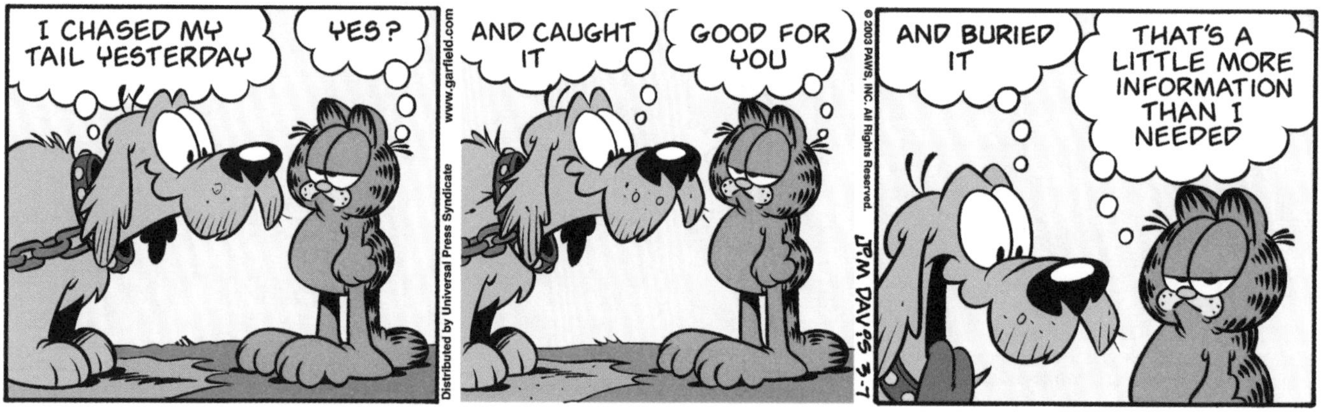
I CHASED MY TAIL YESTERDAY
YES?
www.garfield.com
Distributed by Universal Press Syndicate
AND CAUGHT IT
GOOD FOR YOU
© 2003 PAWS, INC. All Rights Reserved.
JIM DAVIS 3-7
AND BURIED IT
THAT'S A LITTLE MORE INFORMATION THAN I NEEDED

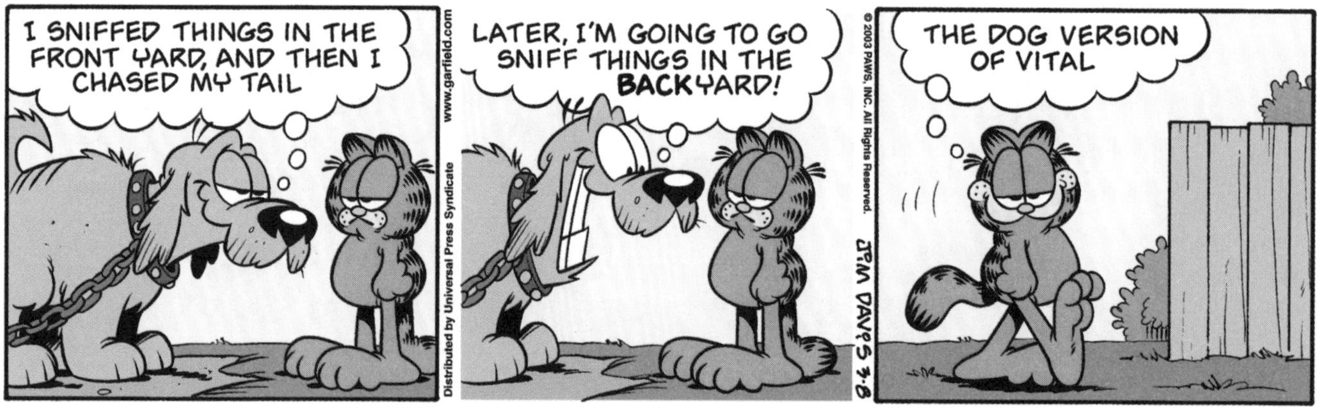
I SNIFFED THINGS IN THE FRONT YARD, AND THEN I CHASED MY TAIL
www.garfield.com
Distributed by Universal Press Syndicate
LATER, I'M GOING TO GO SNIFF THINGS IN THE BACKYARD!
© 2003 PAWS, INC. All Rights Reserved.
JIM DAVIS 3-8
THE DOG VERSION OF VITAL

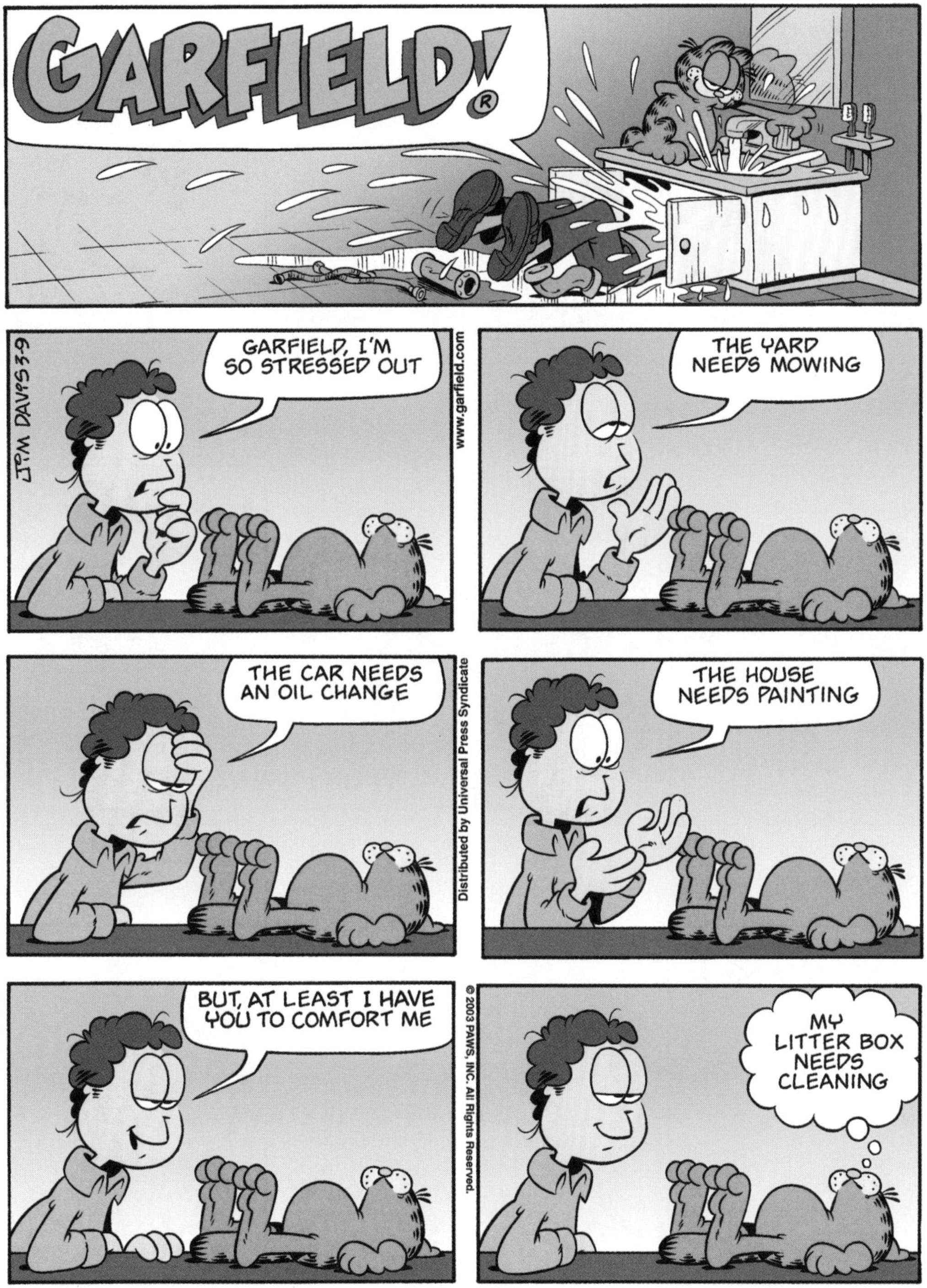
GARFIELD!
JIM DAVIS 3-9
www.garfield.com
GARFIELD, I'M SO STRESSED OUT
THE YARD NEEDS MOWING
Distributed by Universal Press Syndicate
THE CAR NEEDS AN OIL CHANGE
THE HOUSE NEEDS PAINTING
© 2003 PAWS, INC. All Rights Reserved.
BUT, AT LEAST I HAVE YOU TO COMFORT ME
MY LITTER BOX NEEDS CLEANING

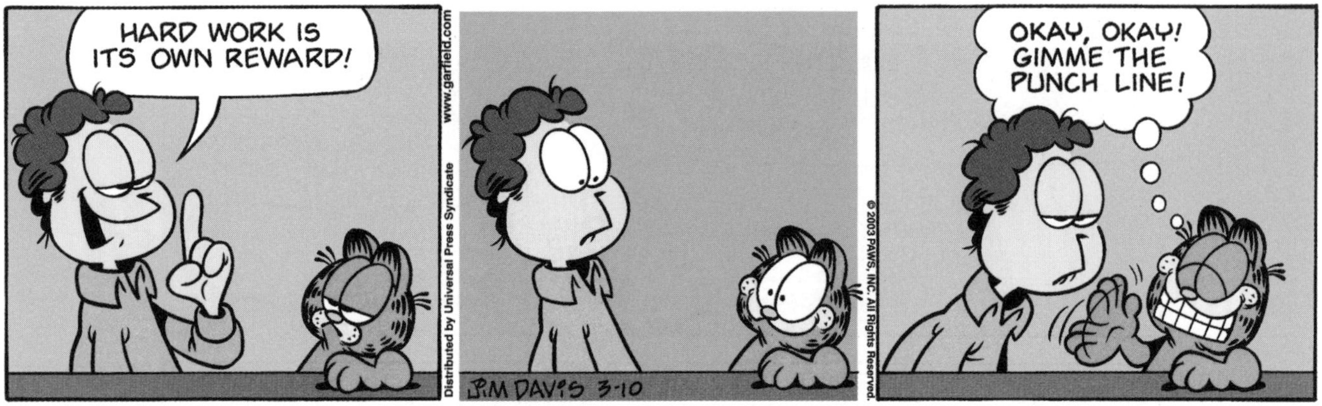
HARD WORK IS ITS OWN REWARD!
OKAY, OKAY! GIMME THE PUNCH LINE!
JIM DAVIS 3-10
Distributed by Universal Press Syndicate www.garfield.com
© 2003 PAWS, INC. All Rights Reserved.

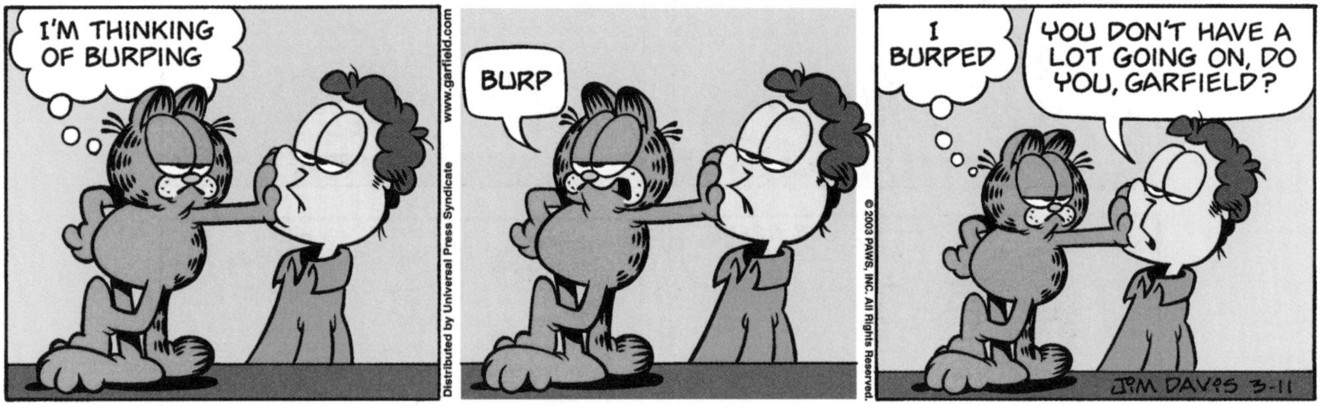
I'M THINKING OF BURPING
BURP
I BURPED
YOU DON'T HAVE A LOT GOING ON, DO YOU, GARFIELD?
JIM DAVIS 3-11
Distributed by Universal Press Syndicate www.garfield.com
© 2003 PAWS, INC. All Rights Reserved.

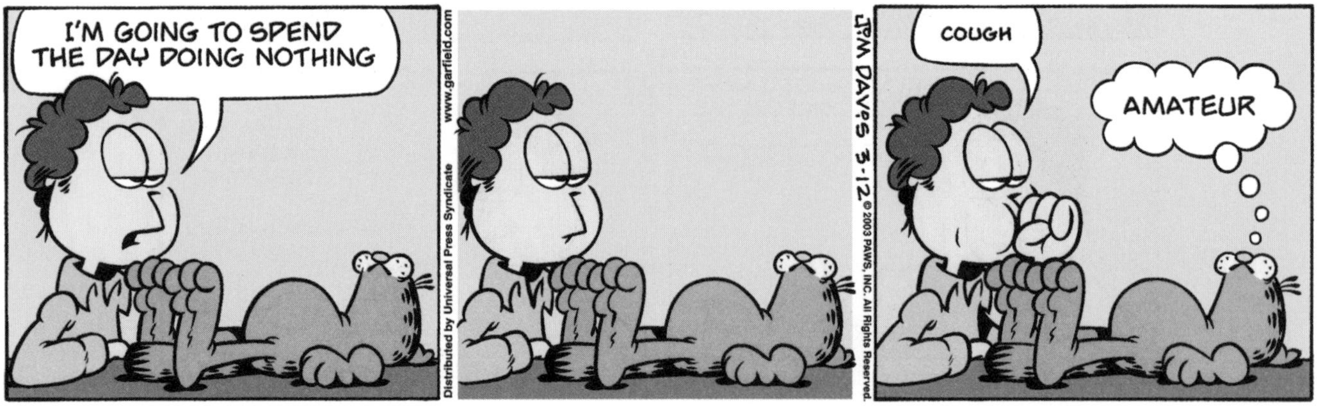
I'M GOING TO SPEND THE DAY DOING NOTHING
COUGH
AMATEUR
JIM DAVIS 3-12
Distributed by Universal Press Syndicate www.garfield.com
© 2003 PAWS, INC. All Rights Reserved.

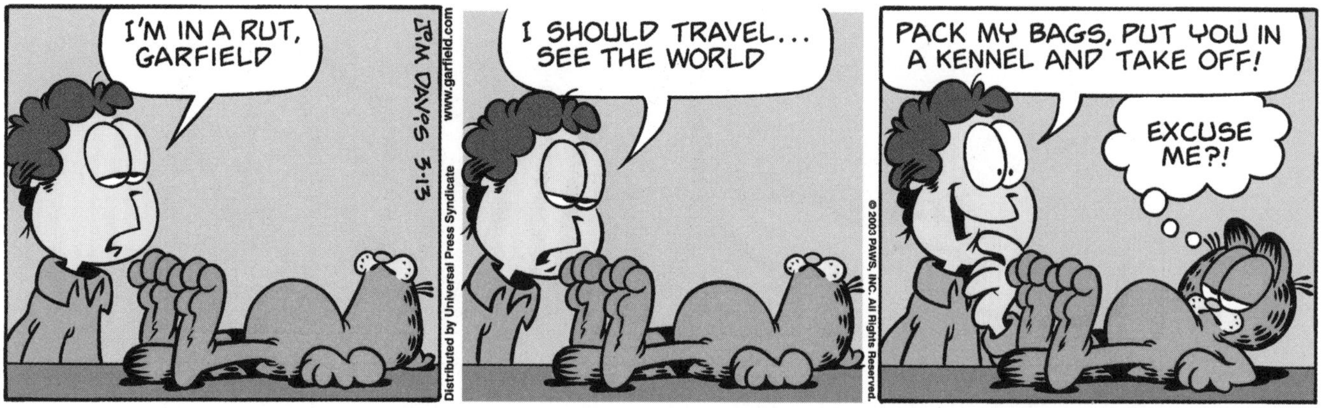
I'M IN A RUT, GARFIELD
JIM DAVIS 3-13
www.garfield.com
Distributed by Universal Press Syndicate
I SHOULD TRAVEL... SEE THE WORLD
© 2003 PAWS, INC. All Rights Reserved.
PACK MY BAGS, PUT YOU IN A KENNEL AND TAKE OFF!
EXCUSE ME?!

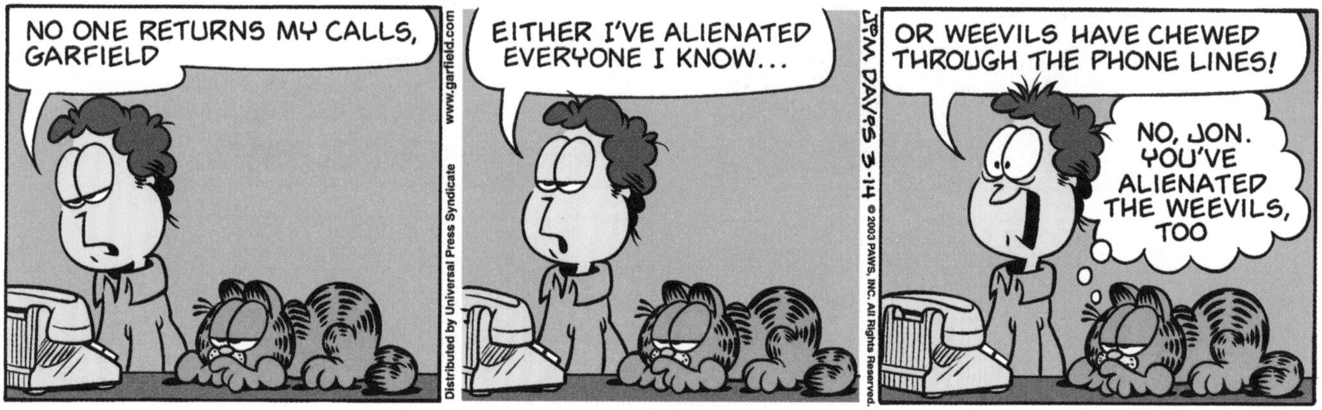
NO ONE RETURNS MY CALLS, GARFIELD
www.garfield.com
Distributed by Universal Press Syndicate
EITHER I'VE ALIENATED EVERYONE I KNOW...
JIM DAVIS 3-14
© 2003 PAWS, INC. All Rights Reserved.
OR WEEVILS HAVE CHEWED THROUGH THE PHONE LINES!
NO, JON. YOU'VE ALIENATED THE WEEVILS, TOO

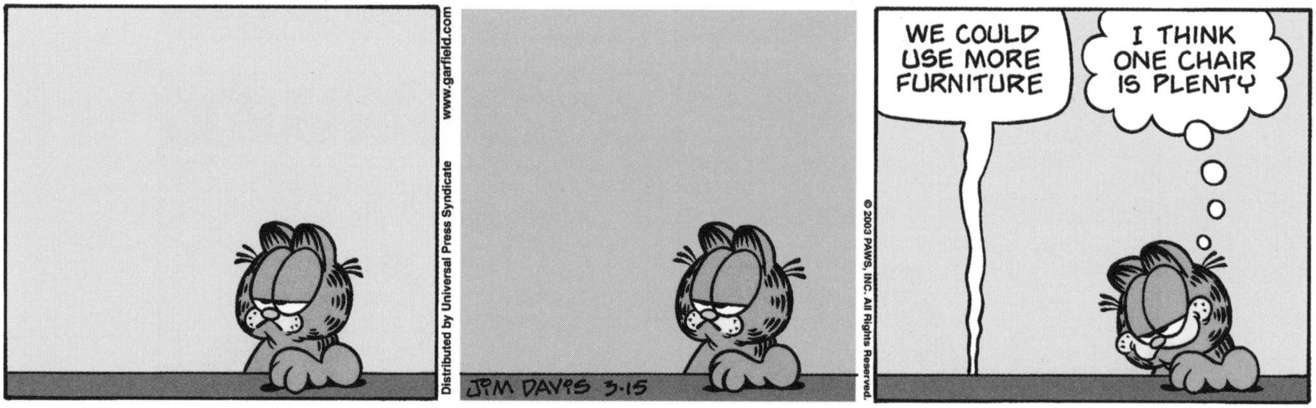
www.garfield.com
Distributed by Universal Press Syndicate
JIM DAVIS 3-15
© 2003 PAWS, INC. All Rights Reserved.
WE COULD USE MORE FURNITURE
I THINK ONE CHAIR IS PLENTY

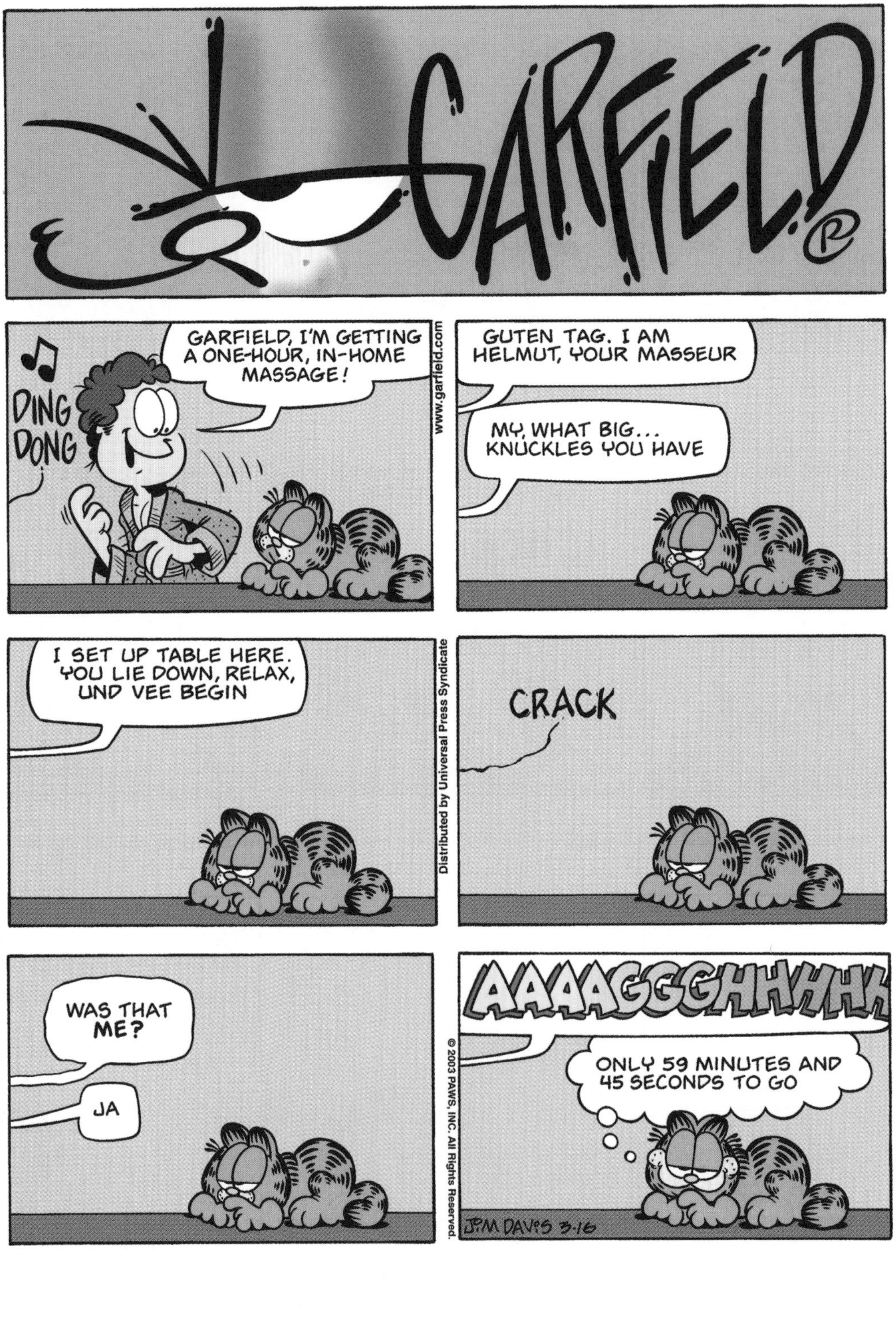
GARFIELD
GARFIELD, I'M GETTING A ONE-HOUR, IN-HOME MASSAGE!
DING DONG
www.garfield.com
GUTEN TAG. I AM HELMUT, YOUR MASSEUR
MY, WHAT BIG... KNUCKLES YOU HAVE
I SET UP TABLE HERE. YOU LIE DOWN, RELAX, UND VEE BEGIN
Distributed by Universal Press Syndicate
CRACK
WAS THAT ME?
JA
© 2003 PAWS, INC. All Rights Reserved.
AAAAGGGHHHHH
ONLY 59 MINUTES AND 45 SECONDS TO GO
JIM DAVIS 3-16

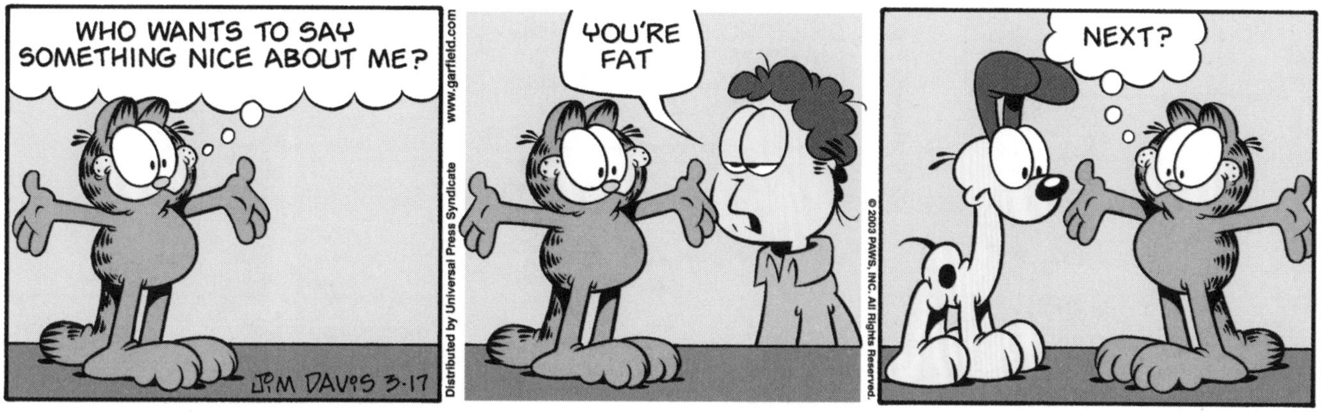
WHO WANTS TO SAY SOMETHING NICE ABOUT ME?
JIM DAVIS 3-17
YOU'RE FAT
NEXT?
www.garfield.com
Distributed by Universal Press Syndicate
© 2003 PAWS, INC. All Rights Reserved.

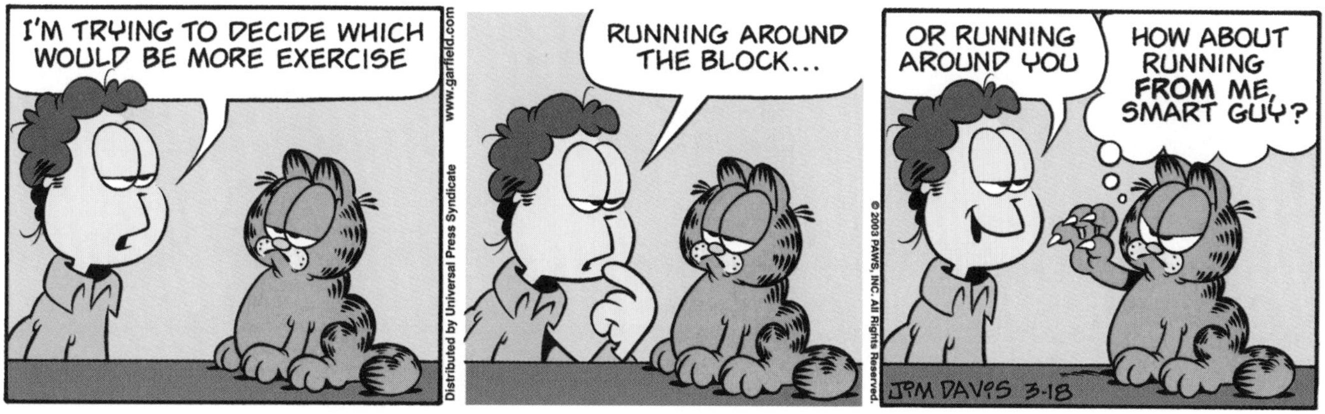
I'M TRYING TO DECIDE WHICH WOULD BE MORE EXERCISE
RUNNING AROUND THE BLOCK...
OR RUNNING AROUND YOU
HOW ABOUT RUNNING **FROM** ME, SMART GUY?
JIM DAVIS 3-18
www.garfield.com
Distributed by Universal Press Syndicate
© 2003 PAWS, INC. All Rights Reserved.

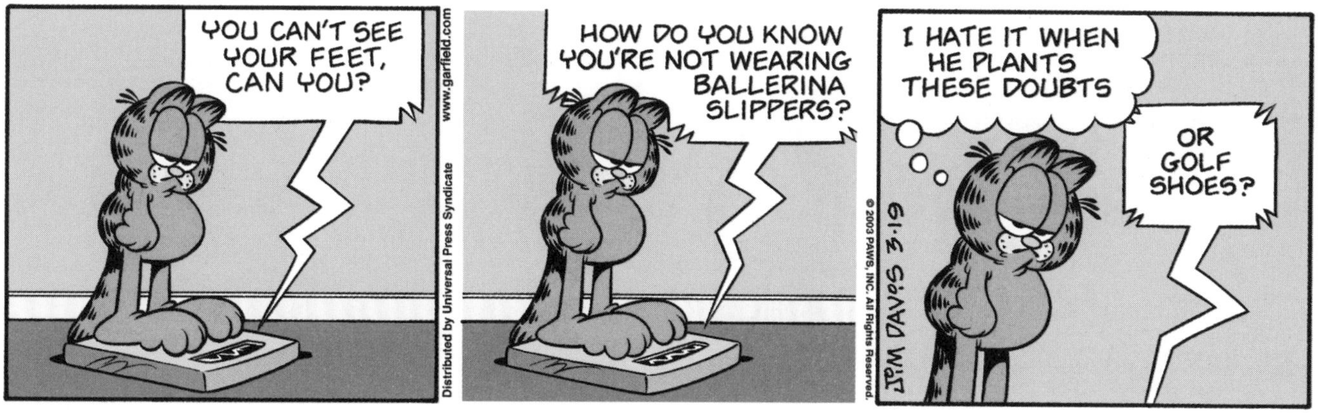
YOU CAN'T SEE YOUR FEET, CAN YOU?
HOW DO YOU KNOW YOU'RE NOT WEARING BALLERINA SLIPPERS?
I HATE IT WHEN HE PLANTS THESE DOUBTS
OR GOLF SHOES?
JIM DAVIS 3-19
www.garfield.com
Distributed by Universal Press Syndicate
© 2003 PAWS, INC. All Rights Reserved.

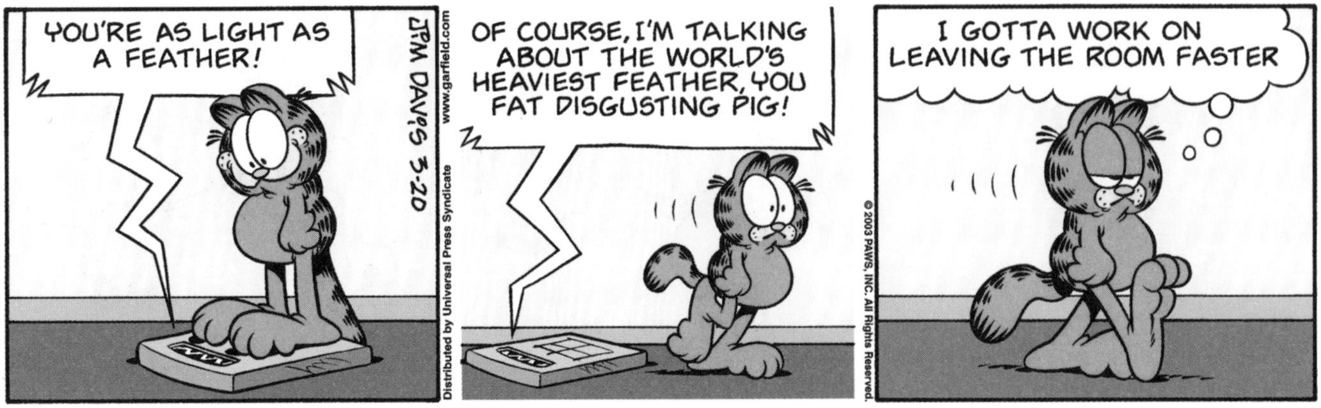
YOU'RE AS LIGHT AS A FEATHER!
JIM DAVIS 3-20
www.garfield.com
Distributed by Universal Press Syndicate
OF COURSE, I'M TALKING ABOUT THE WORLD'S HEAVIEST FEATHER, YOU FAT DISGUSTING PIG!
© 2003 PAWS, INC. All Rights Reserved.
I GOTTA WORK ON LEAVING THE ROOM FASTER

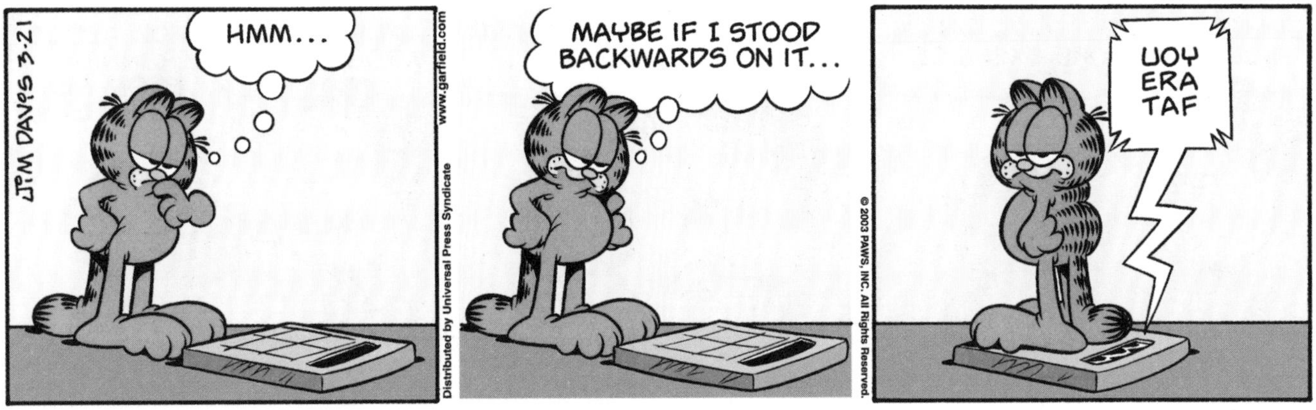
JIM DAVIS 3-21
HMM...
www.garfield.com
Distributed by Universal Press Syndicate
MAYBE IF I STOOD BACKWARDS ON IT...
© 2003 PAWS, INC. All Rights Reserved.
UOY
ERA
TAF

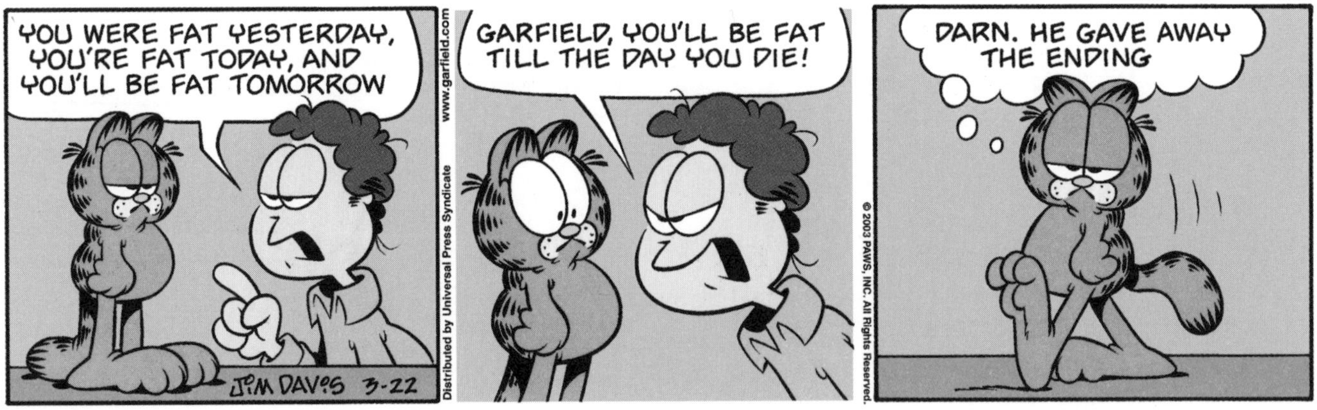
YOU WERE FAT YESTERDAY, YOU'RE FAT TODAY, AND YOU'LL BE FAT TOMORROW
JIM DAVIS 3-22
www.garfield.com
Distributed by Universal Press Syndicate
GARFIELD, YOU'LL BE FAT TILL THE DAY YOU DIE!
© 2003 PAWS, INC. All Rights Reserved.
DARN. HE GAVE AWAY THE ENDING

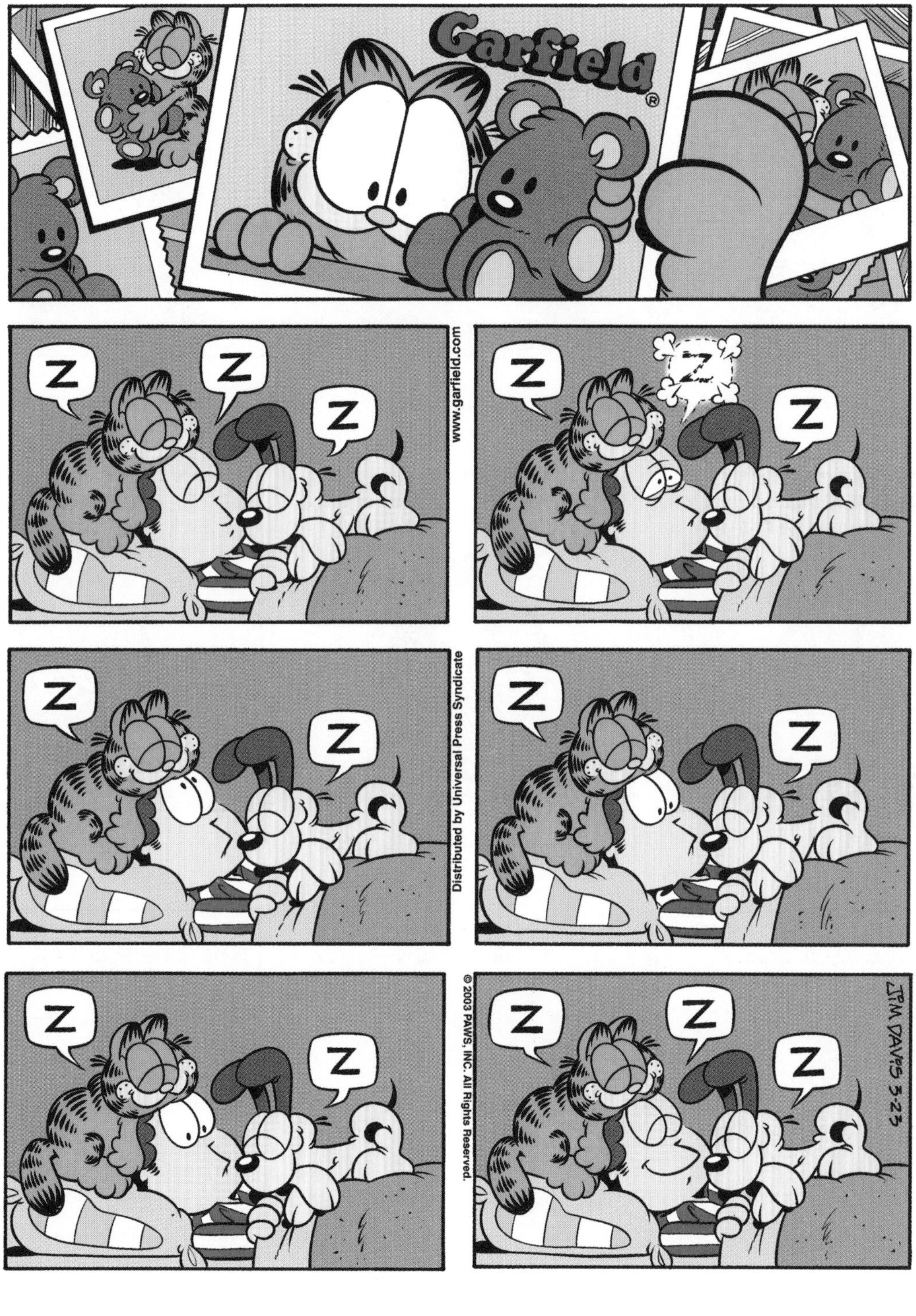
Garfield®
Z
Z
Z
www.garfield.com
Z
Z
Z
Z
Z
Distributed by Universal Press Syndicate
Z
Z
Z
Z
© 2003 PAWS, INC. All Rights Reserved.
JIM DAVIS 3-23
Z
Z
Z

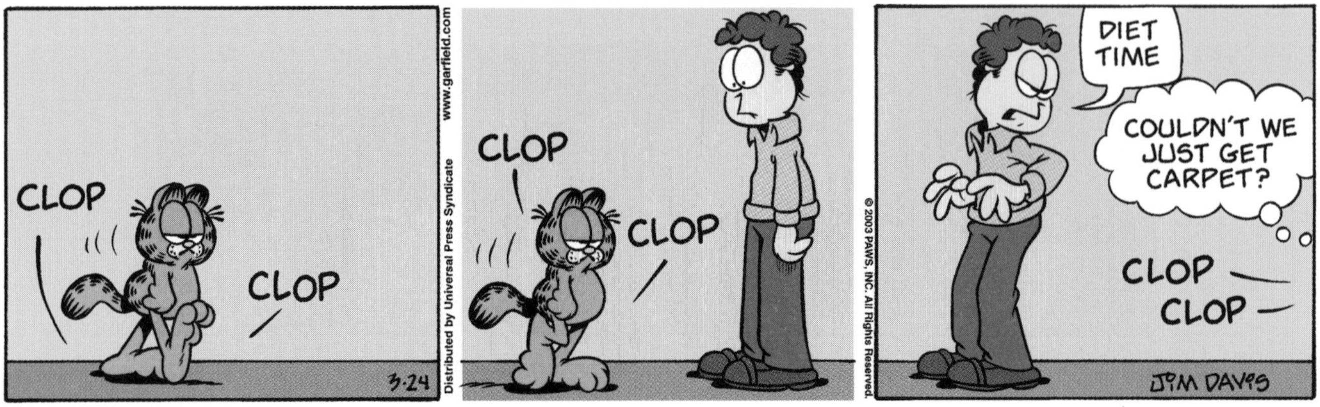
CLOP
CLOP
3-24
www.garfield.com
Distributed by Universal Press Syndicate
CLOP
CLOP
© 2003 PAWS, INC. All Rights Reserved.
DIET TIME
COULDN'T WE JUST GET CARPET?
CLOP
CLOP
JIM DAVIS

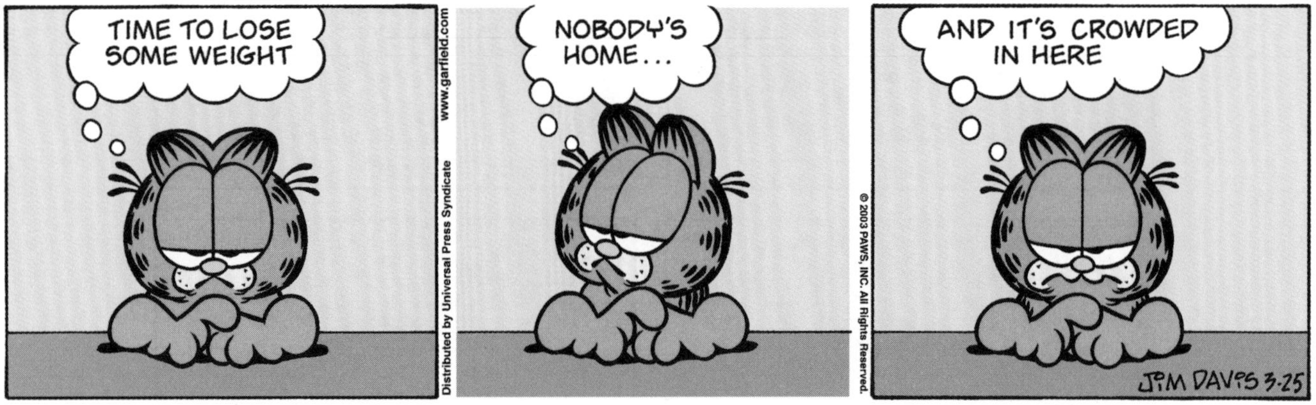
TIME TO LOSE SOME WEIGHT
www.garfield.com
Distributed by Universal Press Syndicate
NOBODY'S HOME...
© 2003 PAWS, INC. All Rights Reserved.
AND IT'S CROWDED IN HERE
JIM DAVIS 3-25

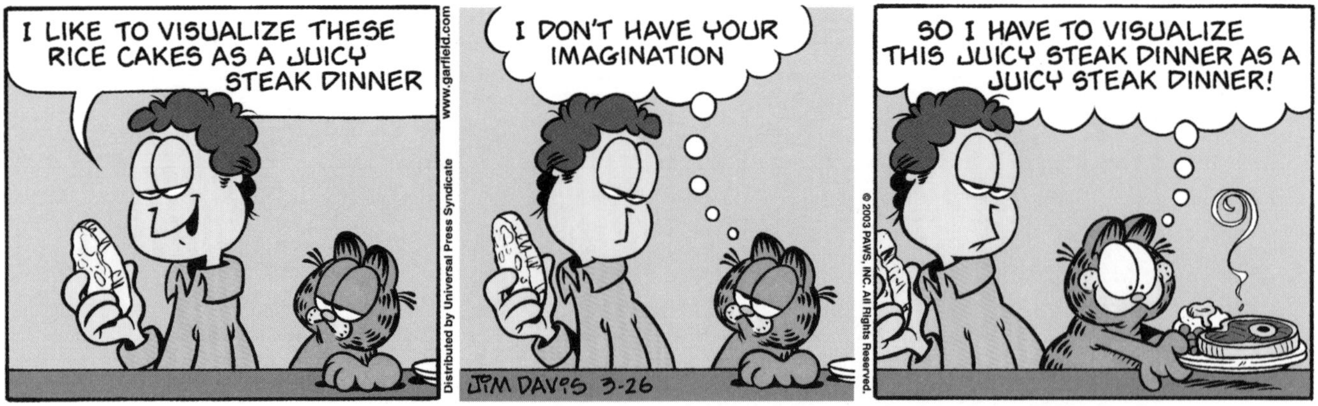
I LIKE TO VISUALIZE THESE RICE CAKES AS A JUICY STEAK DINNER
www.garfield.com
Distributed by Universal Press Syndicate
I DON'T HAVE YOUR IMAGINATION
JIM DAVIS 3-26
© 2003 PAWS, INC. All Rights Reserved.
SO I HAVE TO VISUALIZE THIS JUICY STEAK DINNER AS A JUICY STEAK DINNER!

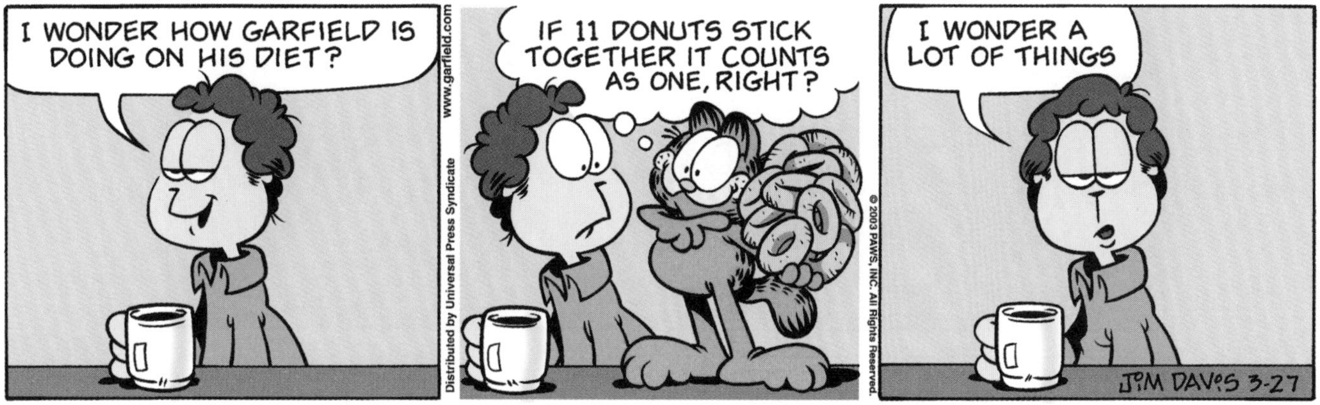
I WONDER HOW GARFIELD IS DOING ON HIS DIET?
IF 11 DONUTS STICK TOGETHER IT COUNTS AS ONE, RIGHT?
I WONDER A LOT OF THINGS
JIM DAVIS 3-27
Distributed by Universal Press Syndicate www.garfield.com
© 2003 PAWS, INC. All Rights Reserved.

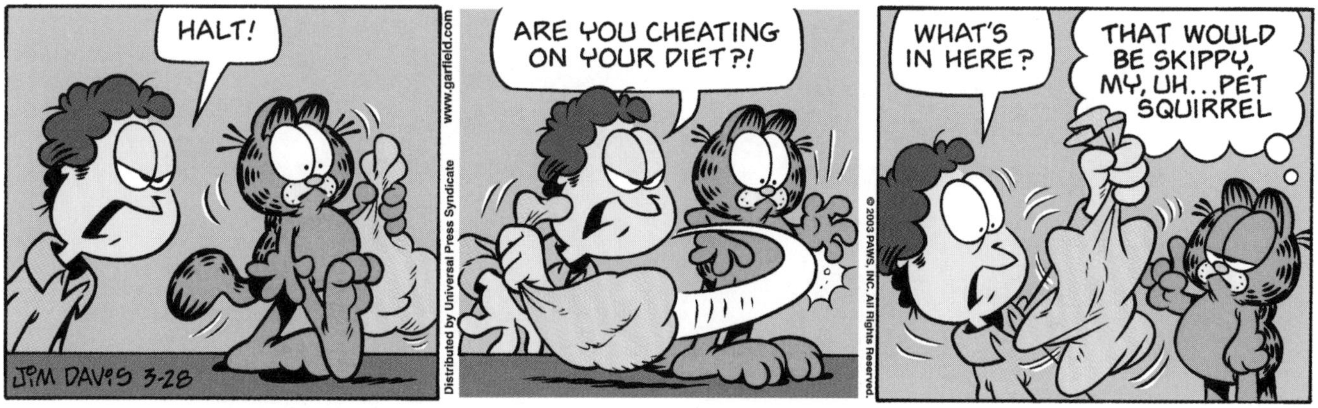
HALT!
JIM DAVIS 3-28
ARE YOU CHEATING ON YOUR DIET?!
WHAT'S IN HERE?
THAT WOULD BE SKIPPY, MY, UH...PET SQUIRREL
Distributed by Universal Press Syndicate www.garfield.com
© 2003 PAWS, INC. All Rights Reserved.

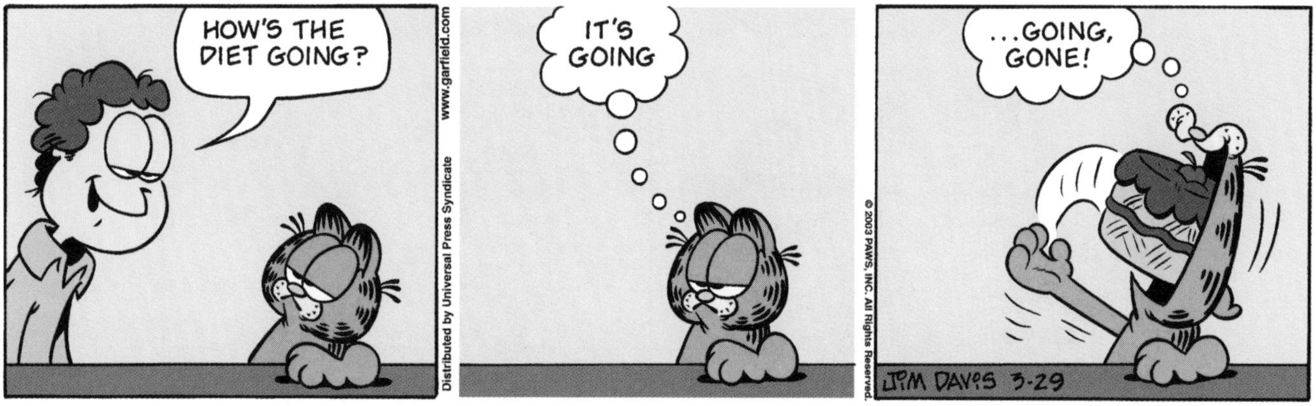
HOW'S THE DIET GOING?
IT'S GOING
...GOING, GONE!
JIM DAVIS 3-29
Distributed by Universal Press Syndicate www.garfield.com
© 2003 PAWS, INC. All Rights Reserved.

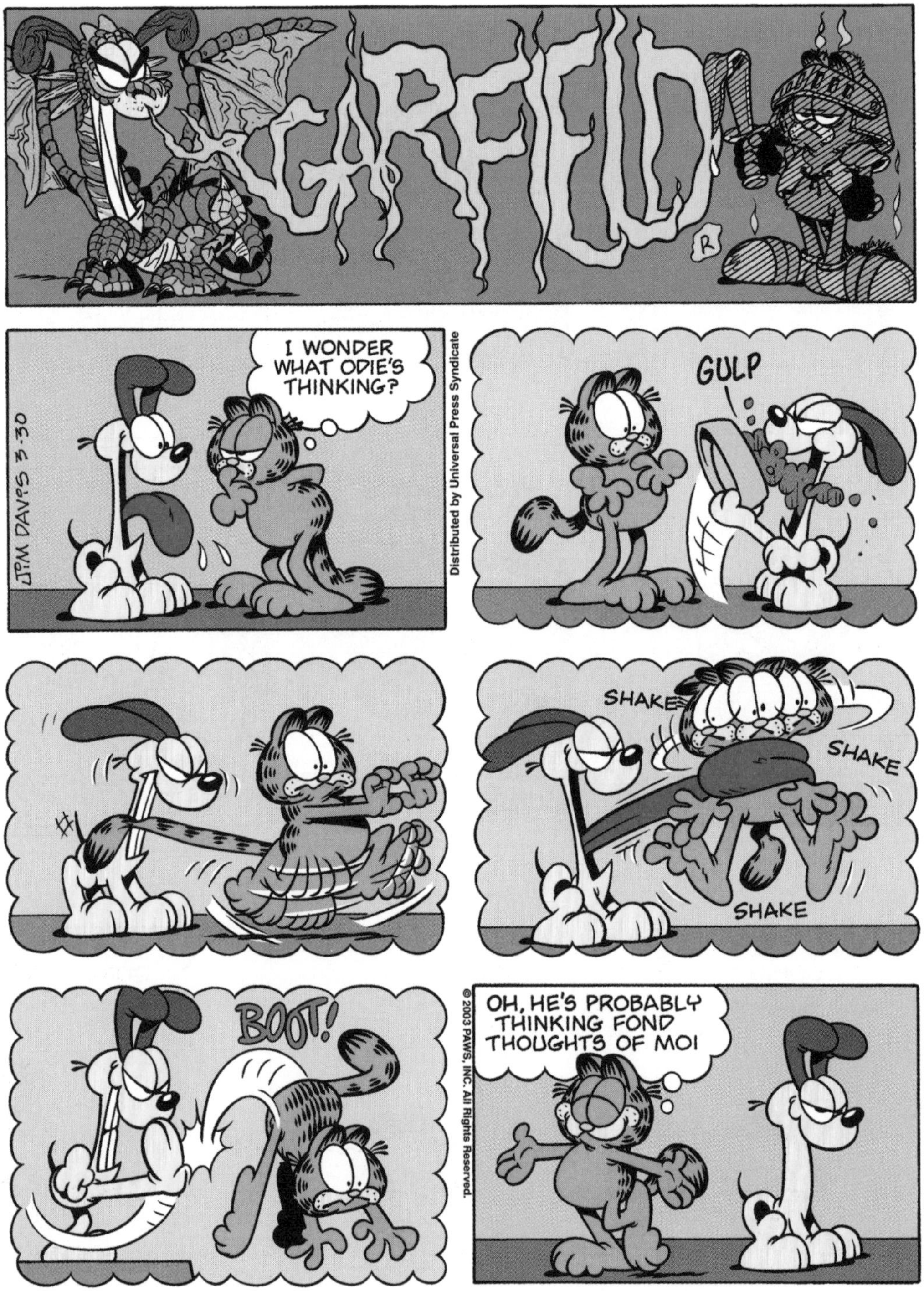
GARFIELD
JIM DAVIS 3-30
I WONDER WHAT ODIE'S THINKING?
Distributed by Universal Press Syndicate
GULP
SHAKE
SHAKE
SHAKE
BOOT!
© 2003 PAWS, INC. All Rights Reserved.
OH, HE'S PROBABLY THINKING FOND THOUGHTS OF MOI

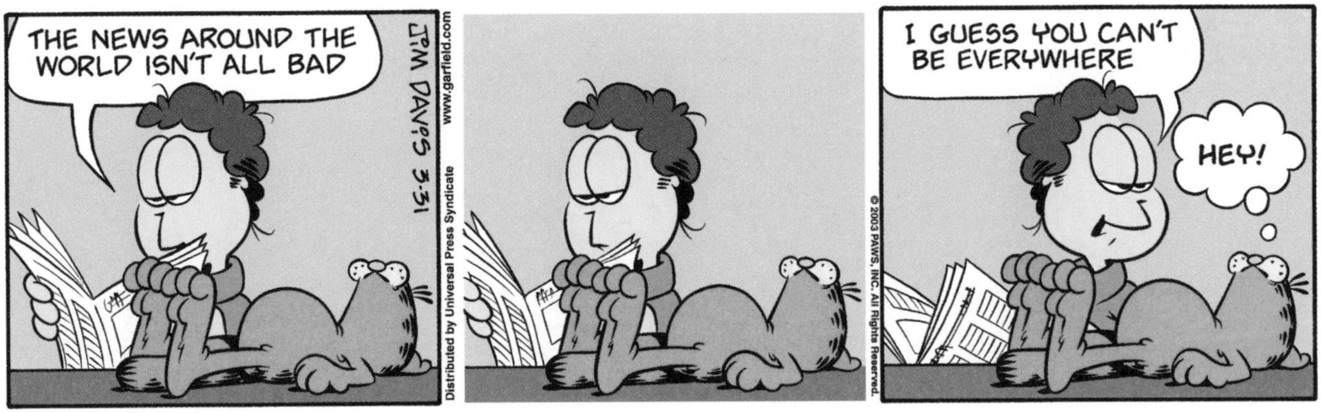
THE NEWS AROUND THE WORLD ISN'T ALL BAD
JIM DAVIS 3-31
www.garfield.com
Distributed by Universal Press Syndicate
I GUESS YOU CAN'T BE EVERYWHERE
HEY!
© 2003 PAWS, INC. All Rights Reserved.

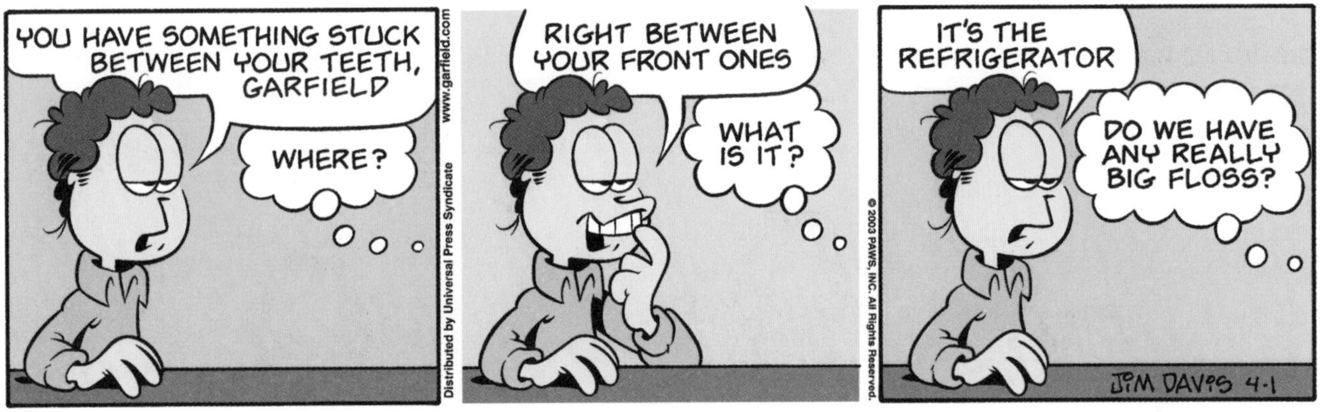
YOU HAVE SOMETHING STUCK BETWEEN YOUR TEETH, GARFIELD
WHERE?
www.garfield.com
Distributed by Universal Press Syndicate
RIGHT BETWEEN YOUR FRONT ONES
WHAT IS IT?
IT'S THE REFRIGERATOR
DO WE HAVE ANY REALLY BIG FLOSS?
© 2003 PAWS, INC. All Rights Reserved.
JIM DAVIS 4-1

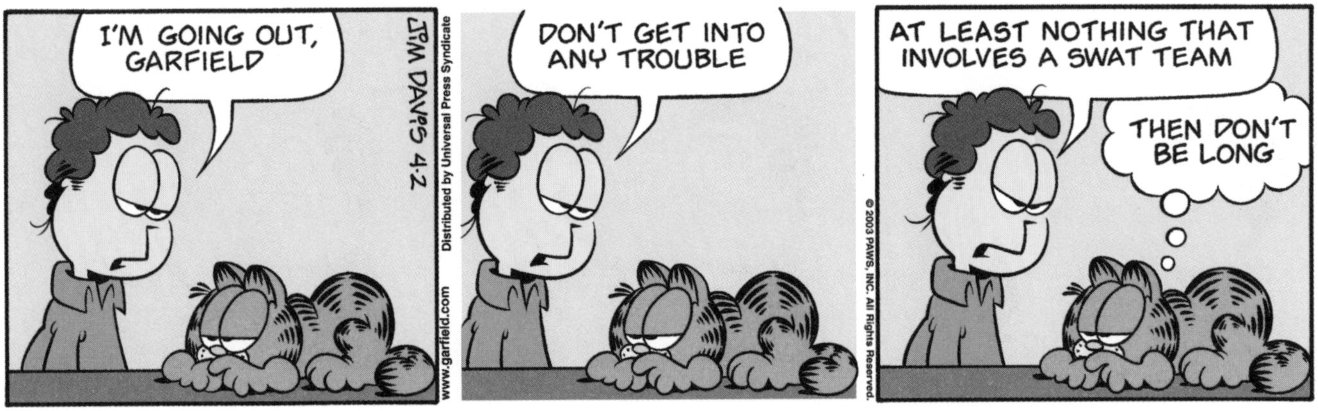
I'M GOING OUT, GARFIELD
JIM DAVIS 4-2
Distributed by Universal Press Syndicate
www.garfield.com
DON'T GET INTO ANY TROUBLE
AT LEAST NOTHING THAT INVOLVES A SWAT TEAM
THEN DON'T BE LONG
© 2003 PAWS, INC. All Rights Reserved.

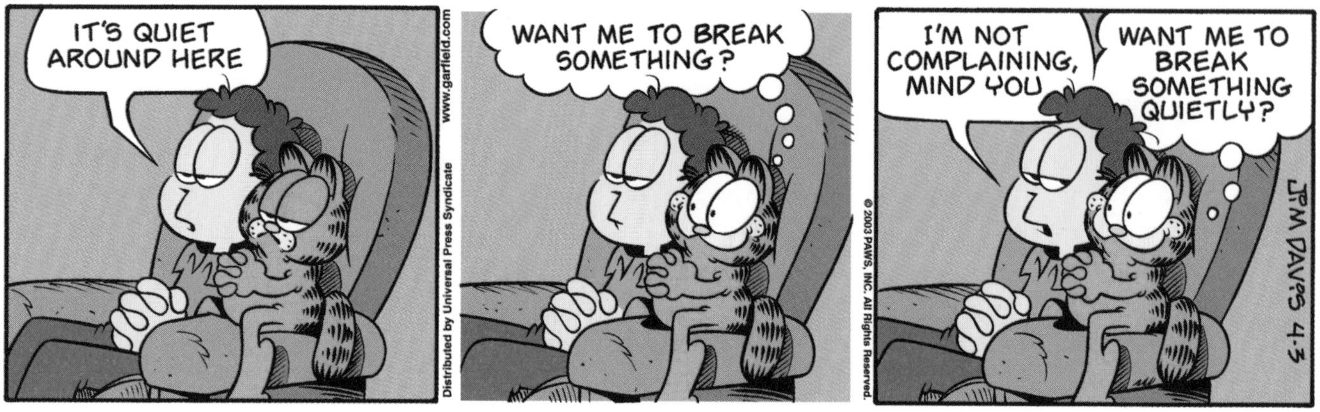
IT'S QUIET AROUND HERE
Distributed by Universal Press Syndicate www.garfield.com
WANT ME TO BREAK SOMETHING?
© 2003 PAWS, INC. All Rights Reserved.
I'M NOT COMPLAINING, MIND YOU
WANT ME TO BREAK SOMETHING QUIETLY?
JIM DAVIS 4-3

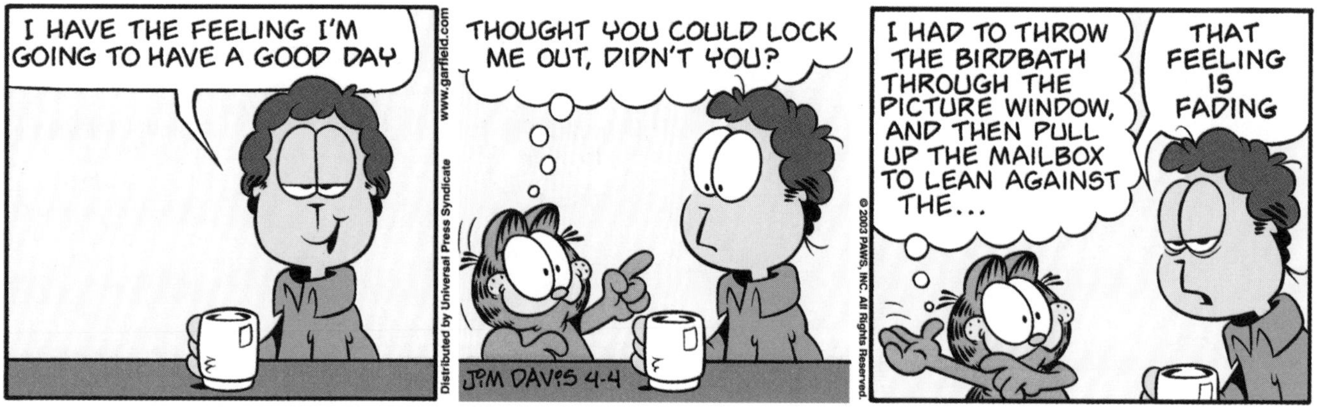
I HAVE THE FEELING I'M GOING TO HAVE A GOOD DAY
Distributed by Universal Press Syndicate www.garfield.com
THOUGHT YOU COULD LOCK ME OUT, DIDN'T YOU?
JIM DAVIS 4-4
© 2003 PAWS, INC. All Rights Reserved.
I HAD TO THROW THE BIRDBATH THROUGH THE PICTURE WINDOW, AND THEN PULL UP THE MAILBOX TO LEAN AGAINST THE...
THAT FEELING IS FADING

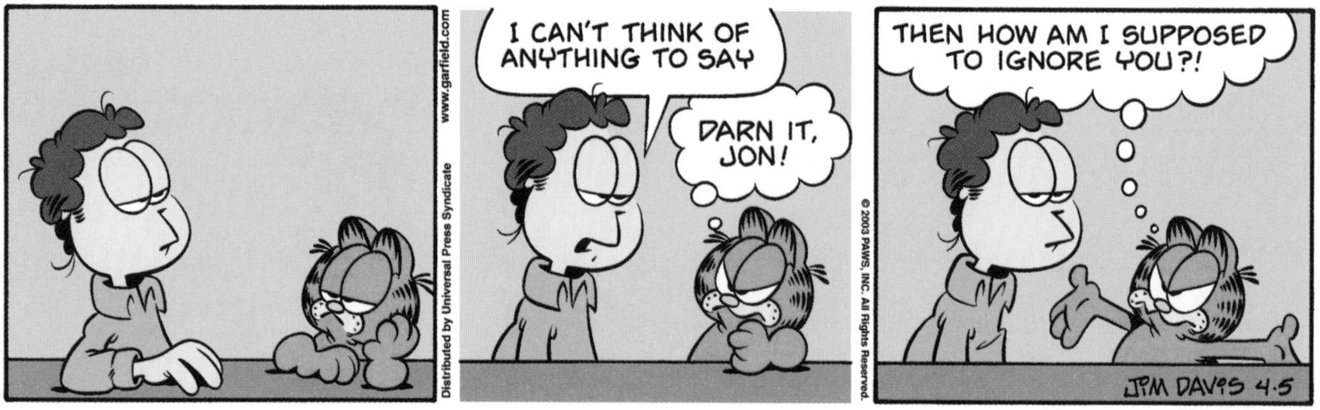
Distributed by Universal Press Syndicate www.garfield.com
I CAN'T THINK OF ANYTHING TO SAY
DARN IT, JON!
© 2003 PAWS, INC. All Rights Reserved.
THEN HOW AM I SUPPOSED TO IGNORE YOU?!
JIM DAVIS 4-5

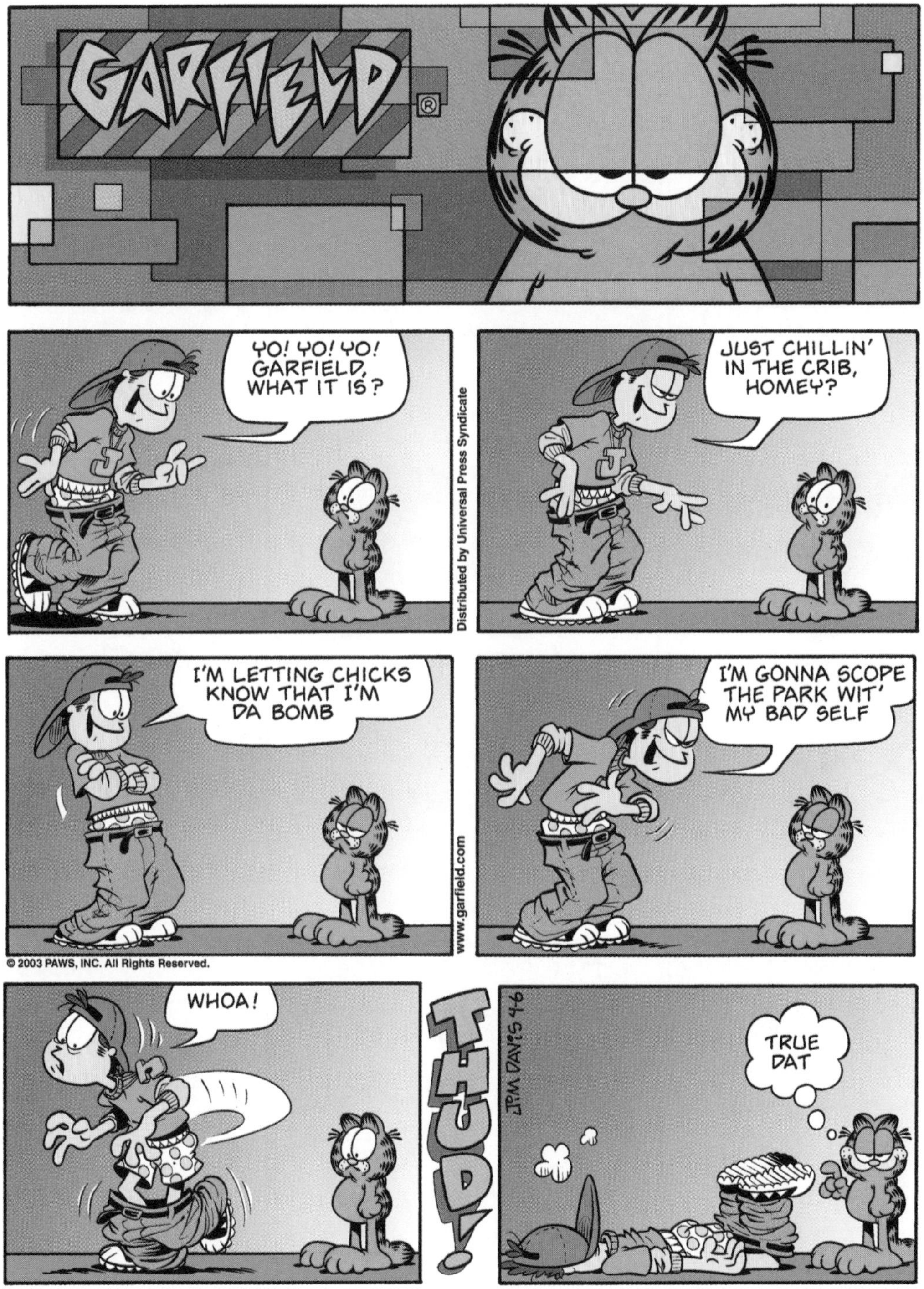
GARFIELD
YO! YO! YO! GARFIELD, WHAT IT IS?
JUST CHILLIN' IN THE CRIB, HOMEY?
Distributed by Universal Press Syndicate
I'M LETTING CHICKS KNOW THAT I'M DA BOMB
I'M GONNA SCOPE THE PARK WIT' MY BAD SELF
www.garfield.com
© 2003 PAWS, INC. All Rights Reserved.
WHOA!
THUD!
JIM DAVIS 4-6
TRUE DAT

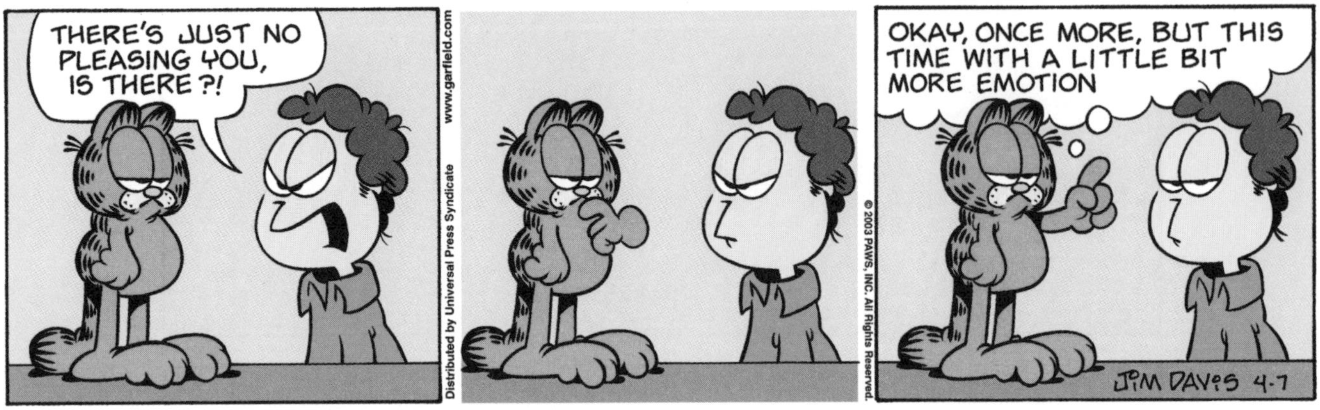
THERE'S JUST NO PLEASING YOU, IS THERE?!
Distributed by Universal Press Syndicate www.garfield.com
© 2003 PAWS, INC. All Rights Reserved.
OKAY, ONCE MORE, BUT THIS TIME WITH A LITTLE BIT MORE EMOTION
JIM DAVIS 4-7

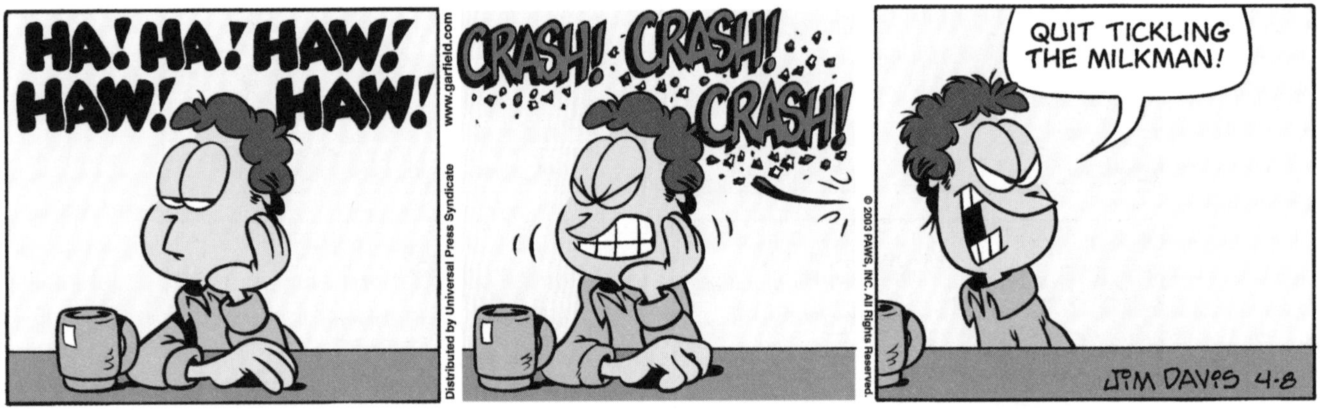
HA! HA! HAW! HAW! HAW!
Distributed by Universal Press Syndicate www.garfield.com
CRASH! CRASH! CRASH!
© 2003 PAWS, INC. All Rights Reserved.
QUIT TICKLING THE MILKMAN!
JIM DAVIS 4-8

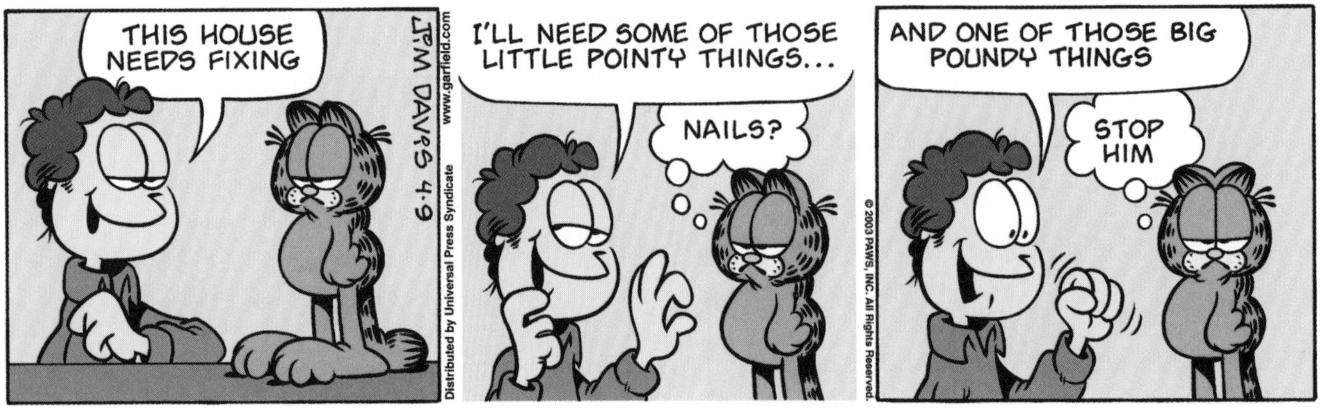
THIS HOUSE NEEDS FIXING
JIM DAVIS 4-9
Distributed by Universal Press Syndicate www.garfield.com
I'LL NEED SOME OF THOSE LITTLE POINTY THINGS...
NAILS?
© 2003 PAWS, INC. All Rights Reserved.
AND ONE OF THOSE BIG POUNDY THINGS
STOP HIM

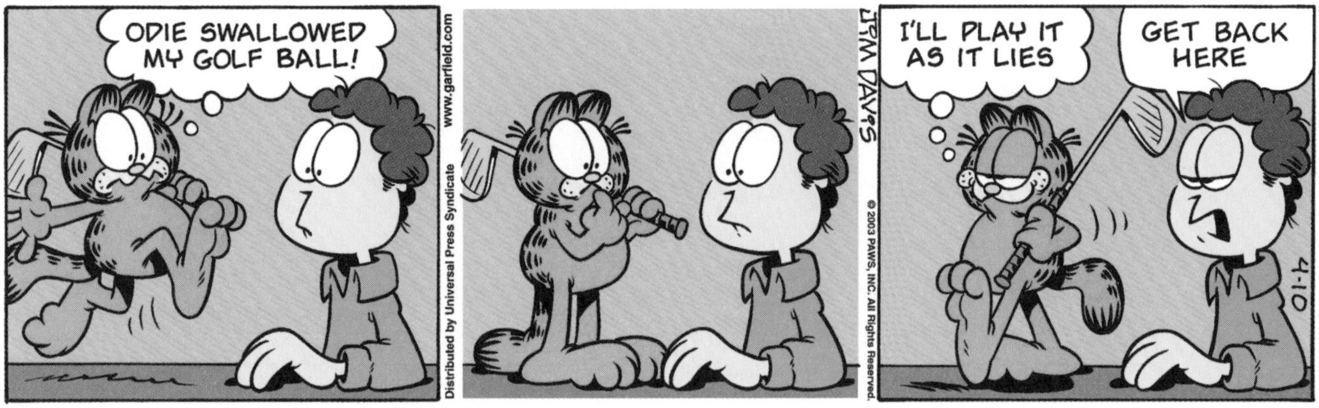
ODIE SWALLOWED MY GOLF BALL!
Distributed by Universal Press Syndicate www.garfield.com
JIM DAVIS
© 2003 PAWS, INC. All Rights Reserved.
I'LL PLAY IT AS IT LIES
GET BACK HERE
4-10

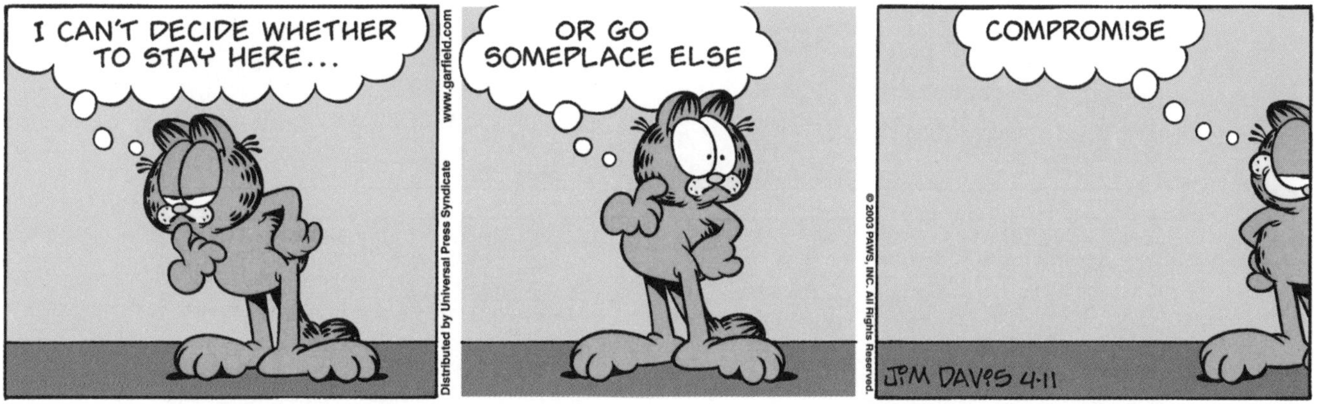
I CAN'T DECIDE WHETHER TO STAY HERE...
Distributed by Universal Press Syndicate www.garfield.com
OR GO SOMEPLACE ELSE
© 2003 PAWS, INC. All Rights Reserved.
COMPROMISE
JIM DAVIS 4-11

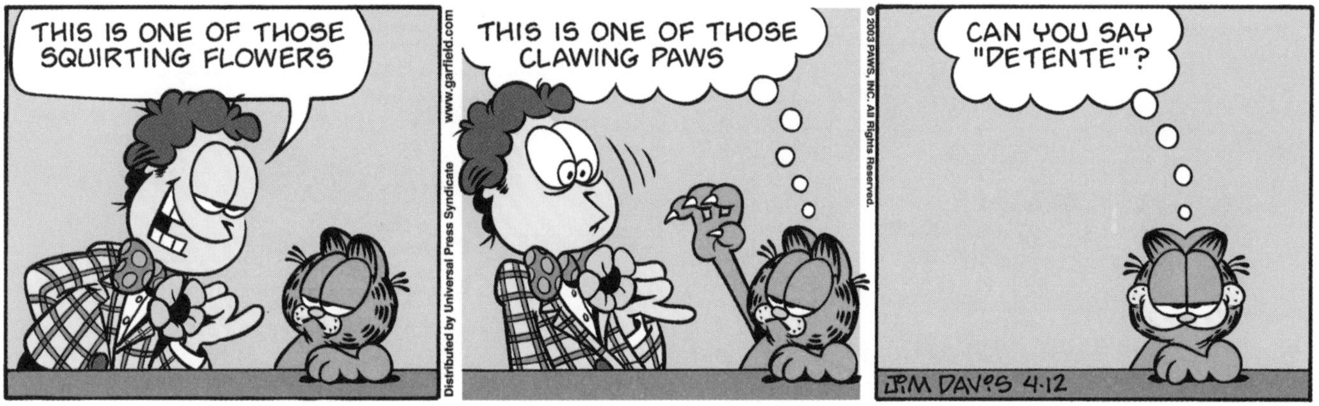
THIS IS ONE OF THOSE SQUIRTING FLOWERS
Distributed by Universal Press Syndicate www.garfield.com
THIS IS ONE OF THOSE CLAWING PAWS
© 2003 PAWS, INC. All Rights Reserved.
CAN YOU SAY "DETENTE"?
JIM DAVIS 4-12

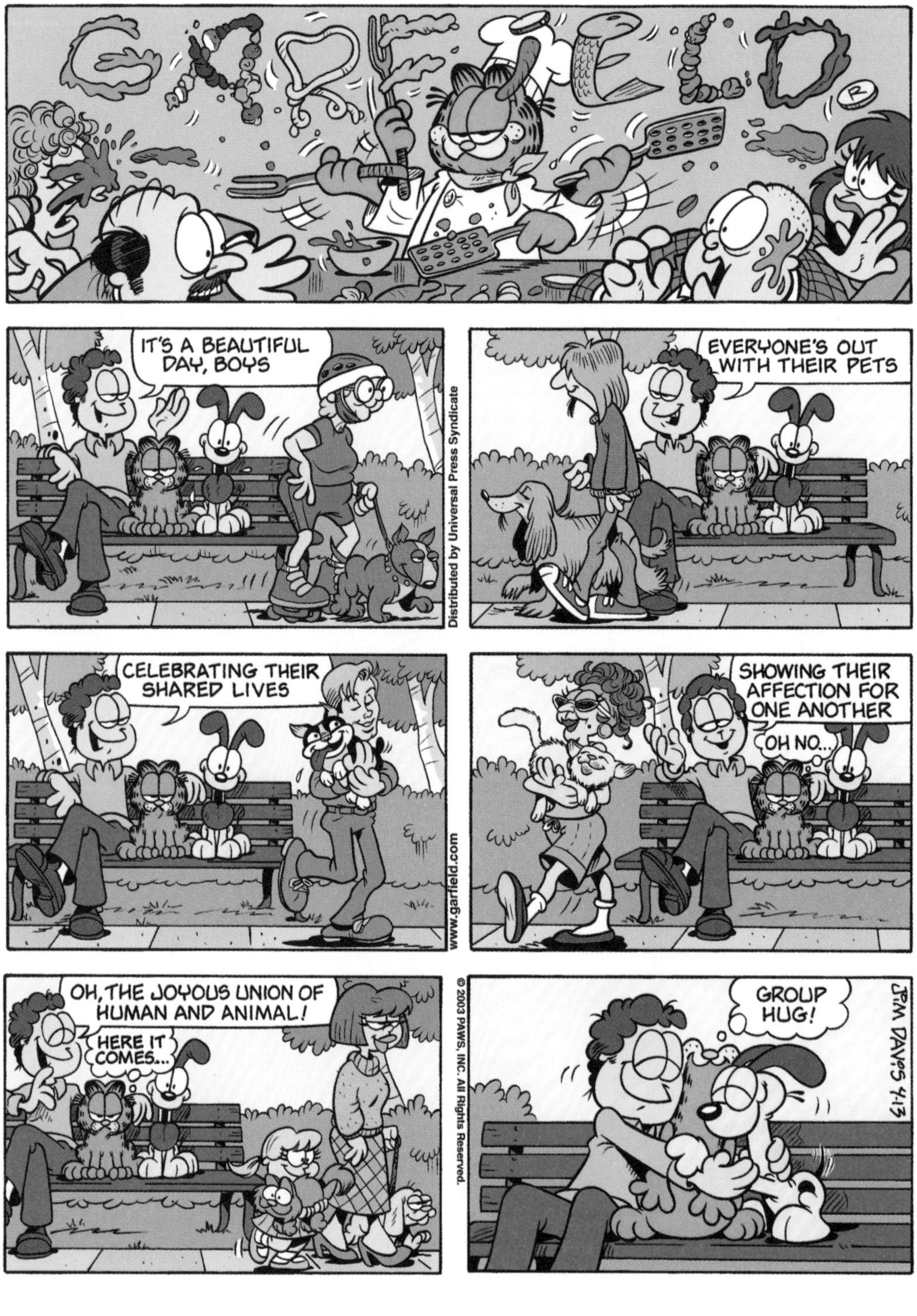
GARFIELD®
IT'S A BEAUTIFUL DAY, BOYS
EVERYONE'S OUT WITH THEIR PETS
Distributed by Universal Press Syndicate
CELEBRATING THEIR SHARED LIVES
SHOWING THEIR AFFECTION FOR ONE ANOTHER
OH NO...
www.garfield.com
OH, THE JOYOUS UNION OF HUMAN AND ANIMAL!
HERE IT COMES...
© 2003 PAWS, INC. All Rights Reserved.
GROUP HUG!
JPM DAVIS 4-13

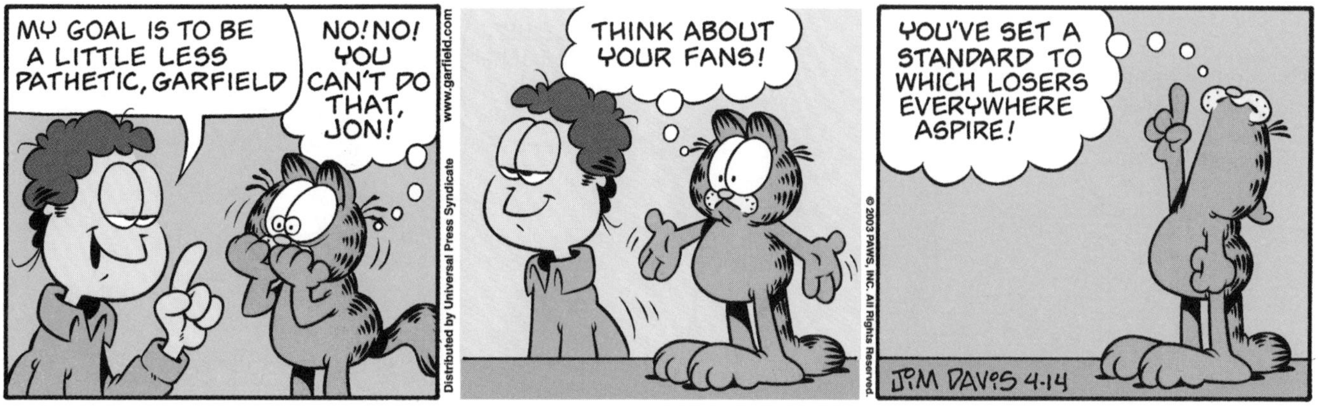
MY GOAL IS TO BE A LITTLE LESS PATHETIC, GARFIELD
NO! NO! YOU CAN'T DO THAT, JON!
www.garfield.com
Distributed by Universal Press Syndicate
THINK ABOUT YOUR FANS!
© 2003 PAWS, INC. All Rights Reserved.
YOU'VE SET A STANDARD TO WHICH LOSERS EVERYWHERE ASPIRE!
JIM DAVIS 4-14

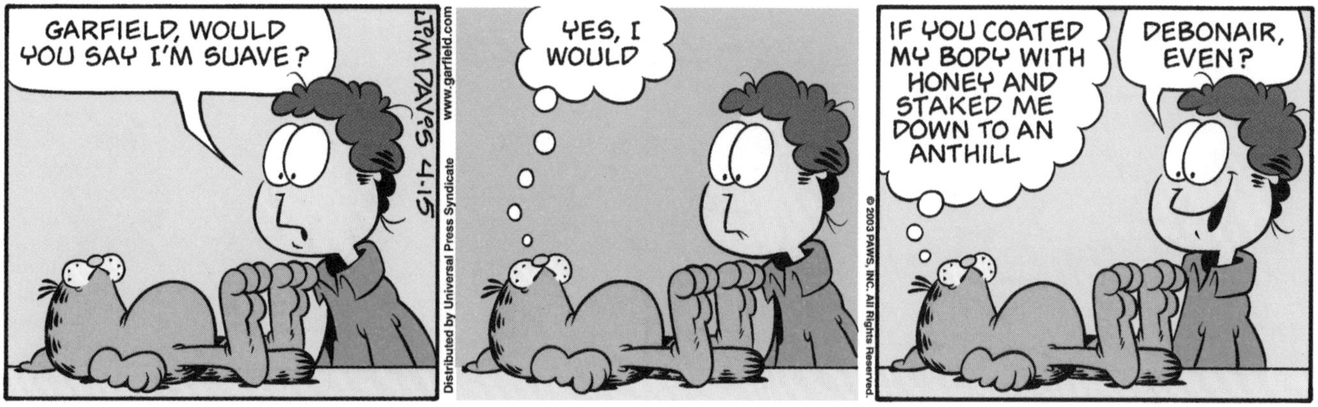
GARFIELD, WOULD YOU SAY I'M SUAVE?
JIM DAVIS 4-15
www.garfield.com
Distributed by Universal Press Syndicate
YES, I WOULD
© 2003 PAWS, INC. All Rights Reserved.
IF YOU COATED MY BODY WITH HONEY AND STAKED ME DOWN TO AN ANTHILL
DEBONAIR, EVEN?

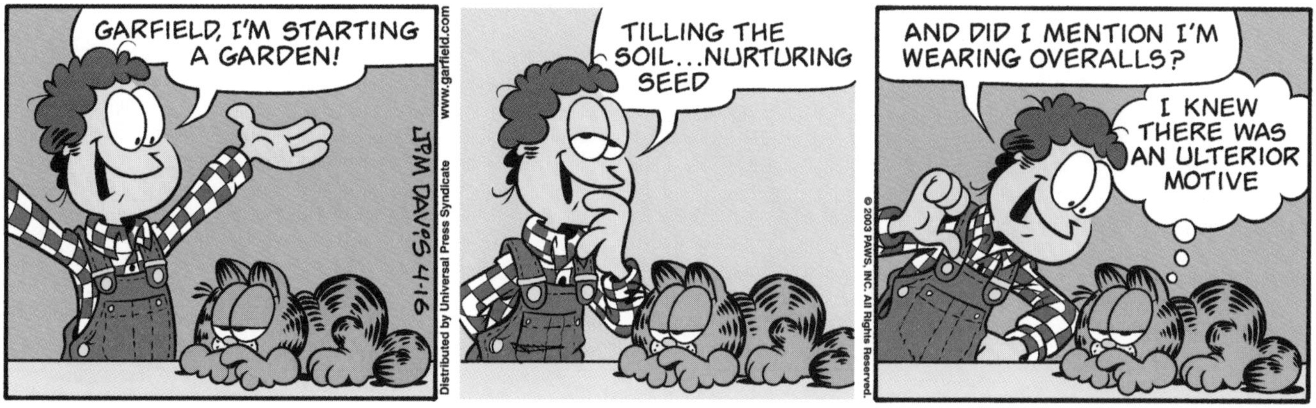
GARFIELD, I'M STARTING A GARDEN!
JIM DAVIS 4-16
www.garfield.com
Distributed by Universal Press Syndicate
TILLING THE SOIL...NURTURING SEED
© 2003 PAWS, INC. All Rights Reserved.
AND DID I MENTION I'M WEARING OVERALLS?
I KNEW THERE WAS AN ULTERIOR MOTIVE

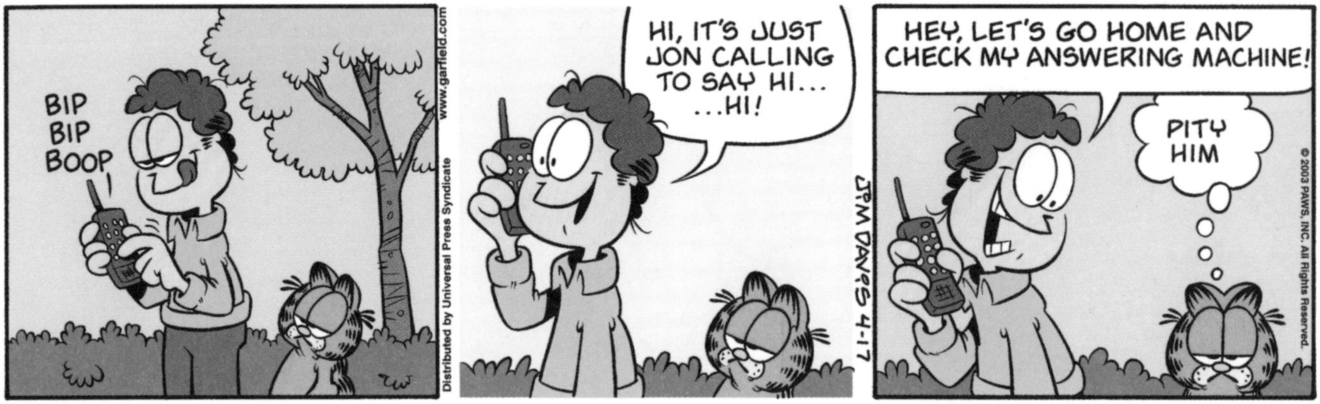
BIP BIP BOOP
www.garfield.com
Distributed by Universal Press Syndicate
HI, IT'S JUST JON CALLING TO SAY HI... ...HI!
JIM DAVIS 4-17
HEY, LET'S GO HOME AND CHECK MY ANSWERING MACHINE!
PITY HIM
© 2003 PAWS, INC. All Rights Reserved.

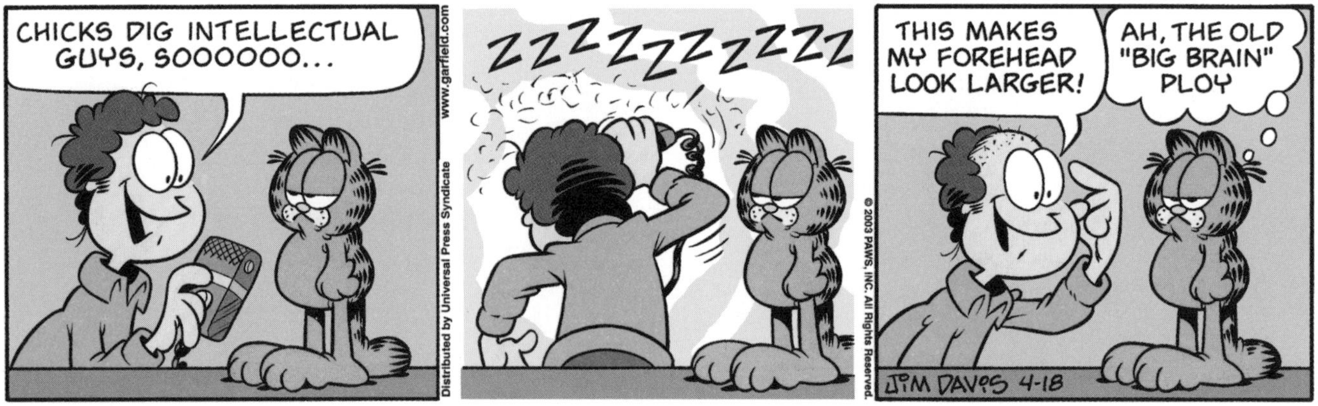
CHICKS DIG INTELLECTUAL GUYS, SOOOOOO...
www.garfield.com
Distributed by Universal Press Syndicate
ZZZZZZZZZZZ
© 2003 PAWS, INC. All Rights Reserved.
THIS MAKES MY FOREHEAD LOOK LARGER!
AH, THE OLD "BIG BRAIN" PLOY
JIM DAVIS 4-18

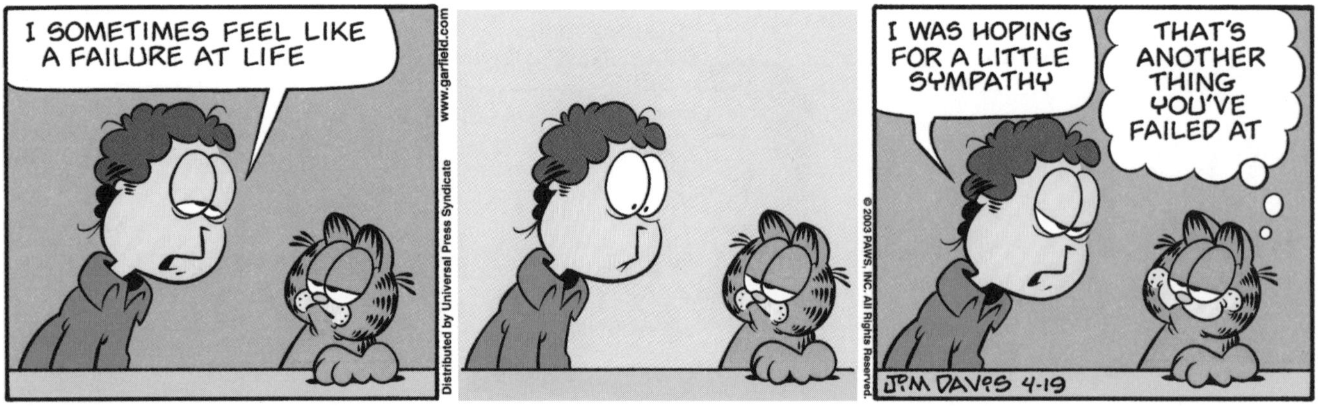
I SOMETIMES FEEL LIKE A FAILURE AT LIFE
www.garfield.com
Distributed by Universal Press Syndicate
© 2003 PAWS, INC. All Rights Reserved.
I WAS HOPING FOR A LITTLE SYMPATHY
THAT'S ANOTHER THING YOU'VE FAILED AT
JIM DAVIS 4-19

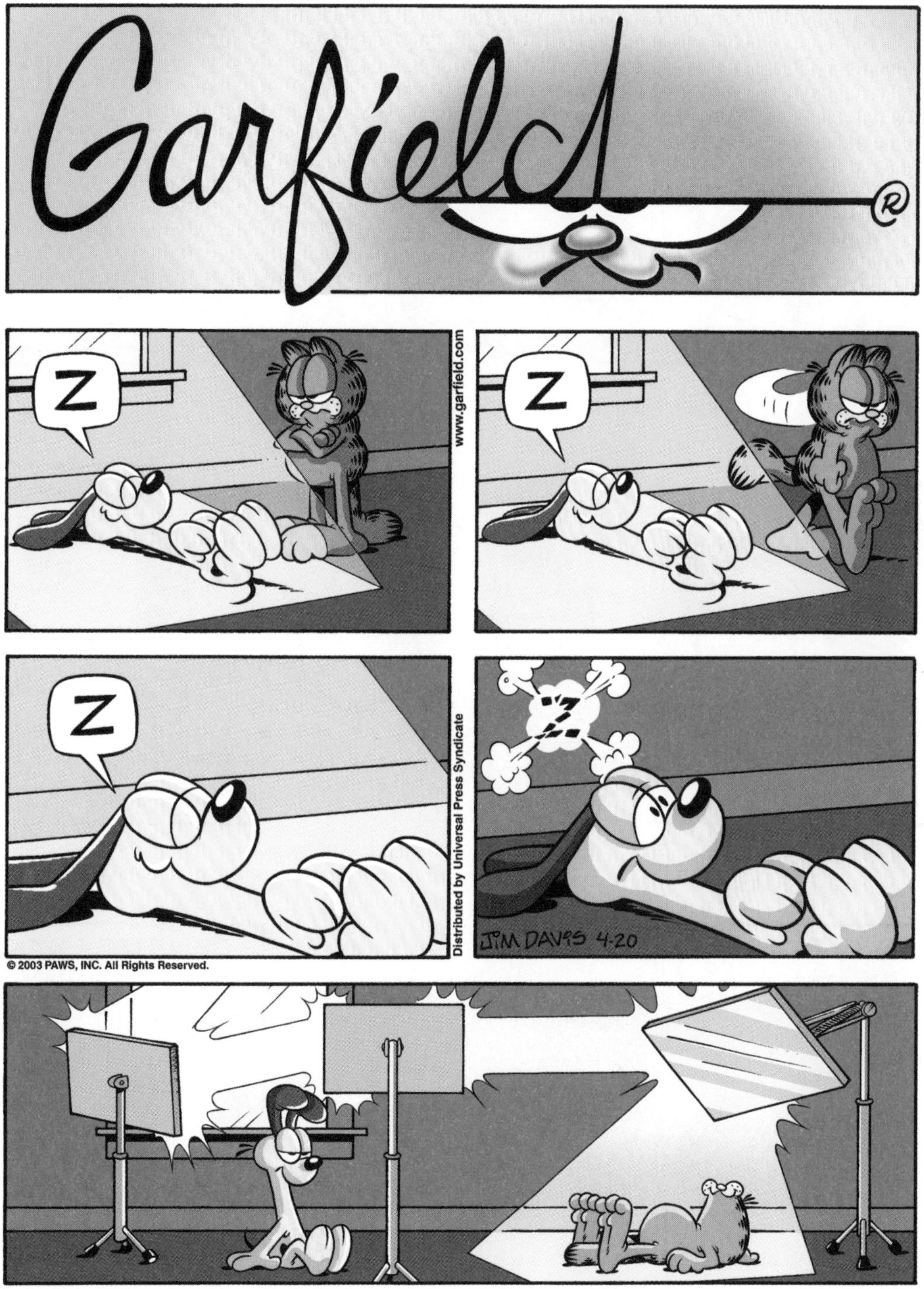
Garfield®
Z
Z
Z
Z
www.garfield.com
Distributed by Universal Press Syndicate
JIM DAVIS 4-20
© 2003 PAWS, INC. All Rights Reserved.

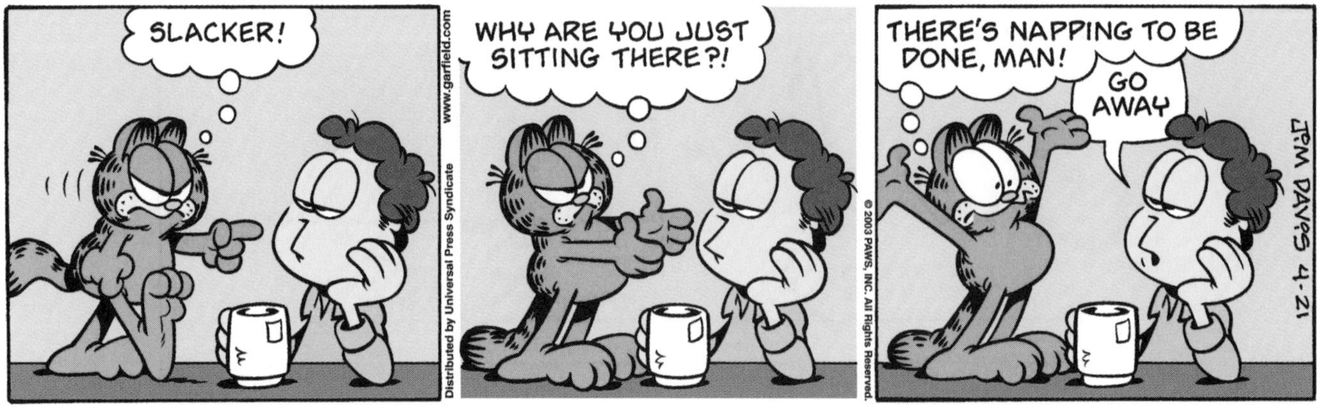
SLACKER!
www.garfield.com
Distributed by Universal Press Syndicate
WHY ARE YOU JUST SITTING THERE?!
© 2003 PAWS, INC. All Rights Reserved.
THERE'S NAPPING TO BE DONE, MAN!
GO AWAY
JIM DAVIS 4-21

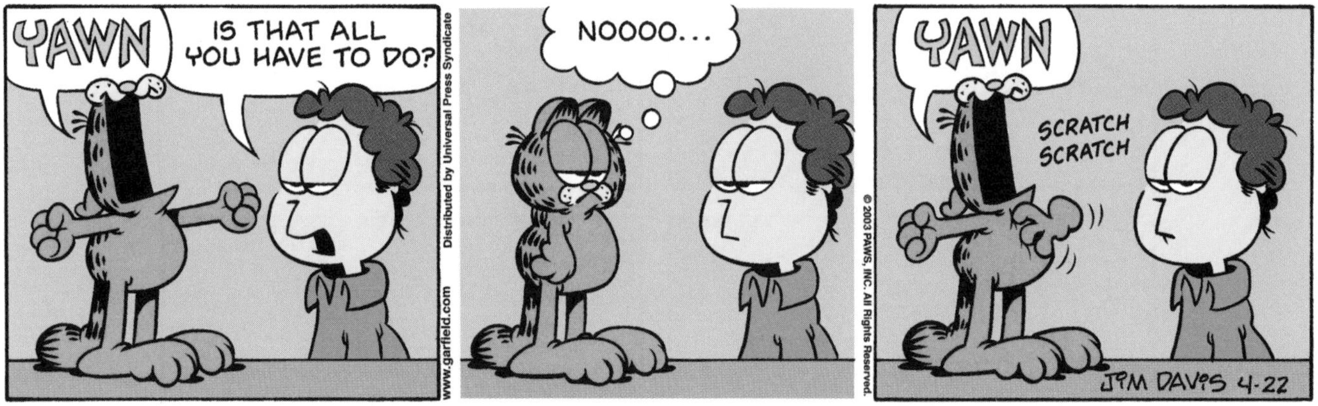
YAWN
IS THAT ALL YOU HAVE TO DO?
Distributed by Universal Press Syndicate
www.garfield.com
NOOOO...
© 2003 PAWS, INC. All Rights Reserved.
YAWN
SCRATCH SCRATCH
JIM DAVIS 4-22

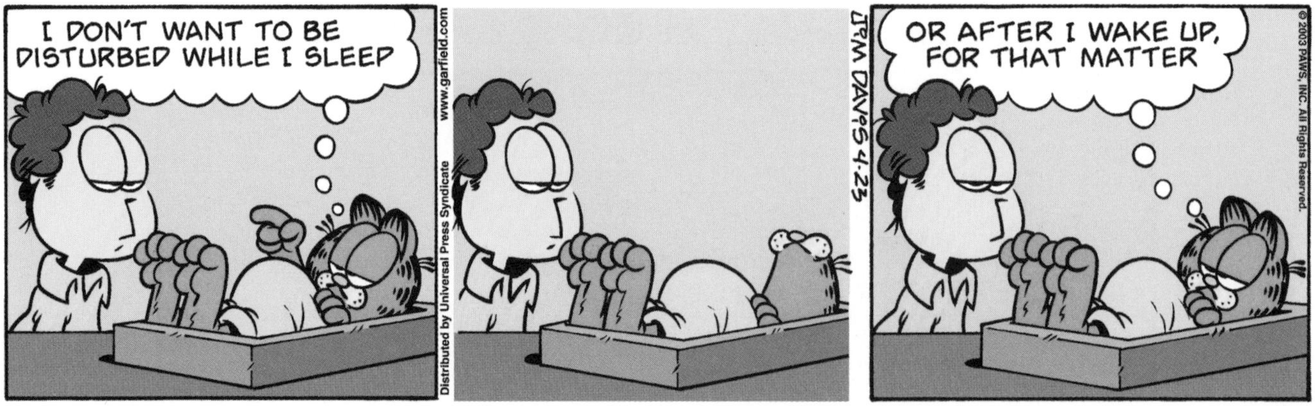
I DON'T WANT TO BE DISTURBED WHILE I SLEEP
www.garfield.com
Distributed by Universal Press Syndicate
JIM DAVIS 4-23
OR AFTER I WAKE UP, FOR THAT MATTER
© 2003 PAWS, INC. All Rights Reserved.

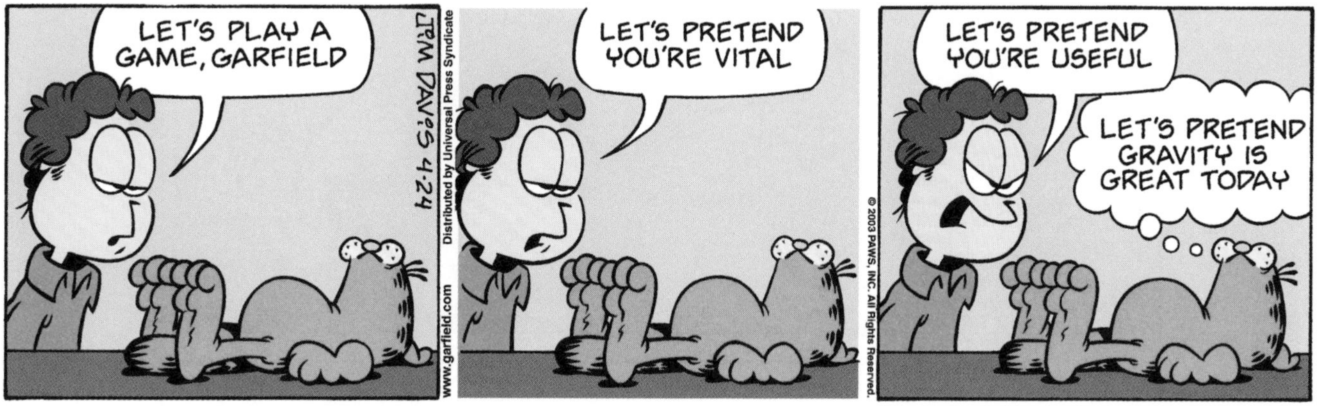
LET'S PLAY A GAME, GARFIELD
Distributed by Universal Press Syndicate
www.garfield.com
LET'S PRETEND YOU'RE VITAL
© 2003 PAWS, INC. All Rights Reserved.
LET'S PRETEND YOU'RE USEFUL
LET'S PRETEND GRAVITY IS GREAT TODAY

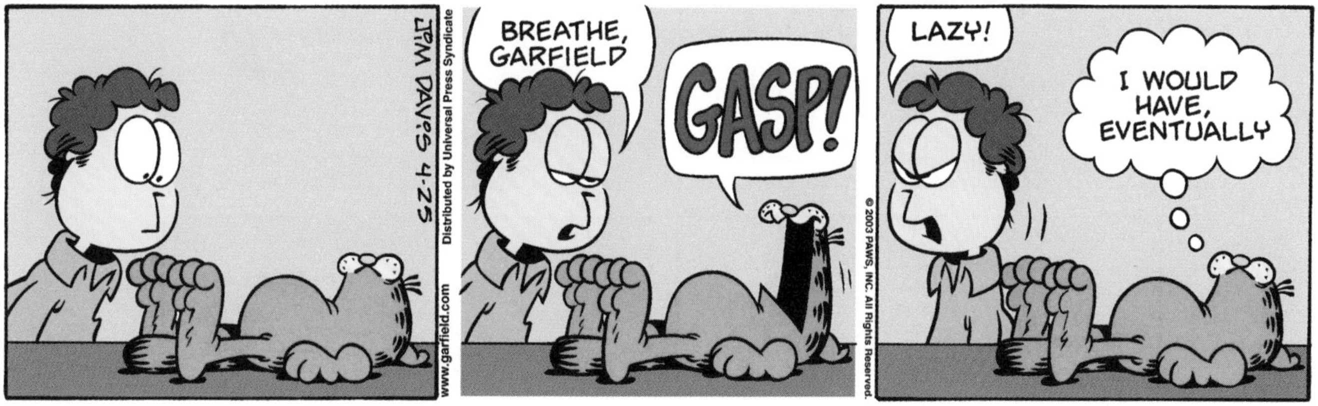
Distributed by Universal Press Syndicate
www.garfield.com
BREATHE, GARFIELD
GASP!
© 2003 PAWS, INC. All Rights Reserved.
LAZY!
I WOULD HAVE, EVENTUALLY

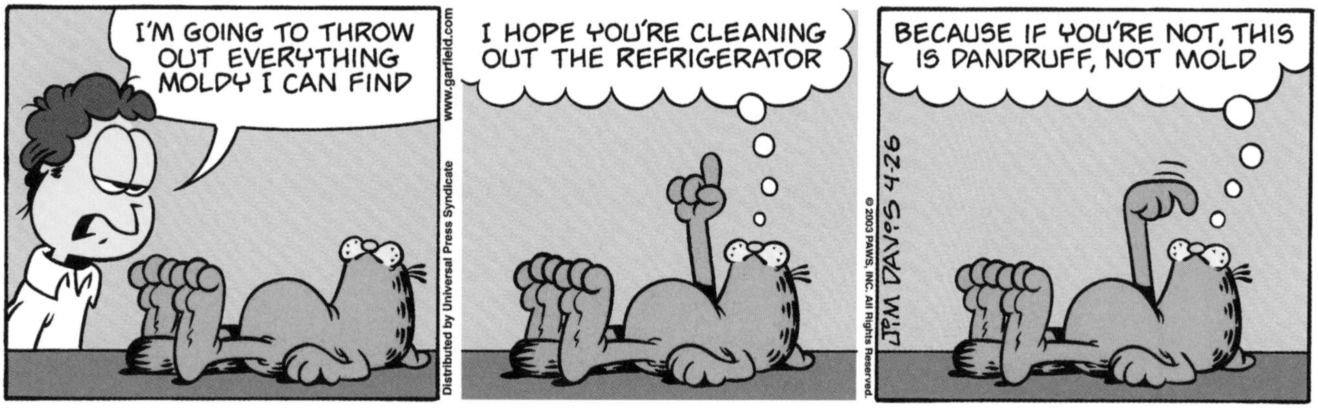
I'M GOING TO THROW OUT EVERYTHING MOLDY I CAN FIND
www.garfield.com
Distributed by Universal Press Syndicate
I HOPE YOU'RE CLEANING OUT THE REFRIGERATOR
© 2003 PAWS, INC. All Rights Reserved.
BECAUSE IF YOU'RE NOT, THIS IS DANDRUFF, NOT MOLD

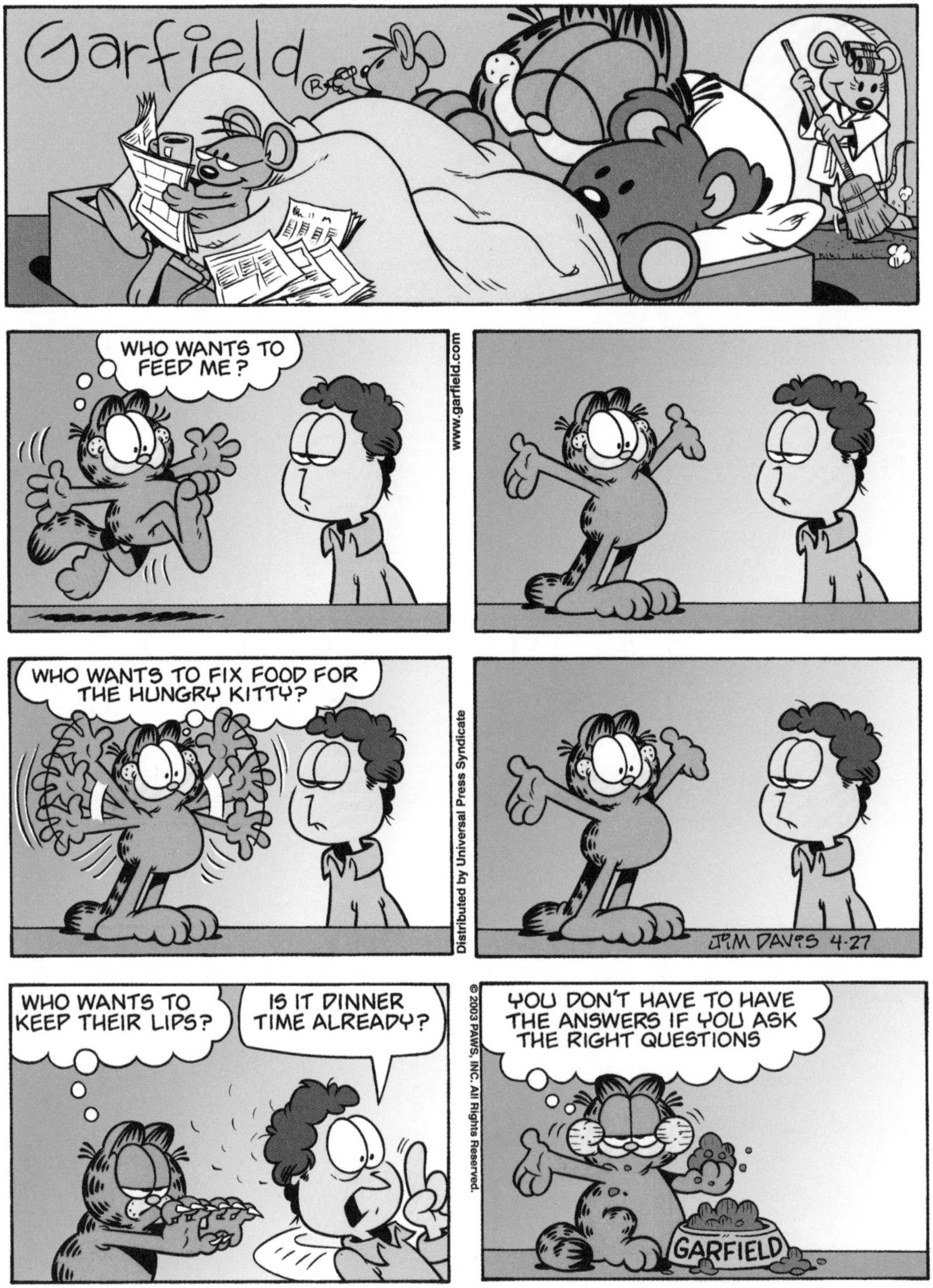
Garfield
WHO WANTS TO FEED ME?
WHO WANTS TO FIX FOOD FOR THE HUNGRY KITTY?
JIM DAVIS 4-27
WHO WANTS TO KEEP THEIR LIPS?
IS IT DINNER TIME ALREADY?
YOU DON'T HAVE TO HAVE THE ANSWERS IF YOU ASK THE RIGHT QUESTIONS
GARFIELD
www.garfield.com
Distributed by Universal Press Syndicate
© 2003 PAWS, INC. All Rights Reserved.

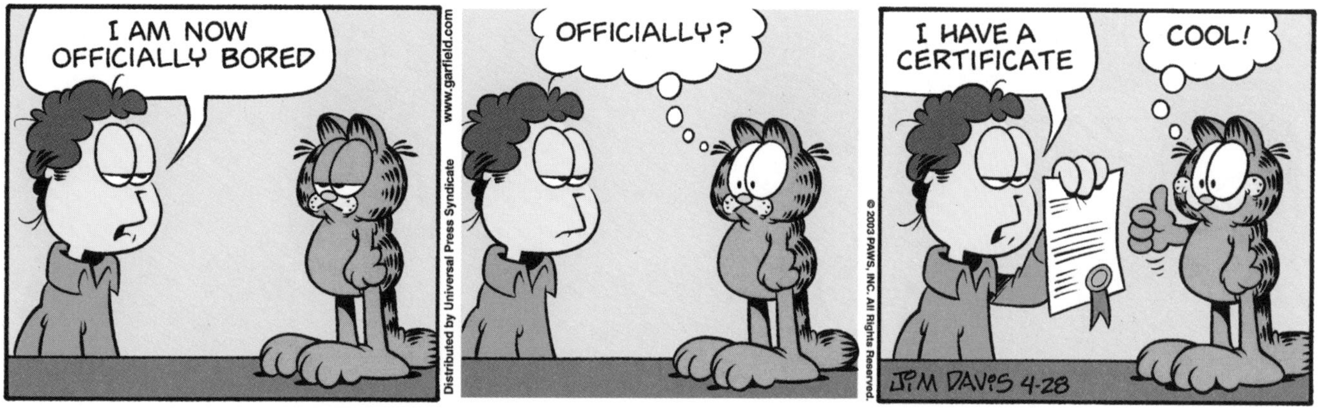
I AM NOW OFFICIALLY BORED
Distributed by Universal Press Syndicate www.garfield.com
OFFICIALLY?
© 2003 PAWS, INC. All Rights Reserved.
I HAVE A CERTIFICATE
COOL!
JIM DAVIS 4-28

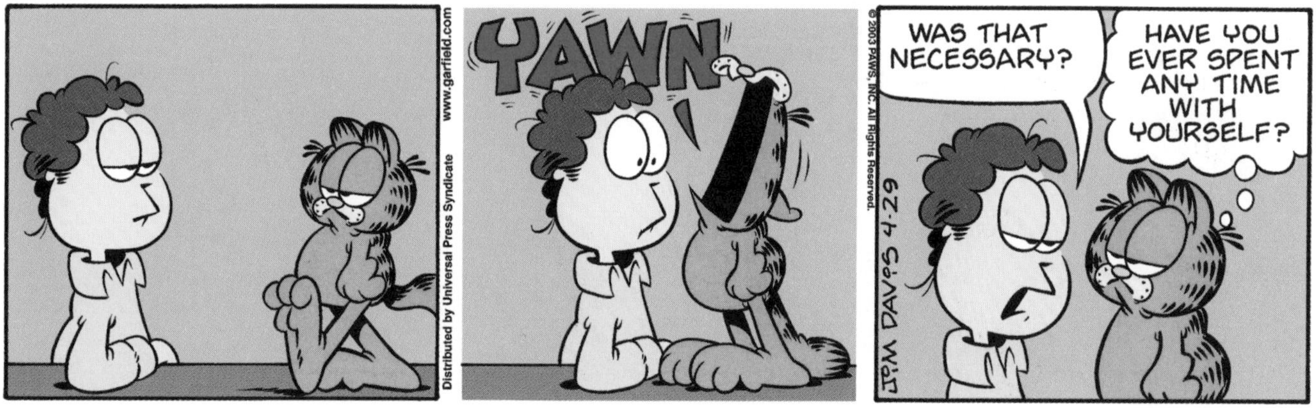
Distributed by Universal Press Syndicate www.garfield.com
YAWN
© 2003 PAWS, INC. All Rights Reserved.
JIM DAVIS 4-29
WAS THAT NECESSARY?
HAVE YOU EVER SPENT ANY TIME WITH YOURSELF?

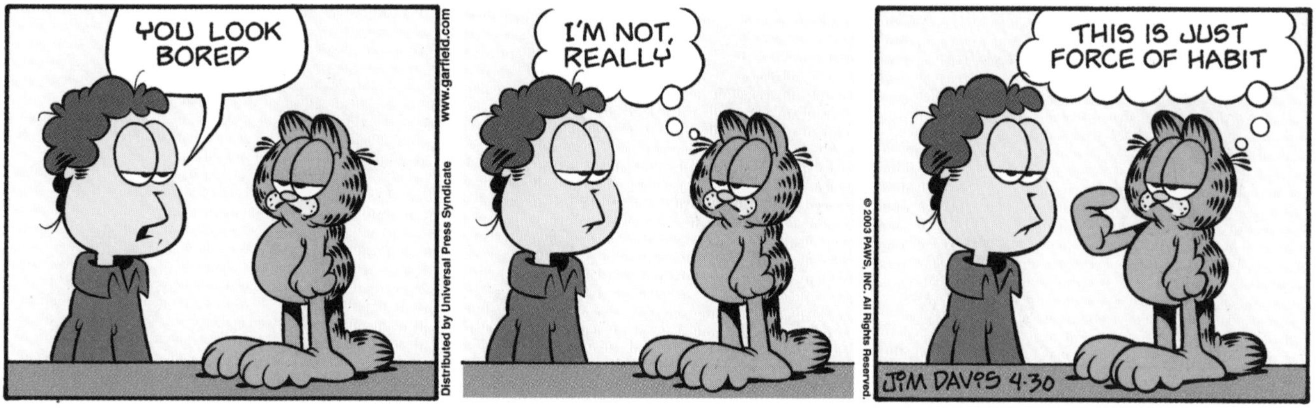
YOU LOOK BORED
Distributed by Universal Press Syndicate www.garfield.com
I'M NOT, REALLY
© 2003 PAWS, INC. All Rights Reserved.
THIS IS JUST FORCE OF HABIT
JIM DAVIS 4-30

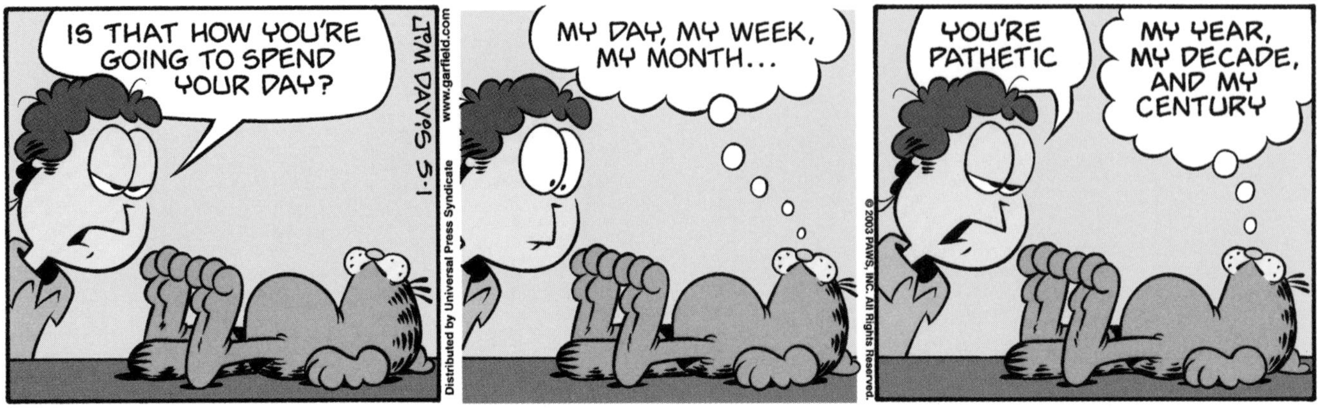
IS THAT HOW YOU'RE GOING TO SPEND YOUR DAY?
JIM DAVIS 5-1
MY DAY, MY WEEK, MY MONTH...
YOU'RE PATHETIC
MY YEAR, MY DECADE, AND MY CENTURY
www.garfield.com Distributed by Universal Press Syndicate
© 2003 PAWS, INC. All Rights Reserved.

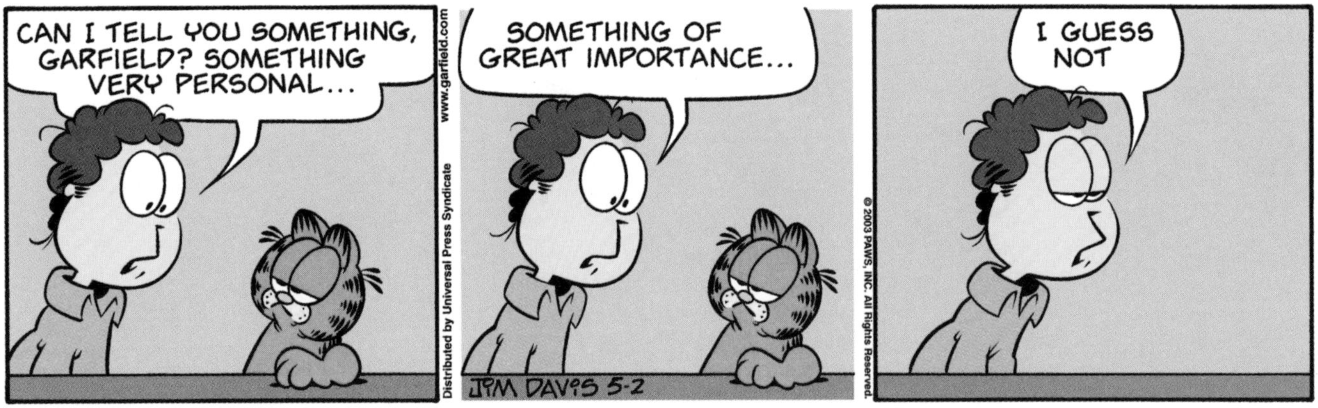
CAN I TELL YOU SOMETHING, GARFIELD? SOMETHING VERY PERSONAL...
SOMETHING OF GREAT IMPORTANCE...
I GUESS NOT
JIM DAVIS 5-2
www.garfield.com Distributed by Universal Press Syndicate
© 2003 PAWS, INC. All Rights Reserved.

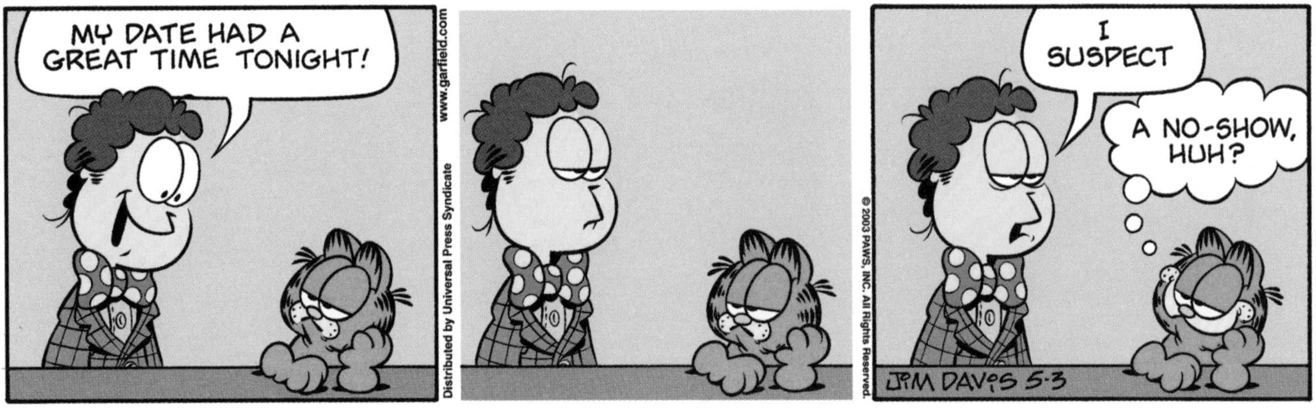
MY DATE HAD A GREAT TIME TONIGHT!
I SUSPECT
A NO-SHOW, HUH?
JIM DAVIS 5-3
www.garfield.com Distributed by Universal Press Syndicate
© 2003 PAWS, INC. All Rights Reserved.

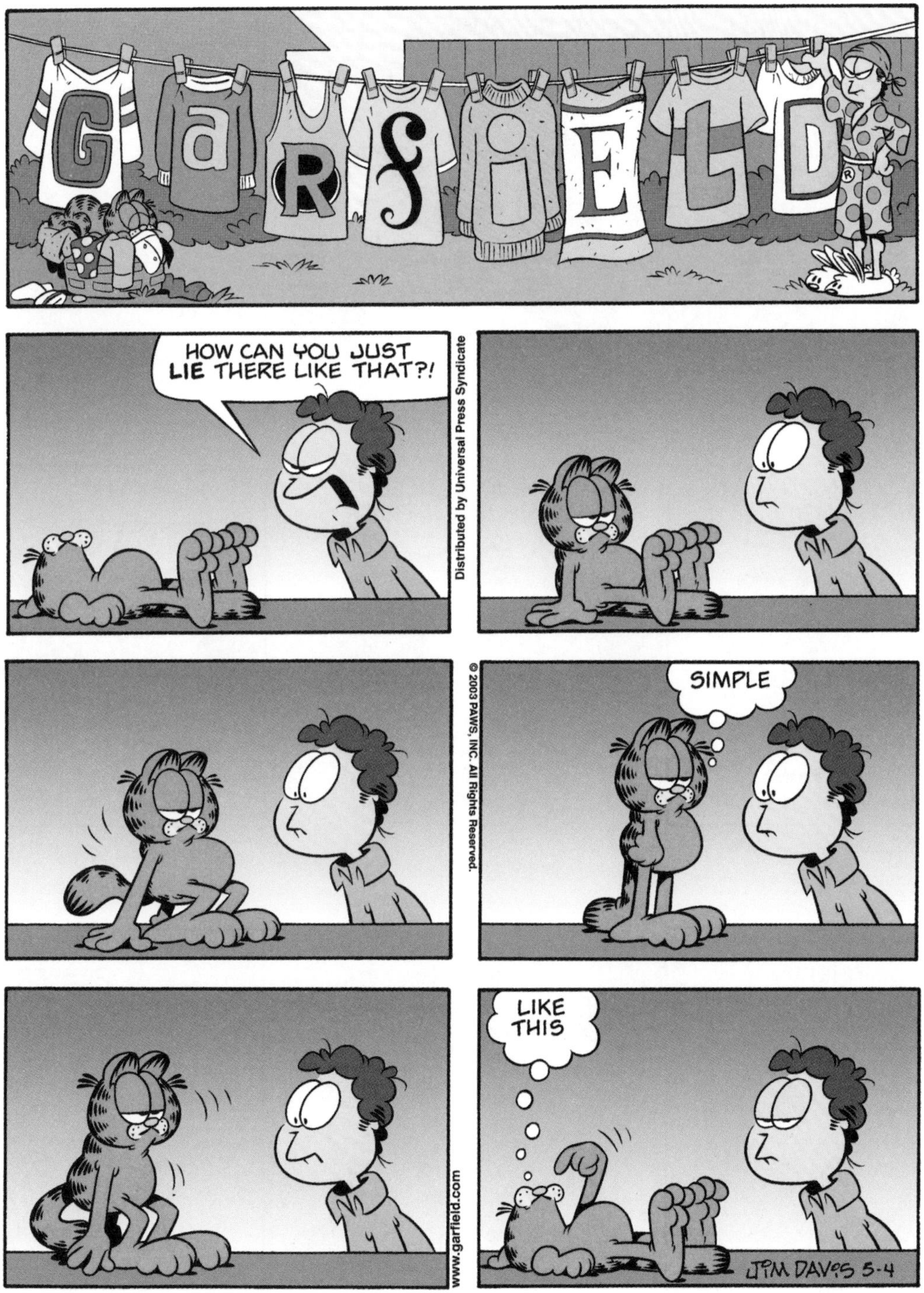
GARFIELD
HOW CAN YOU JUST LIE THERE LIKE THAT?!
SIMPLE
LIKE THIS
JIM DAVIS 5-4
Distributed by Universal Press Syndicate
© 2003 PAWS, INC. All Rights Reserved.
www.garfield.com

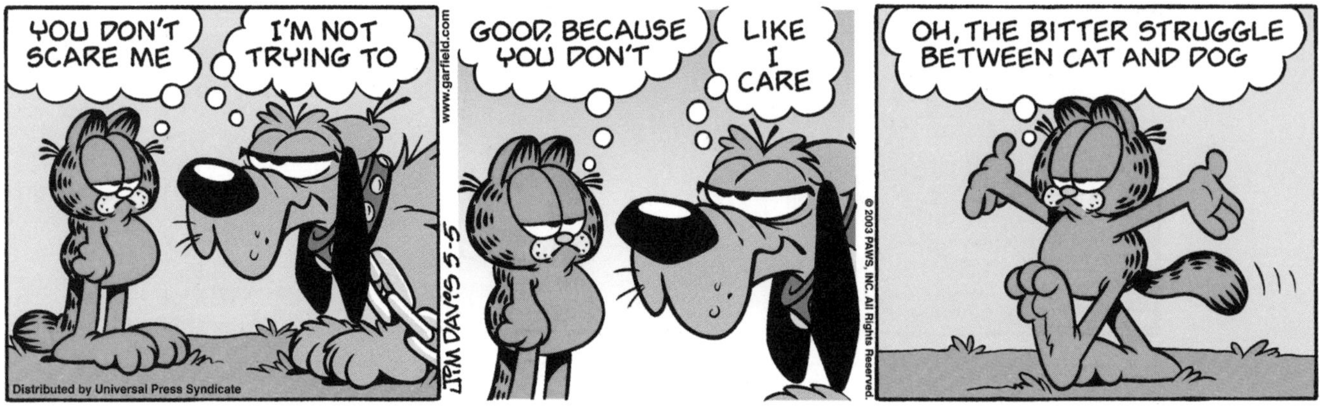
YOU DON'T SCARE ME
I'M NOT TRYING TO
GOOD, BECAUSE YOU DON'T
LIKE I CARE
OH, THE BITTER STRUGGLE BETWEEN CAT AND DOG
Distributed by Universal Press Syndicate
www.garfield.com
JPM DAVIS 5-5
© 2003 PAWS, INC. All Rights Reserved.

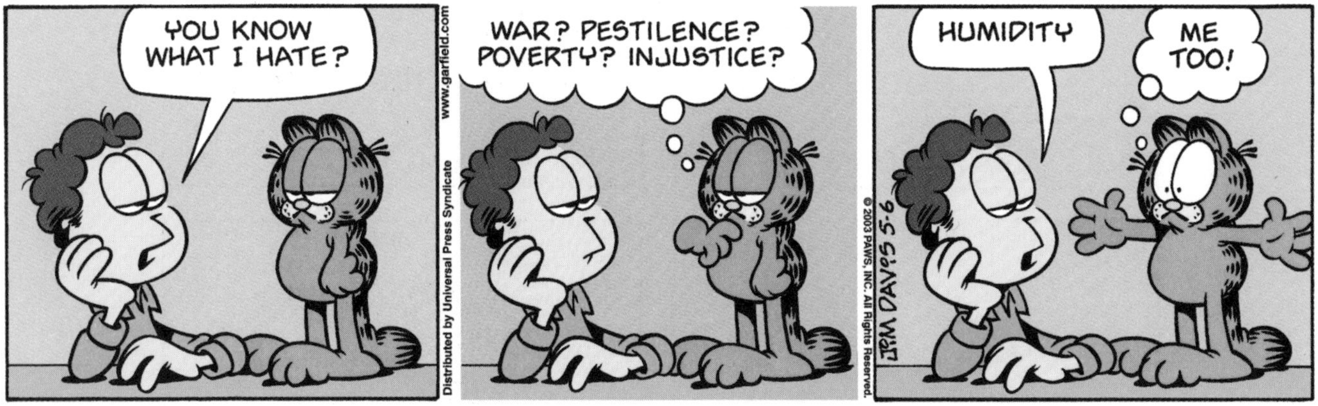
YOU KNOW WHAT I HATE?
WAR? PESTILENCE? POVERTY? INJUSTICE?
HUMIDITY
ME TOO!
www.garfield.com
Distributed by Universal Press Syndicate
JPM DAVIS 5-6
© 2003 PAWS, INC. All Rights Reserved.

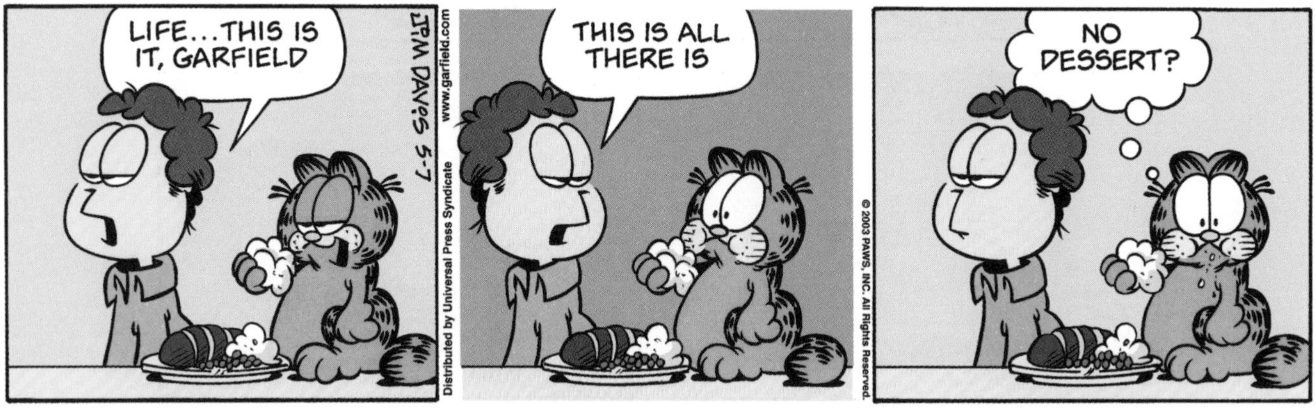
LIFE...THIS IS IT, GARFIELD
THIS IS ALL THERE IS
NO DESSERT?
JPM DAVIS 5-7
www.garfield.com
Distributed by Universal Press Syndicate
© 2003 PAWS, INC. All Rights Reserved.

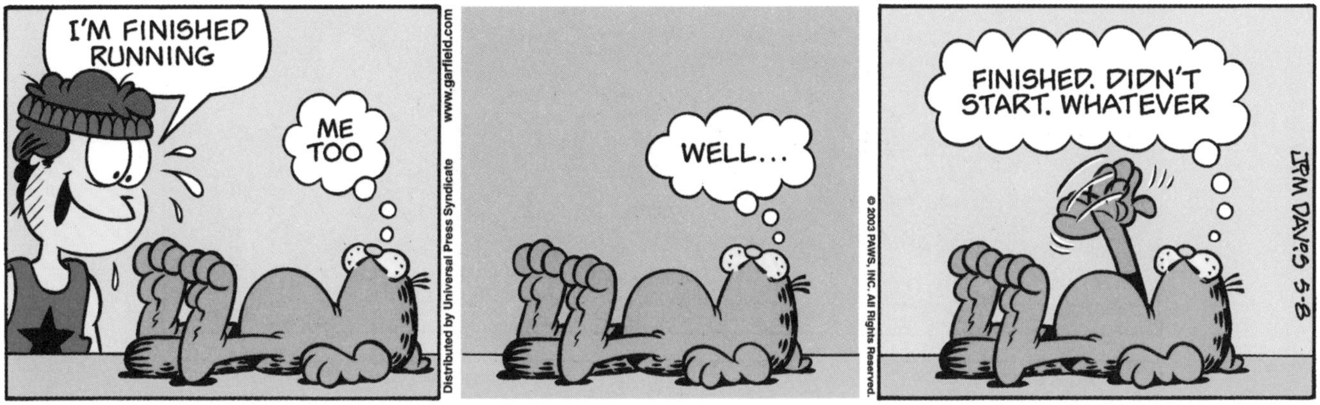
I'M FINISHED RUNNING
ME TOO
WELL...
FINISHED. DIDN'T START. WHATEVER
Distributed by Universal Press Syndicate www.garfield.com
© 2003 PAWS, INC. All Rights Reserved.
JIM DAVIS 5-8

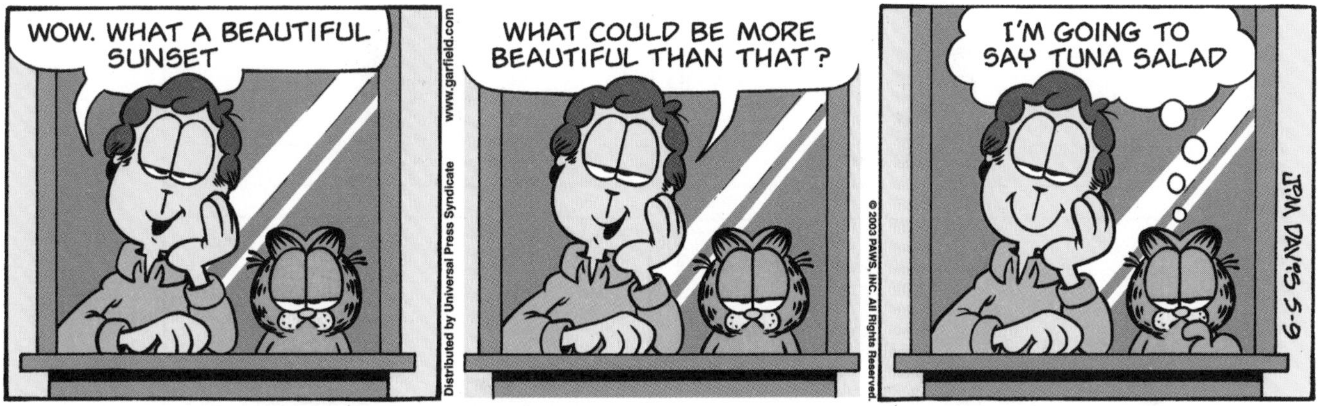
WOW. WHAT A BEAUTIFUL SUNSET
WHAT COULD BE MORE BEAUTIFUL THAN THAT?
I'M GOING TO SAY TUNA SALAD
Distributed by Universal Press Syndicate www.garfield.com
© 2003 PAWS, INC. All Rights Reserved.
JIM DAVIS 5-9

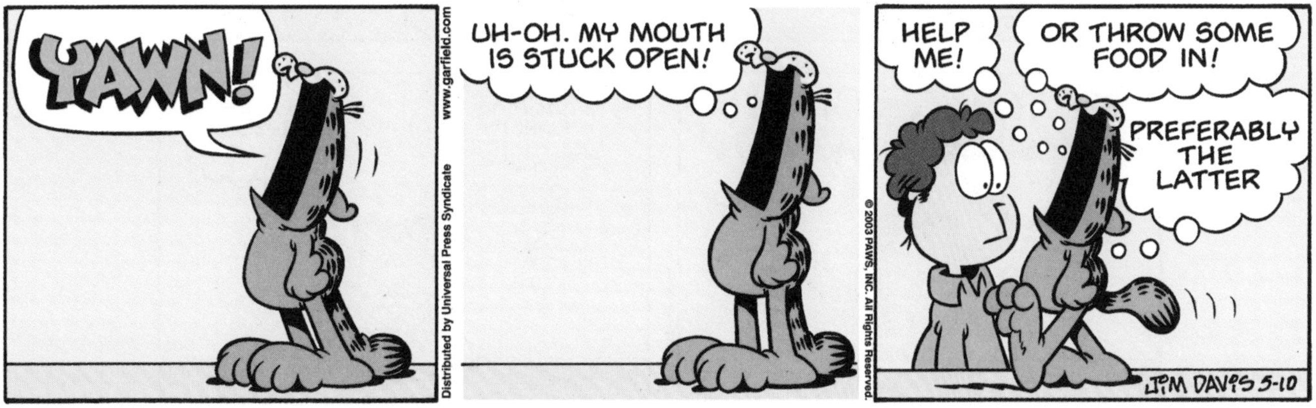
YAWN!
UH-OH. MY MOUTH IS STUCK OPEN!
HELP ME!
OR THROW SOME FOOD IN!
PREFERABLY THE LATTER
Distributed by Universal Press Syndicate www.garfield.com
© 2003 PAWS, INC. All Rights Reserved.
JIM DAVIS 5-10

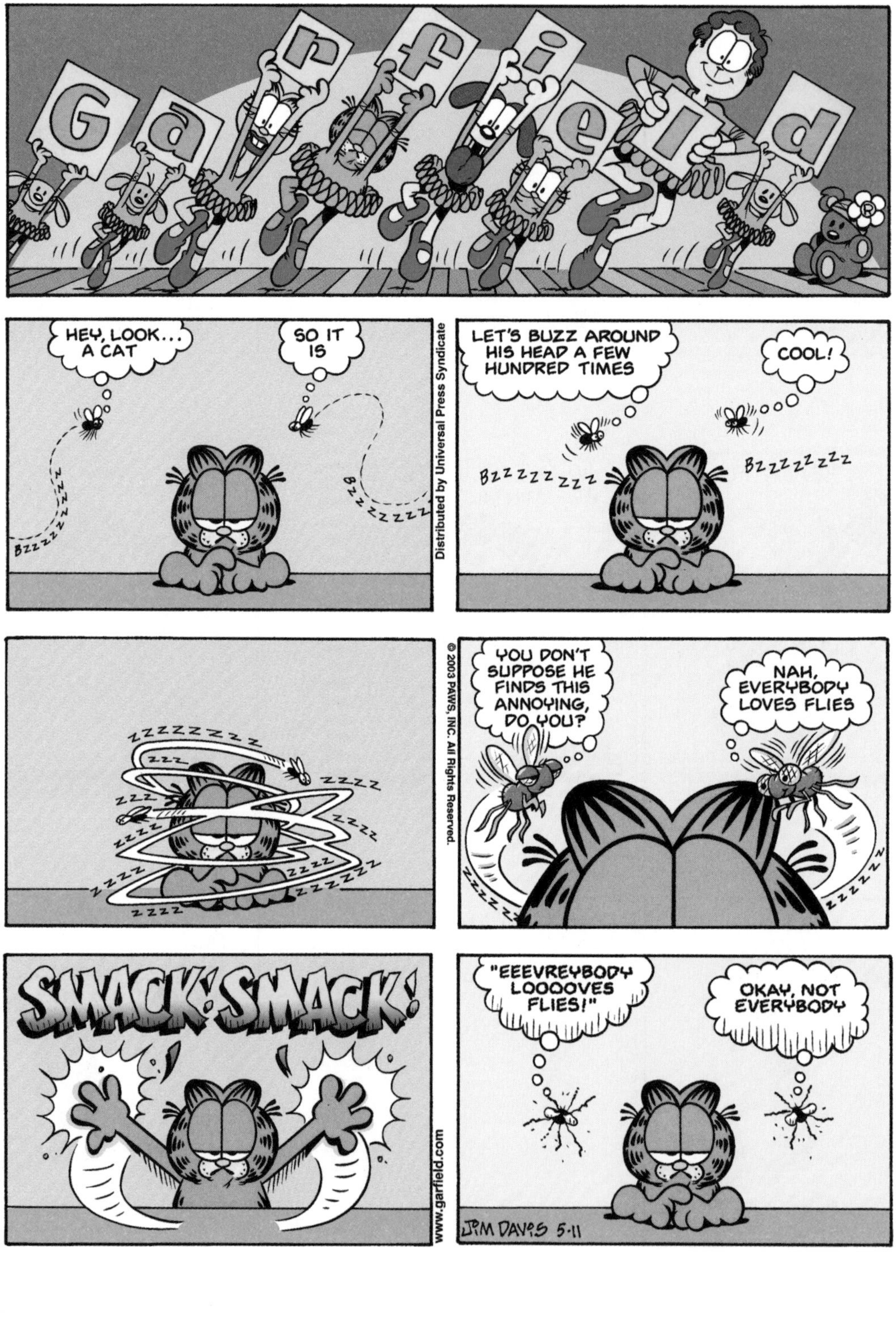
Garfield
HEY, LOOK... A CAT
SO IT IS
Bzzzzzzzz
Bzzzzzzzz
Distributed by Universal Press Syndicate
LET'S BUZZ AROUND HIS HEAD A FEW HUNDRED TIMES
COOL!
Bzzzzzzzzz
Bzzzzzzzz
© 2003 PAWS, INC. All Rights Reserved.
YOU DON'T SUPPOSE HE FINDS THIS ANNOYING, DO YOU?
NAH, EVERYBODY LOVES FLIES
SMACK! SMACK!
www.garfield.com
"EEEVREYBODY LOOOOVES FLIES!"
OKAY, NOT EVERYBODY
JIM DAVIS 5-11

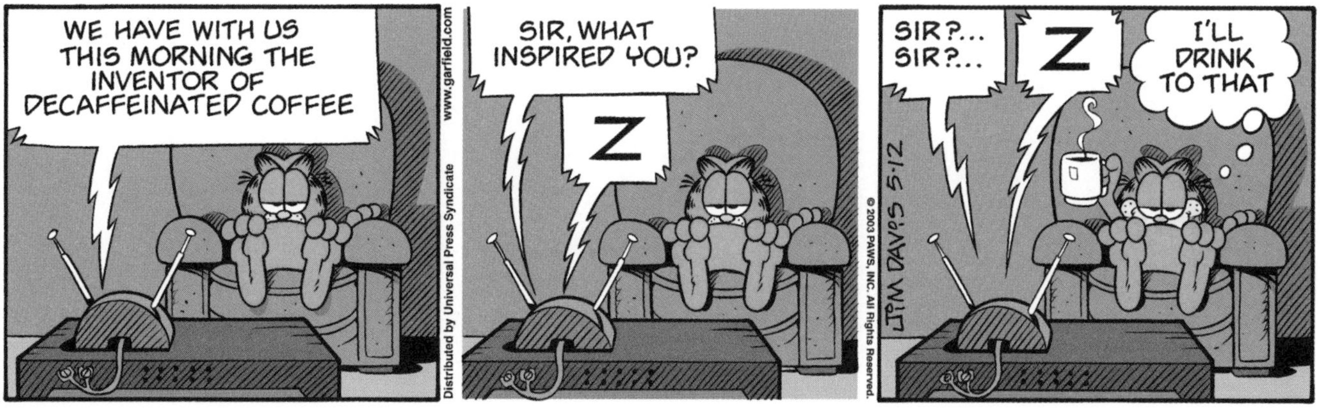
WE HAVE WITH US THIS MORNING THE INVENTOR OF DECAFFEINATED COFFEE
SIR, WHAT INSPIRED YOU?
Z
SIR?... SIR?...
Z
I'LL DRINK TO THAT
JIM DAVIS 5-12
www.garfield.com
Distributed by Universal Press Syndicate
© 2003 PAWS, INC. All Rights Reserved.

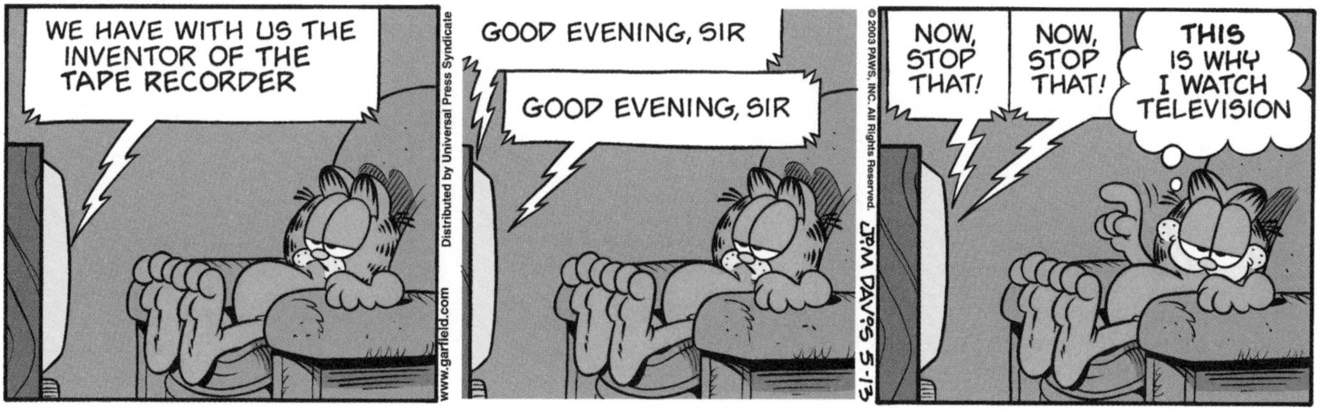
WE HAVE WITH US THE INVENTOR OF THE TAPE RECORDER
GOOD EVENING, SIR
GOOD EVENING, SIR
NOW, STOP THAT!
NOW, STOP THAT!
THIS IS WHY I WATCH TELEVISION
JIM DAVIS 5-13
www.garfield.com
Distributed by Universal Press Syndicate
© 2003 PAWS, INC. All Rights Reserved.

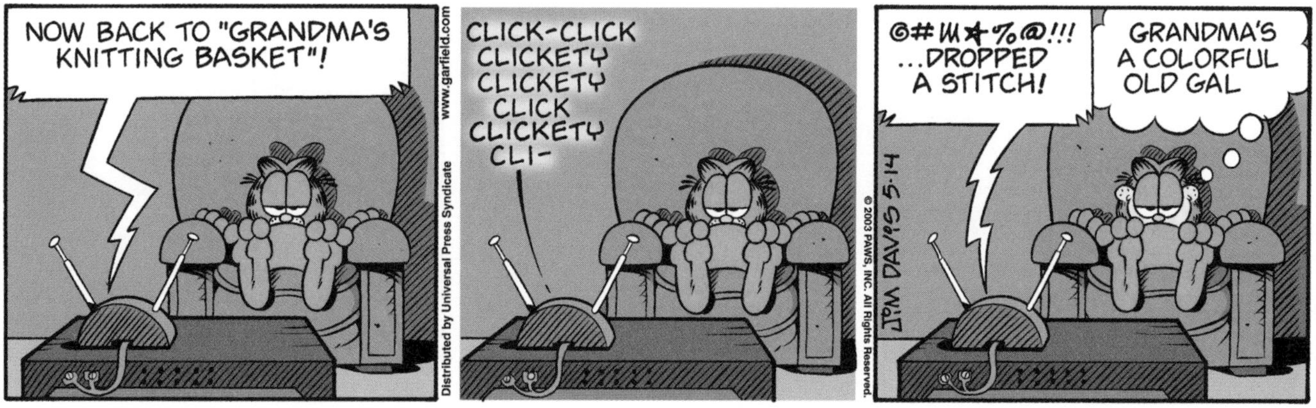
NOW BACK TO "GRANDMA'S KNITTING BASKET"!
CLICK-CLICK CLICKETY CLICKETY CLICK CLICKETY CLI-
@#Ш★%@!!! ...DROPPED A STITCH!
GRANDMA'S A COLORFUL OLD GAL
JIM DAVIS 5-14
www.garfield.com
Distributed by Universal Press Syndicate
© 2003 PAWS, INC. All Rights Reserved.

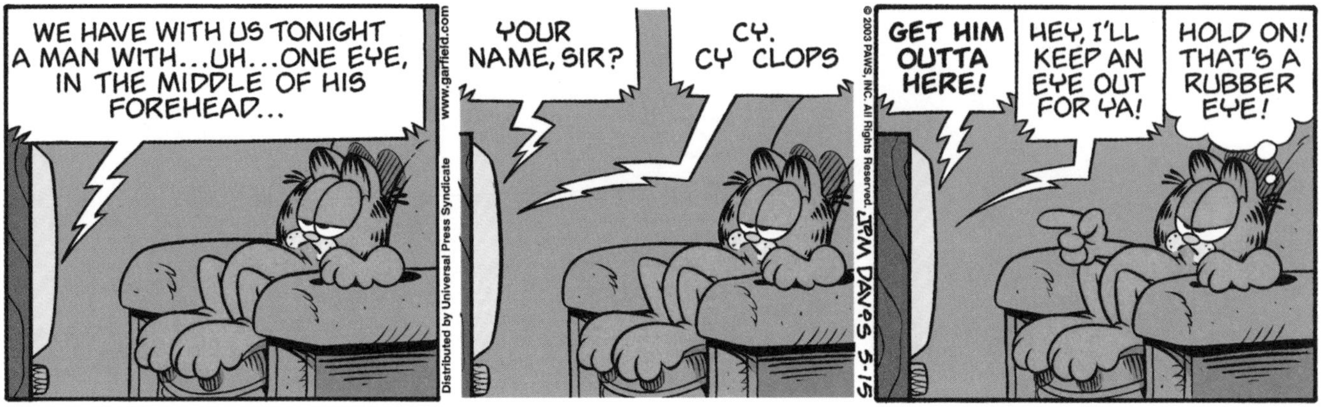
WE HAVE WITH US TONIGHT A MAN WITH...UH...ONE EYE, IN THE MIDDLE OF HIS FOREHEAD...
www.garfield.com
Distributed by Universal Press Syndicate
YOUR NAME, SIR?
CY. CY CLOPS
© 2003 PAWS, INC. All Rights Reserved.
JIM DAVIS 5-15
GET HIM OUTTA HERE!
HEY, I'LL KEEP AN EYE OUT FOR YA!
HOLD ON! THAT'S A RUBBER EYE!

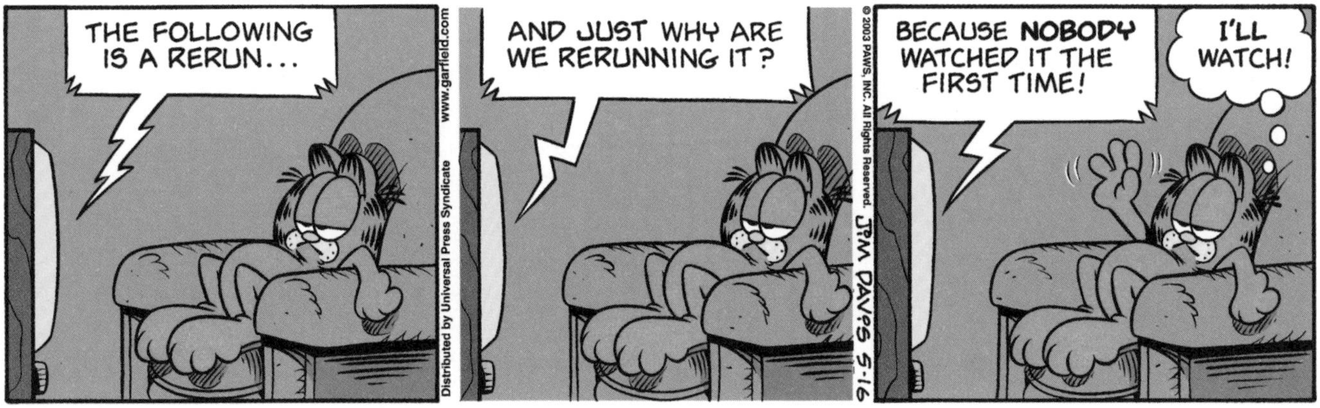
THE FOLLOWING IS A RERUN...
www.garfield.com
Distributed by Universal Press Syndicate
AND JUST WHY ARE WE RERUNNING IT?
© 2003 PAWS, INC. All Rights Reserved.
JIM DAVIS 5-16
BECAUSE NOBODY WATCHED IT THE FIRST TIME!
I'LL WATCH!

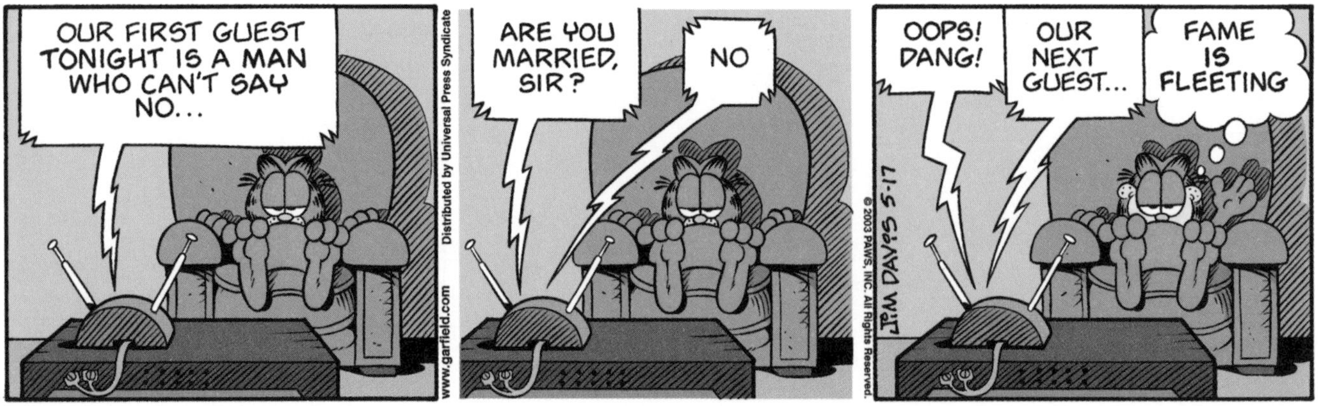
OUR FIRST GUEST TONIGHT IS A MAN WHO CAN'T SAY NO...
Distributed by Universal Press Syndicate
www.garfield.com
ARE YOU MARRIED, SIR?
NO
JIM DAVIS 5-17
© 2003 PAWS, INC. All Rights Reserved.
OOPS! DANG!
OUR NEXT GUEST...
FAME IS FLEETING

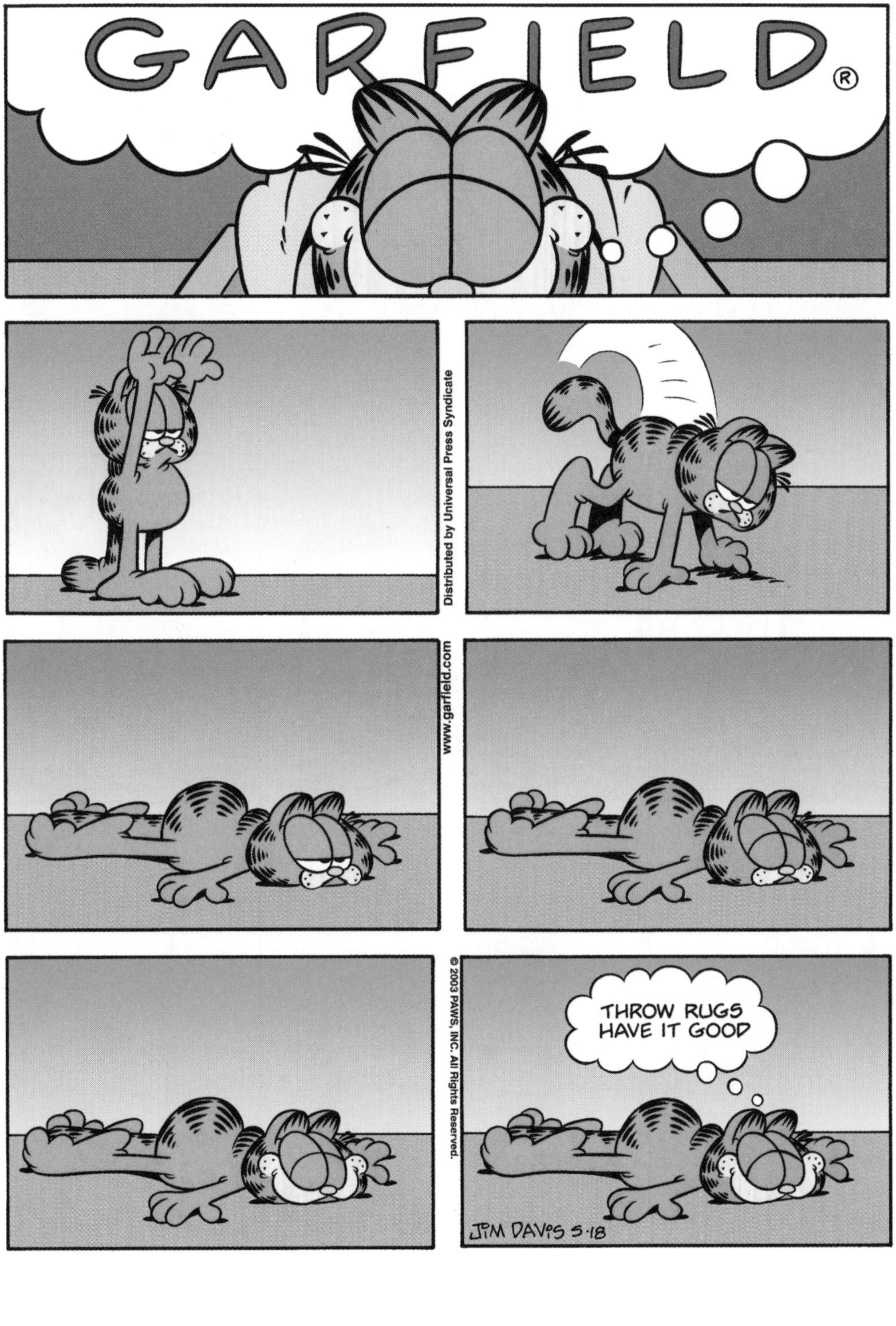
GARFIELD®
Distributed by Universal Press Syndicate
www.garfield.com
© 2003 PAWS, INC. All Rights Reserved.
THROW RUGS HAVE IT GOOD
JIM DAVIS 5-18

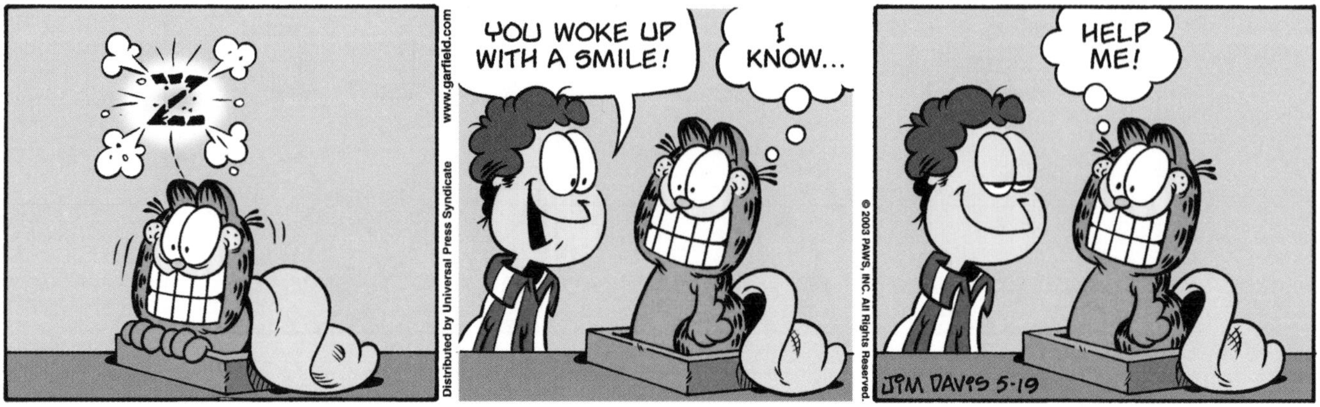
Z
YOU WOKE UP WITH A SMILE!
I KNOW...
HELP ME!
Distributed by Universal Press Syndicate www.garfield.com
© 2003 PAWS, INC. All Rights Reserved.
JIM DAVIS 5-19

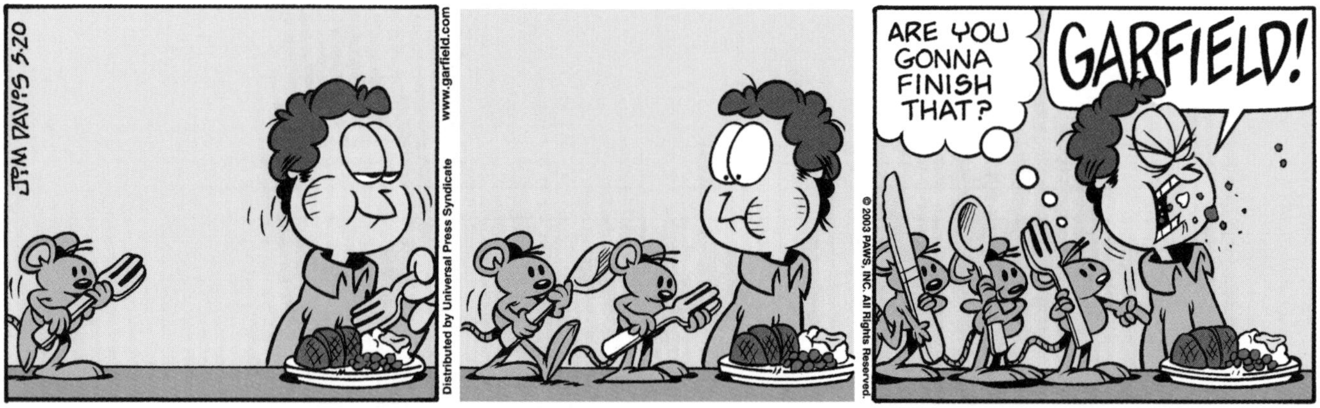
JIM DAVIS 5-20
ARE YOU GONNA FINISH THAT?
GARFIELD!
Distributed by Universal Press Syndicate www.garfield.com
© 2003 PAWS, INC. All Rights Reserved.

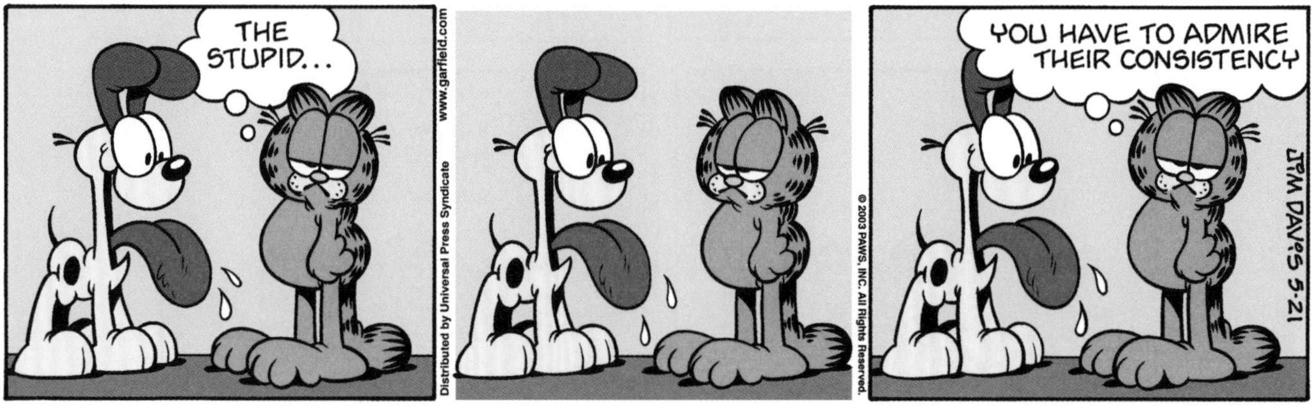
THE STUPID...
YOU HAVE TO ADMIRE THEIR CONSISTENCY
Distributed by Universal Press Syndicate www.garfield.com
© 2003 PAWS, INC. All Rights Reserved.
JIM DAVIS 5-21

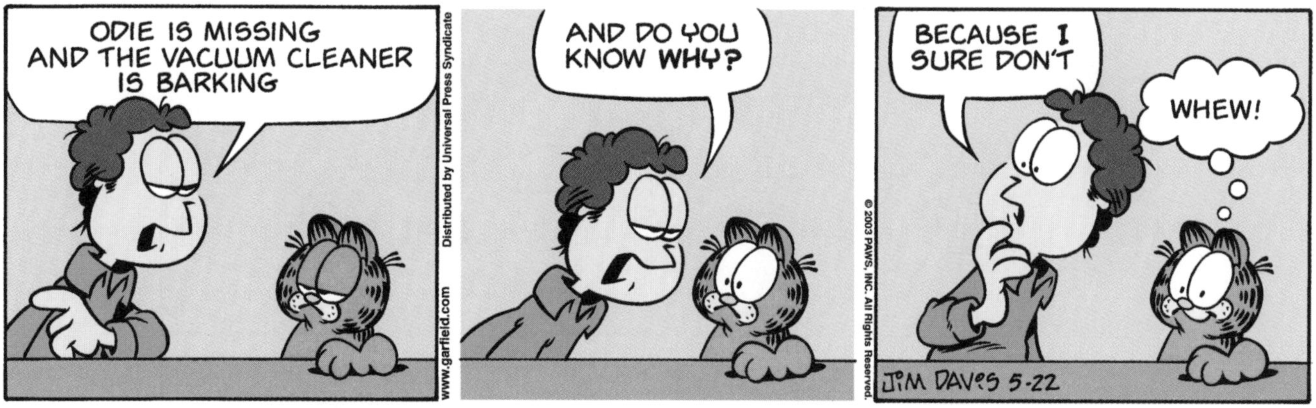
ODIE IS MISSING AND THE VACUUM CLEANER IS BARKING
www.garfield.com Distributed by Universal Press Syndicate
AND DO YOU KNOW WHY?
© 2003 PAWS, INC. All Rights Reserved.
BECAUSE I SURE DON'T
WHEW!
JIM DAVIS 5-22

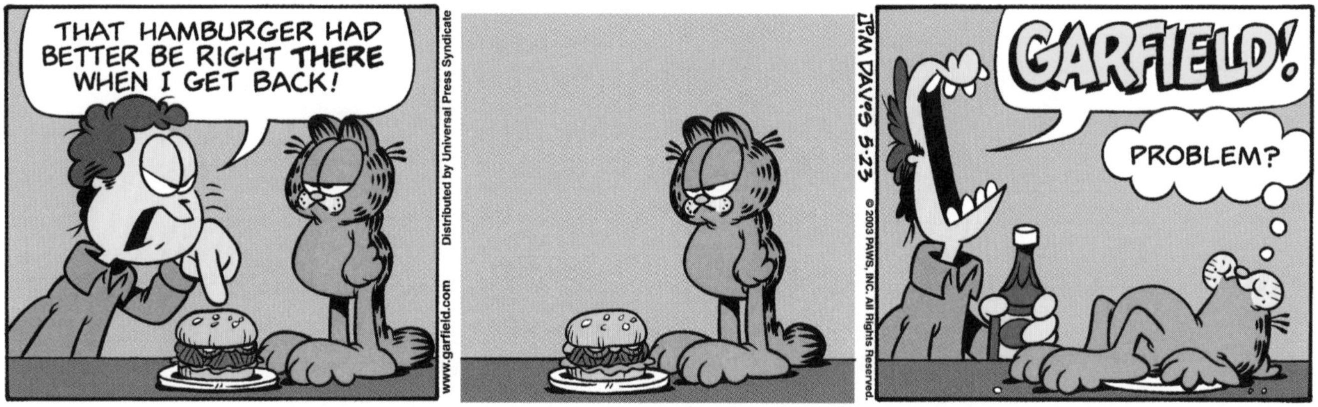
THAT HAMBURGER HAD BETTER BE RIGHT THERE WHEN I GET BACK!
www.garfield.com Distributed by Universal Press Syndicate
JIM DAVIS 5-23
© 2003 PAWS, INC. All Rights Reserved.
GARFIELD!
PROBLEM?

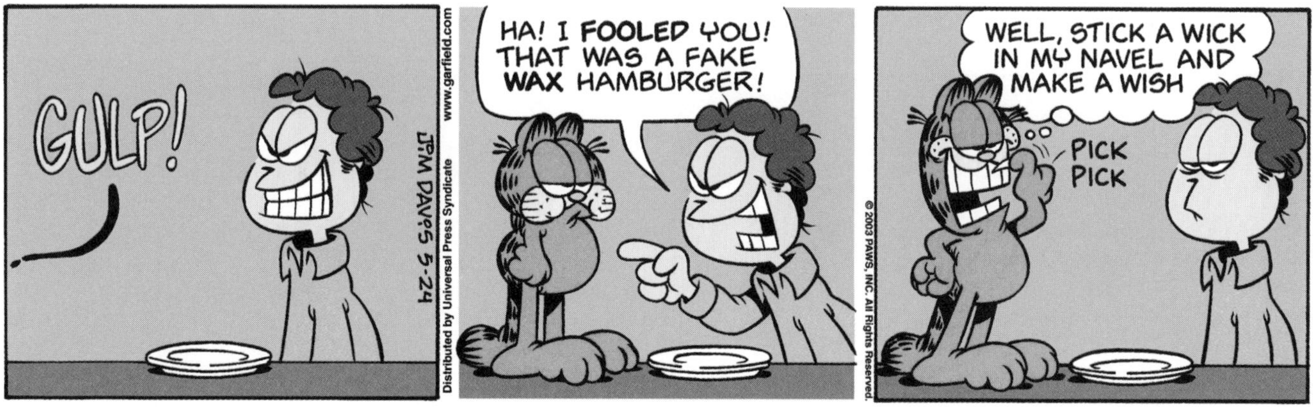
GULP!
JIM DAVIS 5-24
Distributed by Universal Press Syndicate www.garfield.com
HA! I FOOLED YOU! THAT WAS A FAKE WAX HAMBURGER!
© 2003 PAWS, INC. All Rights Reserved.
WELL, STICK A WICK IN MY NAVEL AND MAKE A WISH
PICK PICK

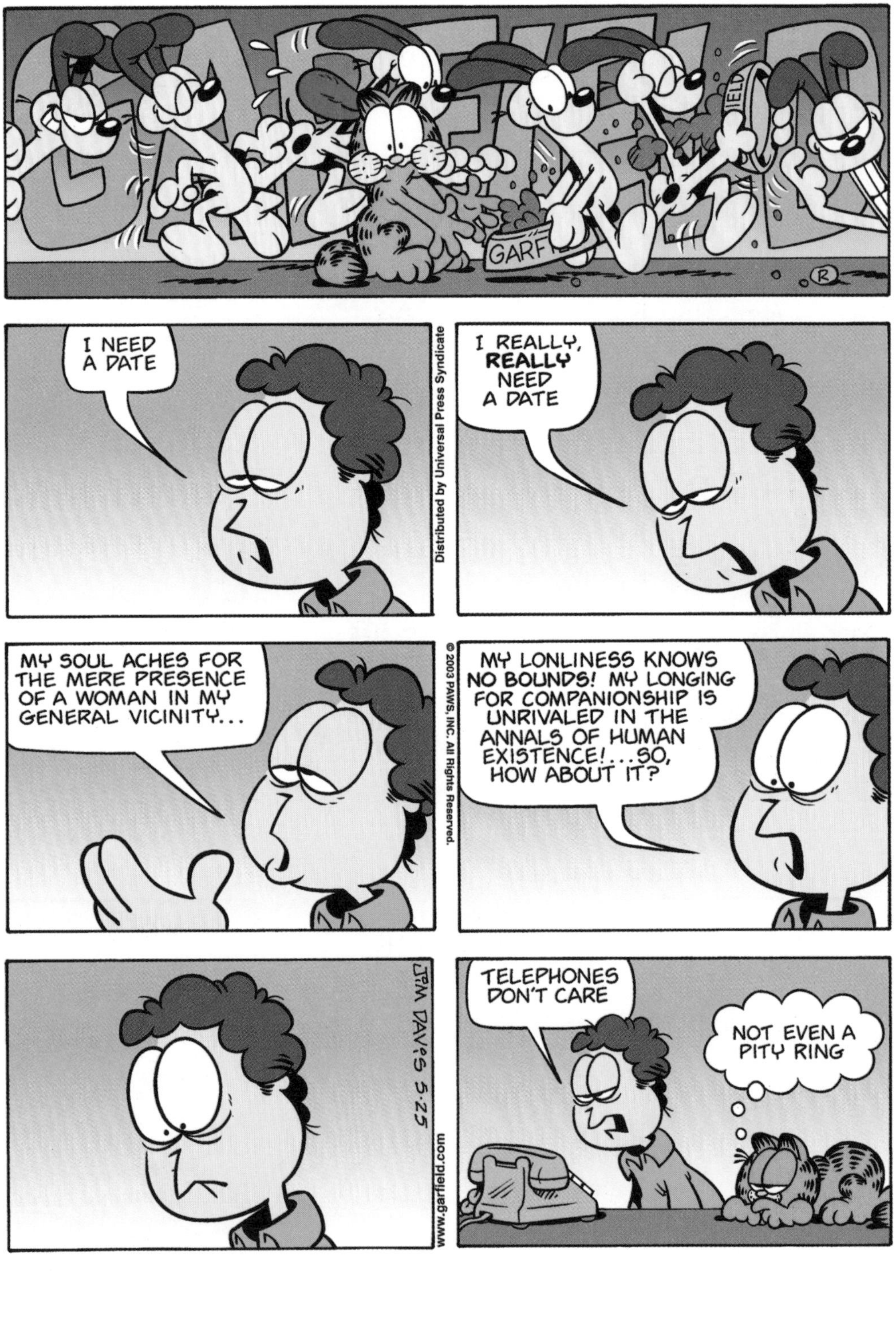
I NEED A DATE
I REALLY, **REALLY** NEED A DATE
Distributed by Universal Press Syndicate
MY SOUL ACHES FOR THE MERE PRESENCE OF A WOMAN IN MY GENERAL VICINITY...
© 2003 PAWS, INC. All Rights Reserved.
MY LONLINESS KNOWS NO BOUNDS! MY LONGING FOR COMPANIONSHIP IS UNRIVALED IN THE ANNALS OF HUMAN EXISTENCE!...SO, HOW ABOUT IT?
JIM DAVIS 5-25
www.garfield.com
TELEPHONES DON'T CARE
NOT EVEN A PITY RING

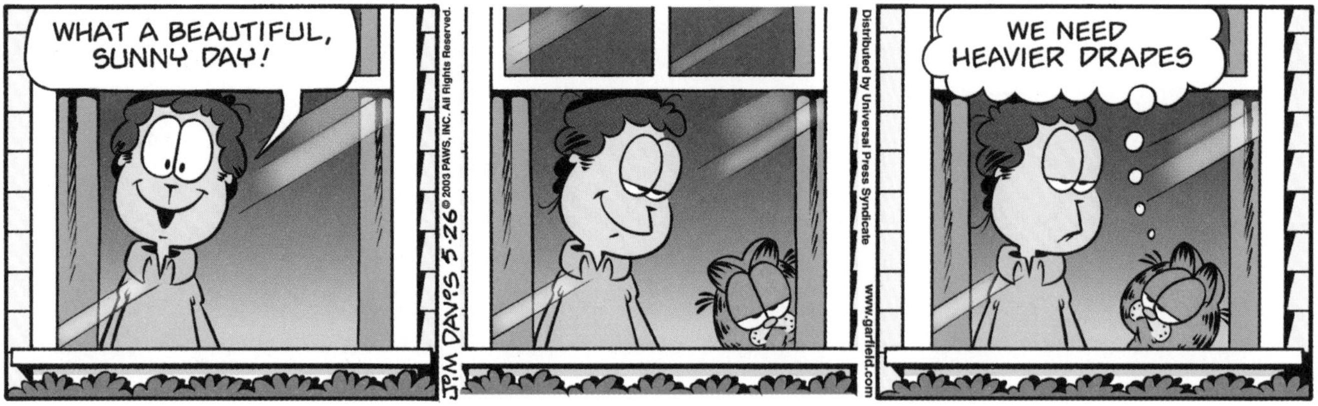
WHAT A BEAUTIFUL, SUNNY DAY!
JIM DAVIS 5·26 © 2003 PAWS, INC. All Rights Reserved.
Distributed by Universal Press Syndicate www.garfield.com
WE NEED HEAVIER DRAPES

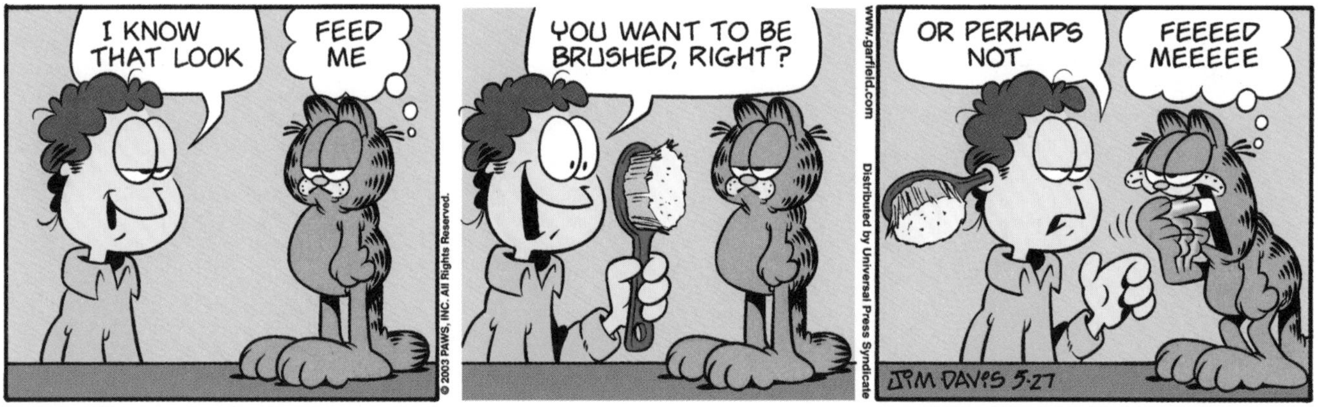
I KNOW THAT LOOK
FEED ME
© 2003 PAWS, INC. All Rights Reserved.
YOU WANT TO BE BRUSHED, RIGHT?
www.garfield.com Distributed by Universal Press Syndicate
OR PERHAPS NOT
FEEEED MEEEEE
JIM DAVIS 5·27

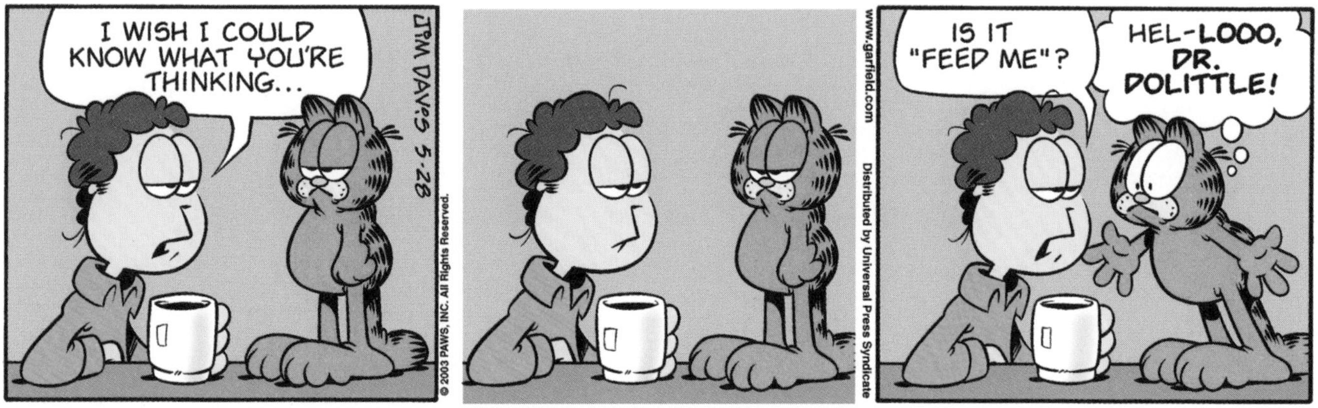
I WISH I COULD KNOW WHAT YOU'RE THINKING...
JIM DAVIS 5·28
© 2003 PAWS, INC. All Rights Reserved.
www.garfield.com Distributed by Universal Press Syndicate
IS IT "FEED ME"?
HEL-**LOOO, DR. DOLITTLE!**

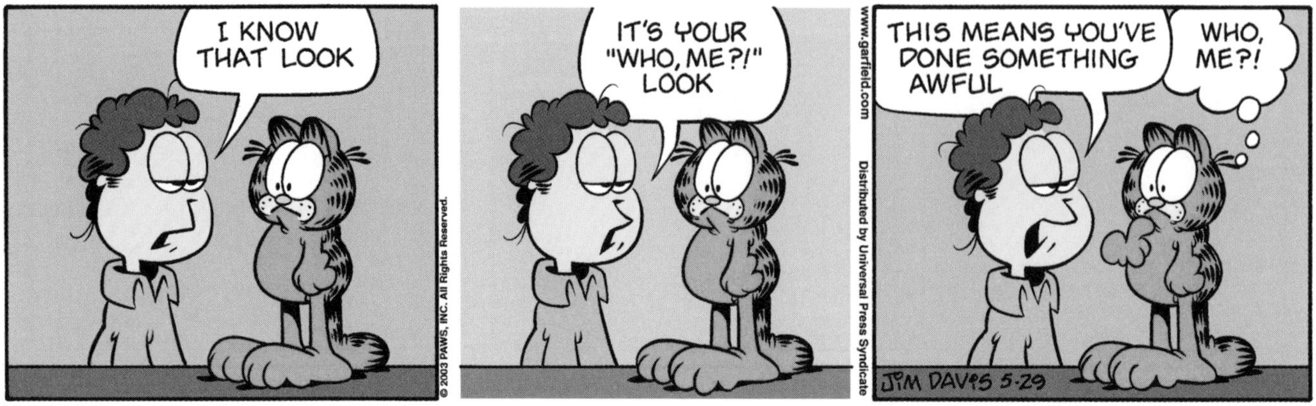
I KNOW THAT LOOK
IT'S YOUR "WHO, ME?!" LOOK
THIS MEANS YOU'VE DONE SOMETHING AWFUL
WHO, ME?!
© 2003 PAWS, INC. All Rights Reserved.
www.garfield.com
Distributed by Universal Press Syndicate
JIM DAVIS 5-29

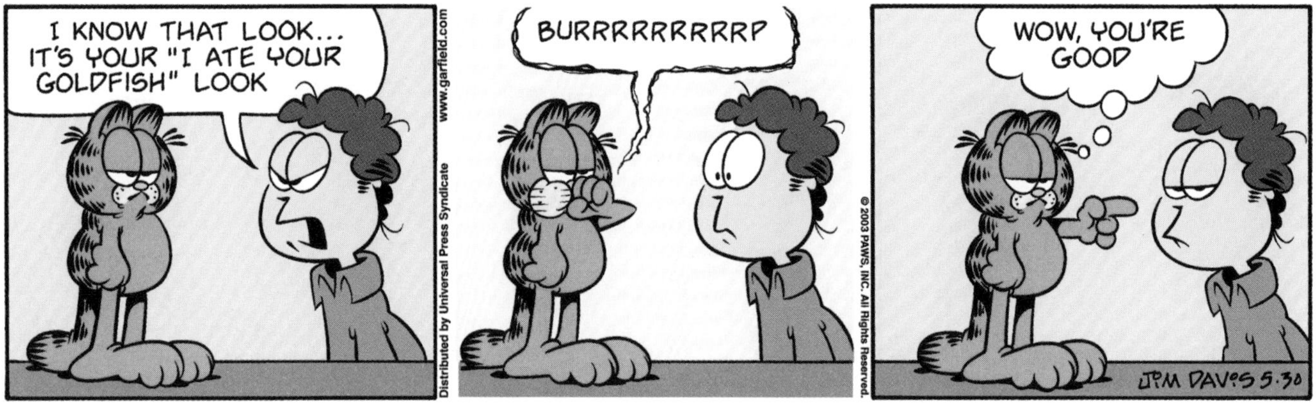
I KNOW THAT LOOK... IT'S YOUR "I ATE YOUR GOLDFISH" LOOK
BURRRRRRRRRP
WOW, YOU'RE GOOD
www.garfield.com
Distributed by Universal Press Syndicate
© 2003 PAWS, INC. All Rights Reserved.
JIM DAVIS 5-30

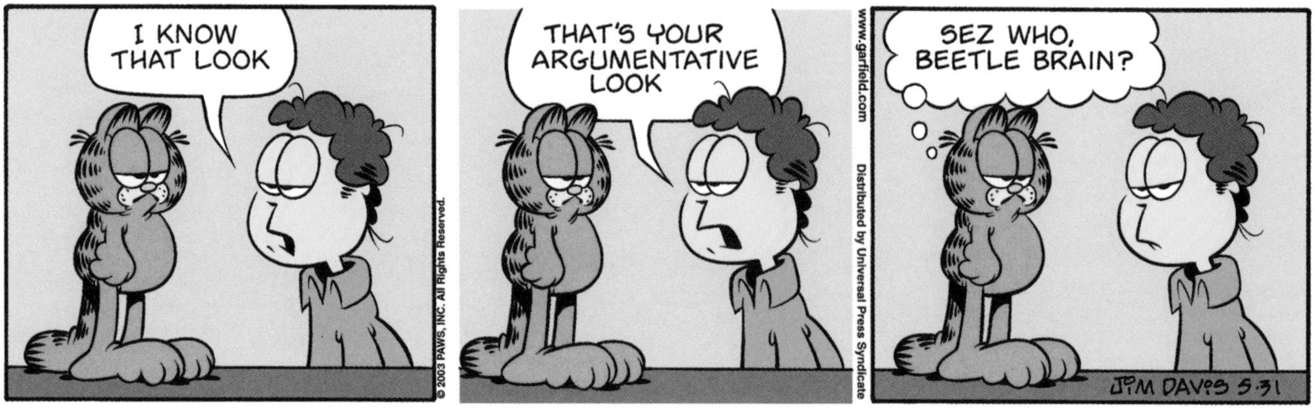
I KNOW THAT LOOK
THAT'S YOUR ARGUMENTATIVE LOOK
SEZ WHO, BEETLE BRAIN?
© 2003 PAWS, INC. All Rights Reserved.
www.garfield.com
Distributed by Universal Press Syndicate
JIM DAVIS 5-31

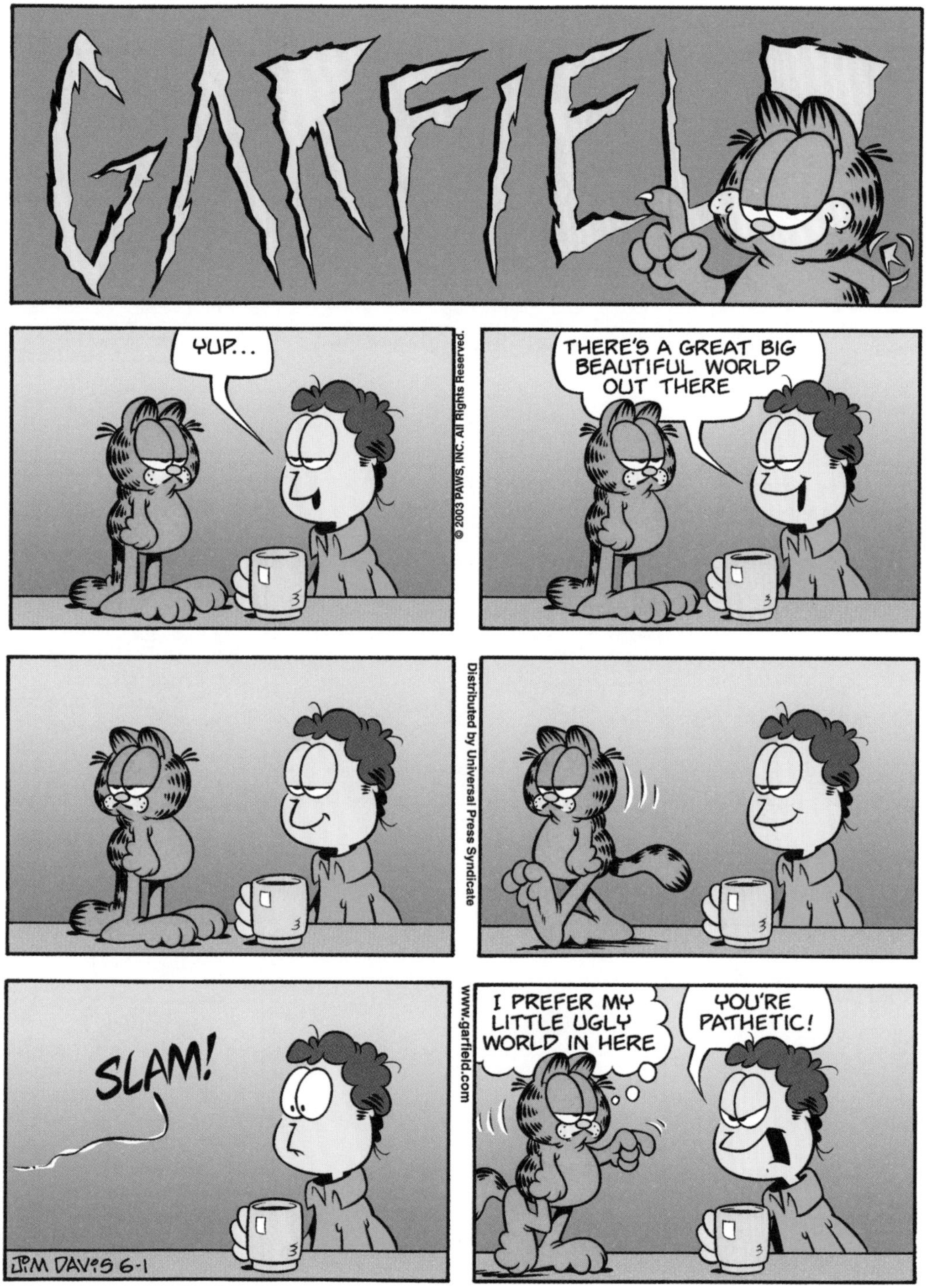
GARFIELD
YUP...
THERE'S A GREAT BIG BEAUTIFUL WORLD OUT THERE
SLAM!
I PREFER MY LITTLE UGLY WORLD IN HERE
YOU'RE PATHETIC!
JIM DAVIS 6-1

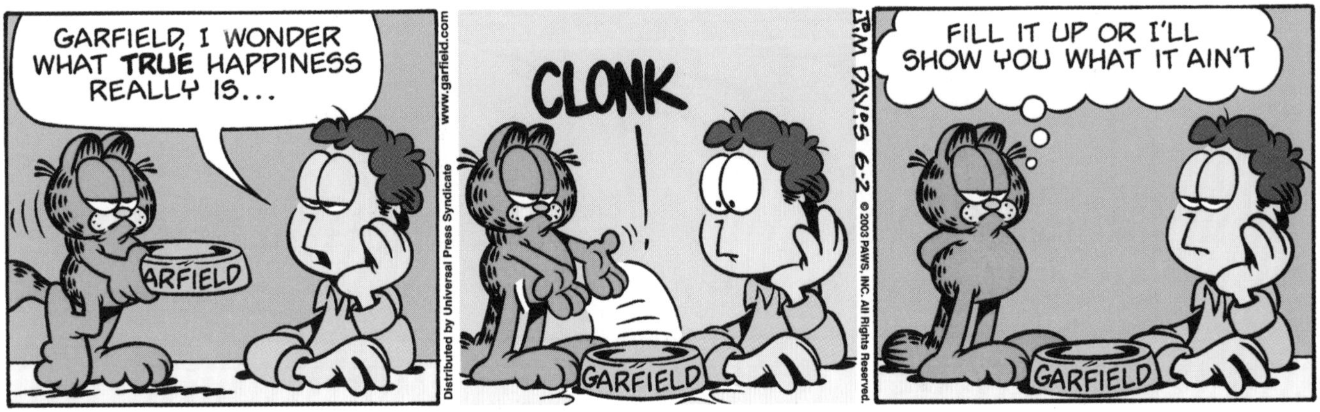
GARFIELD, I WONDER WHAT **TRUE** HAPPINESS REALLY IS...
GARFIELD
CLONK
GARFIELD
FILL IT UP OR I'LL SHOW YOU WHAT IT AIN'T
GARFIELD

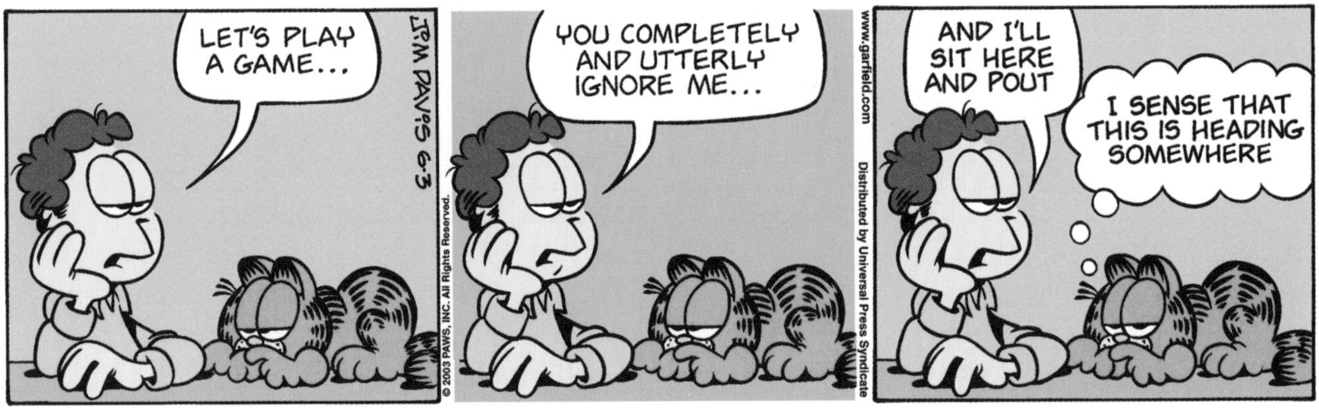
LET'S PLAY A GAME...
YOU COMPLETELY AND UTTERLY IGNORE ME...
AND I'LL SIT HERE AND POUT
I SENSE THAT THIS IS HEADING SOMEWHERE

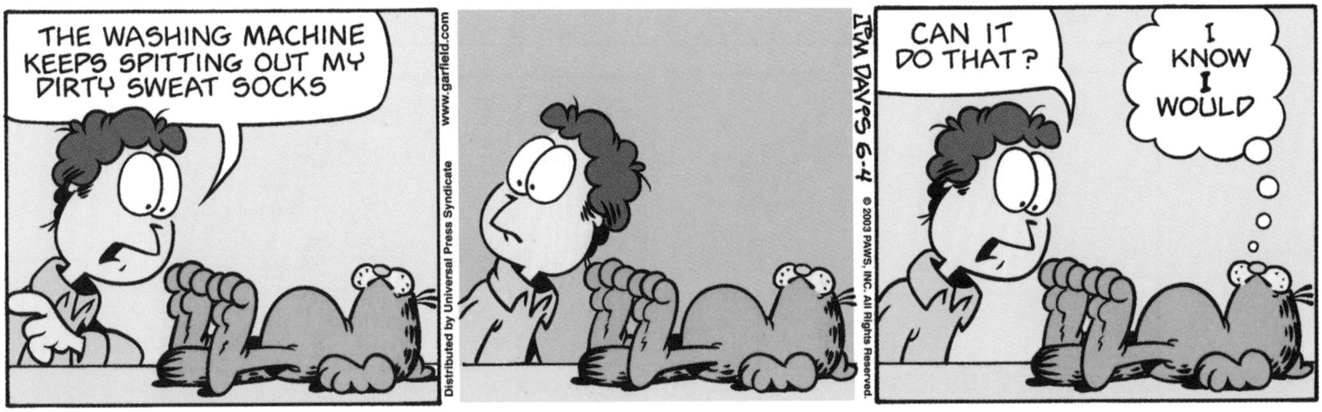
THE WASHING MACHINE KEEPS SPITTING OUT MY DIRTY SWEAT SOCKS
CAN IT DO THAT?
I KNOW **I** WOULD

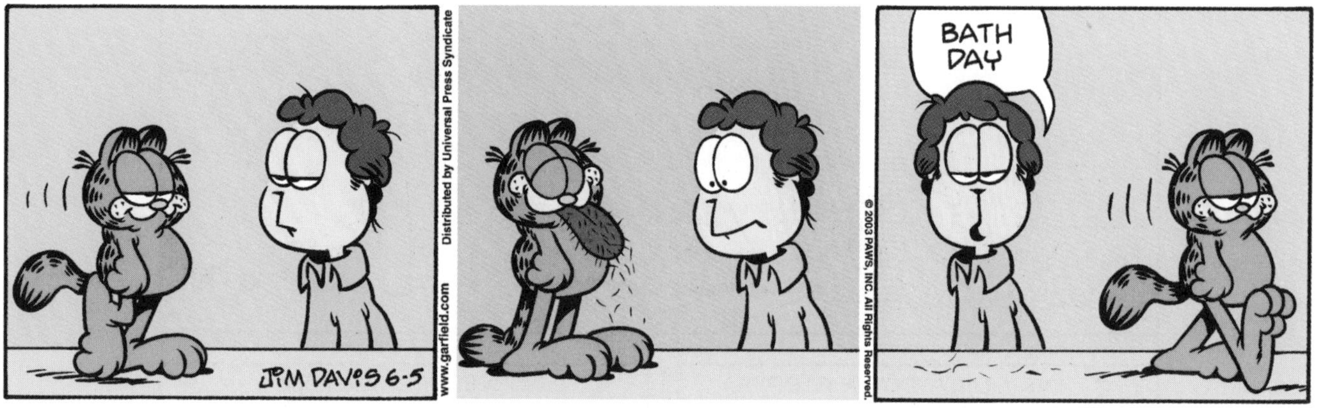
JIM DAVIS 6-5
www.garfield.com
Distributed by Universal Press Syndicate
© 2003 PAWS, INC. All Rights Reserved.
BATH DAY

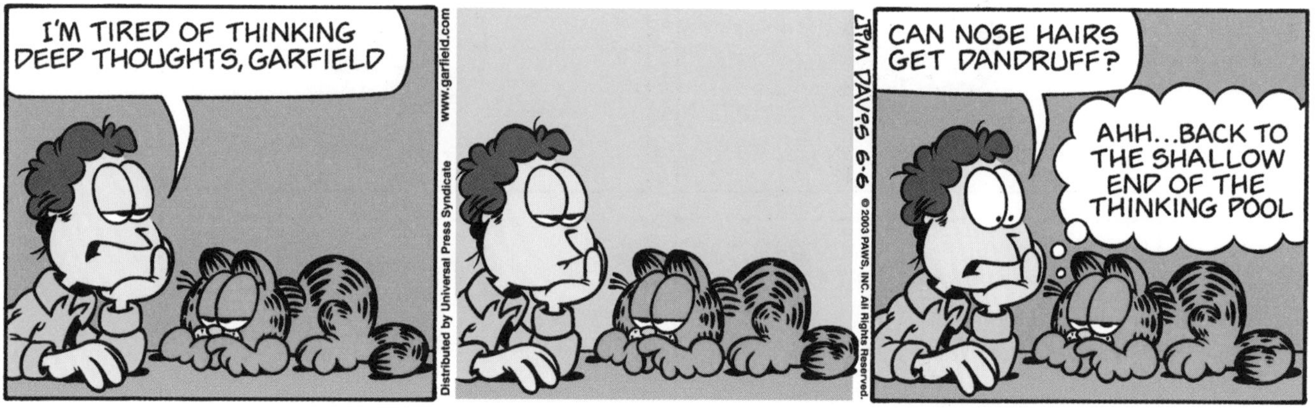
I'M TIRED OF THINKING DEEP THOUGHTS, GARFIELD
www.garfield.com
Distributed by Universal Press Syndicate
JIM DAVIS 6-6
© 2003 PAWS, INC. All Rights Reserved.
CAN NOSE HAIRS GET DANDRUFF?
AHH...BACK TO THE SHALLOW END OF THE THINKING POOL

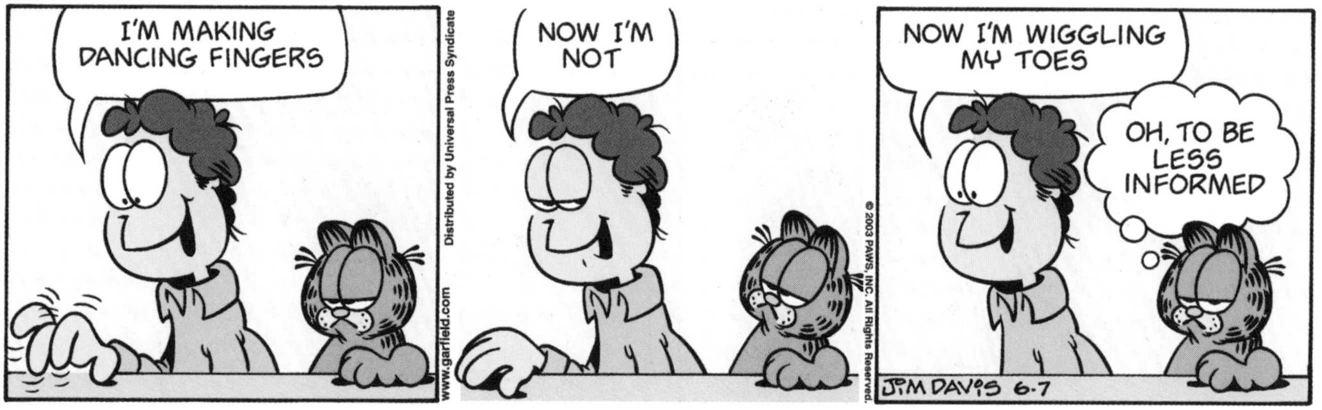
I'M MAKING DANCING FINGERS
Distributed by Universal Press Syndicate
www.garfield.com
NOW I'M NOT
© 2003 PAWS, INC. All Rights Reserved.
NOW I'M WIGGLING MY TOES
OH, TO BE LESS INFORMED
JIM DAVIS 6-7

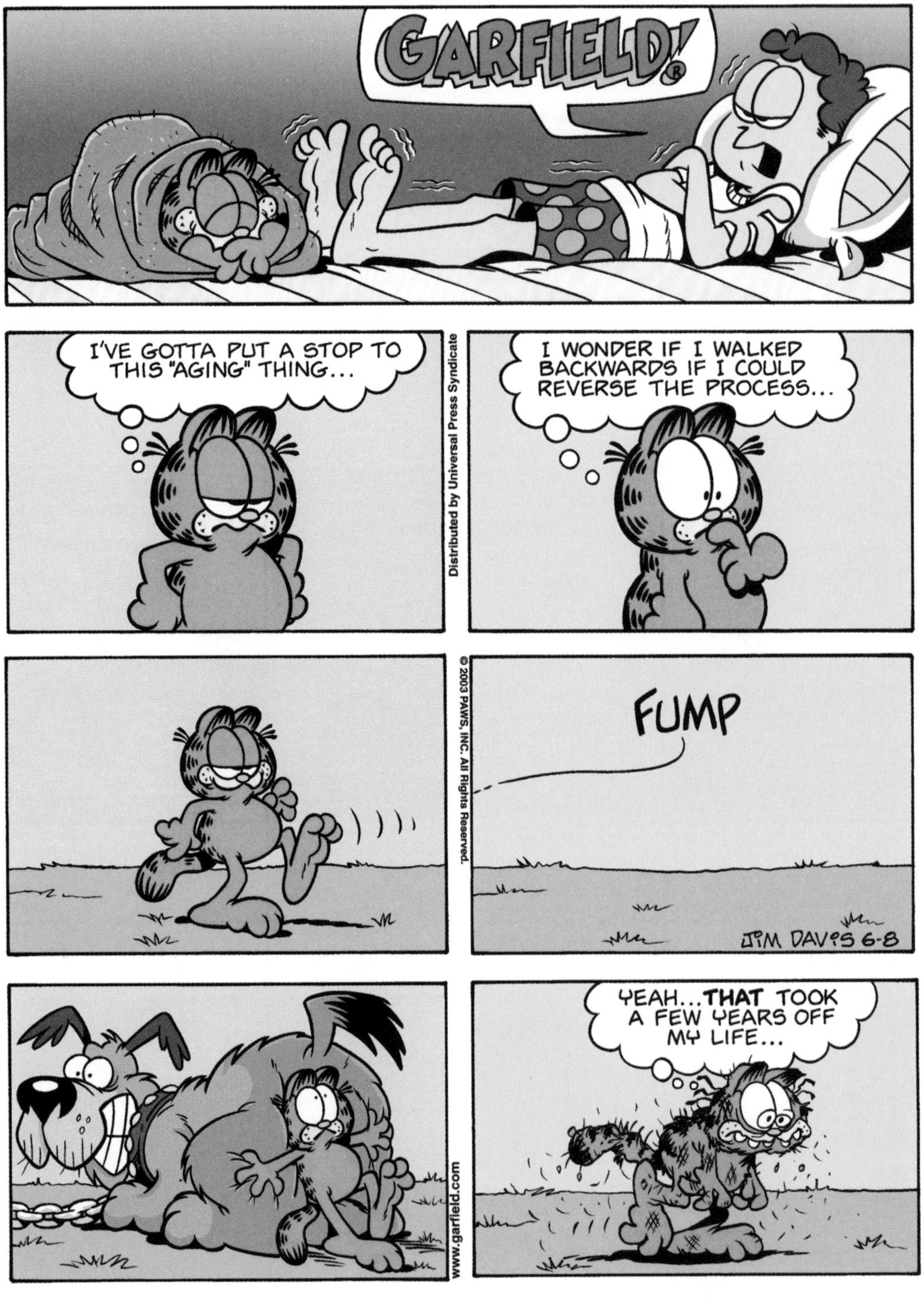
GARFIELD®
I'VE GOTTA PUT A STOP TO THIS "AGING" THING...
Distributed by Universal Press Syndicate
I WONDER IF I WALKED BACKWARDS IF I COULD REVERSE THE PROCESS...
© 2003 PAWS, INC. All Rights Reserved.
FUMP
JIM DAVIS 6-8
www.garfield.com
YEAH...**THAT** TOOK A FEW YEARS OFF MY LIFE...

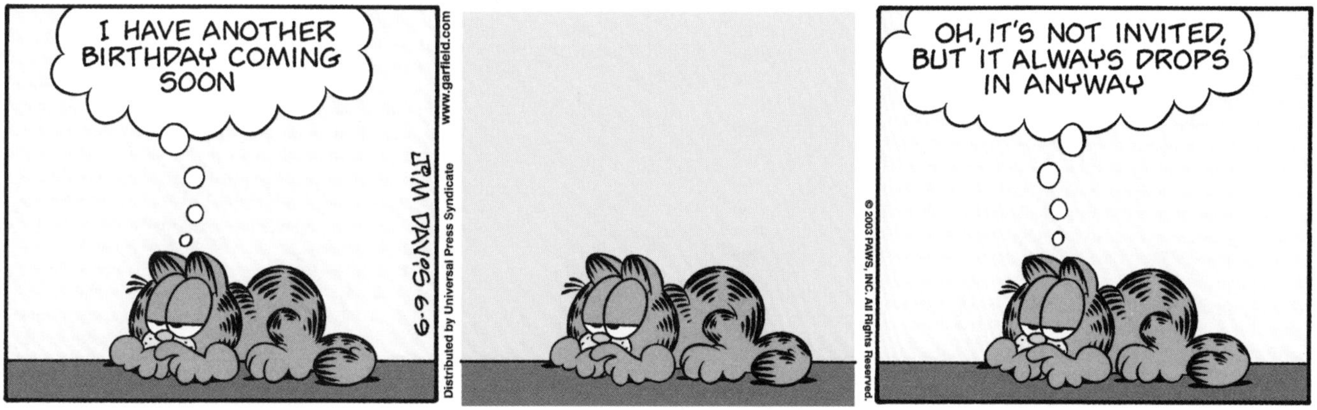
I HAVE ANOTHER BIRTHDAY COMING SOON
OH, IT'S NOT INVITED, BUT IT ALWAYS DROPS IN ANYWAY
JIM DAVIS 6-9
www.garfield.com
Distributed by Universal Press Syndicate
© 2003 PAWS, INC. All Rights Reserved.

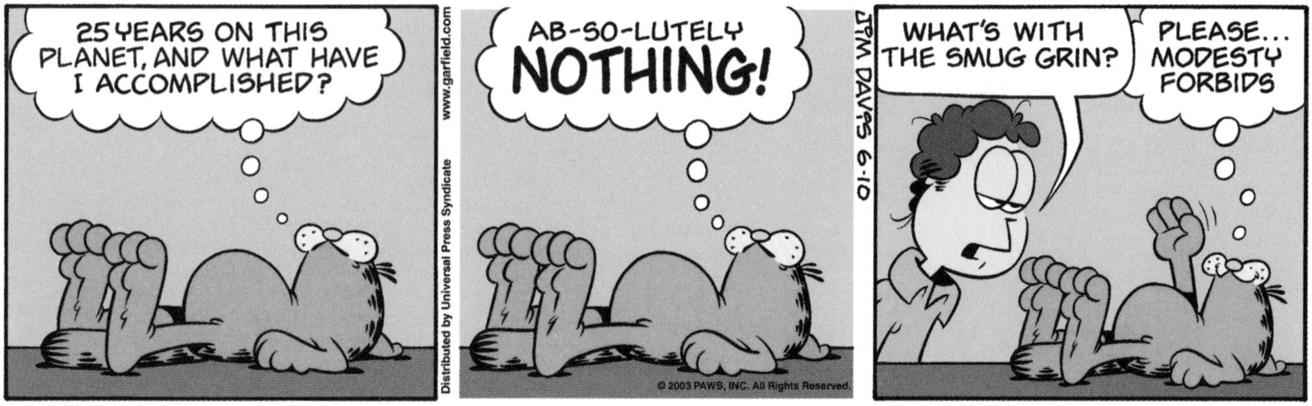
25 YEARS ON THIS PLANET, AND WHAT HAVE I ACCOMPLISHED?
AB-SO-LUTELY
NOTHING!
WHAT'S WITH THE SMUG GRIN?
PLEASE... MODESTY FORBIDS
JIM DAVIS 6-10
www.garfield.com
Distributed by Universal Press Syndicate
© 2003 PAWS, INC. All Rights Reserved.

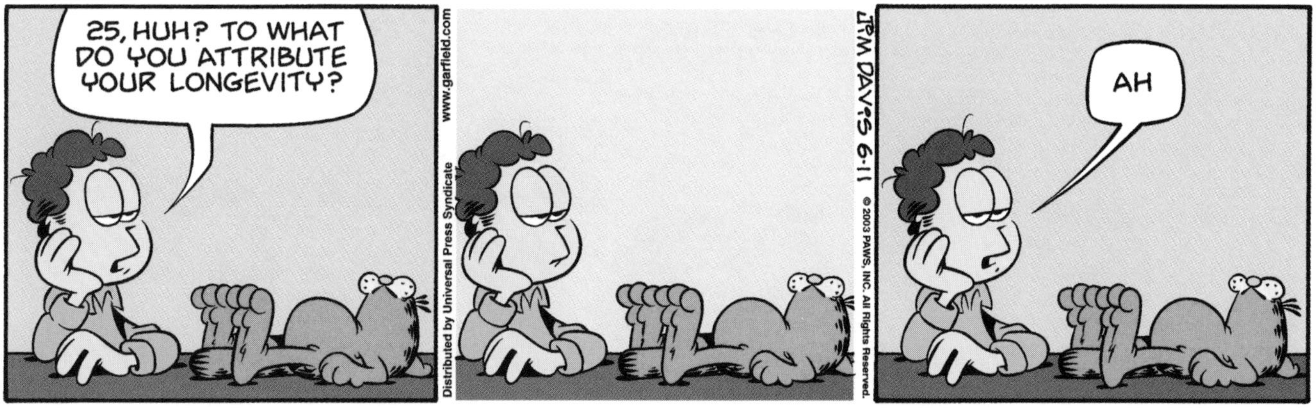
25, HUH? TO WHAT DO YOU ATTRIBUTE YOUR LONGEVITY?
AH
JIM DAVIS 6-11
www.garfield.com
Distributed by Universal Press Syndicate
© 2003 PAWS, INC. All Rights Reserved.

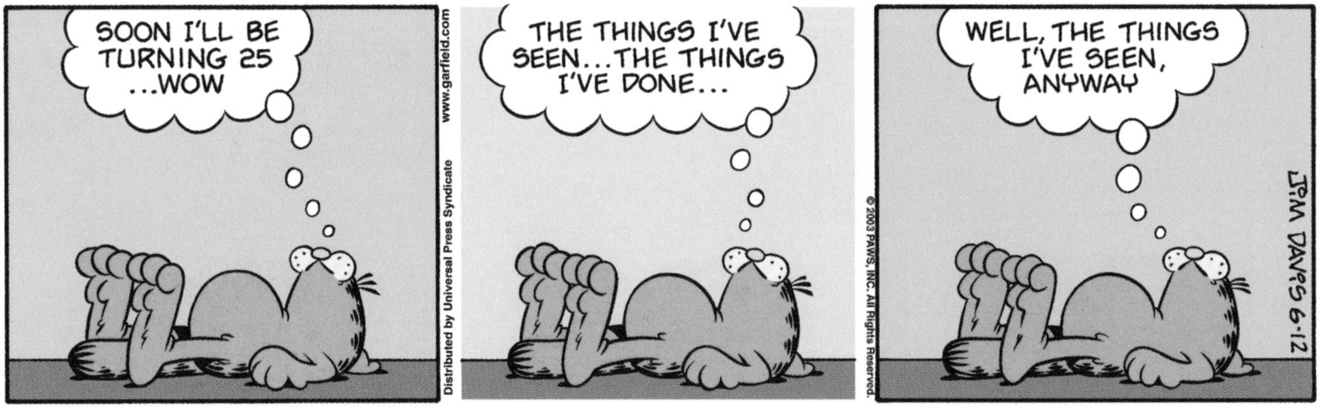
SOON I'LL BE TURNING 25 ...WOW
THE THINGS I'VE SEEN...THE THINGS I'VE DONE...
WELL, THE THINGS I'VE SEEN, ANYWAY
Distributed by Universal Press Syndicate www.garfield.com
© 2003 PAWS, INC. All Rights Reserved.
JIM DAVIS 6-12

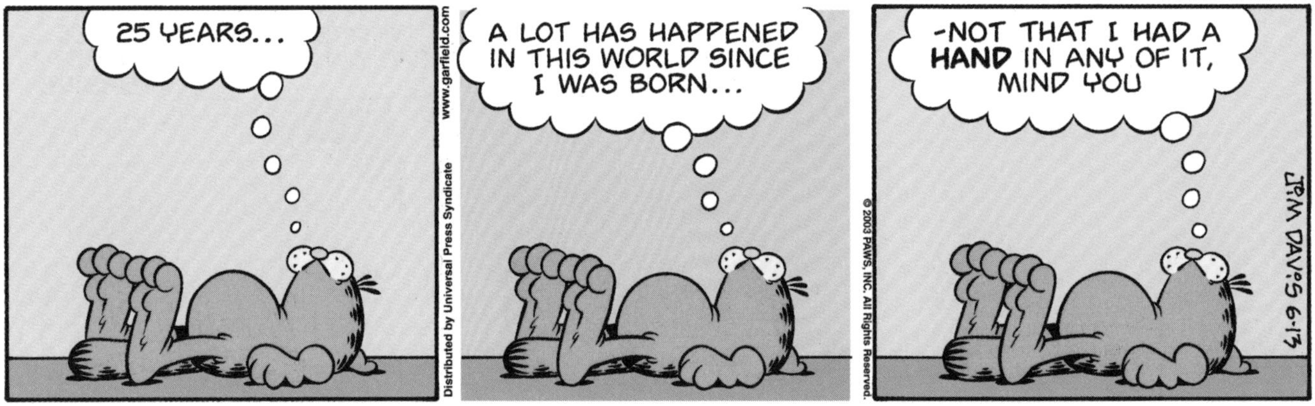
25 YEARS...
A LOT HAS HAPPENED IN THIS WORLD SINCE I WAS BORN...
-NOT THAT I HAD A **HAND** IN ANY OF IT, MIND YOU
Distributed by Universal Press Syndicate www.garfield.com
© 2003 PAWS, INC. All Rights Reserved.
JIM DAVIS 6-13

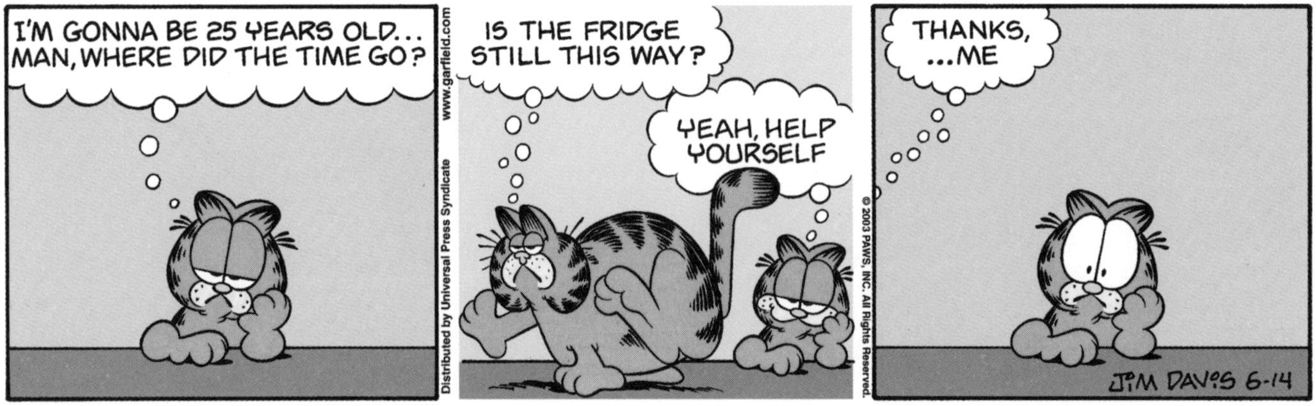
I'M GONNA BE 25 YEARS OLD... MAN, WHERE DID THE TIME GO?
IS THE FRIDGE STILL THIS WAY?
YEAH, HELP YOURSELF
THANKS, ...ME
Distributed by Universal Press Syndicate www.garfield.com
© 2003 PAWS, INC. All Rights Reserved.
JIM DAVIS 6-14

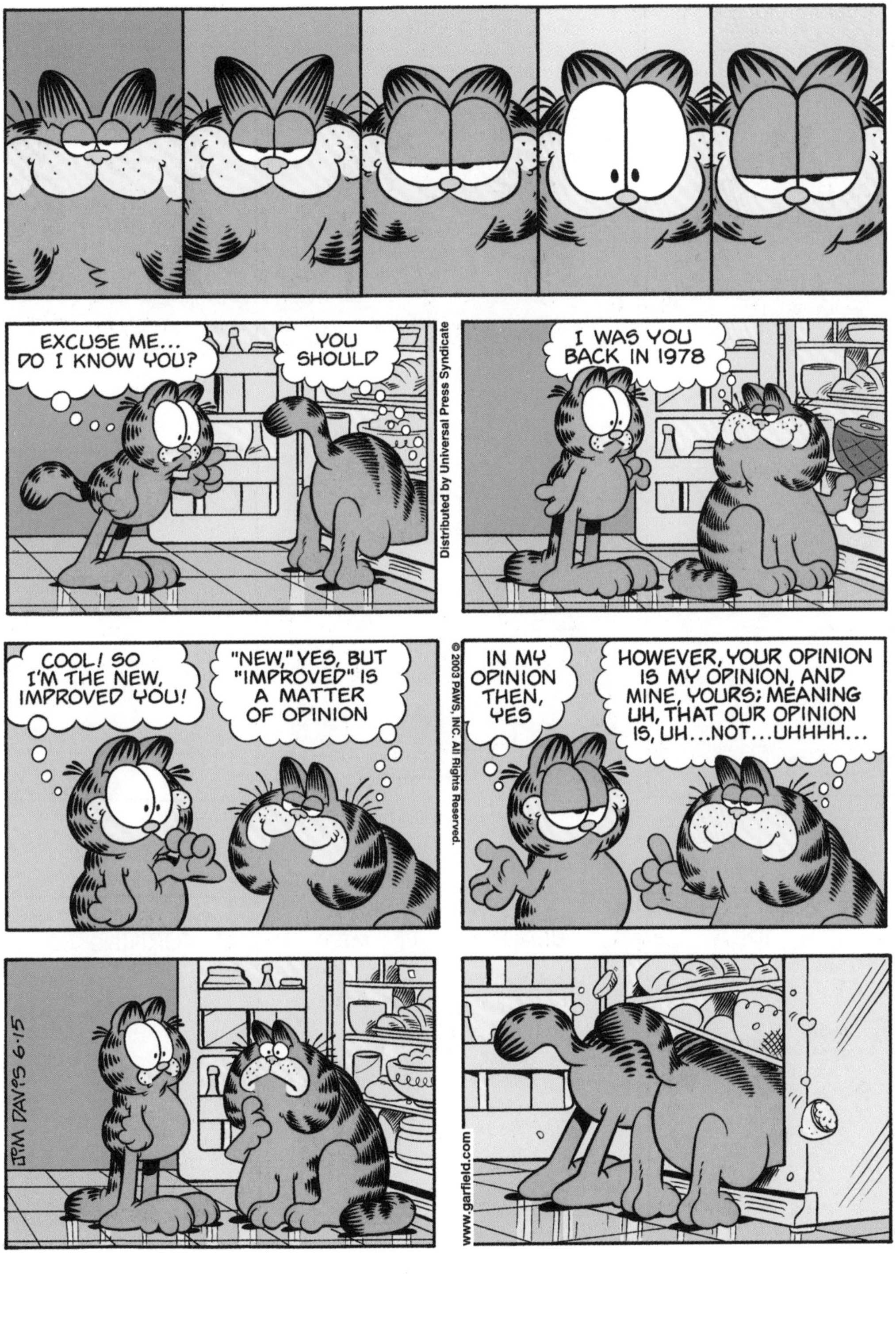

EXCUSE ME... DO I KNOW YOU?
YOU SHOULD
I WAS YOU BACK IN 1978
COOL! SO I'M THE NEW, IMPROVED YOU!
"NEW," YES, BUT "IMPROVED" IS A MATTER OF OPINION
IN MY OPINION THEN, YES
HOWEVER, YOUR OPINION IS MY OPINION, AND MINE, YOURS; MEANING UH, THAT OUR OPINION IS, UH...NOT...UHHHH...
JIM DAVIS 6-15
Distributed by Universal Press Syndicate
© 2003 PAWS, INC. All Rights Reserved.
www.garfield.com

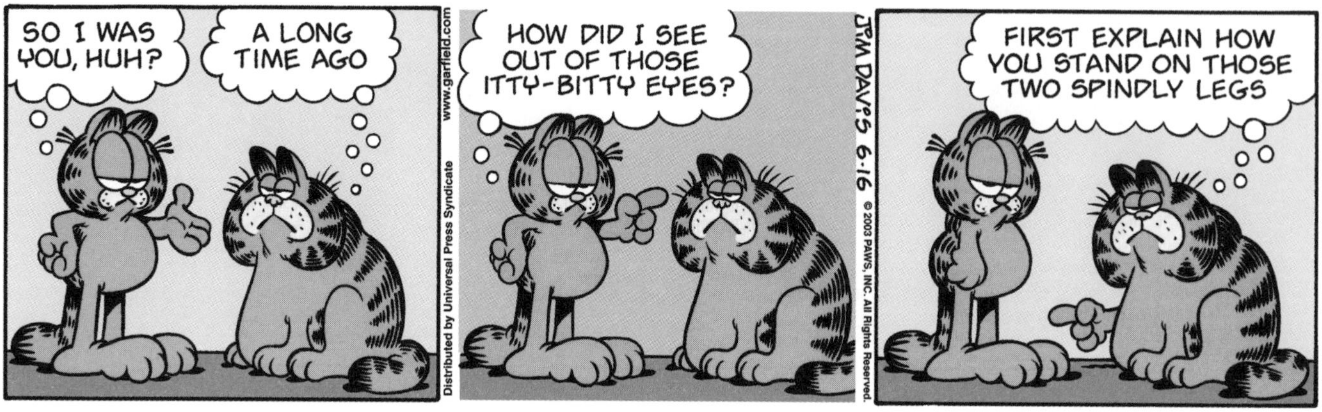
SO I WAS YOU, HUH?
A LONG TIME AGO
HOW DID I SEE OUT OF THOSE ITTY-BITTY EYES?
FIRST EXPLAIN HOW YOU STAND ON THOSE TWO SPINDLY LEGS
JIM DAVIS 6-16
Distributed by Universal Press Syndicate www.garfield.com
© 2003 PAWS, INC. All Rights Reserved.

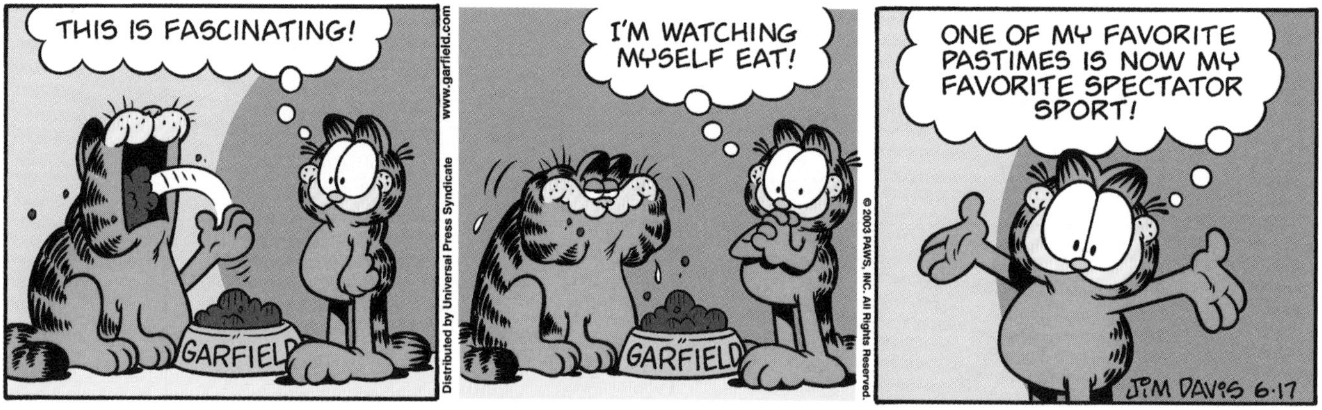
THIS IS FASCINATING!
GARFIELD
I'M WATCHING MYSELF EAT!
GARFIELD
ONE OF MY FAVORITE PASTIMES IS NOW MY FAVORITE SPECTATOR SPORT!
JIM DAVIS 6-17
Distributed by Universal Press Syndicate www.garfield.com
© 2003 PAWS, INC. All Rights Reserved.

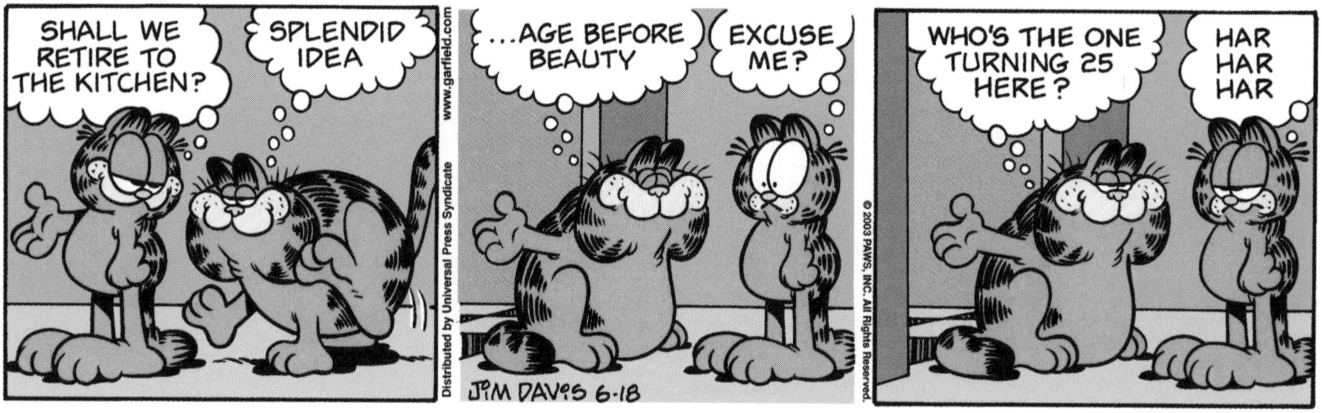
SHALL WE RETIRE TO THE KITCHEN?
SPLENDID IDEA
...AGE BEFORE BEAUTY
EXCUSE ME?
WHO'S THE ONE TURNING 25 HERE?
HAR HAR HAR
JIM DAVIS 6-18
Distributed by Universal Press Syndicate www.garfield.com
© 2003 PAWS, INC. All Rights Reserved.

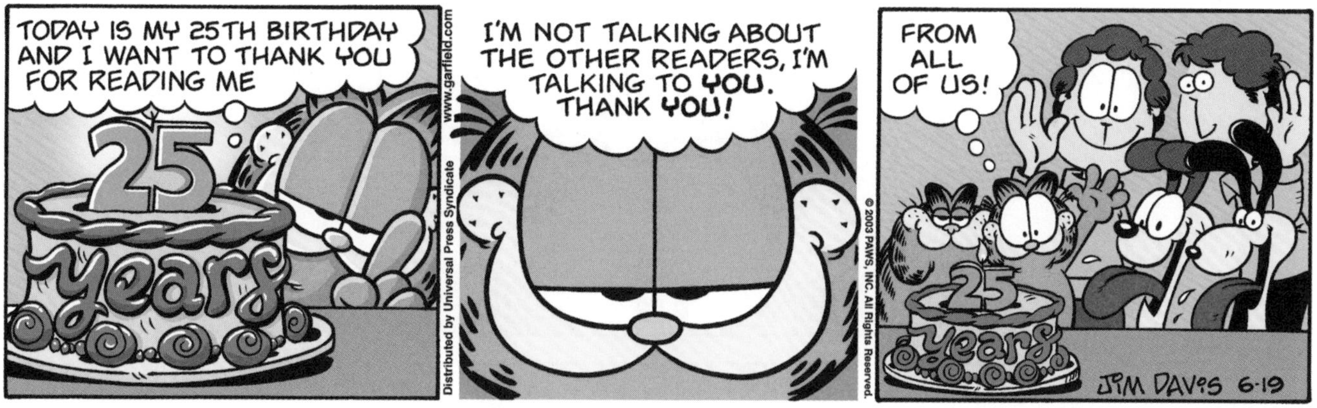
TODAY IS MY 25TH BIRTHDAY AND I WANT TO THANK YOU FOR READING ME
25
years
www.garfield.com
Distributed by Universal Press Syndicate
I'M NOT TALKING ABOUT THE OTHER READERS, I'M TALKING TO **YOU**. THANK **YOU**!
© 2003 PAWS, INC. All Rights Reserved.
FROM ALL OF US!
25
years
JIM DAVIS 6-19

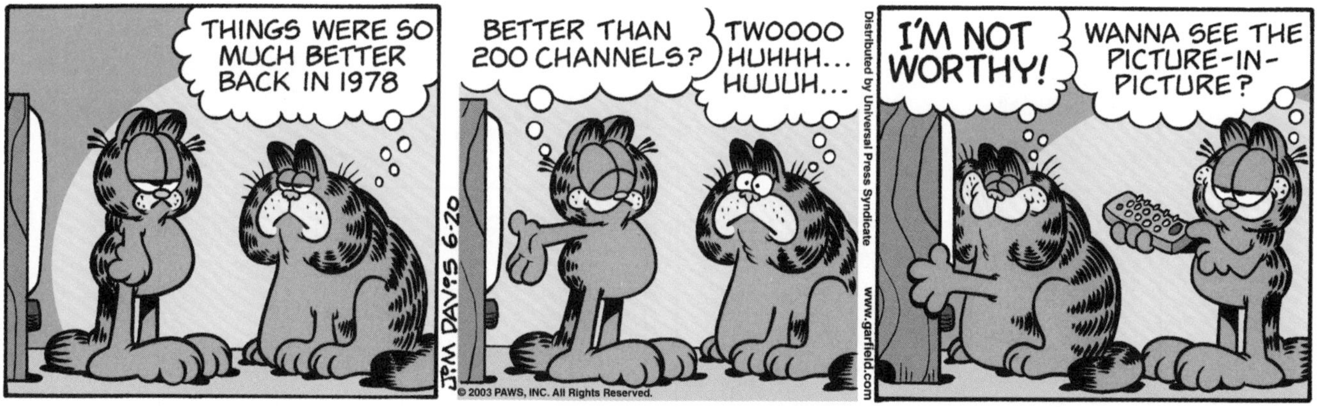
THINGS WERE SO MUCH BETTER BACK IN 1978
JIM DAVIS 6-20
BETTER THAN 200 CHANNELS?
TWOOOO HUHHH... HUUUH...
© 2003 PAWS, INC. All Rights Reserved.
Distributed by Universal Press Syndicate
www.garfield.com
I'M NOT WORTHY!
WANNA SEE THE PICTURE-IN-PICTURE?

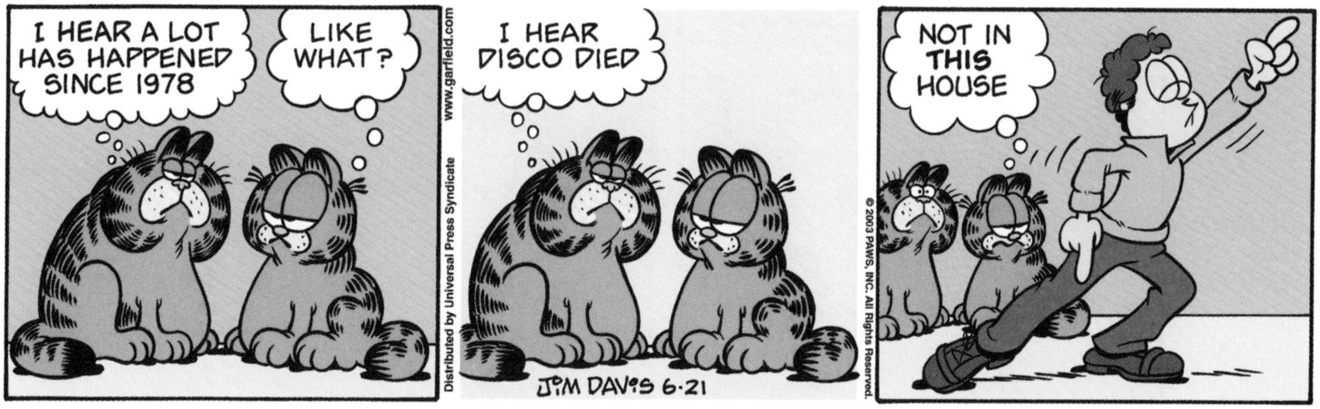
I HEAR A LOT HAS HAPPENED SINCE 1978
LIKE WHAT?
www.garfield.com
Distributed by Universal Press Syndicate
I HEAR DISCO DIED
JIM DAVIS 6-21
© 2003 PAWS, INC. All Rights Reserved.
NOT IN **THIS** HOUSE

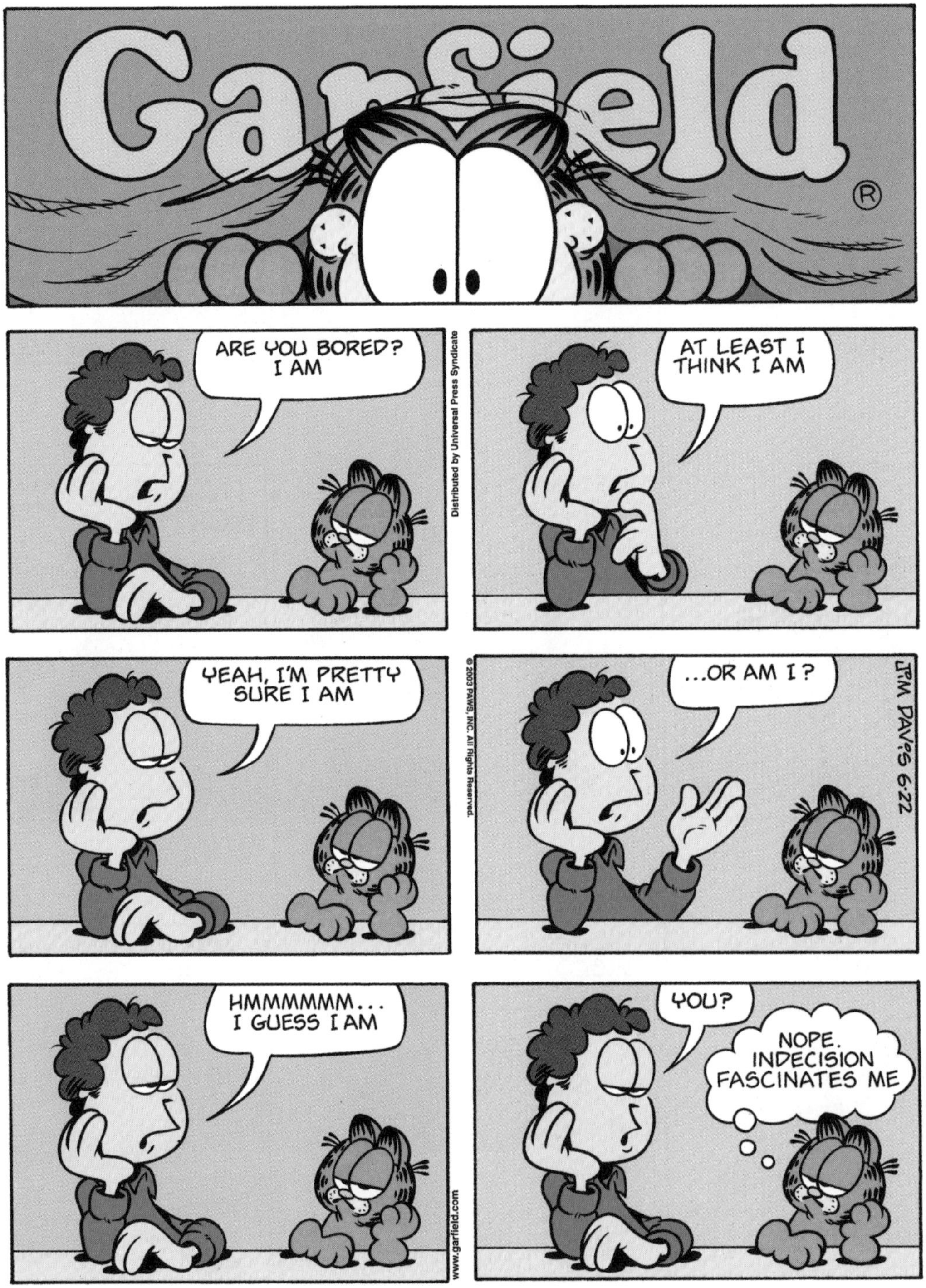
Garfield®
ARE YOU BORED? I AM
AT LEAST I THINK I AM
YEAH, I'M PRETTY SURE I AM
...OR AM I?
HMMMMMM... I GUESS I AM
YOU?
NOPE. INDECISION FASCINATES ME
Distributed by Universal Press Syndicate
© 2003 PAWS, INC. All Rights Reserved.
www.garfield.com
JIM DAVIS 6-22

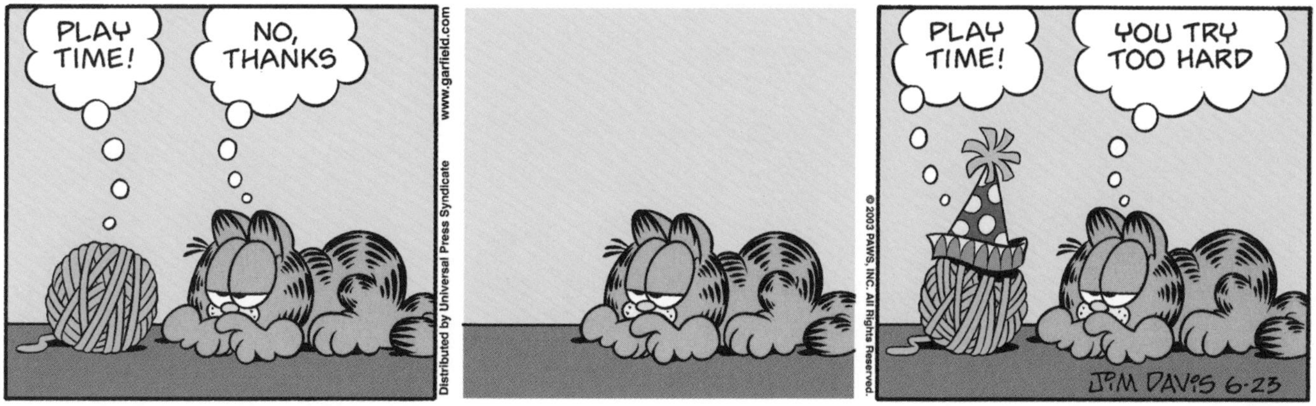
PLAY TIME!
NO, THANKS
PLAY TIME!
YOU TRY TOO HARD
JIM DAVIS 6-23

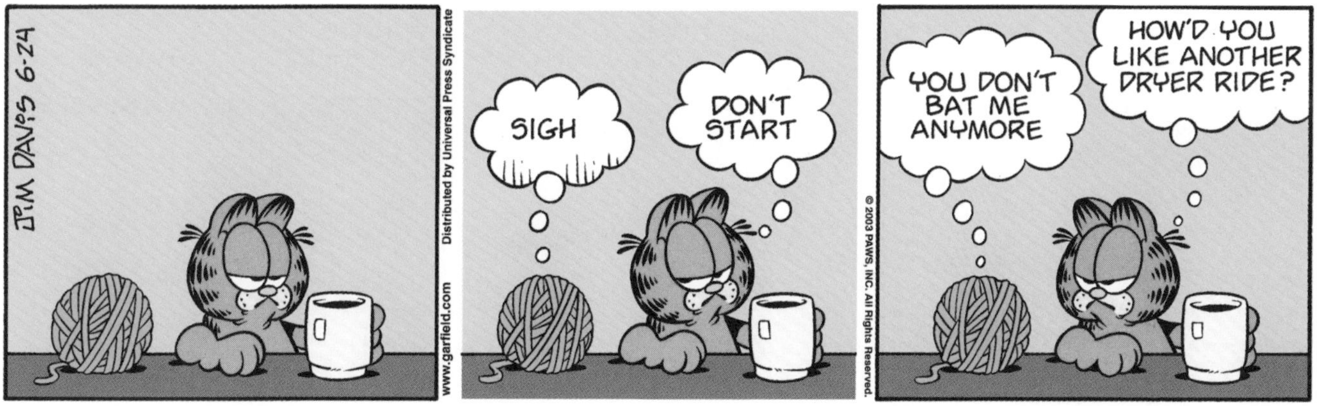
JIM DAVIS 6-24
SIGH
DON'T START
YOU DON'T BAT ME ANYMORE
HOW'D YOU LIKE ANOTHER DRYER RIDE?

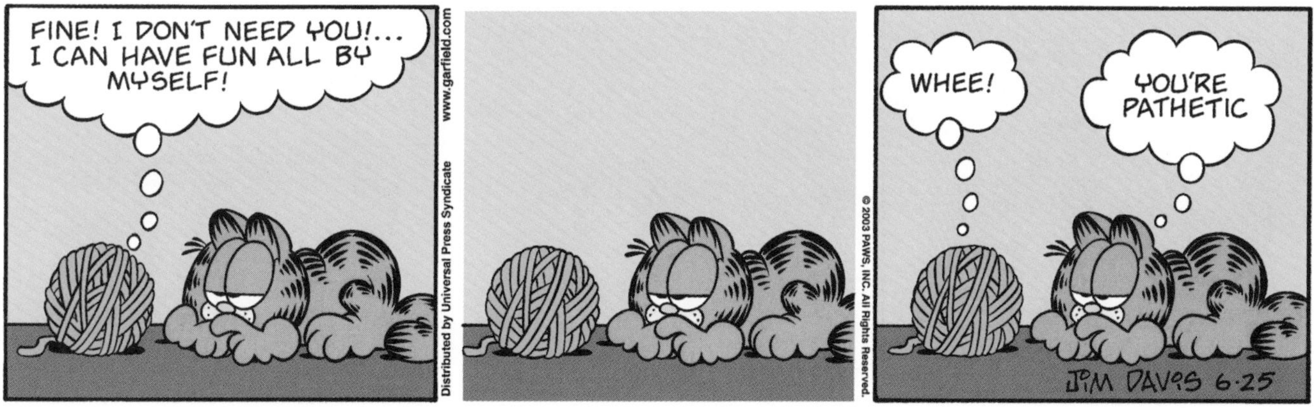
FINE! I DON'T NEED YOU!... I CAN HAVE FUN ALL BY MYSELF!
WHEE!
YOU'RE PATHETIC
JIM DAVIS 6-25

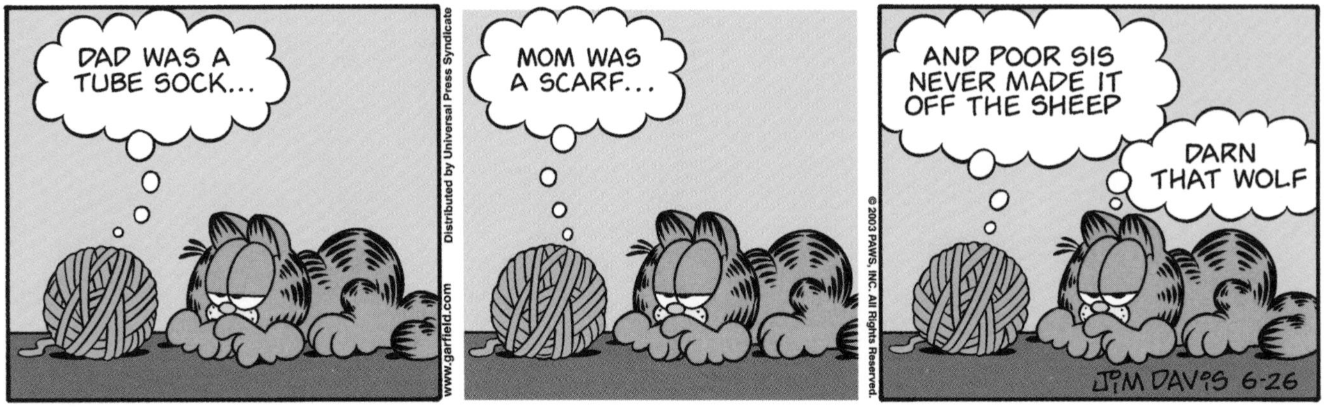
DAD WAS A TUBE SOCK...
MOM WAS A SCARF...
AND POOR SIS NEVER MADE IT OFF THE SHEEP
DARN THAT WOLF
JIM DAVIS 6-26
Distributed by Universal Press Syndicate
www.garfield.com
© 2003 PAWS, INC. All Rights Reserved.

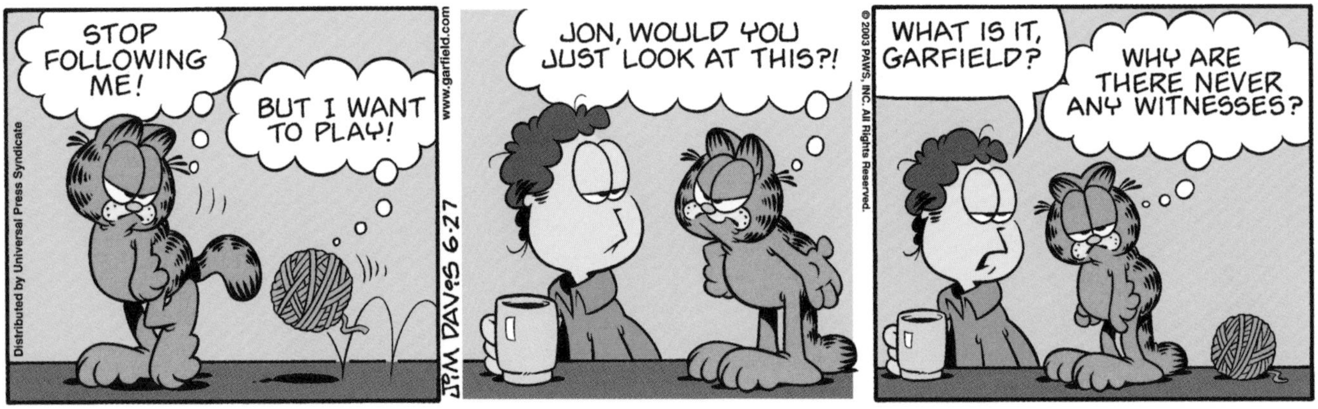
STOP FOLLOWING ME!
BUT I WANT TO PLAY!
JON, WOULD YOU JUST LOOK AT THIS?!
WHAT IS IT, GARFIELD?
WHY ARE THERE NEVER ANY WITNESSES?
JIM DAVIS 6-27
Distributed by Universal Press Syndicate
www.garfield.com
© 2003 PAWS, INC. All Rights Reserved.

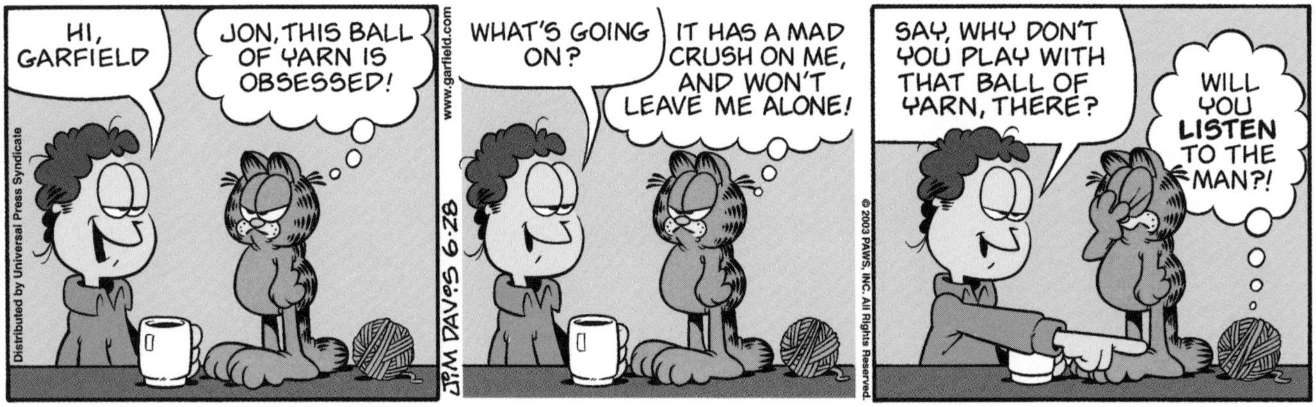
HI, GARFIELD
JON, THIS BALL OF YARN IS OBSESSED!
WHAT'S GOING ON?
IT HAS A MAD CRUSH ON ME, AND WON'T LEAVE ME ALONE!
SAY, WHY DON'T YOU PLAY WITH THAT BALL OF YARN, THERE?
WILL YOU **LISTEN** TO THE MAN?!
JIM DAVIS 6-28
Distributed by Universal Press Syndicate
www.garfield.com
© 2003 PAWS, INC. All Rights Reserved.

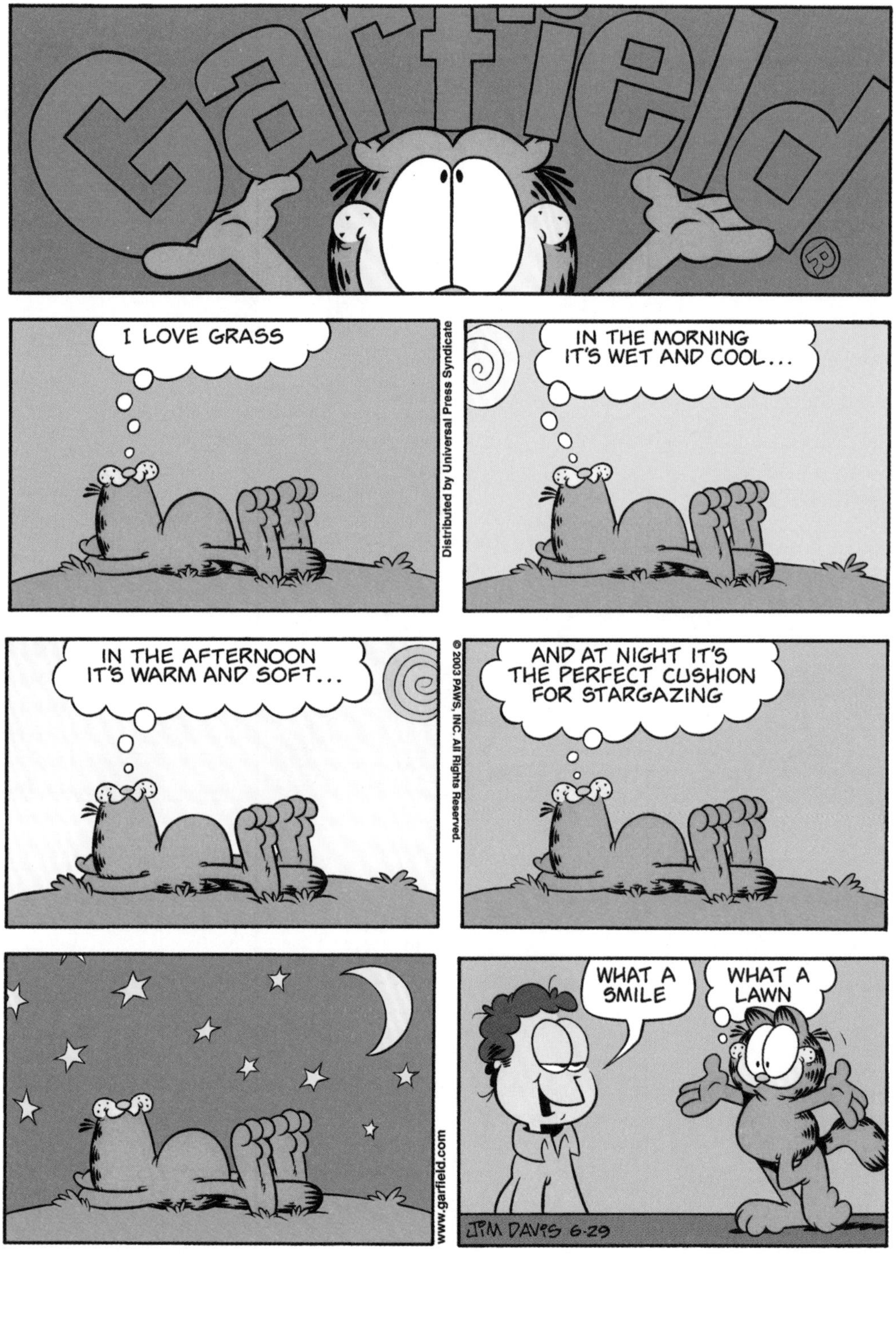
Garfield
I LOVE GRASS
IN THE MORNING IT'S WET AND COOL...
IN THE AFTERNOON IT'S WARM AND SOFT...
AND AT NIGHT IT'S THE PERFECT CUSHION FOR STARGAZING
WHAT A SMILE
WHAT A LAWN
JIM DAVIS 6-29
Distributed by Universal Press Syndicate
© 2003 PAWS, INC. All Rights Reserved.
www.garfield.com

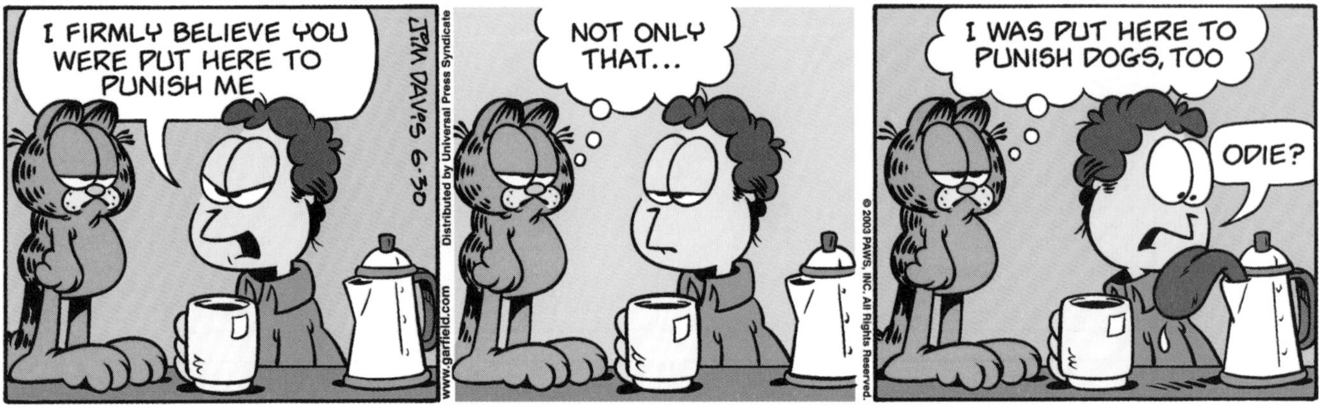
I FIRMLY BELIEVE YOU WERE PUT HERE TO PUNISH ME
JIM DAVIS 6-30
Distributed by Universal Press Syndicate
www.garfield.com
NOT ONLY THAT...
© 2003 PAWS, INC. All Rights Reserved.
I WAS PUT HERE TO PUNISH DOGS, TOO
ODIE?

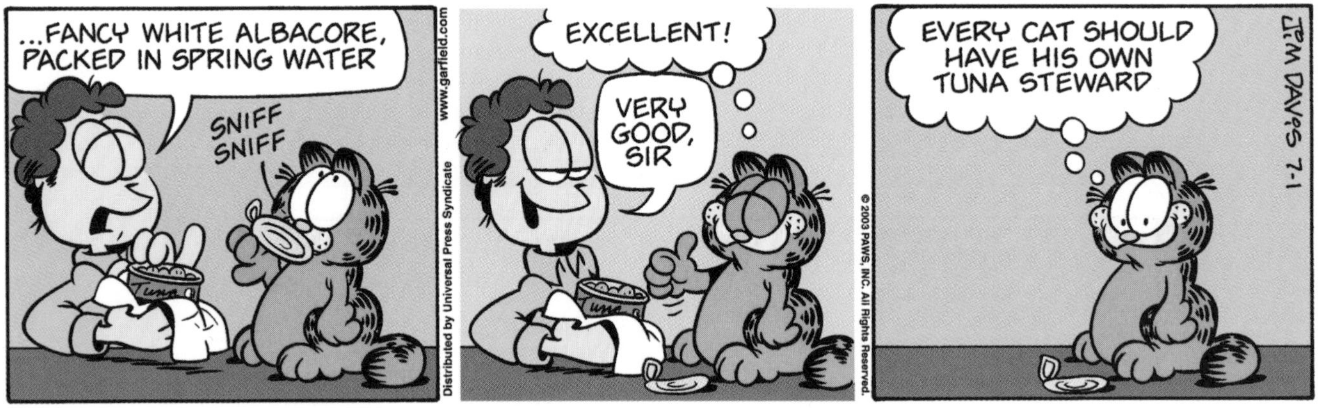
...FANCY WHITE ALBACORE, PACKED IN SPRING WATER
SNIFF SNIFF
TUNA
Distributed by Universal Press Syndicate
www.garfield.com
EXCELLENT!
VERY GOOD, SIR
© 2003 PAWS, INC. All Rights Reserved.
EVERY CAT SHOULD HAVE HIS OWN TUNA STEWARD
JIM DAVIS 7-1

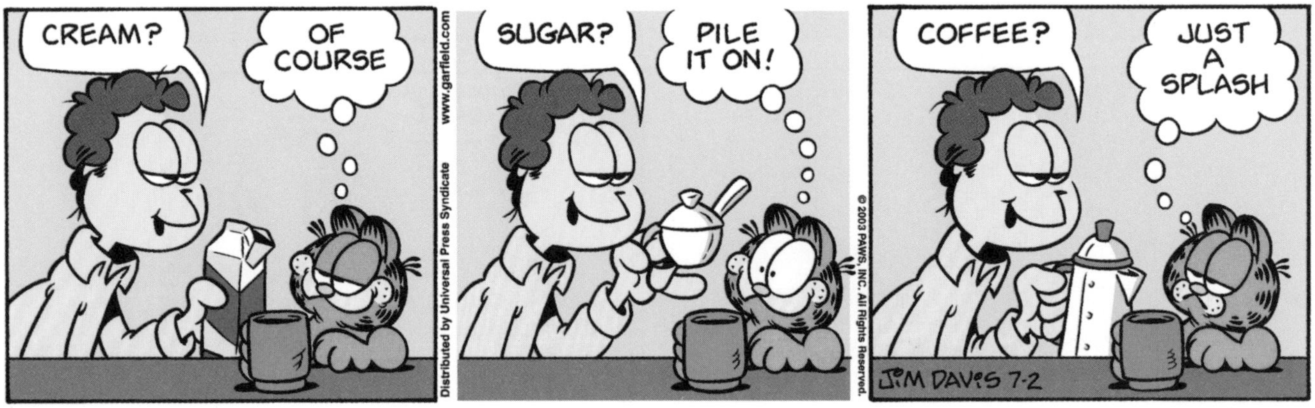
CREAM?
OF COURSE
Distributed by Universal Press Syndicate
www.garfield.com
SUGAR?
PILE IT ON!
© 2003 PAWS, INC. All Rights Reserved.
COFFEE?
JUST A SPLASH
JIM DAVIS 7-2

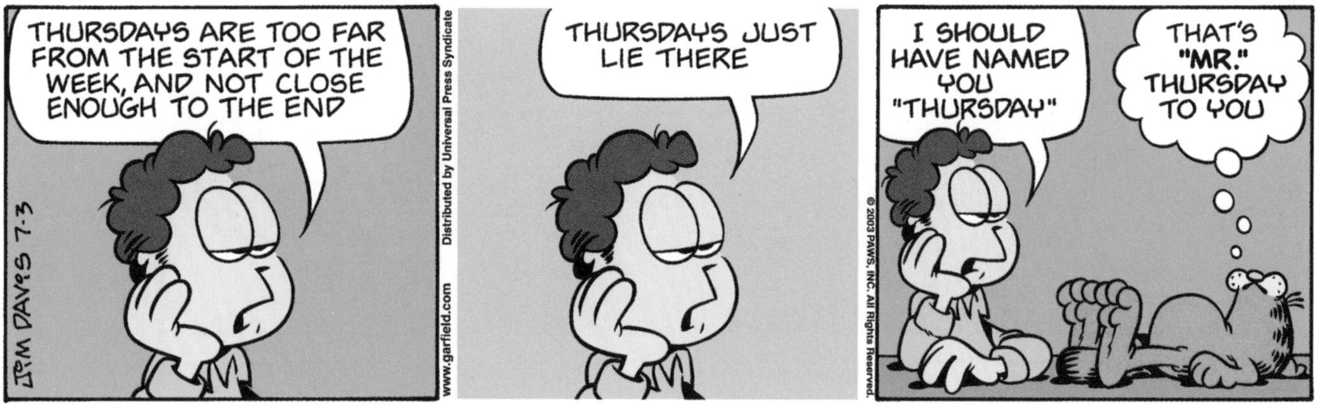
THURSDAYS ARE TOO FAR FROM THE START OF THE WEEK, AND NOT CLOSE ENOUGH TO THE END
JIM DAVIS 7-3
www.garfield.com Distributed by Universal Press Syndicate
THURSDAYS JUST LIE THERE
© 2003 PAWS, INC. All Rights Reserved.
I SHOULD HAVE NAMED YOU "THURSDAY"
THAT'S **"MR."** THURSDAY TO YOU

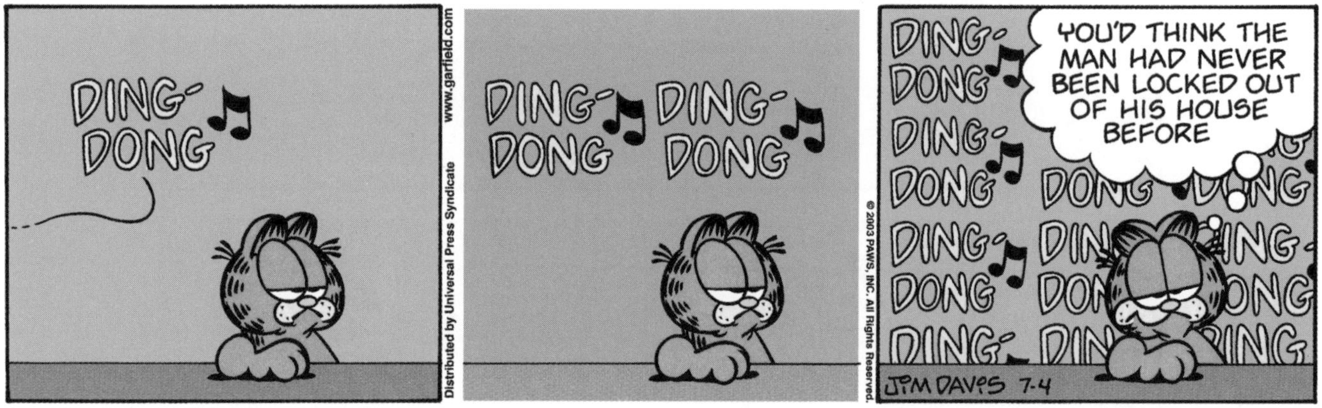
DING-DONG
Distributed by Universal Press Syndicate www.garfield.com
DING-DONG DING-DONG
© 2003 PAWS, INC. All Rights Reserved.
DING-DONG DING-DONG DING-DONG
YOU'D THINK THE MAN HAD NEVER BEEN LOCKED OUT OF HIS HOUSE BEFORE
JIM DAVIS 7-4

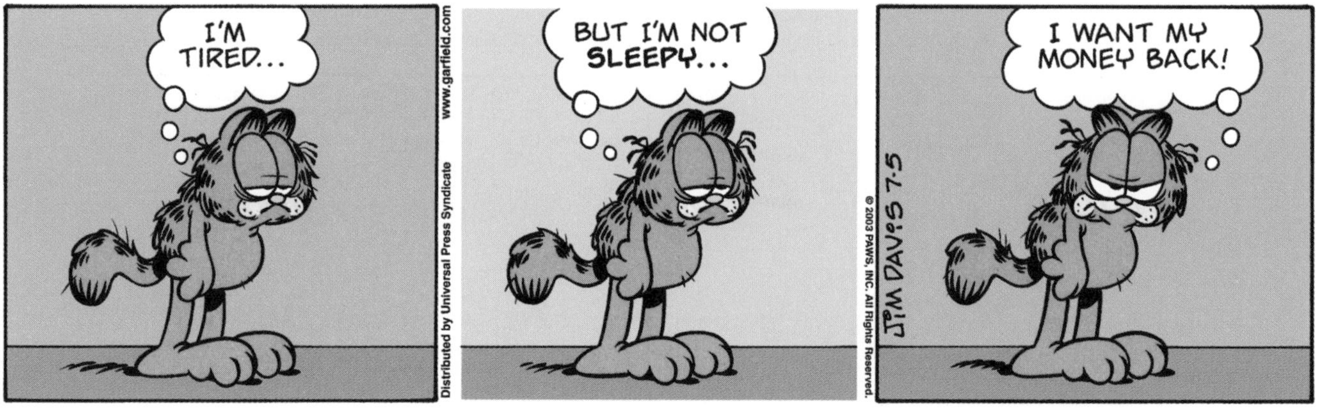
I'M TIRED...
Distributed by Universal Press Syndicate www.garfield.com
BUT I'M NOT **SLEEPY**...
© 2003 PAWS, INC. All Rights Reserved.
JIM DAVIS 7-5
I WANT MY MONEY BACK!

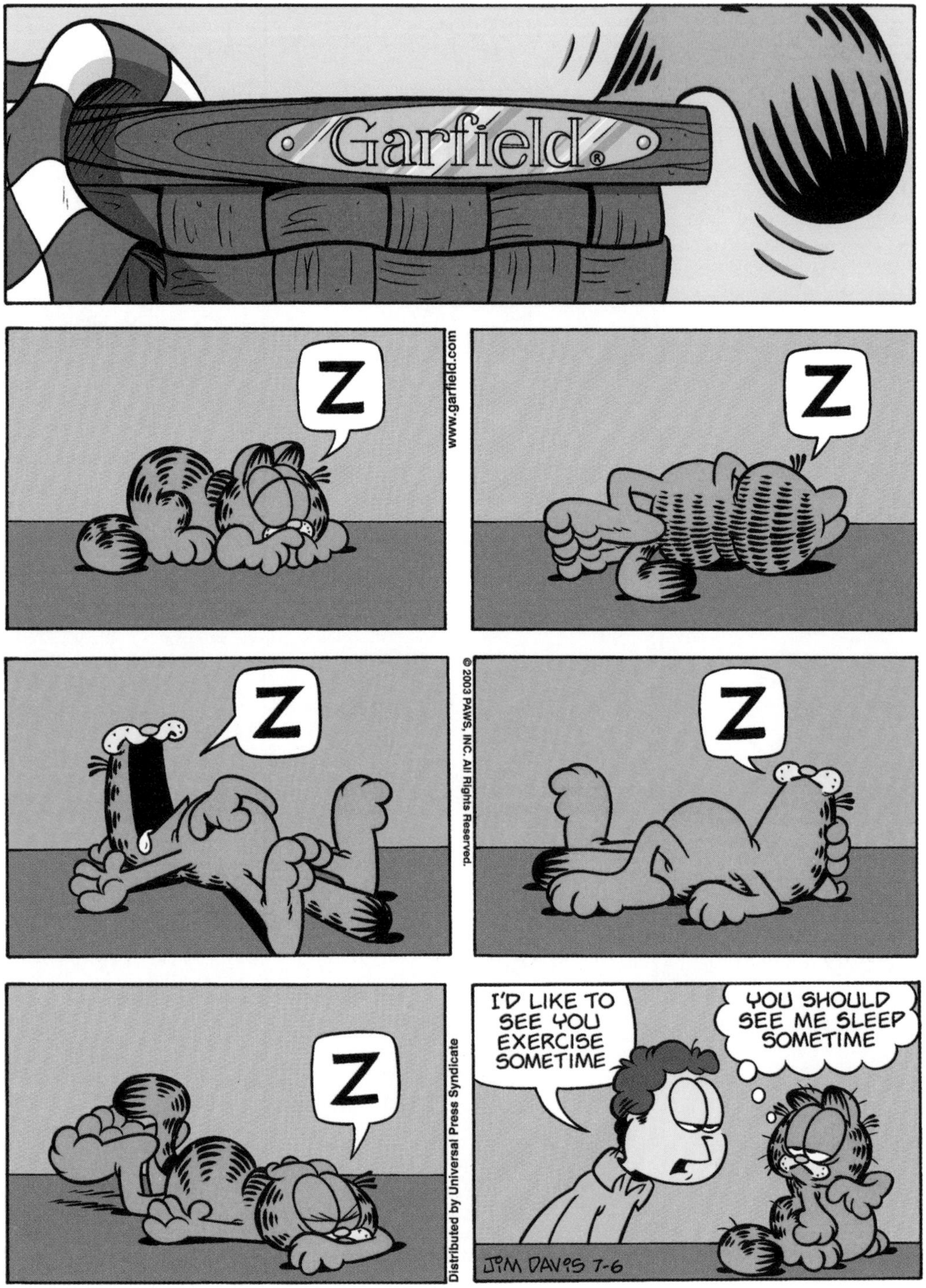
Garfield®
www.garfield.com
Z
Z
© 2003 PAWS, INC. All Rights Reserved.
Z
Z
Distributed by Universal Press Syndicate
Z
I'D LIKE TO SEE YOU EXERCISE SOMETIME
YOU SHOULD SEE ME SLEEP SOMETIME
JIM DAVIS 7-6

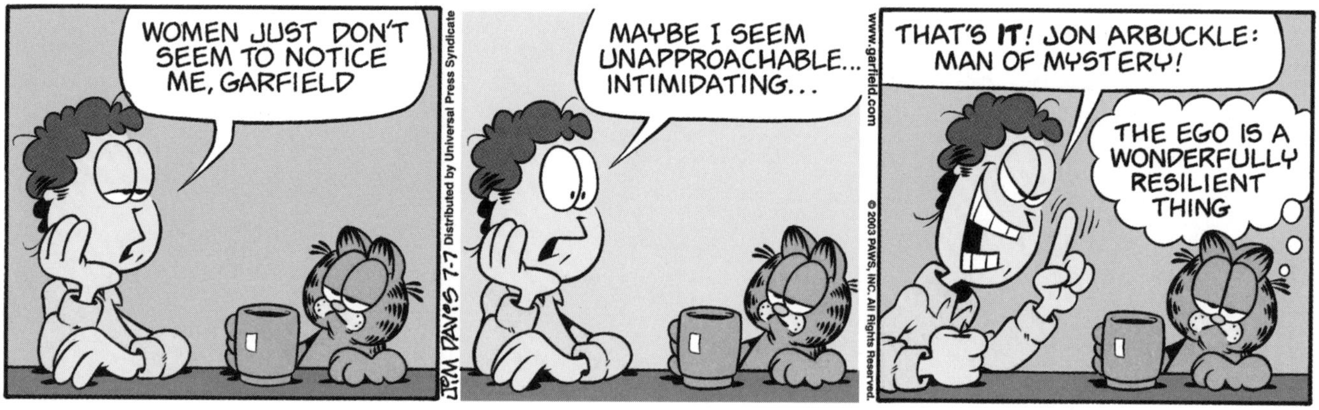
WOMEN JUST DON'T SEEM TO NOTICE ME, GARFIELD
JIM DAVIS 7-7 Distributed by Universal Press Syndicate
MAYBE I SEEM UNAPPROACHABLE... INTIMIDATING...
www.garfield.com © 2003 PAWS, INC. All Rights Reserved.
THAT'S **IT**! JON ARBUCKLE: MAN OF MYSTERY!
THE EGO IS A WONDERFULLY RESILIENT THING

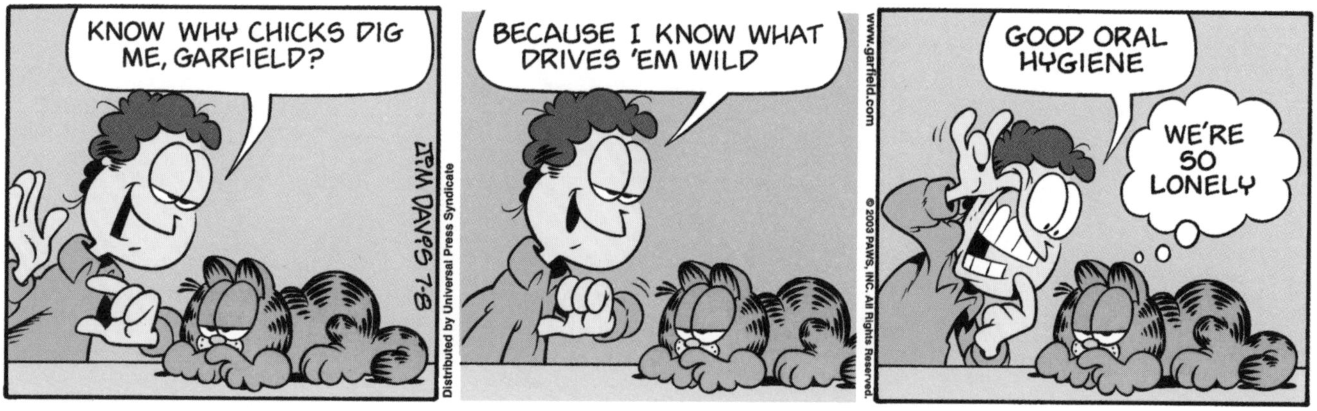
KNOW WHY CHICKS DIG ME, GARFIELD?
JIM DAVIS 7-8
Distributed by Universal Press Syndicate
BECAUSE I KNOW WHAT DRIVES 'EM WILD
www.garfield.com © 2003 PAWS, INC. All Rights Reserved.
GOOD ORAL HYGIENE
WE'RE SO LONELY

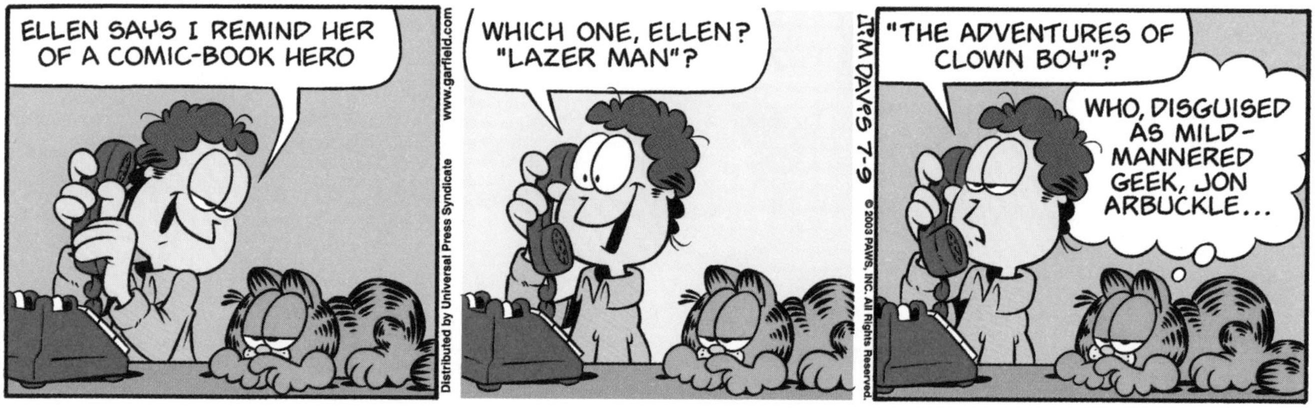
ELLEN SAYS I REMIND HER OF A COMIC-BOOK HERO
www.garfield.com Distributed by Universal Press Syndicate
WHICH ONE, ELLEN? "LAZER MAN"?
JIM DAVIS 7-9 © 2003 PAWS, INC. All Rights Reserved.
"THE ADVENTURES OF CLOWN BOY"?
WHO, DISGUISED AS MILD-MANNERED GEEK, JON ARBUCKLE...

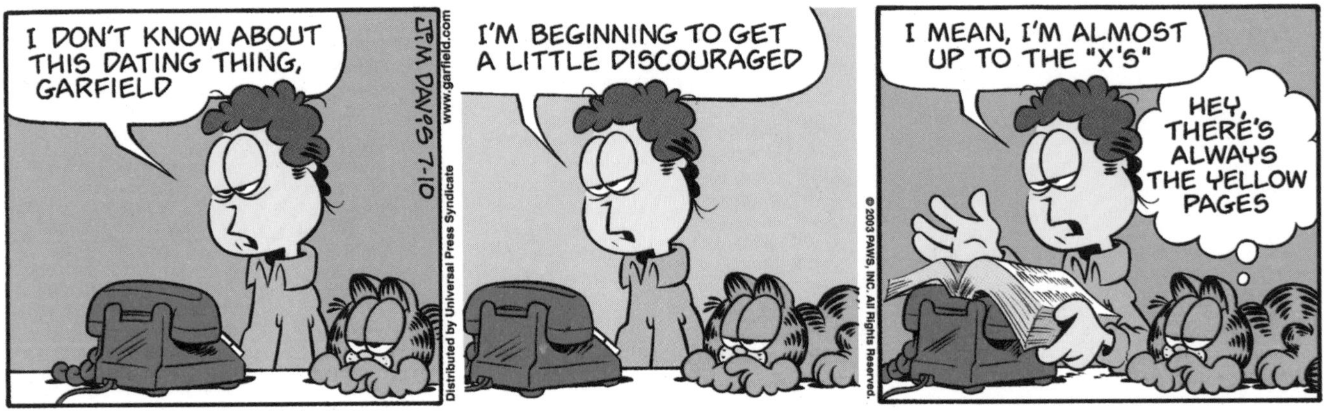
I DON'T KNOW ABOUT THIS DATING THING, GARFIELD
JPM DAVPS 7-10
www.garfield.com
Distributed by Universal Press Syndicate
I'M BEGINNING TO GET A LITTLE DISCOURAGED
© 2003 PAWS, INC. All Rights Reserved.
I MEAN, I'M ALMOST UP TO THE "X'S"
HEY, THERE'S ALWAYS THE YELLOW PAGES

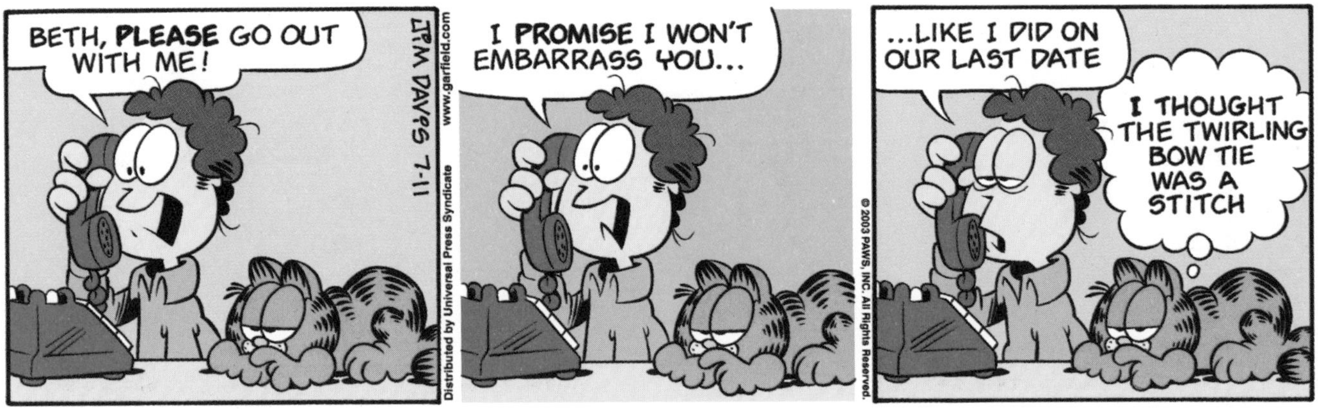
BETH, **PLEASE** GO OUT WITH ME!
JPM DAVPS 7-11
www.garfield.com
Distributed by Universal Press Syndicate
I **PROMISE** I WON'T EMBARRASS YOU...
© 2003 PAWS, INC. All Rights Reserved.
...LIKE I DID ON OUR LAST DATE
I THOUGHT THE TWIRLING BOW TIE WAS A STITCH

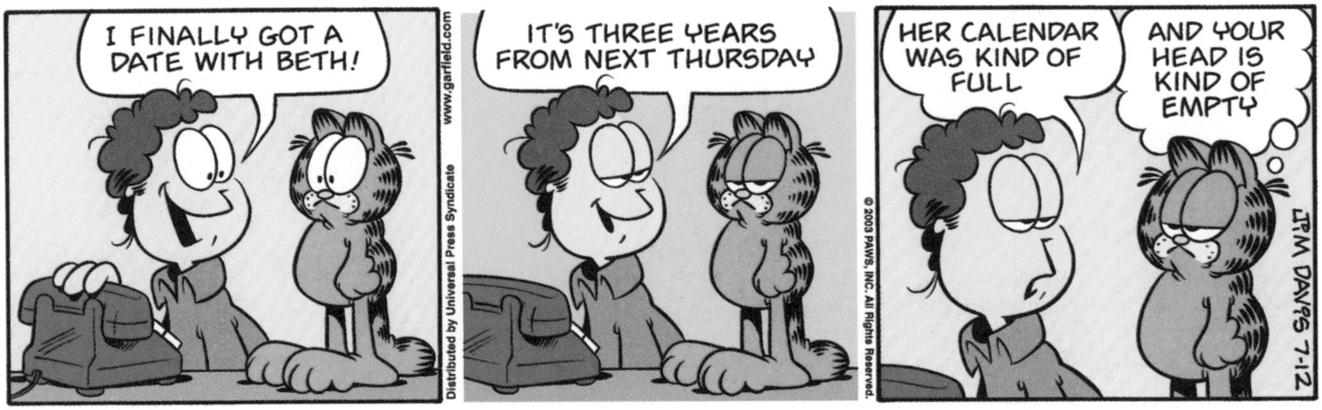
I FINALLY GOT A DATE WITH BETH!
www.garfield.com
Distributed by Universal Press Syndicate
IT'S THREE YEARS FROM NEXT THURSDAY
© 2003 PAWS, INC. All Rights Reserved.
HER CALENDAR WAS KIND OF FULL
AND YOUR HEAD IS KIND OF EMPTY
JPM DAVPS 7-12

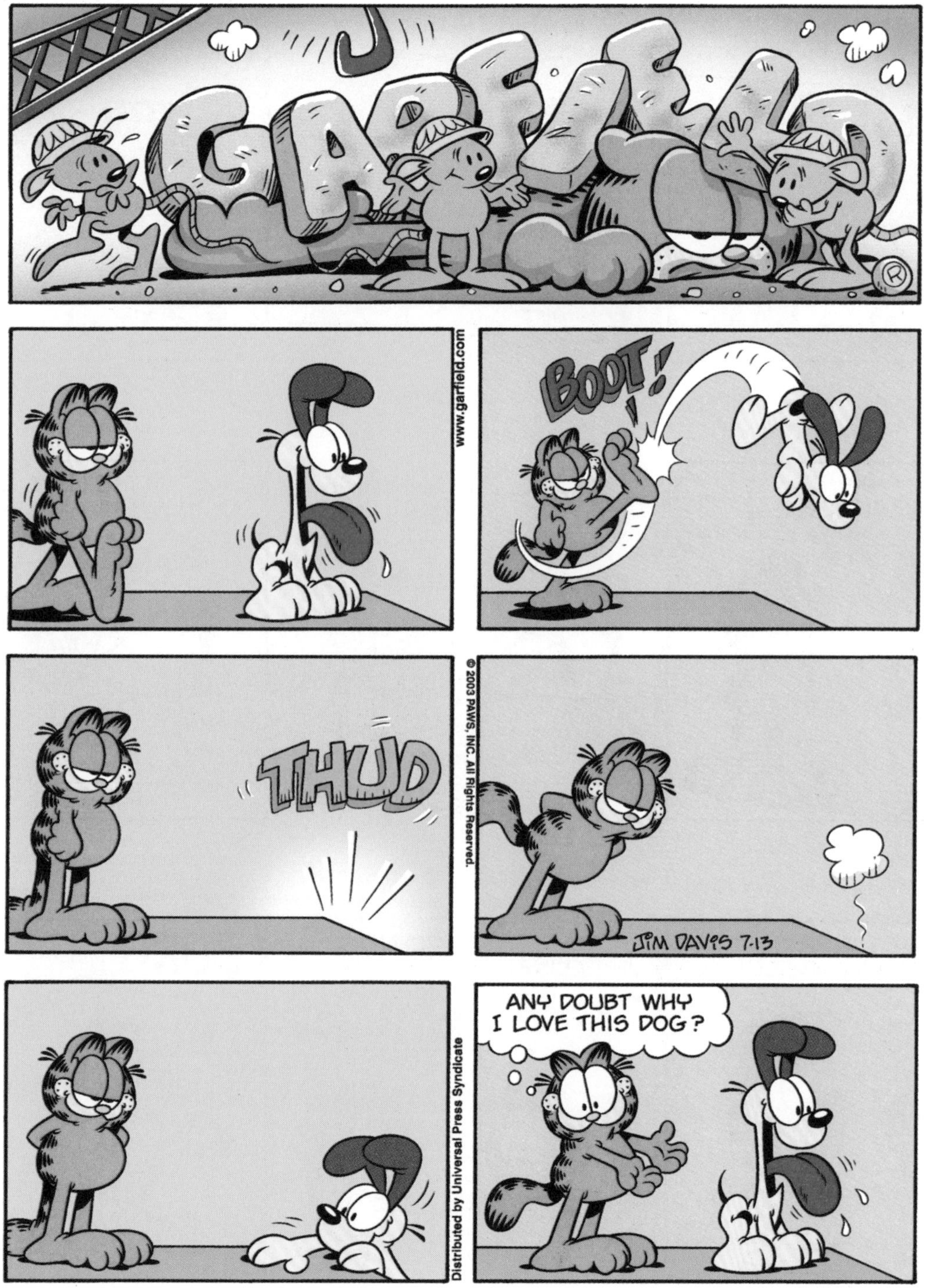
GARFIELD
www.garfield.com
BOOT!
© 2003 PAWS, INC. All Rights Reserved.
THUD
JIM DAVIS 7-13
Distributed by Universal Press Syndicate
ANY DOUBT WHY I LOVE THIS DOG?

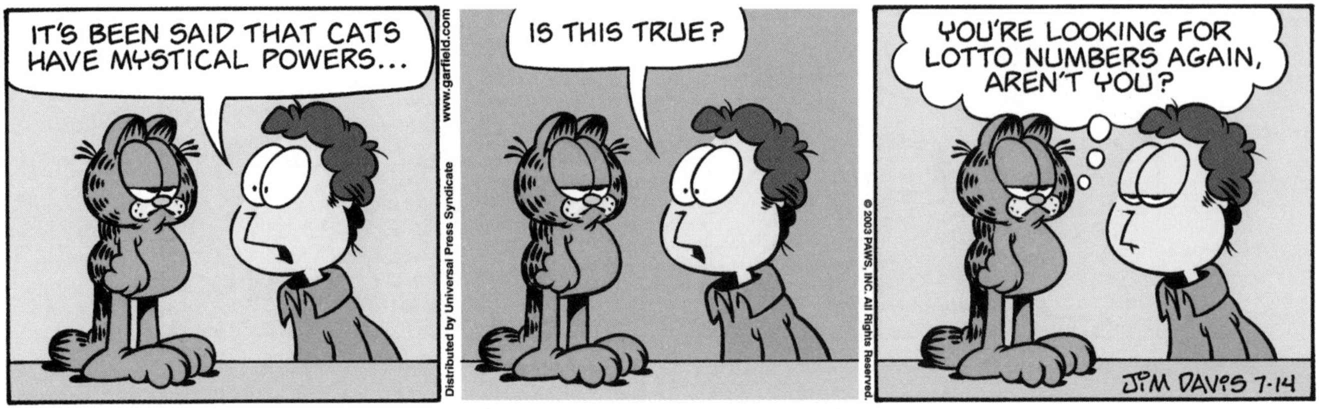
IT'S BEEN SAID THAT CATS HAVE MYSTICAL POWERS...
www.garfield.com
Distributed by Universal Press Syndicate
IS THIS TRUE?
© 2003 PAWS, INC. All Rights Reserved.
YOU'RE LOOKING FOR LOTTO NUMBERS AGAIN, AREN'T YOU?
JIM DAVIS 7-14

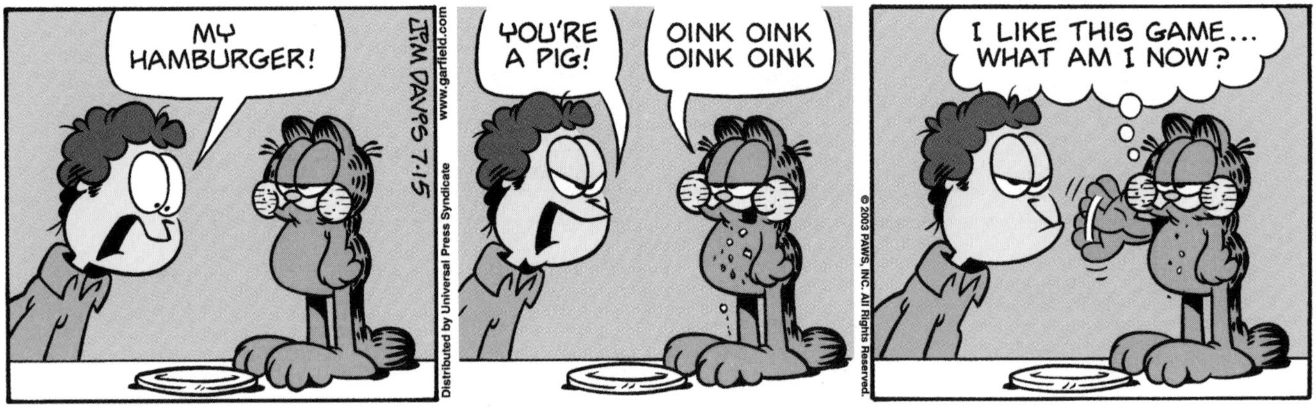
MY HAMBURGER!
JIM DAVIS 7-15
www.garfield.com
Distributed by Universal Press Syndicate
YOU'RE A PIG!
OINK OINK OINK OINK
© 2003 PAWS, INC. All Rights Reserved.
I LIKE THIS GAME... WHAT AM I NOW?

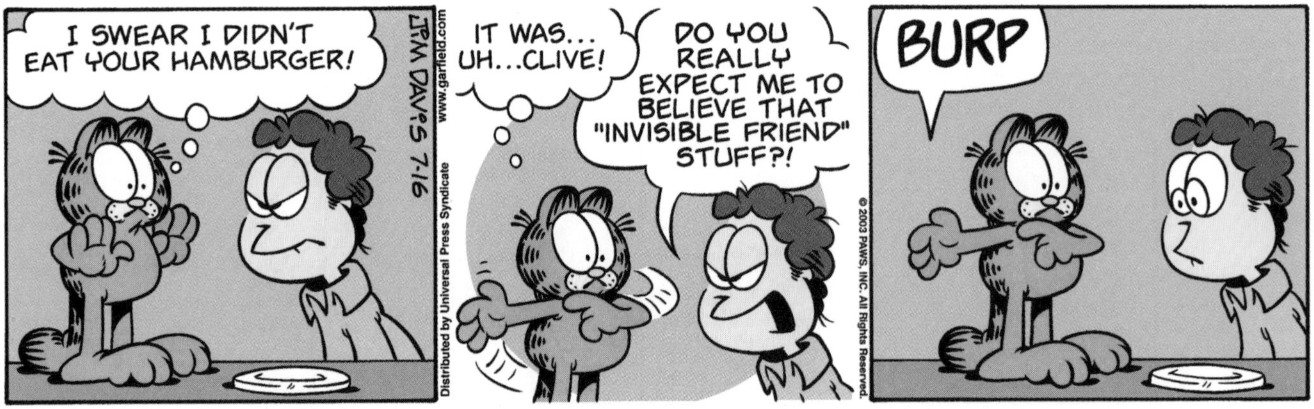
I SWEAR I DIDN'T EAT YOUR HAMBURGER!
JIM DAVIS 7-16
www.garfield.com
Distributed by Universal Press Syndicate
IT WAS... UH...CLIVE!
DO YOU REALLY EXPECT ME TO BELIEVE THAT "INVISIBLE FRIEND" STUFF?!
© 2003 PAWS, INC. All Rights Reserved.
BURP

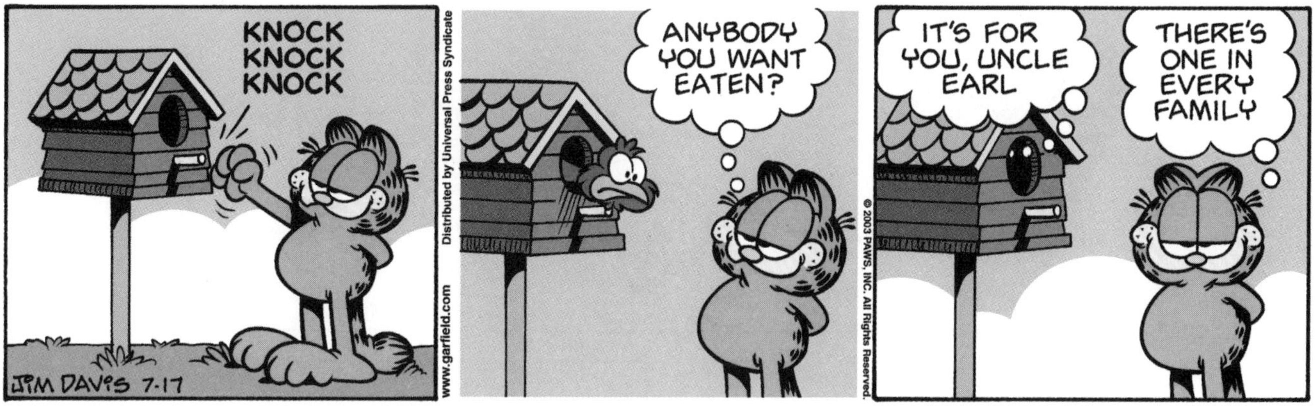
KNOCK KNOCK KNOCK
JIM DAVIS 7-17
www.garfield.com Distributed by Universal Press Syndicate
ANYBODY YOU WANT EATEN?
© 2003 PAWS, INC. All Rights Reserved.
IT'S FOR YOU, UNCLE EARL
THERE'S ONE IN EVERY FAMILY

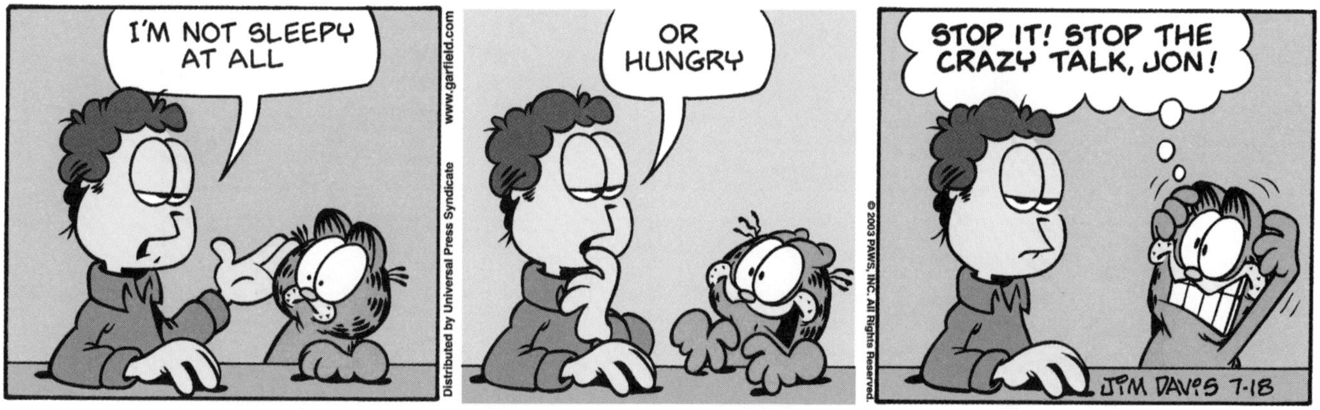
I'M NOT SLEEPY AT ALL
Distributed by Universal Press Syndicate www.garfield.com
OR HUNGRY
© 2003 PAWS, INC. All Rights Reserved.
STOP IT! STOP THE CRAZY TALK, JON!
JIM DAVIS 7-18

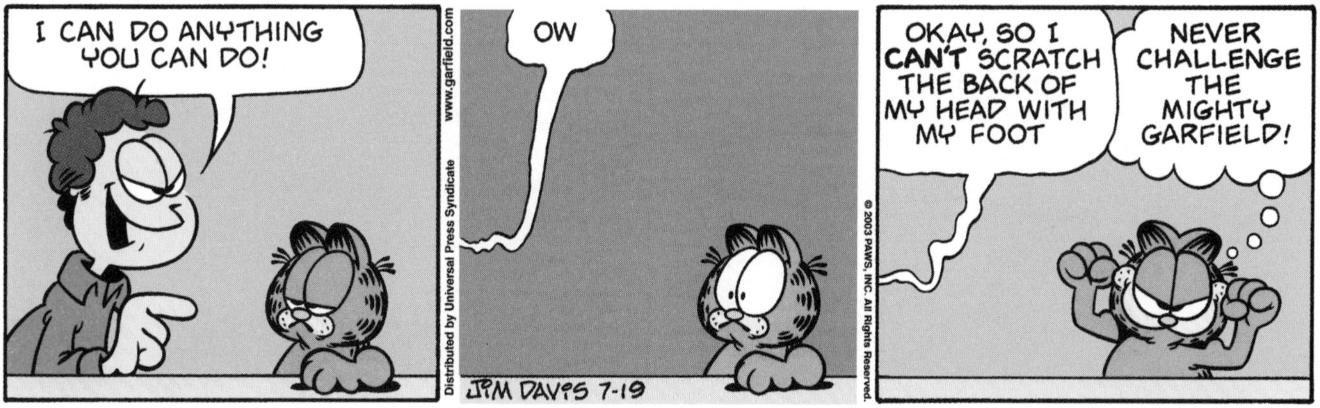
I CAN DO ANYTHING YOU CAN DO!
Distributed by Universal Press Syndicate www.garfield.com
OW
JIM DAVIS 7-19
© 2003 PAWS, INC. All Rights Reserved.
OKAY, SO I CAN'T SCRATCH THE BACK OF MY HEAD WITH MY FOOT
NEVER CHALLENGE THE MIGHTY GARFIELD!

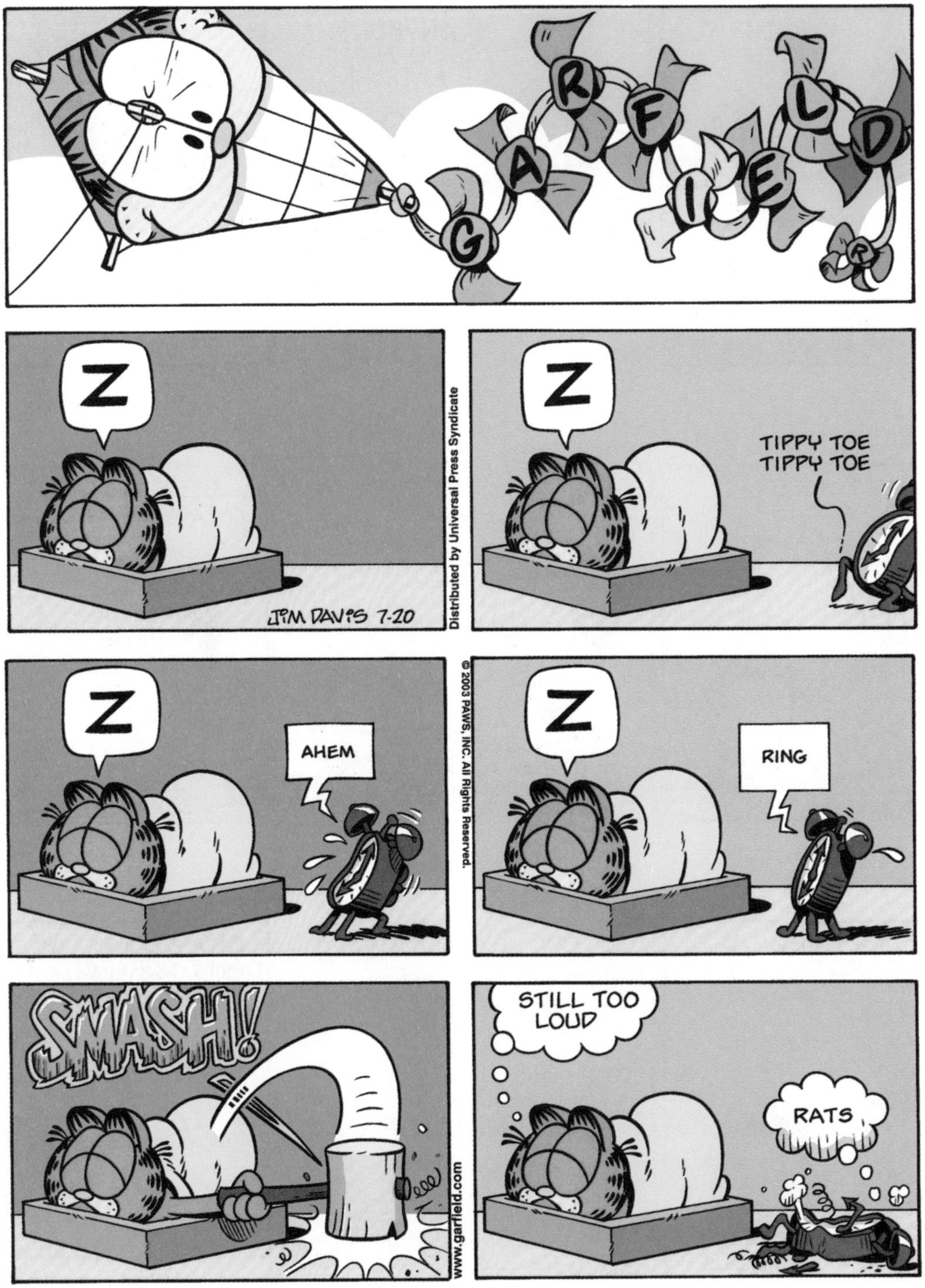
GARFIELD®
Z
JIM DAVIS 7-20
Distributed by Universal Press Syndicate
Z
TIPPY TOE
TIPPY TOE
© 2003 PAWS, INC. All Rights Reserved.
Z
AHEM
Z
RING
SMASH!
www.garfield.com
STILL TOO LOUD
RATS

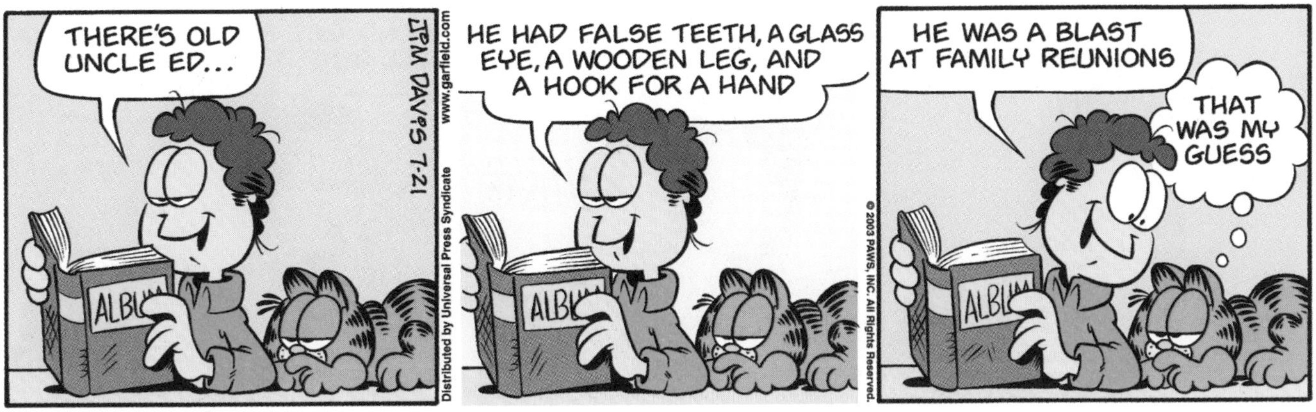
THERE'S OLD UNCLE ED...
JIM DAVIS 7-21
www.garfield.com
Distributed by Universal Press Syndicate
HE HAD FALSE TEETH, A GLASS EYE, A WOODEN LEG, AND A HOOK FOR A HAND
ALBUM
© 2003 PAWS, INC. All Rights Reserved.
HE WAS A BLAST AT FAMILY REUNIONS
THAT WAS MY GUESS

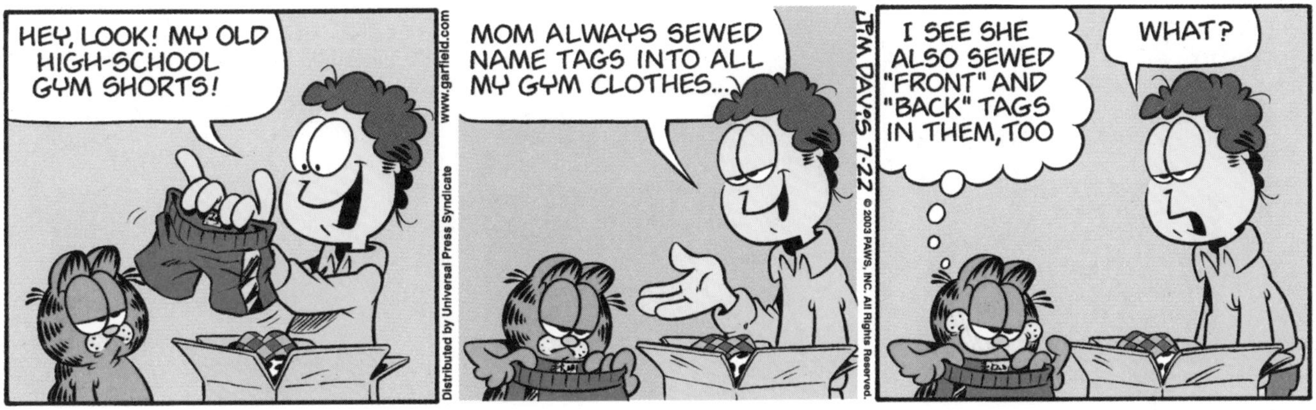
HEY, LOOK! MY OLD HIGH-SCHOOL GYM SHORTS!
www.garfield.com
Distributed by Universal Press Syndicate
MOM ALWAYS SEWED NAME TAGS INTO ALL MY GYM CLOTHES...
JIM DAVIS 7-22
© 2003 PAWS, INC. All Rights Reserved.
I SEE SHE ALSO SEWED "FRONT" AND "BACK" TAGS IN THEM, TOO
WHAT?

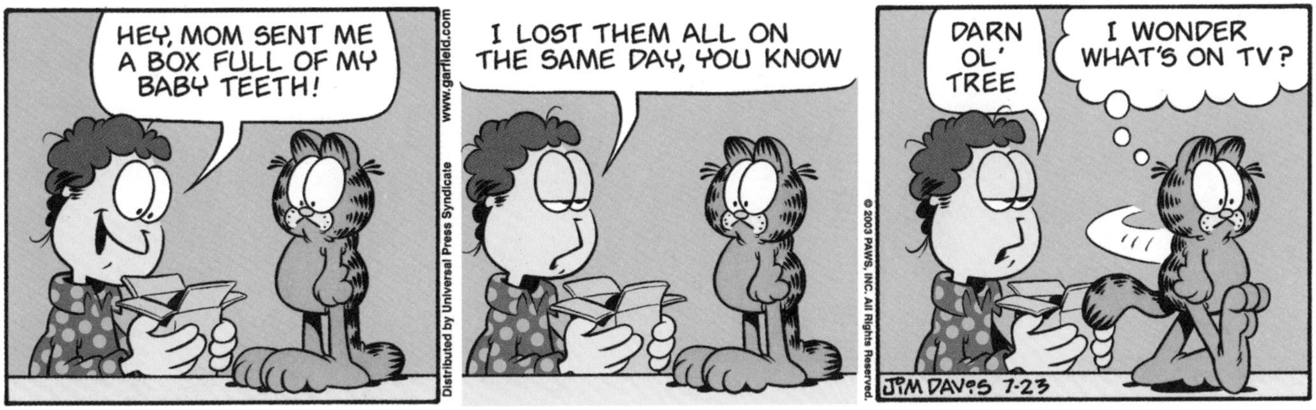
HEY, MOM SENT ME A BOX FULL OF MY BABY TEETH!
www.garfield.com
Distributed by Universal Press Syndicate
I LOST THEM ALL ON THE SAME DAY, YOU KNOW
© 2003 PAWS, INC. All Rights Reserved.
DARN OL' TREE
I WONDER WHAT'S ON TV?
JIM DAVIS 7-23

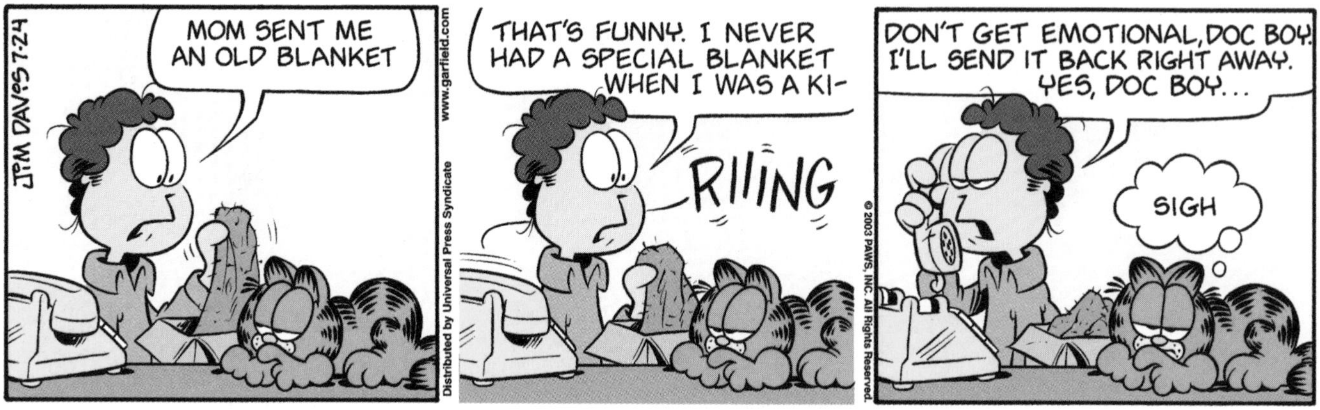
JIM DAVIS 7·24
MOM SENT ME AN OLD BLANKET
www.garfield.com
Distributed by Universal Press Syndicate
THAT'S FUNNY. I NEVER HAD A SPECIAL BLANKET WHEN I WAS A KI-
RIIING
© 2003 PAWS, INC. All Rights Reserved.
DON'T GET EMOTIONAL, DOC BOY. I'LL SEND IT BACK RIGHT AWAY. YES, DOC BOY...
SIGH

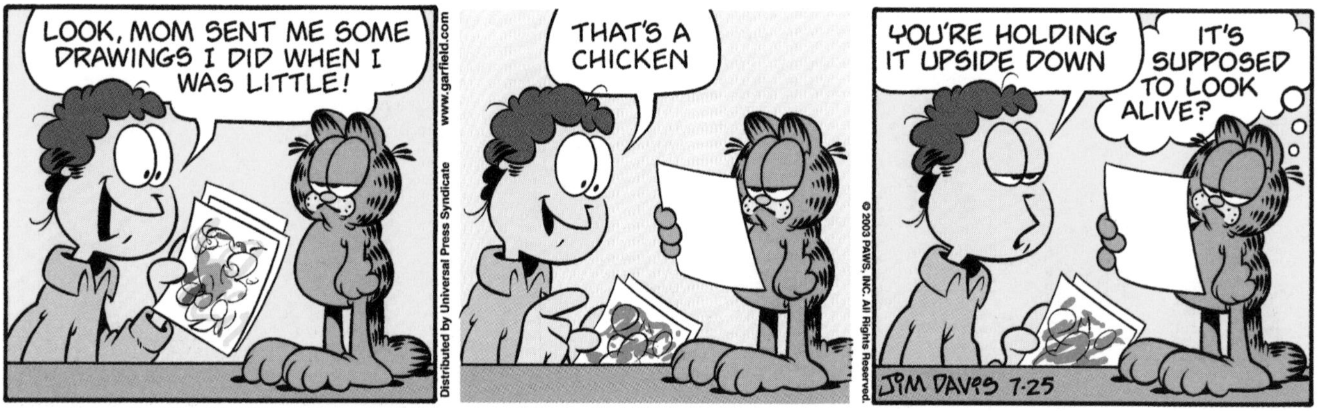
LOOK, MOM SENT ME SOME DRAWINGS I DID WHEN I WAS LITTLE!
www.garfield.com
Distributed by Universal Press Syndicate
THAT'S A CHICKEN
© 2003 PAWS, INC. All Rights Reserved.
YOU'RE HOLDING IT UPSIDE DOWN
IT'S SUPPOSED TO LOOK ALIVE?
JIM DAVIS 7·25

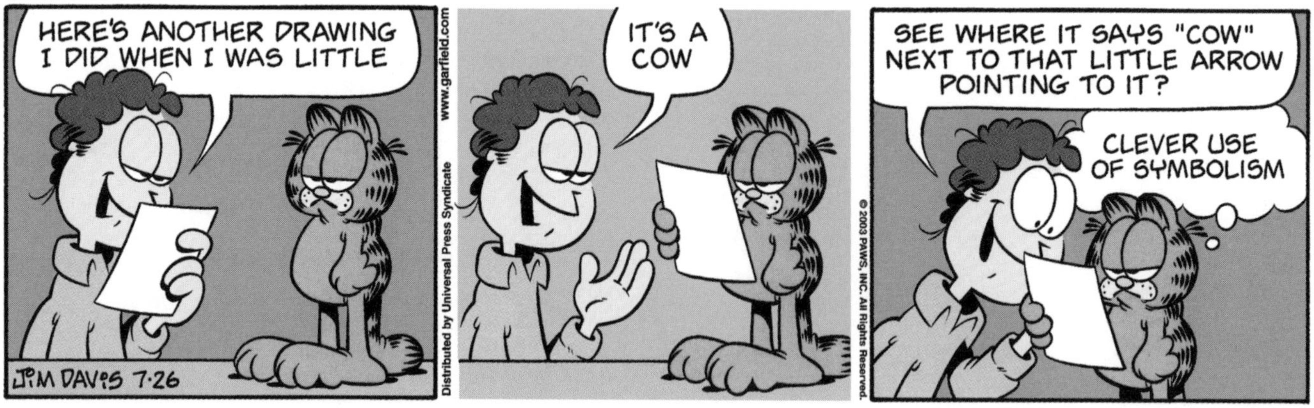
HERE'S ANOTHER DRAWING I DID WHEN I WAS LITTLE
JIM DAVIS 7·26
www.garfield.com
Distributed by Universal Press Syndicate
IT'S A COW
© 2003 PAWS, INC. All Rights Reserved.
SEE WHERE IT SAYS "COW" NEXT TO THAT LITTLE ARROW POINTING TO IT?
CLEVER USE OF SYMBOLISM

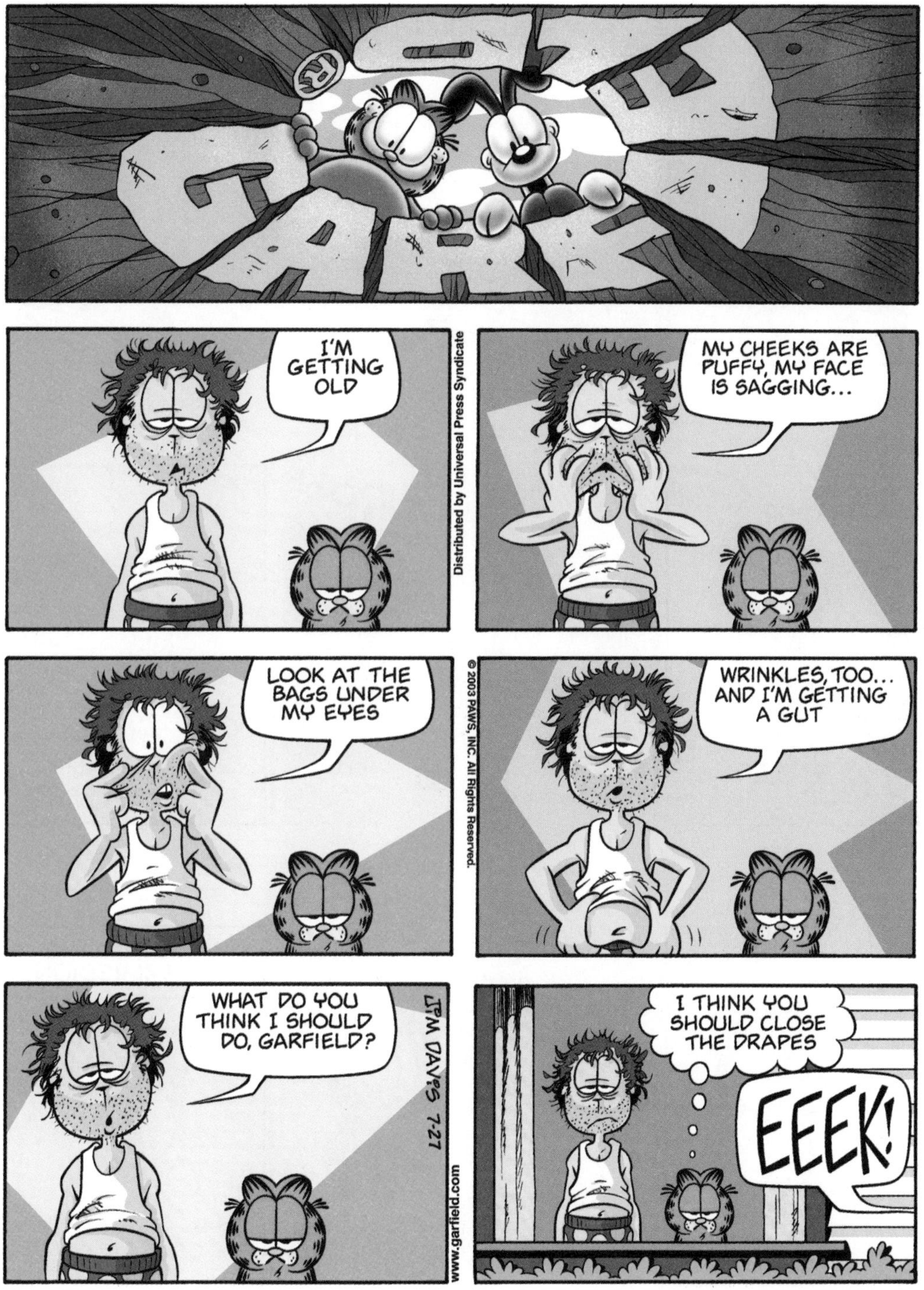
I'M GETTING OLD
MY CHEEKS ARE PUFFY, MY FACE IS SAGGING...
LOOK AT THE BAGS UNDER MY EYES
WRINKLES, TOO... AND I'M GETTING A GUT
WHAT DO YOU THINK I SHOULD DO, GARFIELD?
I THINK YOU SHOULD CLOSE THE DRAPES
EEEK!
JPM DAVIS 7-27
Distributed by Universal Press Syndicate
© 2003 PAWS, INC. All Rights Reserved.
www.garfield.com

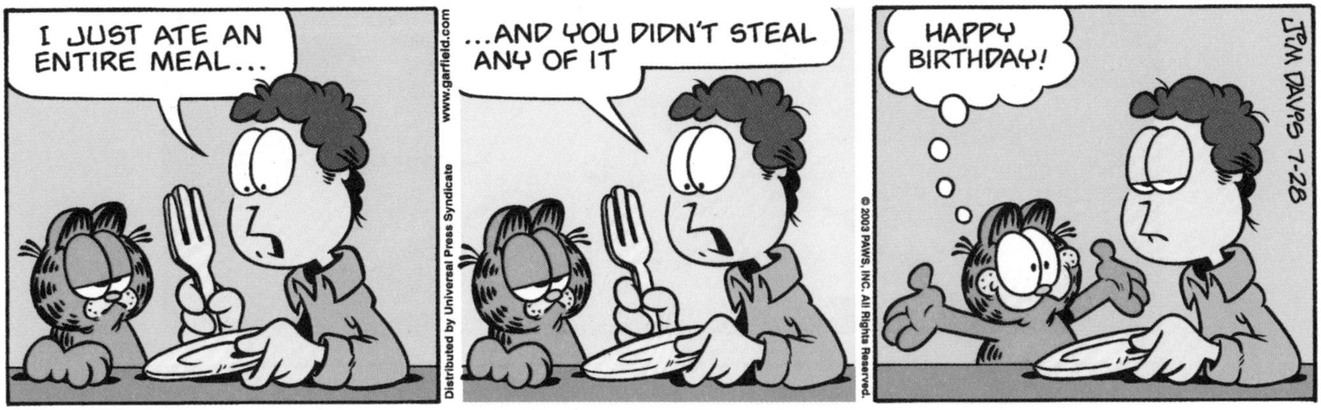
I JUST ATE AN ENTIRE MEAL...
www.garfield.com Distributed by Universal Press Syndicate
...AND YOU DIDN'T STEAL ANY OF IT
© 2003 PAWS, INC. All Rights Reserved.
HAPPY BIRTHDAY!
JIM DAVIS 7-28

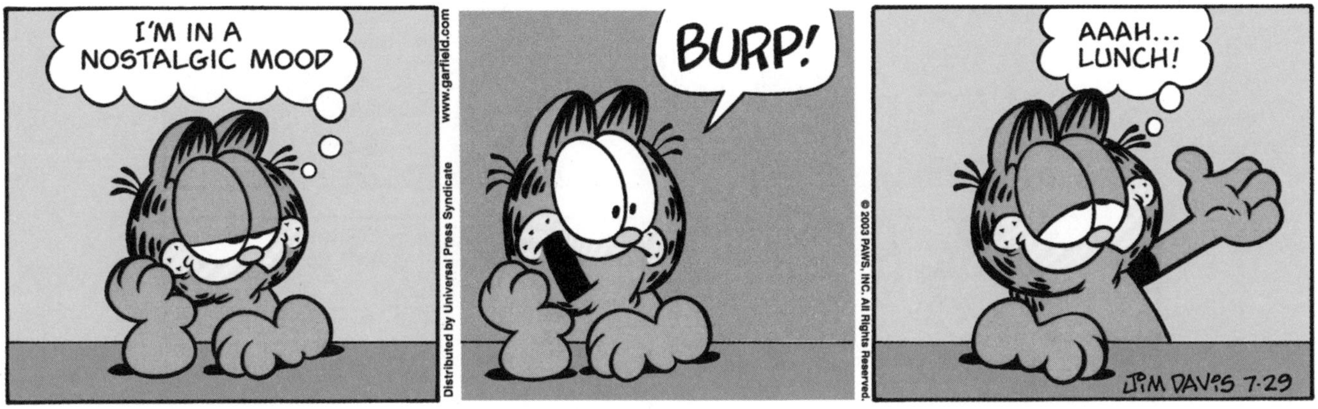
I'M IN A NOSTALGIC MOOD
www.garfield.com Distributed by Universal Press Syndicate
BURP!
© 2003 PAWS, INC. All Rights Reserved.
AAAH... LUNCH!
JIM DAVIS 7-29

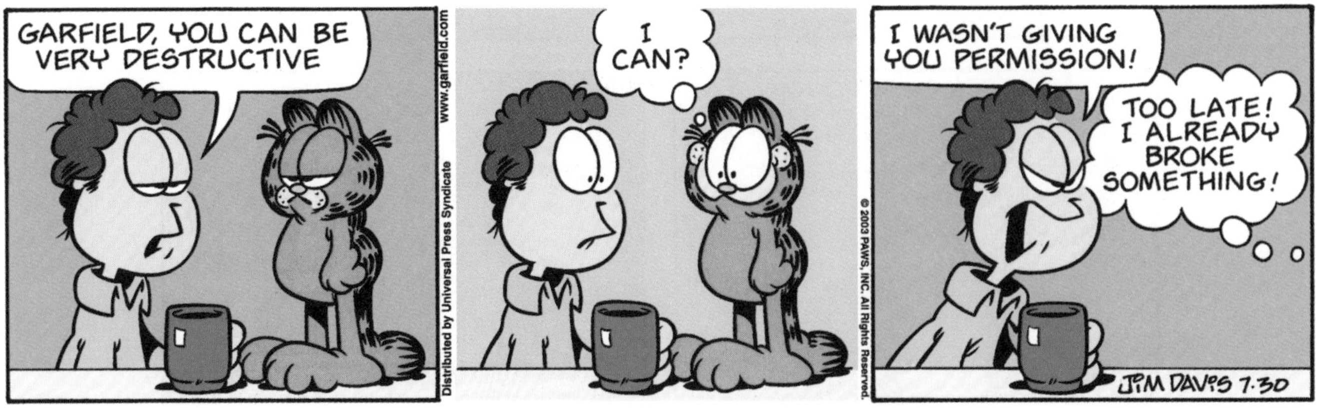
GARFIELD, YOU CAN BE VERY DESTRUCTIVE
www.garfield.com Distributed by Universal Press Syndicate
I CAN?
© 2003 PAWS, INC. All Rights Reserved.
I WASN'T GIVING YOU PERMISSION!
TOO LATE! I ALREADY BROKE SOMETHING!
JIM DAVIS 7-30

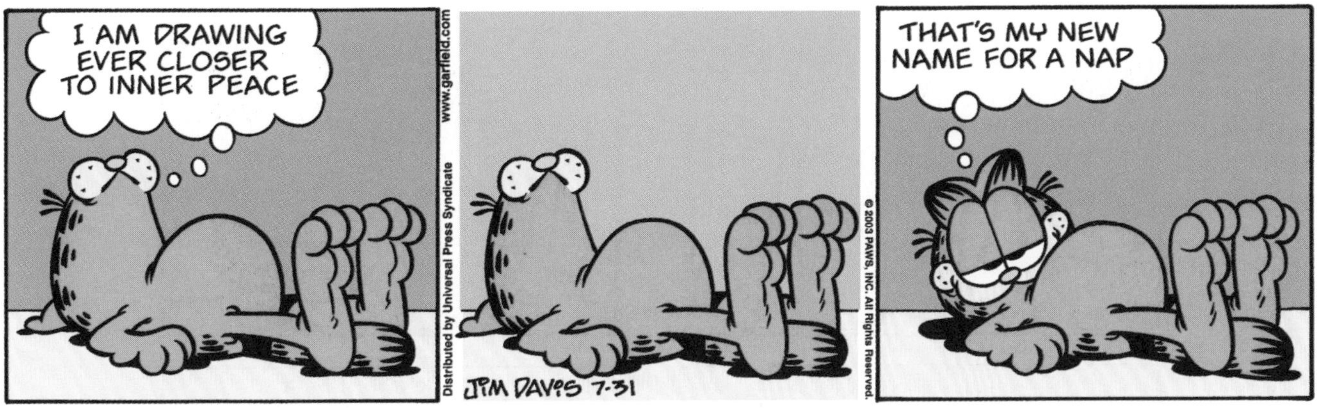
I AM DRAWING EVER CLOSER TO INNER PEACE
THAT'S MY NEW NAME FOR A NAP
JIM DAVIS 7-31
Distributed by Universal Press Syndicate www.garfield.com
© 2003 PAWS, INC. All Rights Reserved.

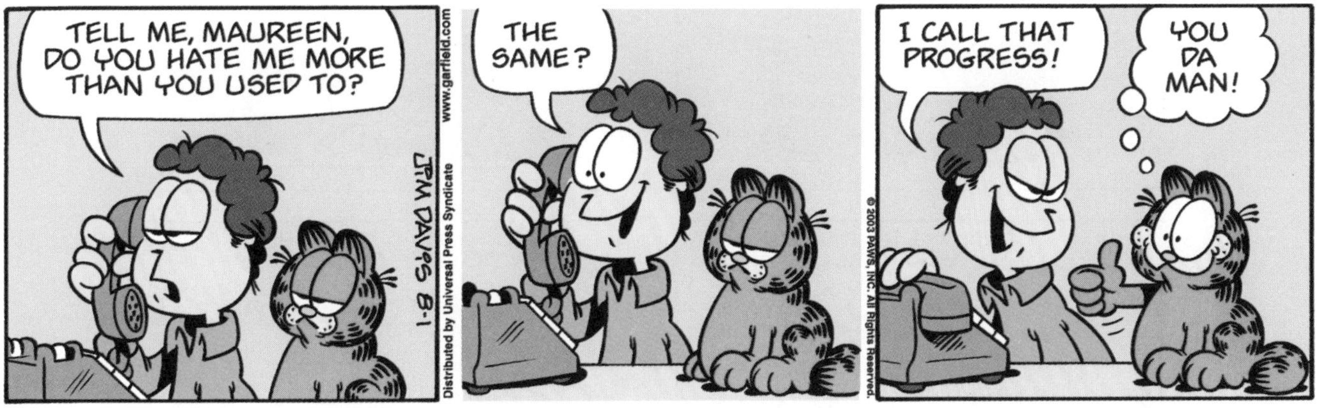
TELL ME, MAUREEN, DO YOU HATE ME MORE THAN YOU USED TO?
THE SAME?
I CALL THAT PROGRESS!
YOU DA MAN!
JIM DAVIS 8-1
Distributed by Universal Press Syndicate www.garfield.com
© 2003 PAWS, INC. All Rights Reserved.

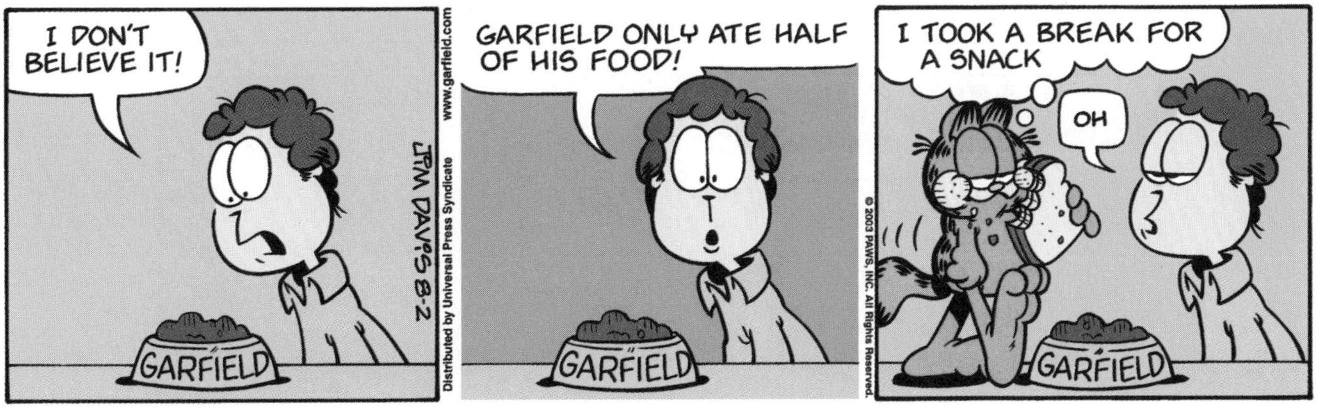
I DON'T BELIEVE IT!
GARFIELD ONLY ATE HALF OF HIS FOOD!
I TOOK A BREAK FOR A SNACK
OH
GARFIELD
JIM DAVIS 8-2
Distributed by Universal Press Syndicate www.garfield.com
© 2003 PAWS, INC. All Rights Reserved.

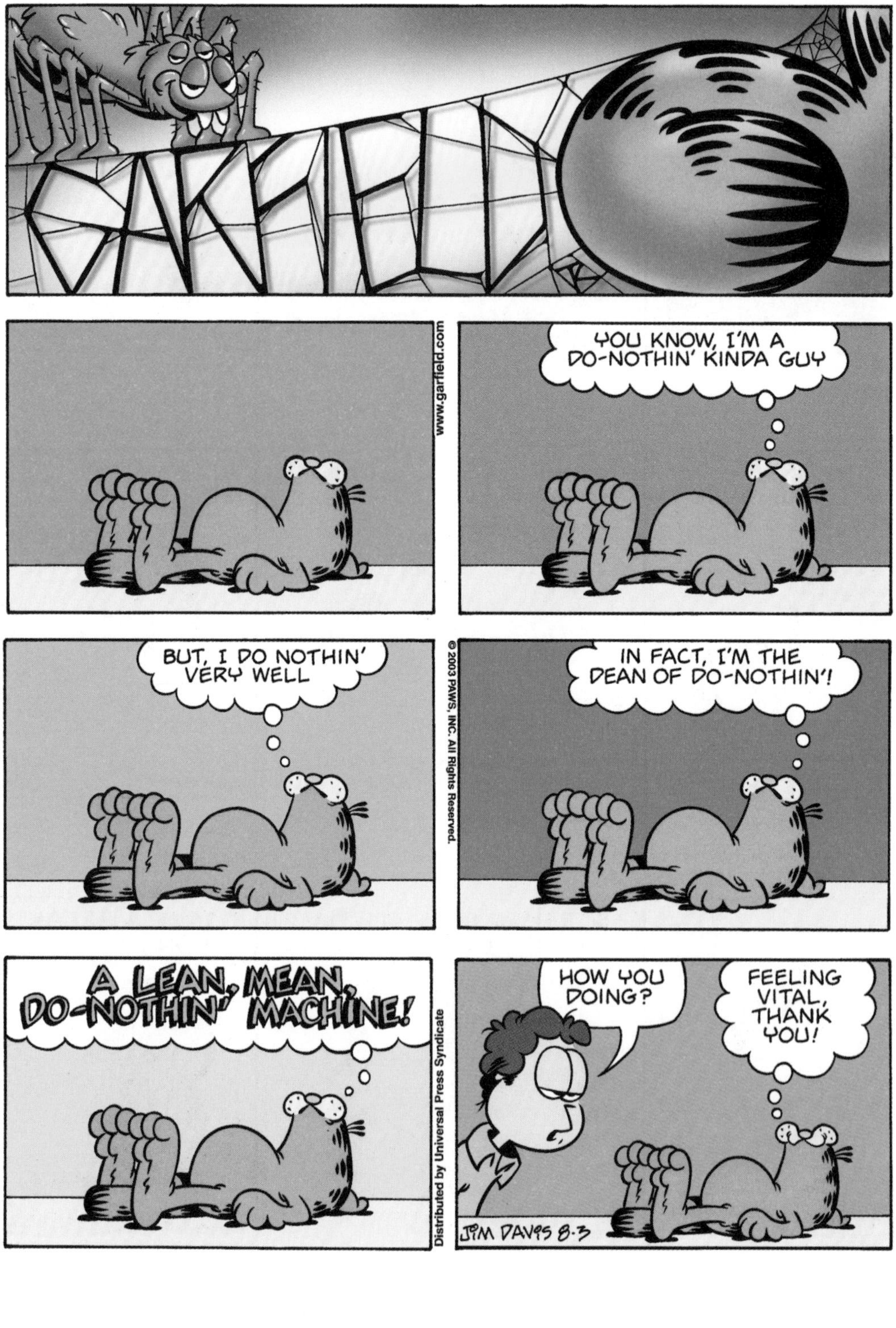
GARFIELD
www.garfield.com
YOU KNOW, I'M A DO-NOTHIN' KINDA GUY
BUT, I DO NOTHIN' VERY WELL
© 2003 PAWS, INC. All Rights Reserved.
IN FACT, I'M THE DEAN OF DO-NOTHIN'!
A LEAN, MEAN, DO-NOTHIN' MACHINE!
Distributed by Universal Press Syndicate
HOW YOU DOING?
FEELING VITAL, THANK YOU!
JIM DAVIS 8-3

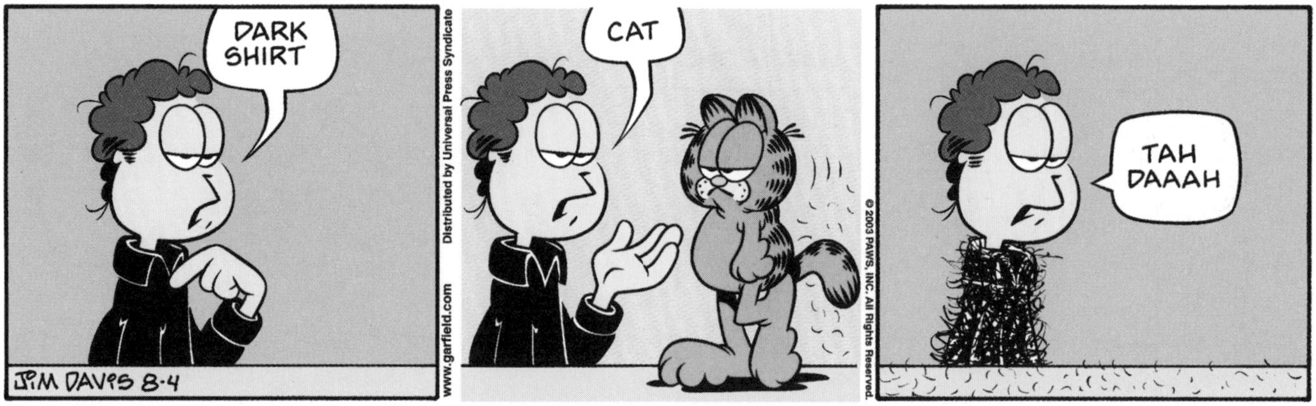
DARK SHIRT
CAT
TAH DAAAH
JIM DAVIS 8-4
www.garfield.com Distributed by Universal Press Syndicate
© 2003 PAWS, INC. All Rights Reserved.

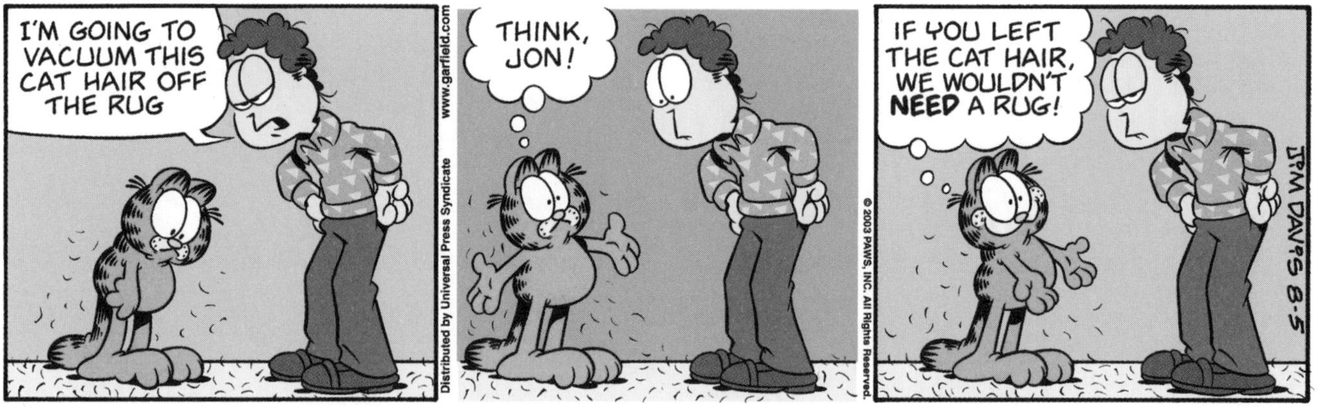
I'M GOING TO VACUUM THIS CAT HAIR OFF THE RUG
THINK, JON!
IF YOU LEFT THE CAT HAIR, WE WOULDN'T **NEED** A RUG!
JIM DAVIS 8-5
Distributed by Universal Press Syndicate www.garfield.com
© 2003 PAWS, INC. All Rights Reserved.

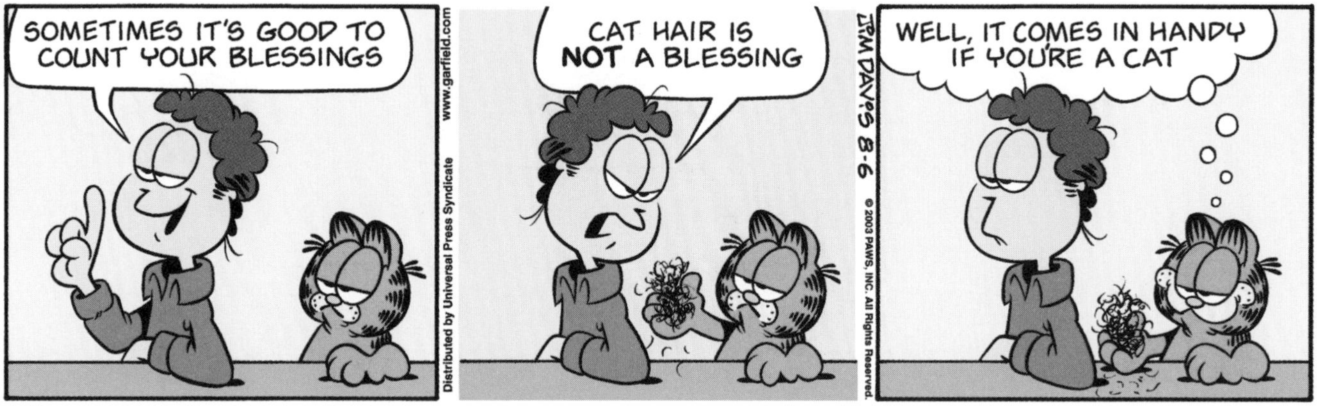
SOMETIMES IT'S GOOD TO COUNT YOUR BLESSINGS
CAT HAIR IS **NOT** A BLESSING
WELL, IT COMES IN HANDY IF YOU'RE A CAT
JIM DAVIS 8-6
Distributed by Universal Press Syndicate www.garfield.com
© 2003 PAWS, INC. All Rights Reserved.

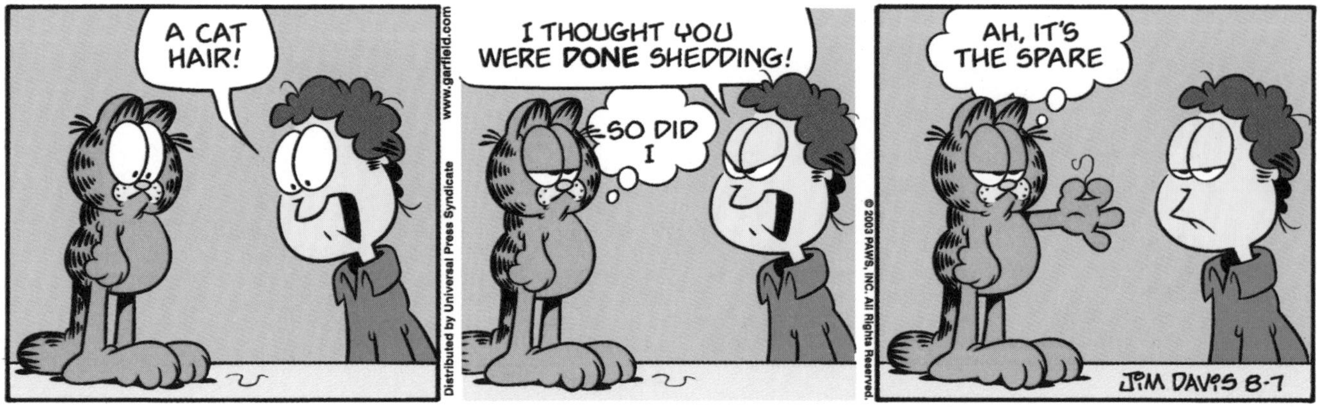
A CAT HAIR!
I THOUGHT YOU WERE DONE SHEDDING!
SO DID I
AH, IT'S THE SPARE
www.garfield.com
Distributed by Universal Press Syndicate
© 2003 PAWS, INC. All Rights Reserved.
JIM DAVIS 8-7

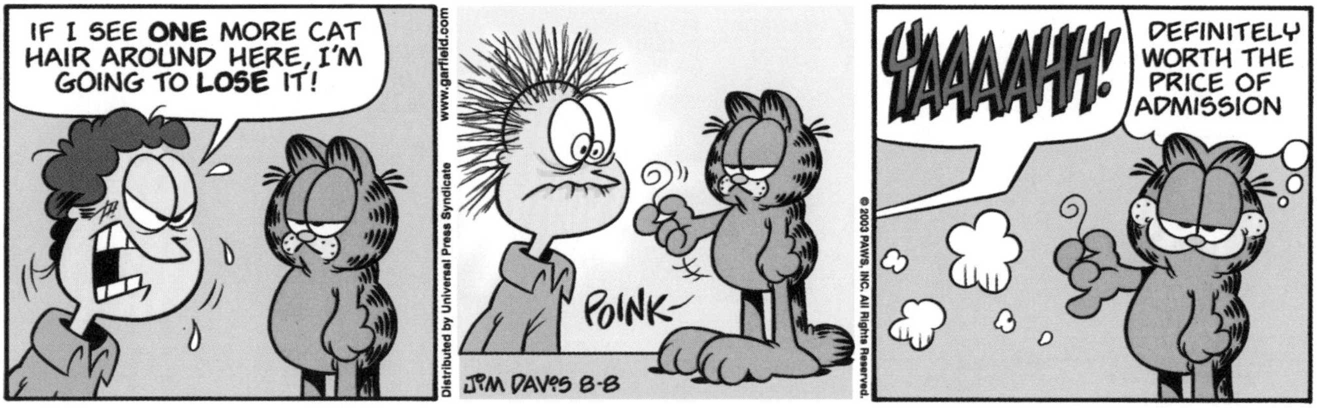
IF I SEE ONE MORE CAT HAIR AROUND HERE, I'M GOING TO LOSE IT!
POINK
YAAAAHH!
DEFINITELY WORTH THE PRICE OF ADMISSION
www.garfield.com
Distributed by Universal Press Syndicate
© 2003 PAWS, INC. All Rights Reserved.
JIM DAVIS 8-8

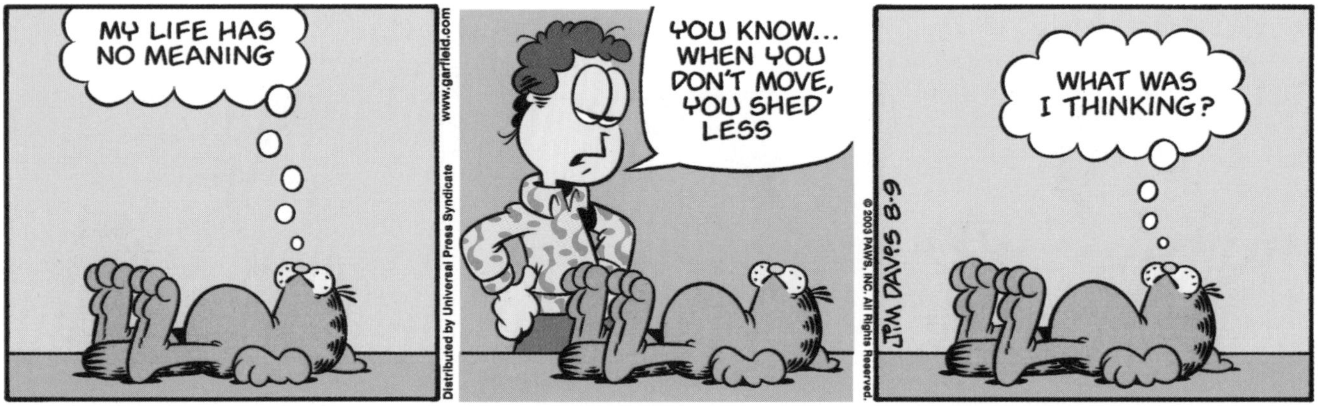
MY LIFE HAS NO MEANING
YOU KNOW... WHEN YOU DON'T MOVE, YOU SHED LESS
WHAT WAS I THINKING?
www.garfield.com
Distributed by Universal Press Syndicate
© 2003 PAWS, INC. All Rights Reserved.
JIM DAVIS 8-9

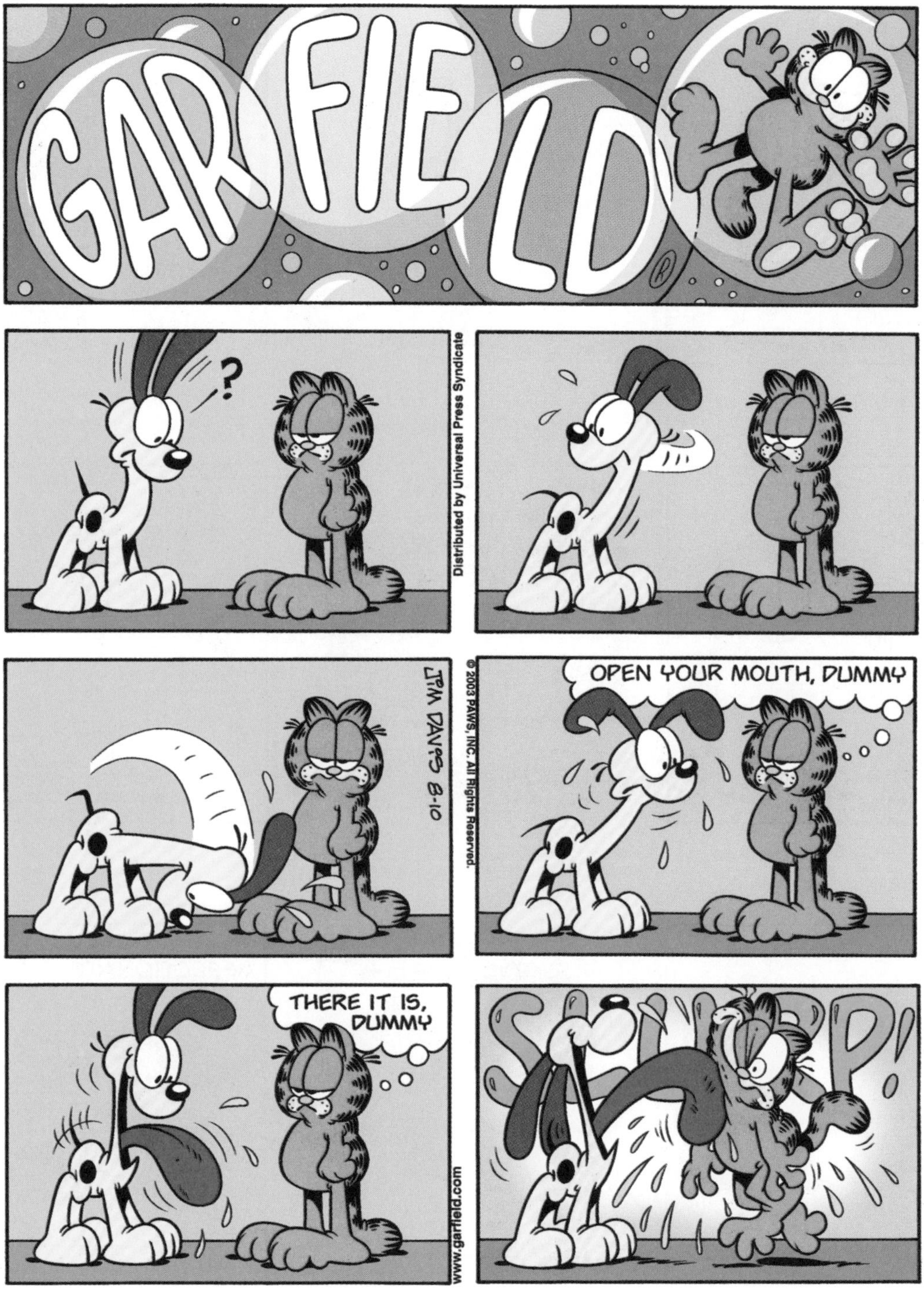
GARFIELD
Distributed by Universal Press Syndicate
JIM DAVIS 8-10
© 2003 PAWS, INC. All Rights Reserved.
OPEN YOUR MOUTH, DUMMY
THERE IT IS, DUMMY
www.garfield.com

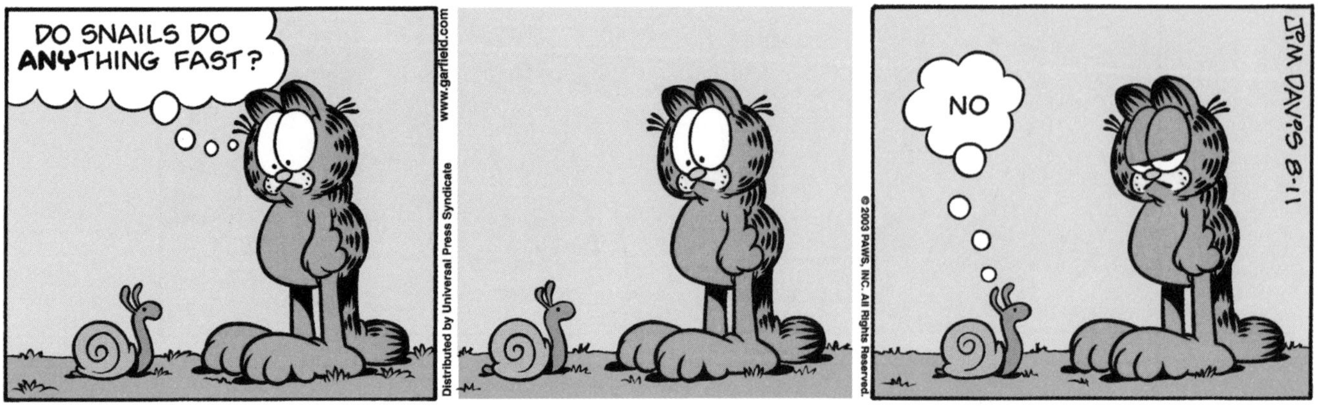
DO SNAILS DO ANYTHING FAST?
NO
JIM DAVIS 8-11
www.garfield.com Distributed by Universal Press Syndicate
© 2003 PAWS, INC. All Rights Reserved.

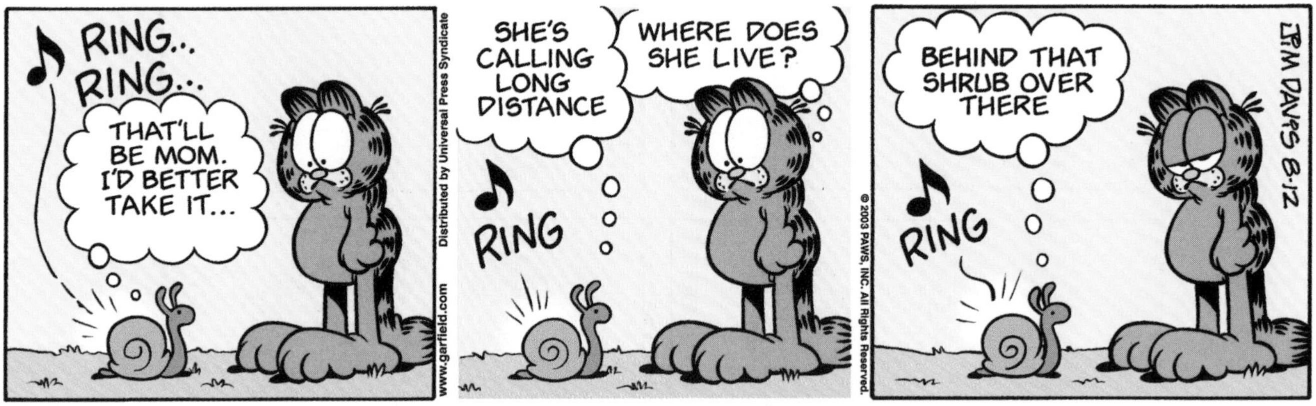
RING... RING...
THAT'LL BE MOM. I'D BETTER TAKE IT...
SHE'S CALLING LONG DISTANCE
RING
WHERE DOES SHE LIVE?
BEHIND THAT SHRUB OVER THERE
RING
JIM DAVIS 8-12
www.garfield.com Distributed by Universal Press Syndicate
© 2003 PAWS, INC. All Rights Reserved.

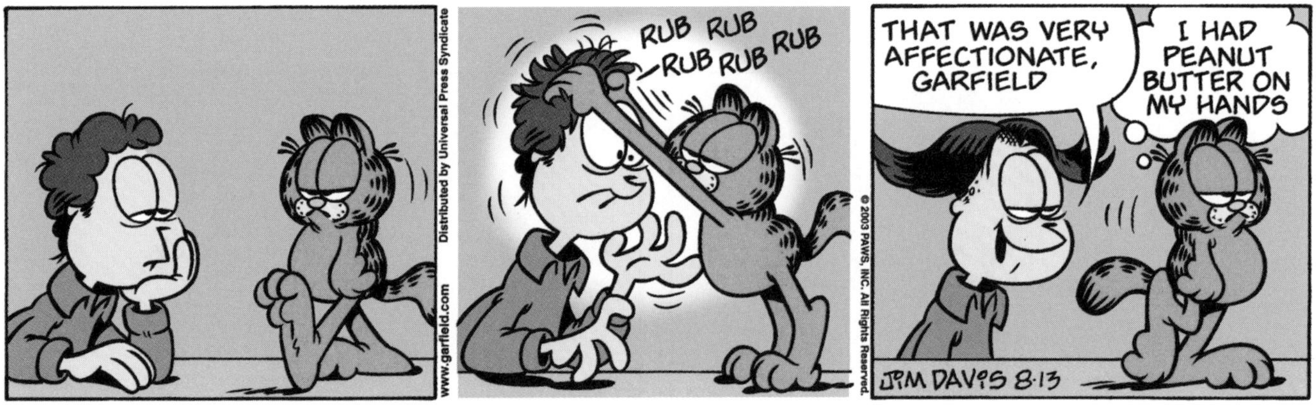
RUB RUB RUB RUB RUB
THAT WAS VERY AFFECTIONATE, GARFIELD
I HAD PEANUT BUTTER ON MY HANDS
JIM DAVIS 8-13
www.garfield.com Distributed by Universal Press Syndicate
© 2003 PAWS, INC. All Rights Reserved.

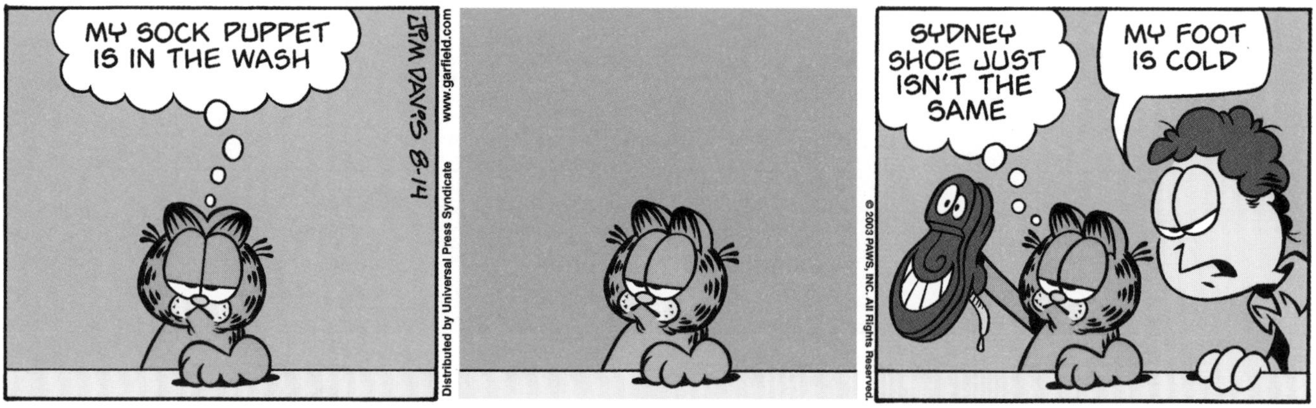
MY SOCK PUPPET IS IN THE WASH
JIM DAVIS 8-14
Distributed by Universal Press Syndicate www.garfield.com
SYDNEY SHOE JUST ISN'T THE SAME
MY FOOT IS COLD
© 2003 PAWS, INC. All Rights Reserved.

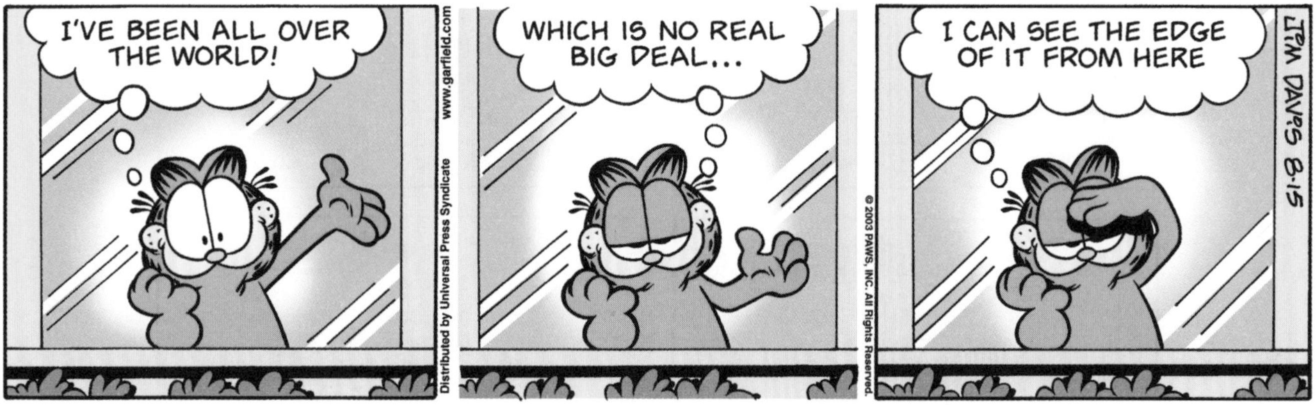
I'VE BEEN ALL OVER THE WORLD!
Distributed by Universal Press Syndicate www.garfield.com
WHICH IS NO REAL BIG DEAL...
© 2003 PAWS, INC. All Rights Reserved.
I CAN SEE THE EDGE OF IT FROM HERE
JIM DAVIS 8-15

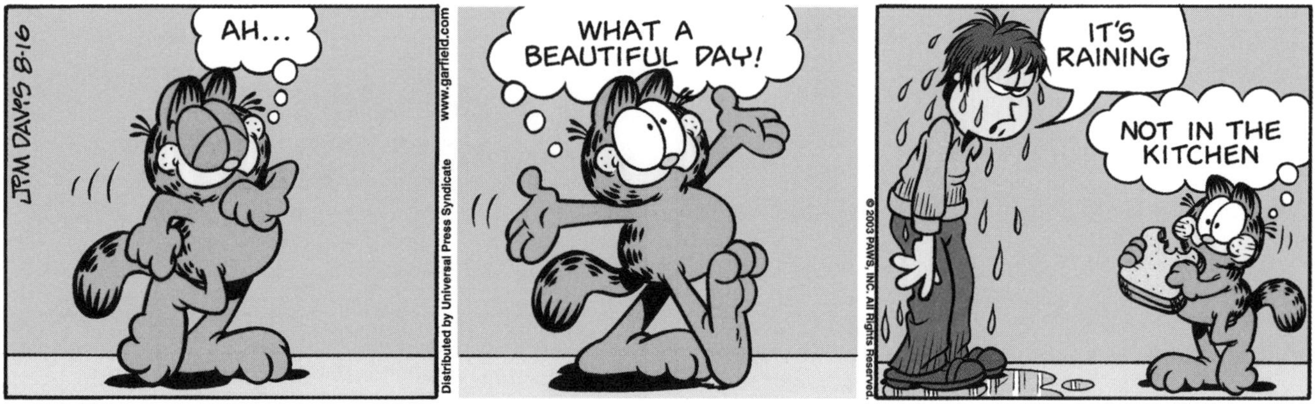
JIM DAVIS 8-16
AH...
Distributed by Universal Press Syndicate www.garfield.com
WHAT A BEAUTIFUL DAY!
© 2003 PAWS, INC. All Rights Reserved.
IT'S RAINING
NOT IN THE KITCHEN

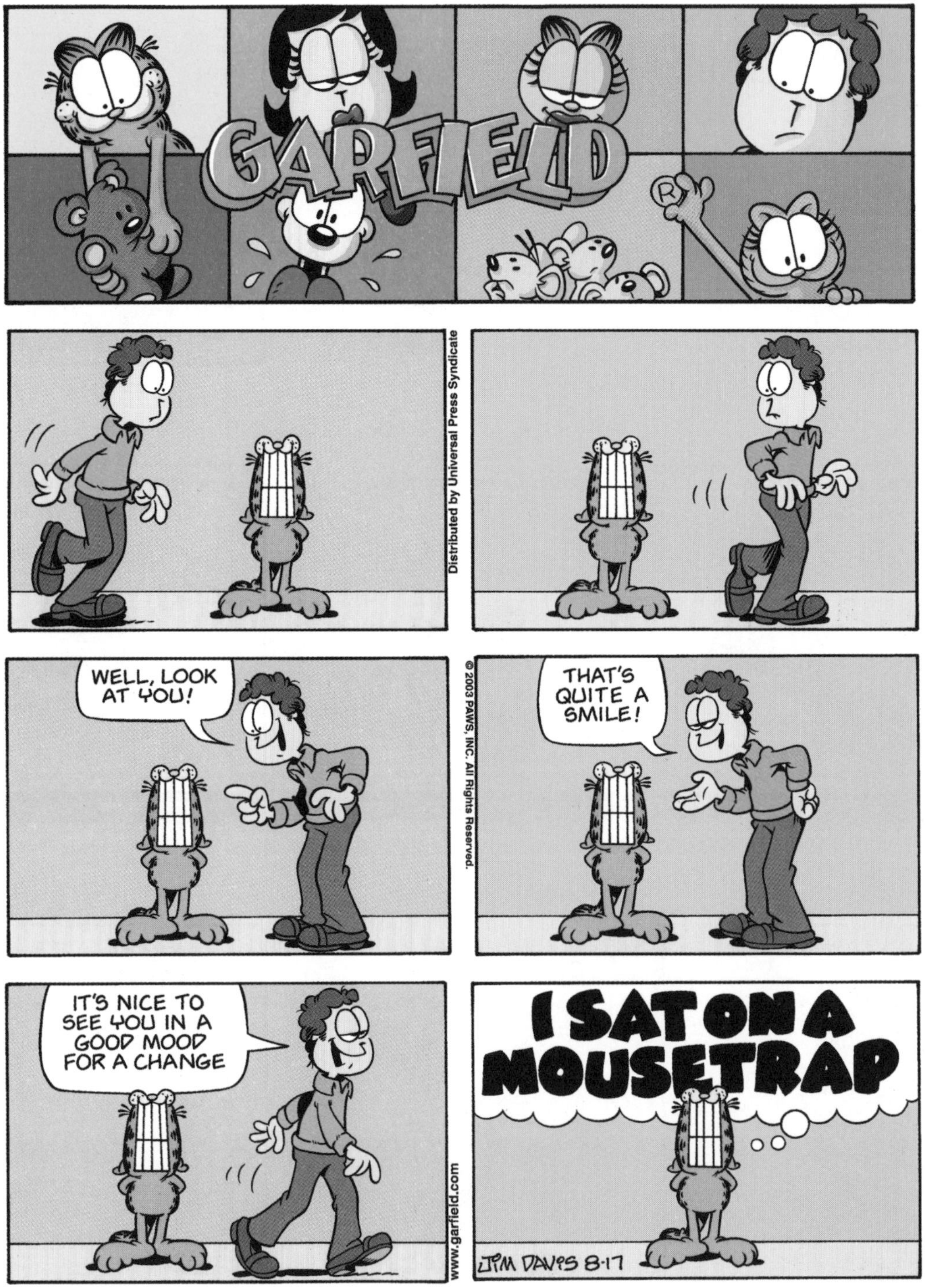
GARFIELD
Distributed by Universal Press Syndicate
WELL, LOOK AT YOU!
© 2003 PAWS, INC. All Rights Reserved.
THAT'S QUITE A SMILE!
IT'S NICE TO SEE YOU IN A GOOD MOOD FOR A CHANGE
www.garfield.com
I SAT ON A MOUSETRAP
JIM DAVIS 8-17

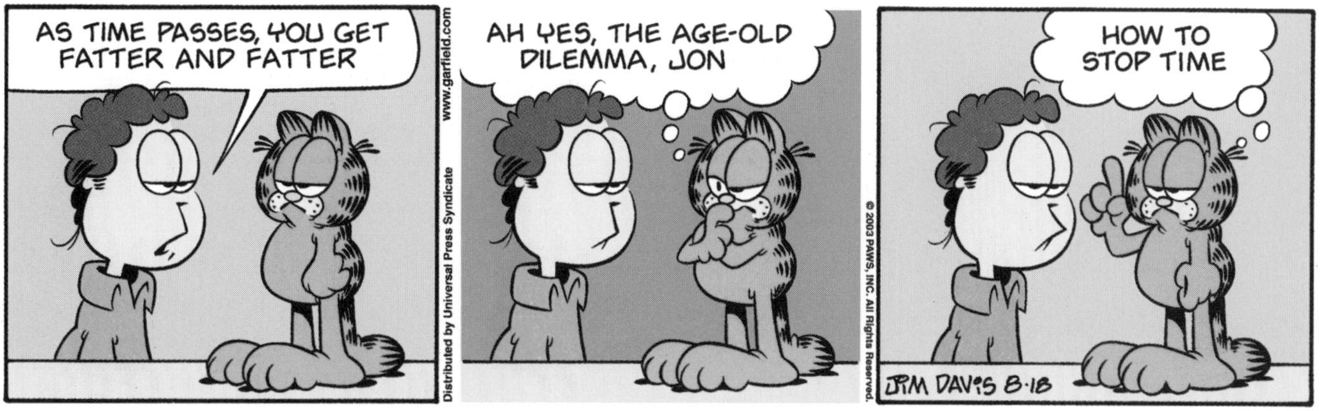
AS TIME PASSES, YOU GET FATTER AND FATTER
AH YES, THE AGE-OLD DILEMMA, JON
HOW TO STOP TIME
JIM DAVIS 8-18
www.garfield.com
Distributed by Universal Press Syndicate
© 2003 PAWS, INC. All Rights Reserved.

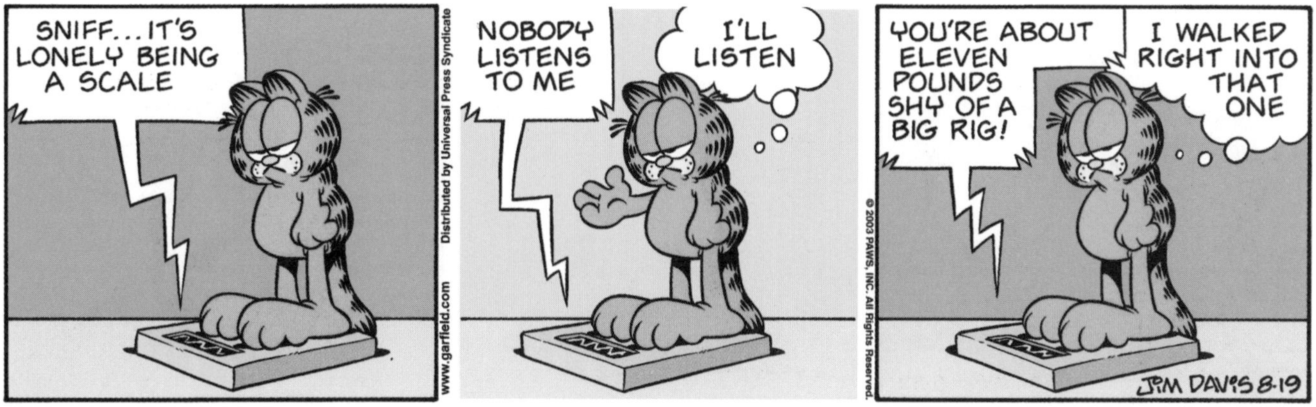
SNIFF... IT'S LONELY BEING A SCALE
NOBODY LISTENS TO ME
I'LL LISTEN
YOU'RE ABOUT ELEVEN POUNDS SHY OF A BIG RIG!
I WALKED RIGHT INTO THAT ONE
JIM DAVIS 8-19
Distributed by Universal Press Syndicate
www.garfield.com
© 2003 PAWS, INC. All Rights Reserved.

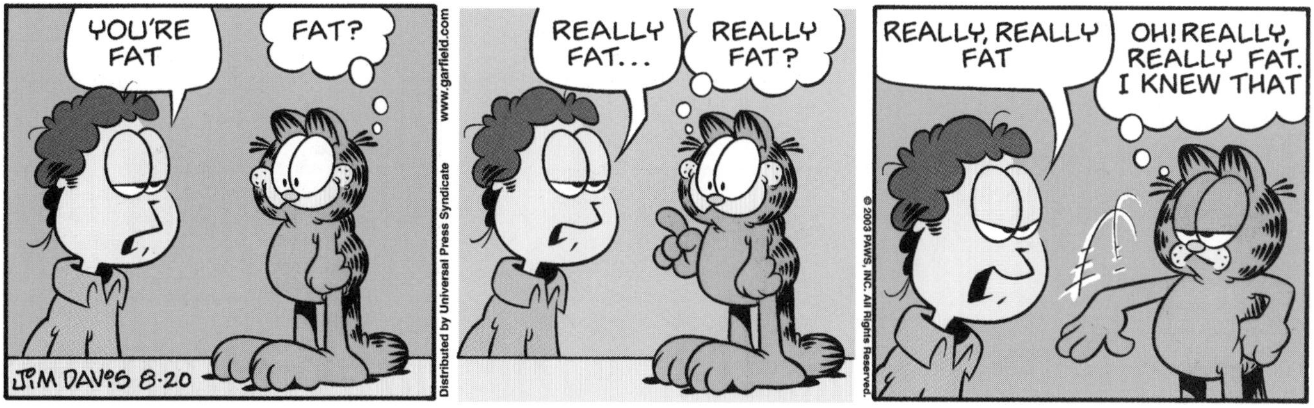
YOU'RE FAT
FAT?
REALLY FAT...
REALLY FAT?
REALLY, REALLY FAT
OH! REALLY, REALLY FAT. I KNEW THAT
JIM DAVIS 8-20
www.garfield.com
Distributed by Universal Press Syndicate
© 2003 PAWS, INC. All Rights Reserved.

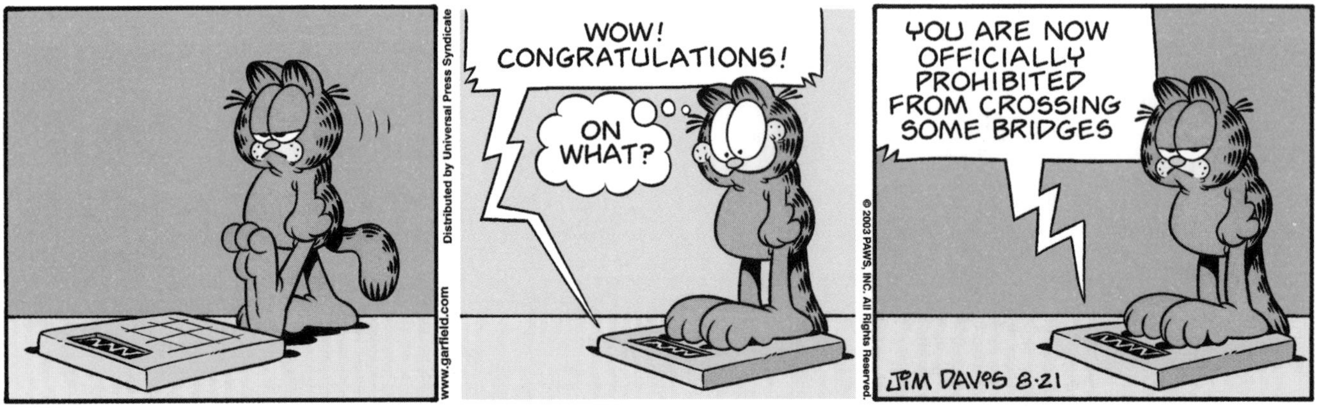
WOW! CONGRATULATIONS!
ON WHAT?
YOU ARE NOW OFFICIALLY PROHIBITED FROM CROSSING SOME BRIDGES
JIM DAVIS 8-21
www.garfield.com
Distributed by Universal Press Syndicate
© 2003 PAWS, INC. All Rights Reserved.

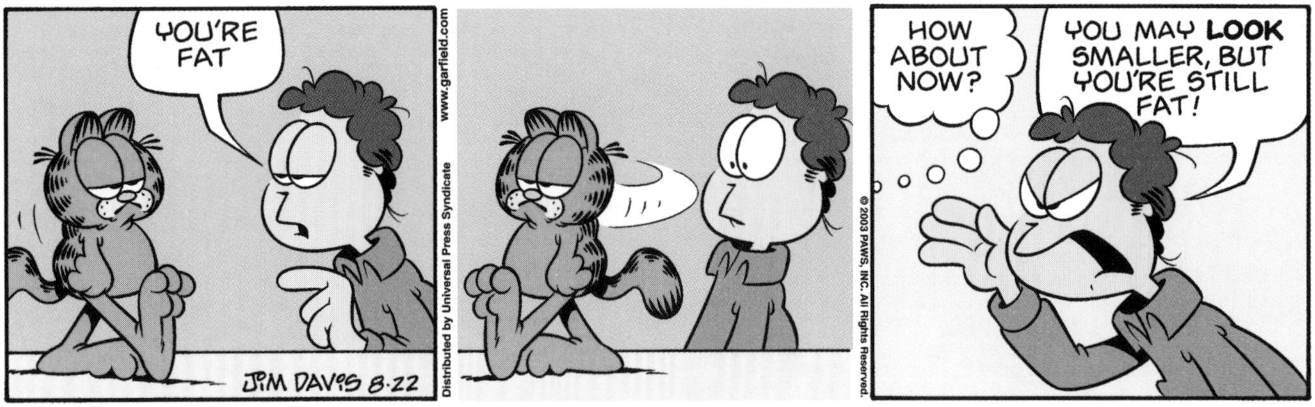
YOU'RE FAT
JIM DAVIS 8-22
HOW ABOUT NOW?
YOU MAY **LOOK** SMALLER, BUT YOU'RE STILL FAT!
www.garfield.com
Distributed by Universal Press Syndicate
© 2003 PAWS, INC. All Rights Reserved.

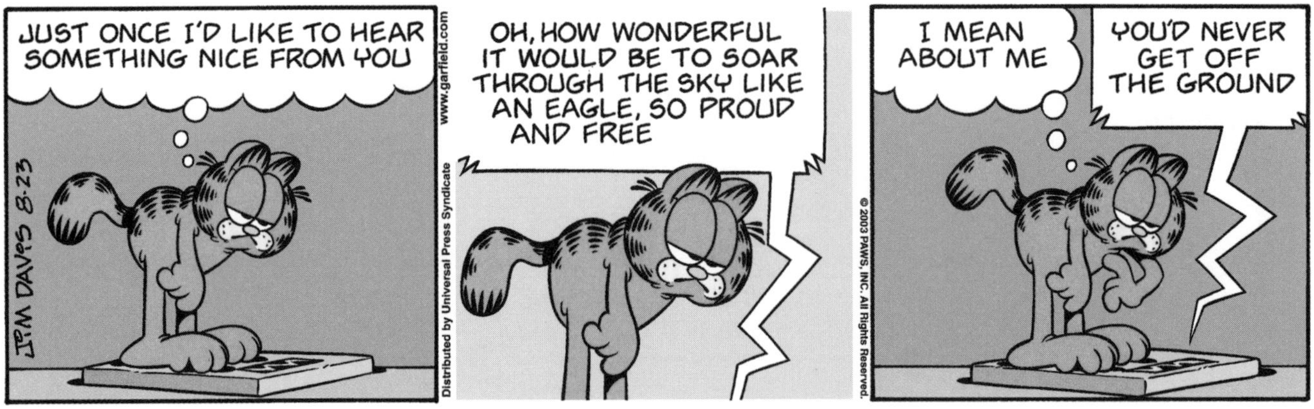
JUST ONCE I'D LIKE TO HEAR SOMETHING NICE FROM YOU
JIM DAVIS 8-23
OH, HOW WONDERFUL IT WOULD BE TO SOAR THROUGH THE SKY LIKE AN EAGLE, SO PROUD AND FREE
I MEAN ABOUT ME
YOU'D NEVER GET OFF THE GROUND
www.garfield.com
Distributed by Universal Press Syndicate
© 2003 PAWS, INC. All Rights Reserved.

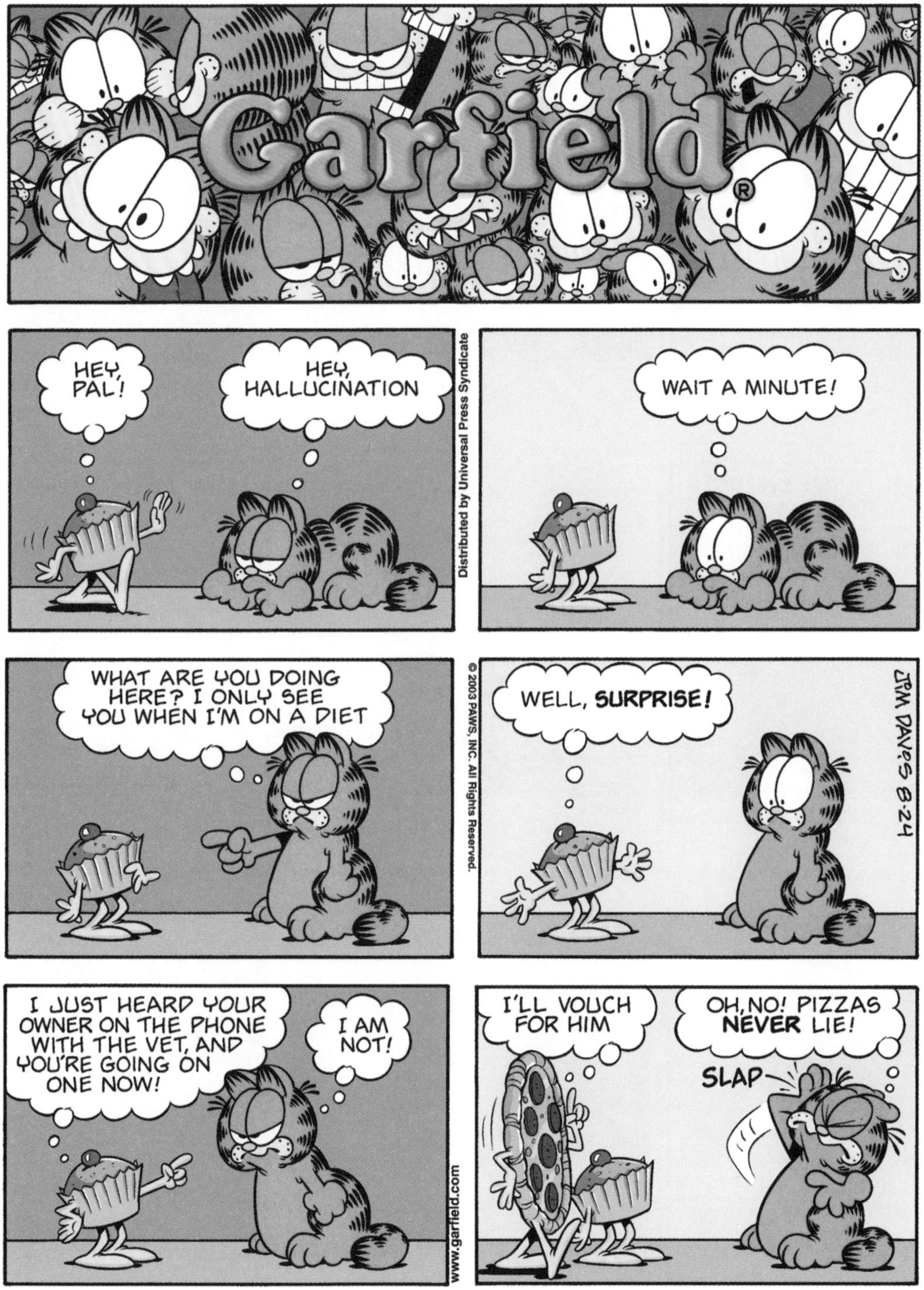
Garfield
HEY, PAL!
HEY, HALLUCINATION
WAIT A MINUTE!
WHAT ARE YOU DOING HERE? I ONLY SEE YOU WHEN I'M ON A DIET
WELL, SURPRISE!
JPM DAVIS 8-24
I JUST HEARD YOUR OWNER ON THE PHONE WITH THE VET, AND YOU'RE GOING ON ONE NOW!
I AM NOT!
I'LL VOUCH FOR HIM
OH, NO! PIZZAS NEVER LIE!
SLAP
Distributed by Universal Press Syndicate
© 2003 PAWS, INC. All Rights Reserved.
www.garfield.com

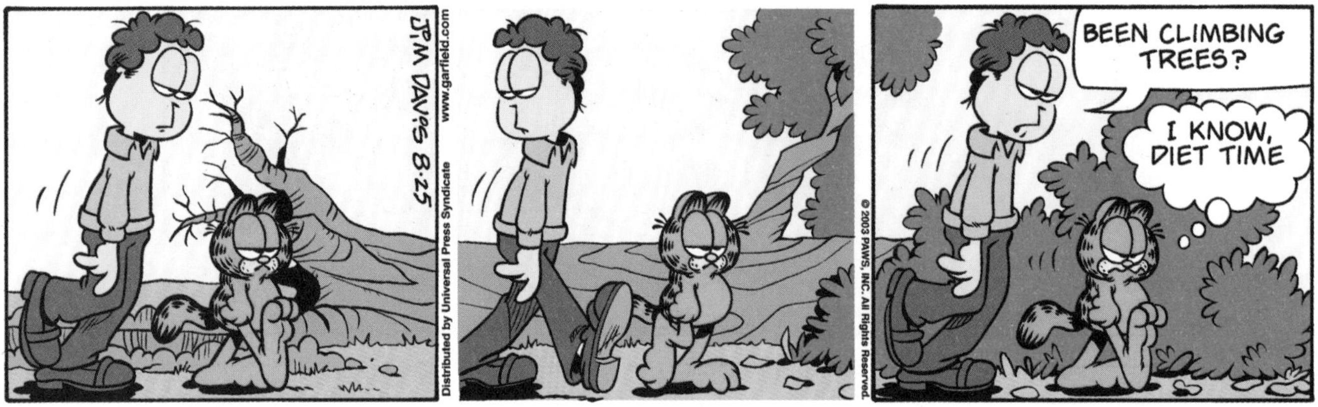
JIM DAVIS 8-25
www.garfield.com
Distributed by Universal Press Syndicate
BEEN CLIMBING TREES?
I KNOW, DIET TIME
© 2003 PAWS, INC. All Rights Reserved.

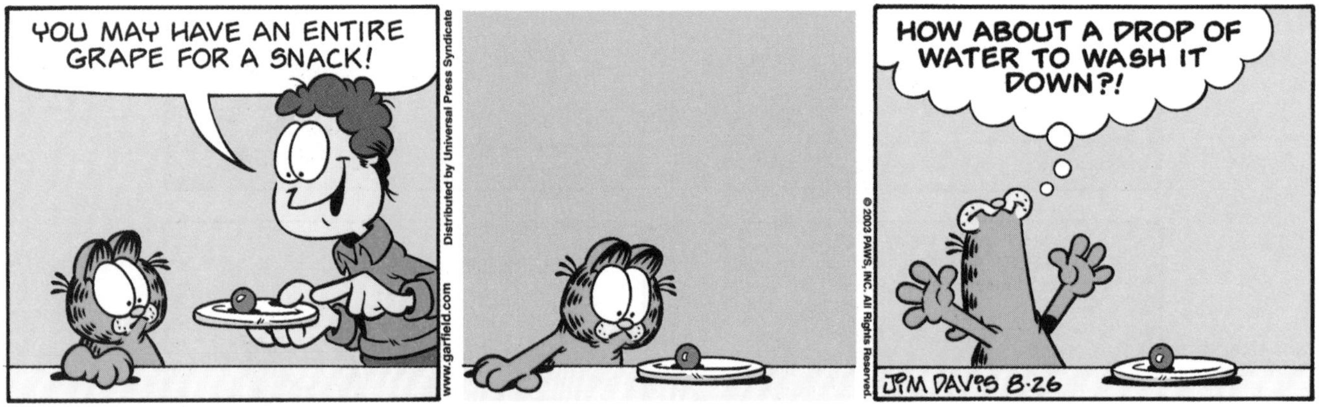
YOU MAY HAVE AN ENTIRE GRAPE FOR A SNACK!
Distributed by Universal Press Syndicate
www.garfield.com
HOW ABOUT A DROP OF WATER TO WASH IT DOWN?!
© 2003 PAWS, INC. All Rights Reserved.
JIM DAVIS 8-26

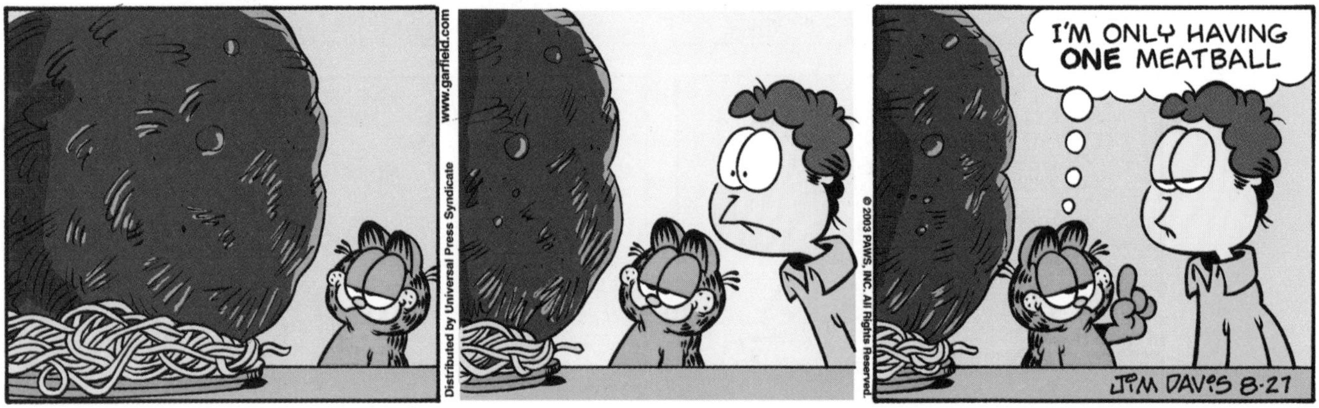
www.garfield.com
Distributed by Universal Press Syndicate
I'M ONLY HAVING ONE MEATBALL
© 2003 PAWS, INC. All Rights Reserved.
JIM DAVIS 8-27

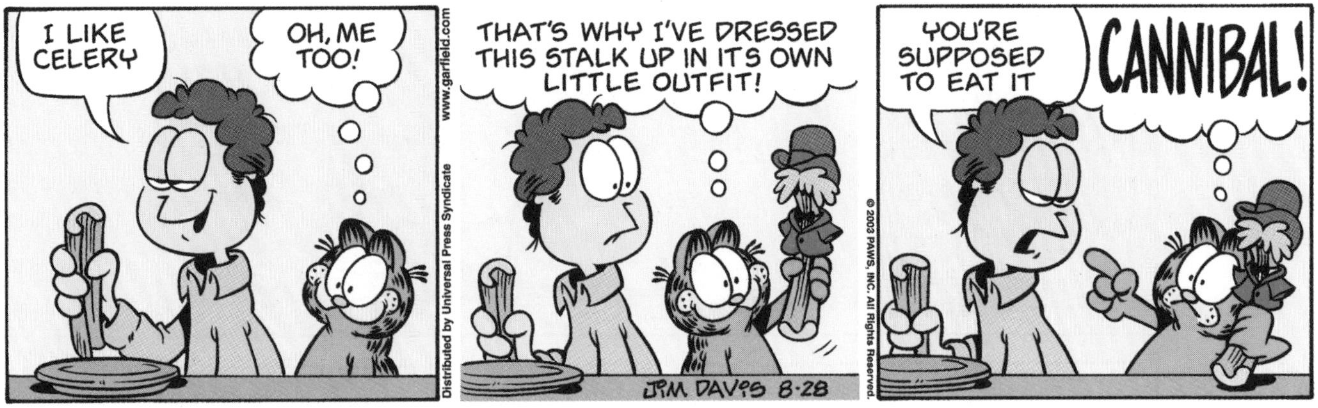
I LIKE CELERY
OH, ME TOO!
THAT'S WHY I'VE DRESSED THIS STALK UP IN ITS OWN LITTLE OUTFIT!
YOU'RE SUPPOSED TO EAT IT
CANNIBAL!
JIM DAVIS 8-28
www.garfield.com
Distributed by Universal Press Syndicate
© 2003 PAWS, INC. All Rights Reserved.

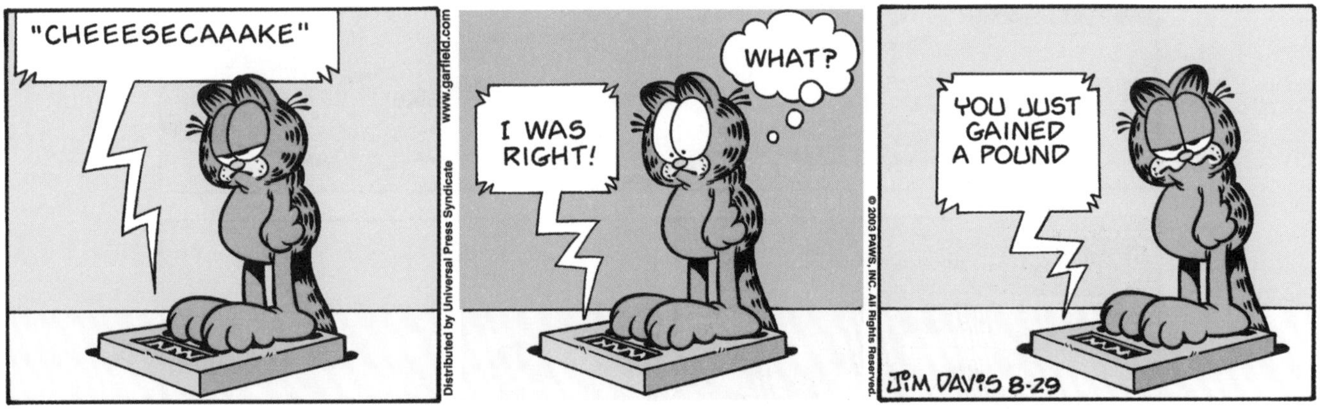
"CHEEESECAAAKE"
I WAS RIGHT!
WHAT?
YOU JUST GAINED A POUND
JIM DAVIS 8-29
www.garfield.com
Distributed by Universal Press Syndicate
© 2003 PAWS, INC. All Rights Reserved.

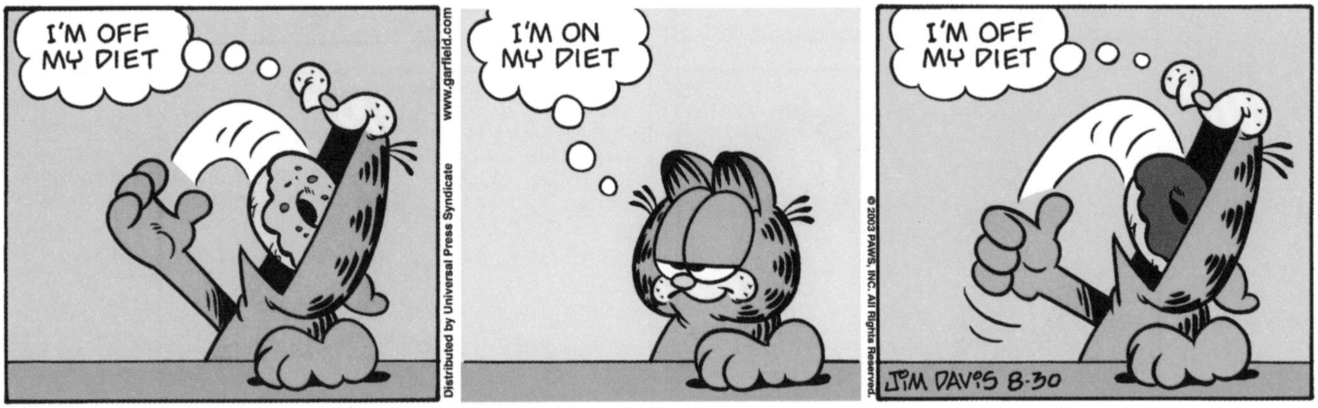
I'M OFF MY DIET
I'M ON MY DIET
I'M OFF MY DIET
JIM DAVIS 8-30
www.garfield.com
Distributed by Universal Press Syndicate
© 2003 PAWS, INC. All Rights Reserved.

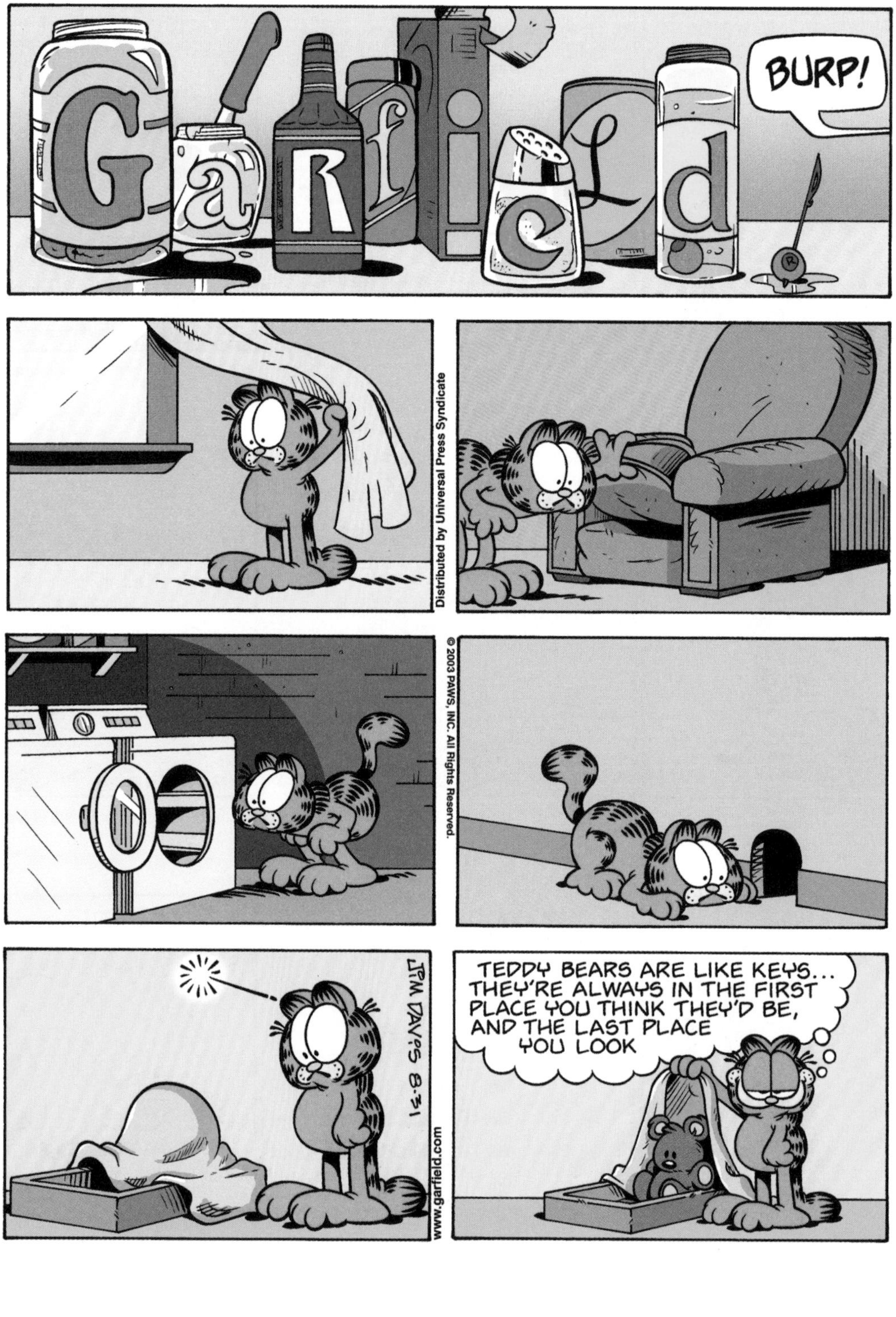
Garfield
BURP!
Distributed by Universal Press Syndicate
© 2003 PAWS, INC. All Rights Reserved.
JIM DAVIS 8-31
www.garfield.com
TEDDY BEARS ARE LIKE KEYS... THEY'RE ALWAYS IN THE FIRST PLACE YOU THINK THEY'D BE, AND THE LAST PLACE YOU LOOK

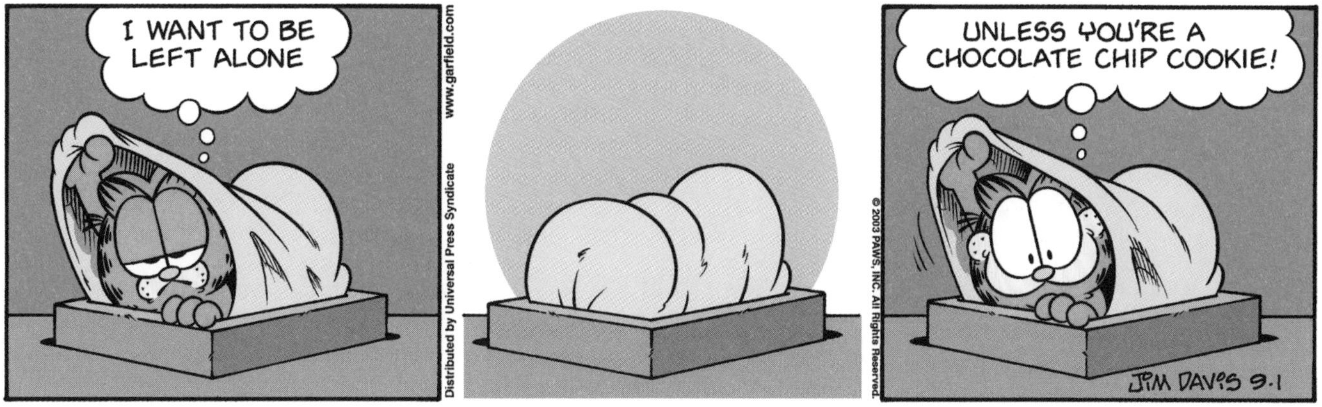
I WANT TO BE LEFT ALONE
UNLESS YOU'RE A CHOCOLATE CHIP COOKIE!
JIM DAVIS 9.1
www.garfield.com
Distributed by Universal Press Syndicate
© 2003 PAWS, INC. All Rights Reserved.

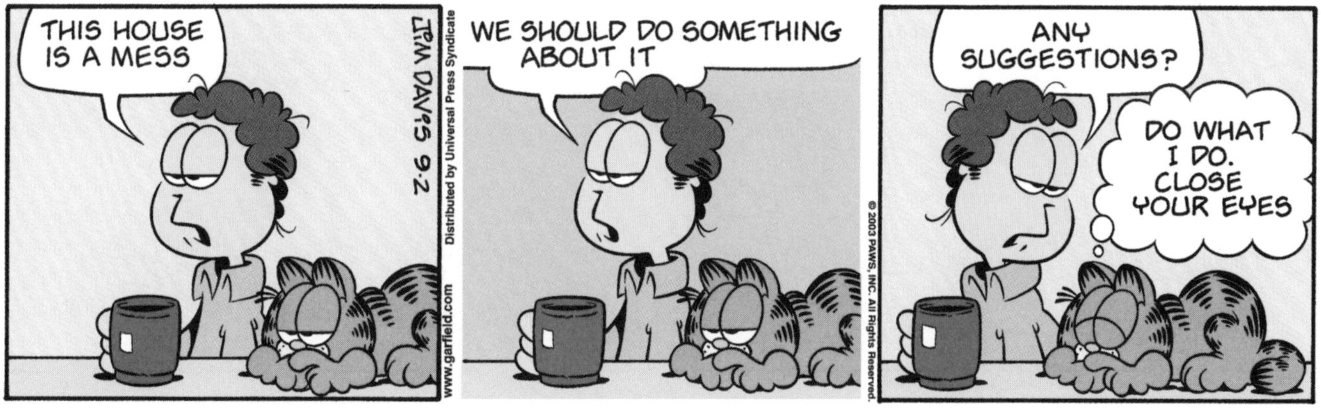
THIS HOUSE IS A MESS
WE SHOULD DO SOMETHING ABOUT IT
ANY SUGGESTIONS?
DO WHAT I DO. CLOSE YOUR EYES
JIM DAVIS 9.2
Distributed by Universal Press Syndicate
www.garfield.com
© 2003 PAWS, INC. All Rights Reserved.

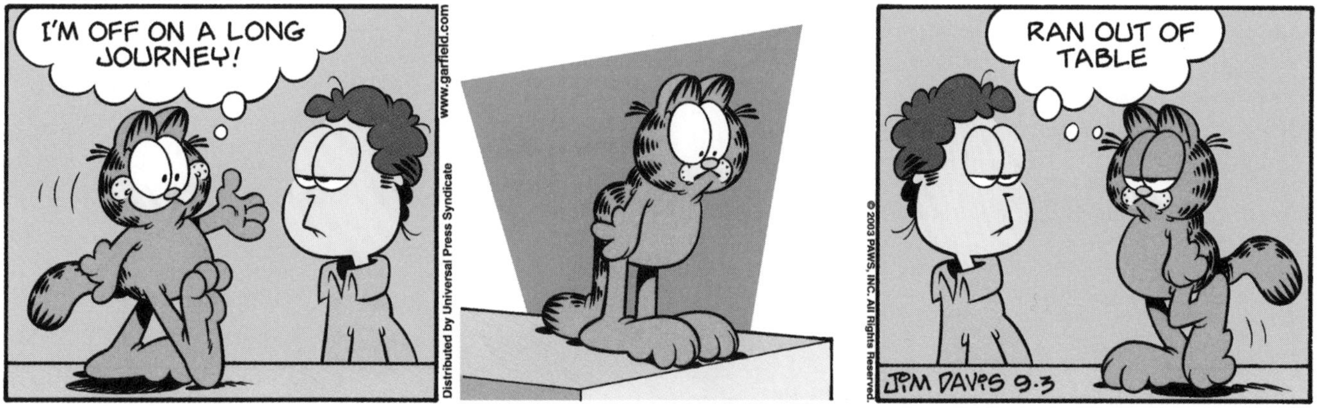
I'M OFF ON A LONG JOURNEY!
RAN OUT OF TABLE
JIM DAVIS 9.3
www.garfield.com
Distributed by Universal Press Syndicate
© 2003 PAWS, INC. All Rights Reserved.

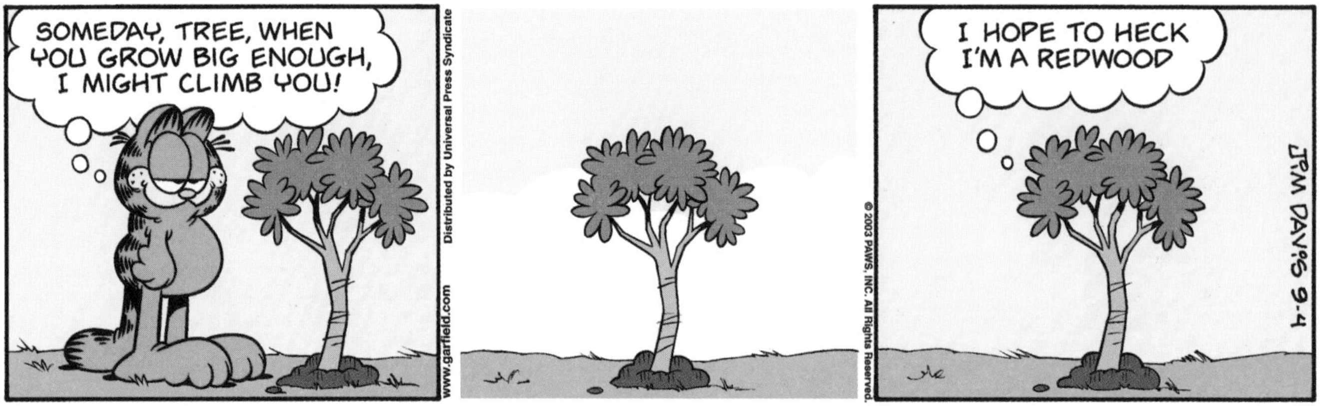
SOMEDAY, TREE, WHEN YOU GROW BIG ENOUGH, I MIGHT CLIMB YOU!
I HOPE TO HECK I'M A REDWOOD
JIM DAVIS 9-4
www.garfield.com Distributed by Universal Press Syndicate
© 2003 PAWS, INC. All Rights Reserved.

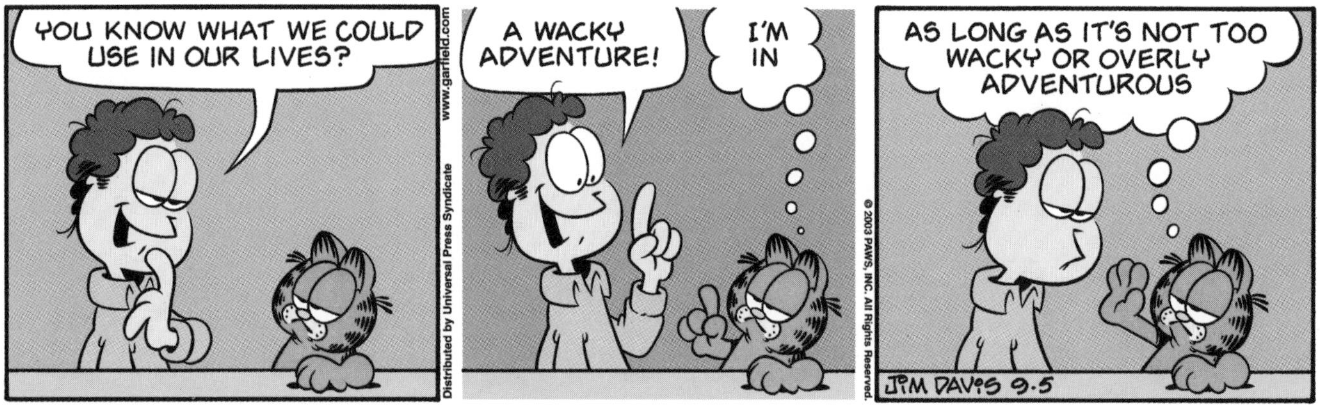
YOU KNOW WHAT WE COULD USE IN OUR LIVES?
A WACKY ADVENTURE!
I'M IN
AS LONG AS IT'S NOT TOO WACKY OR OVERLY ADVENTUROUS
JIM DAVIS 9-5
www.garfield.com Distributed by Universal Press Syndicate
© 2003 PAWS, INC. All Rights Reserved.

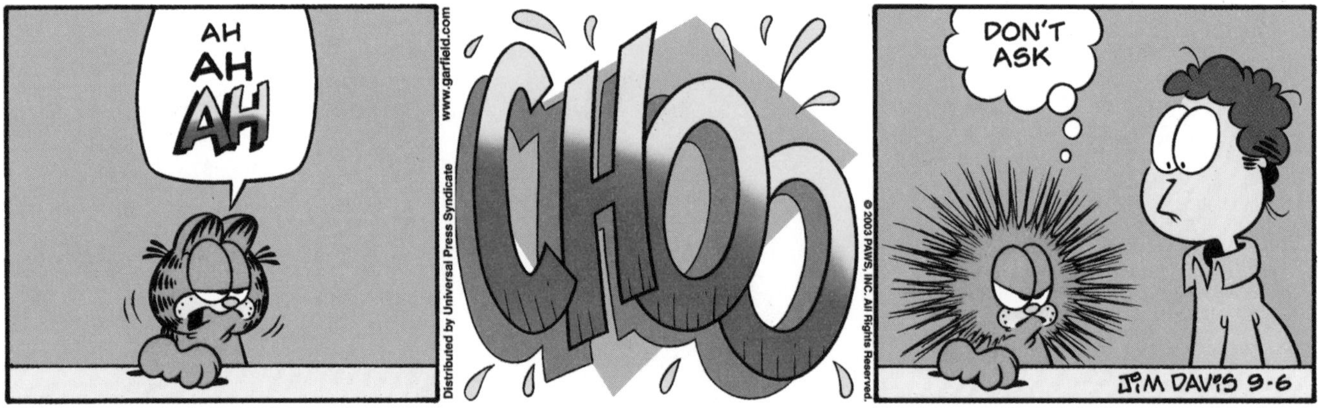
AH AH AH
CHOO
DON'T ASK
JIM DAVIS 9-6
www.garfield.com Distributed by Universal Press Syndicate
© 2003 PAWS, INC. All Rights Reserved.

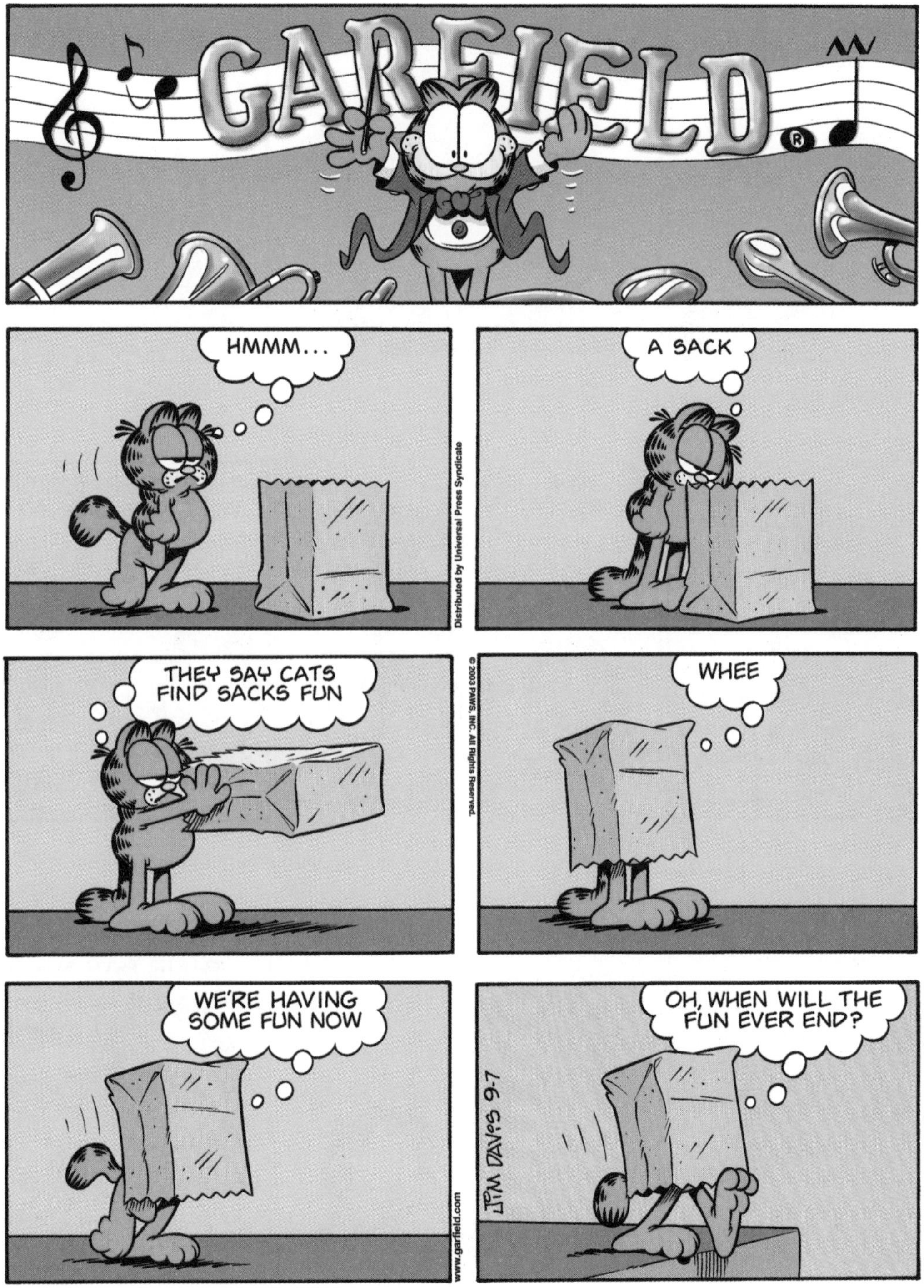
GARFIELD®
HMMM...
A SACK
THEY SAY CATS FIND SACKS FUN
WHEE
WE'RE HAVING SOME FUN NOW
OH, WHEN WILL THE FUN EVER END?
JIM DAVIS 9-7
Distributed by Universal Press Syndicate
© 2003 PAWS, INC. All Rights Reserved.
www.garfield.com

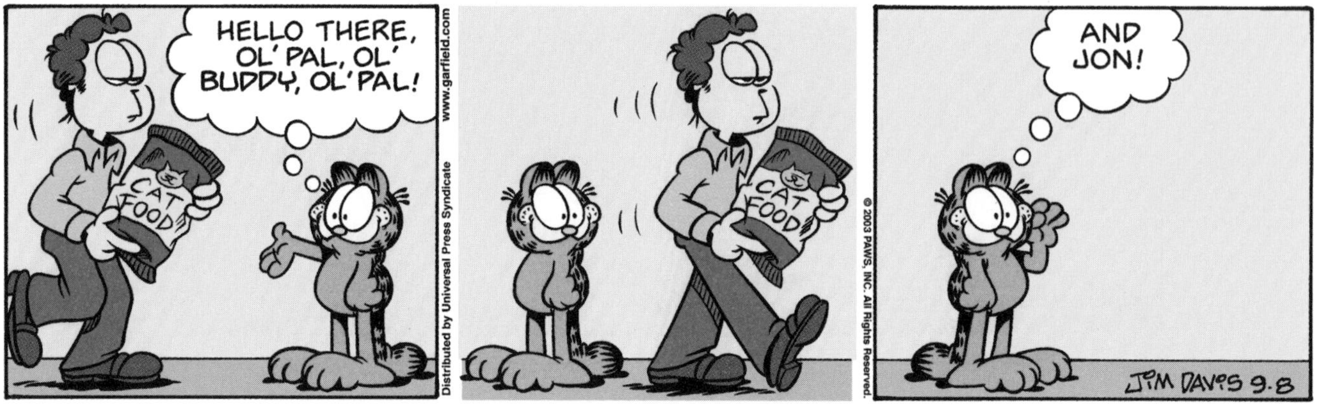
HELLO THERE, OL' PAL, OL' BUDDY, OL' PAL!
Distributed by Universal Press Syndicate www.garfield.com
CAT FOOD
© 2003 PAWS, INC. All Rights Reserved.
AND JON!
JIM DAVIS 9.8

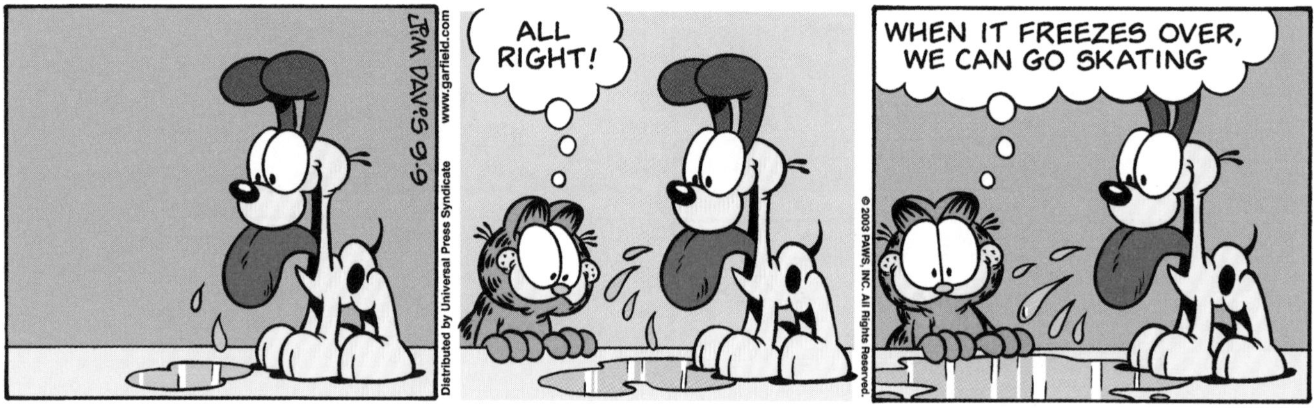
JIM DAVIS 9.9
Distributed by Universal Press Syndicate www.garfield.com
ALL RIGHT!
© 2003 PAWS, INC. All Rights Reserved.
WHEN IT FREEZES OVER, WE CAN GO SKATING

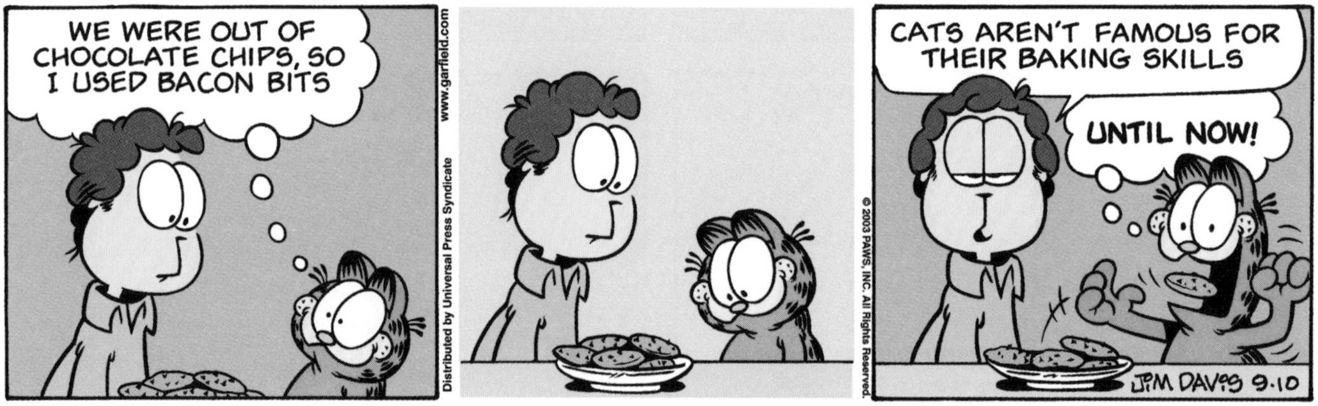
WE WERE OUT OF CHOCOLATE CHIPS, SO I USED BACON BITS
Distributed by Universal Press Syndicate www.garfield.com
© 2003 PAWS, INC. All Rights Reserved.
CATS AREN'T FAMOUS FOR THEIR BAKING SKILLS
UNTIL NOW!
JIM DAVIS 9.10

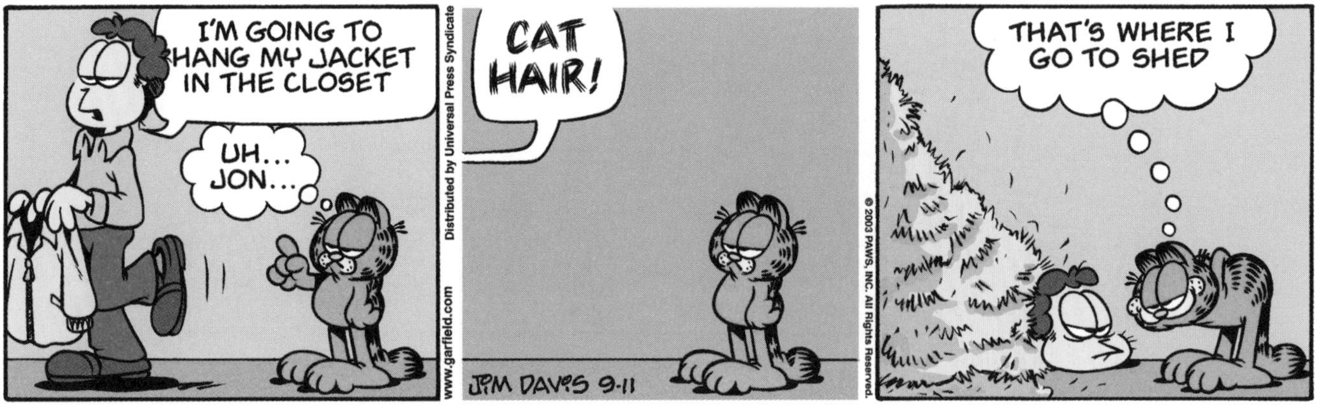
I'M GOING TO HANG MY JACKET IN THE CLOSET
UH... JON...
Distributed by Universal Press Syndicate
www.garfield.com
CAT HAIR!
JIM DAVIS 9-11
THAT'S WHERE I GO TO SHED
© 2003 PAWS, INC. All Rights Reserved.

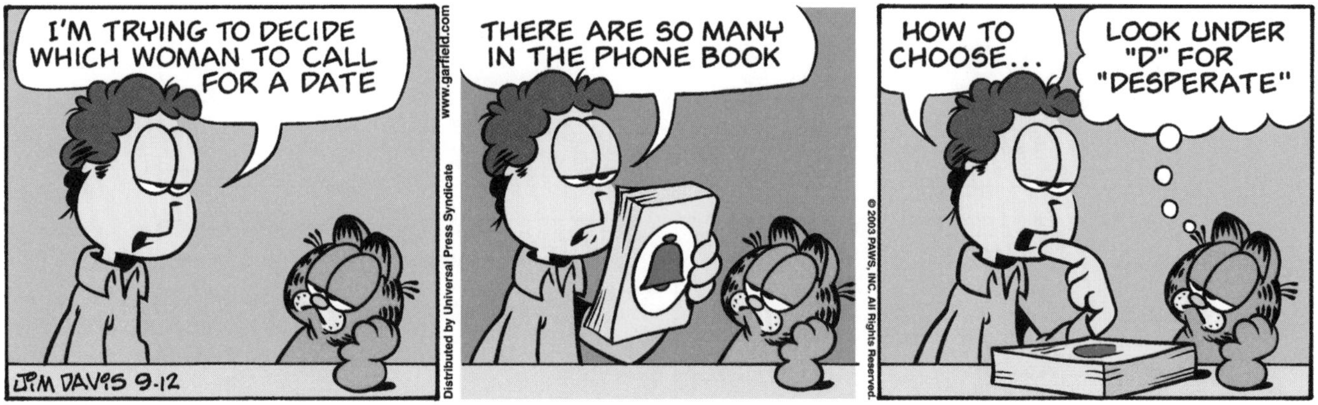
I'M TRYING TO DECIDE WHICH WOMAN TO CALL FOR A DATE
JIM DAVIS 9-12
www.garfield.com
Distributed by Universal Press Syndicate
THERE ARE SO MANY IN THE PHONE BOOK
HOW TO CHOOSE...
LOOK UNDER "D" FOR "DESPERATE"
© 2003 PAWS, INC. All Rights Reserved.

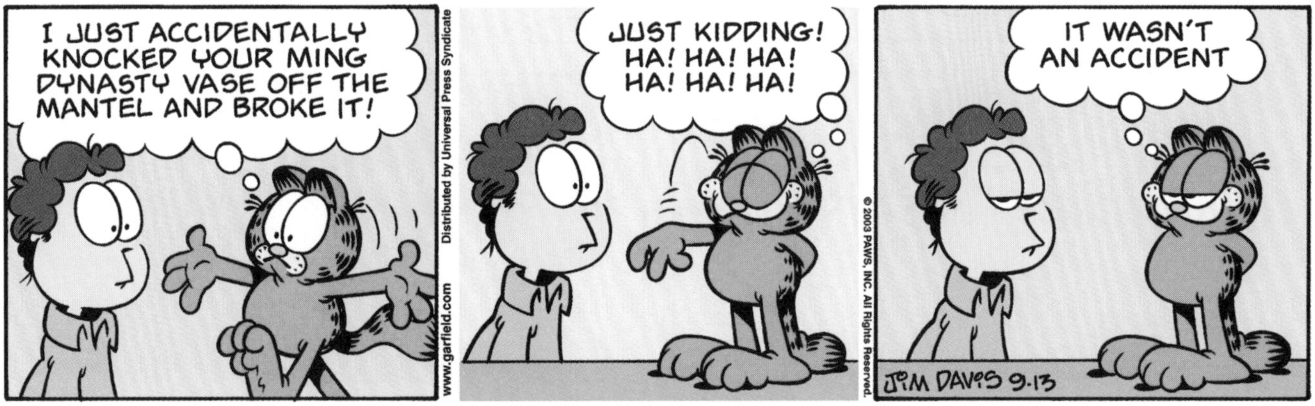
I JUST ACCIDENTALLY KNOCKED YOUR MING DYNASTY VASE OFF THE MANTEL AND BROKE IT!
Distributed by Universal Press Syndicate
www.garfield.com
JUST KIDDING! HA! HA! HA! HA! HA! HA!
IT WASN'T AN ACCIDENT
© 2003 PAWS, INC. All Rights Reserved.
JIM DAVIS 9-13

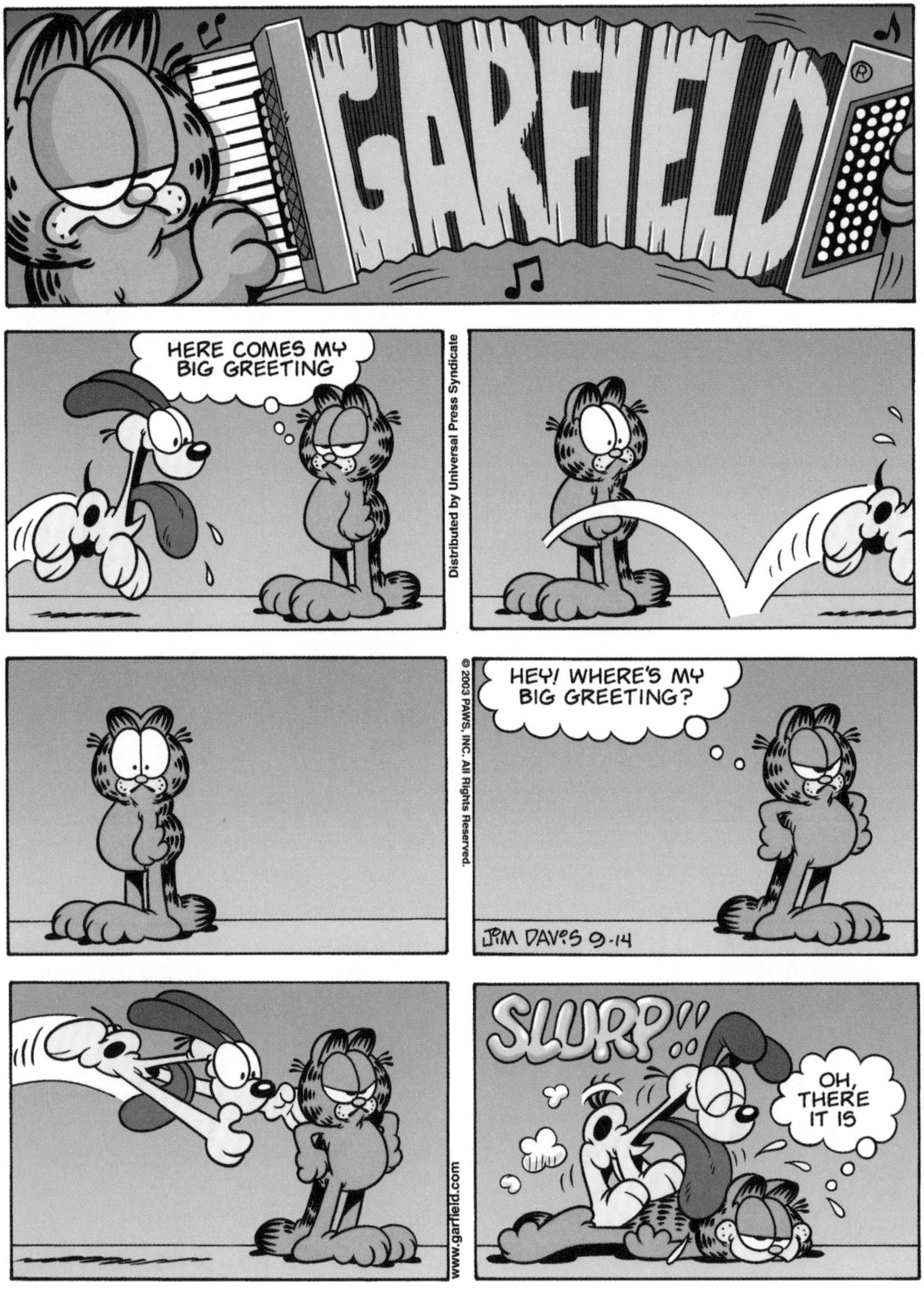
GARFIELD®
HERE COMES MY BIG GREETING
Distributed by Universal Press Syndicate
© 2003 PAWS, INC. All Rights Reserved.
HEY! WHERE'S MY BIG GREETING?
JIM DAVIS 9-14
SLURP!!
OH, THERE IT IS
www.garfield.com

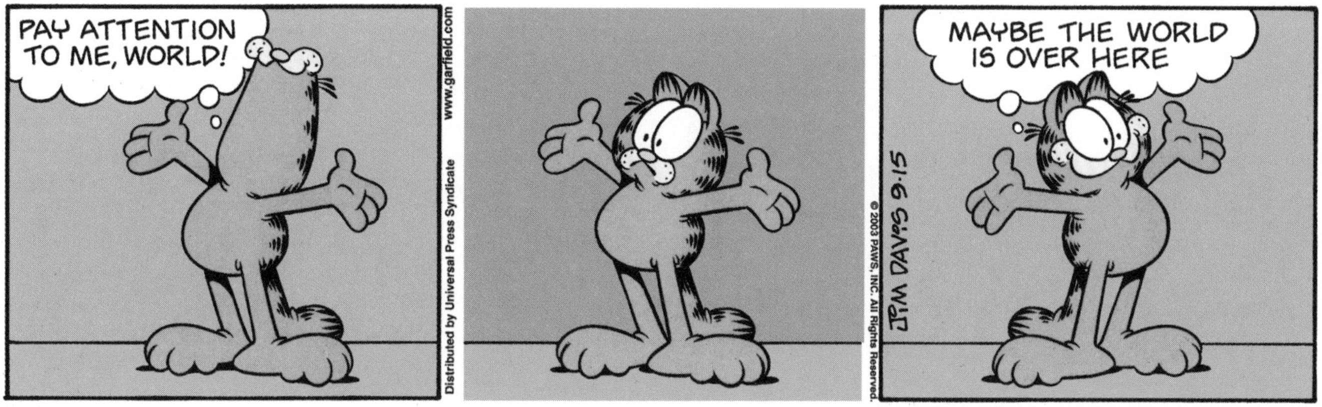
PAY ATTENTION TO ME, WORLD!
MAYBE THE WORLD IS OVER HERE
Distributed by Universal Press Syndicate www.garfield.com
© 2003 PAWS, INC. All Rights Reserved.
JIM DAVIS 9.15

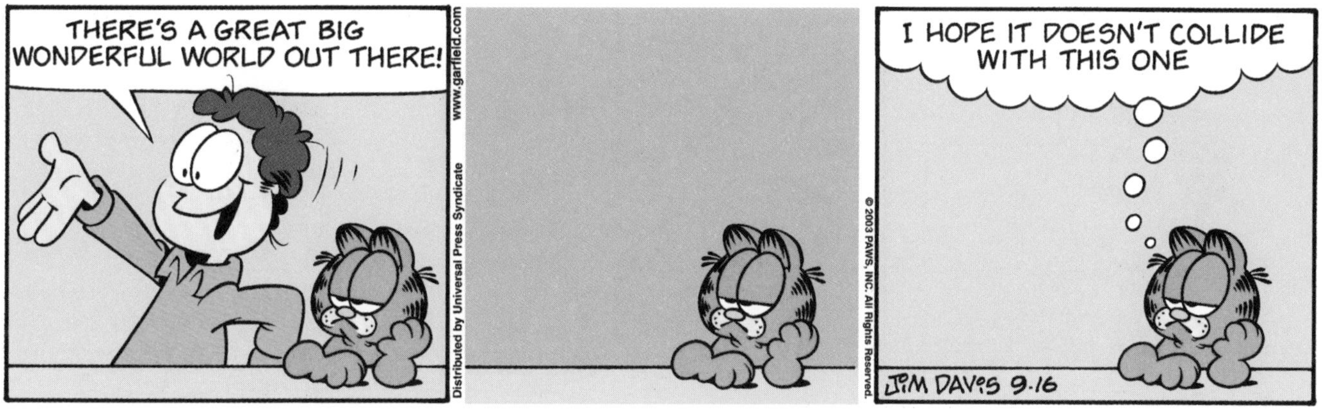
THERE'S A GREAT BIG WONDERFUL WORLD OUT THERE!
I HOPE IT DOESN'T COLLIDE WITH THIS ONE
Distributed by Universal Press Syndicate www.garfield.com
© 2003 PAWS, INC. All Rights Reserved.
JIM DAVIS 9.16

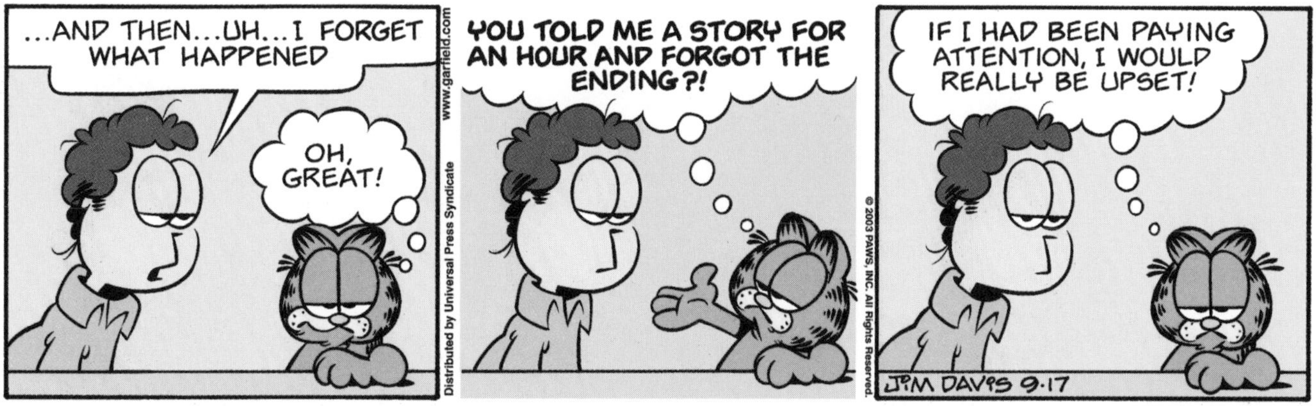
...AND THEN...UH...I FORGET WHAT HAPPENED
OH, GREAT!
YOU TOLD ME A STORY FOR AN HOUR AND FORGOT THE ENDING?!
IF I HAD BEEN PAYING ATTENTION, I WOULD REALLY BE UPSET!
Distributed by Universal Press Syndicate www.garfield.com
© 2003 PAWS, INC. All Rights Reserved.
JIM DAVIS 9.17

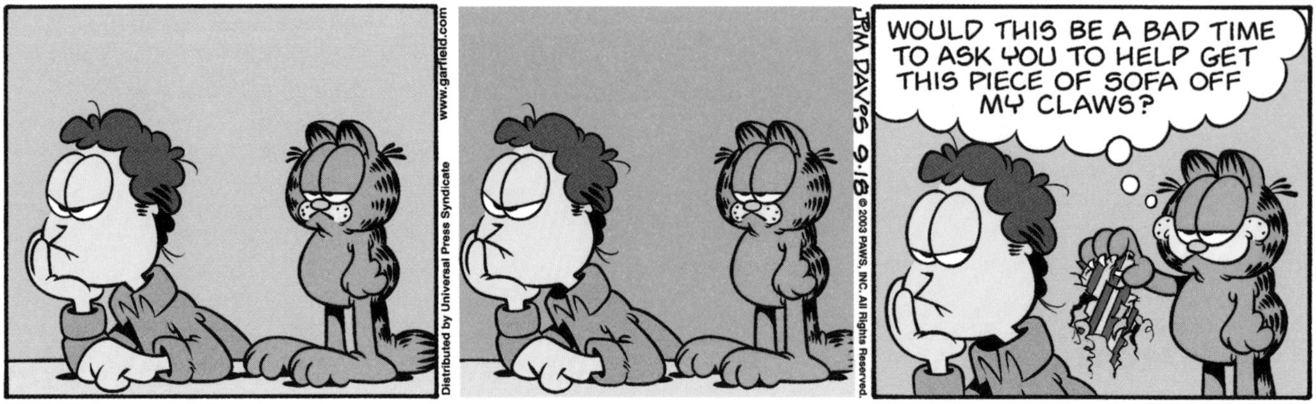
www.garfield.com
Distributed by Universal Press Syndicate
JIM DAVIS 9-18
© 2003 PAWS, INC. All Rights Reserved.
WOULD THIS BE A BAD TIME TO ASK YOU TO HELP GET THIS PIECE OF SOFA OFF MY CLAWS?

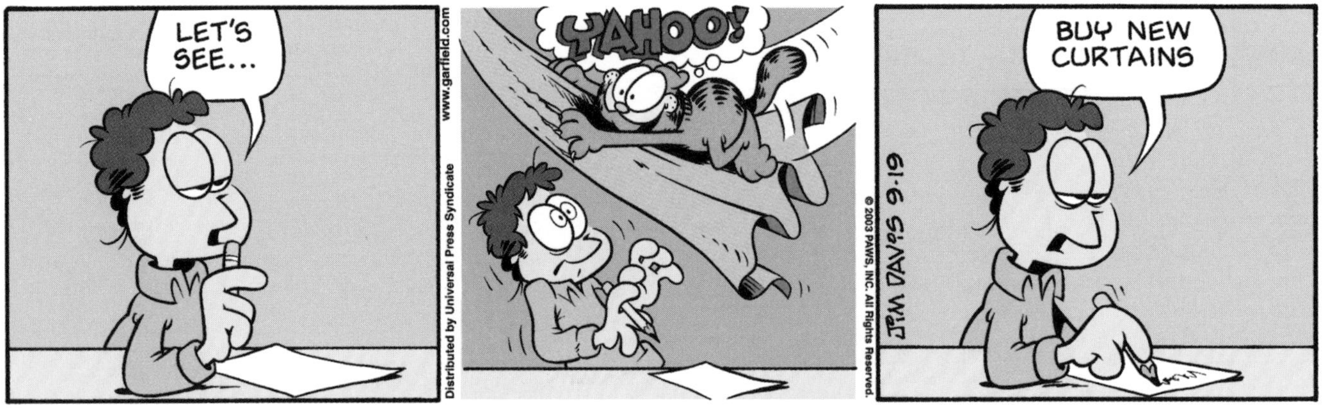
LET'S SEE...
www.garfield.com
Distributed by Universal Press Syndicate
YAHOO!
© 2003 PAWS, INC. All Rights Reserved.
JIM DAVIS 9-19
BUY NEW CURTAINS

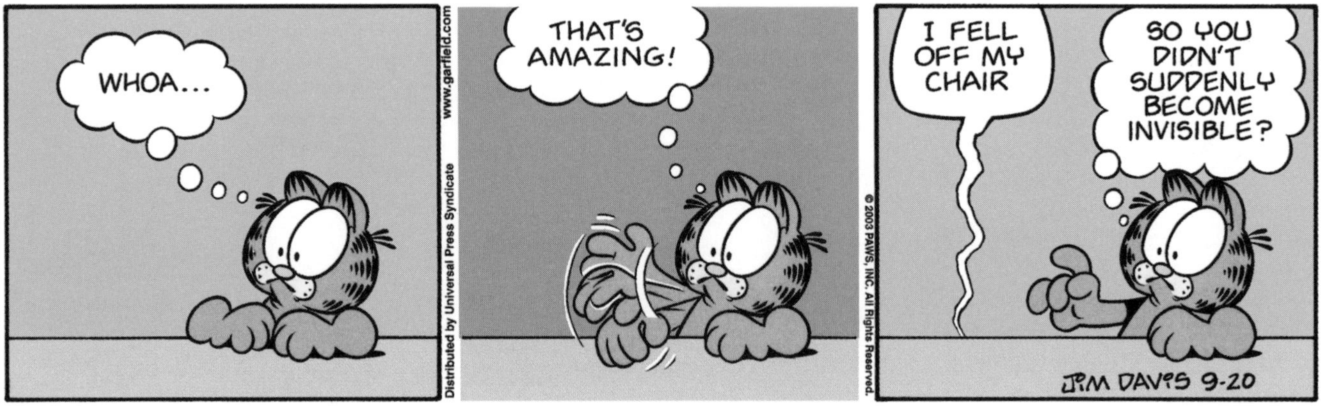
WHOA...
www.garfield.com
Distributed by Universal Press Syndicate
THAT'S AMAZING!
© 2003 PAWS, INC. All Rights Reserved.
I FELL OFF MY CHAIR
SO YOU DIDN'T SUDDENLY BECOME INVISIBLE?
JIM DAVIS 9-20

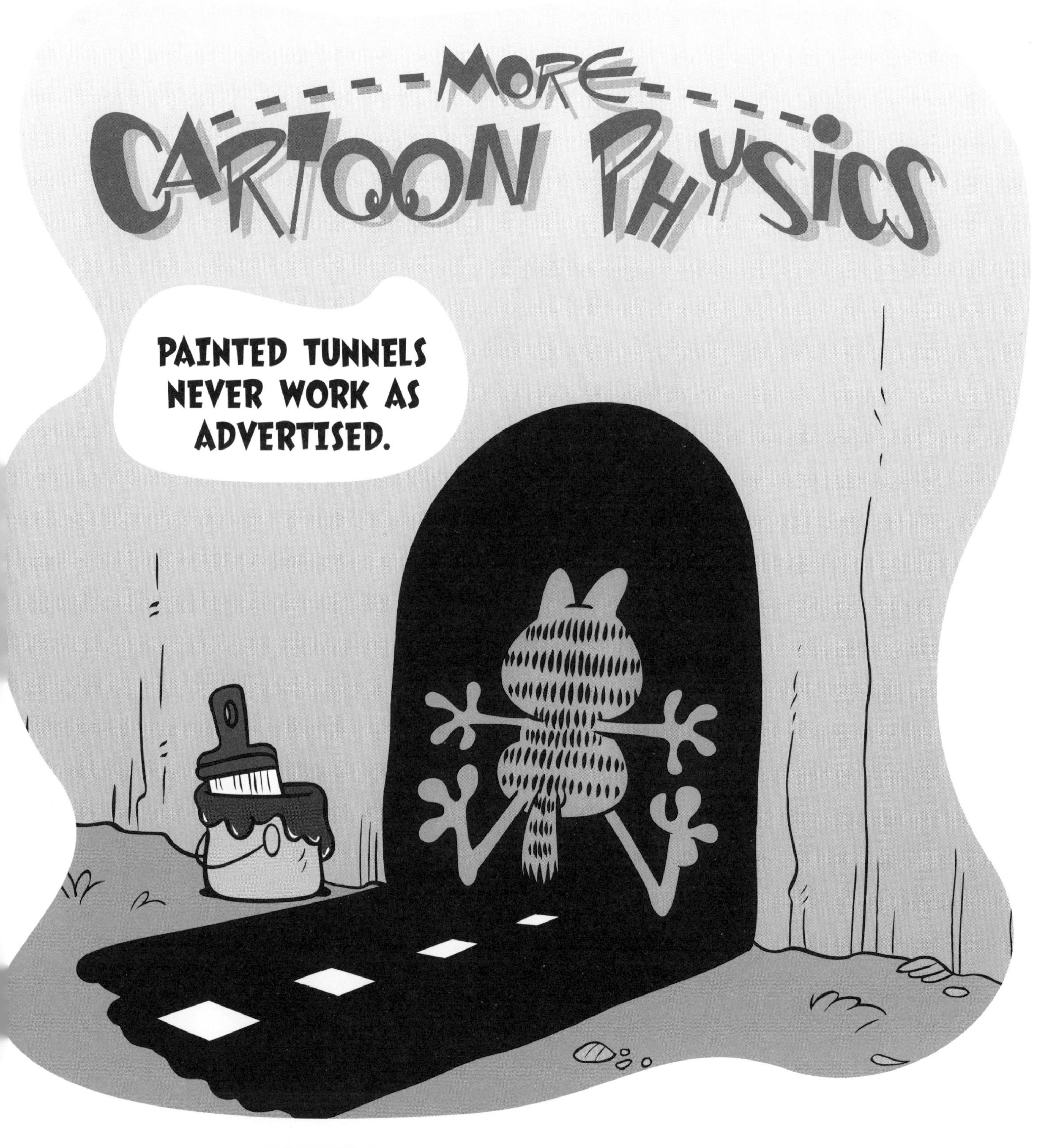
MORE
CARTOON PHYSICS
PAINTED TUNNELS NEVER WORK AS ADVERTISED.

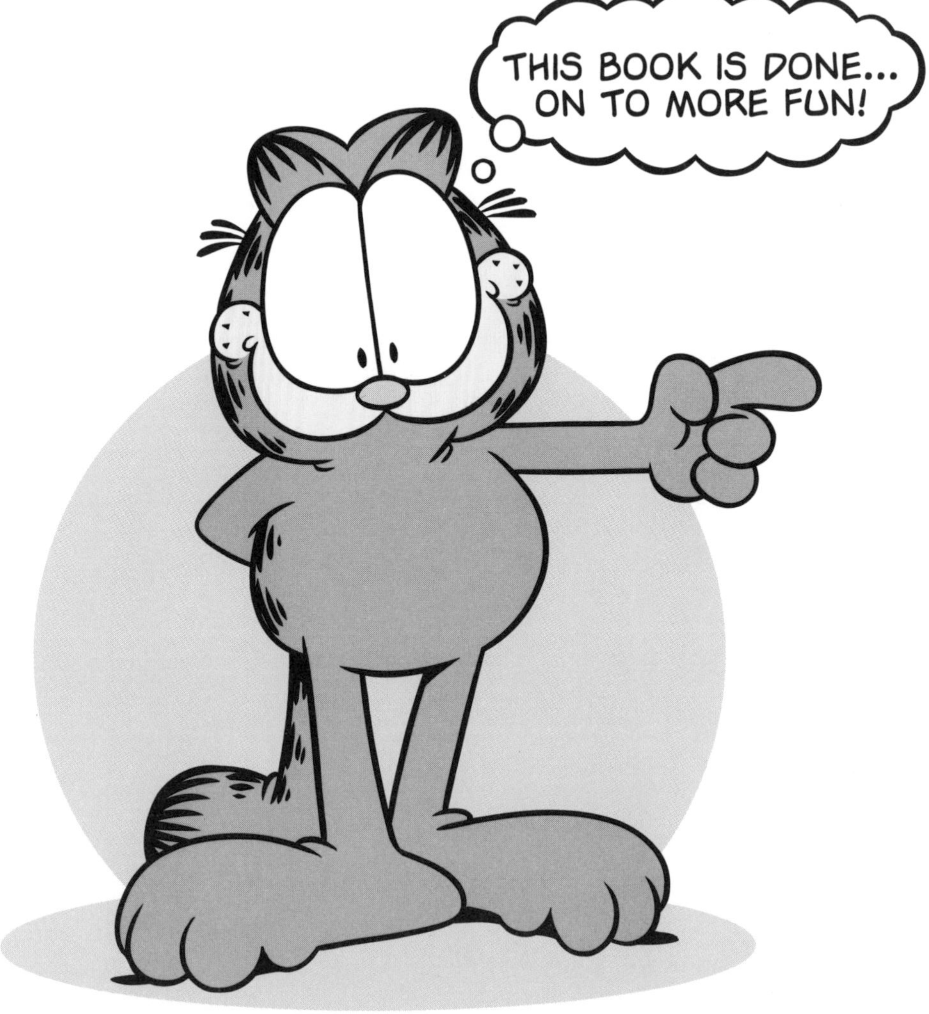
THIS BOOK IS DONE...
ON TO MORE FUN!

Garfield GOES BANANAS

BY JIM DAVIS

Ballantine Books • New York

Cats Rule Dogs Drool

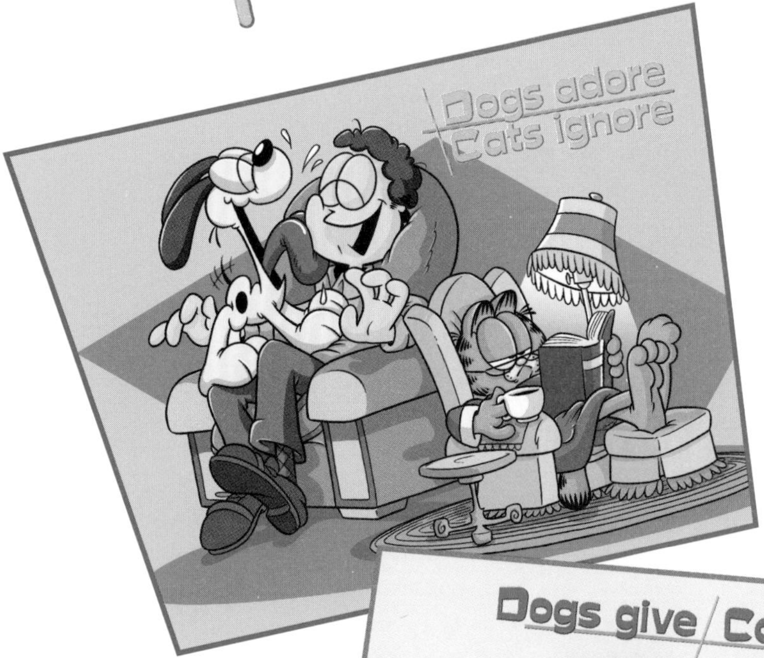
Dogs adore
Cats ignore

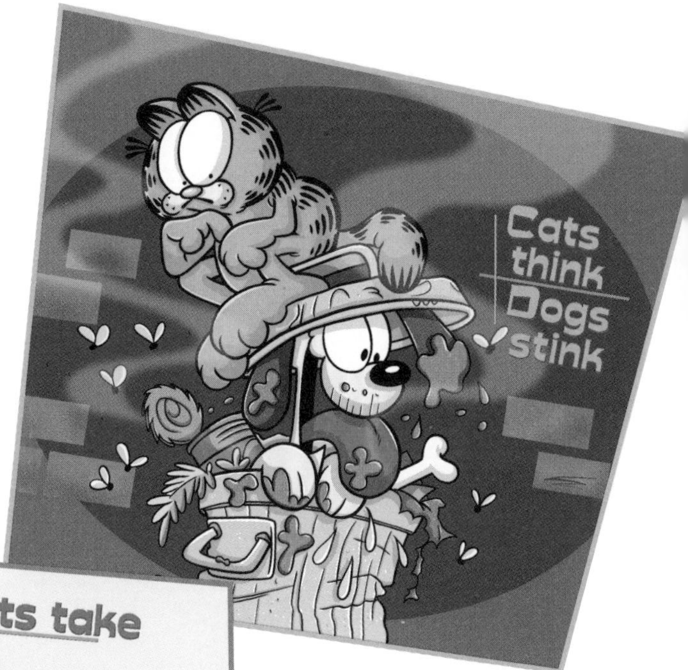
Cats think
Dogs stink

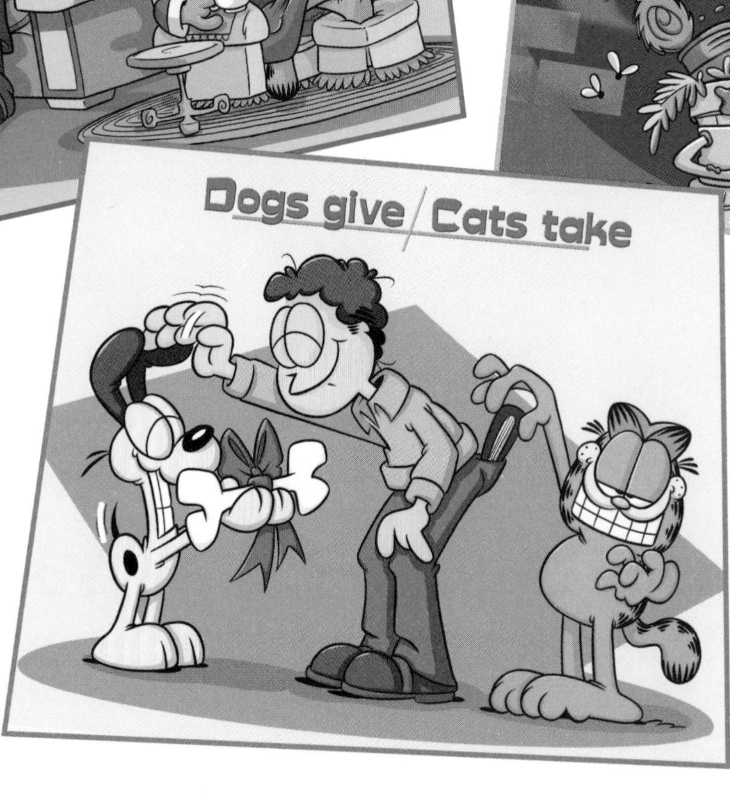
Dogs give/Cats take

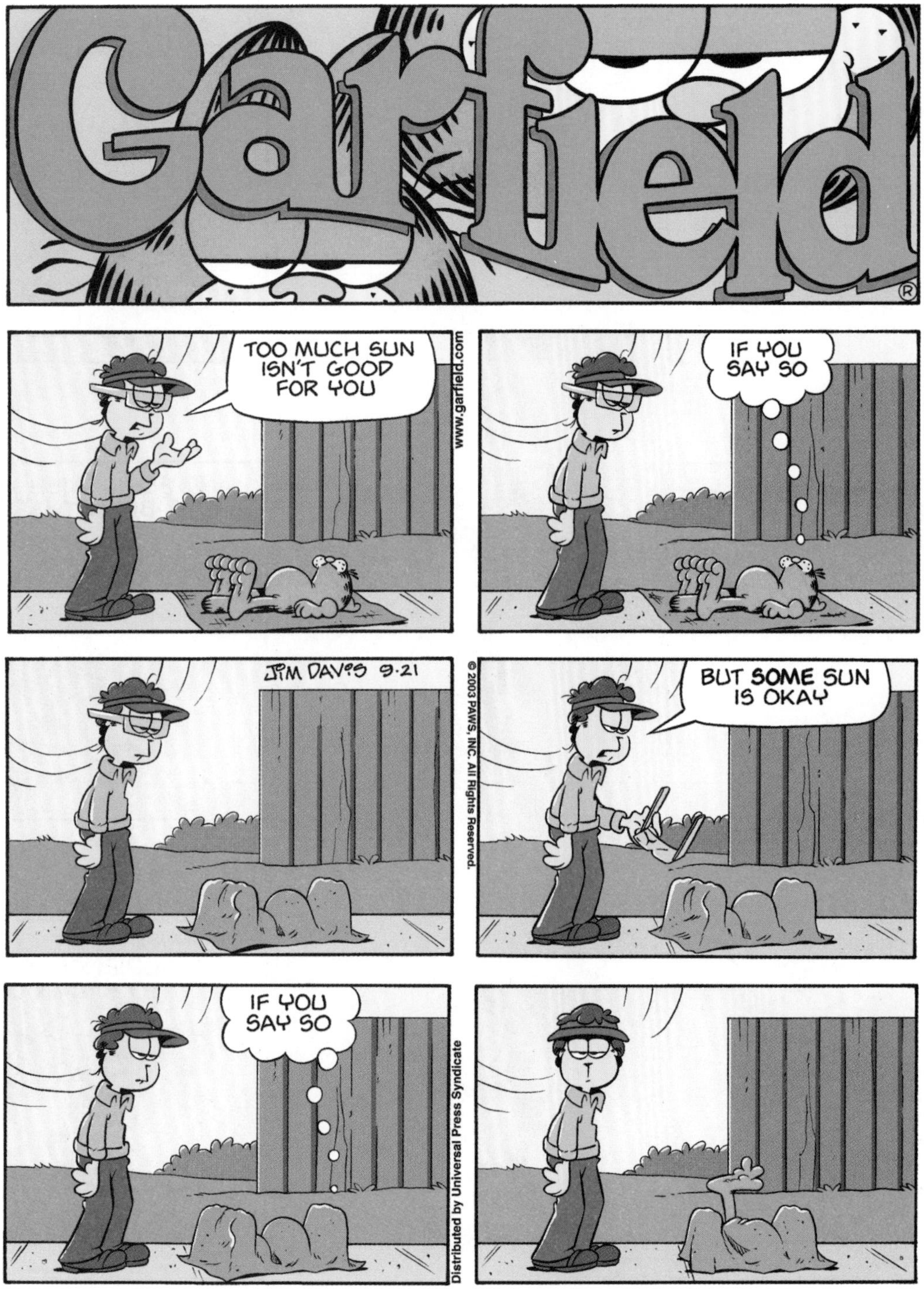
Garfield
TOO MUCH SUN ISN'T GOOD FOR YOU
www.garfield.com
IF YOU SAY SO
JIM DAVIS 9-21
© 2003 PAWS, INC. All Rights Reserved.
BUT SOME SUN IS OKAY
IF YOU SAY SO
Distributed by Universal Press Syndicate

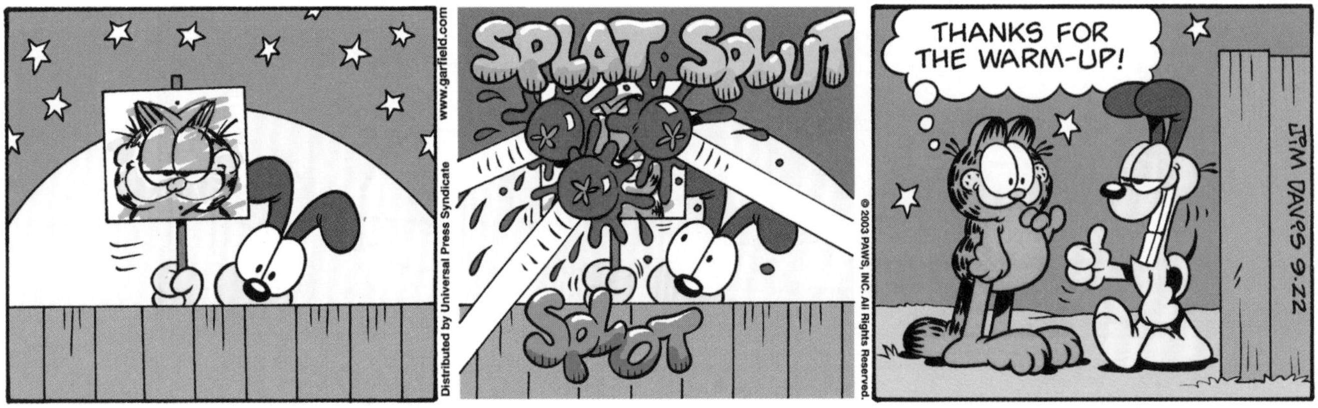
www.garfield.com
Distributed by Universal Press Syndicate
SPLAT SPLUT
SPLOT
© 2003 PAWS, INC. All Rights Reserved.
THANKS FOR THE WARM-UP!
JPM DAVPS 9.22

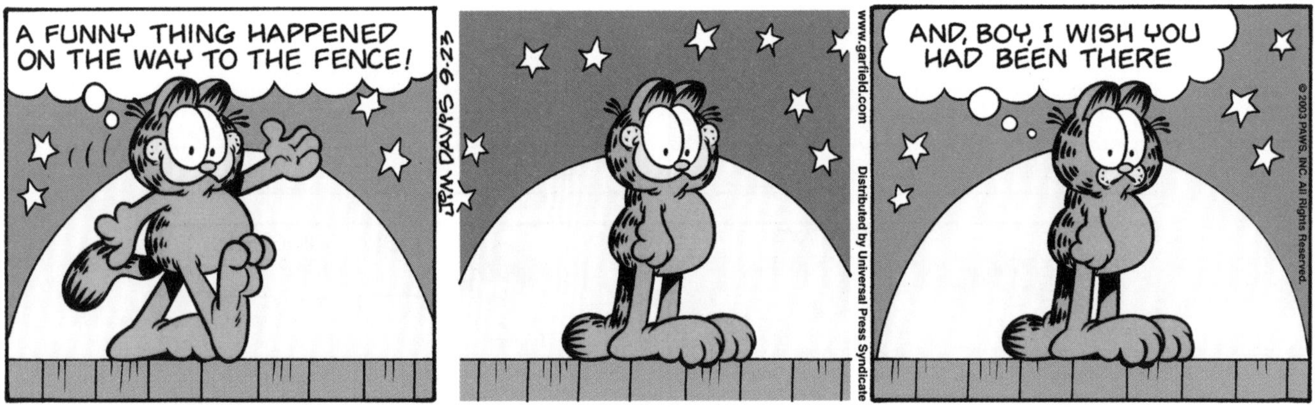
A FUNNY THING HAPPENED ON THE WAY TO THE FENCE!
JPM DAVPS 9.23
www.garfield.com
Distributed by Universal Press Syndicate
AND, BOY, I WISH YOU HAD BEEN THERE
© 2003 PAWS, INC. All Rights Reserved.

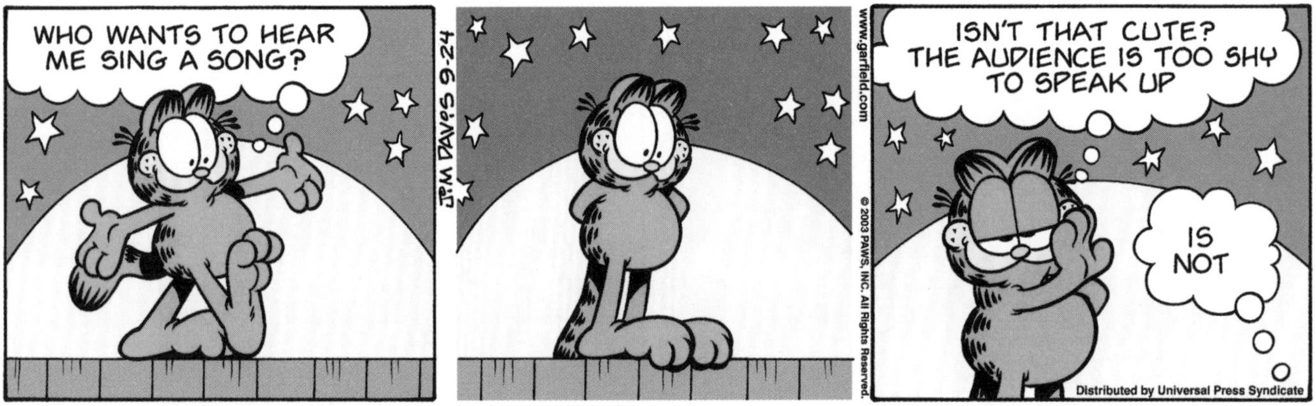
WHO WANTS TO HEAR ME SING A SONG?
JPM DAVPS 9.24
www.garfield.com
© 2003 PAWS, INC. All Rights Reserved.
ISN'T THAT CUTE? THE AUDIENCE IS TOO SHY TO SPEAK UP
IS NOT
Distributed by Universal Press Syndicate

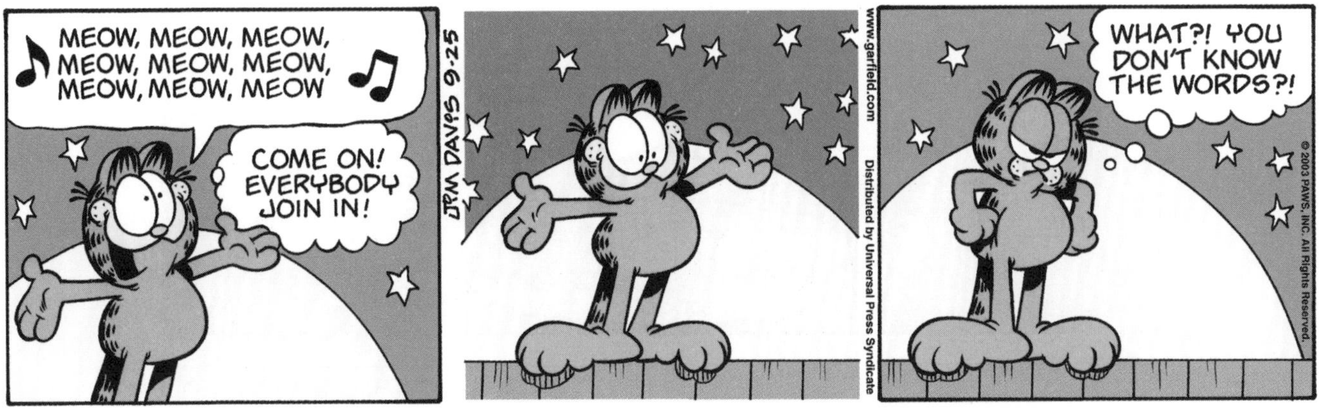
MEOW, MEOW, MEOW, MEOW, MEOW, MEOW, MEOW, MEOW, MEOW
COME ON! EVERYBODY JOIN IN!
JIM DAVIS 9-25
www.garfield.com
Distributed by Universal Press Syndicate
WHAT?! YOU DON'T KNOW THE WORDS?!
© 2003 PAWS, INC. All Rights Reserved.

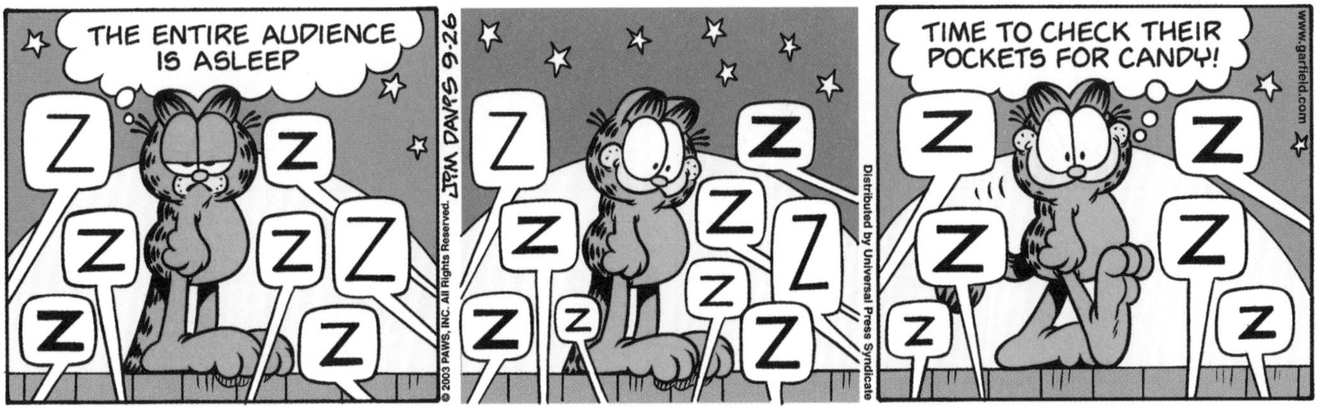
THE ENTIRE AUDIENCE IS ASLEEP
Z
JIM DAVIS 9-26
© 2003 PAWS, INC. All Rights Reserved.
Distributed by Universal Press Syndicate
TIME TO CHECK THEIR POCKETS FOR CANDY!
www.garfield.com

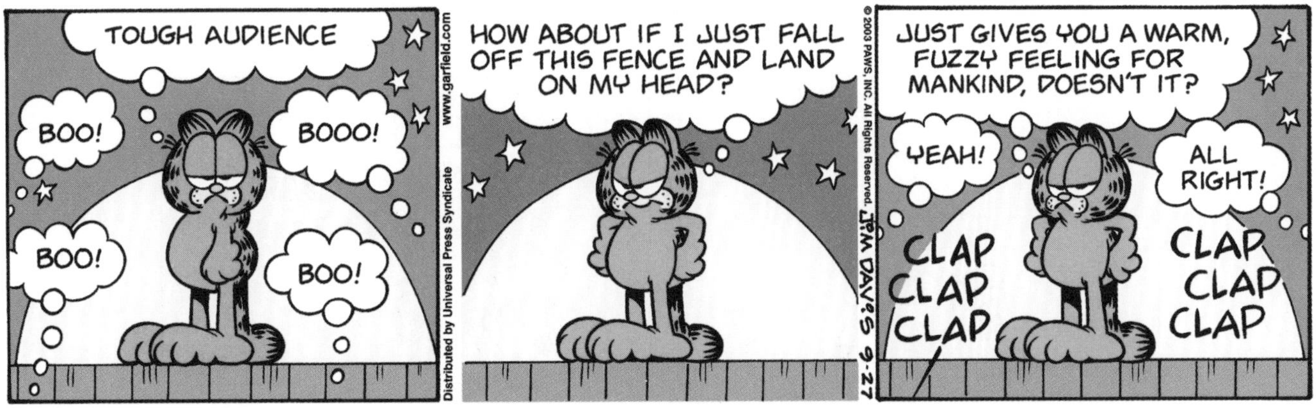
TOUGH AUDIENCE
BOO!
BOOO!
BOO!
BOO!
www.garfield.com
Distributed by Universal Press Syndicate
HOW ABOUT IF I JUST FALL OFF THIS FENCE AND LAND ON MY HEAD?
© 2003 PAWS, INC. All Rights Reserved.
JIM DAVIS 9-27
JUST GIVES YOU A WARM, FUZZY FEELING FOR MANKIND, DOESN'T IT?
YEAH!
ALL RIGHT!
CLAP CLAP CLAP
CLAP CLAP CLAP

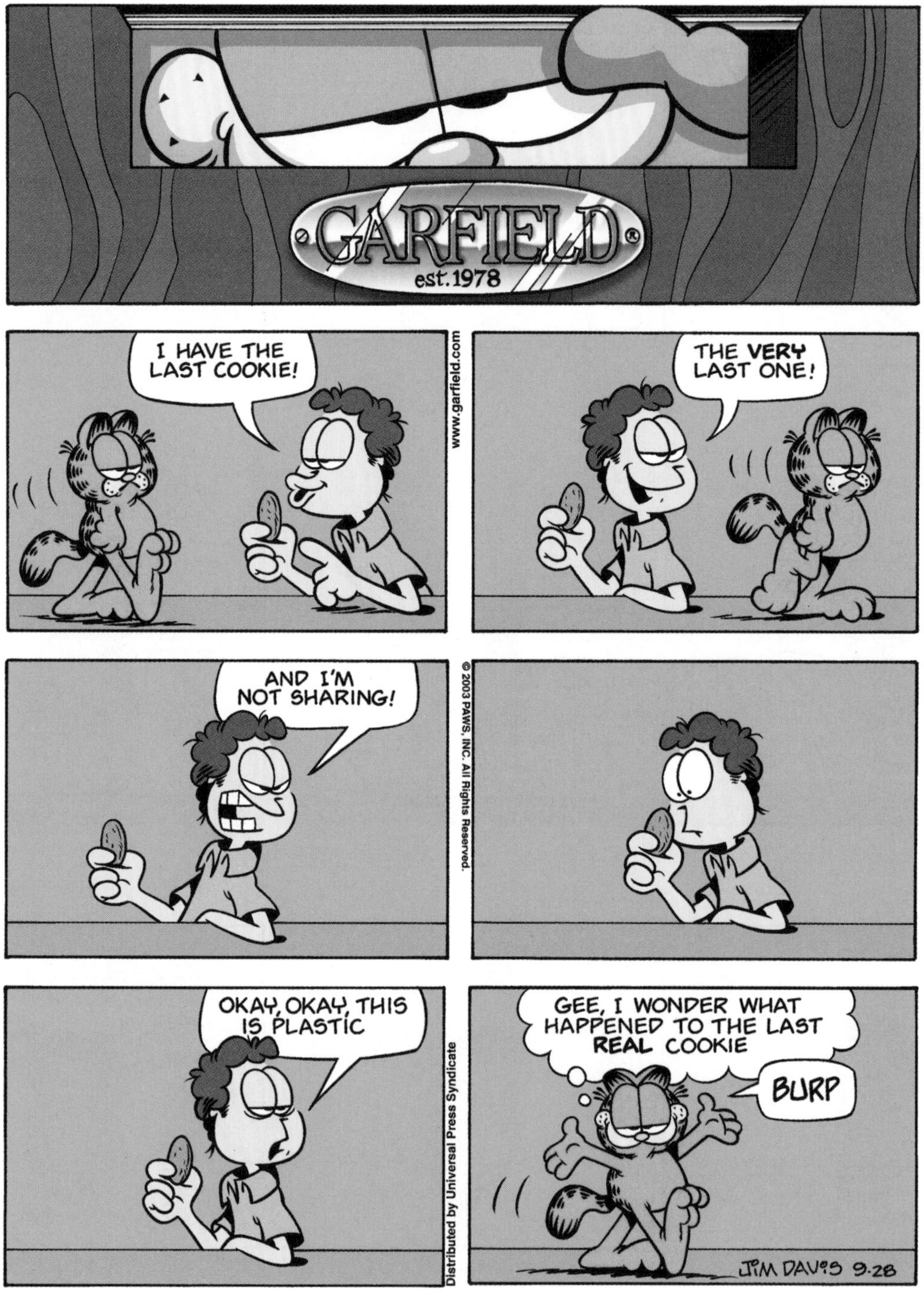
GARFIELD
est. 1978
I HAVE THE LAST COOKIE!
www.garfield.com
THE VERY LAST ONE!
AND I'M NOT SHARING!
© 2003 PAWS, INC. All Rights Reserved.
OKAY, OKAY, THIS IS PLASTIC
Distributed by Universal Press Syndicate
GEE, I WONDER WHAT HAPPENED TO THE LAST REAL COOKIE
BURP
JIM DAVIS 9.28

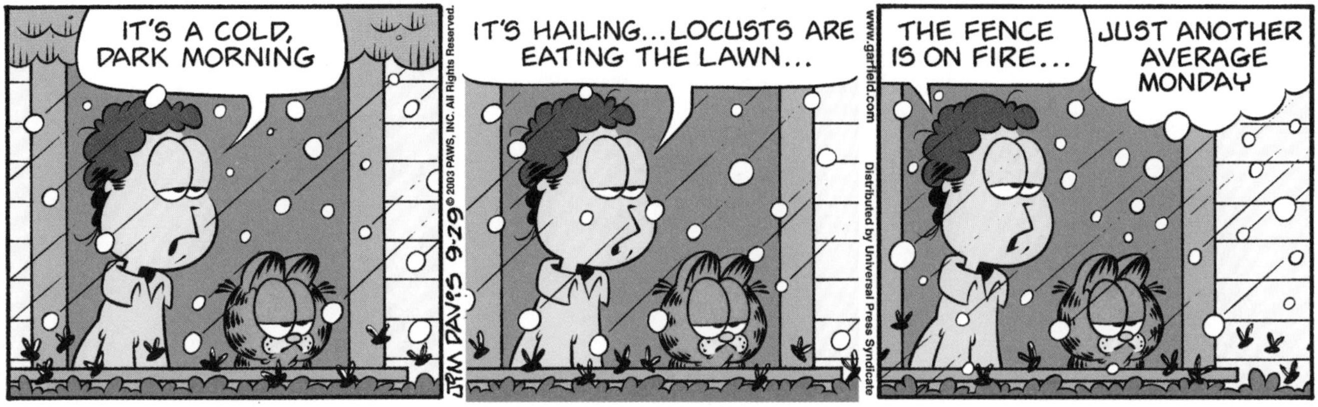
IT'S A COLD, DARK MORNING
IT'S HAILING...LOCUSTS ARE EATING THE LAWN...
THE FENCE IS ON FIRE...
JUST ANOTHER AVERAGE MONDAY

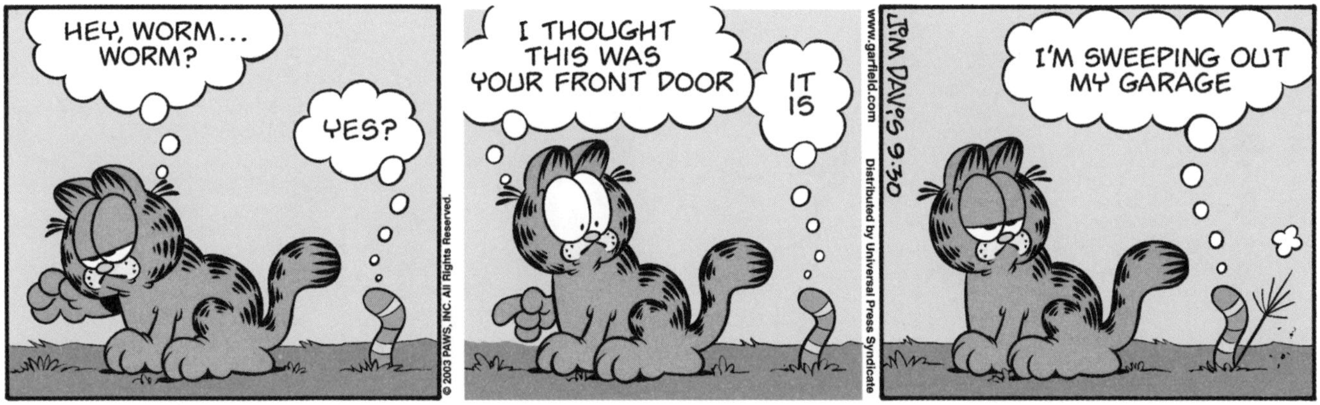
HEY, WORM... WORM?
YES?
I THOUGHT THIS WAS YOUR FRONT DOOR
IT IS
I'M SWEEPING OUT MY GARAGE

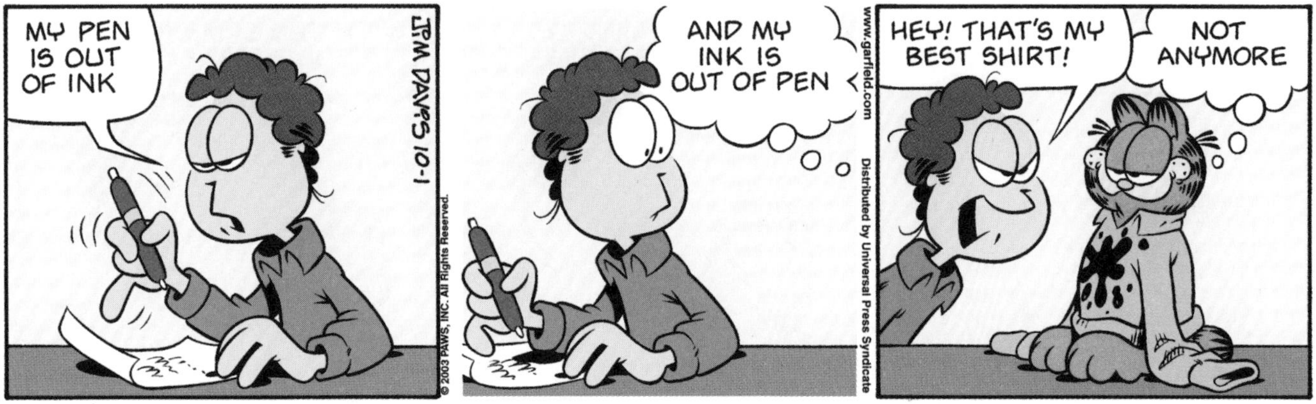
MY PEN IS OUT OF INK
AND MY INK IS OUT OF PEN
HEY! THAT'S MY BEST SHIRT!
NOT ANYMORE

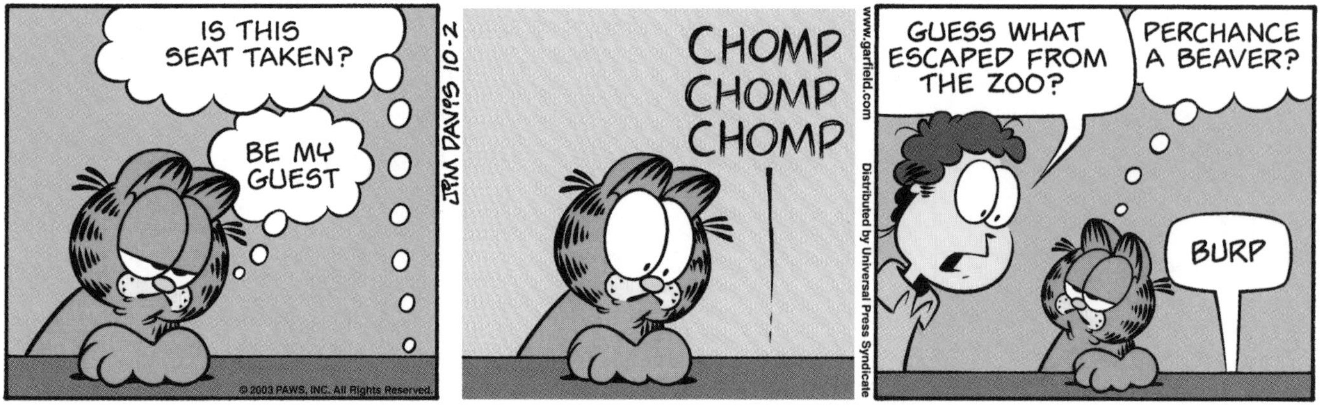
IS THIS SEAT TAKEN?
BE MY GUEST
JPM DAVPS 10·2
© 2003 PAWS, INC. All Rights Reserved.
CHOMP CHOMP CHOMP
www.garfield.com Distributed by Universal Press Syndicate
GUESS WHAT ESCAPED FROM THE ZOO?
PERCHANCE A BEAVER?
BURP

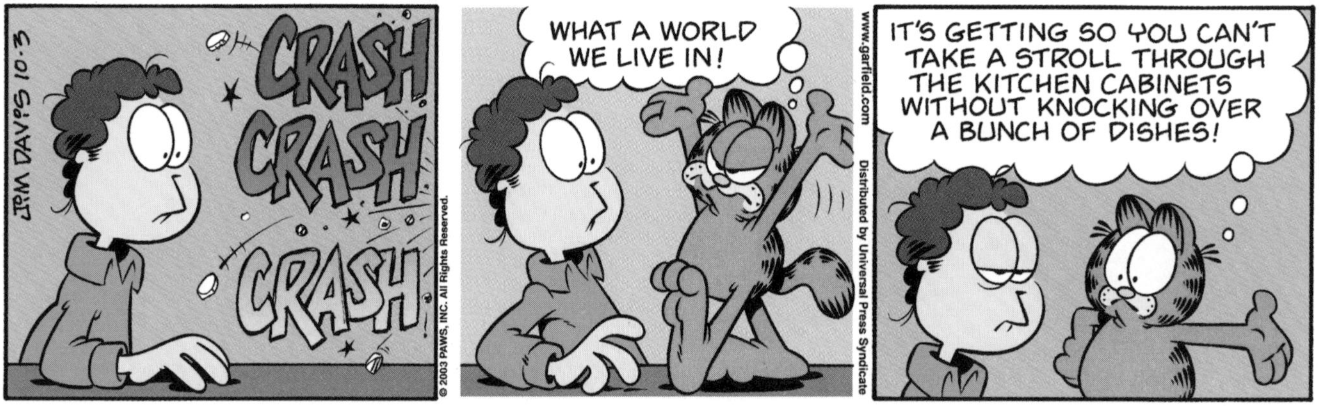
JPM DAVPS 10·3
CRASH CRASH CRASH
© 2003 PAWS, INC. All Rights Reserved.
WHAT A WORLD WE LIVE IN!
www.garfield.com Distributed by Universal Press Syndicate
IT'S GETTING SO YOU CAN'T TAKE A STROLL THROUGH THE KITCHEN CABINETS WITHOUT KNOCKING OVER A BUNCH OF DISHES!

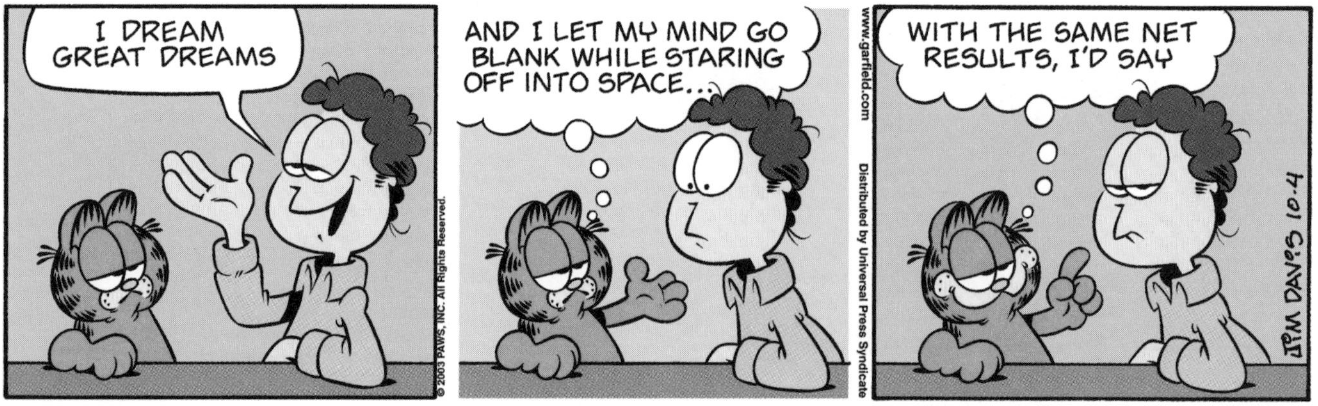
I DREAM GREAT DREAMS
© 2003 PAWS, INC. All Rights Reserved.
AND I LET MY MIND GO BLANK WHILE STARING OFF INTO SPACE...
www.garfield.com Distributed by Universal Press Syndicate
WITH THE SAME NET RESULTS, I'D SAY
JPM DAVPS 10·4

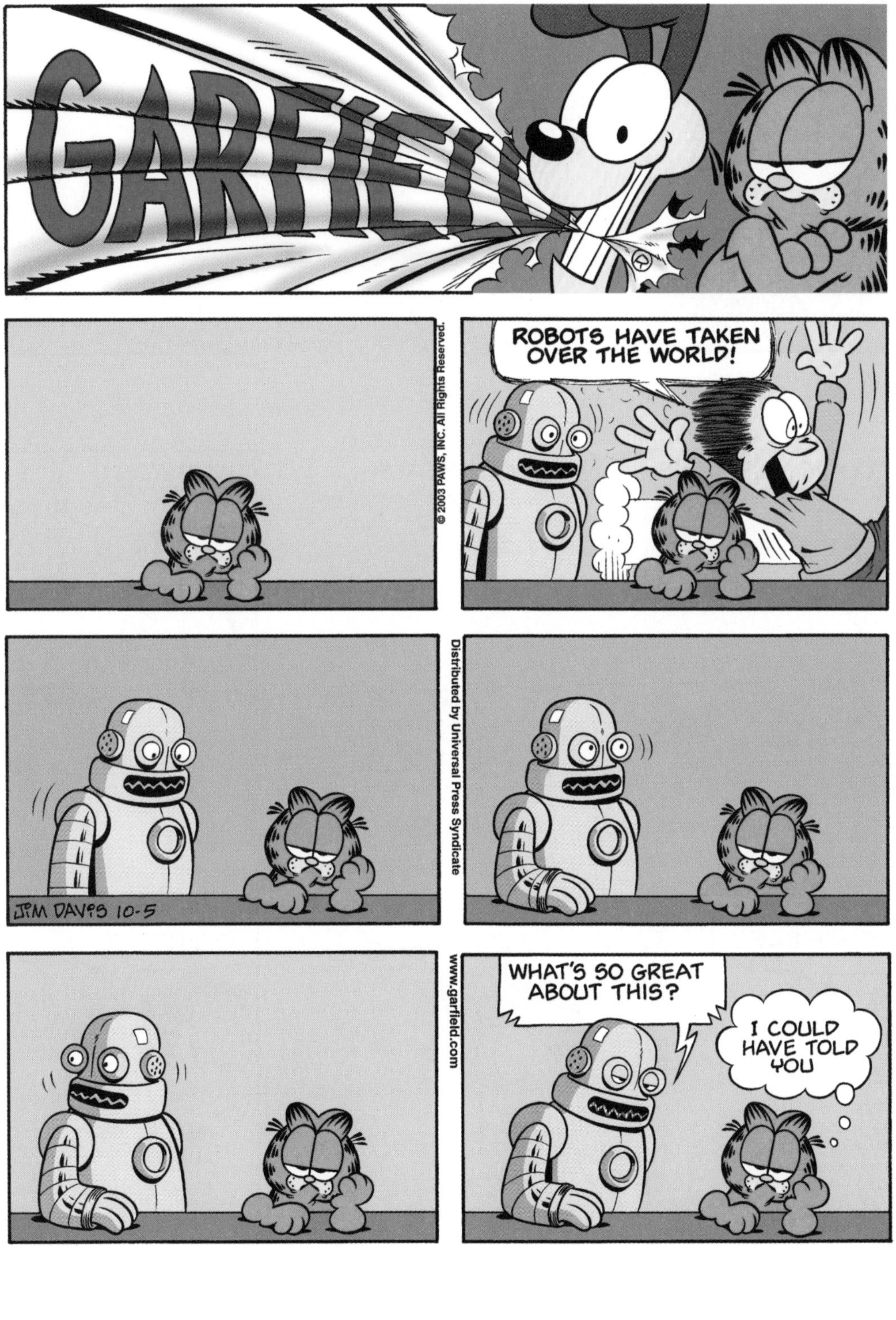
GARFIELD
© 2003 PAWS, INC. All Rights Reserved.
ROBOTS HAVE TAKEN OVER THE WORLD!
Distributed by Universal Press Syndicate
JIM DAVIS 10-5
www.garfield.com
WHAT'S SO GREAT ABOUT THIS?
I COULD HAVE TOLD YOU

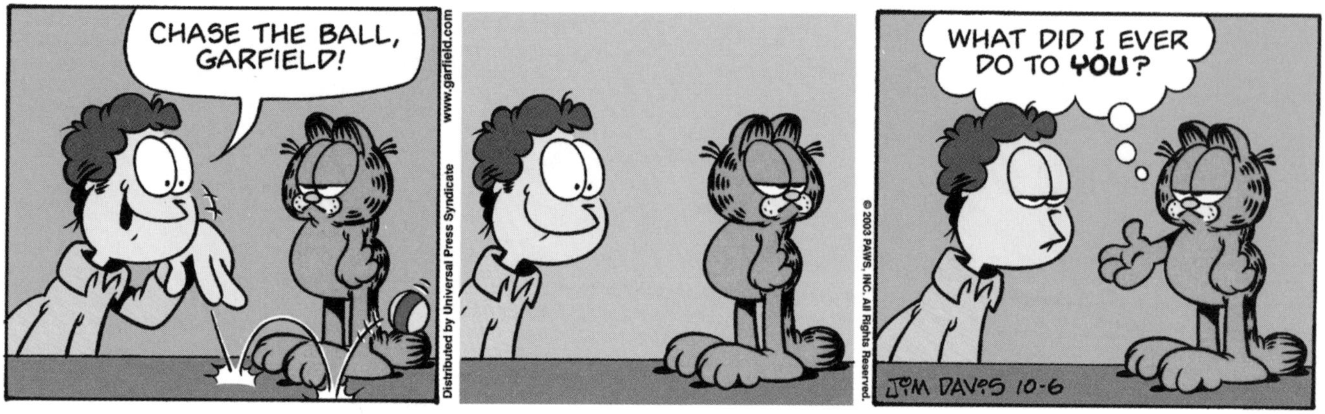
CHASE THE BALL, GARFIELD!
WHAT DID I EVER DO TO **YOU**?
JIM DAVIS 10-6
www.garfield.com
Distributed by Universal Press Syndicate
© 2003 PAWS, INC. All Rights Reserved.

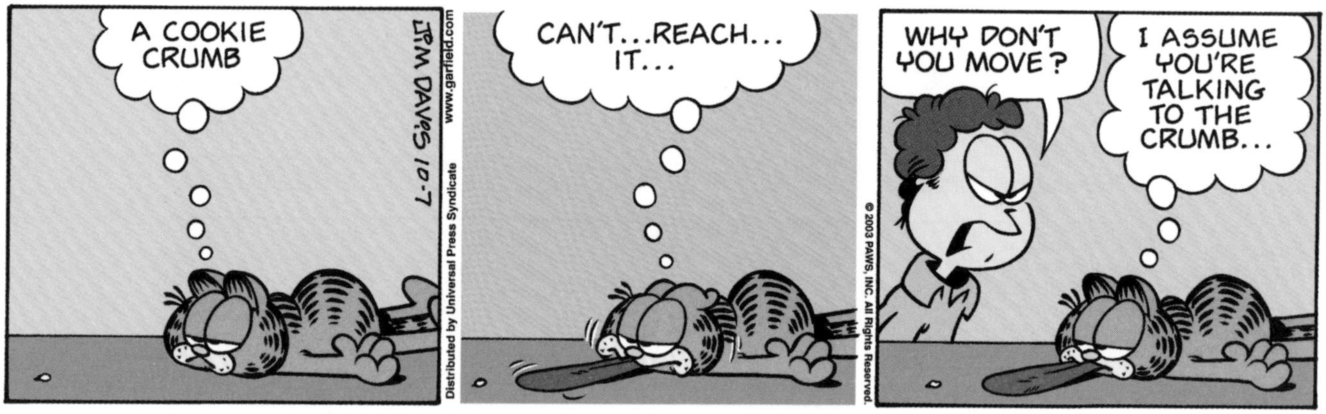
A COOKIE CRUMB
CAN'T...REACH... IT...
WHY DON'T YOU MOVE?
I ASSUME YOU'RE TALKING TO THE CRUMB...
JIM DAVIS 10-7
www.garfield.com
Distributed by Universal Press Syndicate
© 2003 PAWS, INC. All Rights Reserved.

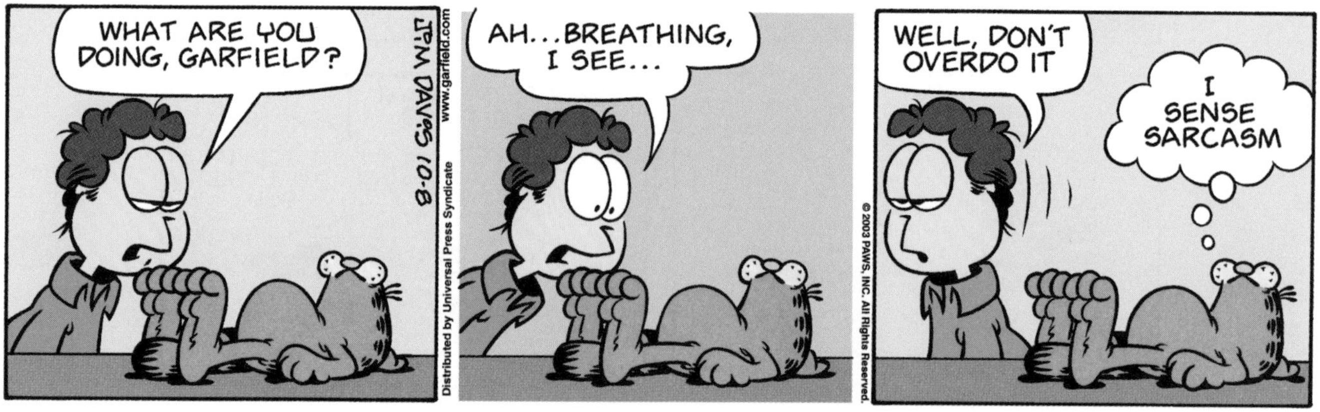
WHAT ARE YOU DOING, GARFIELD?
AH...BREATHING, I SEE...
WELL, DON'T OVERDO IT
I SENSE SARCASM
JIM DAVIS 10-8
www.garfield.com
Distributed by Universal Press Syndicate
© 2003 PAWS, INC. All Rights Reserved.

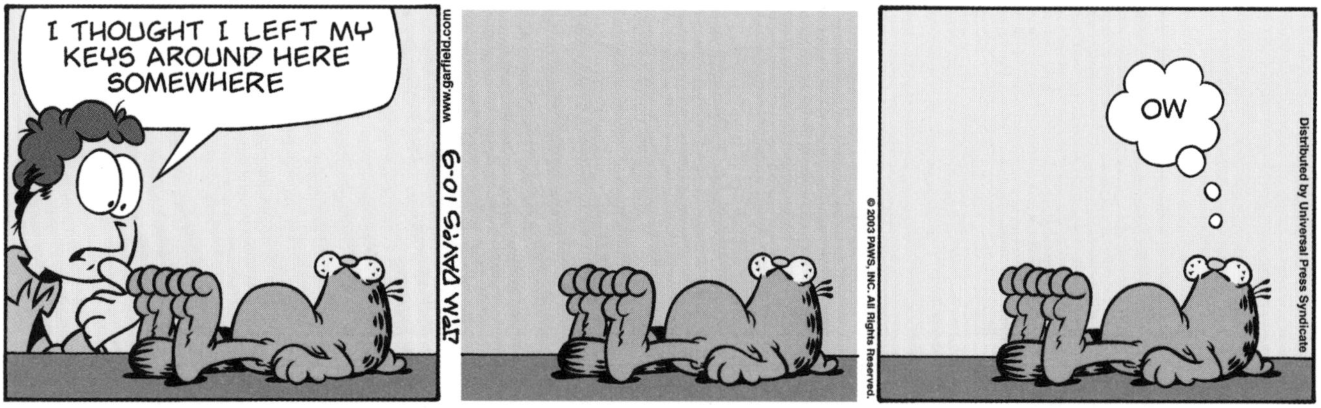
I THOUGHT I LEFT MY KEYS AROUND HERE SOMEWHERE
OW
www.garfield.com
JPM DAVIS 10-9
© 2003 PAWS, INC. All Rights Reserved.
Distributed by Universal Press Syndicate

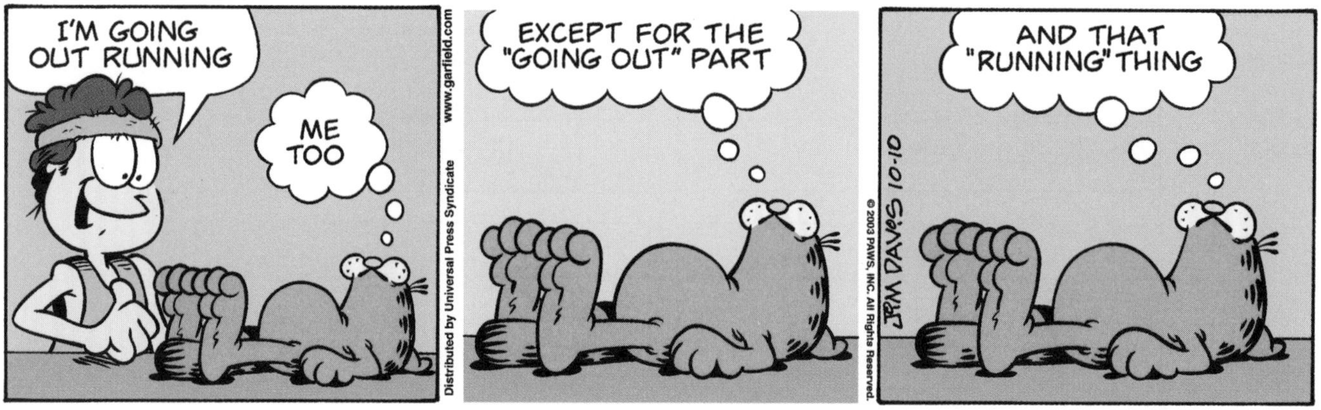
I'M GOING OUT RUNNING
ME TOO
EXCEPT FOR THE "GOING OUT" PART
AND THAT "RUNNING" THING
www.garfield.com
Distributed by Universal Press Syndicate
JPM DAVIS 10-10
© 2003 PAWS, INC. All Rights Reserved.

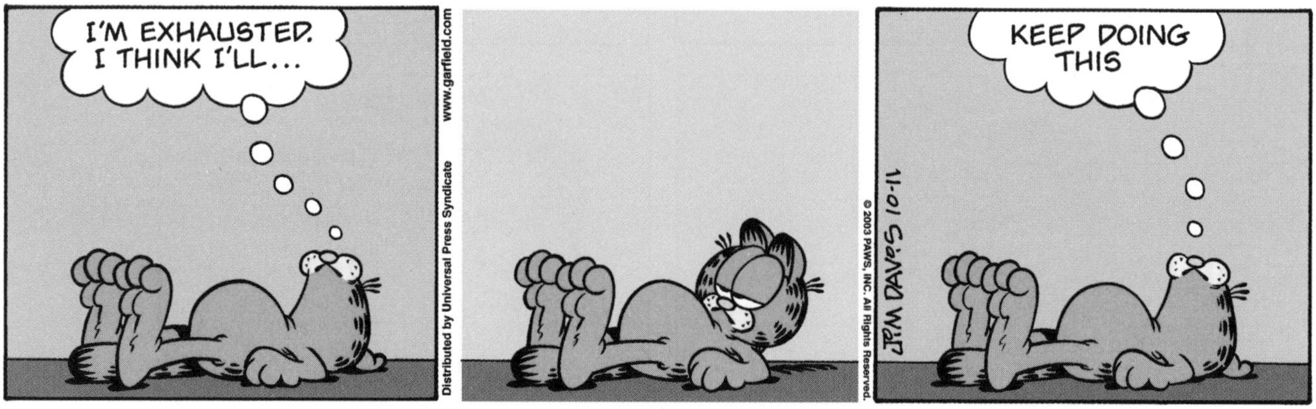
I'M EXHAUSTED. I THINK I'LL...
KEEP DOING THIS
www.garfield.com
Distributed by Universal Press Syndicate
JPM DAVIS 10-11
© 2003 PAWS, INC. All Rights Reserved.

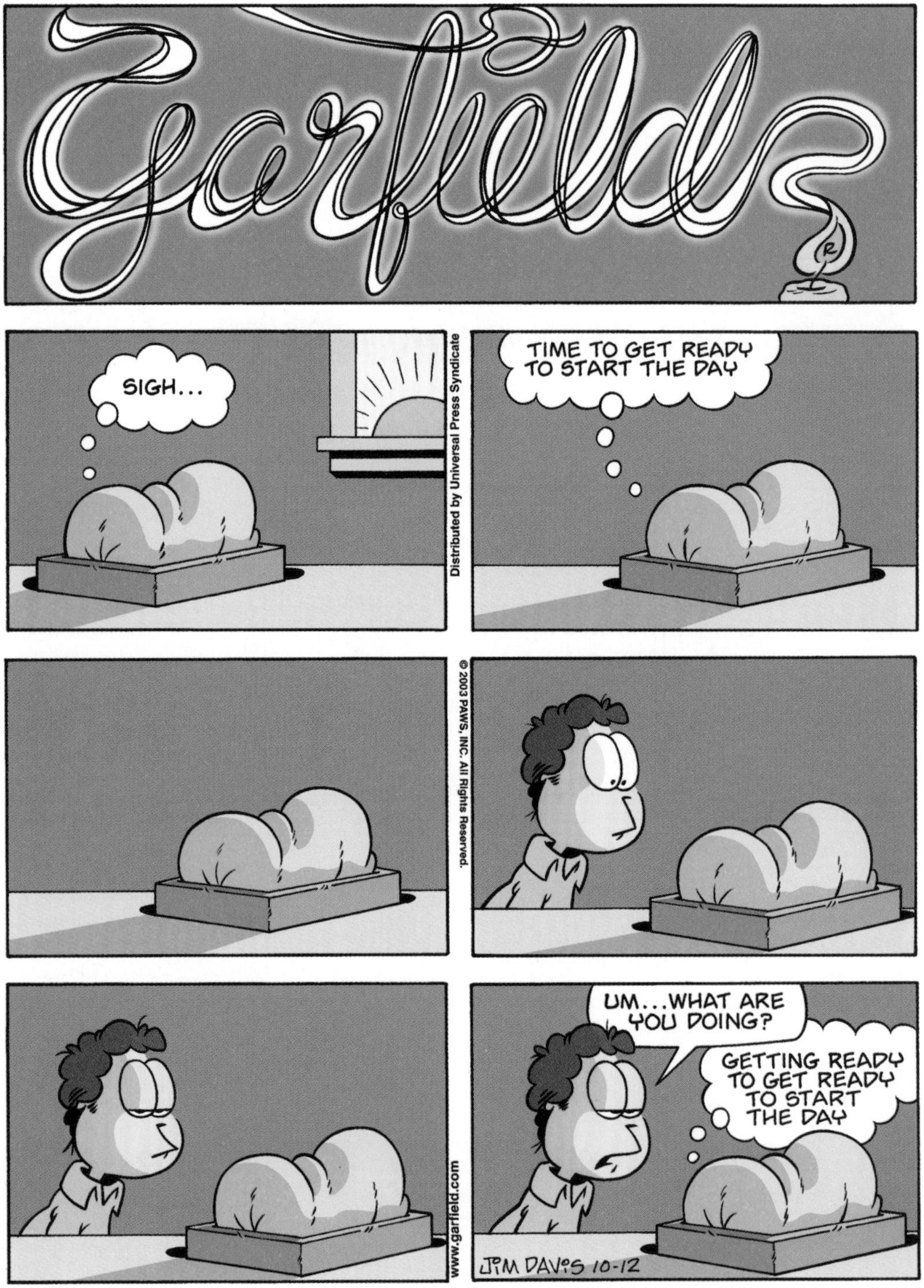
Garfield
SIGH...
TIME TO GET READY TO START THE DAY
UM...WHAT ARE YOU DOING?
GETTING READY TO GET READY TO START THE DAY
Distributed by Universal Press Syndicate
© 2003 PAWS, INC. All Rights Reserved.
www.garfield.com
JIM DAVIS 10-12

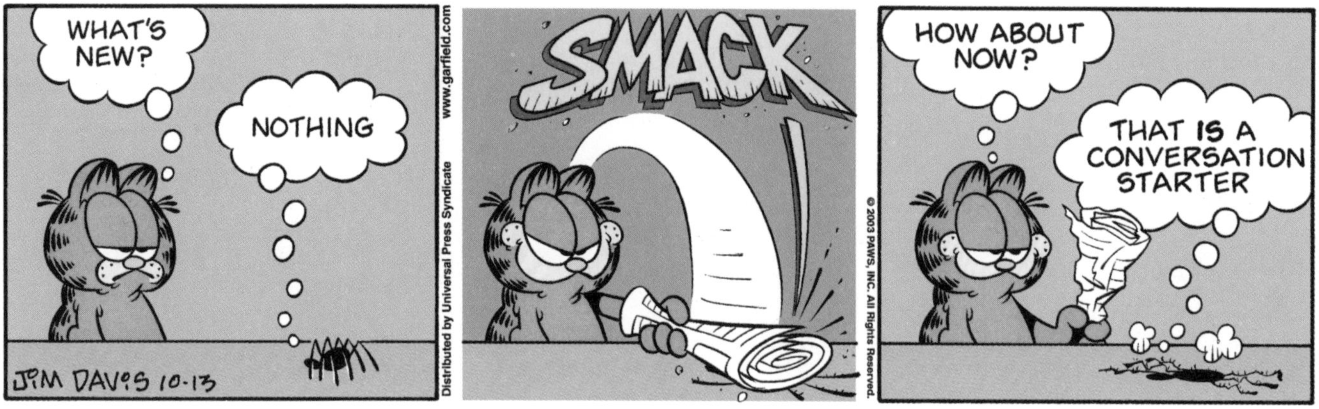
WHAT'S NEW?
NOTHING
JIM DAVIS 10-13
www.garfield.com
Distributed by Universal Press Syndicate
SMACK
© 2003 PAWS, INC. All Rights Reserved.
HOW ABOUT NOW?
THAT IS A CONVERSATION STARTER

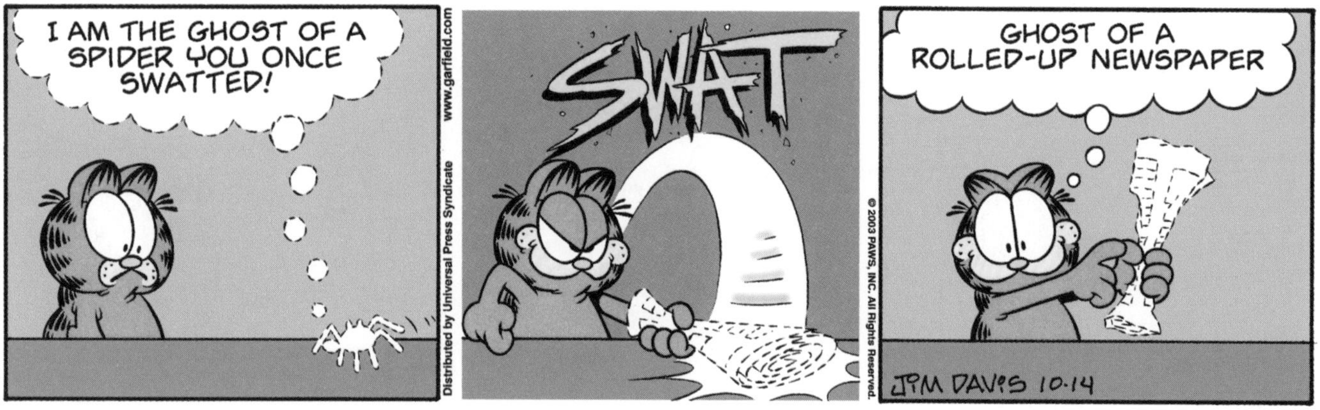
I AM THE GHOST OF A SPIDER YOU ONCE SWATTED!
www.garfield.com
Distributed by Universal Press Syndicate
SWAT
© 2003 PAWS, INC. All Rights Reserved.
GHOST OF A ROLLED-UP NEWSPAPER
JIM DAVIS 10-14

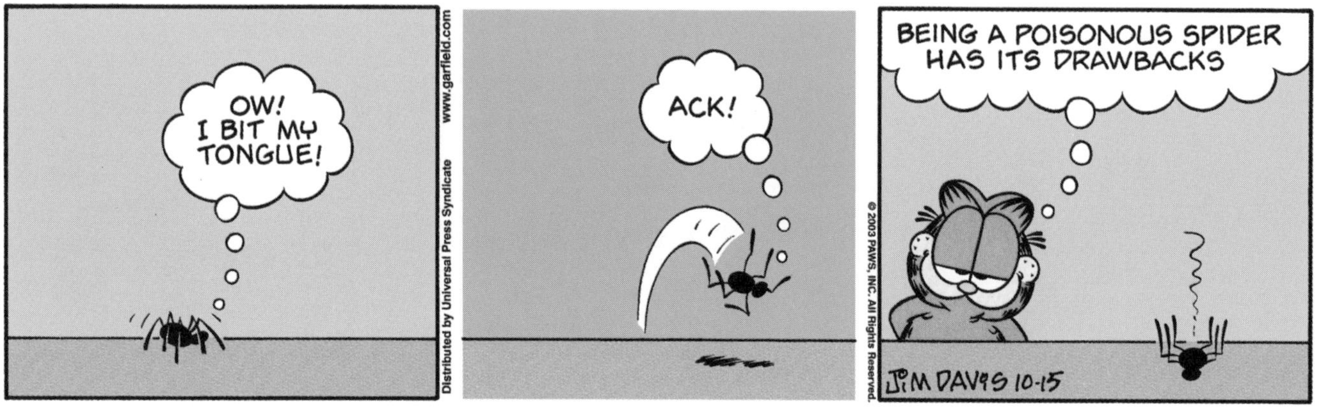
OW! I BIT MY TONGUE!
www.garfield.com
Distributed by Universal Press Syndicate
ACK!
© 2003 PAWS, INC. All Rights Reserved.
BEING A POISONOUS SPIDER HAS ITS DRAWBACKS
JIM DAVIS 10-15

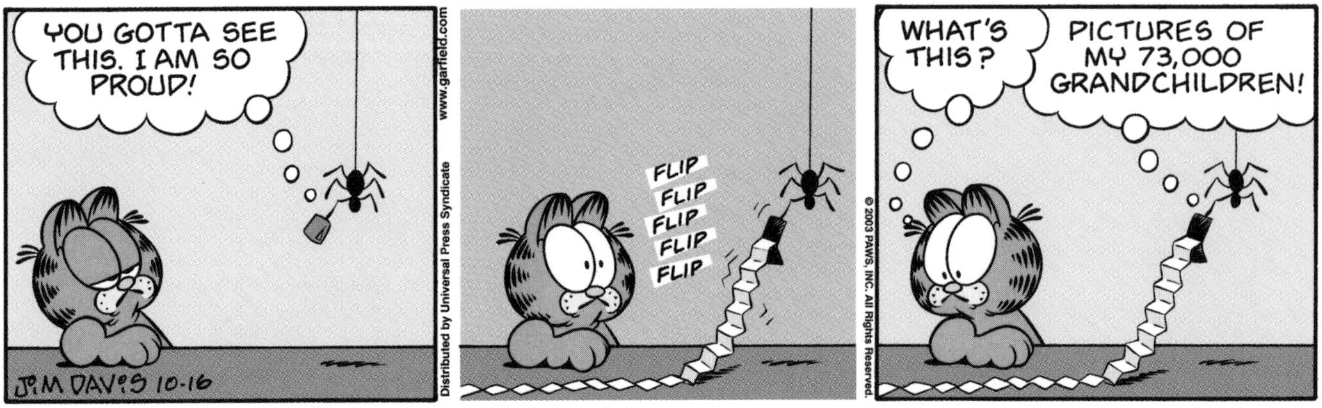
YOU GOTTA SEE THIS. I AM SO PROUD!
JIM DAVIS 10-16
www.garfield.com
Distributed by Universal Press Syndicate
FLIP
FLIP
FLIP
FLIP
FLIP
© 2003 PAWS, INC. All Rights Reserved.
WHAT'S THIS?
PICTURES OF MY 73,000 GRANDCHILDREN!

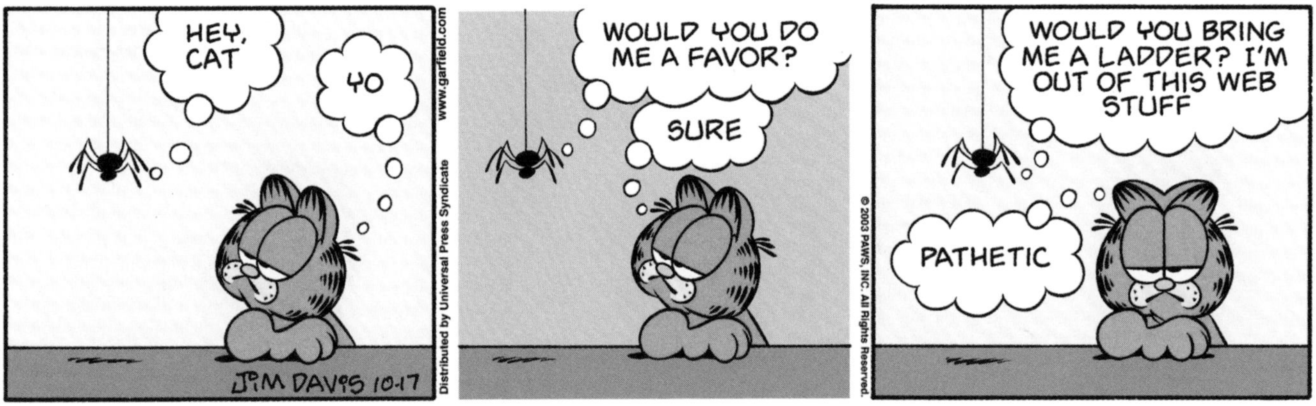
HEY, CAT
YO
JIM DAVIS 10-17
www.garfield.com
Distributed by Universal Press Syndicate
WOULD YOU DO ME A FAVOR?
SURE
© 2003 PAWS, INC. All Rights Reserved.
WOULD YOU BRING ME A LADDER? I'M OUT OF THIS WEB STUFF
PATHETIC

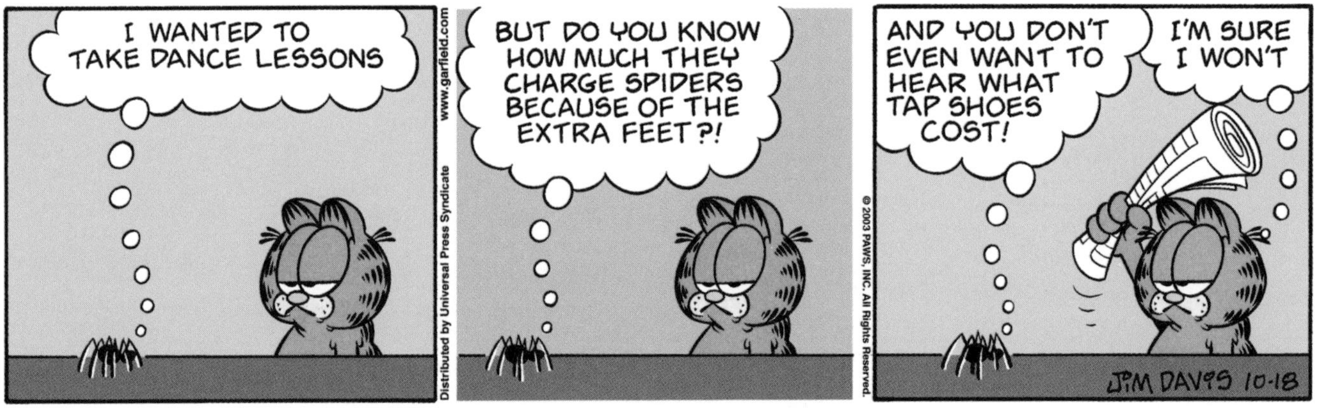
I WANTED TO TAKE DANCE LESSONS
www.garfield.com
Distributed by Universal Press Syndicate
BUT DO YOU KNOW HOW MUCH THEY CHARGE SPIDERS BECAUSE OF THE EXTRA FEET?!
© 2003 PAWS, INC. All Rights Reserved.
AND YOU DON'T EVEN WANT TO HEAR WHAT TAP SHOES COST!
I'M SURE I WON'T
JIM DAVIS 10-18

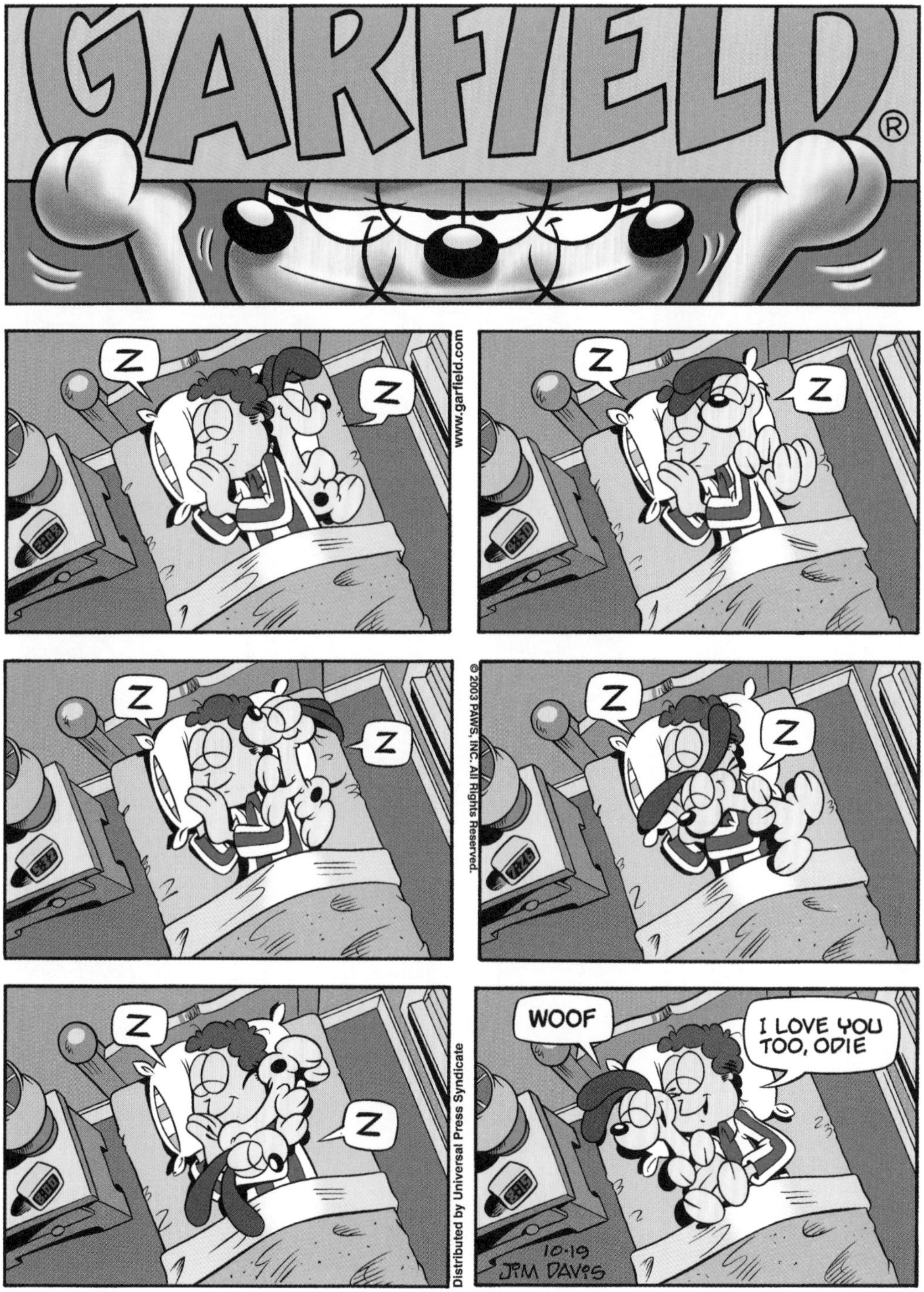
GARFIELD®
www.garfield.com
Z
Z
Z
Z
© 2003 PAWS, INC. All Rights Reserved.
Z
Z
Z
Z
Distributed by Universal Press Syndicate
Z
Z
WOOF
I LOVE YOU TOO, ODIE
10-19
JIM DAVIS

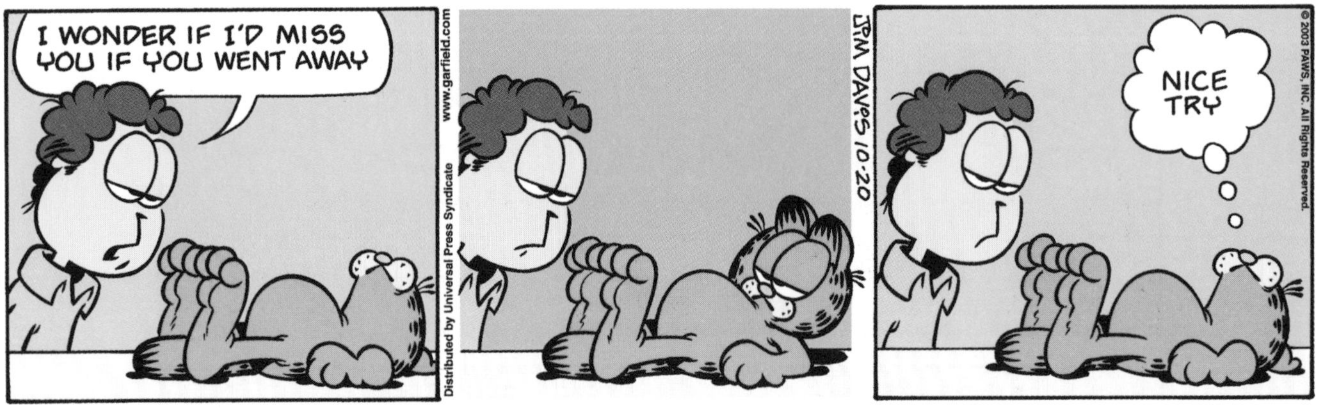
I WONDER IF I'D MISS YOU IF YOU WENT AWAY
NICE TRY
JIM DAVIS 10-20
www.garfield.com
Distributed by Universal Press Syndicate
© 2003 PAWS, INC. All Rights Reserved.

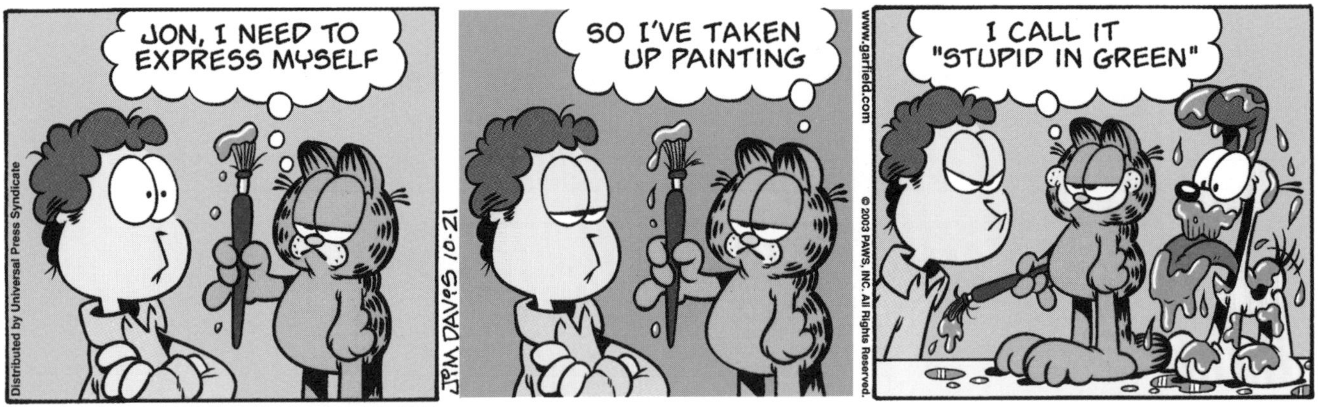
JON, I NEED TO EXPRESS MYSELF
SO I'VE TAKEN UP PAINTING
I CALL IT "STUPID IN GREEN"
JIM DAVIS 10-21
Distributed by Universal Press Syndicate
www.garfield.com
© 2003 PAWS, INC. All Rights Reserved.

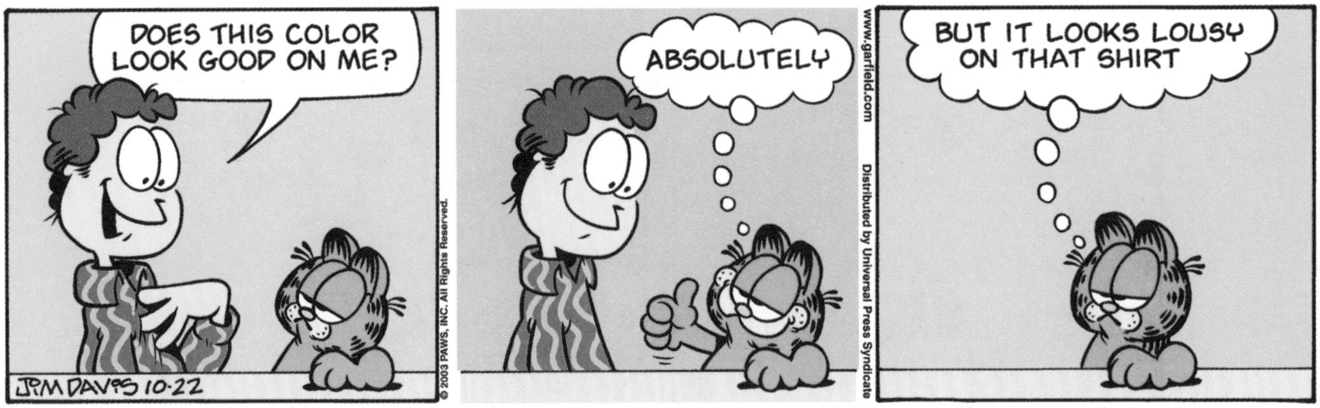
DOES THIS COLOR LOOK GOOD ON ME?
ABSOLUTELY
BUT IT LOOKS LOUSY ON THAT SHIRT
JIM DAVIS 10-22
© 2003 PAWS, INC. All Rights Reserved.
www.garfield.com
Distributed by Universal Press Syndicate

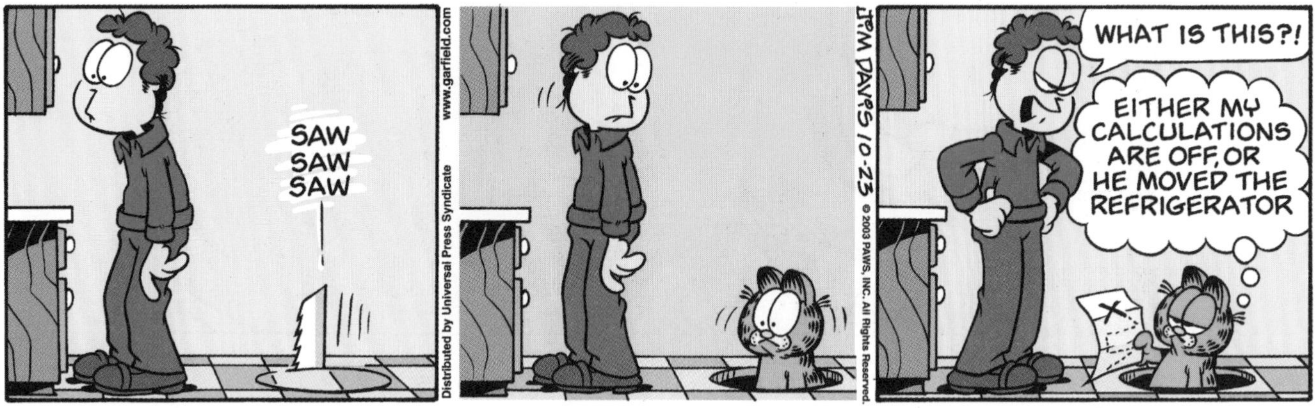
SAW
SAW
SAW
www.garfield.com
Distributed by Universal Press Syndicate
JPM DAVIS 10-23
© 2003 PAWS, INC. All Rights Reserved.
WHAT IS THIS?!
EITHER MY CALCULATIONS ARE OFF, OR HE MOVED THE REFRIGERATOR

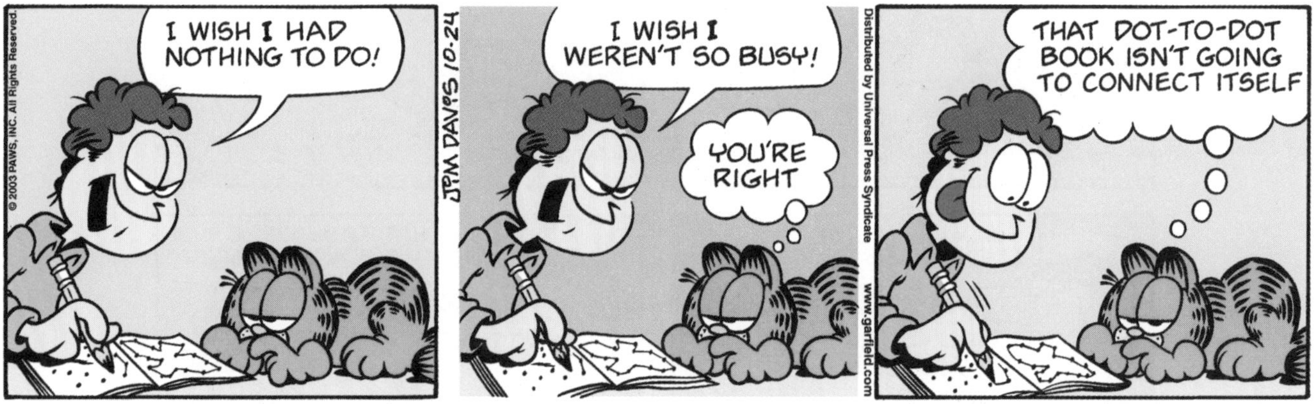
© 2003 PAWS, INC. All Rights Reserved.
I WISH I HAD NOTHING TO DO!
JPM DAVIS 10-24
I WISH I WEREN'T SO BUSY!
YOU'RE RIGHT
Distributed by Universal Press Syndicate
www.garfield.com
THAT DOT-TO-DOT BOOK ISN'T GOING TO CONNECT ITSELF

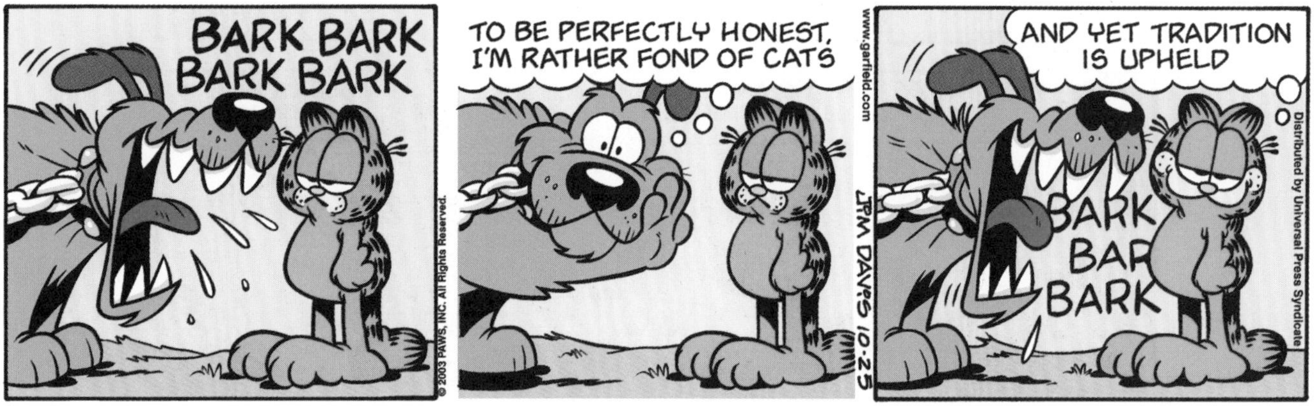
BARK BARK
BARK BARK
© 2003 PAWS, INC. All Rights Reserved.
TO BE PERFECTLY HONEST, I'M RATHER FOND OF CATS
www.garfield.com
JPM DAVIS 10-25
AND YET TRADITION IS UPHELD
BARK
BAR
BARK
Distributed by Universal Press Syndicate

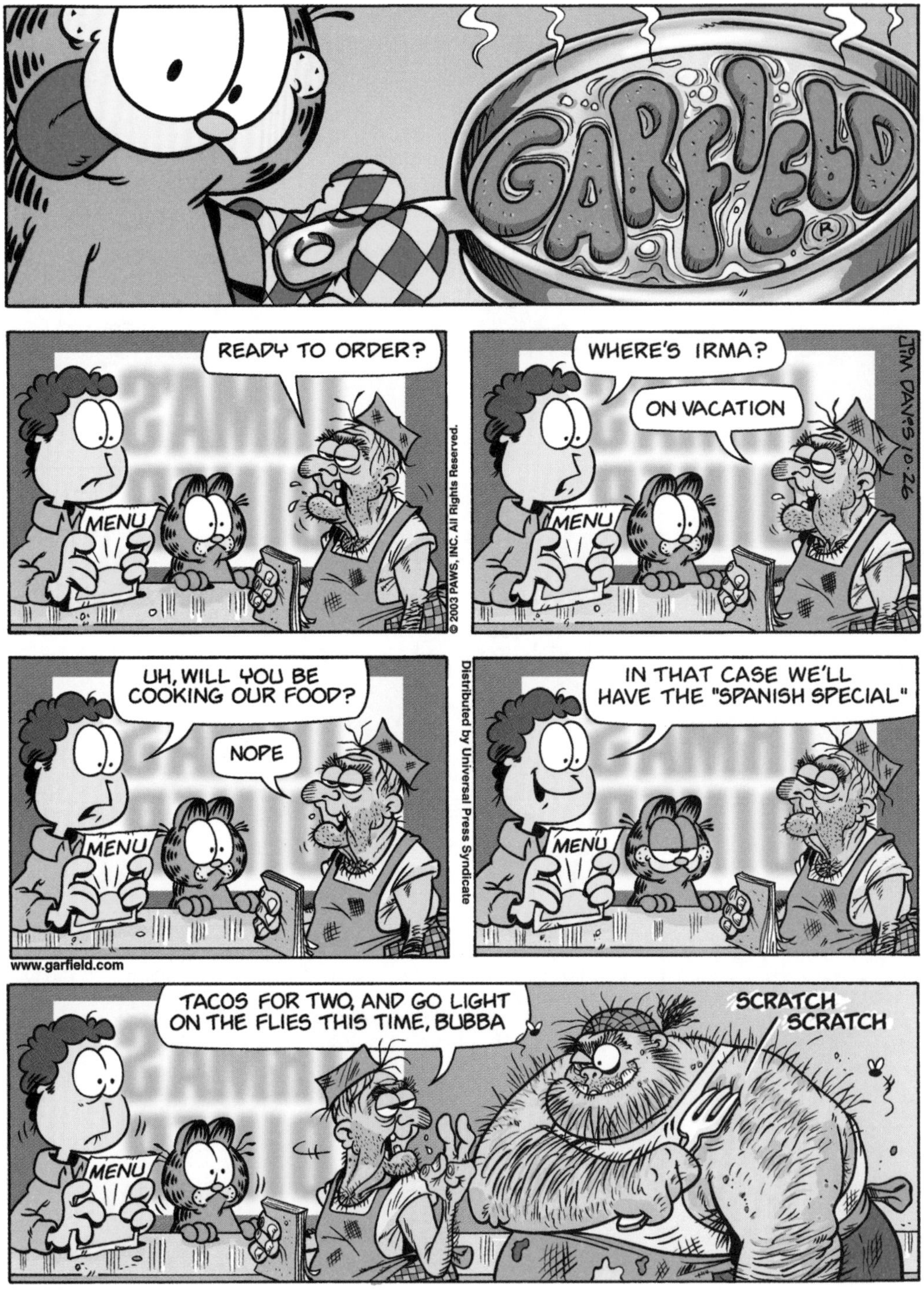
GARFIELD®
READY TO ORDER?
WHERE'S IRMA?
ON VACATION
JIM DAVIS 10-26
© 2003 PAWS, INC. All Rights Reserved.
UH, WILL YOU BE COOKING OUR FOOD?
NOPE
Distributed by Universal Press Syndicate
IN THAT CASE WE'LL HAVE THE "SPANISH SPECIAL"
www.garfield.com
TACOS FOR TWO, AND GO LIGHT ON THE FLIES THIS TIME, BUBBA
SCRATCH
SCRATCH

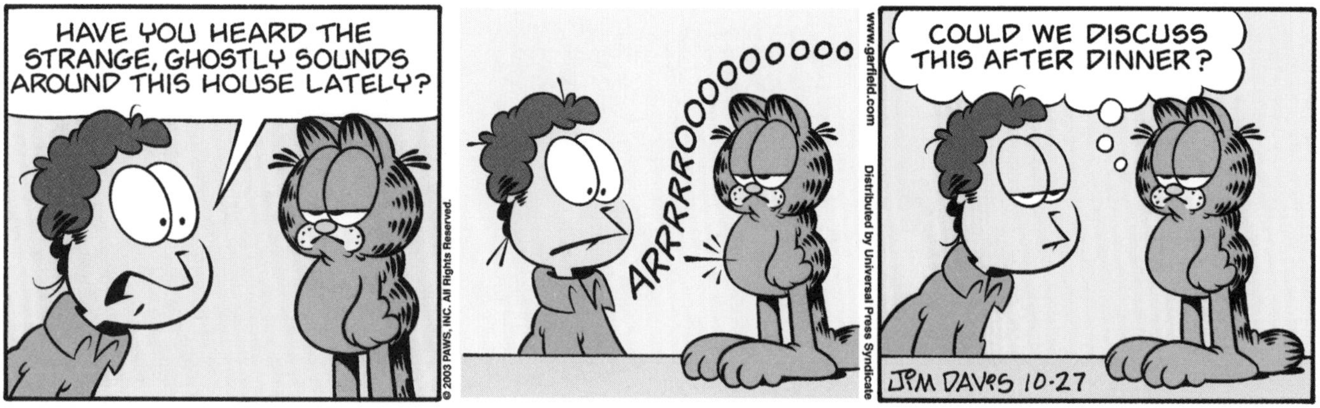
HAVE YOU HEARD THE STRANGE, GHOSTLY SOUNDS AROUND THIS HOUSE LATELY?
© 2003 PAWS, INC. All Rights Reserved.
ARRRROOOOOOOOOOO
www.garfield.com Distributed by Universal Press Syndicate
COULD WE DISCUSS THIS AFTER DINNER?
JIM DAVIS 10-27

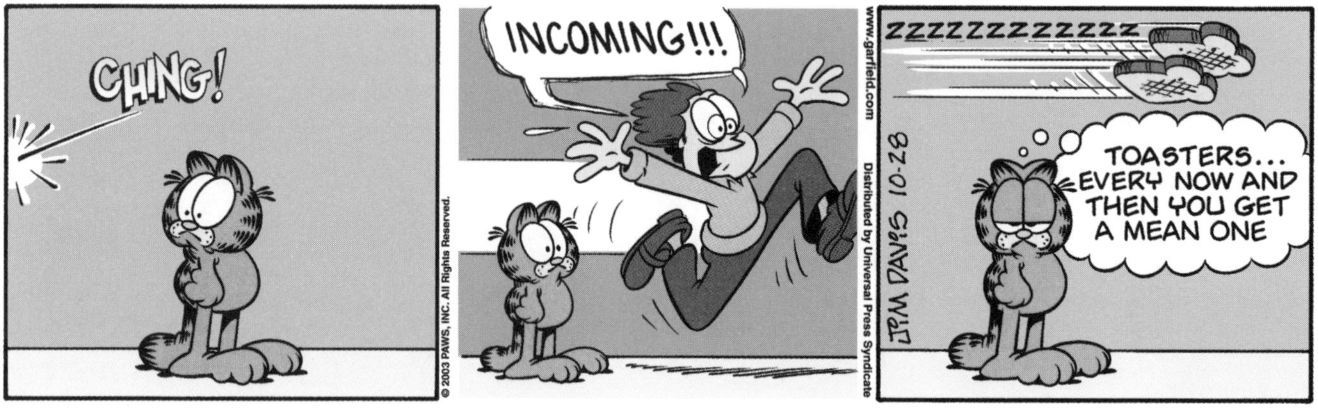
CHING!
© 2003 PAWS, INC. All Rights Reserved.
INCOMING!!!
www.garfield.com Distributed by Universal Press Syndicate
ZZZZZZZZZZZZ
TOASTERS... EVERY NOW AND THEN YOU GET A MEAN ONE
JIM DAVIS 10-28

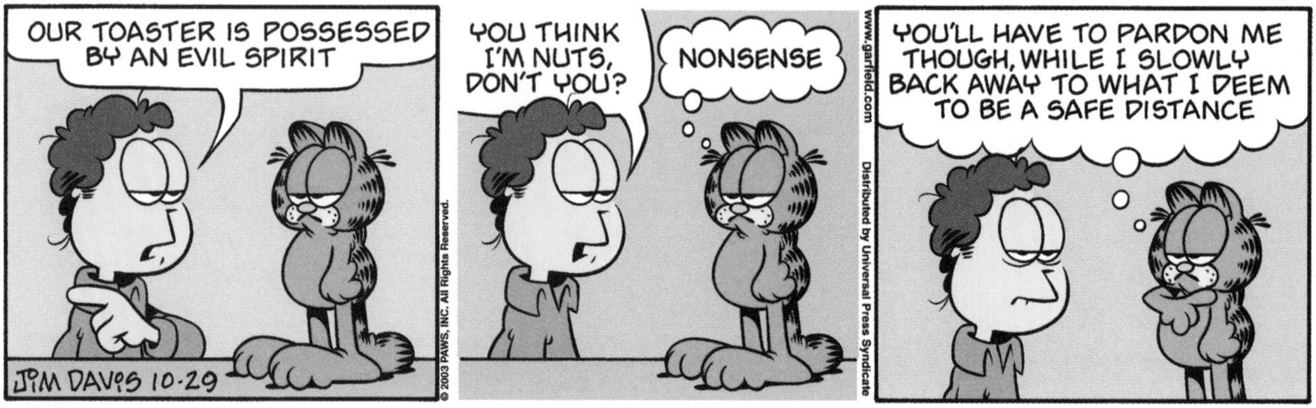
OUR TOASTER IS POSSESSED BY AN EVIL SPIRIT
JIM DAVIS 10-29
© 2003 PAWS, INC. All Rights Reserved.
YOU THINK I'M NUTS, DON'T YOU?
NONSENSE
www.garfield.com Distributed by Universal Press Syndicate
YOU'LL HAVE TO PARDON ME THOUGH, WHILE I SLOWLY BACK AWAY TO WHAT I DEEM TO BE A SAFE DISTANCE

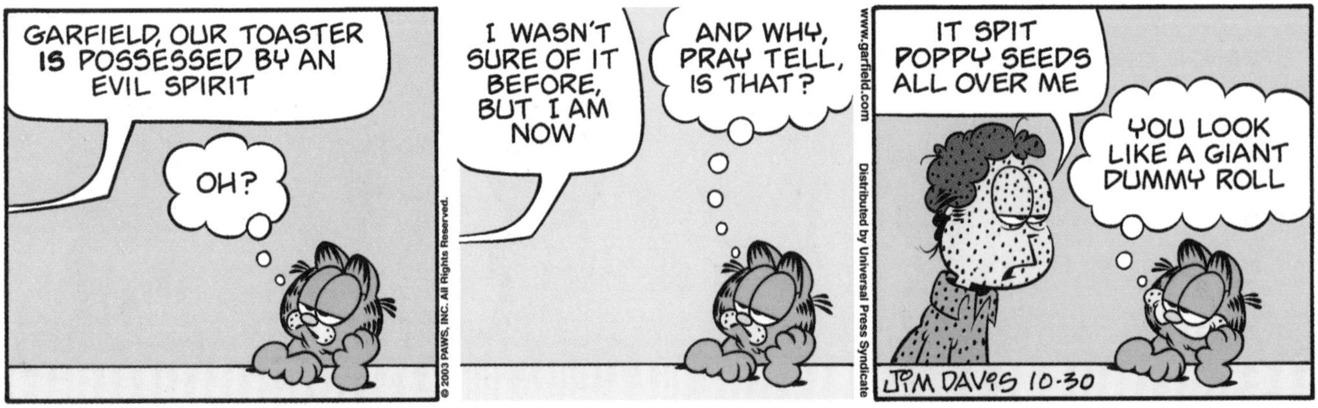
GARFIELD, OUR TOASTER IS POSSESSED BY AN EVIL SPIRIT
OH?
© 2003 PAWS, INC. All Rights Reserved.
I WASN'T SURE OF IT BEFORE, BUT I AM NOW
AND WHY, PRAY TELL, IS THAT?
www.garfield.com
Distributed by Universal Press Syndicate
IT SPIT POPPY SEEDS ALL OVER ME
YOU LOOK LIKE A GIANT DUMMY ROLL
JIM DAVIS 10-30

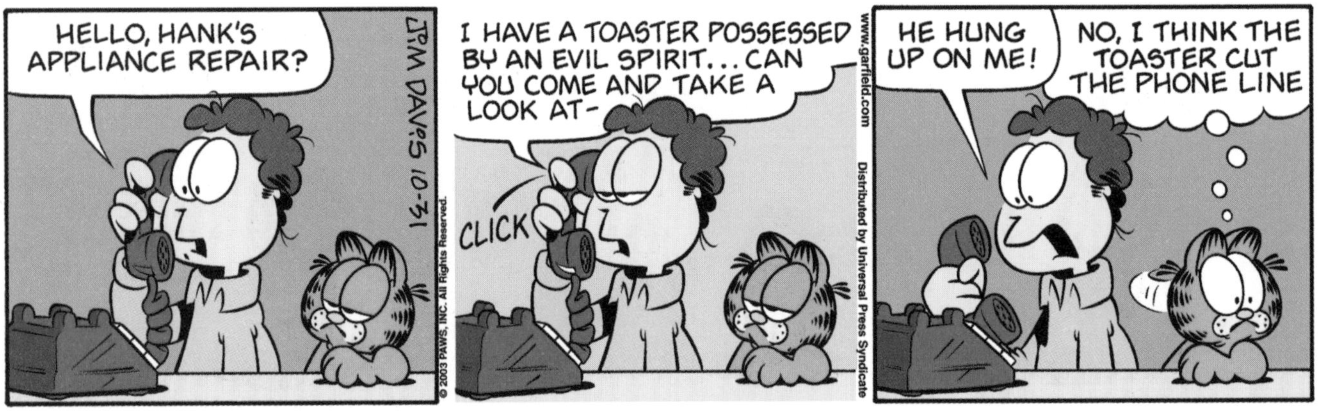
HELLO, HANK'S APPLIANCE REPAIR?
JIM DAVIS 10-31
© 2003 PAWS, INC. All Rights Reserved.
I HAVE A TOASTER POSSESSED BY AN EVIL SPIRIT... CAN YOU COME AND TAKE A LOOK AT-
CLICK
www.garfield.com
Distributed by Universal Press Syndicate
HE HUNG UP ON ME!
NO, I THINK THE TOASTER CUT THE PHONE LINE

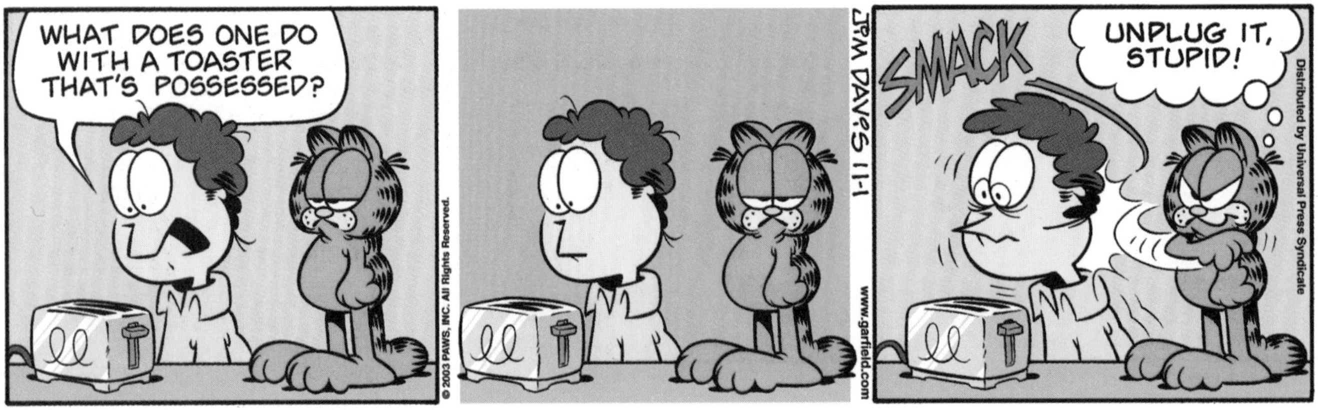
WHAT DOES ONE DO WITH A TOASTER THAT'S POSSESSED?
© 2003 PAWS, INC. All Rights Reserved.
JIM DAVIS 11-1
www.garfield.com
SMACK
UNPLUG IT, STUPID!
Distributed by Universal Press Syndicate

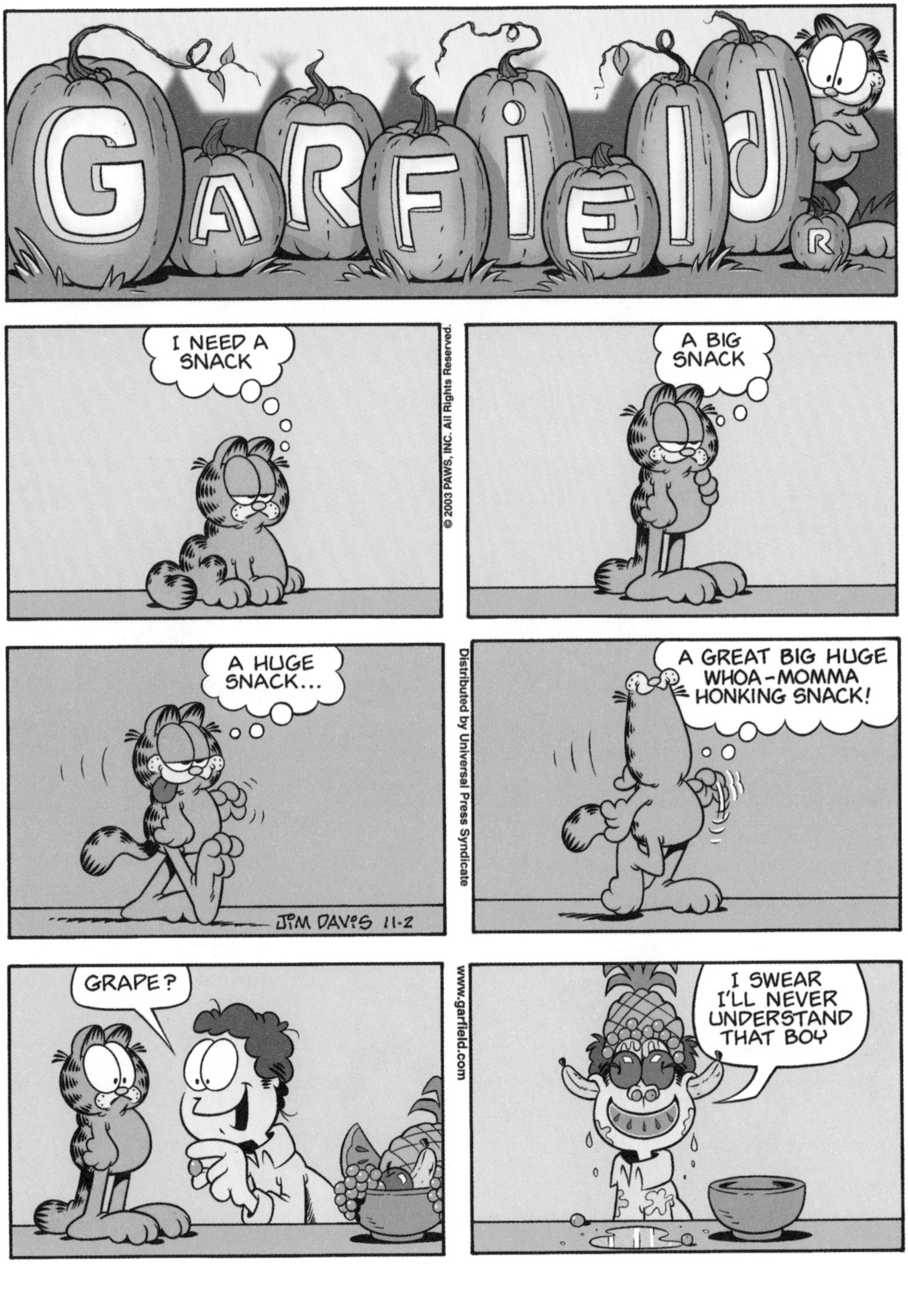
GARFIELD
I NEED A SNACK
A BIG SNACK
A HUGE SNACK...
A GREAT BIG HUGE WHOA-MOMMA HONKING SNACK!
JIM DAVIS 11-2
GRAPE?
I SWEAR I'LL NEVER UNDERSTAND THAT BOY

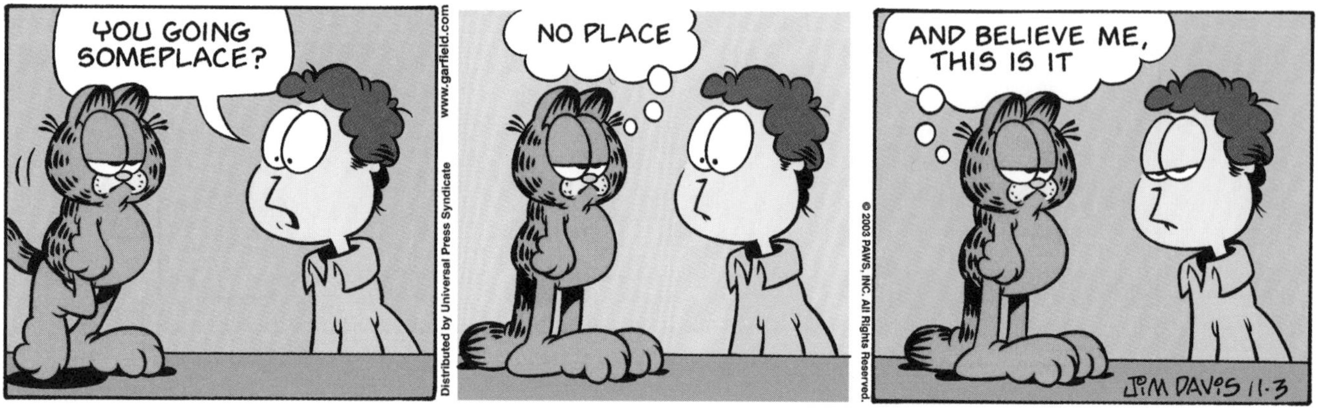
YOU GOING SOMEPLACE?
www.garfield.com
Distributed by Universal Press Syndicate
NO PLACE
© 2003 PAWS, INC. All Rights Reserved.
AND BELIEVE ME, THIS IS IT
JIM DAVIS 11-3

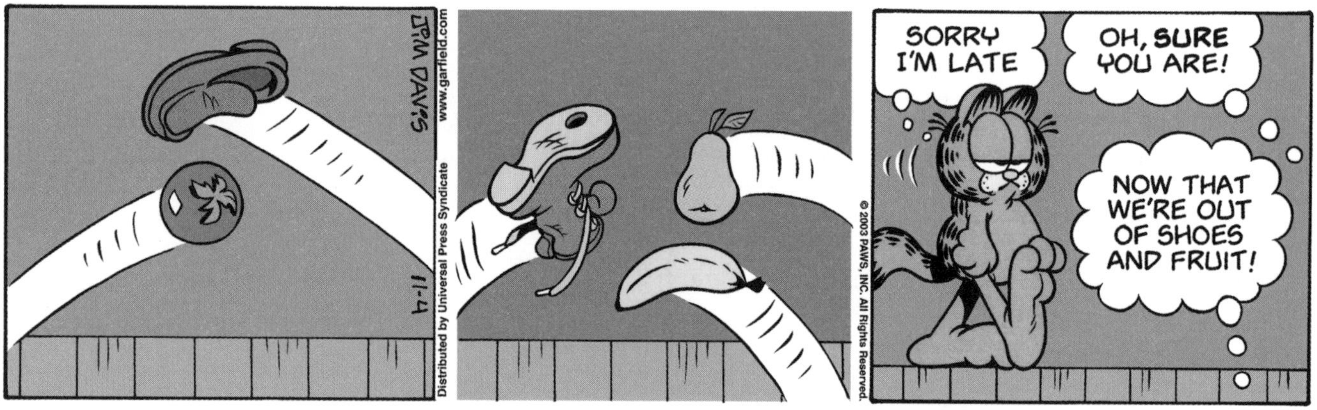
JIM DAVIS
11-4
www.garfield.com
Distributed by Universal Press Syndicate
© 2003 PAWS, INC. All Rights Reserved.
SORRY I'M LATE
OH, **SURE** YOU ARE!
NOW THAT WE'RE OUT OF SHOES AND FRUIT!

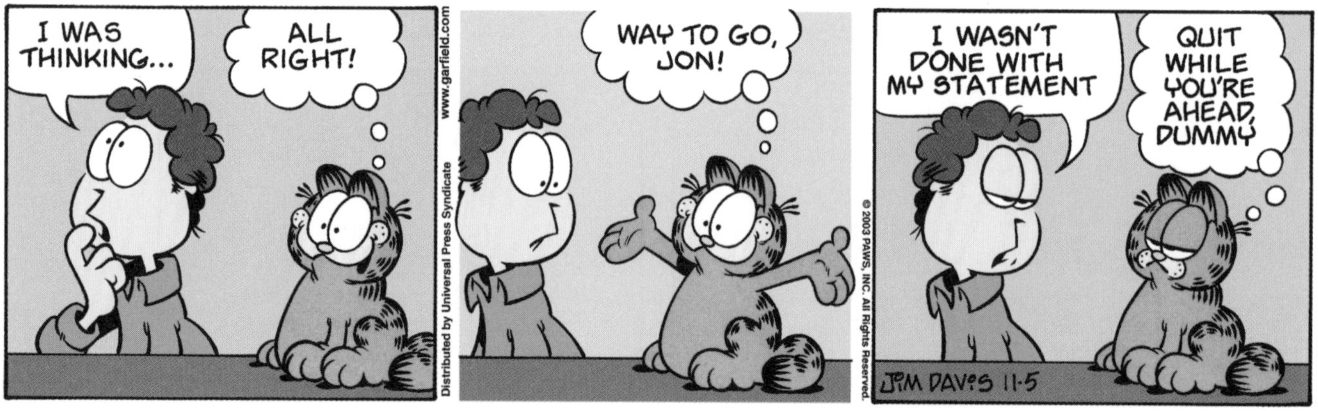
I WAS THINKING...
ALL RIGHT!
www.garfield.com
Distributed by Universal Press Syndicate
WAY TO GO, JON!
© 2003 PAWS, INC. All Rights Reserved.
I WASN'T DONE WITH MY STATEMENT
QUIT WHILE YOU'RE AHEAD, DUMMY
JIM DAVIS 11-5

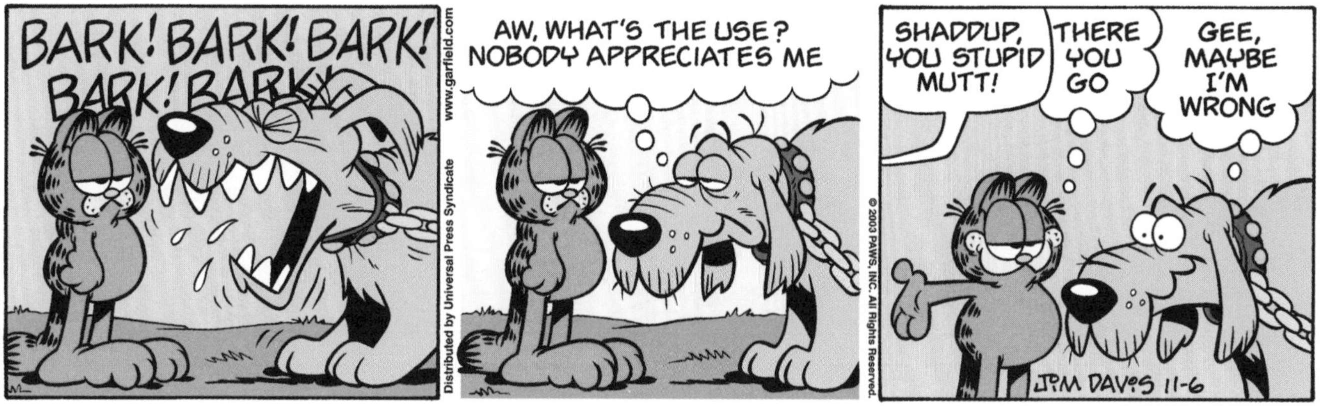
BARK! BARK! BARK! BARK! BARK!
AW, WHAT'S THE USE? NOBODY APPRECIATES ME
SHADDUP, YOU STUPID MUTT!
THERE YOU GO
GEE, MAYBE I'M WRONG
JIM DAVIS 11-6
Distributed by Universal Press Syndicate www.garfield.com
© 2003 PAWS, INC. All Rights Reserved.

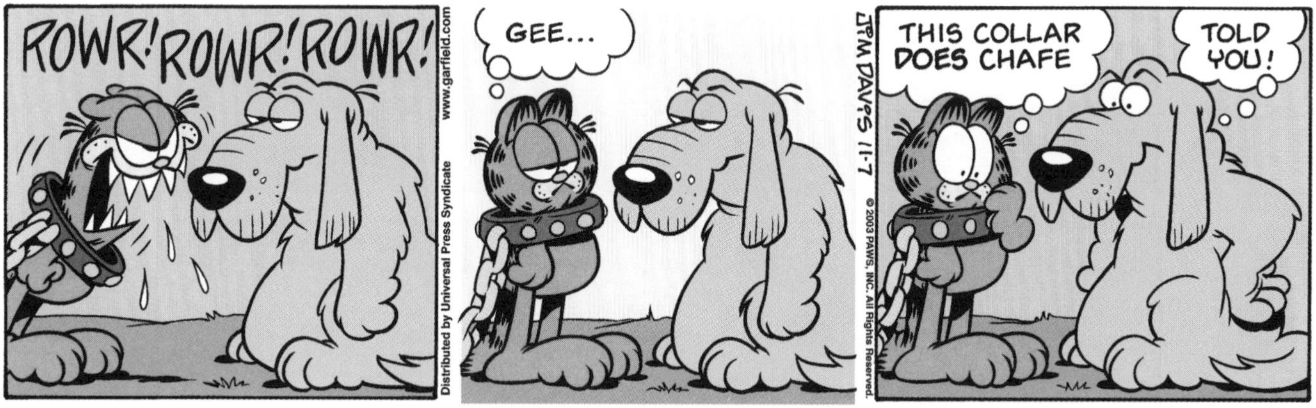
ROWR! ROWR! ROWR!
GEE...
THIS COLLAR DOES CHAFE
TOLD YOU!
JIM DAVIS 11-7
Distributed by Universal Press Syndicate www.garfield.com
© 2003 PAWS, INC. All Rights Reserved.

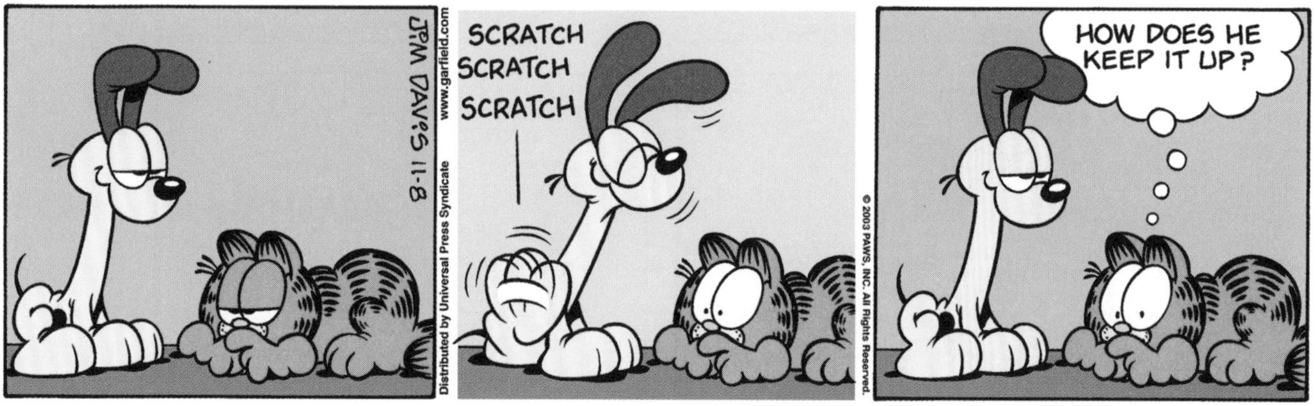
JIM DAVIS 11-8
SCRATCH
SCRATCH
SCRATCH
HOW DOES HE KEEP IT UP?
Distributed by Universal Press Syndicate www.garfield.com
© 2003 PAWS, INC. All Rights Reserved.

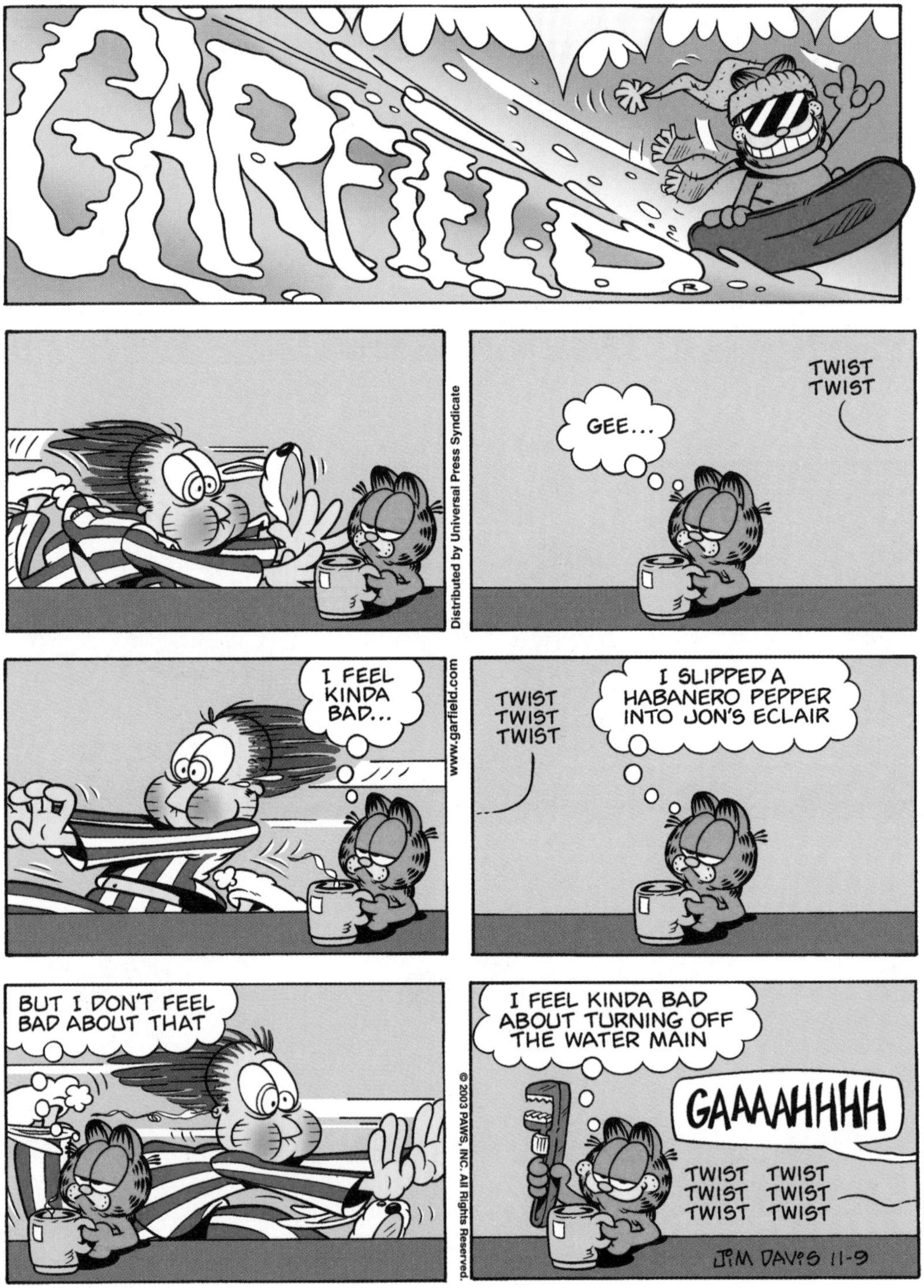
GARFIELD
Distributed by Universal Press Syndicate
GEE...
TWIST
TWIST
I FEEL KINDA BAD...
www.garfield.com
TWIST
TWIST
TWIST
I SLIPPED A HABANERO PEPPER INTO JON'S ECLAIR
BUT I DON'T FEEL BAD ABOUT THAT
© 2003 PAWS, INC. All Rights Reserved.
I FEEL KINDA BAD ABOUT TURNING OFF THE WATER MAIN
GAAAAHHHH
TWIST TWIST
TWIST TWIST
TWIST TWIST
JIM DAVIS 11-9

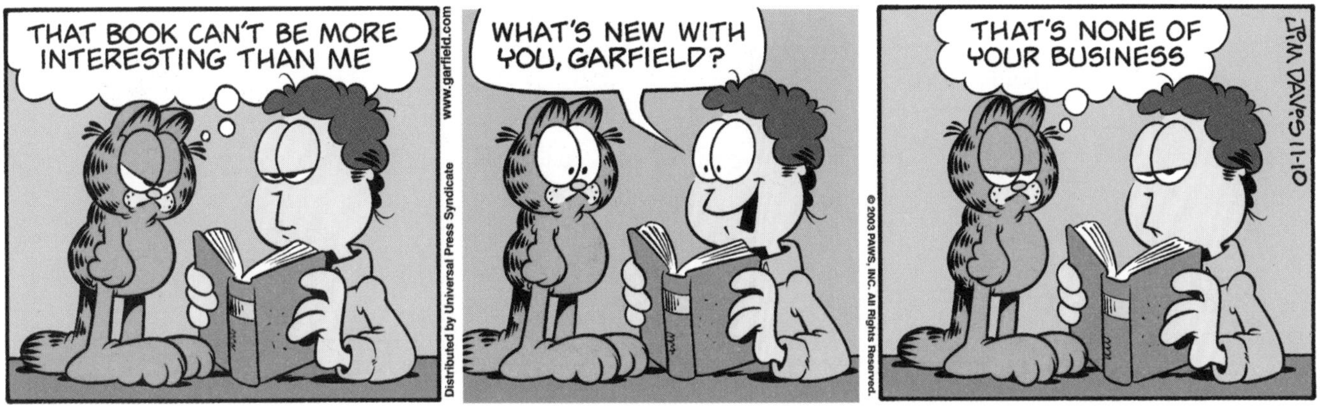
THAT BOOK CAN'T BE MORE INTERESTING THAN ME
WHAT'S NEW WITH YOU, GARFIELD?
THAT'S NONE OF YOUR BUSINESS
JIM DAVIS 11-10
www.garfield.com
Distributed by Universal Press Syndicate
© 2003 PAWS, INC. All Rights Reserved.

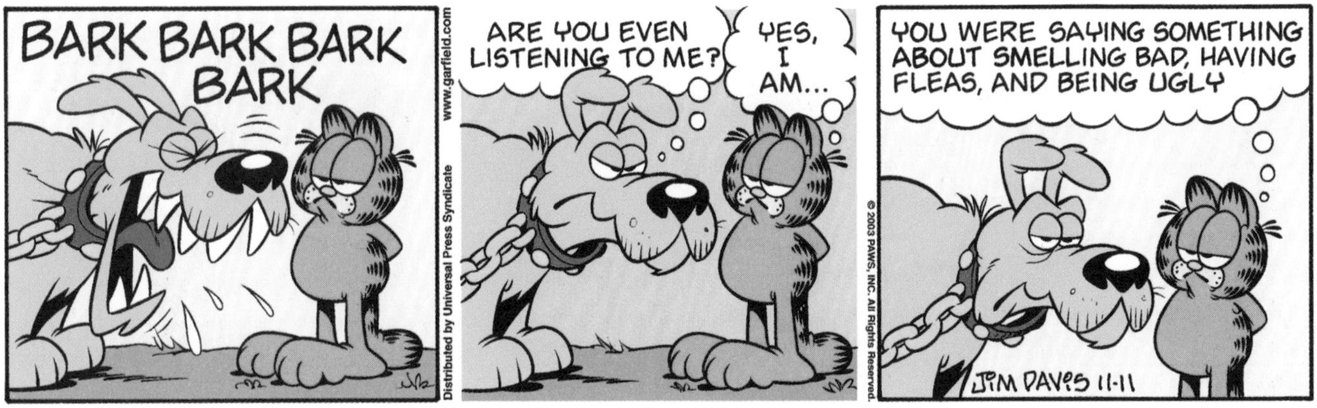
BARK BARK BARK BARK
ARE YOU EVEN LISTENING TO ME?
YES, I AM...
YOU WERE SAYING SOMETHING ABOUT SMELLING BAD, HAVING FLEAS, AND BEING UGLY
JIM DAVIS 11-11
www.garfield.com
Distributed by Universal Press Syndicate
© 2003 PAWS, INC. All Rights Reserved.

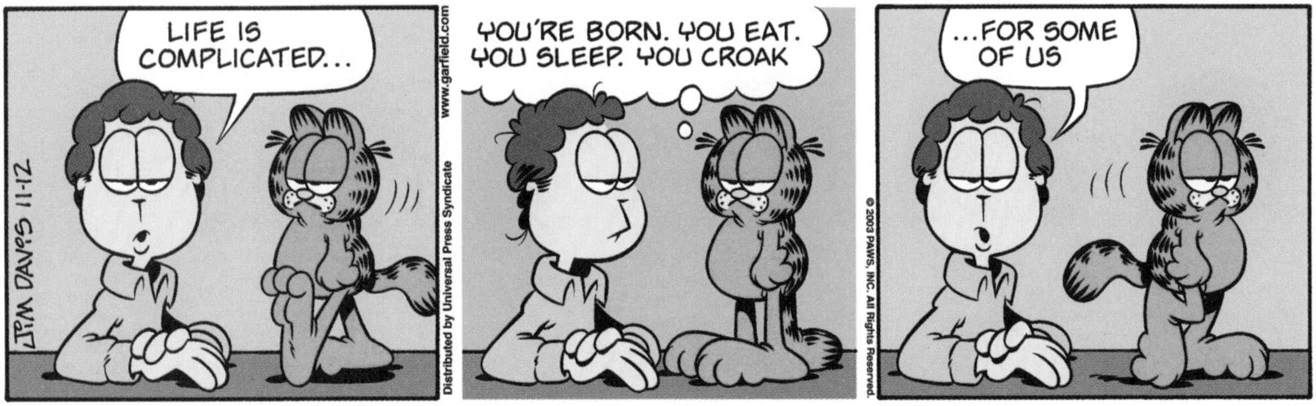
LIFE IS COMPLICATED...
YOU'RE BORN. YOU EAT. YOU SLEEP. YOU CROAK
...FOR SOME OF US
JIM DAVIS 11-12
www.garfield.com
Distributed by Universal Press Syndicate
© 2003 PAWS, INC. All Rights Reserved.

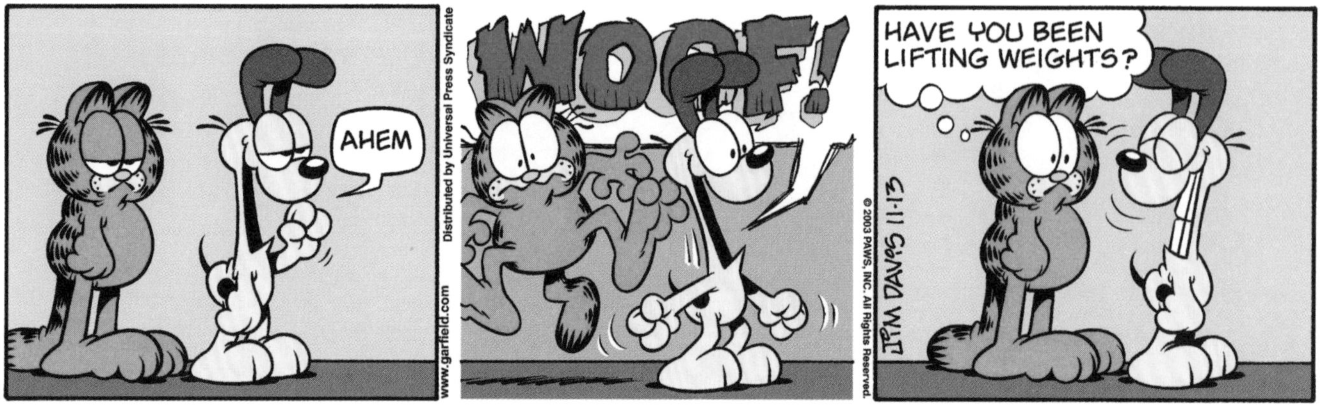
AHEM
www.garfield.com
Distributed by Universal Press Syndicate
WOOF!
© 2003 PAWS, INC. All Rights Reserved.
JIM DAVIS 11-13
HAVE YOU BEEN LIFTING WEIGHTS?

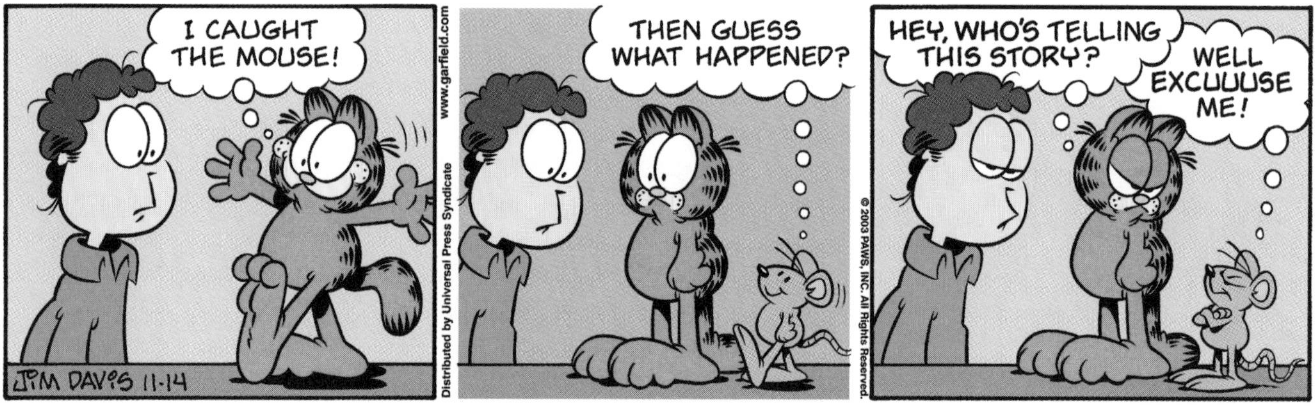
I CAUGHT THE MOUSE!
JIM DAVIS 11-14
Distributed by Universal Press Syndicate
www.garfield.com
THEN GUESS WHAT HAPPENED?
© 2003 PAWS, INC. All Rights Reserved.
HEY, WHO'S TELLING THIS STORY?
WELL EXCUUUSE ME!

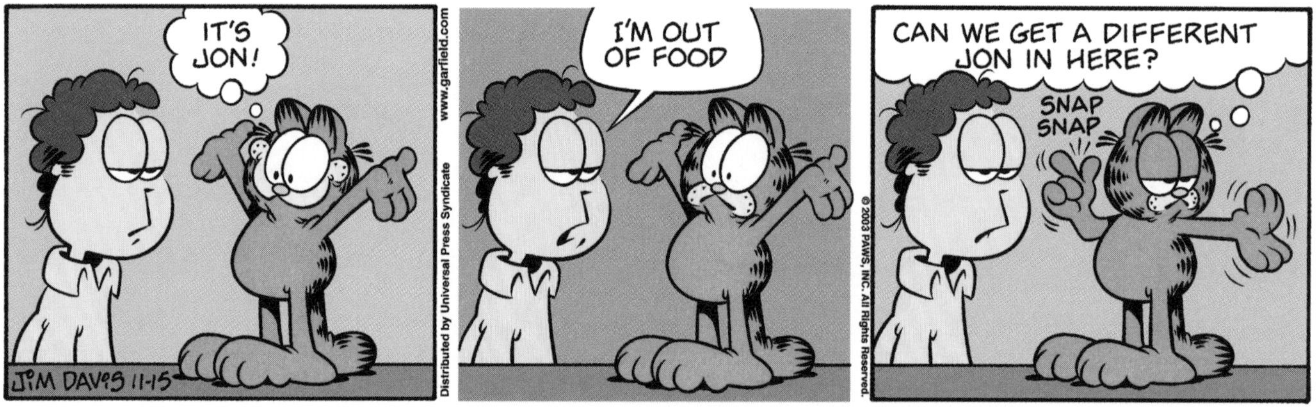
IT'S JON!
JIM DAVIS 11-15
Distributed by Universal Press Syndicate
www.garfield.com
I'M OUT OF FOOD
© 2003 PAWS, INC. All Rights Reserved.
CAN WE GET A DIFFERENT JON IN HERE?
SNAP SNAP

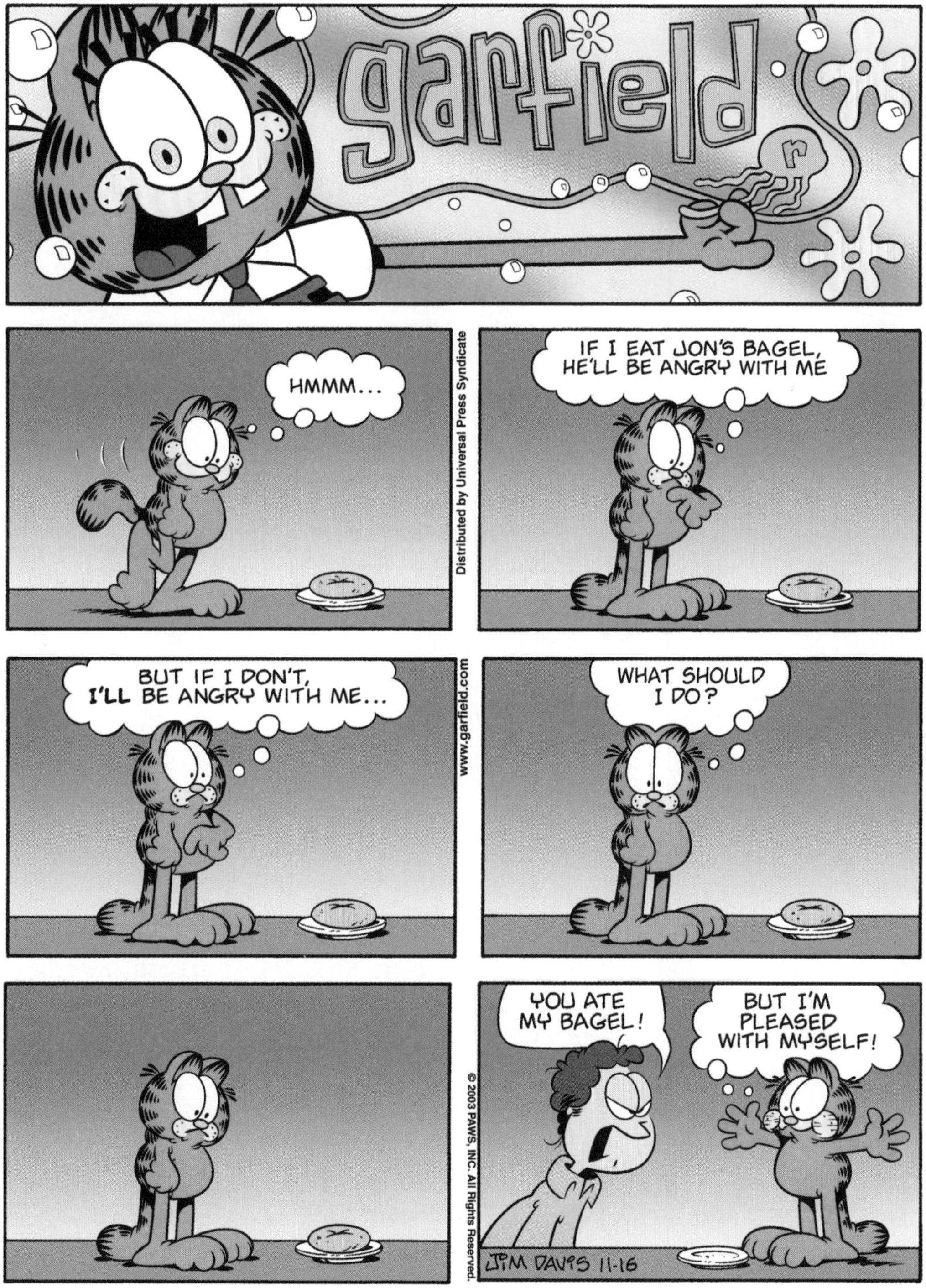
garfield
Distributed by Universal Press Syndicate
HMMM...
IF I EAT JON'S BAGEL, HE'LL BE ANGRY WITH ME
www.garfield.com
BUT IF I DON'T, **I'LL** BE ANGRY WITH ME...
WHAT SHOULD I DO?
© 2003 PAWS, INC. All Rights Reserved.
YOU ATE MY BAGEL!
BUT I'M PLEASED WITH MYSELF!
JIM DAVIS 11-16

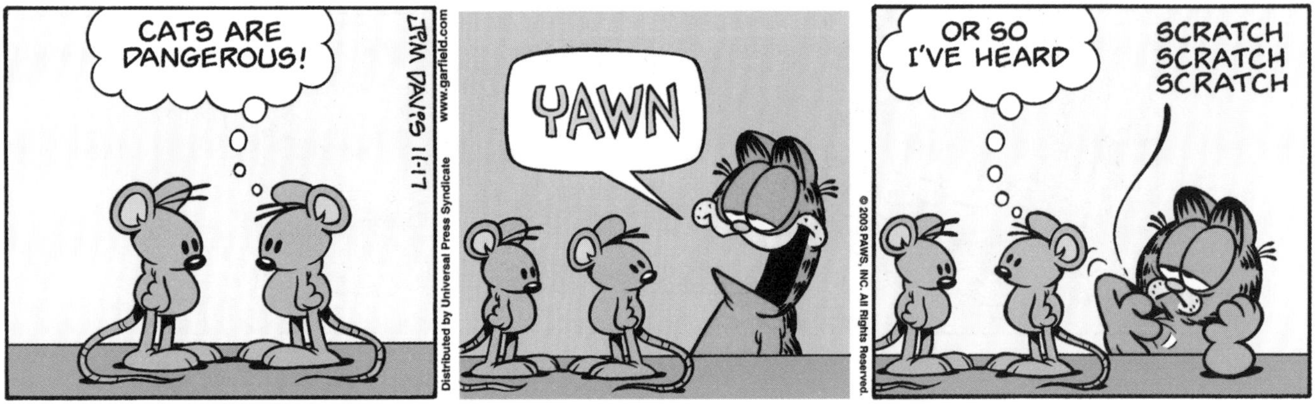
CATS ARE DANGEROUS!
JIM DAVIS 11-17
www.garfield.com
Distributed by Universal Press Syndicate
YAWN
© 2003 PAWS, INC. All Rights Reserved.
OR SO I'VE HEARD
SCRATCH SCRATCH SCRATCH

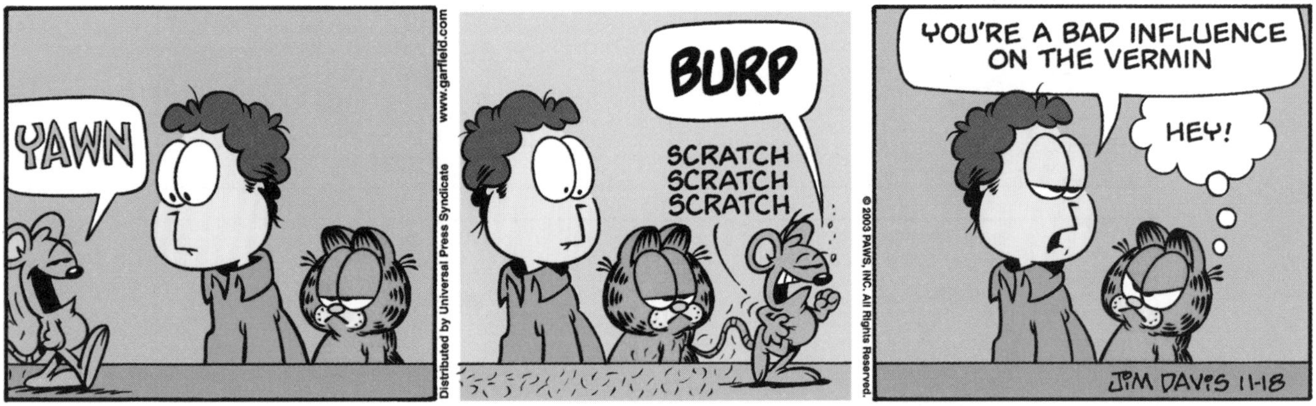
YAWN
www.garfield.com
Distributed by Universal Press Syndicate
BURP
SCRATCH SCRATCH SCRATCH
© 2003 PAWS, INC. All Rights Reserved.
YOU'RE A BAD INFLUENCE ON THE VERMIN
HEY!
JIM DAVIS 11-18

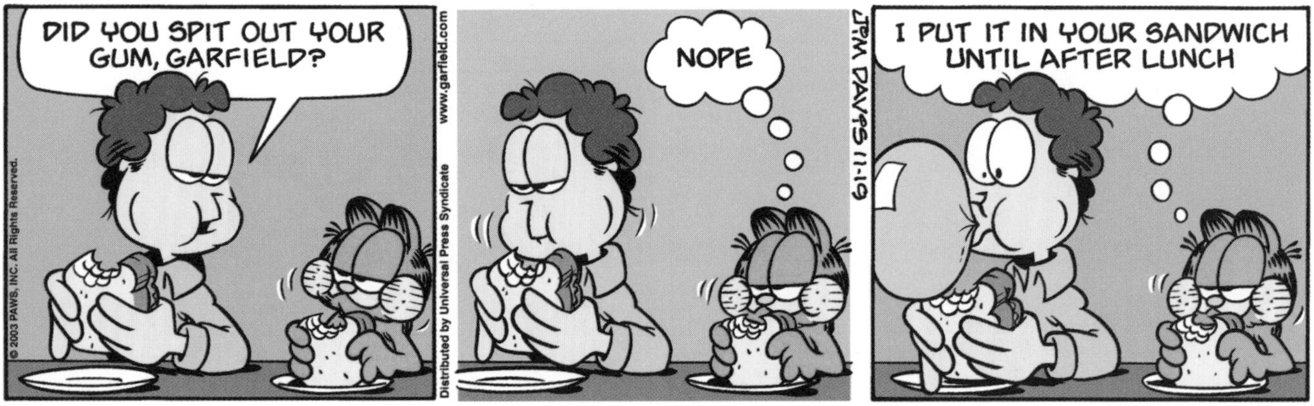
DID YOU SPIT OUT YOUR GUM, GARFIELD?
© 2003 PAWS, INC. All Rights Reserved.
www.garfield.com
Distributed by Universal Press Syndicate
NOPE
JIM DAVIS 11-19
I PUT IT IN YOUR SANDWICH UNTIL AFTER LUNCH

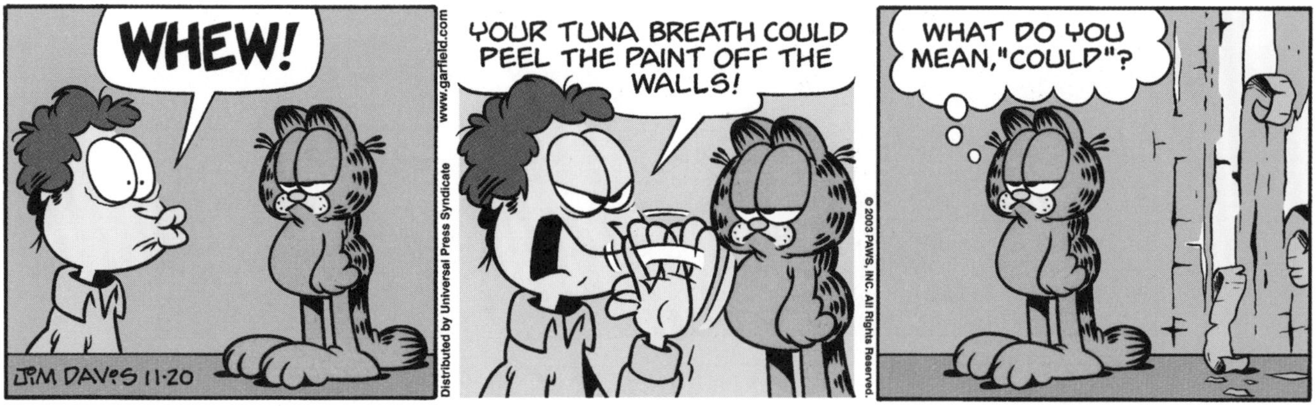
WHEW!
JIM DAVIS 11·20
YOUR TUNA BREATH COULD PEEL THE PAINT OFF THE WALLS!
WHAT DO YOU MEAN, "COULD"?

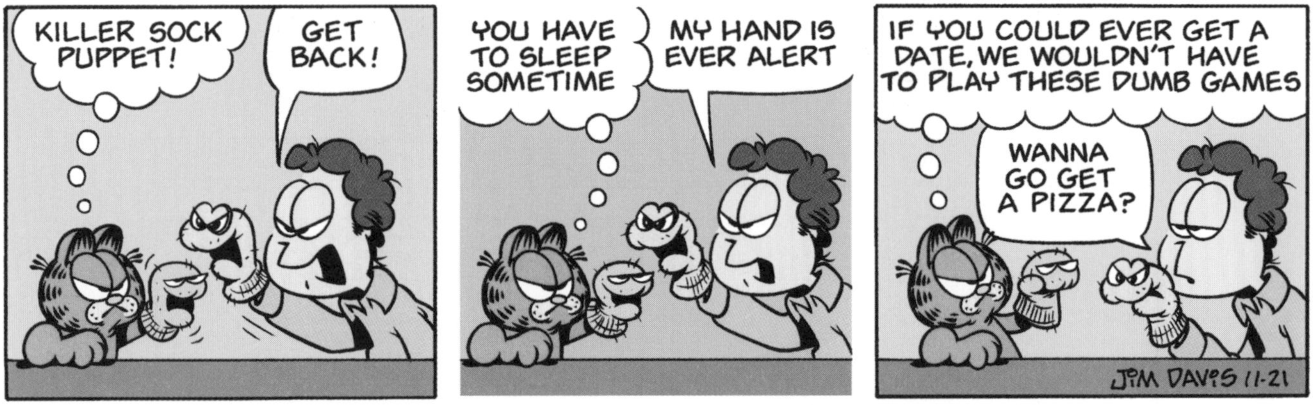
KILLER SOCK PUPPET!
GET BACK!
YOU HAVE TO SLEEP SOMETIME
MY HAND IS EVER ALERT
IF YOU COULD EVER GET A DATE, WE WOULDN'T HAVE TO PLAY THESE DUMB GAMES
WANNA GO GET A PIZZA?
JIM DAVIS 11·21

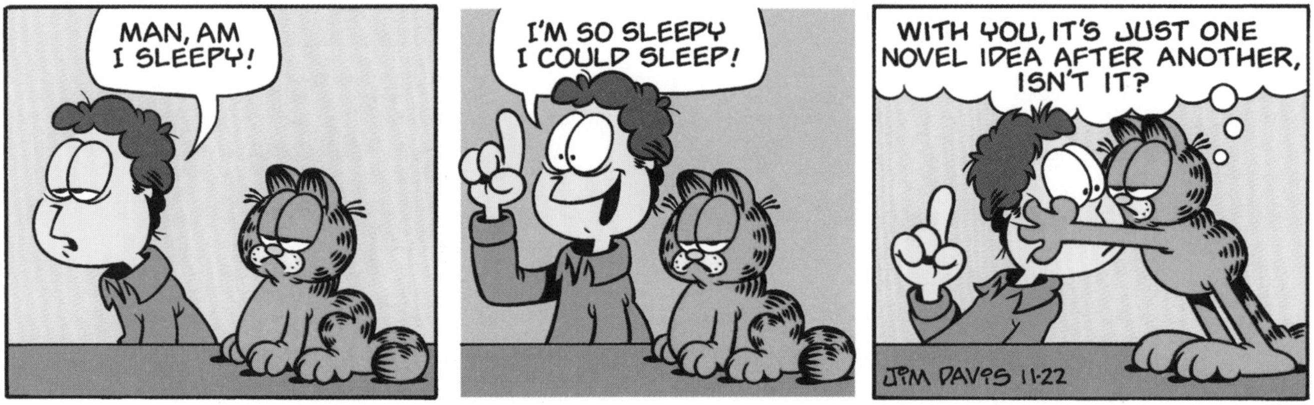
MAN, AM I SLEEPY!
I'M SO SLEEPY I COULD SLEEP!
WITH YOU, IT'S JUST ONE NOVEL IDEA AFTER ANOTHER, ISN'T IT?
JIM DAVIS 11·22

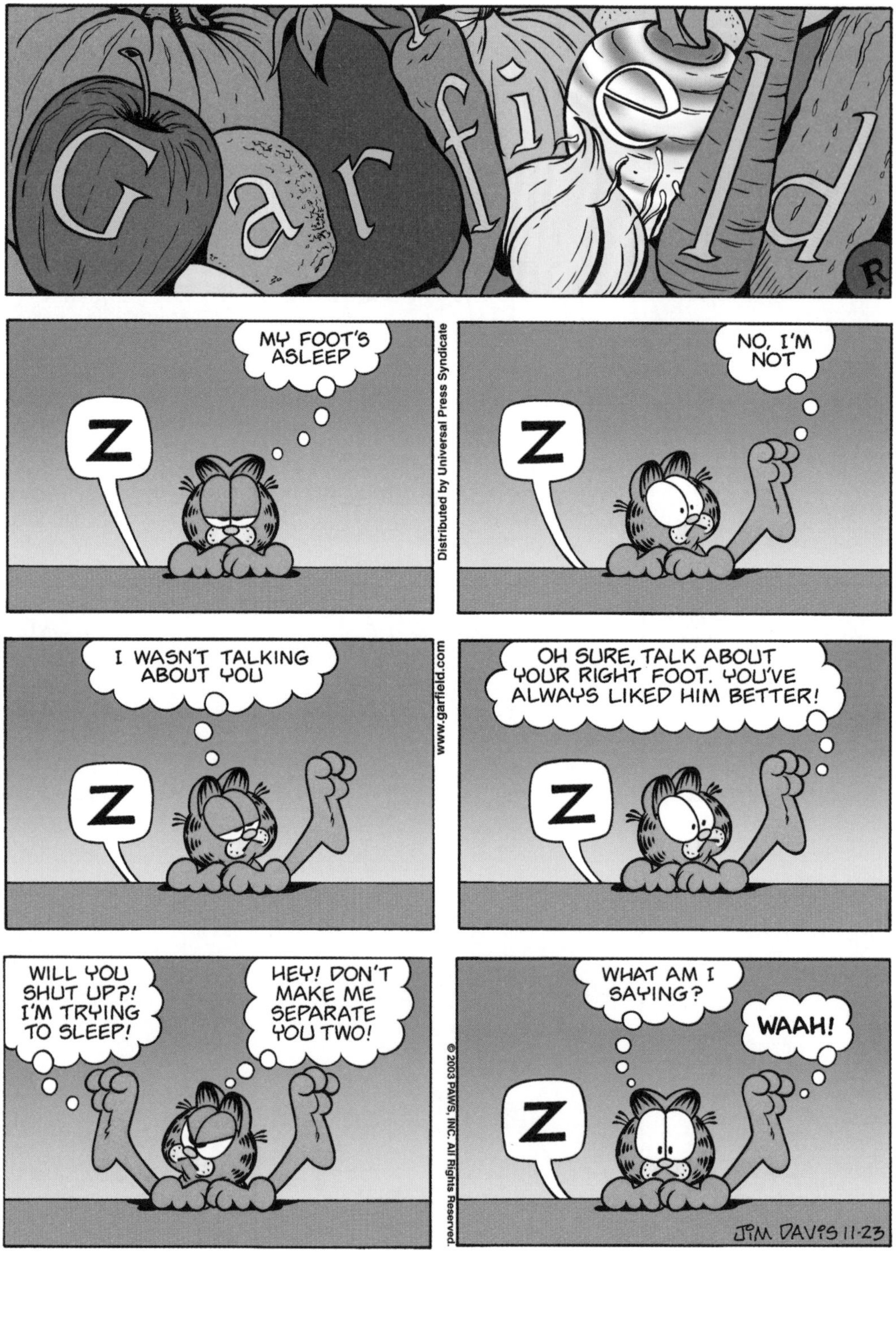
Garfield
MY FOOT'S ASLEEP
Z
NO, I'M NOT
Z
I WASN'T TALKING ABOUT YOU
Z
OH SURE, TALK ABOUT YOUR RIGHT FOOT. YOU'VE ALWAYS LIKED HIM BETTER!
Z
WILL YOU SHUT UP?! I'M TRYING TO SLEEP!
HEY! DON'T MAKE ME SEPARATE YOU TWO!
WHAT AM I SAYING?
WAAH!
Z
JIM DAVIS 11-23
Distributed by Universal Press Syndicate
www.garfield.com
© 2003 PAWS, INC. All Rights Reserved.

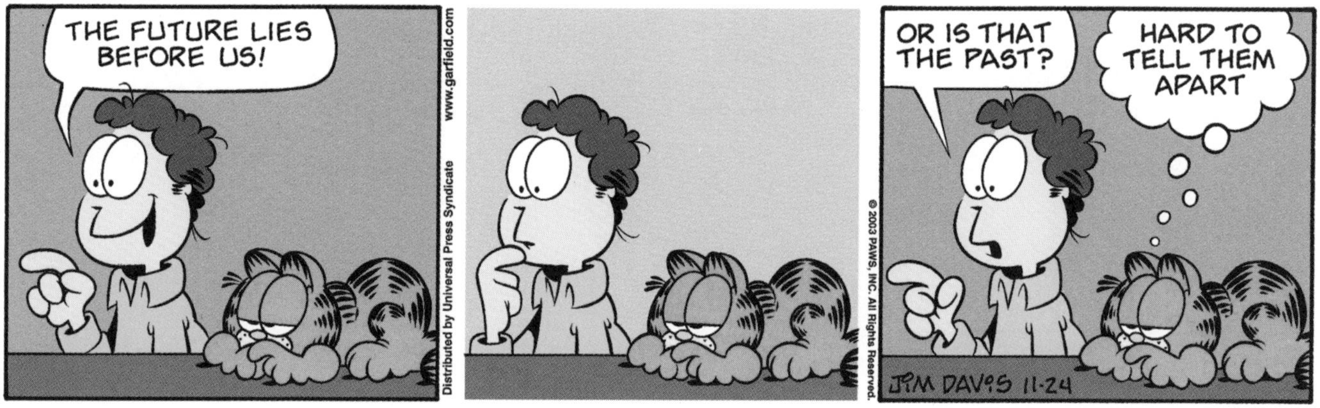
THE FUTURE LIES BEFORE US!
OR IS THAT THE PAST?
HARD TO TELL THEM APART
JIM DAVIS 11-24
Distributed by Universal Press Syndicate www.garfield.com
© 2003 PAWS, INC. All Rights Reserved.

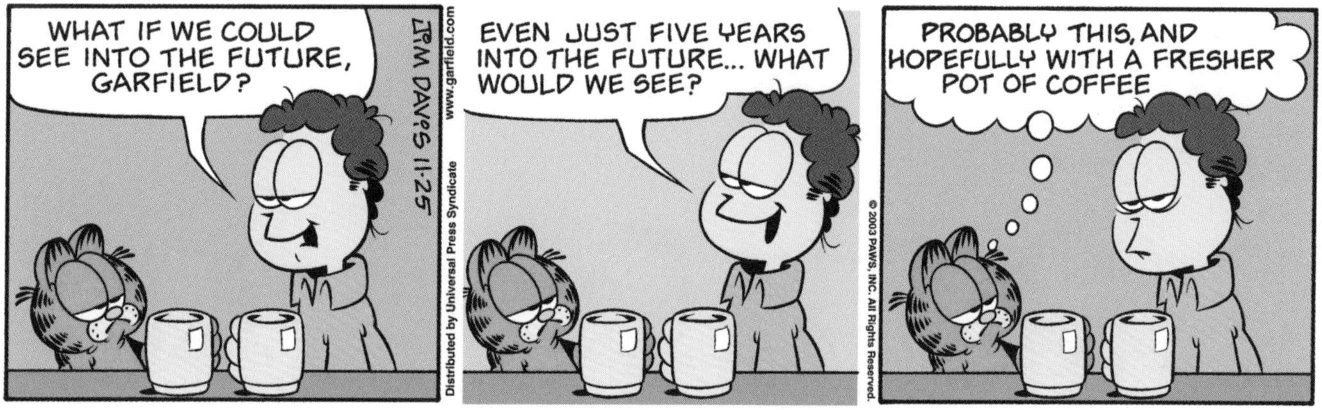
WHAT IF WE COULD SEE INTO THE FUTURE, GARFIELD?
EVEN JUST FIVE YEARS INTO THE FUTURE... WHAT WOULD WE SEE?
PROBABLY THIS, AND HOPEFULLY WITH A FRESHER POT OF COFFEE
JIM DAVIS 11-25
Distributed by Universal Press Syndicate www.garfield.com
© 2003 PAWS, INC. All Rights Reserved.

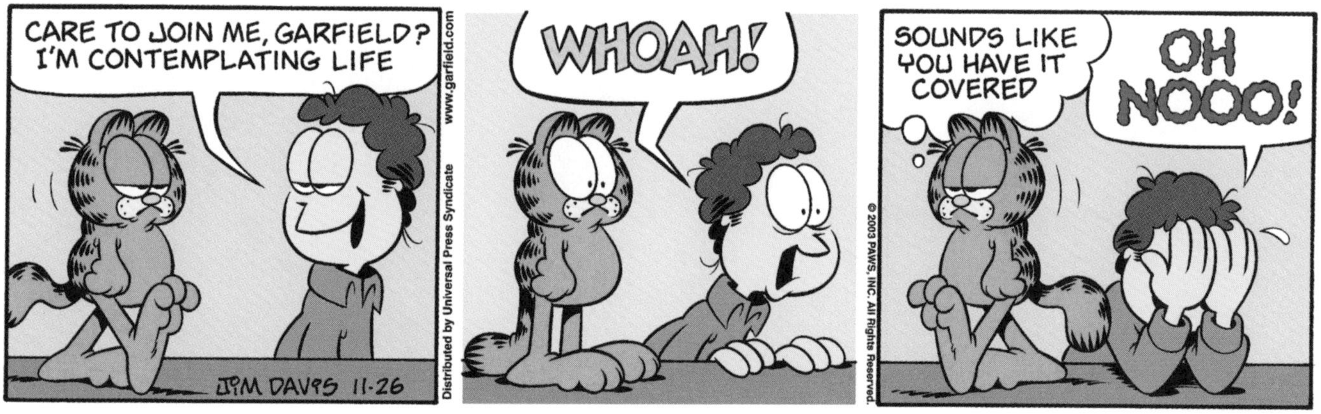
CARE TO JOIN ME, GARFIELD? I'M CONTEMPLATING LIFE
WHOAH!
SOUNDS LIKE YOU HAVE IT COVERED
OH NOOO!
JIM DAVIS 11-26
Distributed by Universal Press Syndicate www.garfield.com
© 2003 PAWS, INC. All Rights Reserved.

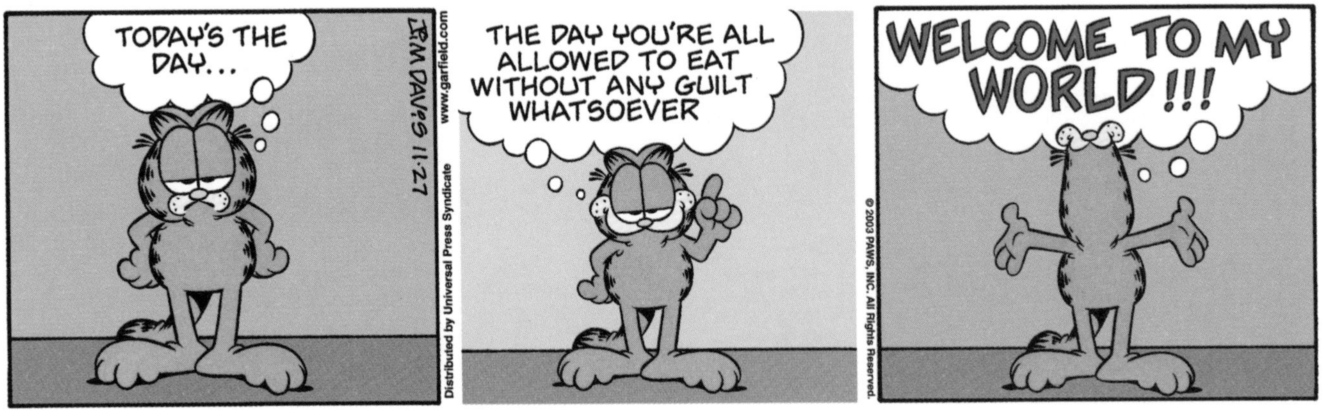

TODAY'S THE DAY...
JIM DAVIS 11-27
www.garfield.com
Distributed by Universal Press Syndicate
THE DAY YOU'RE ALL ALLOWED TO EAT WITHOUT ANY GUILT WHATSOEVER
© 2003 PAWS, INC. All Rights Reserved.
WELCOME TO MY WORLD!!!

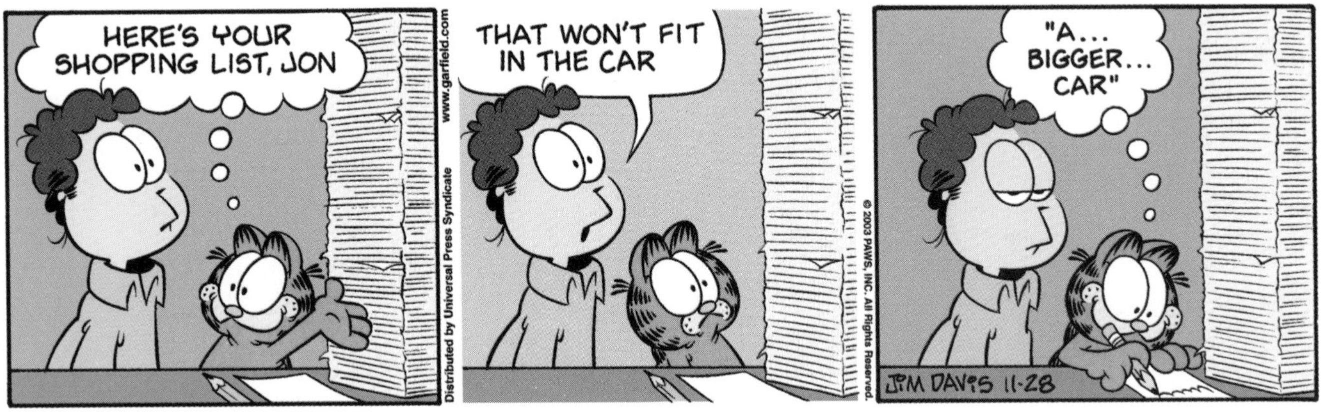

HERE'S YOUR SHOPPING LIST, JON
www.garfield.com
Distributed by Universal Press Syndicate
THAT WON'T FIT IN THE CAR
© 2003 PAWS, INC. All Rights Reserved.
"A... BIGGER... CAR"
JIM DAVIS 11-28

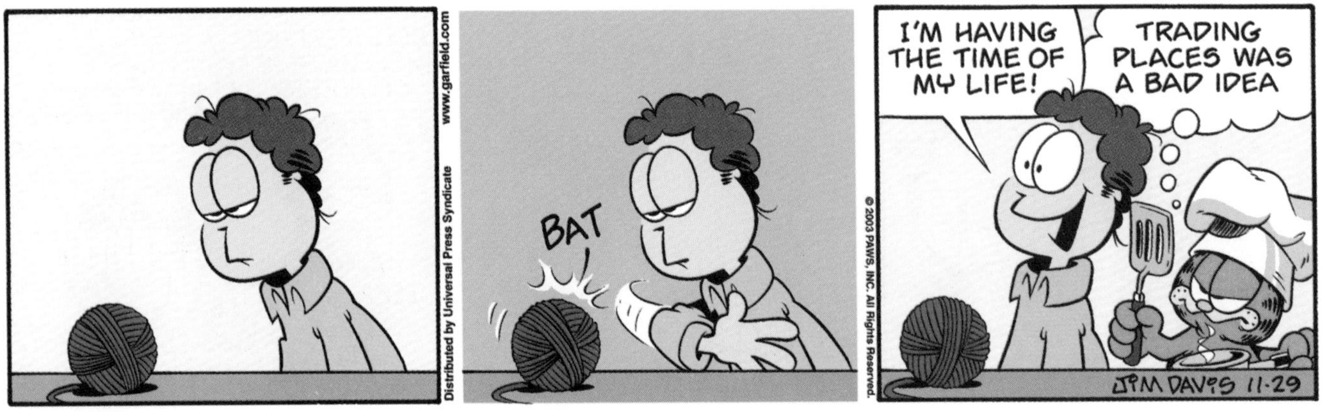

www.garfield.com
Distributed by Universal Press Syndicate
BAT
© 2003 PAWS, INC. All Rights Reserved.
I'M HAVING THE TIME OF MY LIFE!
TRADING PLACES WAS A BAD IDEA
JIM DAVIS 11-29

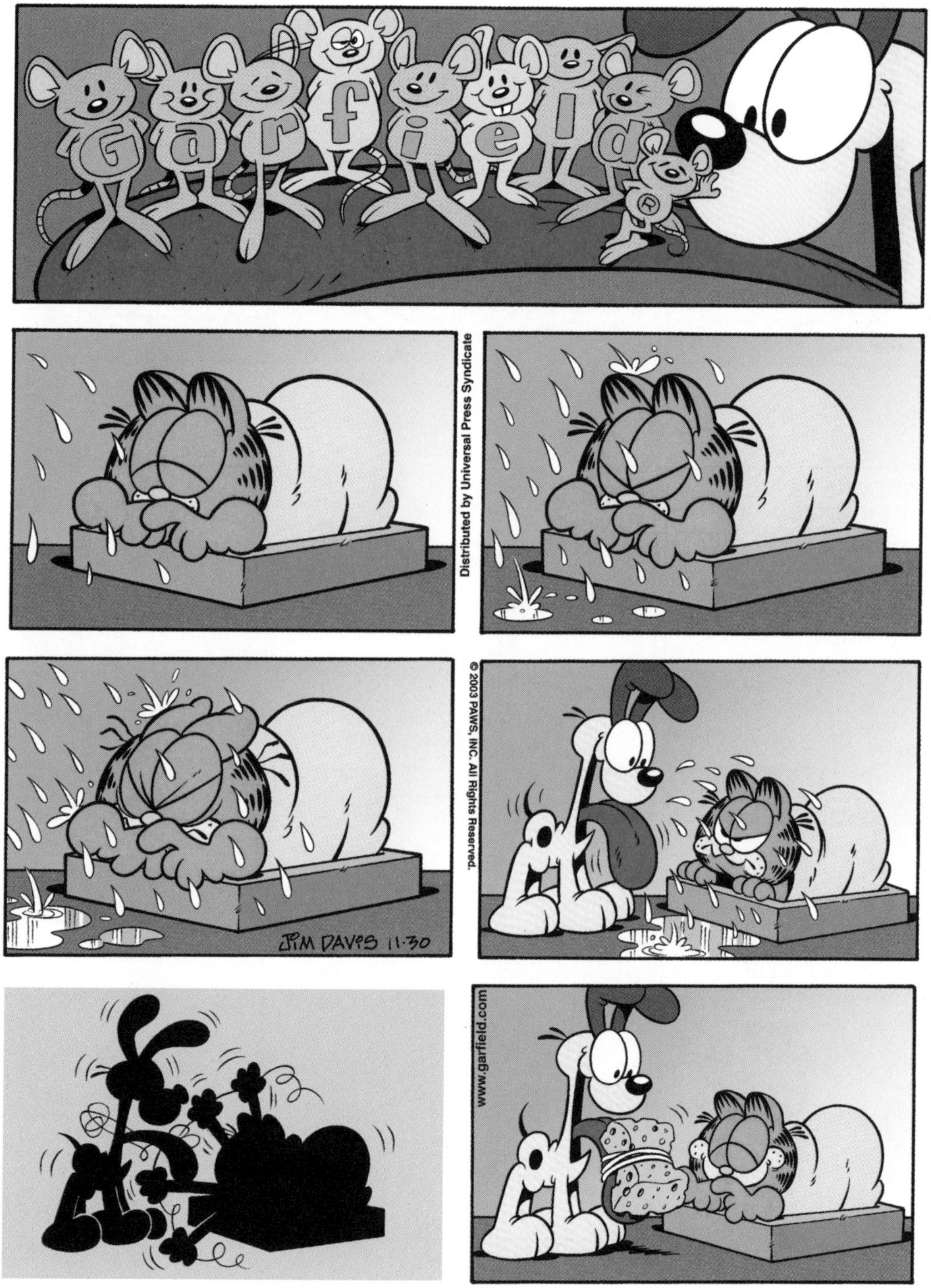
Garfield
Distributed by Universal Press Syndicate
© 2003 PAWS, INC. All Rights Reserved.
JIM DAVIS 11-30
www.garfield.com

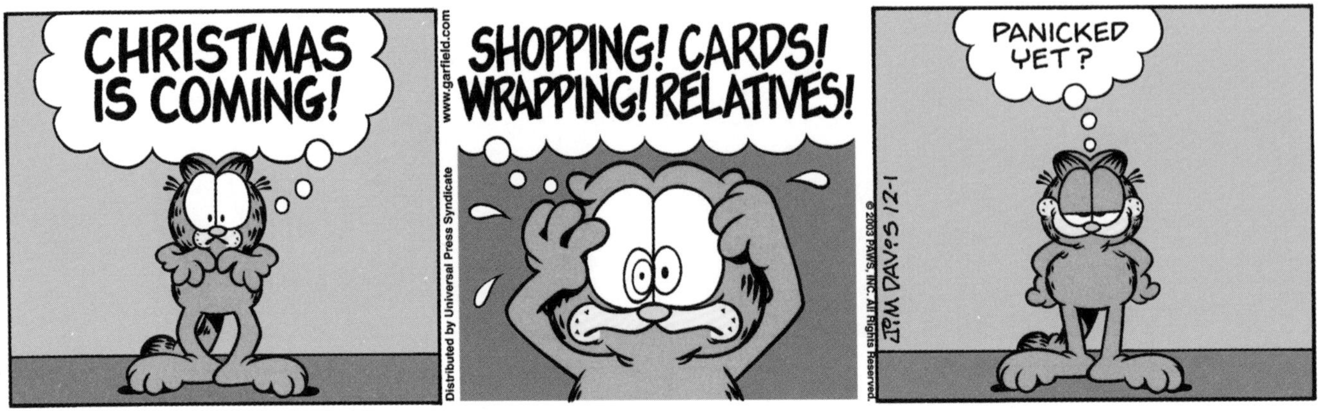
CHRISTMAS IS COMING!
SHOPPING! CARDS! WRAPPING! RELATIVES!
PANICKED YET?
www.garfield.com
Distributed by Universal Press Syndicate
© 2003 PAWS, INC. All Rights Reserved.
JIM DAVIS 12-1

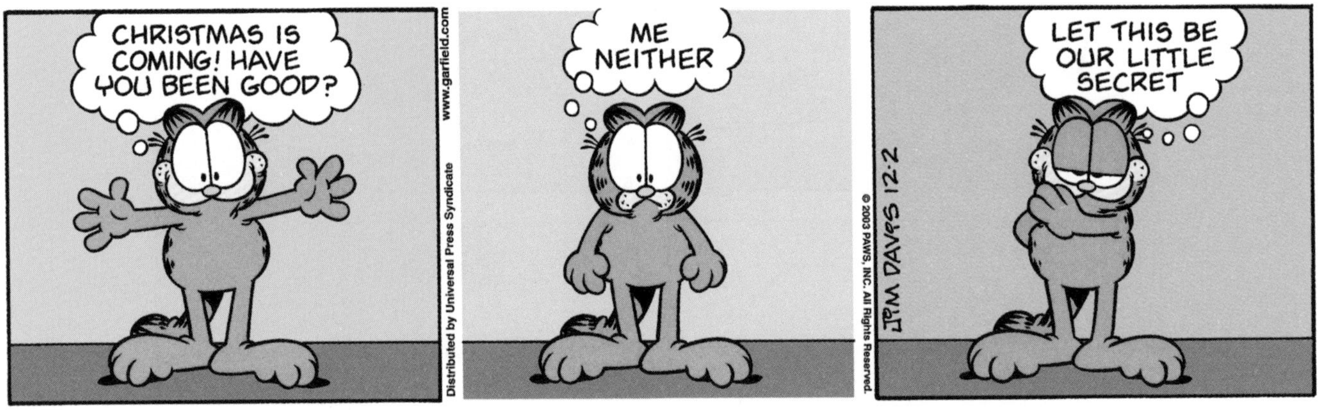
CHRISTMAS IS COMING! HAVE YOU BEEN GOOD?
ME NEITHER
LET THIS BE OUR LITTLE SECRET
www.garfield.com
Distributed by Universal Press Syndicate
© 2003 PAWS, INC. All Rights Reserved.
JIM DAVIS 12-2

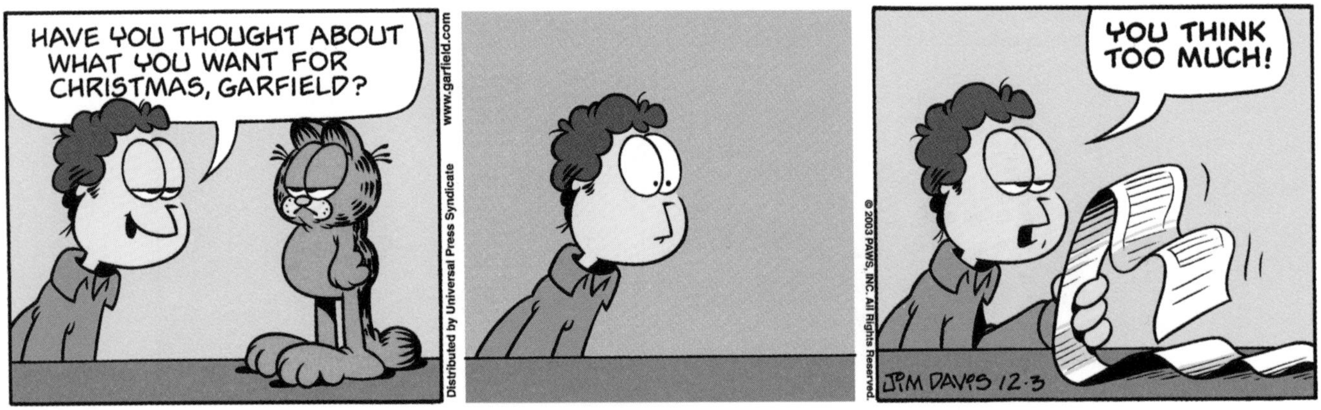
HAVE YOU THOUGHT ABOUT WHAT YOU WANT FOR CHRISTMAS, GARFIELD?
YOU THINK TOO MUCH!
www.garfield.com
Distributed by Universal Press Syndicate
© 2003 PAWS, INC. All Rights Reserved.
JIM DAVIS 12-3

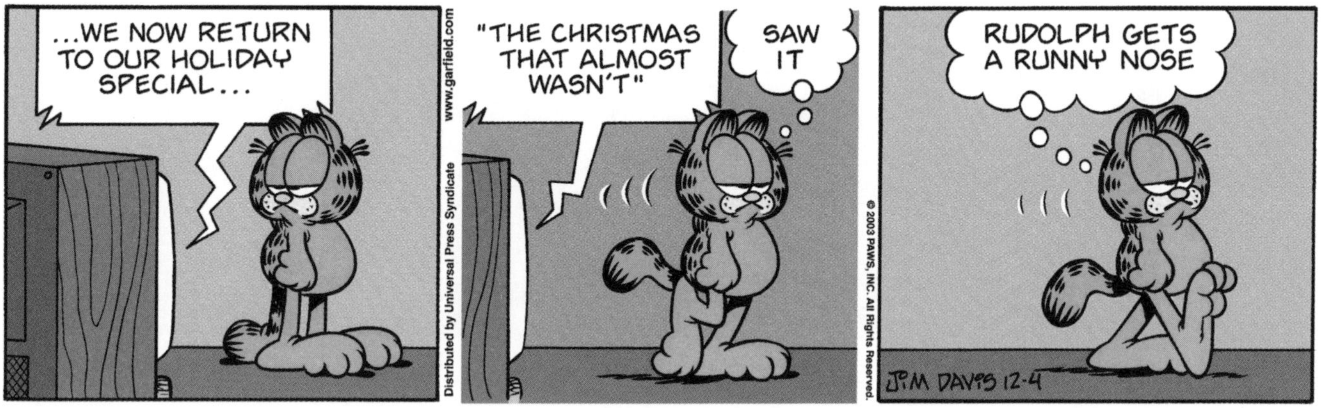
...WE NOW RETURN TO OUR HOLIDAY SPECIAL...
"THE CHRISTMAS THAT ALMOST WASN'T"
SAW IT
RUDOLPH GETS A RUNNY NOSE
www.garfield.com
Distributed by Universal Press Syndicate
© 2003 PAWS, INC. All Rights Reserved.
JIM DAVIS 12-4

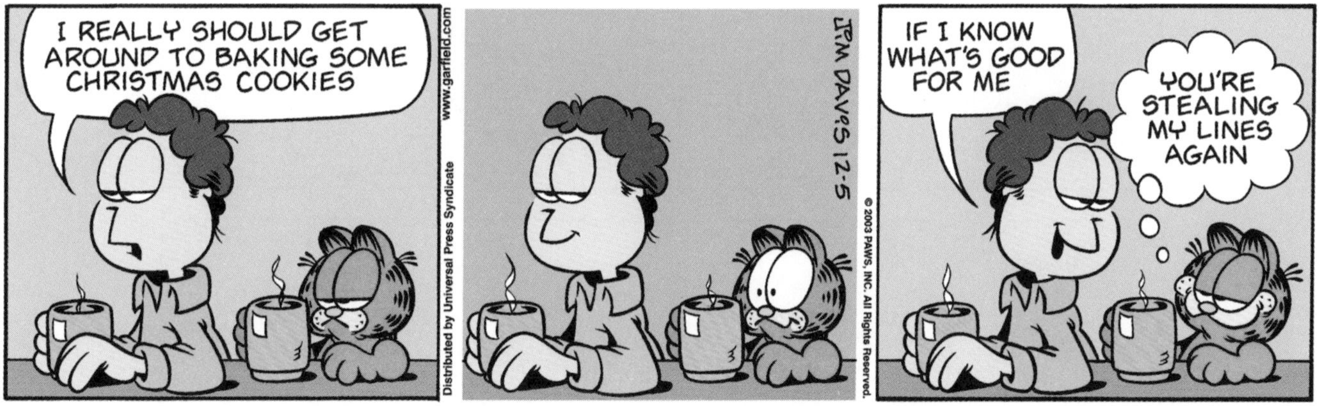
I REALLY SHOULD GET AROUND TO BAKING SOME CHRISTMAS COOKIES
IF I KNOW WHAT'S GOOD FOR ME
YOU'RE STEALING MY LINES AGAIN
www.garfield.com
Distributed by Universal Press Syndicate
© 2003 PAWS, INC. All Rights Reserved.
JIM DAVIS 12-5

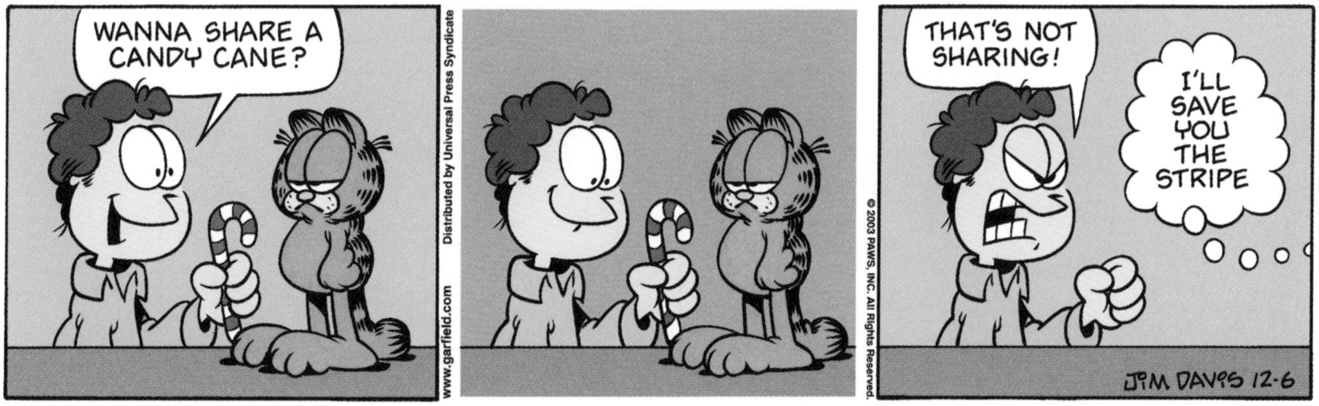
WANNA SHARE A CANDY CANE?
THAT'S NOT SHARING!
I'LL SAVE YOU THE STRIPE
Distributed by Universal Press Syndicate
www.garfield.com
© 2003 PAWS, INC. All Rights Reserved.
JIM DAVIS 12-6

GARFIELD
www.garfield.com
I LOVE CHRISTMAS
Distributed by Universal Press Syndicate
I LOVE CHRISTMAS
© 2003 PAWS, INC. All Rights Reserved.
I'M A CARRIER
JIM DAVIS 12-7

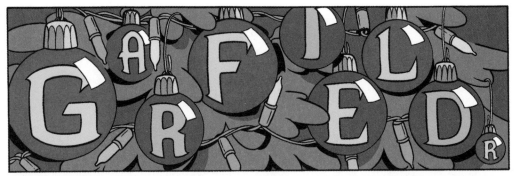

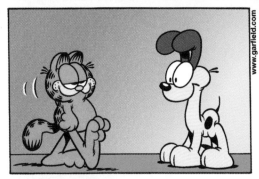

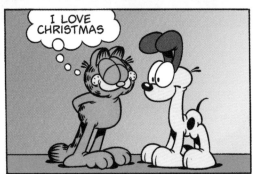

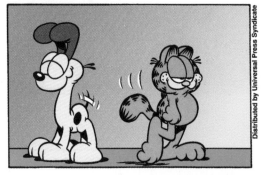

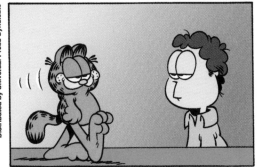

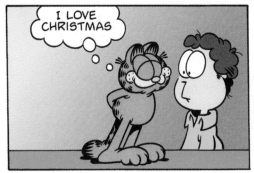

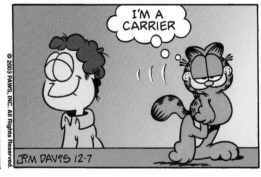

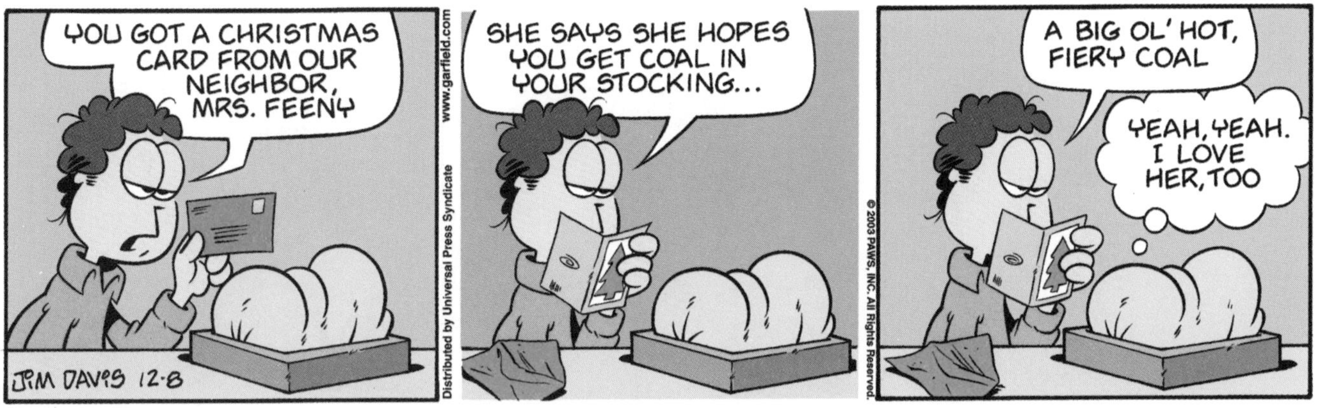
YOU GOT A CHRISTMAS CARD FROM OUR NEIGHBOR, MRS. FEENY
JIM DAVIS 12-8
www.garfield.com
Distributed by Universal Press Syndicate
SHE SAYS SHE HOPES YOU GET COAL IN YOUR STOCKING...
A BIG OL' HOT, FIERY COAL
YEAH, YEAH. I LOVE HER, TOO
© 2003 PAWS, INC. All Rights Reserved.

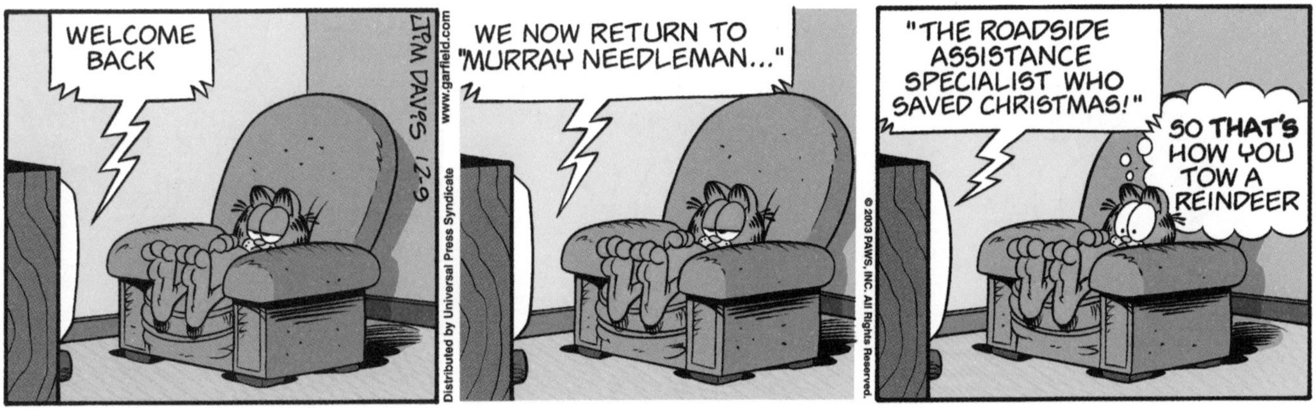
WELCOME BACK
JIM DAVIS 12-9
www.garfield.com
Distributed by Universal Press Syndicate
WE NOW RETURN TO "MURRAY NEEDLEMAN..."
"THE ROADSIDE ASSISTANCE SPECIALIST WHO SAVED CHRISTMAS!"
SO THAT'S HOW YOU TOW A REINDEER
© 2003 PAWS, INC. All Rights Reserved.

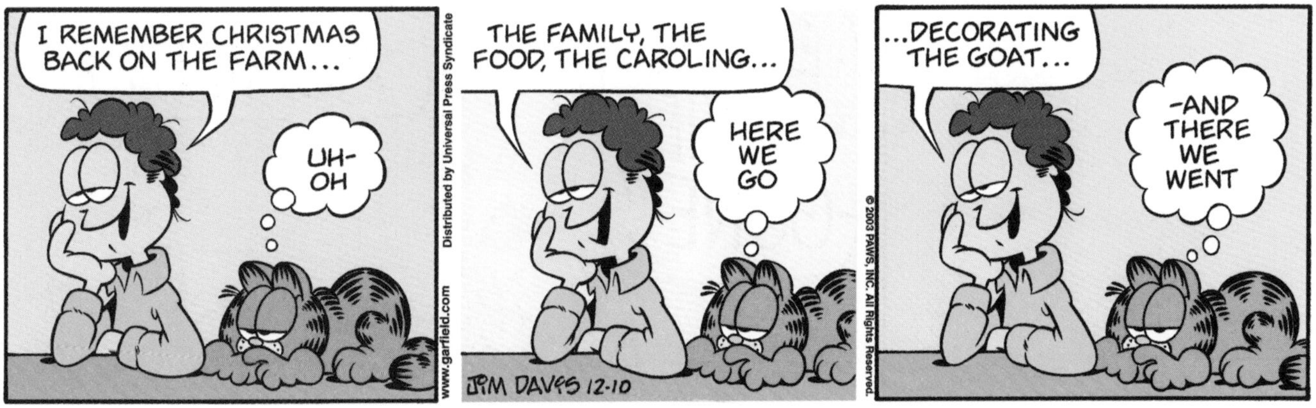
I REMEMBER CHRISTMAS BACK ON THE FARM...
UH-OH
Distributed by Universal Press Syndicate
www.garfield.com
THE FAMILY, THE FOOD, THE CAROLING...
HERE WE GO
JIM DAVIS 12-10
...DECORATING THE GOAT...
-AND THERE WE WENT
© 2003 PAWS, INC. All Rights Reserved.

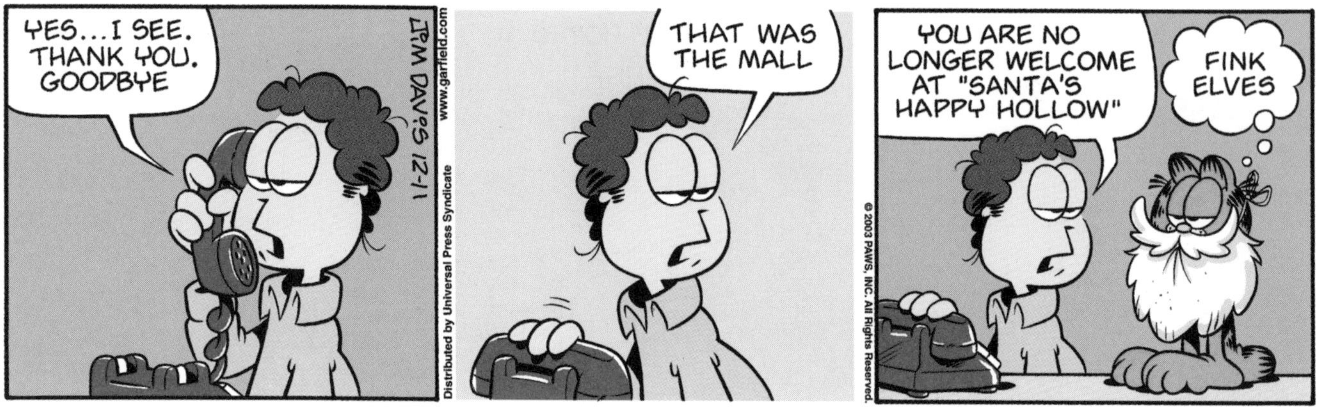
YES... I SEE. THANK YOU. GOODBYE
JIM DAVIS 12-11
www.garfield.com
Distributed by Universal Press Syndicate
THAT WAS THE MALL
YOU ARE NO LONGER WELCOME AT "SANTA'S HAPPY HOLLOW"
FINK ELVES
© 2003 PAWS, INC. All Rights Reserved.

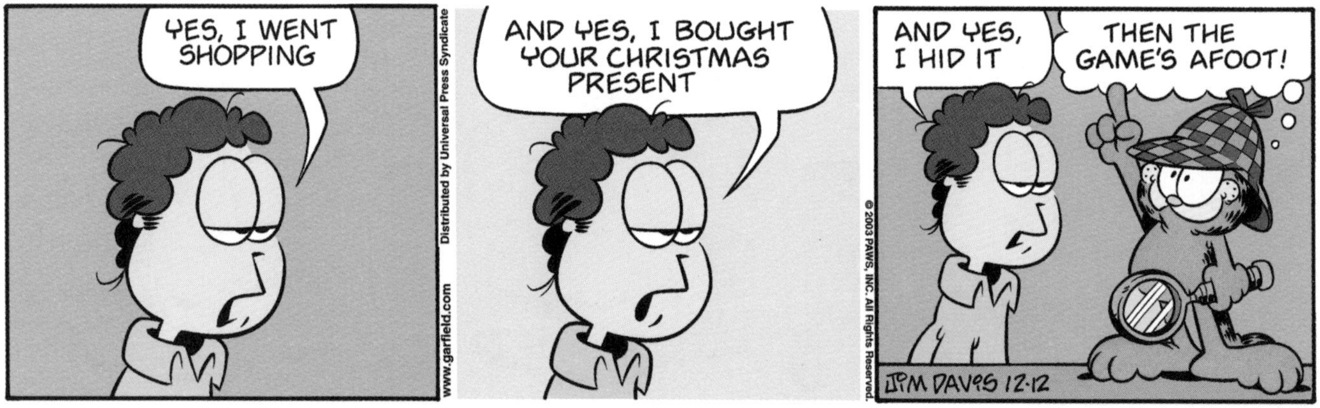
YES, I WENT SHOPPING
www.garfield.com
Distributed by Universal Press Syndicate
AND YES, I BOUGHT YOUR CHRISTMAS PRESENT
AND YES, I HID IT
THEN THE GAME'S AFOOT!
© 2003 PAWS, INC. All Rights Reserved.
JIM DAVIS 12-12

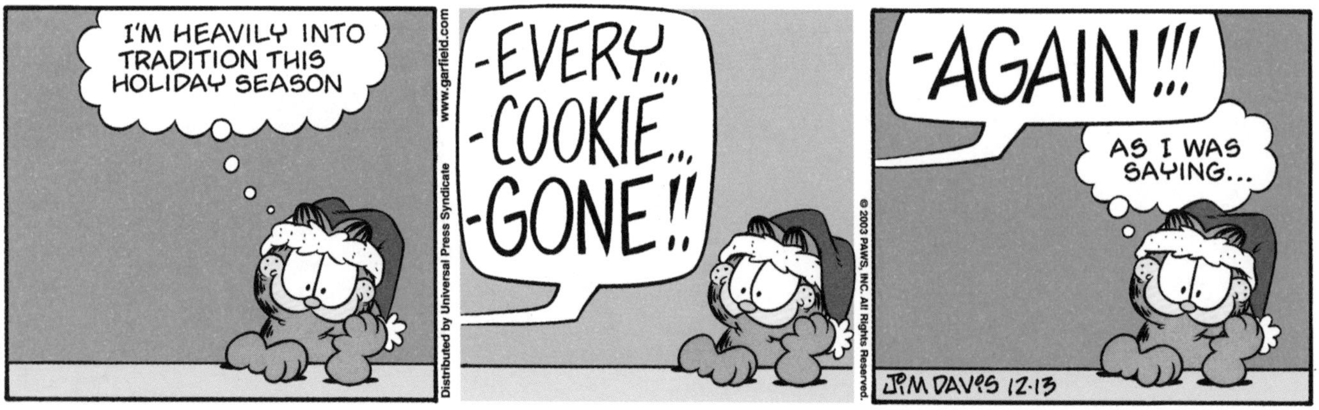
I'M HEAVILY INTO TRADITION THIS HOLIDAY SEASON
www.garfield.com
Distributed by Universal Press Syndicate
-EVERY... -COOKIE... -GONE!!
-AGAIN!!!
AS I WAS SAYING...
© 2003 PAWS, INC. All Rights Reserved.
JIM DAVIS 12-13

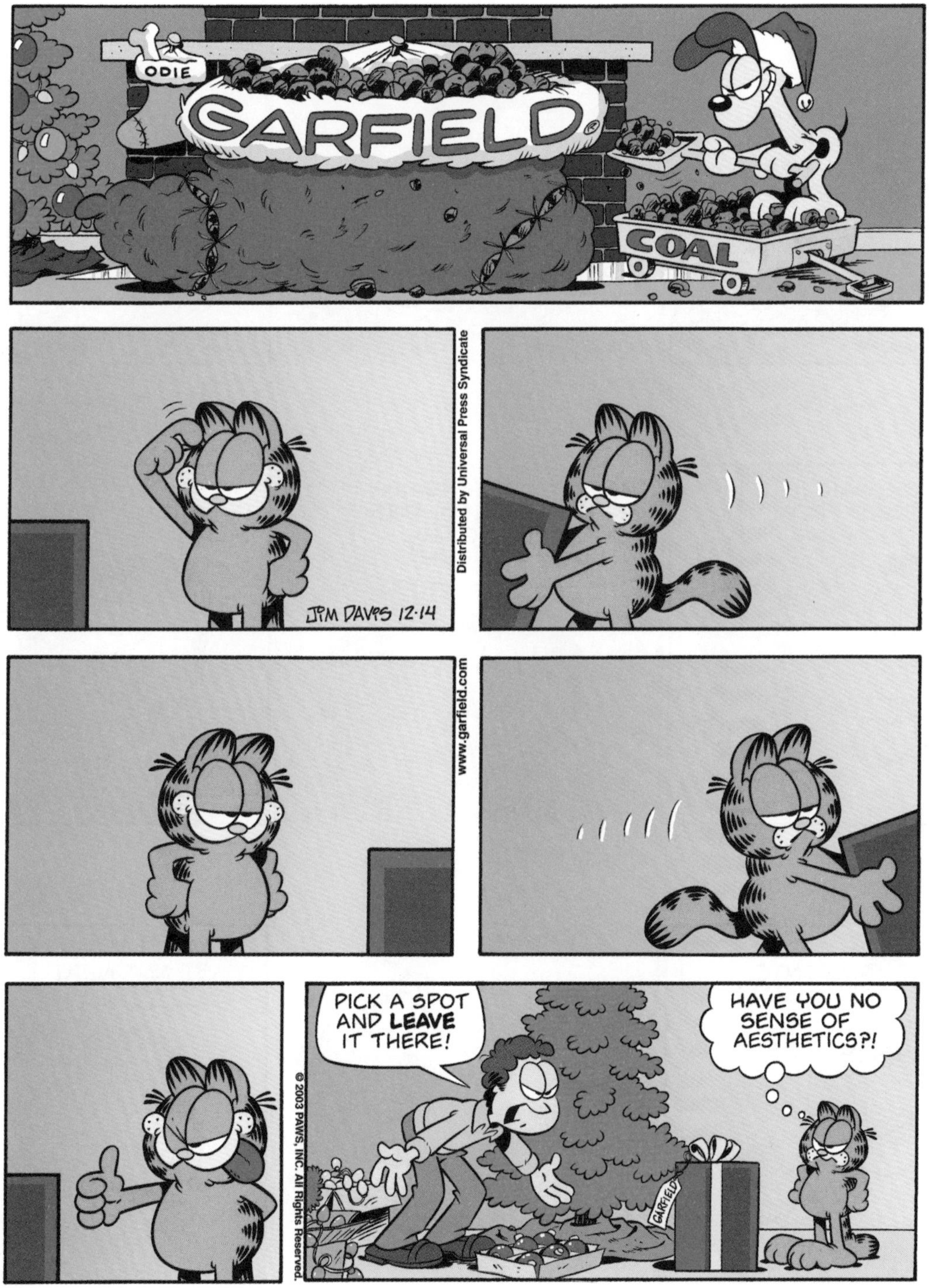
ODIE
GARFIELD®
COAL
JIM DAVIS 12·14
Distributed by Universal Press Syndicate
www.garfield.com
© 2003 PAWS, INC. All Rights Reserved.
PICK A SPOT AND **LEAVE** IT THERE!
HAVE YOU NO SENSE OF AESTHETICS?!
GARFIELD

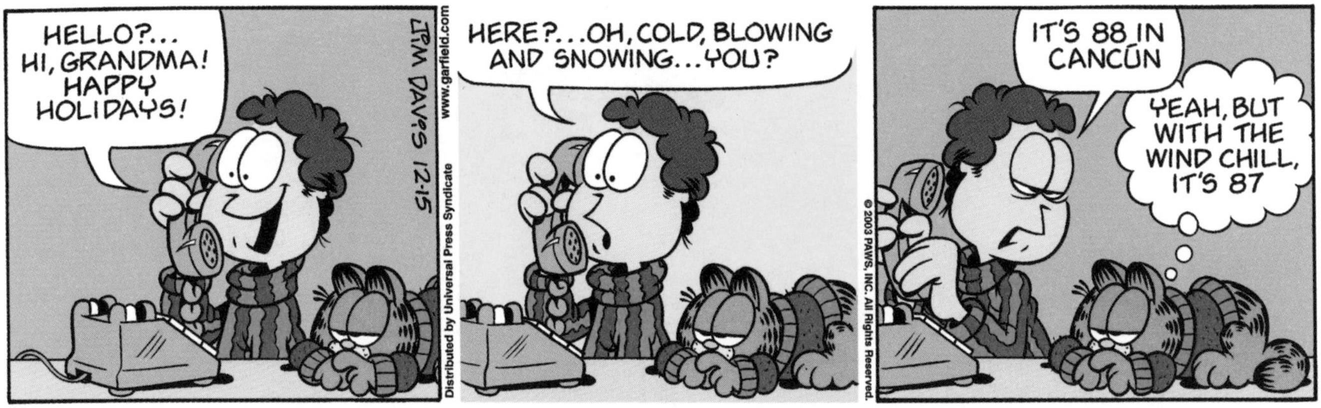
HELLO?... HI, GRANDMA! HAPPY HOLIDAYS!
JIM DAVIS 12-15
Distributed by Universal Press Syndicate www.garfield.com
HERE?...OH, COLD, BLOWING AND SNOWING...YOU?
© 2003 PAWS, INC. All Rights Reserved.
IT'S 88 IN CANCÚN
YEAH, BUT WITH THE WIND CHILL, IT'S 87

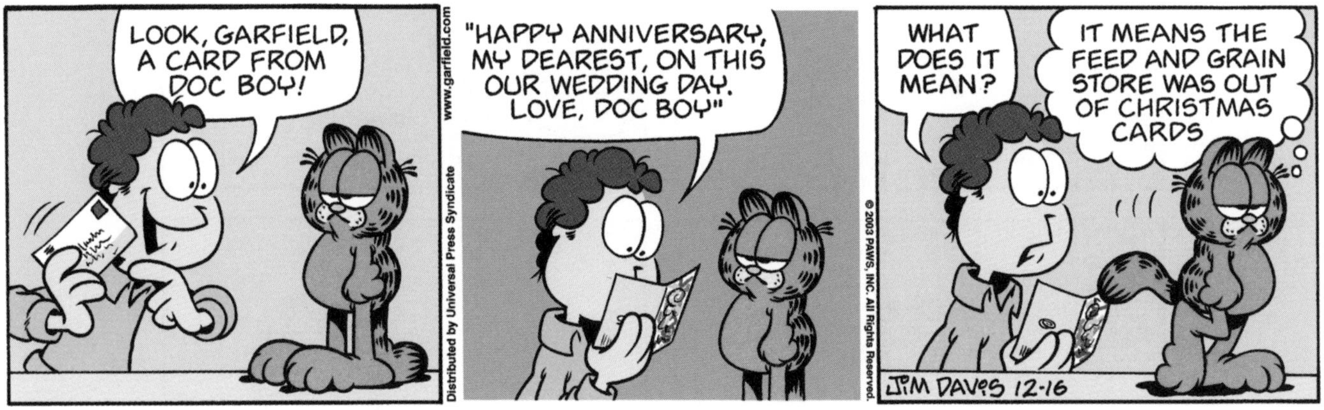
LOOK, GARFIELD, A CARD FROM DOC BOY!
Distributed by Universal Press Syndicate www.garfield.com
"HAPPY ANNIVERSARY, MY DEAREST, ON THIS OUR WEDDING DAY. LOVE, DOC BOY"
© 2003 PAWS, INC. All Rights Reserved.
WHAT DOES IT MEAN?
IT MEANS THE FEED AND GRAIN STORE WAS OUT OF CHRISTMAS CARDS
JIM DAVIS 12-16

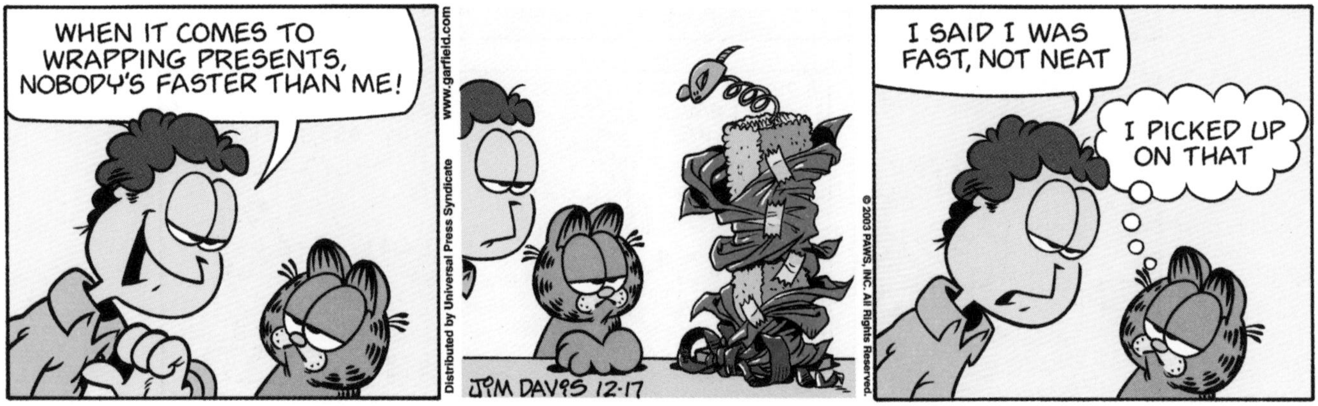
WHEN IT COMES TO WRAPPING PRESENTS, NOBODY'S FASTER THAN ME!
Distributed by Universal Press Syndicate www.garfield.com
JIM DAVIS 12-17
© 2003 PAWS, INC. All Rights Reserved.
I SAID I WAS FAST, NOT NEAT
I PICKED UP ON THAT

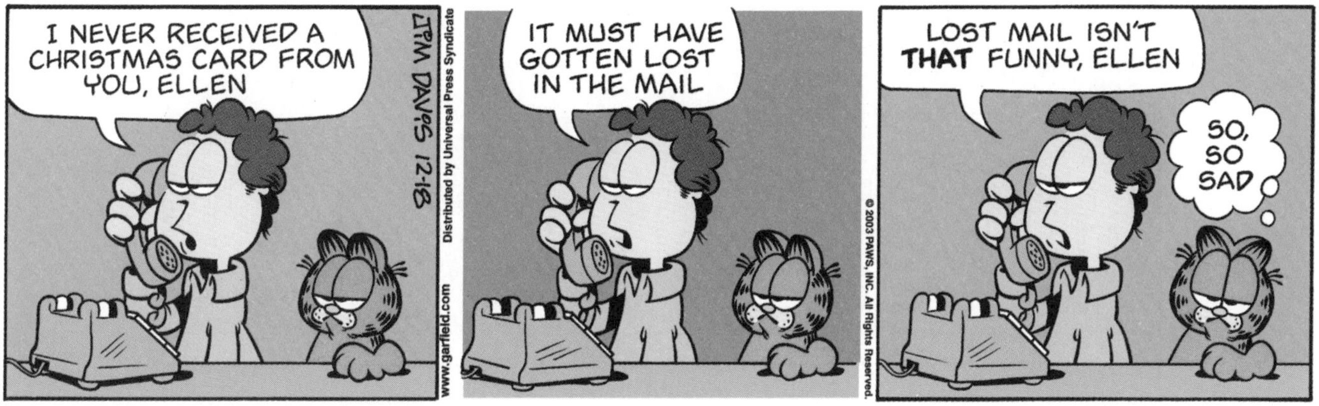
I NEVER RECEIVED A CHRISTMAS CARD FROM YOU, ELLEN
IT MUST HAVE GOTTEN LOST IN THE MAIL
LOST MAIL ISN'T **THAT** FUNNY, ELLEN
SO, SO SAD

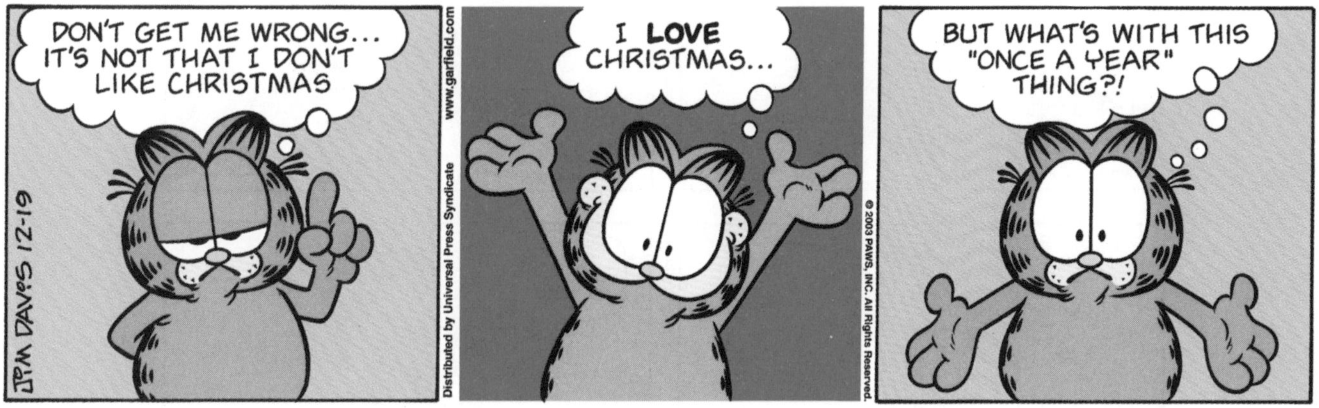
DON'T GET ME WRONG... IT'S NOT THAT I DON'T LIKE CHRISTMAS
I **LOVE** CHRISTMAS...
BUT WHAT'S WITH THIS "ONCE A YEAR" THING?!

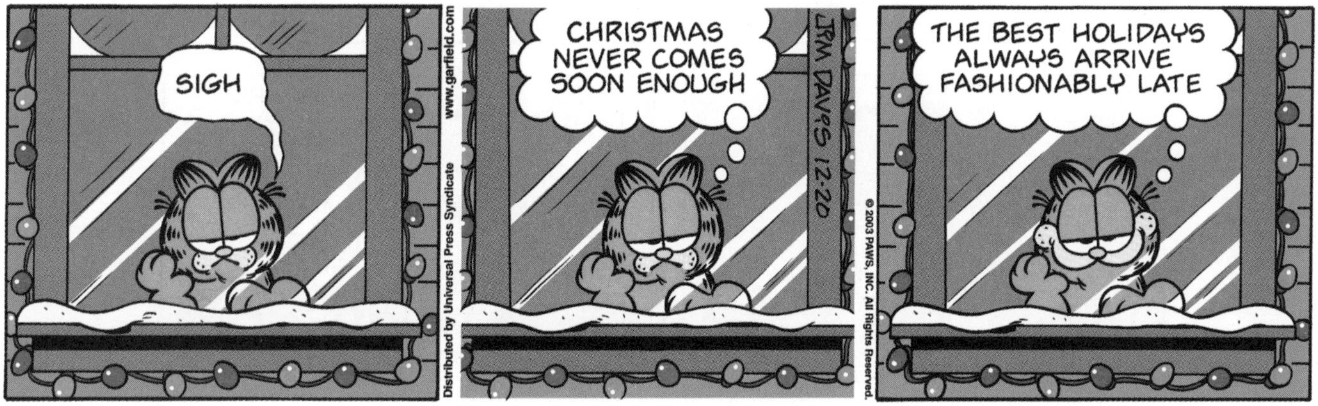
SIGH
CHRISTMAS NEVER COMES SOON ENOUGH
THE BEST HOLIDAYS ALWAYS ARRIVE FASHIONABLY LATE

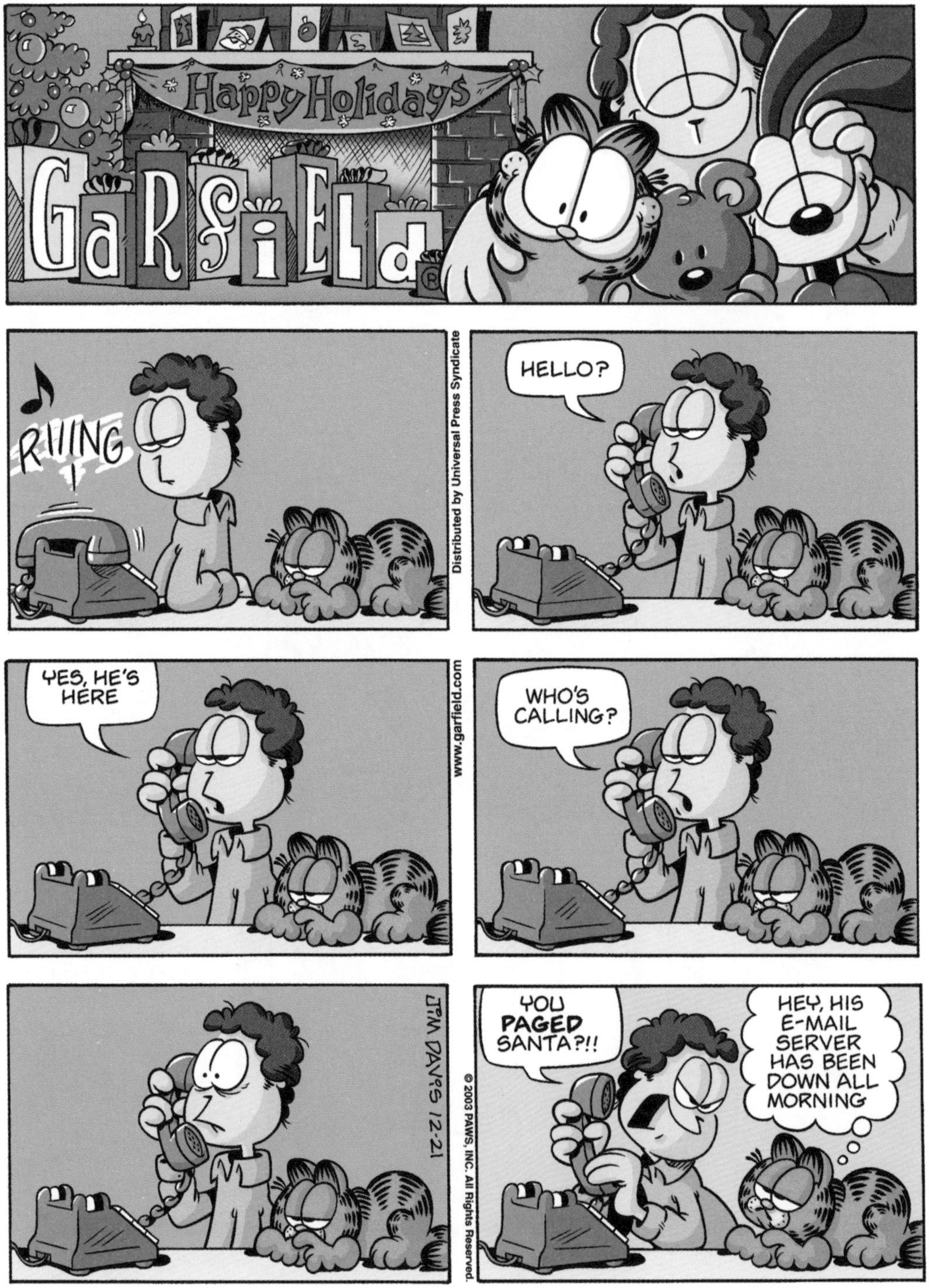
Happy Holidays
GARFIELD
RIIING
HELLO?
YES, HE'S HERE
WHO'S CALLING?
YOU PAGED SANTA?!!
HEY, HIS E-MAIL SERVER HAS BEEN DOWN ALL MORNING
JIM DAVIS 12-21
Distributed by Universal Press Syndicate
www.garfield.com
© 2003 PAWS, INC. All Rights Reserved.

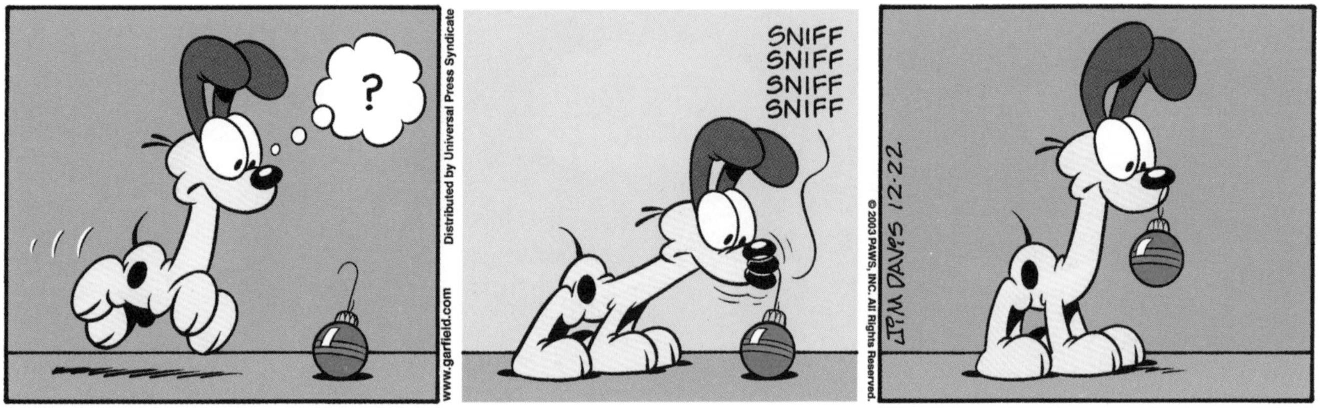
?
www.garfield.com
Distributed by Universal Press Syndicate
SNIFF
SNIFF
SNIFF
SNIFF
JIM DAVIS 12-22
© 2003 PAWS, INC. All Rights Reserved.

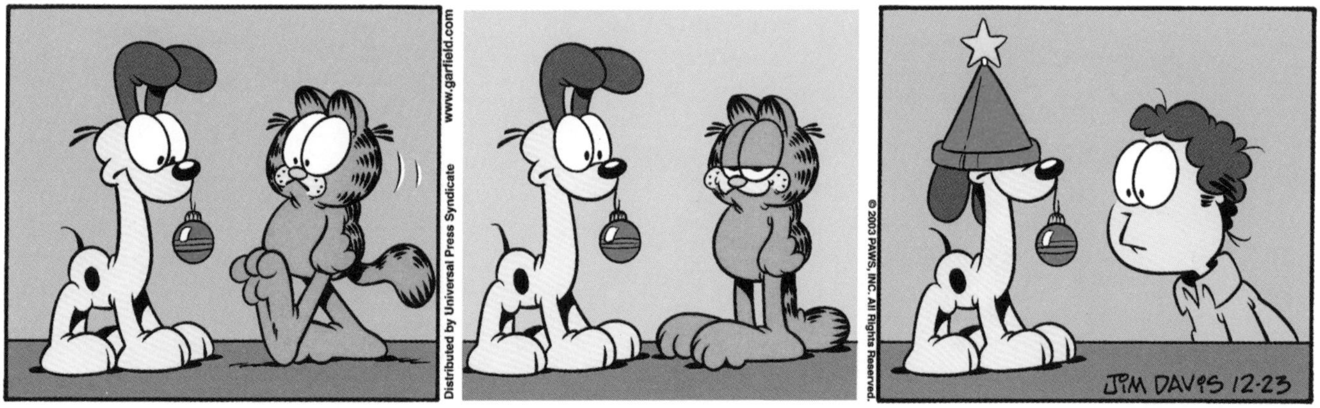
www.garfield.com
Distributed by Universal Press Syndicate
© 2003 PAWS, INC. All Rights Reserved.
JIM DAVIS 12-23

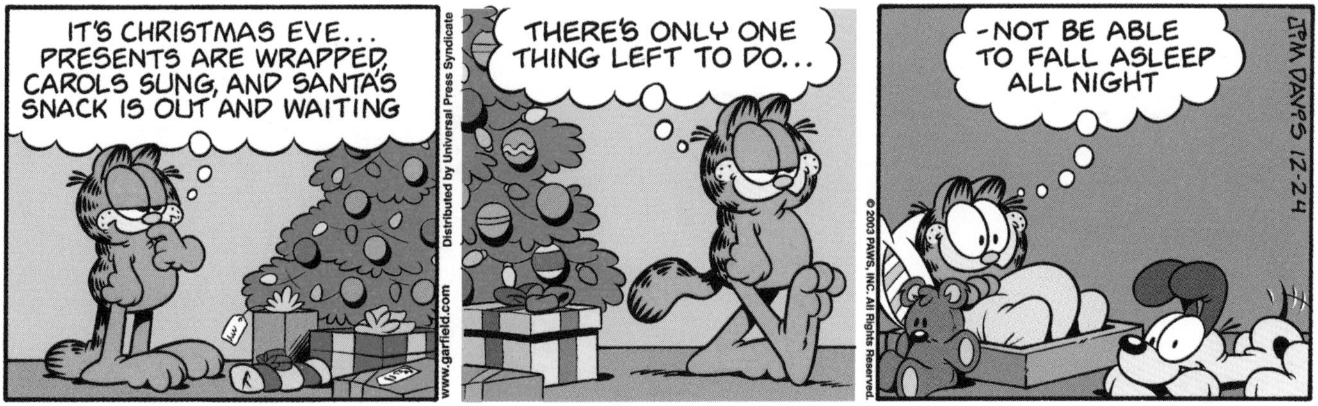
IT'S CHRISTMAS EVE... PRESENTS ARE WRAPPED, CAROLS SUNG, AND SANTA'S SNACK IS OUT AND WAITING
www.garfield.com
Distributed by Universal Press Syndicate
THERE'S ONLY ONE THING LEFT TO DO...
© 2003 PAWS, INC. All Rights Reserved.
-NOT BE ABLE TO FALL ASLEEP ALL NIGHT
JIM DAVIS 12-24

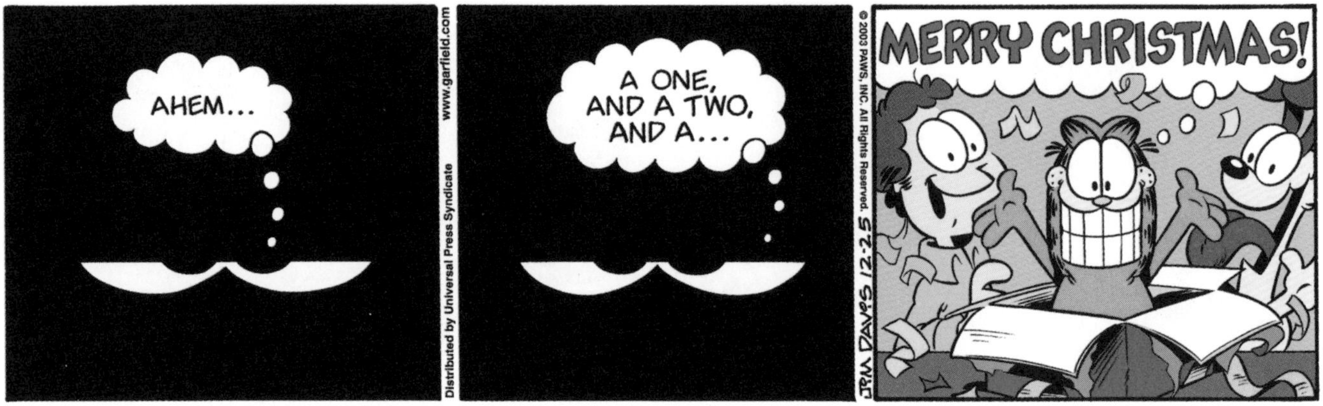
AHEM...
A ONE, AND A TWO, AND A...
MERRY CHRISTMAS!
www.garfield.com
Distributed by Universal Press Syndicate
© 2003 PAWS, INC. All Rights Reserved.
JIM DAVIS 12-25

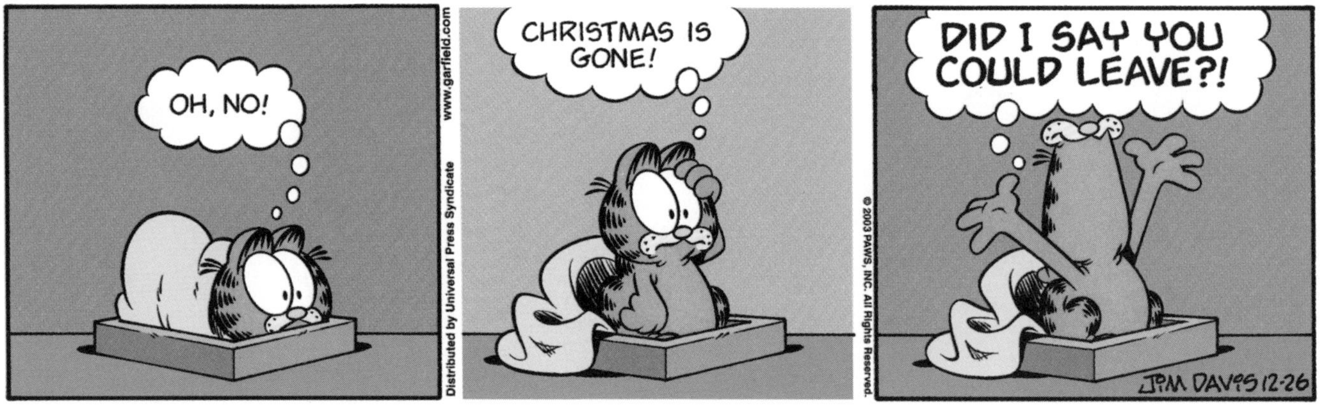
OH, NO!
CHRISTMAS IS GONE!
DID I SAY YOU COULD LEAVE?!
www.garfield.com
Distributed by Universal Press Syndicate
© 2003 PAWS, INC. All Rights Reserved.
JIM DAVIS 12-26

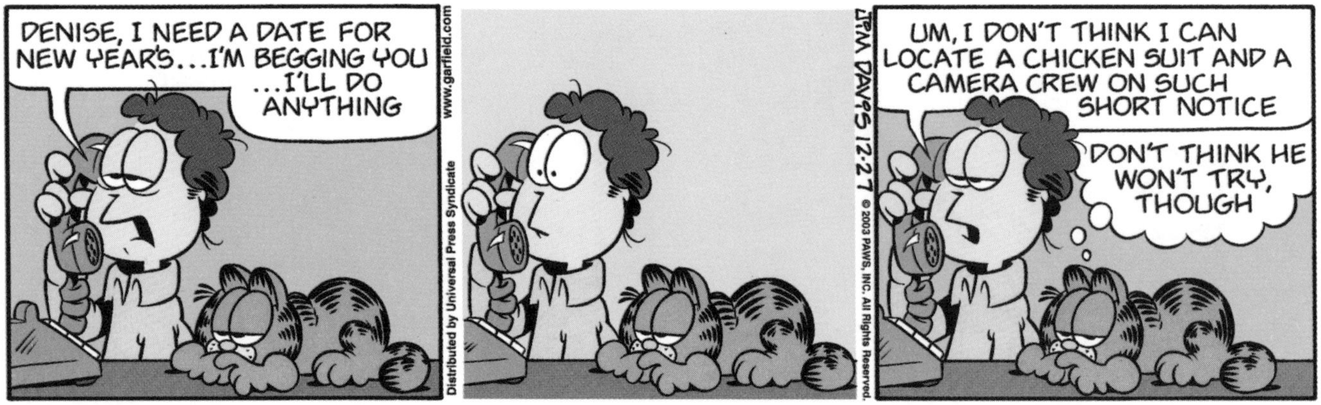
DENISE, I NEED A DATE FOR NEW YEAR'S...I'M BEGGING YOU ...I'LL DO ANYTHING
UM, I DON'T THINK I CAN LOCATE A CHICKEN SUIT AND A CAMERA CREW ON SUCH SHORT NOTICE
DON'T THINK HE WON'T TRY, THOUGH
www.garfield.com
Distributed by Universal Press Syndicate
JIM DAVIS 12-27
© 2003 PAWS, INC. All Rights Reserved.

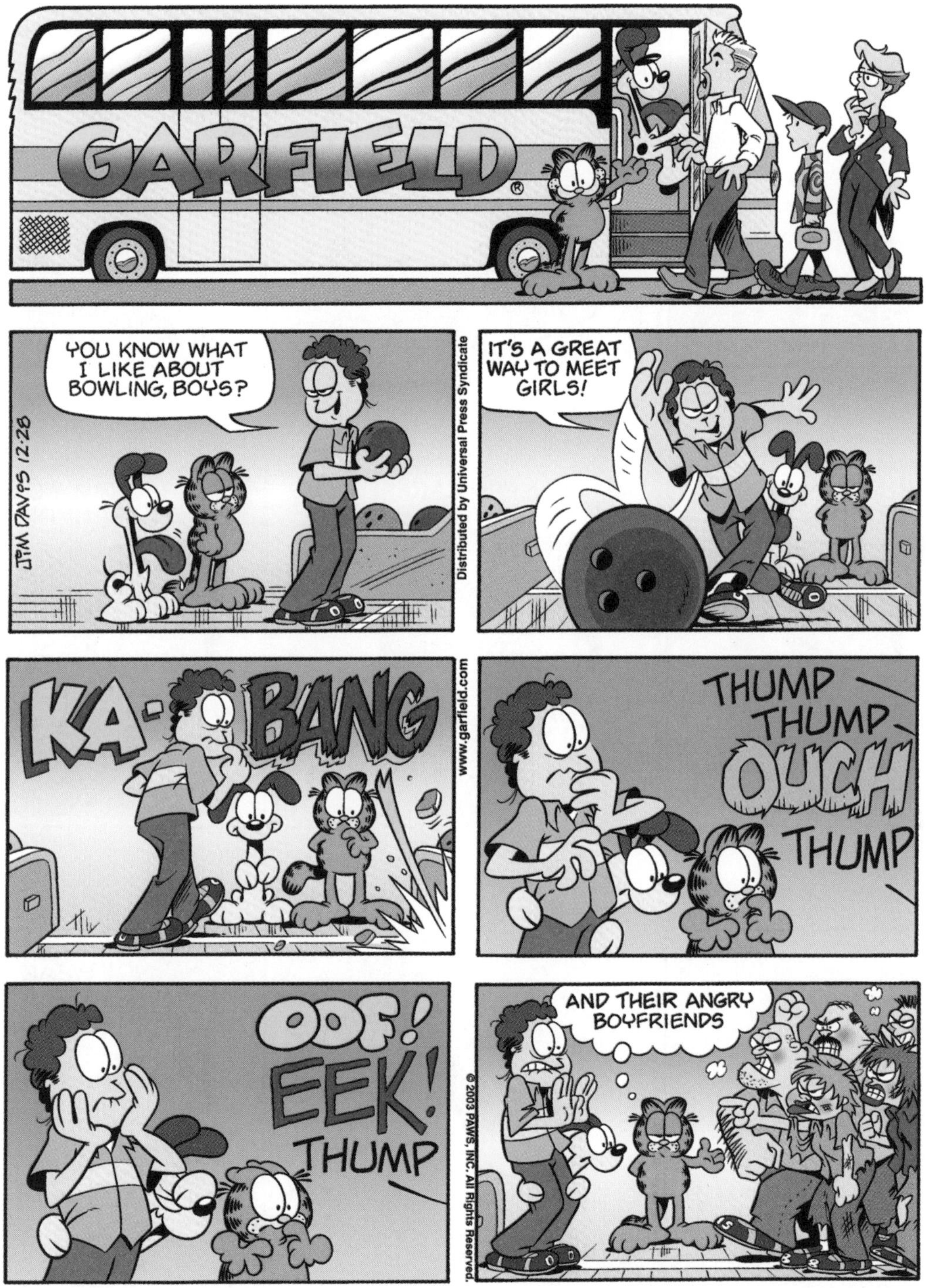
GARFIELD®
JIM DAVIS 12-28
YOU KNOW WHAT I LIKE ABOUT BOWLING, BOYS?
Distributed by Universal Press Syndicate
IT'S A GREAT WAY TO MEET GIRLS!
KA-BANG
www.garfield.com
THUMP
THUMP
OUCH
THUMP
OOF!
EEK!
THUMP
© 2003 PAWS, INC. All Rights Reserved.
AND THEIR ANGRY BOYFRIENDS

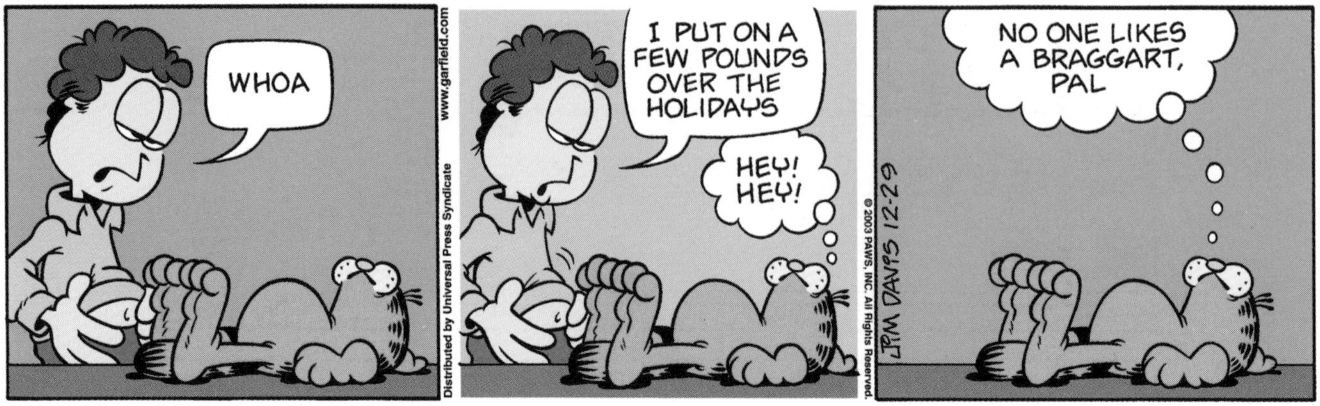
WHOA
I PUT ON A FEW POUNDS OVER THE HOLIDAYS
HEY! HEY!
NO ONE LIKES A BRAGGART, PAL
JIM DAVIS 12-29
www.garfield.com
Distributed by Universal Press Syndicate
© 2003 PAWS, INC. All Rights Reserved.

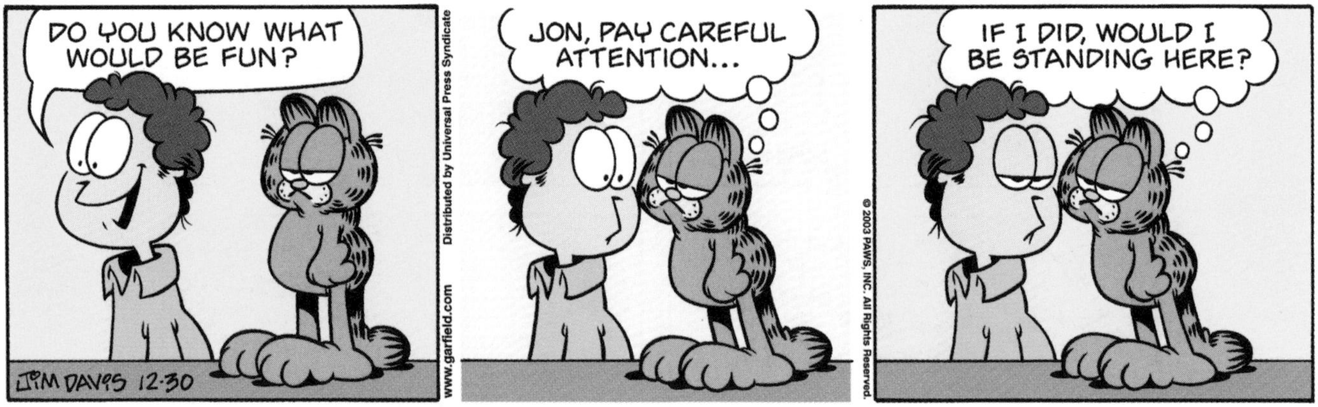
DO YOU KNOW WHAT WOULD BE FUN?
JON, PAY CAREFUL ATTENTION...
IF I DID, WOULD I BE STANDING HERE?
JIM DAVIS 12-30
www.garfield.com
Distributed by Universal Press Syndicate
© 2003 PAWS, INC. All Rights Reserved.

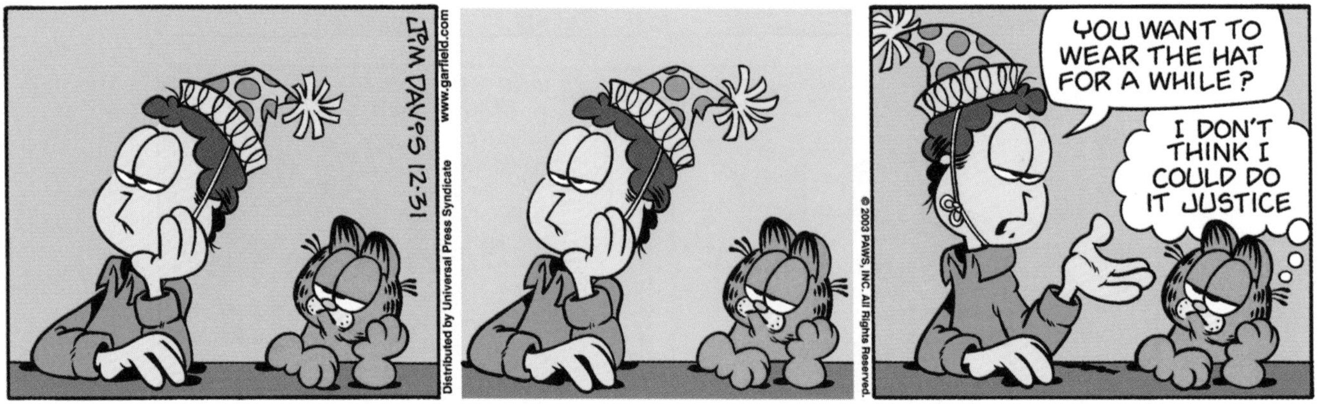
YOU WANT TO WEAR THE HAT FOR A WHILE?
I DON'T THINK I COULD DO IT JUSTICE
JIM DAVIS 12-31
www.garfield.com
Distributed by Universal Press Syndicate
© 2003 PAWS, INC. All Rights Reserved.

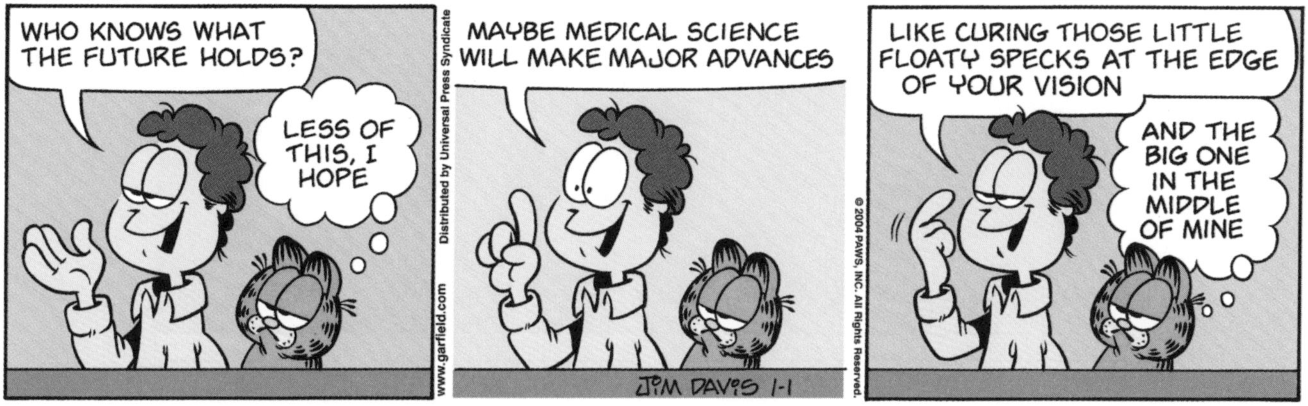
WHO KNOWS WHAT THE FUTURE HOLDS?
LESS OF THIS, I HOPE
MAYBE MEDICAL SCIENCE WILL MAKE MAJOR ADVANCES
LIKE CURING THOSE LITTLE FLOATY SPECKS AT THE EDGE OF YOUR VISION
AND THE BIG ONE IN THE MIDDLE OF MINE
JIM DAVIS 1-1

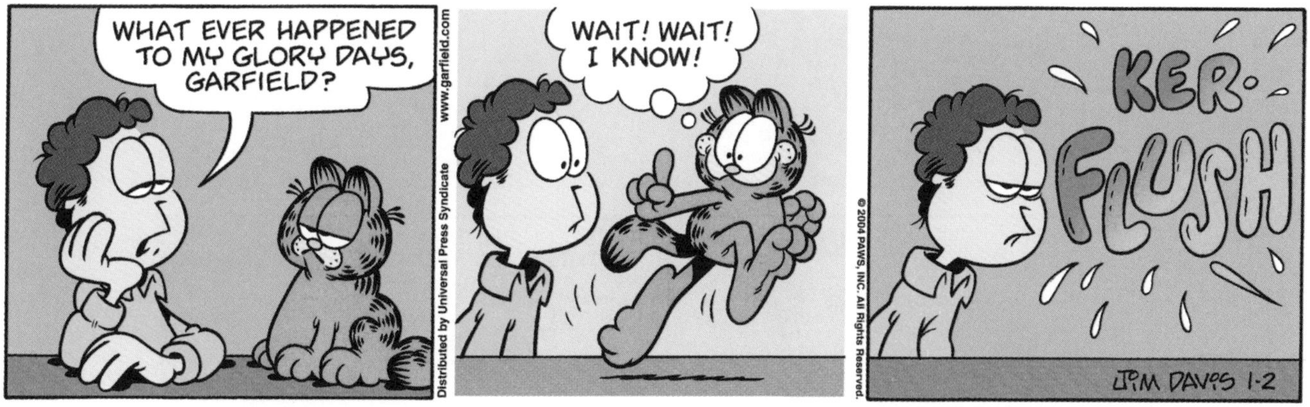
WHAT EVER HAPPENED TO MY GLORY DAYS, GARFIELD?
WAIT! WAIT! I KNOW!
KER-FLUSH
JIM DAVIS 1-2

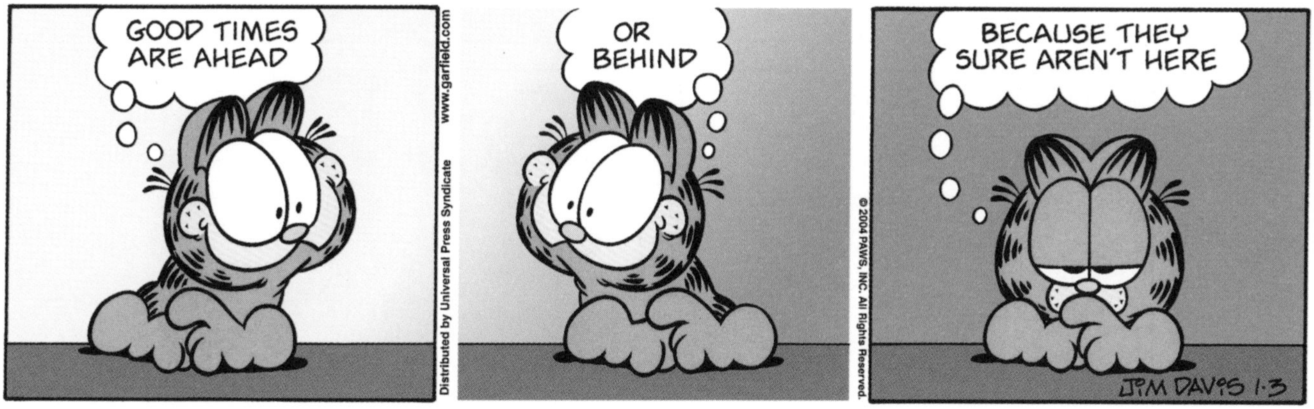
GOOD TIMES ARE AHEAD
OR BEHIND
BECAUSE THEY SURE AREN'T HERE
JIM DAVIS 1-3

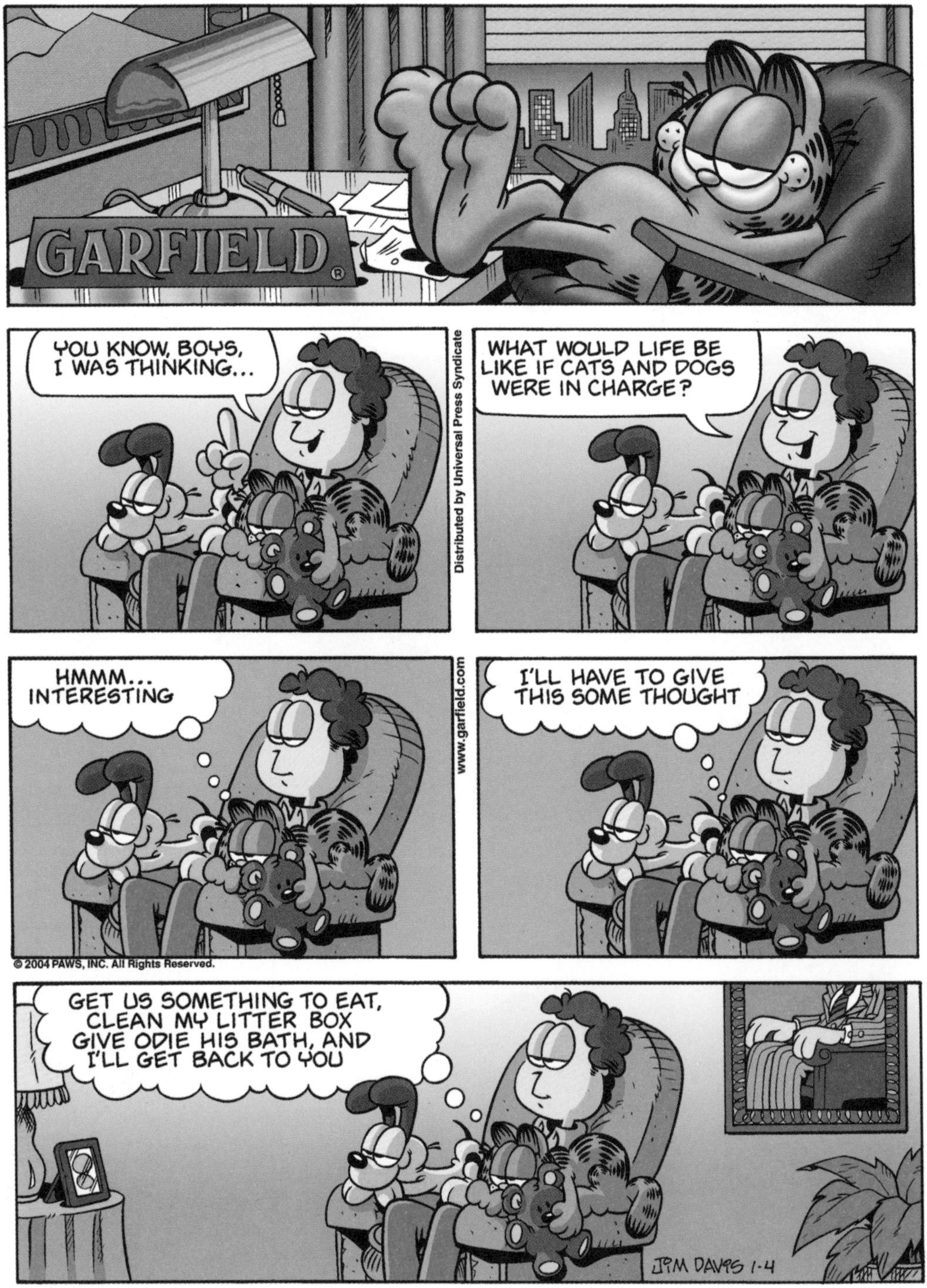
GARFIELD®
YOU KNOW, BOYS, I WAS THINKING...
WHAT WOULD LIFE BE LIKE IF CATS AND DOGS WERE IN CHARGE?
HMMM... INTERESTING
I'LL HAVE TO GIVE THIS SOME THOUGHT
GET US SOMETHING TO EAT, CLEAN MY LITTER BOX GIVE ODIE HIS BATH, AND I'LL GET BACK TO YOU
JIM DAVIS 1-4

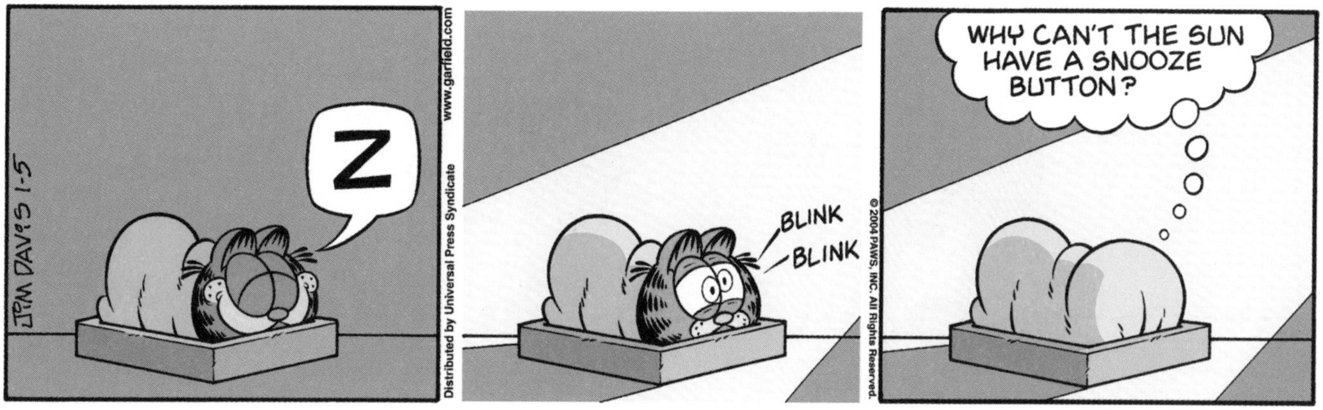
JIM DAVIS 1-5
Z
Distributed by Universal Press Syndicate www.garfield.com
BLINK
BLINK
© 2004 PAWS, INC. All Rights Reserved.
WHY CAN'T THE SUN HAVE A SNOOZE BUTTON?

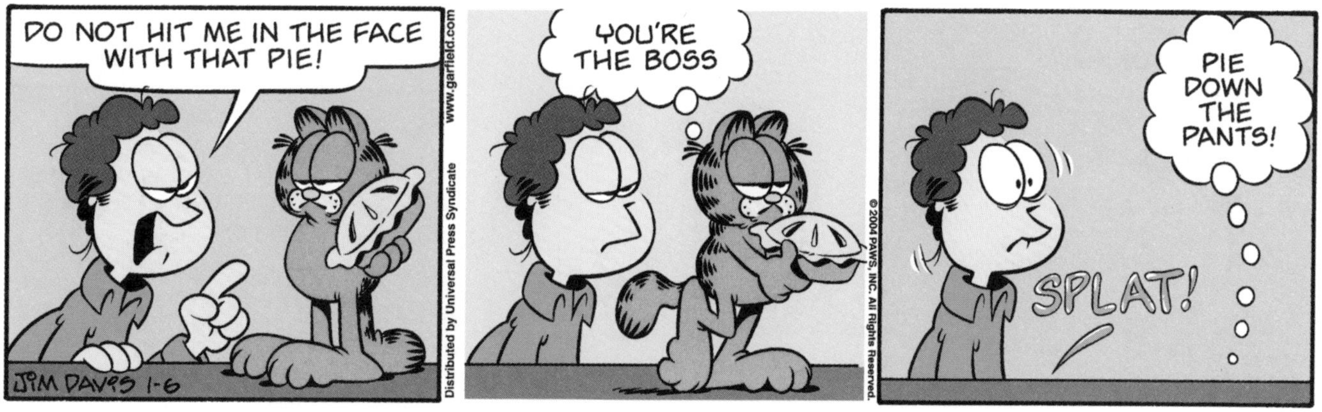
DO NOT HIT ME IN THE FACE WITH THAT PIE!
JIM DAVIS 1-6
Distributed by Universal Press Syndicate www.garfield.com
YOU'RE THE BOSS
© 2004 PAWS, INC. All Rights Reserved.
PIE DOWN THE PANTS!
SPLAT!

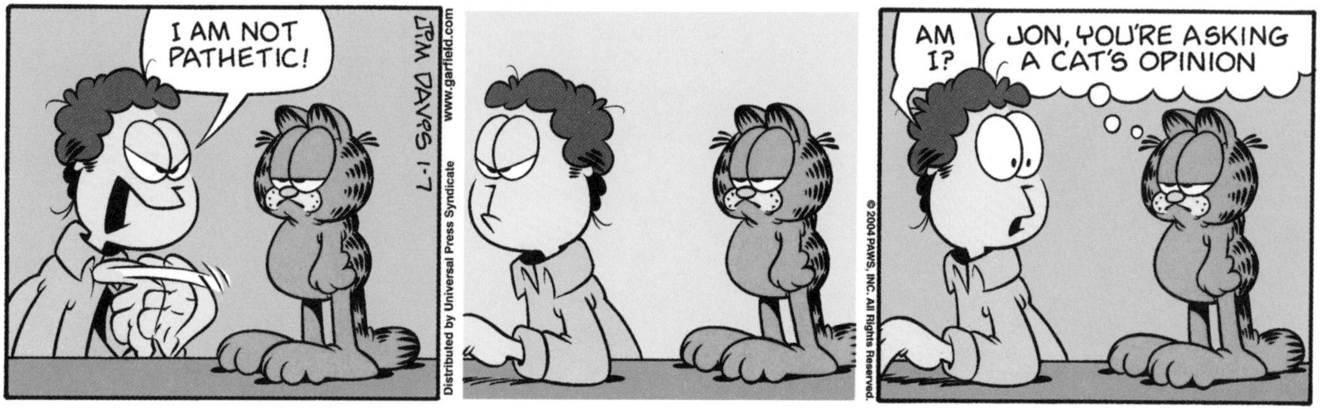
I AM NOT PATHETIC!
JIM DAVIS 1-7
Distributed by Universal Press Syndicate www.garfield.com
© 2004 PAWS, INC. All Rights Reserved.
AM I?
JON, YOU'RE ASKING A CAT'S OPINION

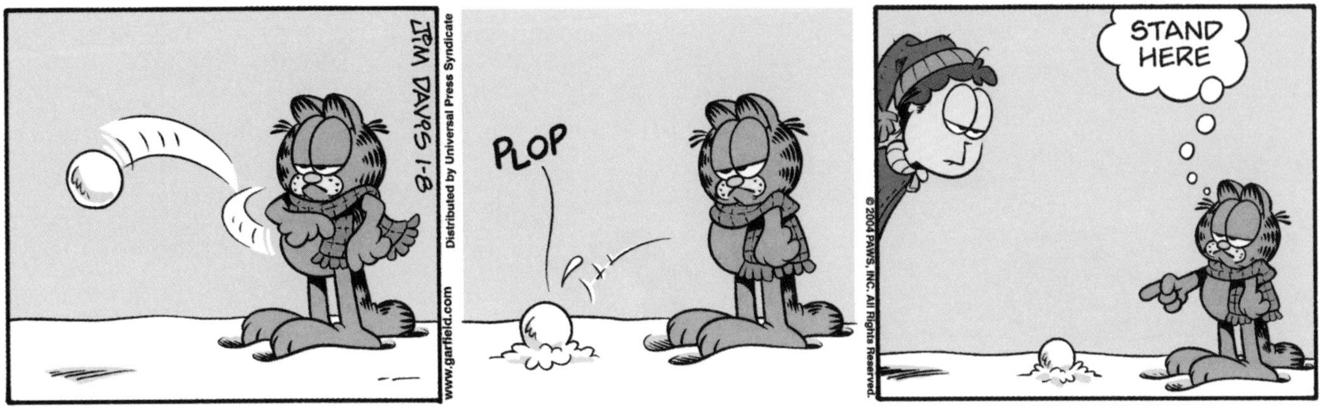
JPM DAVIS 1-8
Distributed by Universal Press Syndicate
www.garfield.com
PLOP
© 2004 PAWS, INC. All Rights Reserved.
STAND HERE

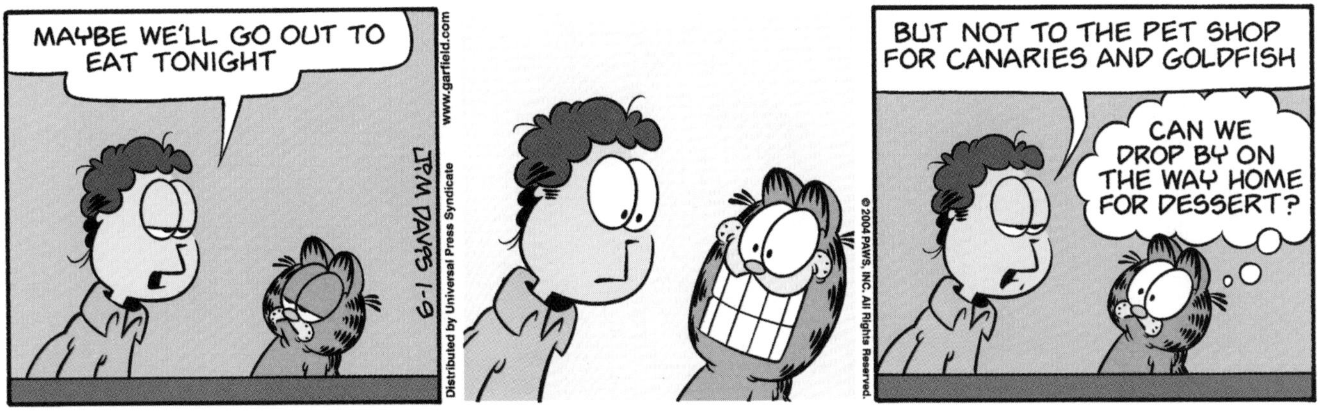
MAYBE WE'LL GO OUT TO EAT TONIGHT
JPM DAVIS 1-9
Distributed by Universal Press Syndicate
www.garfield.com
© 2004 PAWS, INC. All Rights Reserved.
BUT NOT TO THE PET SHOP FOR CANARIES AND GOLDFISH
CAN WE DROP BY ON THE WAY HOME FOR DESSERT?

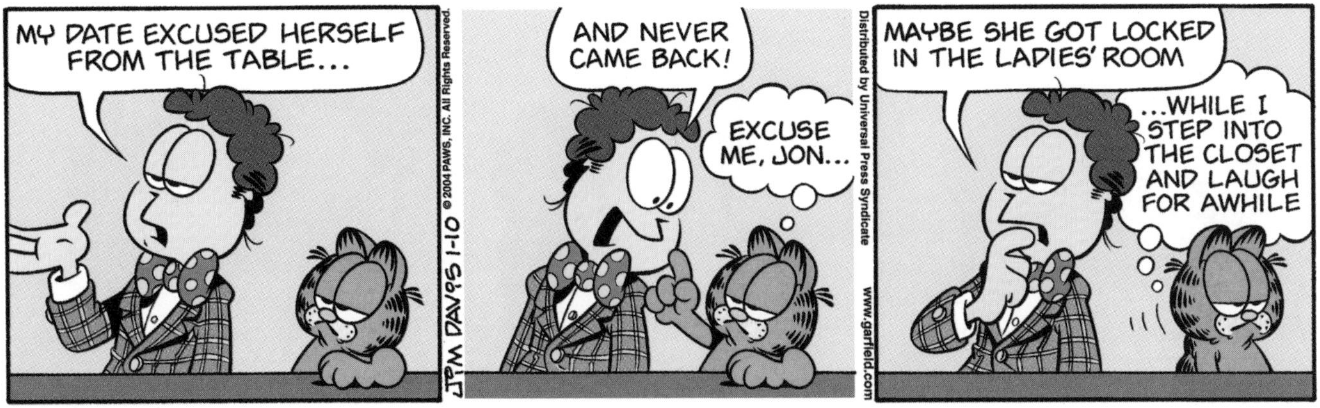
MY DATE EXCUSED HERSELF FROM THE TABLE...
© 2004 PAWS, INC. All Rights Reserved.
JPM DAVIS 1-10
AND NEVER CAME BACK!
EXCUSE ME, JON...
Distributed by Universal Press Syndicate
www.garfield.com
MAYBE SHE GOT LOCKED IN THE LADIES' ROOM
...WHILE I STEP INTO THE CLOSET AND LAUGH FOR AWHILE

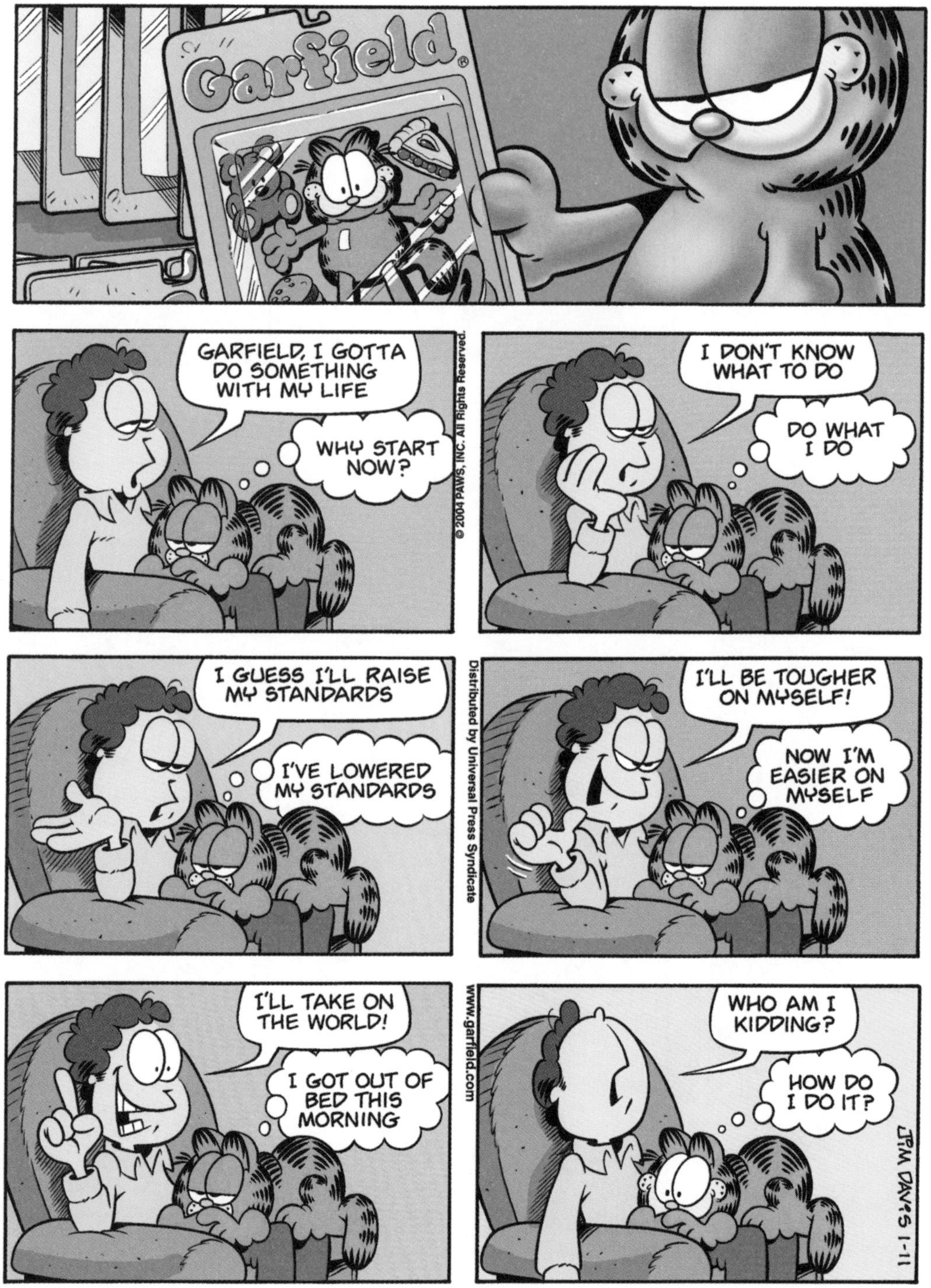
Garfield®
GARFIELD, I GOTTA DO SOMETHING WITH MY LIFE
WHY START NOW?
I DON'T KNOW WHAT TO DO
DO WHAT I DO
I GUESS I'LL RAISE MY STANDARDS
I'VE LOWERED MY STANDARDS
I'LL BE TOUGHER ON MYSELF!
NOW I'M EASIER ON MYSELF
I'LL TAKE ON THE WORLD!
I GOT OUT OF BED THIS MORNING
WHO AM I KIDDING?
HOW DO I DO IT?
JIM DAVIS 1-11
© 2004 PAWS, INC. All Rights Reserved.
Distributed by Universal Press Syndicate
www.garfield.com

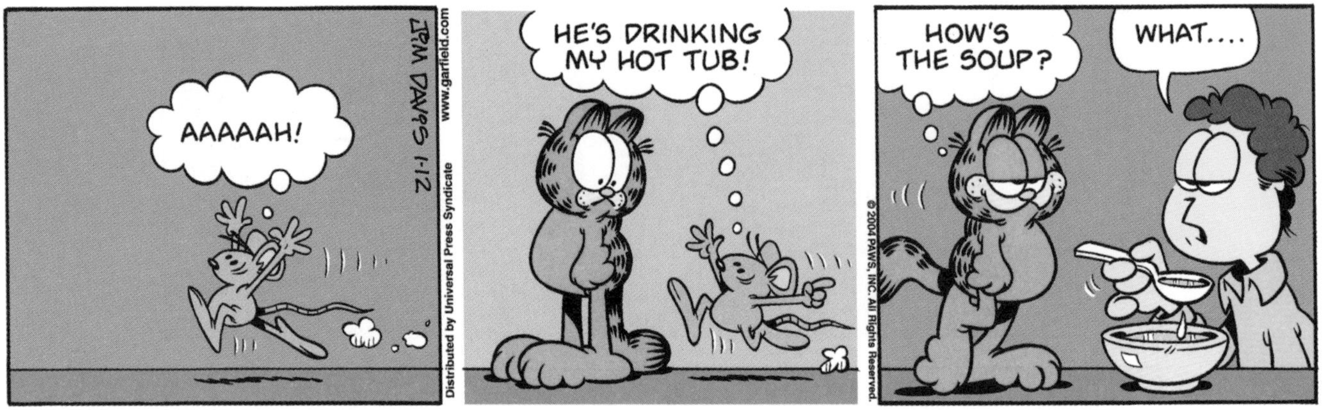
AAAAAH!
JIM DAVIS 1-12
www.garfield.com
Distributed by Universal Press Syndicate
HE'S DRINKING MY HOT TUB!
© 2004 PAWS, INC. All Rights Reserved.
HOW'S THE SOUP?
WHAT....

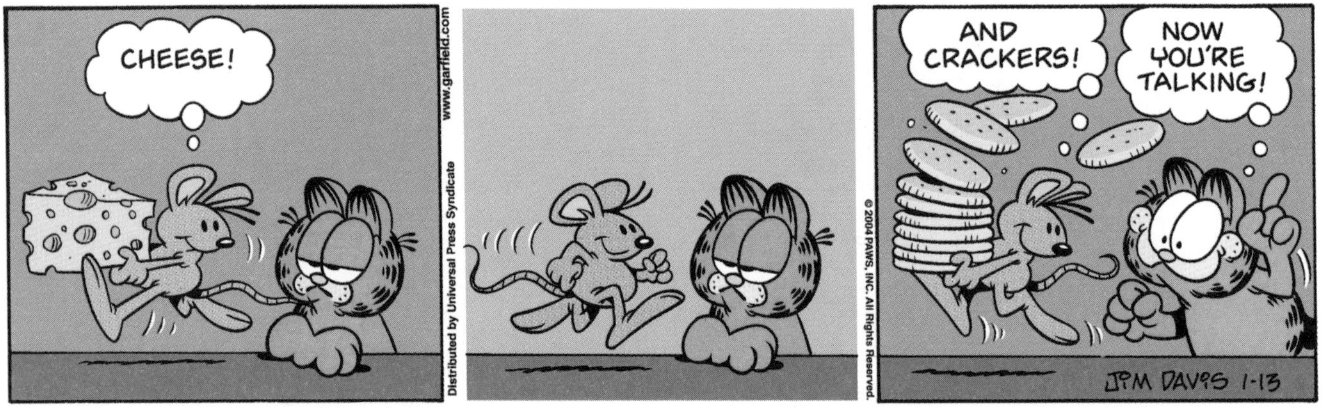
CHEESE!
www.garfield.com
Distributed by Universal Press Syndicate
© 2004 PAWS, INC. All Rights Reserved.
AND CRACKERS!
NOW YOU'RE TALKING!
JIM DAVIS 1-13

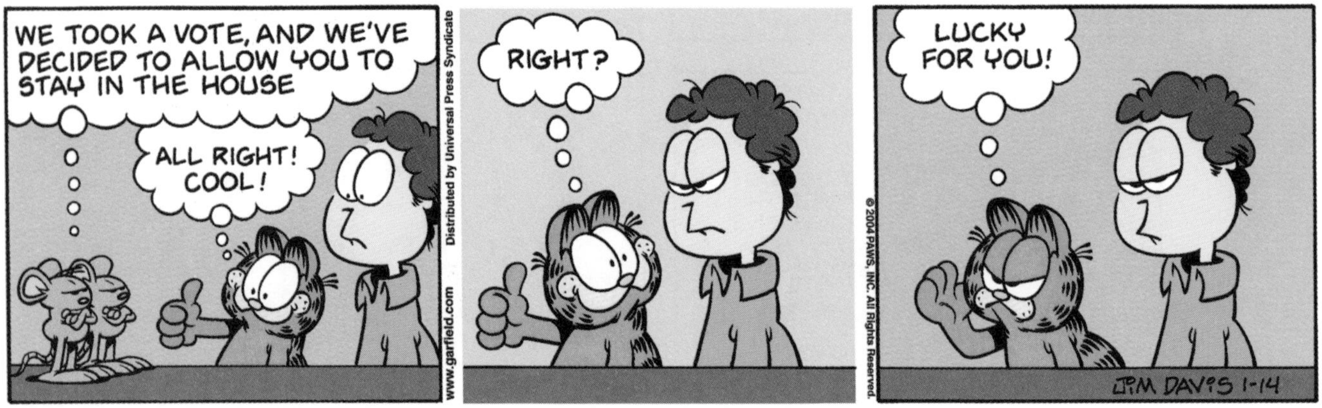
WE TOOK A VOTE, AND WE'VE DECIDED TO ALLOW YOU TO STAY IN THE HOUSE
ALL RIGHT! COOL!
Distributed by Universal Press Syndicate
www.garfield.com
RIGHT?
© 2004 PAWS, INC. All Rights Reserved.
LUCKY FOR YOU!
JIM DAVIS 1-14

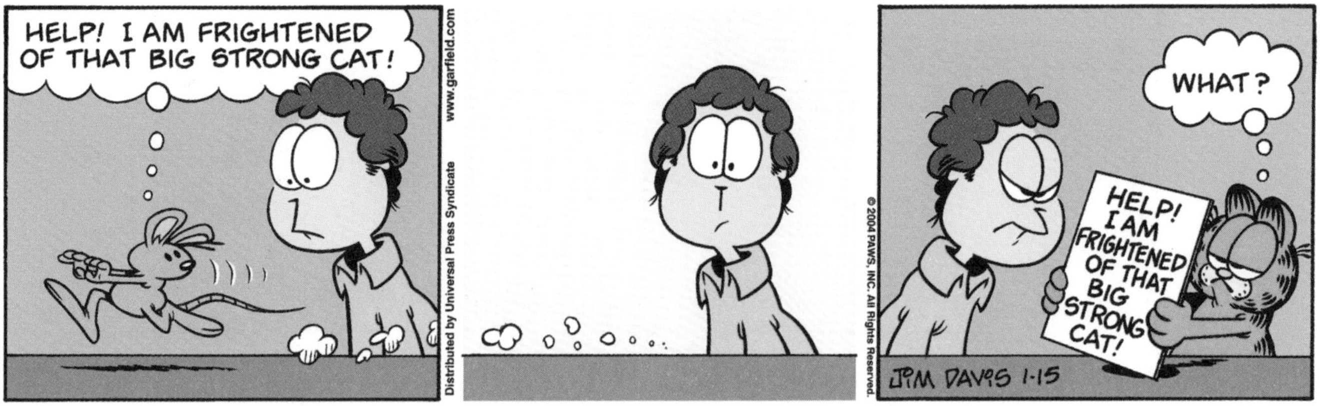
HELP! I AM FRIGHTENED OF THAT BIG STRONG CAT!
www.garfield.com
Distributed by Universal Press Syndicate
© 2004 PAWS, INC. All Rights Reserved.
WHAT?
HELP! I AM FRIGHTENED OF THAT BIG STRONG CAT!
JIM DAVIS 1-15

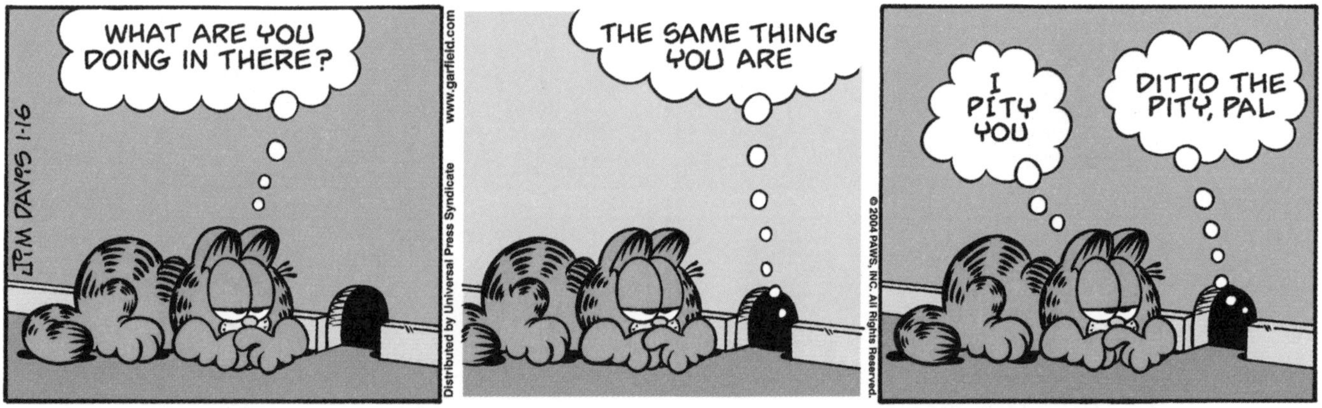
WHAT ARE YOU DOING IN THERE?
JIM DAVIS 1-16
www.garfield.com
Distributed by Universal Press Syndicate
THE SAME THING YOU ARE
© 2004 PAWS, INC. All Rights Reserved.
I PITY YOU
DITTO THE PITY, PAL

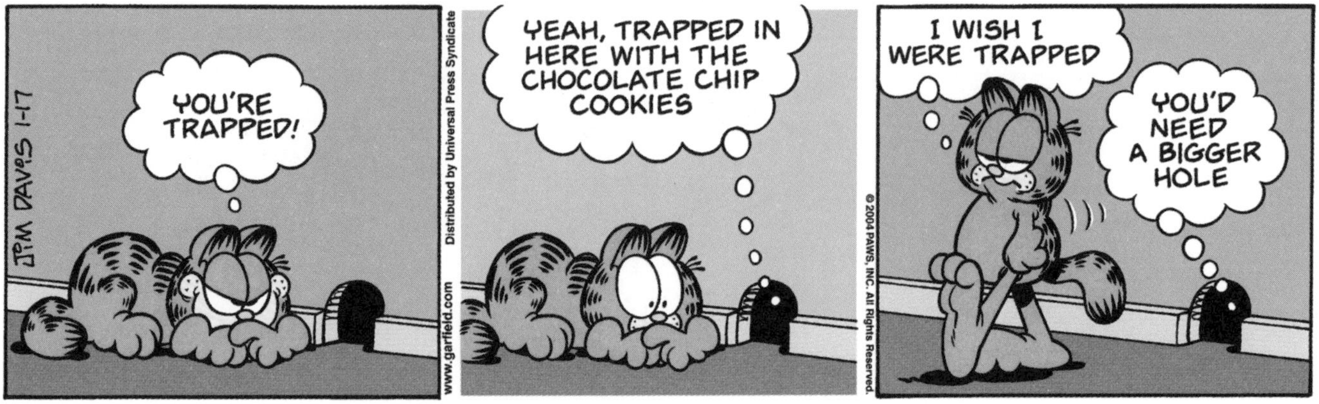
JIM DAVIS 1-17
YOU'RE TRAPPED!
Distributed by Universal Press Syndicate
www.garfield.com
YEAH, TRAPPED IN HERE WITH THE CHOCOLATE CHIP COOKIES
© 2004 PAWS, INC. All Rights Reserved.
I WISH I WERE TRAPPED
YOU'D NEED A BIGGER HOLE

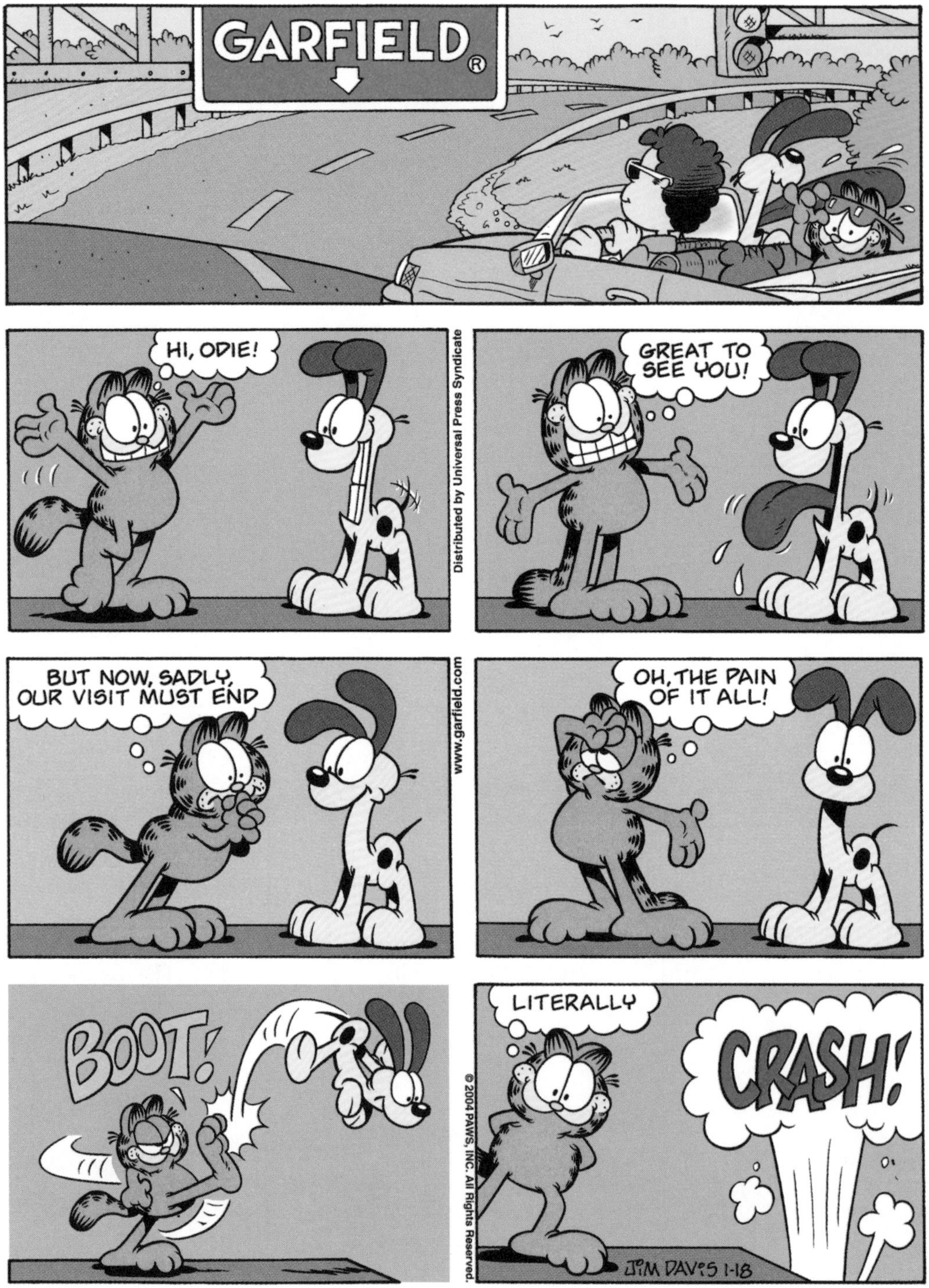
GARFIELD®
HI, ODIE!
GREAT TO SEE YOU!
BUT NOW, SADLY, OUR VISIT MUST END
OH, THE PAIN OF IT ALL!
BOOT!
LITERALLY
CRASH!
JIM DAVIS 1-18
Distributed by Universal Press Syndicate
www.garfield.com

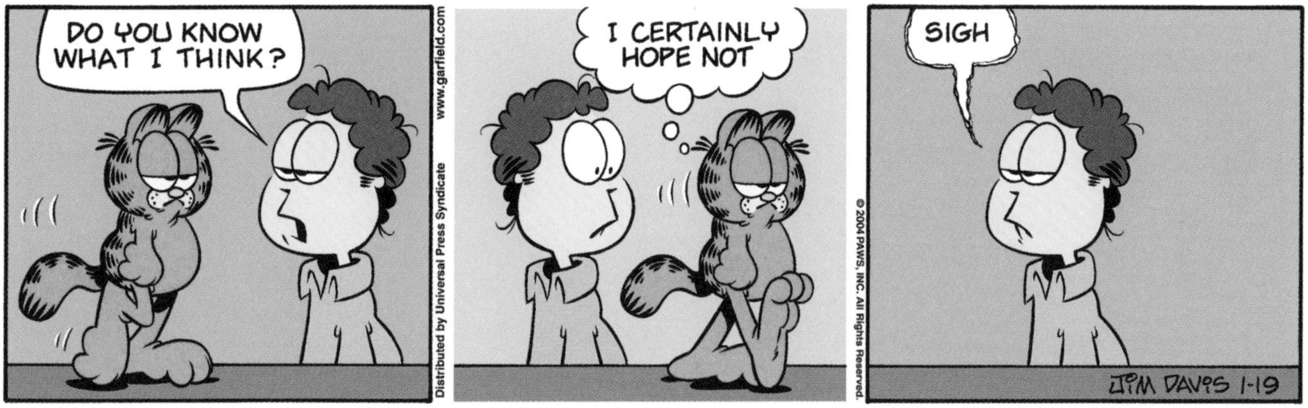
DO YOU KNOW WHAT I THINK?
I CERTAINLY HOPE NOT
SIGH
JIM DAVIS 1-19
www.garfield.com Distributed by Universal Press Syndicate
© 2004 PAWS, INC. All Rights Reserved.

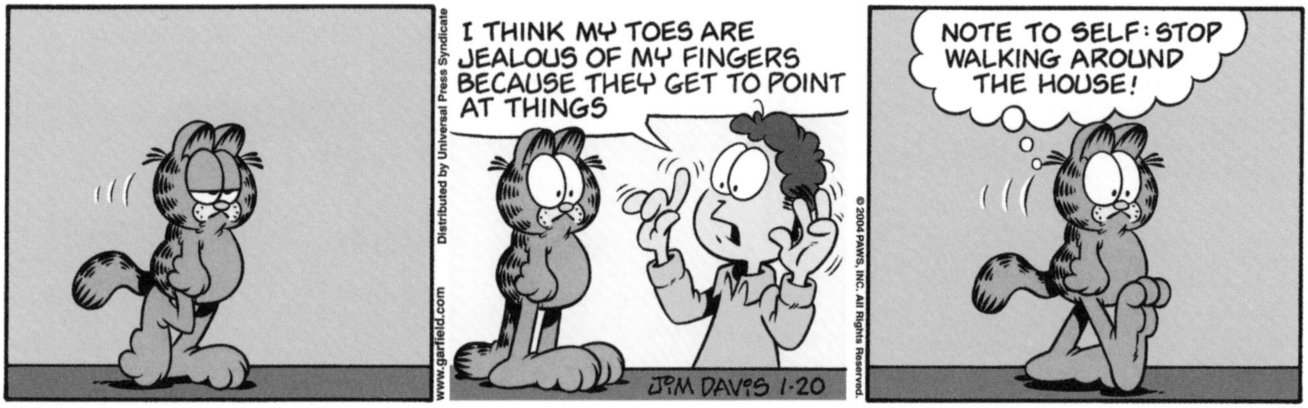
I THINK MY TOES ARE JEALOUS OF MY FINGERS BECAUSE THEY GET TO POINT AT THINGS
NOTE TO SELF: STOP WALKING AROUND THE HOUSE!
JIM DAVIS 1-20
www.garfield.com Distributed by Universal Press Syndicate
© 2004 PAWS, INC. All Rights Reserved.

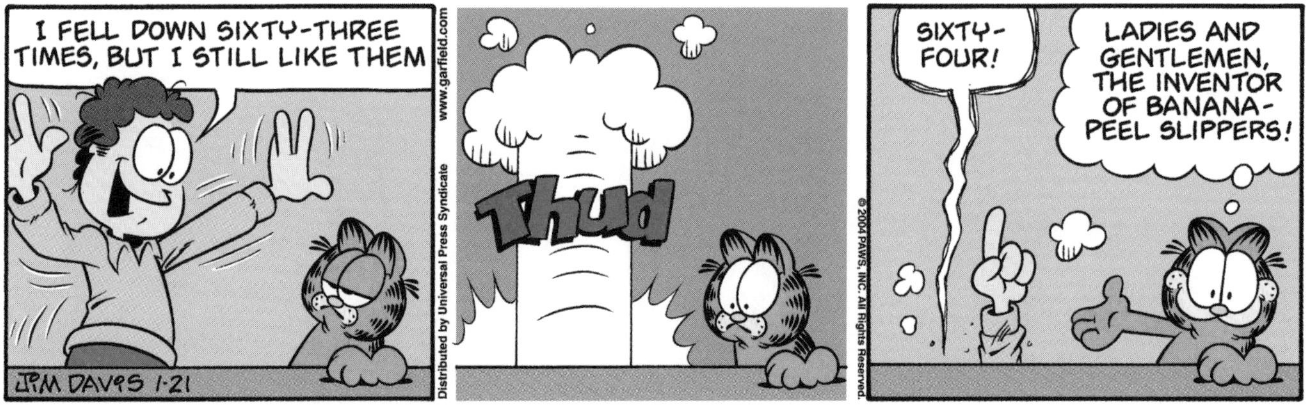
I FELL DOWN SIXTY-THREE TIMES, BUT I STILL LIKE THEM
Thud
SIXTY-FOUR!
LADIES AND GENTLEMEN, THE INVENTOR OF BANANA-PEEL SLIPPERS!
JIM DAVIS 1-21
www.garfield.com Distributed by Universal Press Syndicate
© 2004 PAWS, INC. All Rights Reserved.

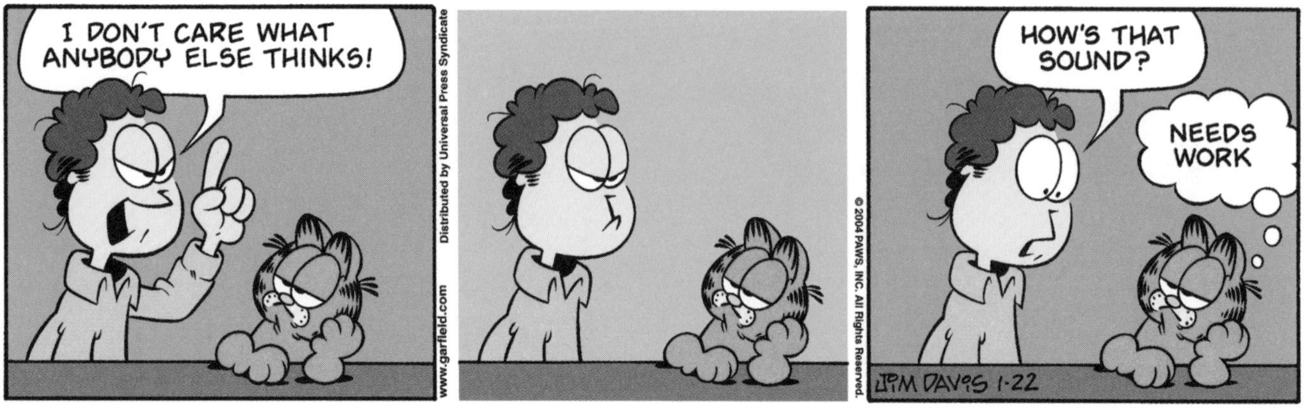
I DON'T CARE WHAT ANYBODY ELSE THINKS!
HOW'S THAT SOUND?
NEEDS WORK
JIM DAVIS 1-22
www.garfield.com Distributed by Universal Press Syndicate
© 2004 PAWS, INC. All Rights Reserved.

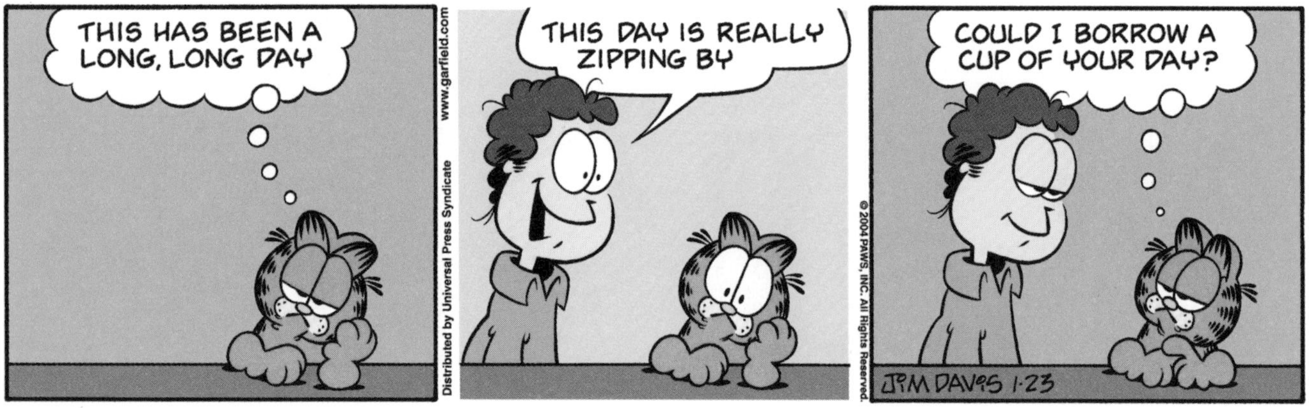
THIS HAS BEEN A LONG, LONG DAY
THIS DAY IS REALLY ZIPPING BY
COULD I BORROW A CUP OF YOUR DAY?
JIM DAVIS 1-23
Distributed by Universal Press Syndicate www.garfield.com
© 2004 PAWS, INC. All Rights Reserved.

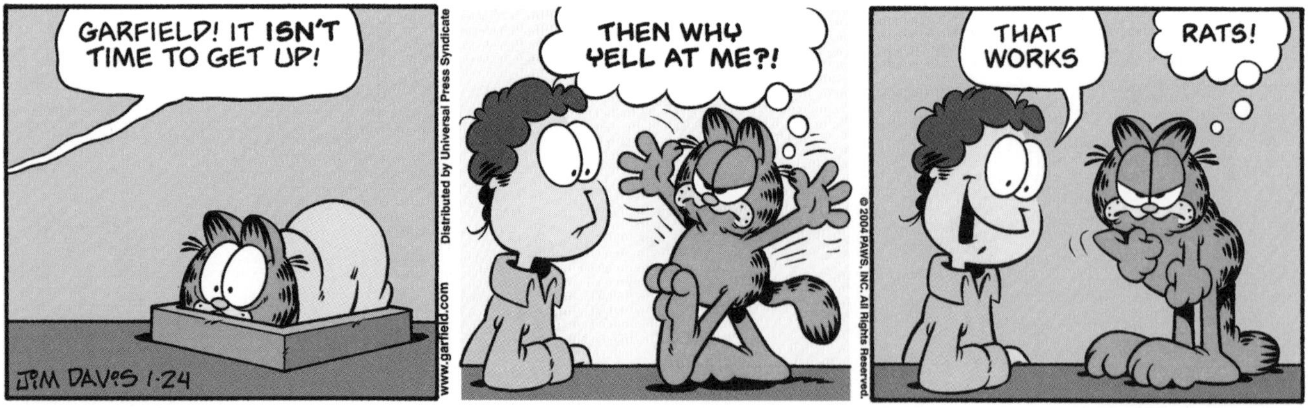
GARFIELD! IT ISN'T TIME TO GET UP!
THEN WHY YELL AT ME?!
THAT WORKS
RATS!
JIM DAVIS 1-24
www.garfield.com Distributed by Universal Press Syndicate
© 2004 PAWS, INC. All Rights Reserved.

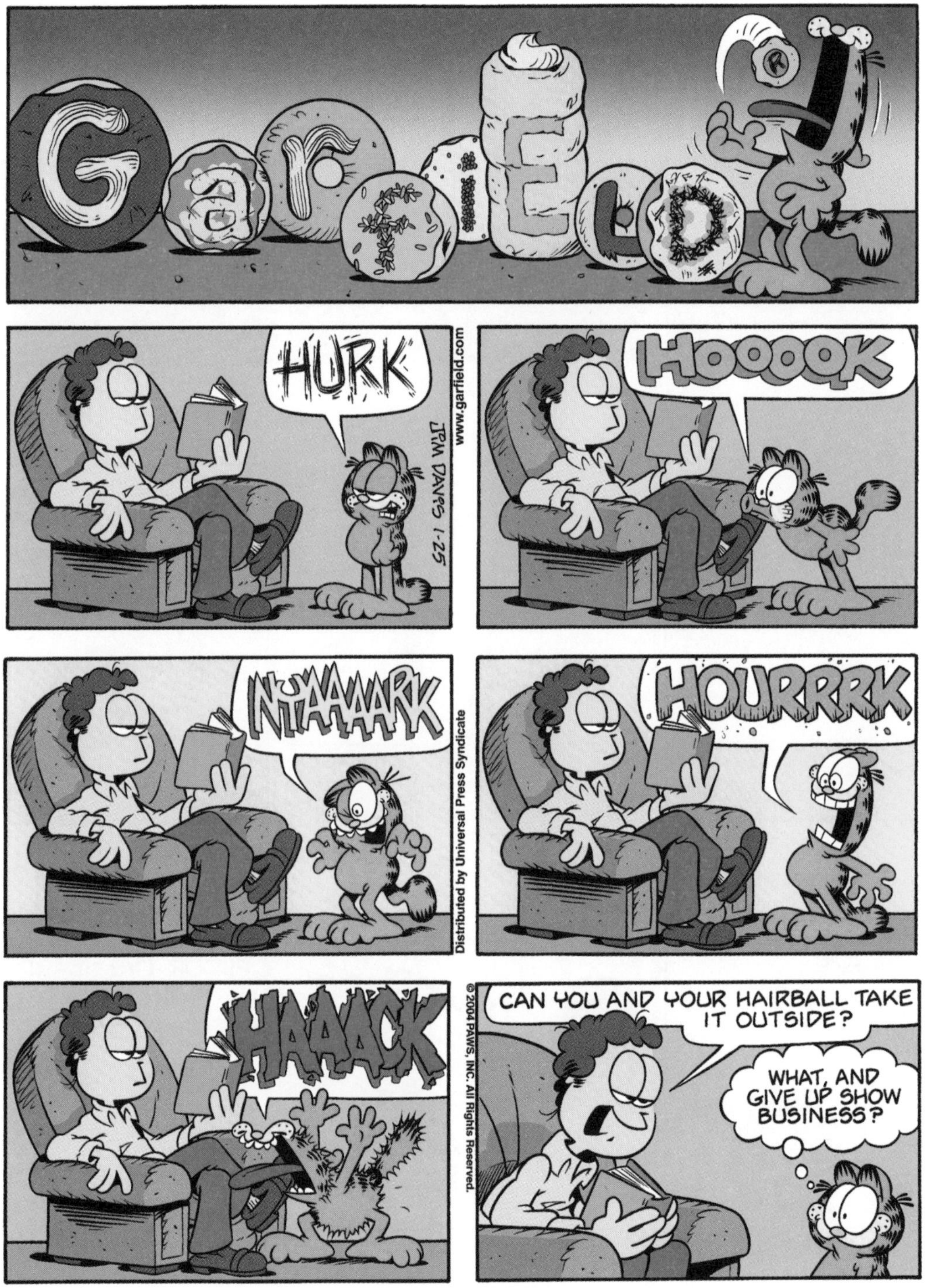

Garfield
HURK
JIM DAVIS 1-25
www.garfield.com
HOOOOK
NIAAAARK
Distributed by Universal Press Syndicate
HOURRRK
HAAACK
© 2004 PAWS, INC. All Rights Reserved.
CAN YOU AND YOUR HAIRBALL TAKE IT OUTSIDE?
WHAT, AND GIVE UP SHOW BUSINESS?

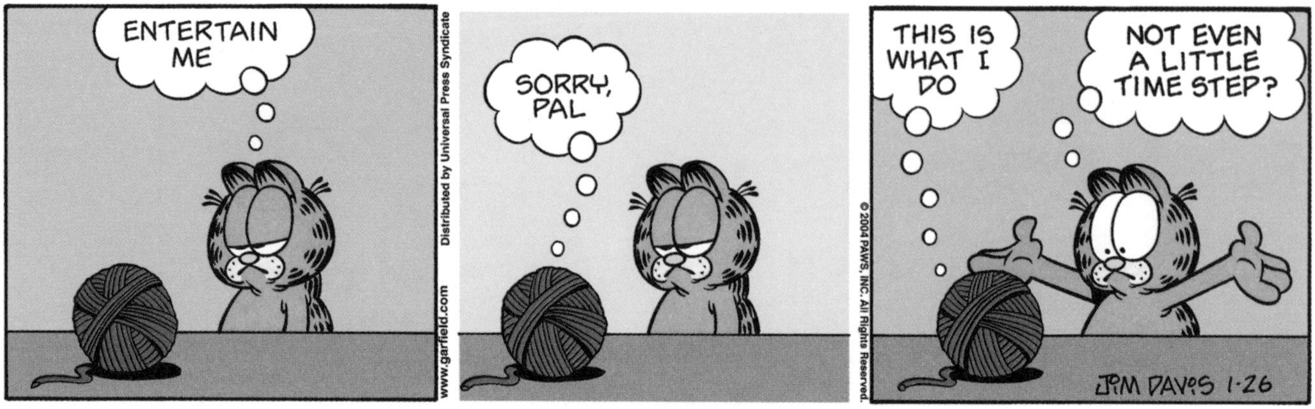
ENTERTAIN ME
SORRY, PAL
THIS IS WHAT I DO
NOT EVEN A LITTLE TIME STEP?
JIM DAVIS 1-26
www.garfield.com Distributed by Universal Press Syndicate
© 2004 PAWS, INC. All Rights Reserved.

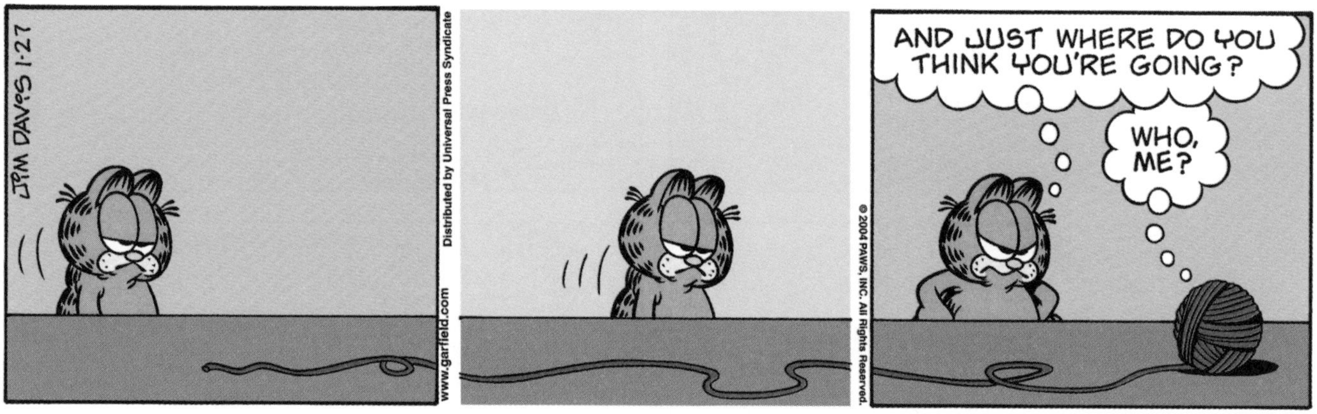
JIM DAVIS 1-27
AND JUST WHERE DO YOU THINK YOU'RE GOING?
WHO, ME?
www.garfield.com Distributed by Universal Press Syndicate
© 2004 PAWS, INC. All Rights Reserved.

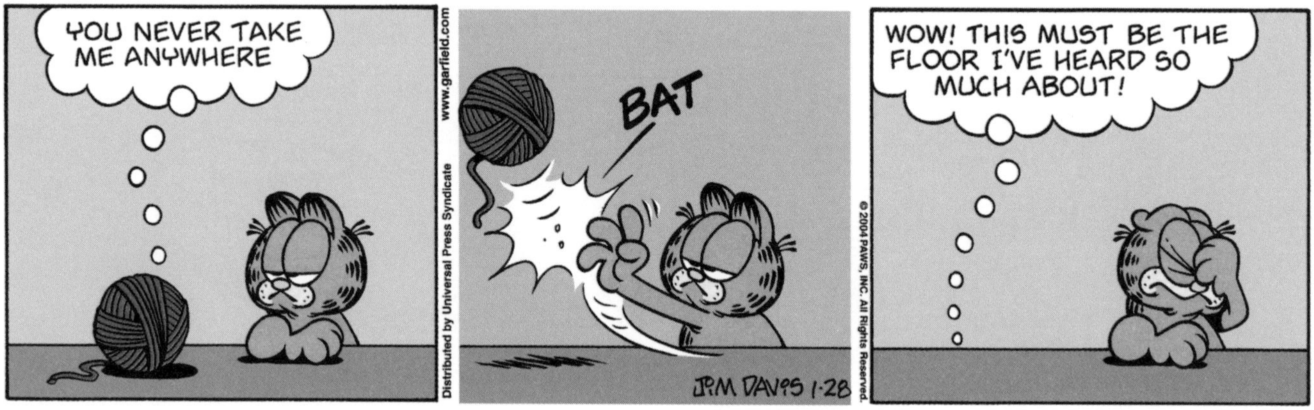
YOU NEVER TAKE ME ANYWHERE
BAT
JIM DAVIS 1-28
WOW! THIS MUST BE THE FLOOR I'VE HEARD SO MUCH ABOUT!
Distributed by Universal Press Syndicate www.garfield.com
© 2004 PAWS, INC. All Rights Reserved.

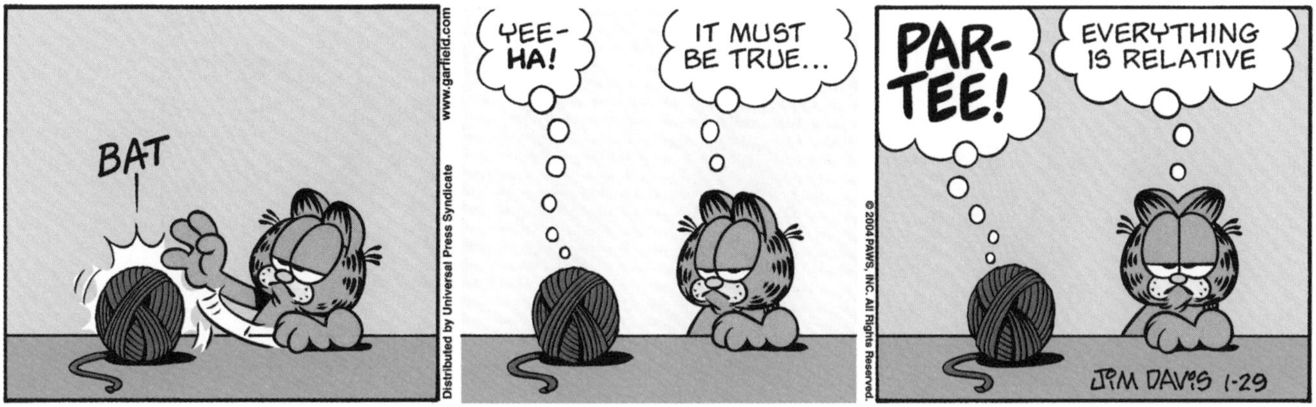
BAT
YEE-HA!
IT MUST BE TRUE...
PAR-TEE!
EVERYTHING IS RELATIVE
JIM DAVIS 1-29
www.garfield.com
Distributed by Universal Press Syndicate
© 2004 PAWS, INC. All Rights Reserved.

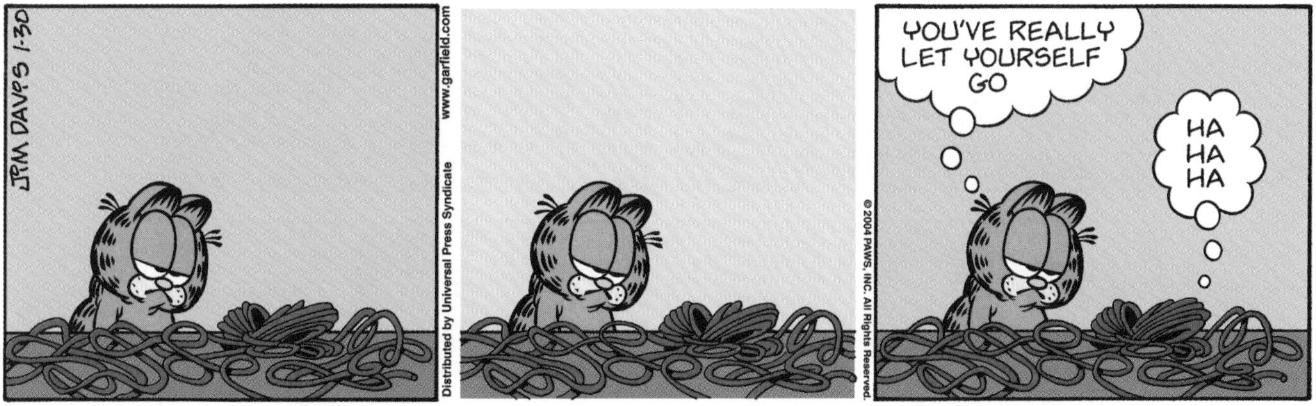
JIM DAVIS 1-30
www.garfield.com
Distributed by Universal Press Syndicate
YOU'VE REALLY LET YOURSELF GO
HA HA HA
© 2004 PAWS, INC. All Rights Reserved.

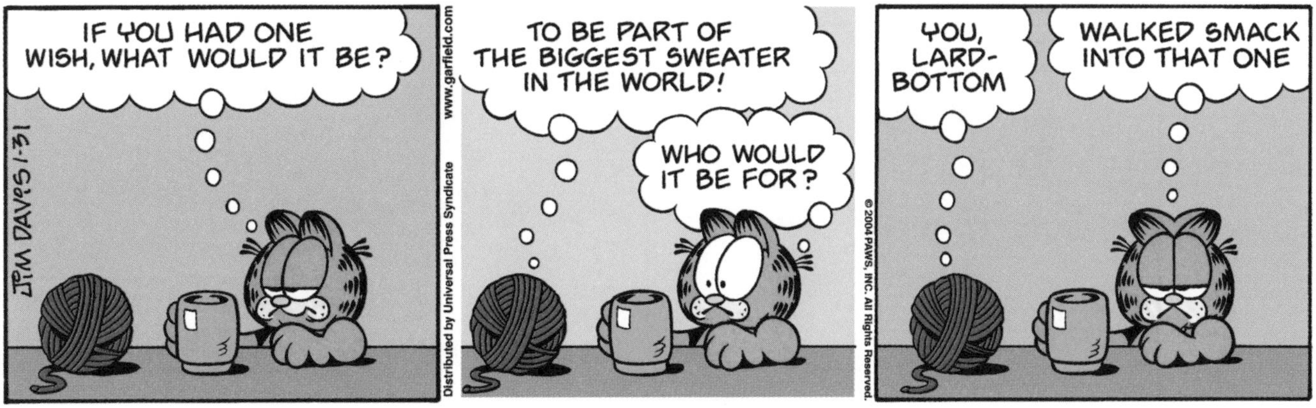
IF YOU HAD ONE WISH, WHAT WOULD IT BE?
JIM DAVIS 1-31
www.garfield.com
Distributed by Universal Press Syndicate
TO BE PART OF THE BIGGEST SWEATER IN THE WORLD!
WHO WOULD IT BE FOR?
YOU, LARD-BOTTOM
WALKED SMACK INTO THAT ONE
© 2004 PAWS, INC. All Rights Reserved.

Garfield
Distributed by Universal Press Syndicate
www.garfield.com
JIM DAVIS 2-1
© 2004 PAWS, INC. All Rights Reserved.
I'M ON THE "I HAVE PETS" DIET

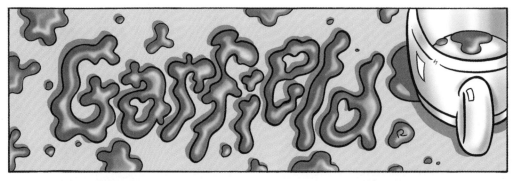

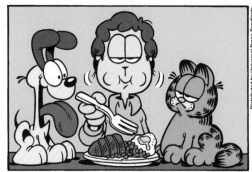

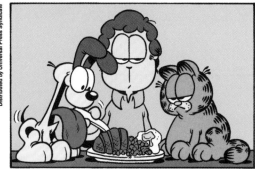

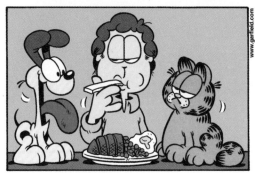

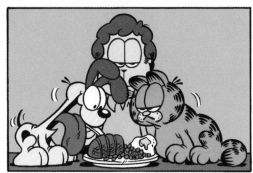

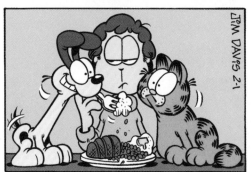

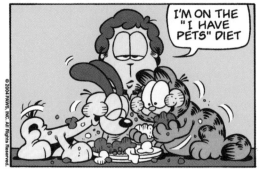

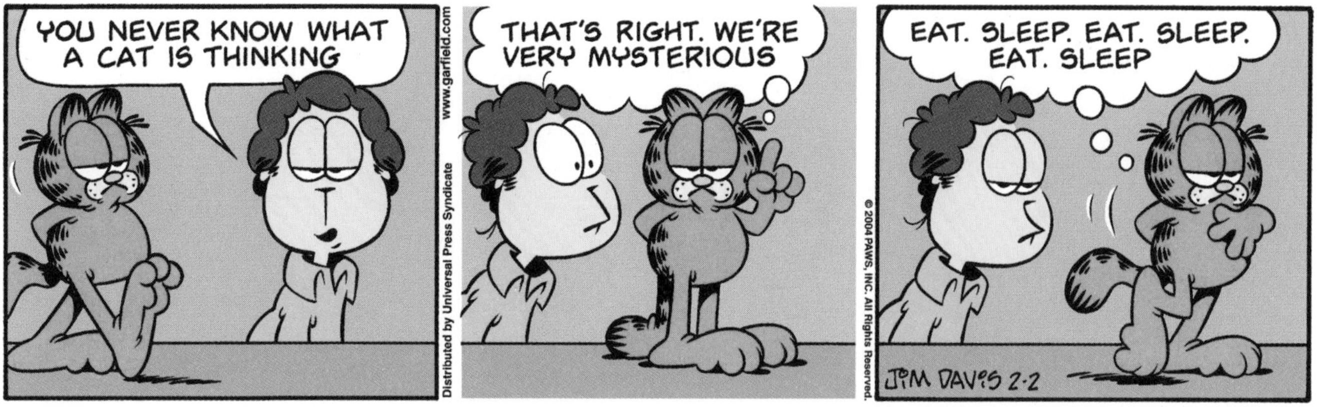
YOU NEVER KNOW WHAT A CAT IS THINKING
www.garfield.com
Distributed by Universal Press Syndicate
THAT'S RIGHT. WE'RE VERY MYSTERIOUS
© 2004 PAWS, INC. All Rights Reserved.
EAT. SLEEP. EAT. SLEEP. EAT. SLEEP
JIM DAVIS 2·2

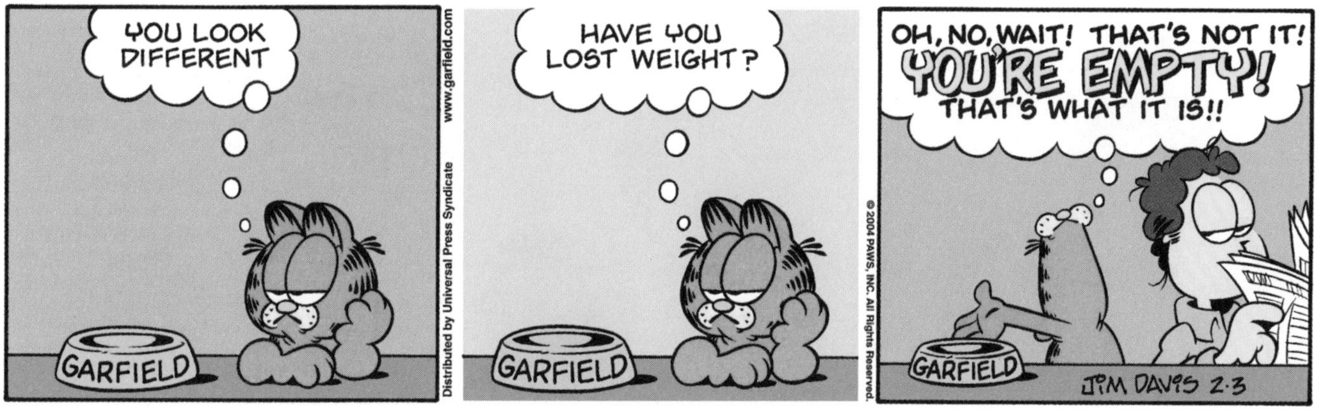
YOU LOOK DIFFERENT
GARFIELD
www.garfield.com
Distributed by Universal Press Syndicate
HAVE YOU LOST WEIGHT?
GARFIELD
© 2004 PAWS, INC. All Rights Reserved.
OH, NO, WAIT! THAT'S NOT IT! YOU'RE EMPTY! THAT'S WHAT IT IS!!
GARFIELD
JIM DAVIS 2·3

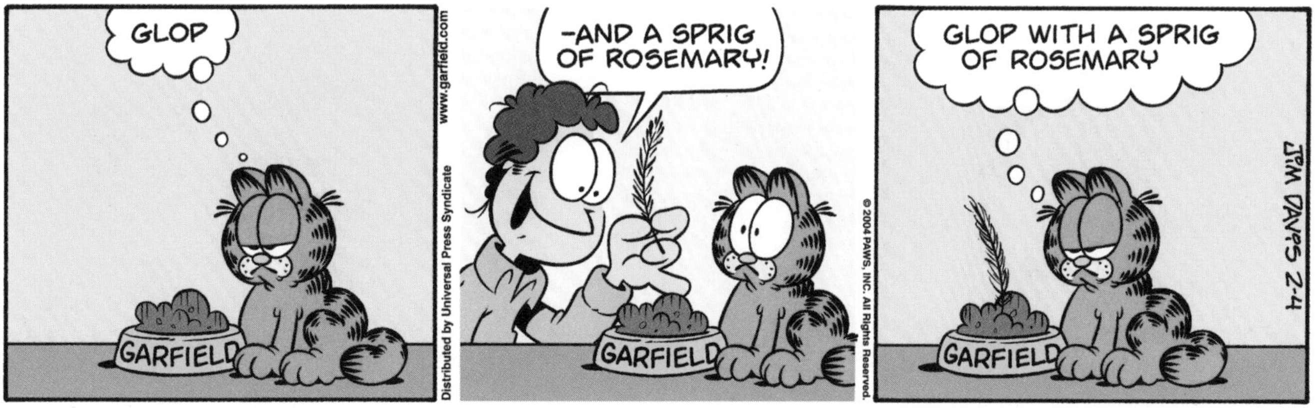
GLOP
GARFIELD
www.garfield.com
Distributed by Universal Press Syndicate
–AND A SPRIG OF ROSEMARY!
GARFIELD
© 2004 PAWS, INC. All Rights Reserved.
GLOP WITH A SPRIG OF ROSEMARY
GARFIELD
JIM DAVIS 2·4

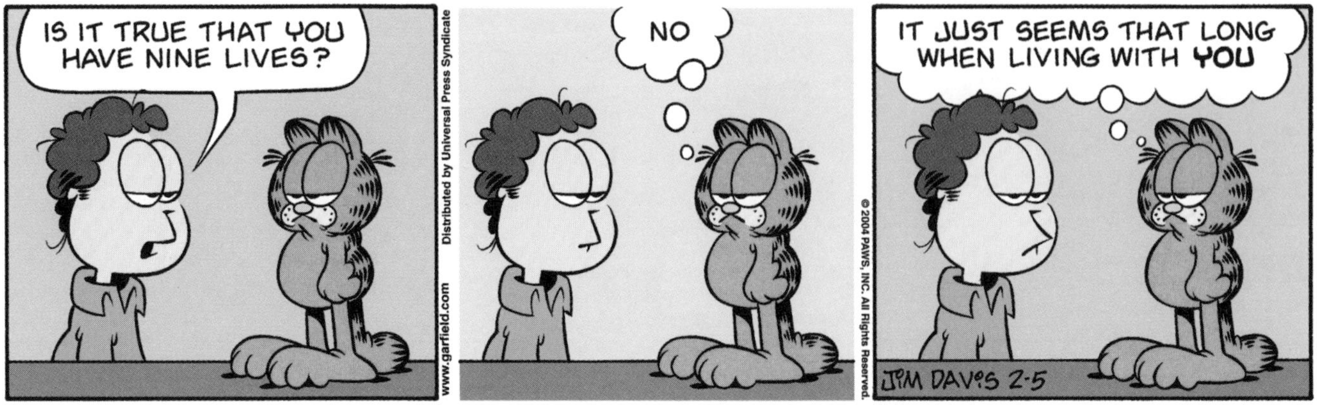
IS IT TRUE THAT YOU HAVE NINE LIVES?
NO
IT JUST SEEMS THAT LONG WHEN LIVING WITH **YOU**
JIM DAVIS 2-5
www.garfield.com Distributed by Universal Press Syndicate
© 2004 PAWS, INC. All Rights Reserved.

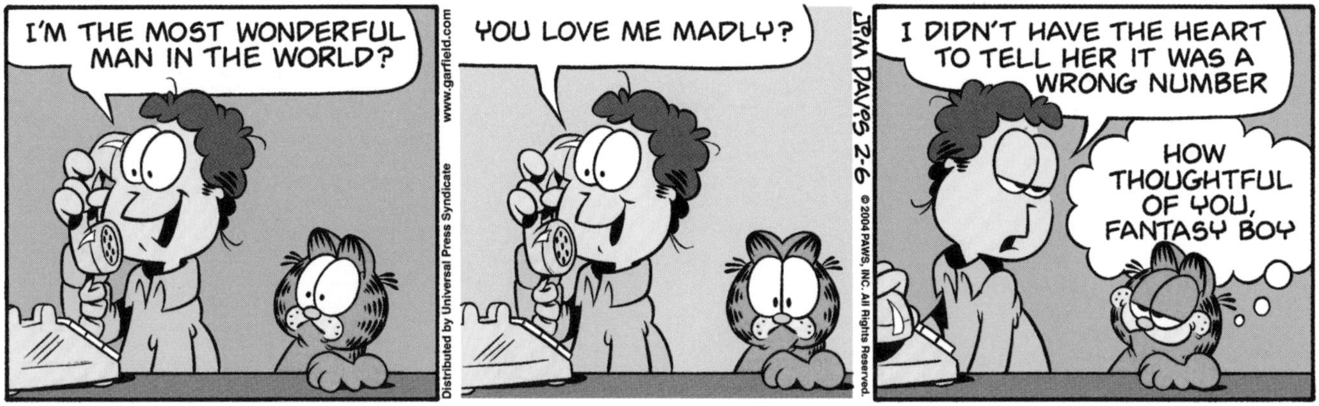
I'M THE MOST WONDERFUL MAN IN THE WORLD?
YOU LOVE ME MADLY?
I DIDN'T HAVE THE HEART TO TELL HER IT WAS A WRONG NUMBER
HOW THOUGHTFUL OF YOU, FANTASY BOY
JIM DAVIS 2-6
Distributed by Universal Press Syndicate www.garfield.com
© 2004 PAWS, INC. All Rights Reserved.

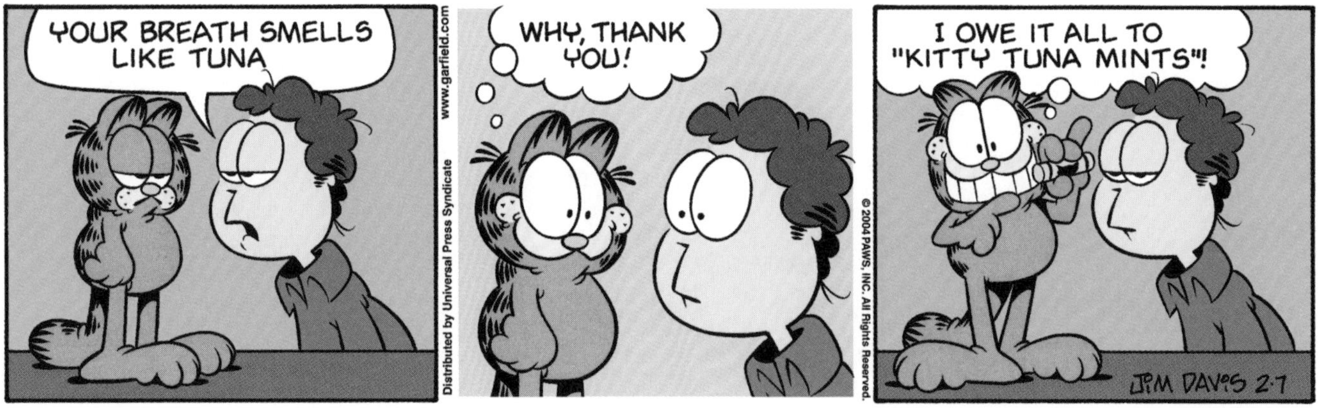
YOUR BREATH SMELLS LIKE TUNA
WHY, THANK YOU!
I OWE IT ALL TO "KITTY TUNA MINTS"!
JIM DAVIS 2-7
Distributed by Universal Press Syndicate www.garfield.com
© 2004 PAWS, INC. All Rights Reserved.

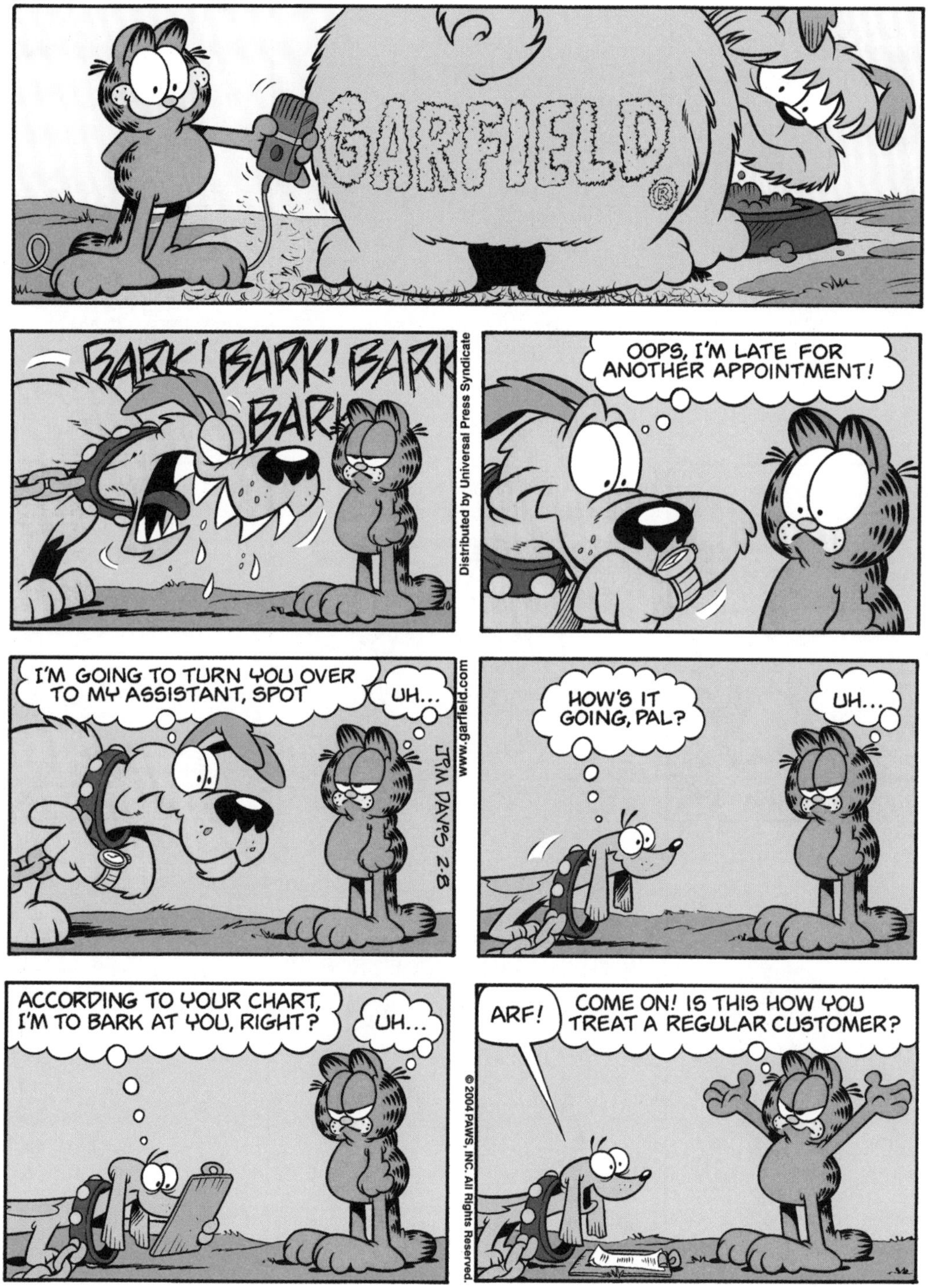
GARFIELD®
BARK! BARK! BARK
BARK
OOPS, I'M LATE FOR ANOTHER APPOINTMENT!
Distributed by Universal Press Syndicate
I'M GOING TO TURN YOU OVER TO MY ASSISTANT, SPOT
UH...
JIM DAVIS 2-8
www.garfield.com
HOW'S IT GOING, PAL?
UH...
ACCORDING TO YOUR CHART, I'M TO BARK AT YOU, RIGHT?
UH...
© 2004 PAWS, INC. All Rights Reserved.
ARF!
COME ON! IS THIS HOW YOU TREAT A REGULAR CUSTOMER?

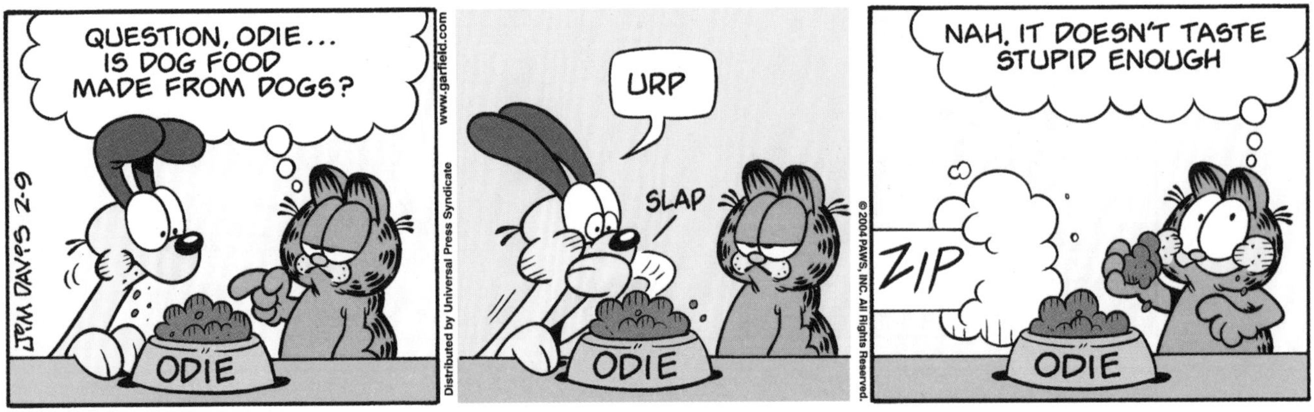
QUESTION, ODIE... IS DOG FOOD MADE FROM DOGS?
JIM DAVIS 2-9
ODIE
URP
SLAP
ODIE
NAH, IT DOESN'T TASTE STUPID ENOUGH
ZIP
ODIE
www.garfield.com
Distributed by Universal Press Syndicate
© 2004 PAWS, INC. All Rights Reserved.

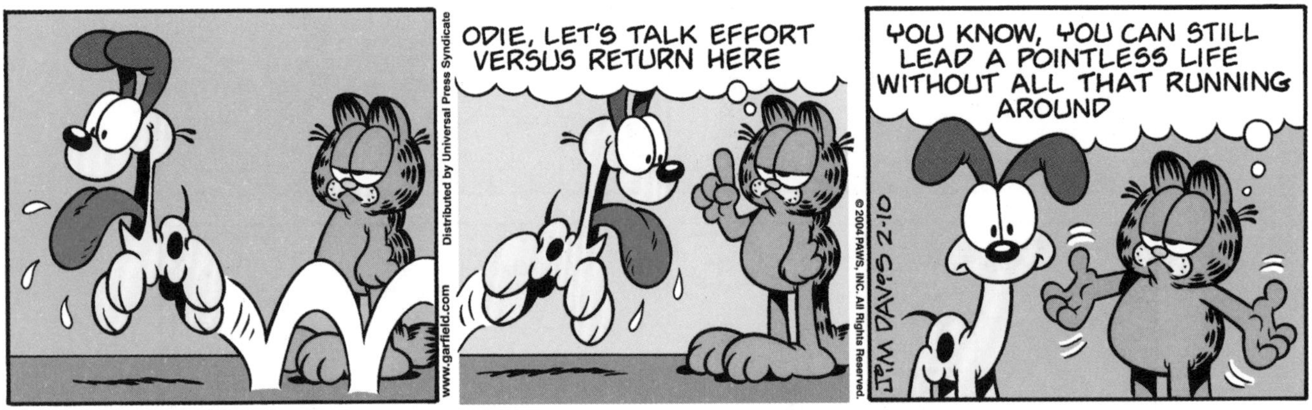
ODIE, LET'S TALK EFFORT VERSUS RETURN HERE
YOU KNOW, YOU CAN STILL LEAD A POINTLESS LIFE WITHOUT ALL THAT RUNNING AROUND
JIM DAVIS 2-10
www.garfield.com
Distributed by Universal Press Syndicate
© 2004 PAWS, INC. All Rights Reserved.

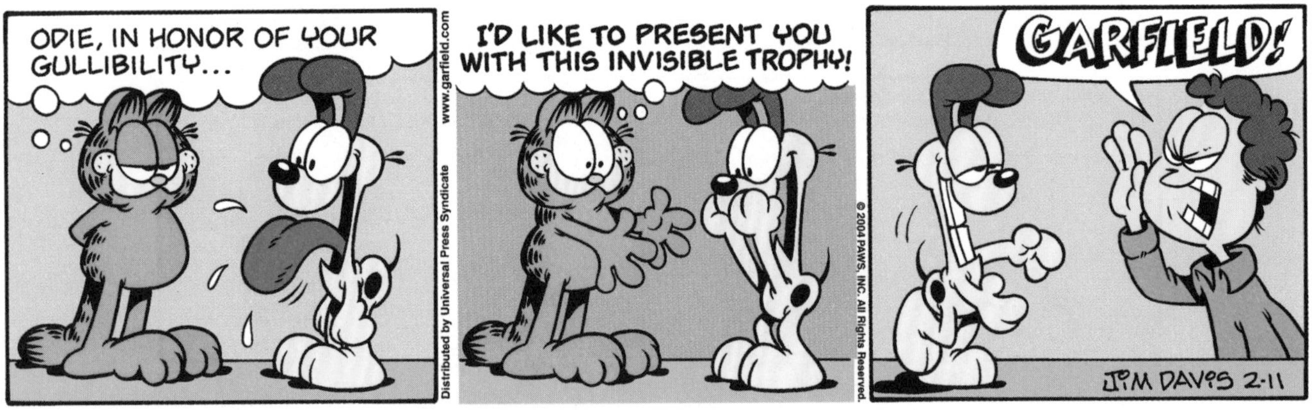
ODIE, IN HONOR OF YOUR GULLIBILITY...
I'D LIKE TO PRESENT YOU WITH THIS INVISIBLE TROPHY!
GARFIELD!
JIM DAVIS 2-11
www.garfield.com
Distributed by Universal Press Syndicate
© 2004 PAWS, INC. All Rights Reserved.

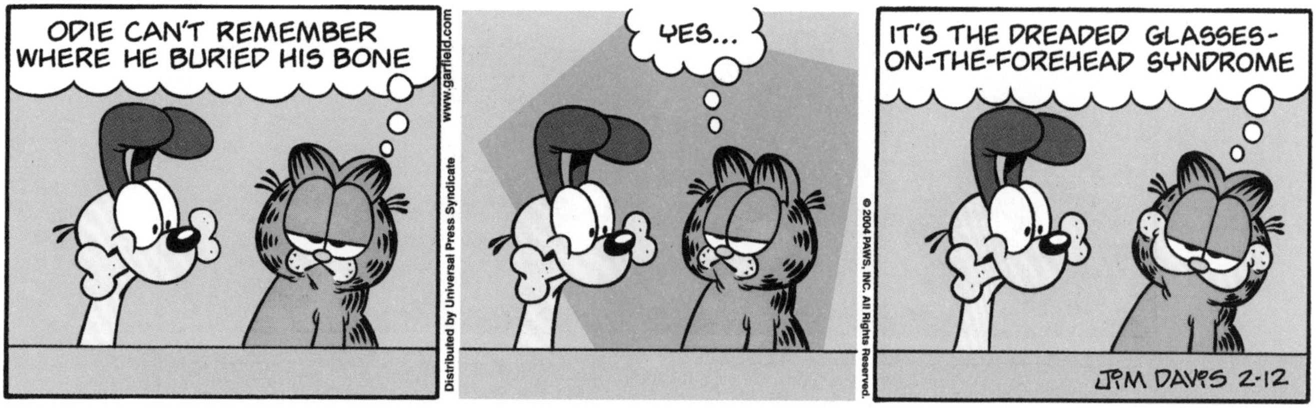
ODIE CAN'T REMEMBER WHERE HE BURIED HIS BONE
YES...
IT'S THE DREADED GLASSES-ON-THE-FOREHEAD SYNDROME
JIM DAVIS 2-12
www.garfield.com
Distributed by Universal Press Syndicate
© 2004 PAWS, INC. All Rights Reserved.

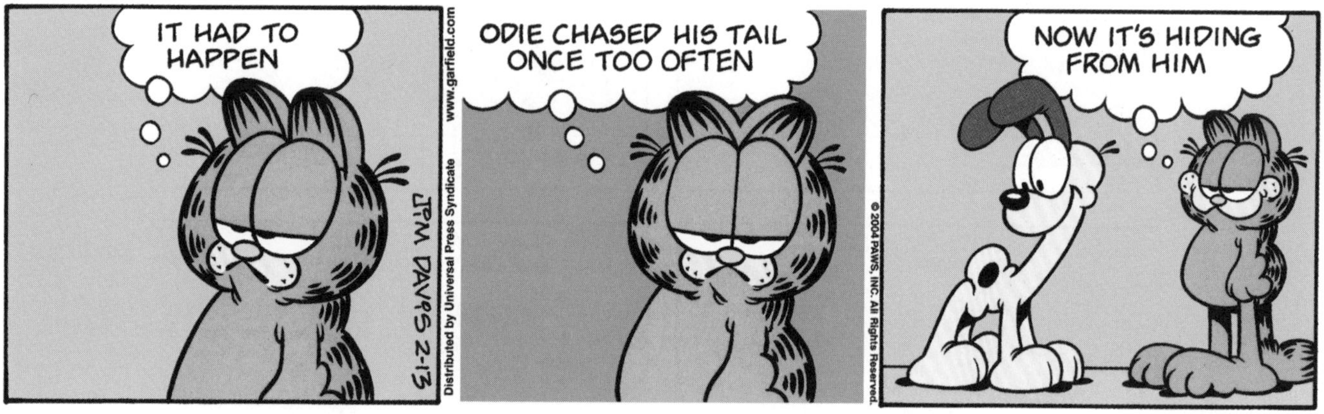
IT HAD TO HAPPEN
ODIE CHASED HIS TAIL ONCE TOO OFTEN
NOW IT'S HIDING FROM HIM
JIM DAVIS 2-13
www.garfield.com
Distributed by Universal Press Syndicate
© 2004 PAWS, INC. All Rights Reserved.

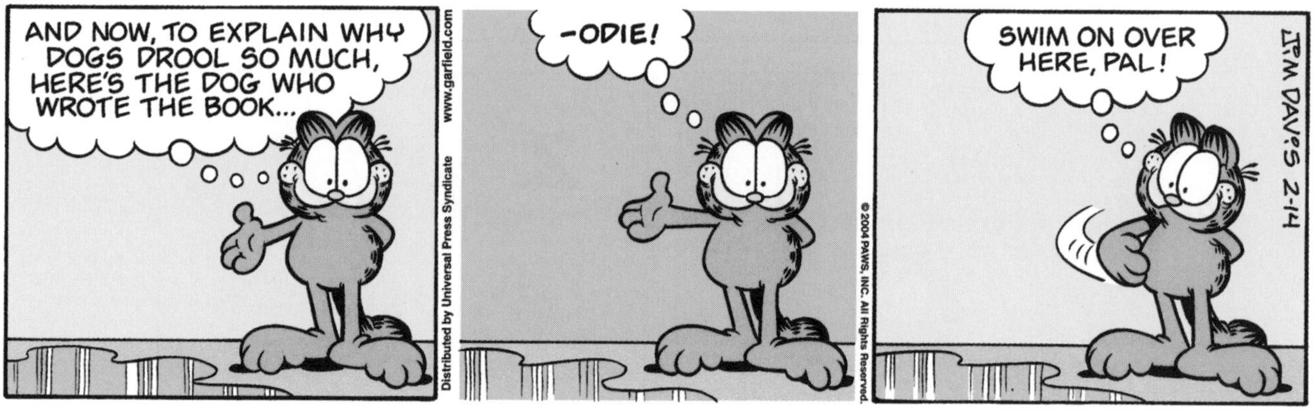
AND NOW, TO EXPLAIN WHY DOGS DROOL SO MUCH, HERE'S THE DOG WHO WROTE THE BOOK...
-ODIE!
SWIM ON OVER HERE, PAL!
JIM DAVIS 2-14
www.garfield.com
Distributed by Universal Press Syndicate
© 2004 PAWS, INC. All Rights Reserved.

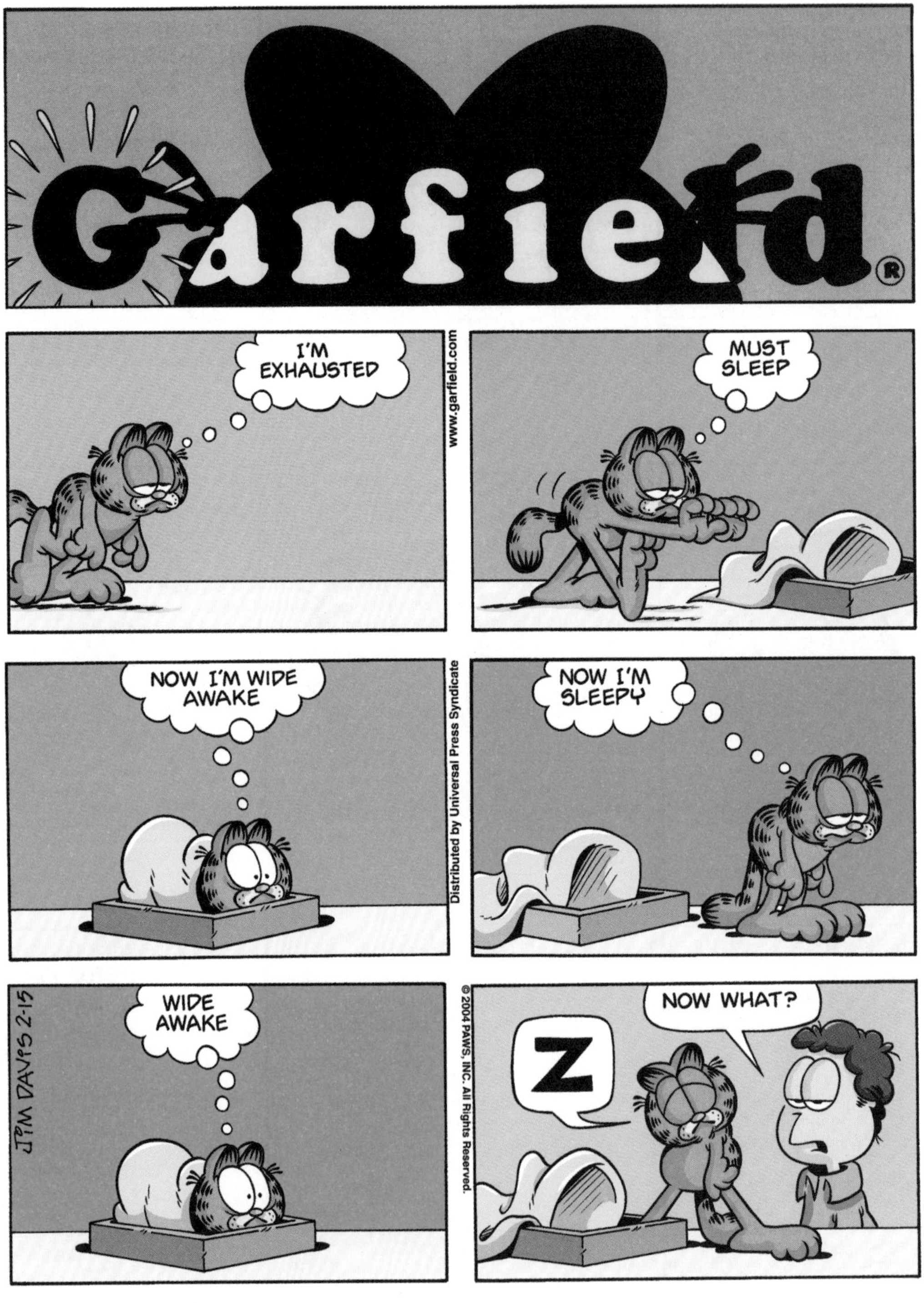

Garfield®
I'M EXHAUSTED
MUST SLEEP
NOW I'M WIDE AWAKE
NOW I'M SLEEPY
WIDE AWAKE
Z
NOW WHAT?
JIM DAVIS 2-15
www.garfield.com
Distributed by Universal Press Syndicate
© 2004 PAWS, INC. All Rights Reserved.

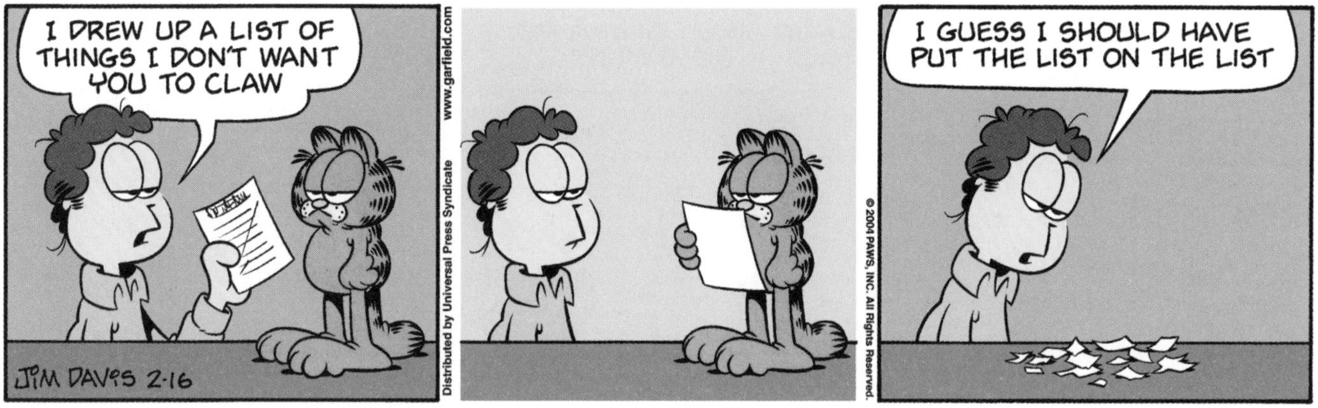
I DREW UP A LIST OF THINGS I DON'T WANT YOU TO CLAW
JIM DAVIS 2-16
Distributed by Universal Press Syndicate www.garfield.com
© 2004 PAWS, INC. All Rights Reserved.
I GUESS I SHOULD HAVE PUT THE LIST ON THE LIST

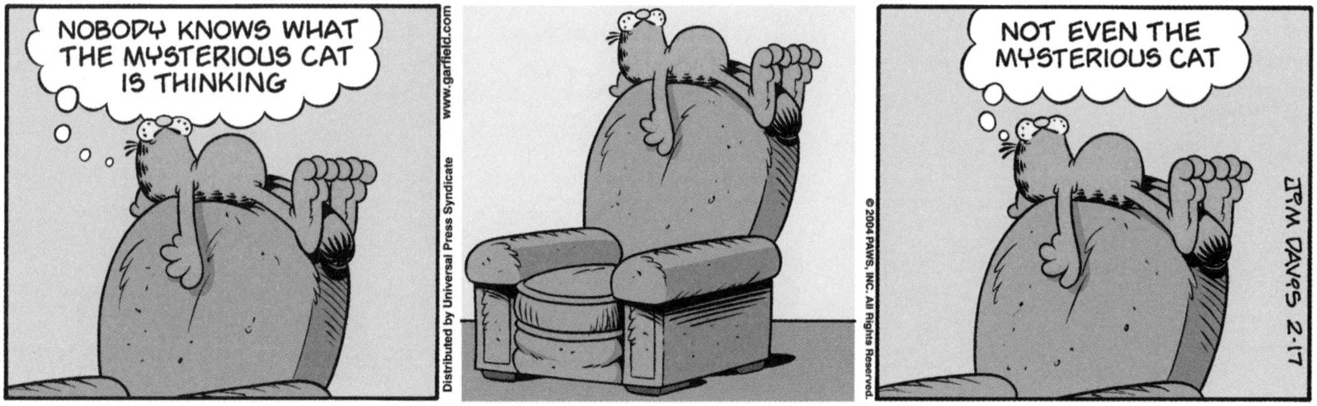
NOBODY KNOWS WHAT THE MYSTERIOUS CAT IS THINKING
Distributed by Universal Press Syndicate www.garfield.com
© 2004 PAWS, INC. All Rights Reserved.
NOT EVEN THE MYSTERIOUS CAT
JIM DAVIS 2-17

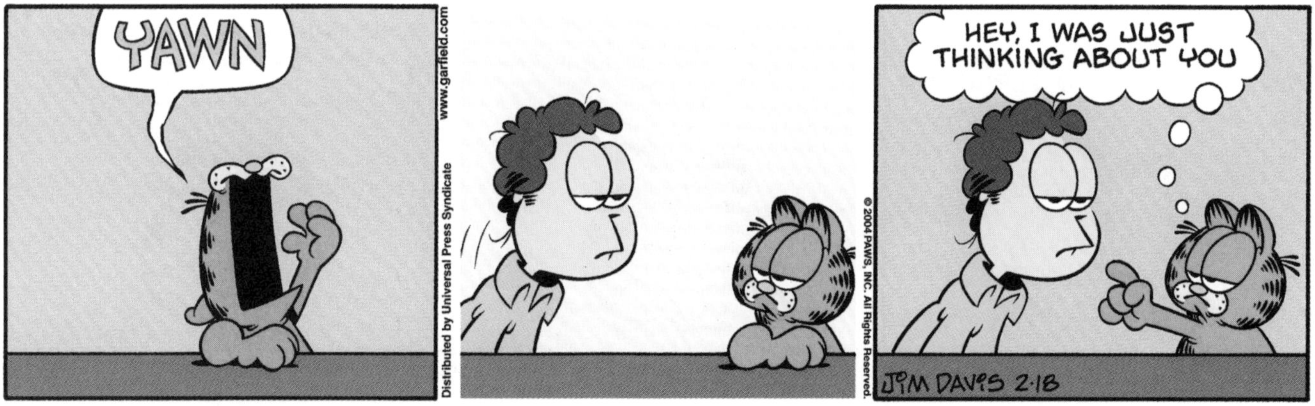
YAWN
Distributed by Universal Press Syndicate www.garfield.com
© 2004 PAWS, INC. All Rights Reserved.
HEY, I WAS JUST THINKING ABOUT YOU
JIM DAVIS 2-18

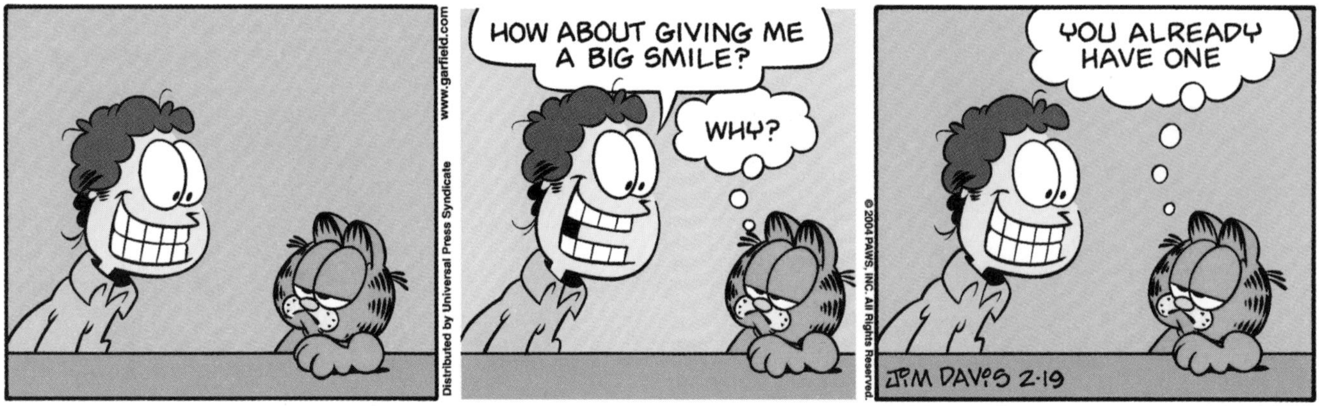
HOW ABOUT GIVING ME A BIG SMILE?
WHY?
YOU ALREADY HAVE ONE
www.garfield.com
Distributed by Universal Press Syndicate
© 2004 PAWS, INC. All Rights Reserved.
JIM DAVIS 2-19

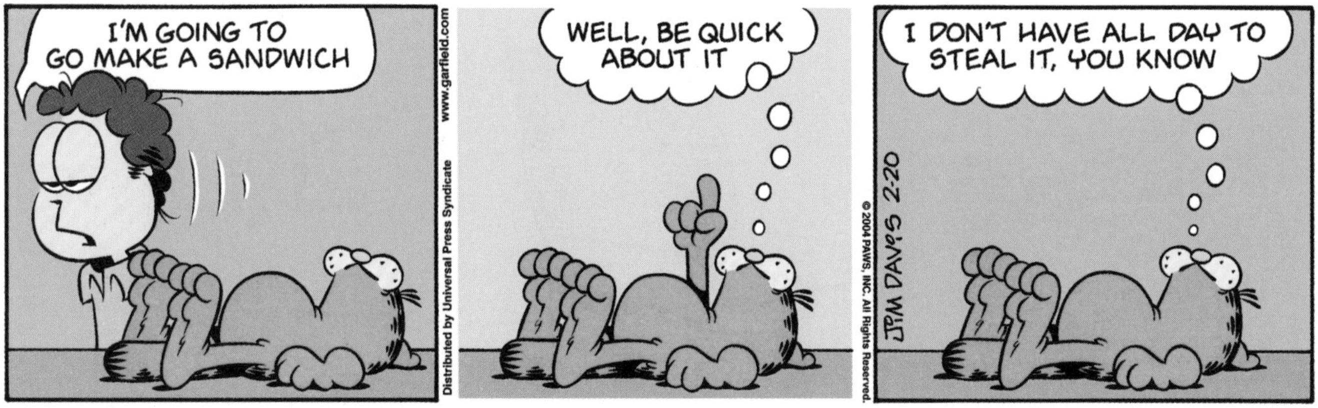
I'M GOING TO GO MAKE A SANDWICH
WELL, BE QUICK ABOUT IT
I DON'T HAVE ALL DAY TO STEAL IT, YOU KNOW
www.garfield.com
Distributed by Universal Press Syndicate
© 2004 PAWS, INC. All Rights Reserved.
JIM DAVIS 2-20

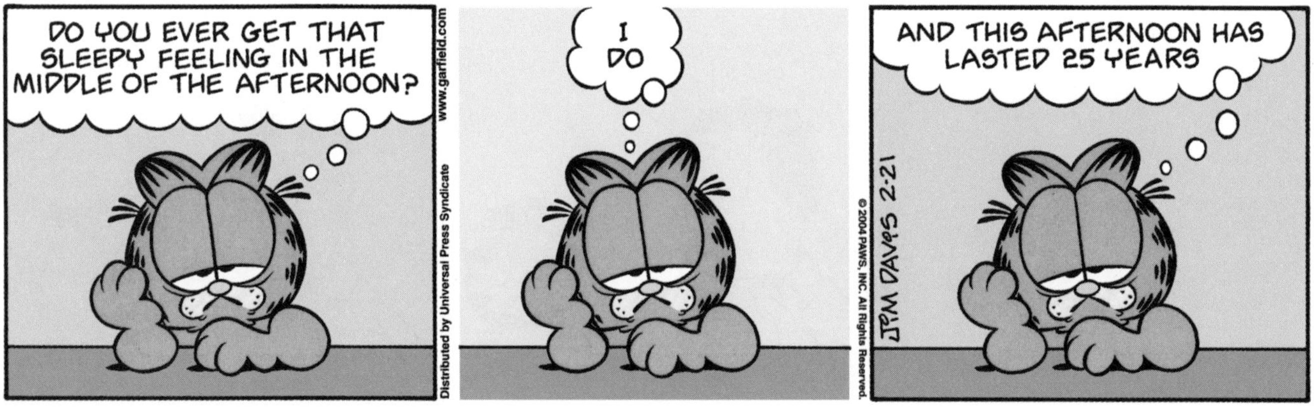
DO YOU EVER GET THAT SLEEPY FEELING IN THE MIDDLE OF THE AFTERNOON?
I DO
AND THIS AFTERNOON HAS LASTED 25 YEARS
www.garfield.com
Distributed by Universal Press Syndicate
© 2004 PAWS, INC. All Rights Reserved.
JIM DAVIS 2-21

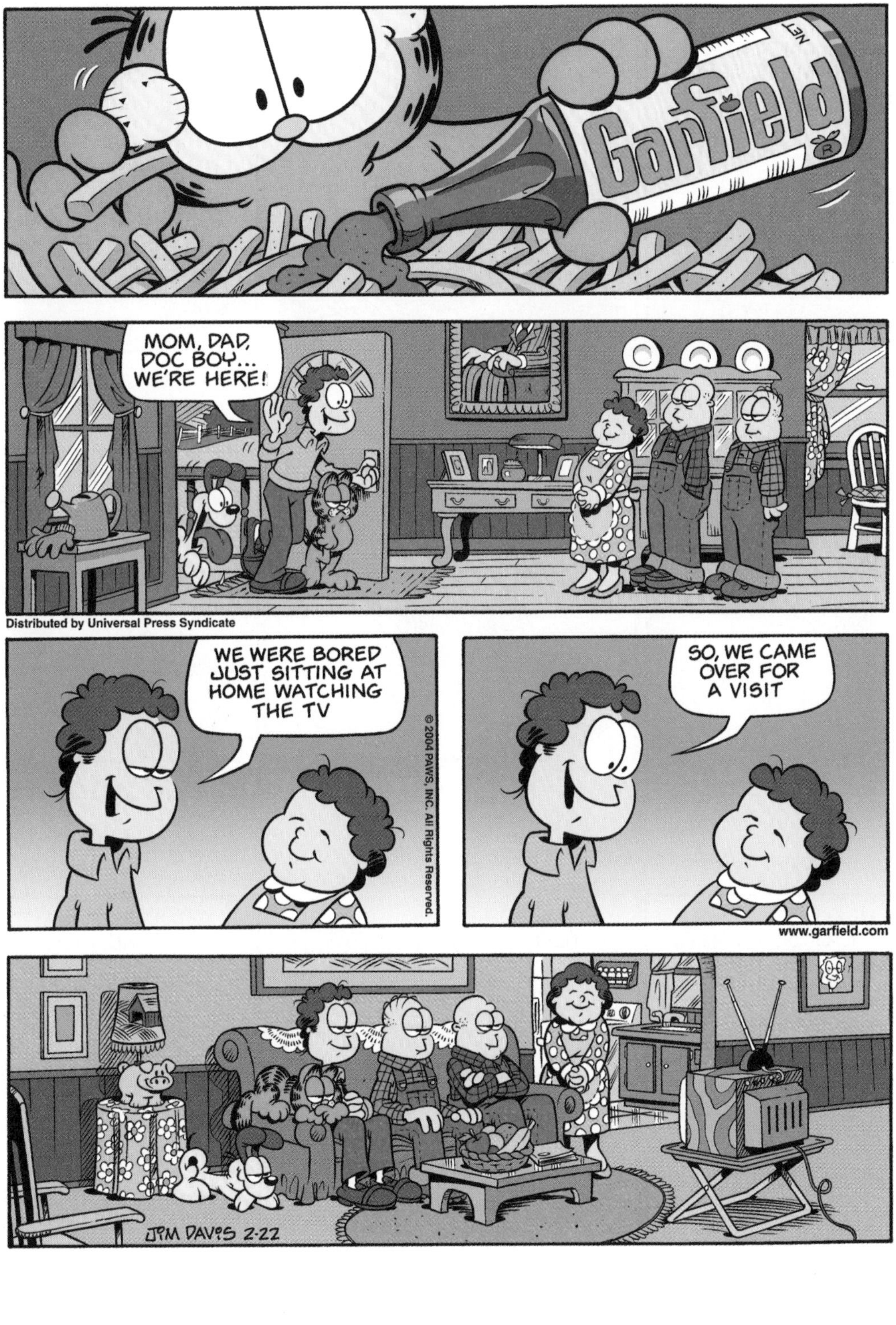
Garfield
MOM, DAD, DOC BOY... WE'RE HERE!
WE WERE BORED JUST SITTING AT HOME WATCHING THE TV
SO, WE CAME OVER FOR A VISIT
JIM DAVIS 2-22

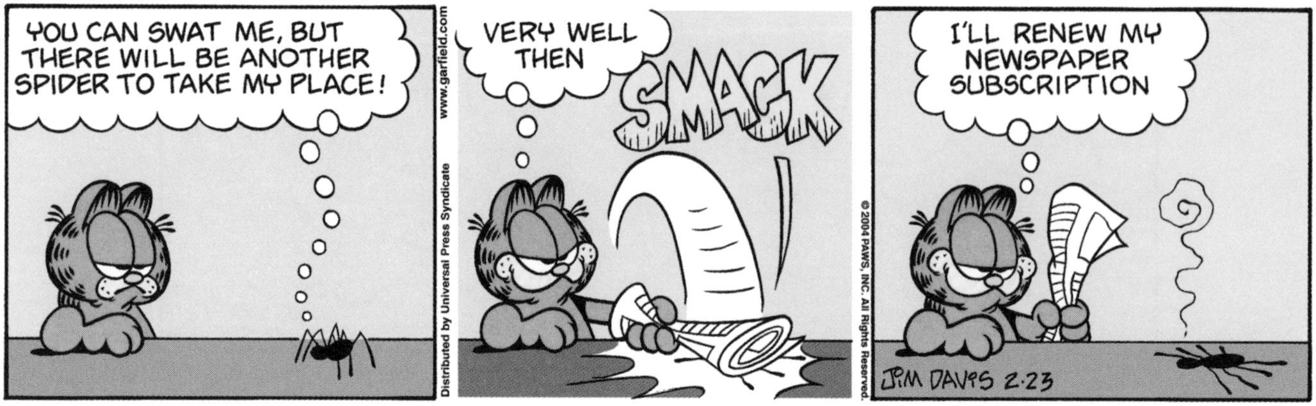
YOU CAN SWAT ME, BUT THERE WILL BE ANOTHER SPIDER TO TAKE MY PLACE!
www.garfield.com
Distributed by Universal Press Syndicate
VERY WELL THEN
SMACK
© 2004 PAWS, INC. All Rights Reserved.
I'LL RENEW MY NEWSPAPER SUBSCRIPTION
JIM DAVIS 2·23

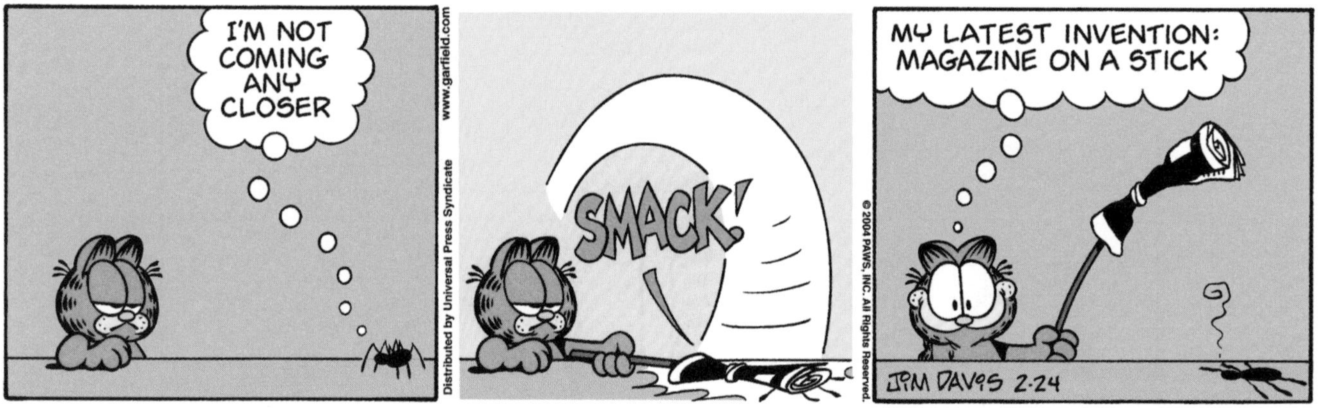
I'M NOT COMING ANY CLOSER
www.garfield.com
Distributed by Universal Press Syndicate
SMACK!
© 2004 PAWS, INC. All Rights Reserved.
MY LATEST INVENTION: MAGAZINE ON A STICK
JIM DAVIS 2·24

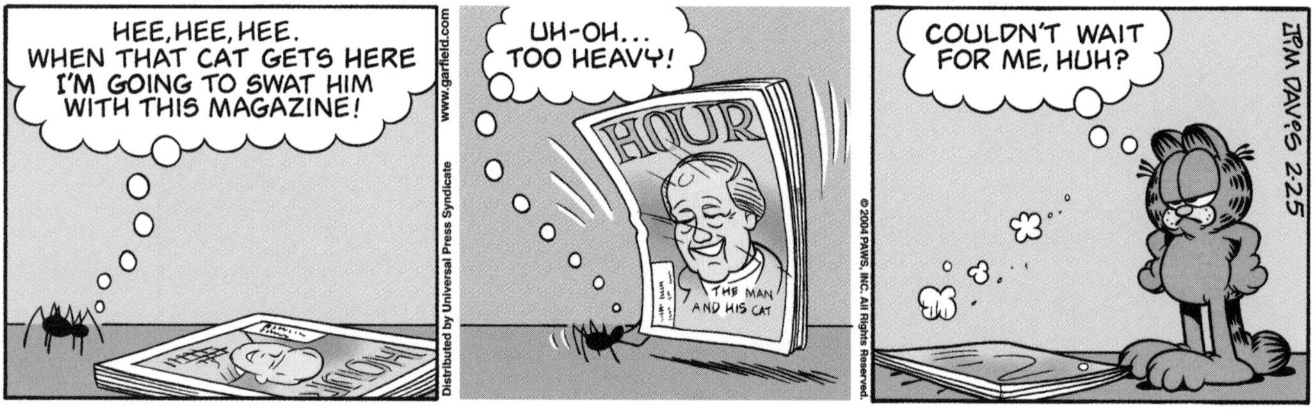
HEE, HEE, HEE. WHEN THAT CAT GETS HERE I'M GOING TO SWAT HIM WITH THIS MAGAZINE!
www.garfield.com
Distributed by Universal Press Syndicate
UH-OH... TOO HEAVY!
HOUR
THE MAN AND HIS CAT
© 2004 PAWS, INC. All Rights Reserved.
COULDN'T WAIT FOR ME, HUH?
JIM DAVIS 2·25

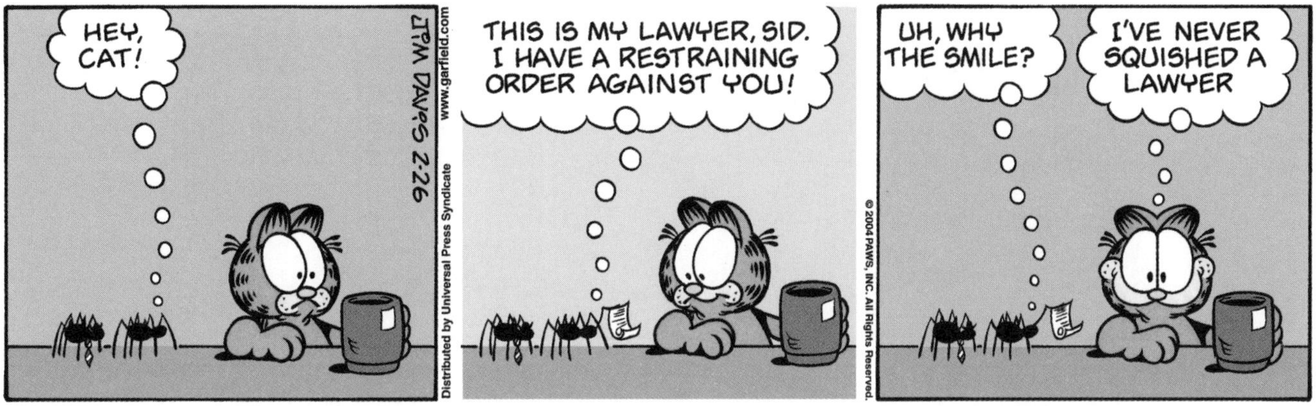
JIM DAVIS 2-26
www.garfield.com
Distributed by Universal Press Syndicate
HEY, CAT!
THIS IS MY LAWYER, SID. I HAVE A RESTRAINING ORDER AGAINST YOU!
© 2004 PAWS, INC. All Rights Reserved.
UH, WHY THE SMILE?
I'VE NEVER SQUISHED A LAWYER

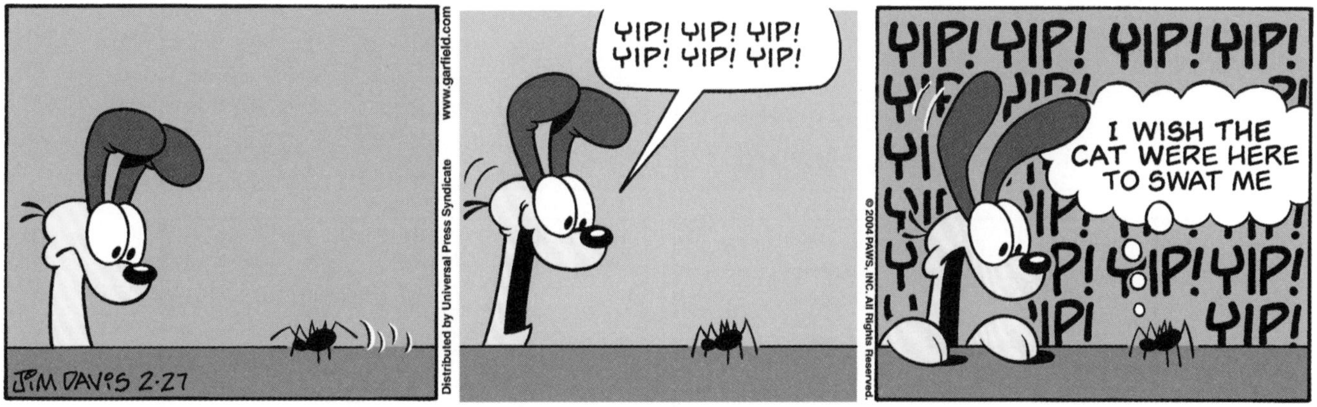
JIM DAVIS 2-27
www.garfield.com
Distributed by Universal Press Syndicate
YIP! YIP! YIP! YIP! YIP! YIP!
© 2004 PAWS, INC. All Rights Reserved.
YIP! YIP! YIP! YIP!
I WISH THE CAT WERE HERE TO SWAT ME
YIP! YIP!
YIP!

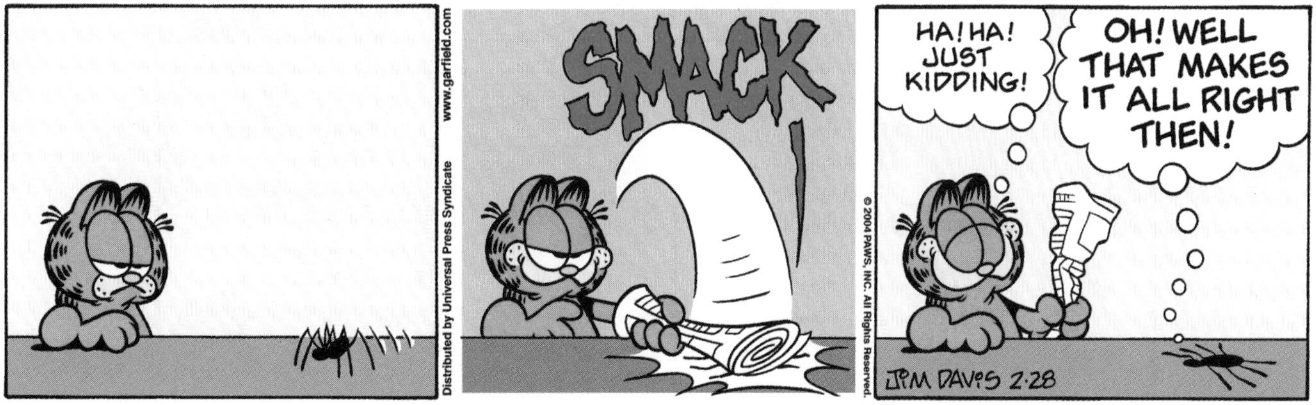
www.garfield.com
Distributed by Universal Press Syndicate
SMACK
© 2004 PAWS, INC. All Rights Reserved.
HA! HA! JUST KIDDING!
OH! WELL THAT MAKES IT ALL RIGHT THEN!
JIM DAVIS 2-28

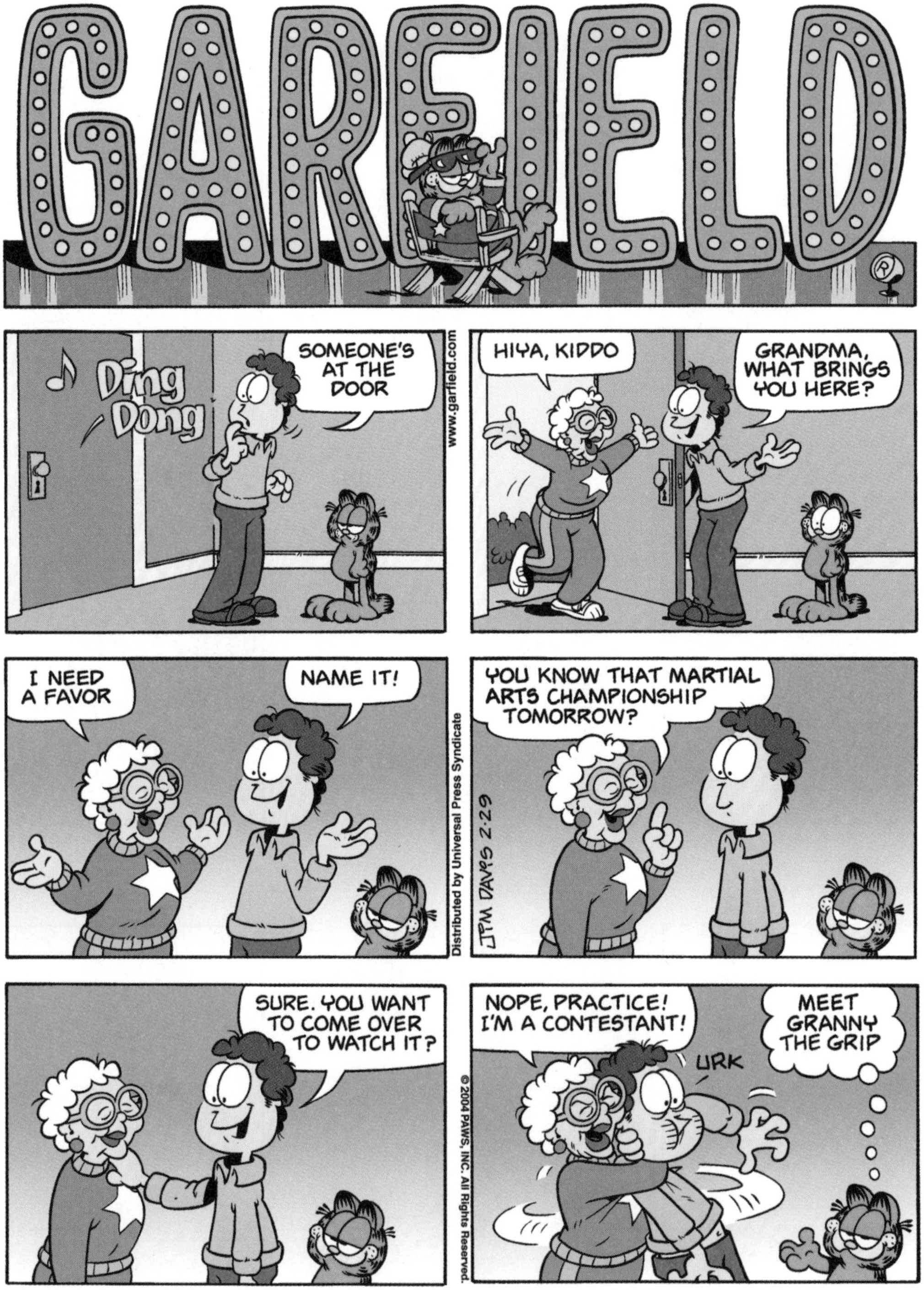
GARFIELD
Ding Dong
SOMEONE'S AT THE DOOR
www.garfield.com
HIYA, KIDDO
GRANDMA, WHAT BRINGS YOU HERE?
I NEED A FAVOR
NAME IT!
Distributed by Universal Press Syndicate
JPM DAVIS 2·29
YOU KNOW THAT MARTIAL ARTS CHAMPIONSHIP TOMORROW?
SURE. YOU WANT TO COME OVER TO WATCH IT?
© 2004 PAWS, INC. All Rights Reserved.
NOPE, PRACTICE! I'M A CONTESTANT!
URK
MEET GRANNY THE GRIP

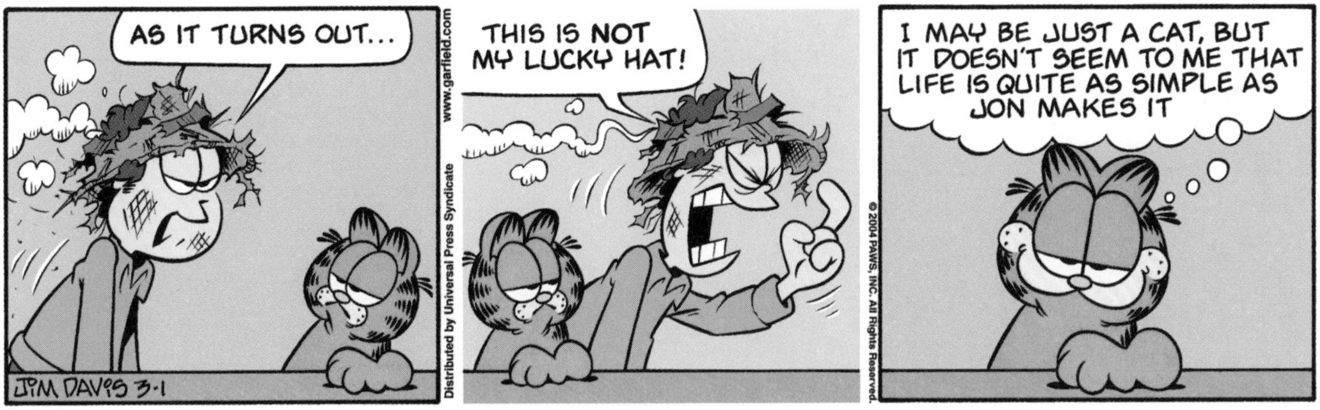
AS IT TURNS OUT...
JIM DAVIS 3-1
THIS IS NOT MY LUCKY HAT!
I MAY BE JUST A CAT, BUT IT DOESN'T SEEM TO ME THAT LIFE IS QUITE AS SIMPLE AS JON MAKES IT
Distributed by Universal Press Syndicate www.garfield.com
© 2004 PAWS, INC. All Rights Reserved.

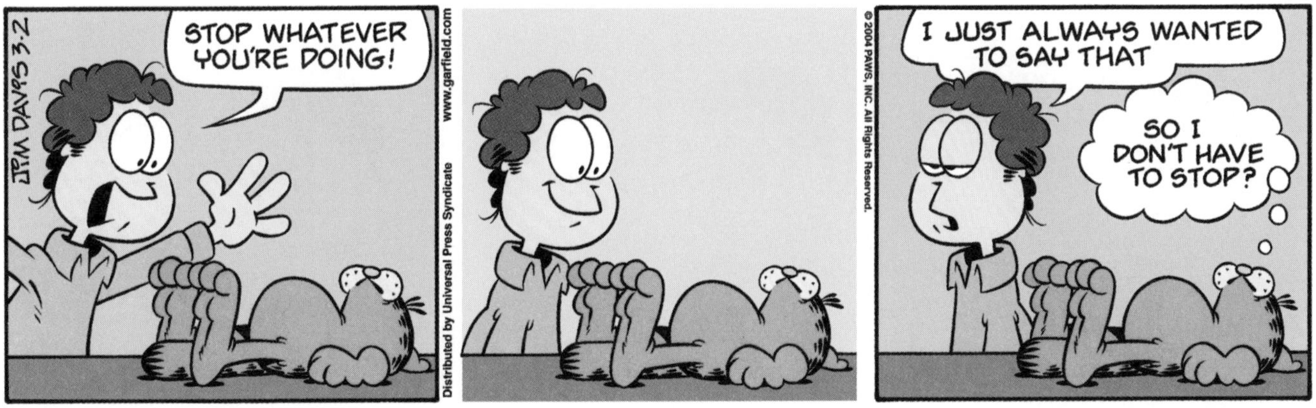
JIM DAVIS 3-2
STOP WHATEVER YOU'RE DOING!
I JUST ALWAYS WANTED TO SAY THAT
SO I DON'T HAVE TO STOP?
Distributed by Universal Press Syndicate www.garfield.com
© 2004 PAWS, INC. All Rights Reserved.

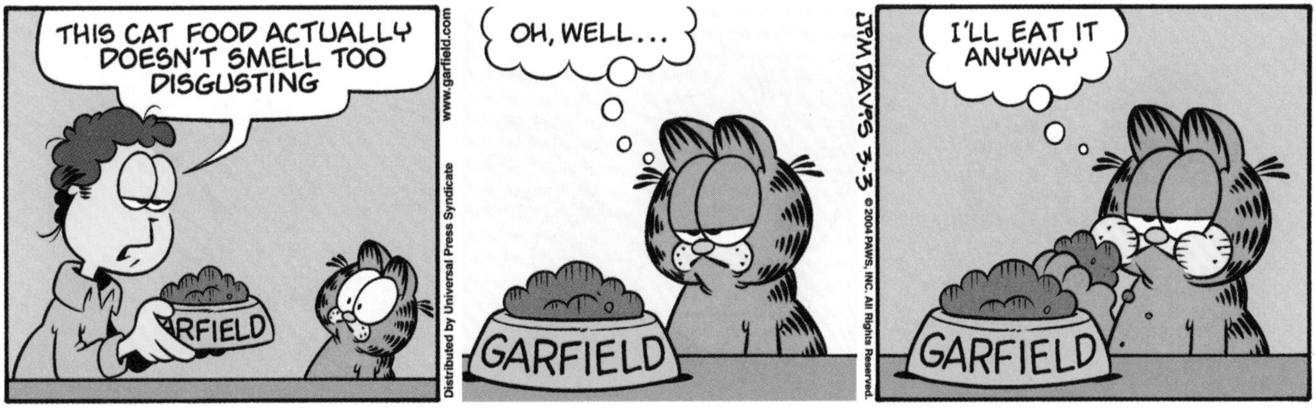
THIS CAT FOOD ACTUALLY DOESN'T SMELL TOO DISGUSTING
RFIELD
OH, WELL...
GARFIELD
JIM DAVIS 3-3
I'LL EAT IT ANYWAY
GARFIELD
Distributed by Universal Press Syndicate www.garfield.com
© 2004 PAWS, INC. All Rights Reserved.

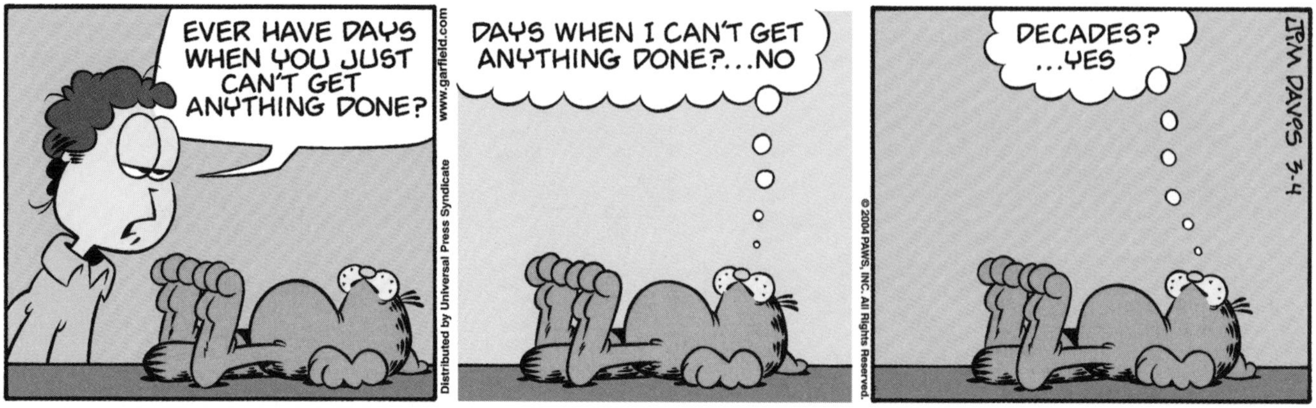
EVER HAVE DAYS WHEN YOU JUST CAN'T GET ANYTHING DONE?
DAYS WHEN I CAN'T GET ANYTHING DONE?...NO
DECADES? ...YES
JIM DAVIS 3-4
Distributed by Universal Press Syndicate www.garfield.com
© 2004 PAWS, INC. All Rights Reserved.

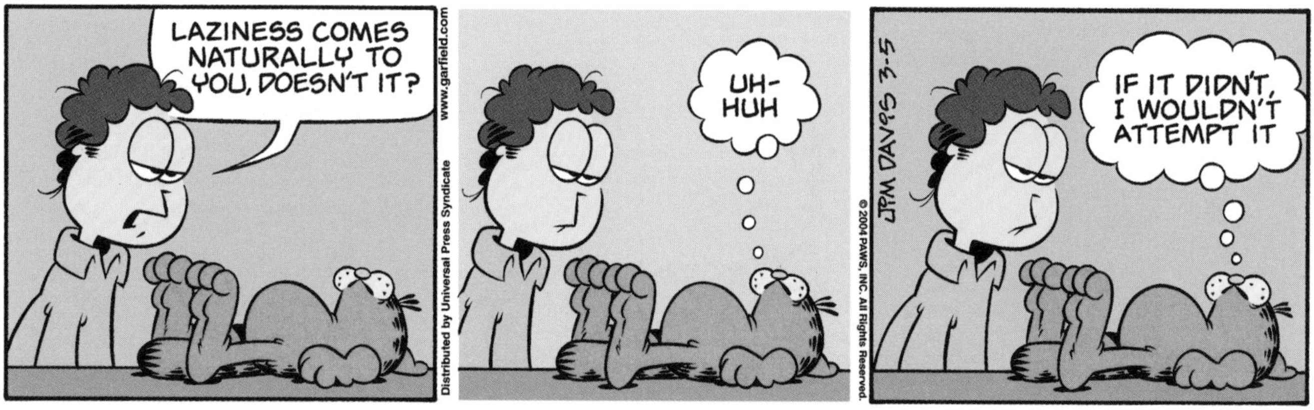
LAZINESS COMES NATURALLY TO YOU, DOESN'T IT?
UH-HUH
IF IT DIDN'T, I WOULDN'T ATTEMPT IT
JIM DAVIS 3-5
Distributed by Universal Press Syndicate www.garfield.com
© 2004 PAWS, INC. All Rights Reserved.

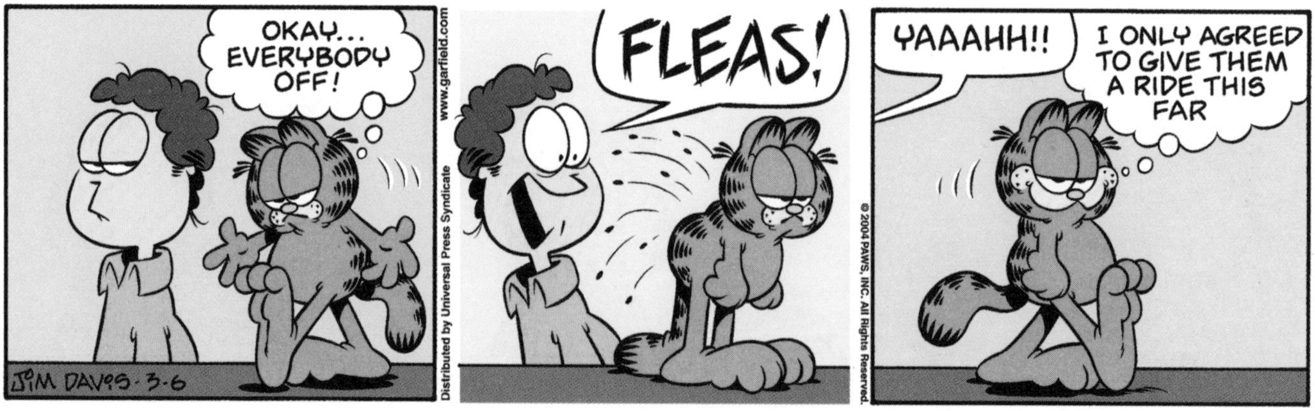
OKAY... EVERYBODY OFF!
FLEAS!
YAAAHH!!
I ONLY AGREED TO GIVE THEM A RIDE THIS FAR
JIM DAVIS 3-6
Distributed by Universal Press Syndicate www.garfield.com
© 2004 PAWS, INC. All Rights Reserved.

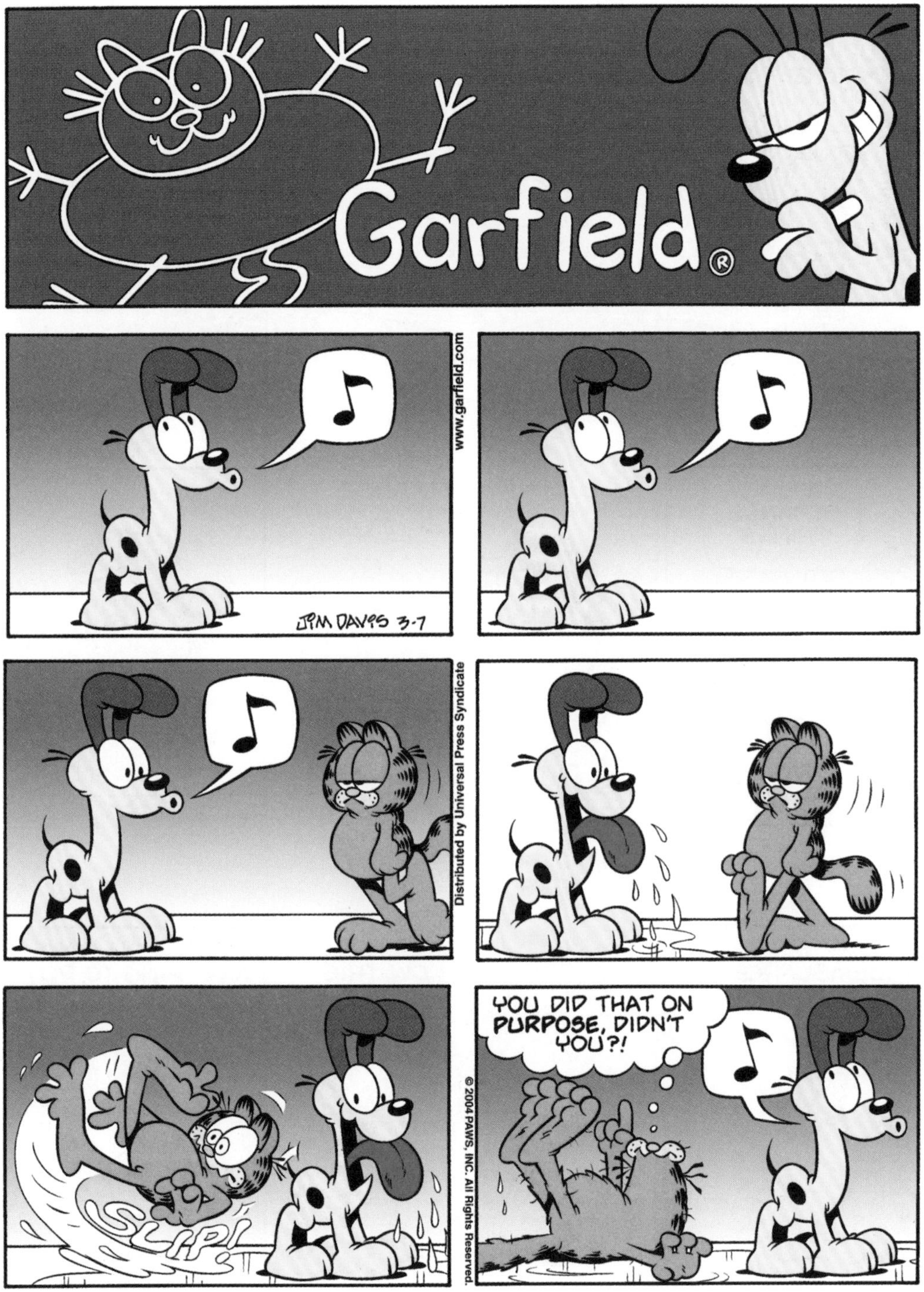
Garfield®
www.garfield.com
JIM DAVIS 3-7
Distributed by Universal Press Syndicate
SLIP!
© 2004 PAWS, INC. All Rights Reserved.
YOU DID THAT ON **PURPOSE**, DIDN'T YOU?!

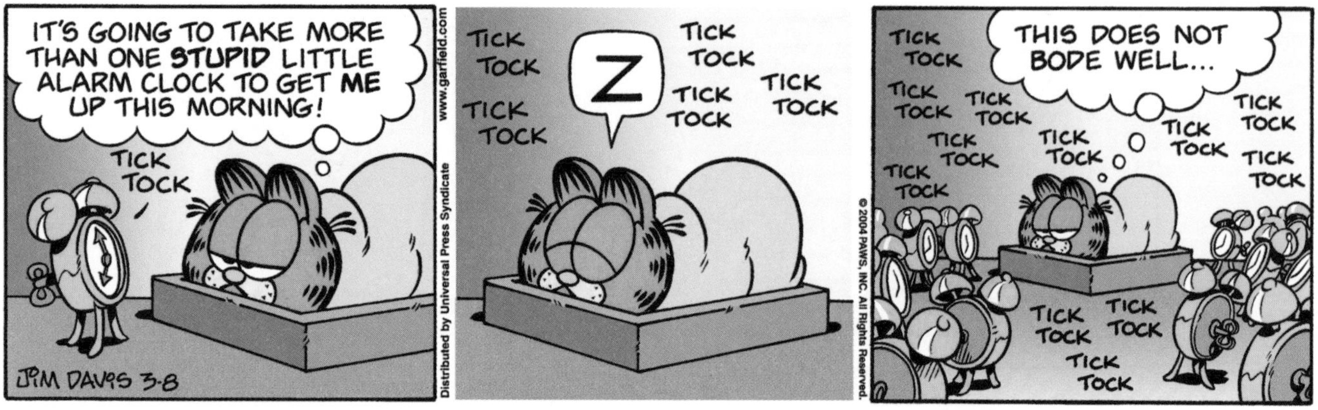

IT'S GOING TO TAKE MORE THAN ONE **STUPID** LITTLE ALARM CLOCK TO GET **ME** UP THIS MORNING!
TICK TOCK
JIM DAVIS 3-8
www.garfield.com
Distributed by Universal Press Syndicate
TICK TOCK
TICK TOCK
Z
TICK TOCK
TICK TOCK
TICK TOCK
© 2004 PAWS, INC. All Rights Reserved.
TICK TOCK
THIS DOES NOT BODE WELL...
TICK TOCK

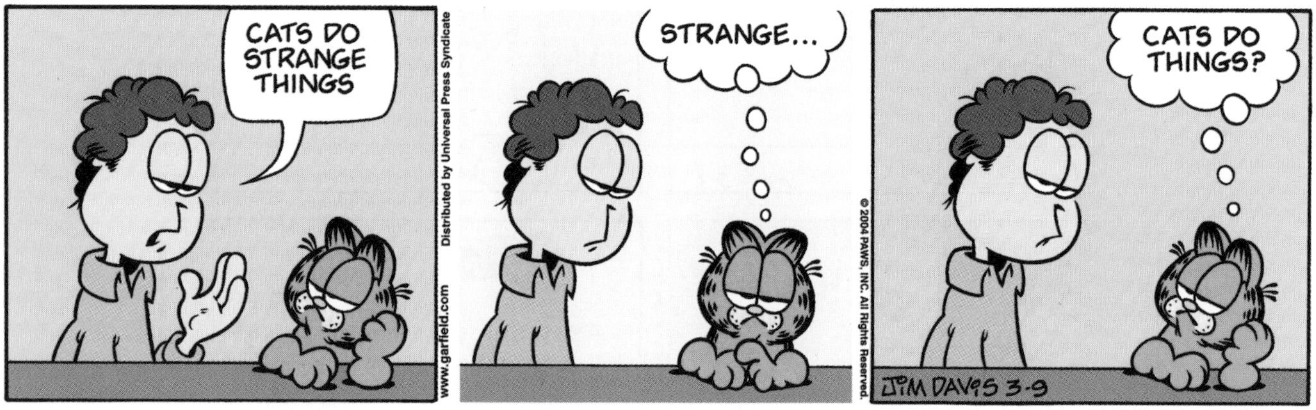

CATS DO STRANGE THINGS
www.garfield.com
Distributed by Universal Press Syndicate
STRANGE...
© 2004 PAWS, INC. All Rights Reserved.
CATS DO THINGS?
JIM DAVIS 3-9

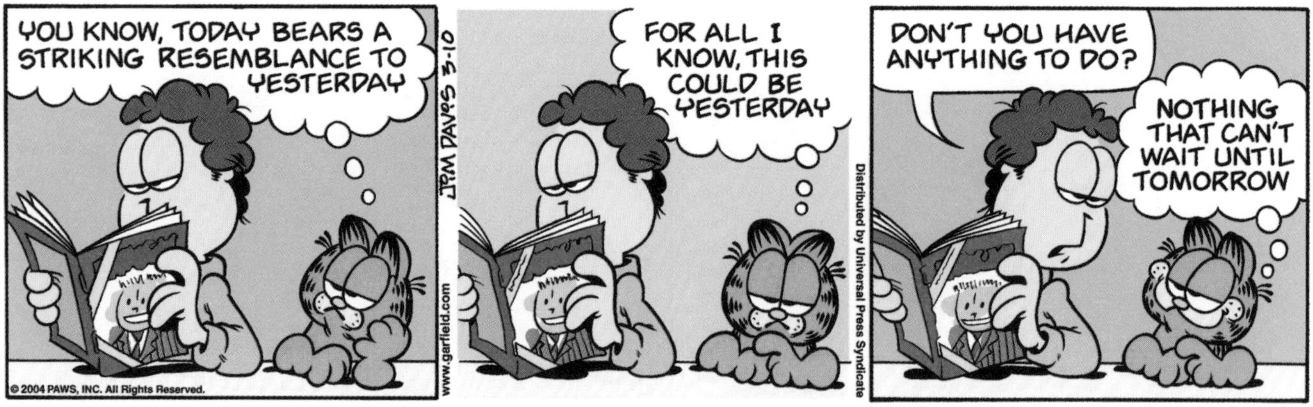

YOU KNOW, TODAY BEARS A STRIKING RESEMBLANCE TO YESTERDAY
© 2004 PAWS, INC. All Rights Reserved.
JIM DAVIS 3-10
www.garfield.com
FOR ALL I KNOW, THIS COULD BE YESTERDAY
Distributed by Universal Press Syndicate
DON'T YOU HAVE ANYTHING TO DO?
NOTHING THAT CAN'T WAIT UNTIL TOMORROW

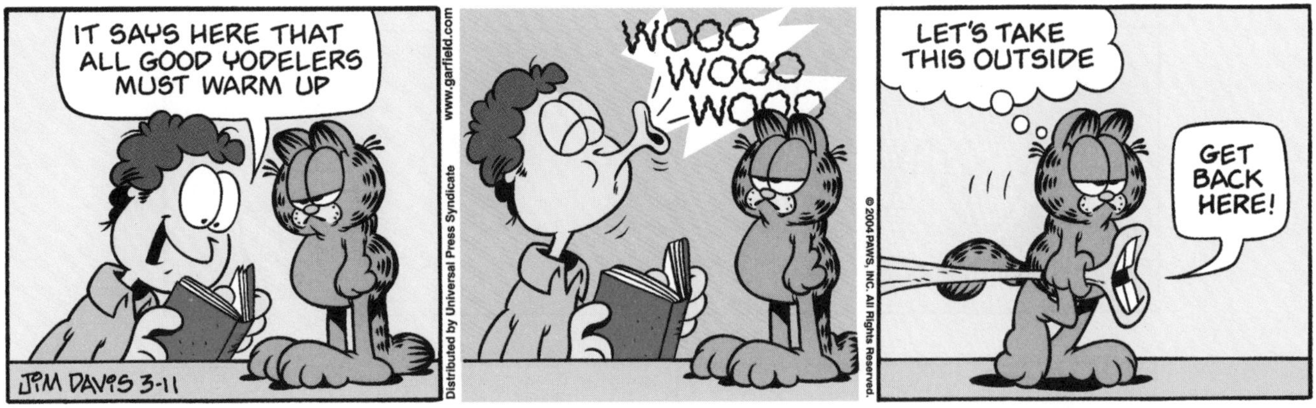
IT SAYS HERE THAT ALL GOOD YODELERS MUST WARM UP
JIM DAVIS 3-11
www.garfield.com
Distributed by Universal Press Syndicate
WOOO WOOO WOOO
© 2004 PAWS, INC. All Rights Reserved.
LET'S TAKE THIS OUTSIDE
GET BACK HERE!

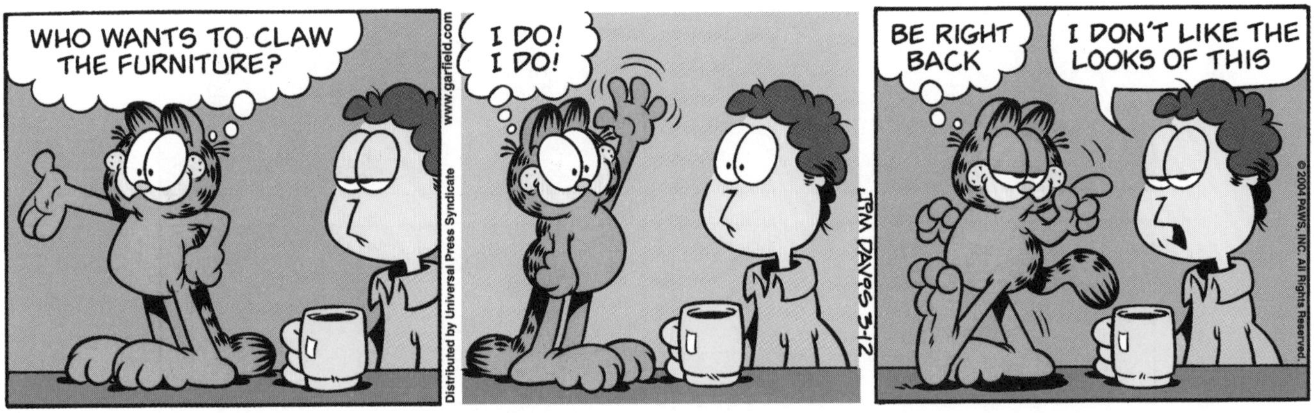
WHO WANTS TO CLAW THE FURNITURE?
www.garfield.com
Distributed by Universal Press Syndicate
I DO! I DO!
JIM DAVIS 3-12
BE RIGHT BACK
I DON'T LIKE THE LOOKS OF THIS
© 2004 PAWS, INC. All Rights Reserved.

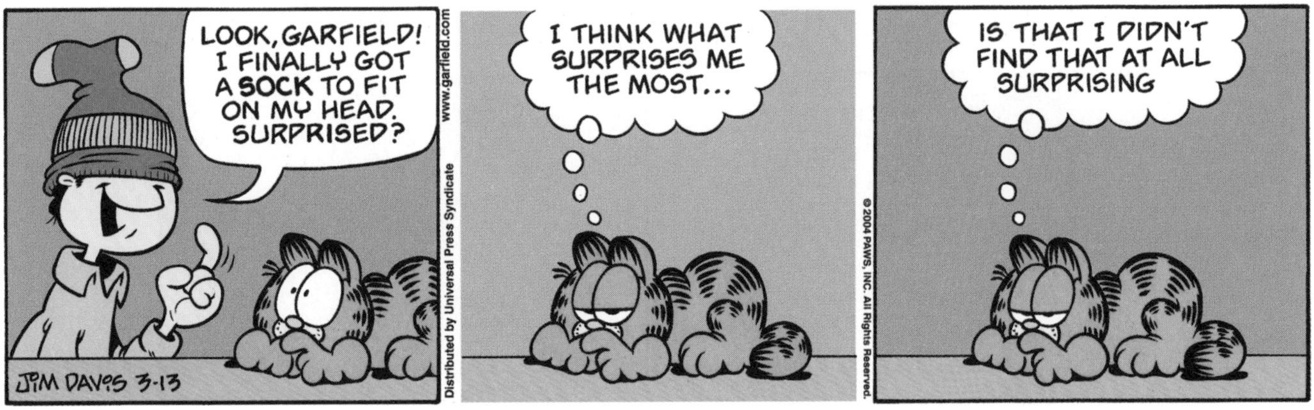
LOOK, GARFIELD! I FINALLY GOT A **SOCK** TO FIT ON MY HEAD. SURPRISED?
JIM DAVIS 3-13
www.garfield.com
Distributed by Universal Press Syndicate
I THINK WHAT SURPRISES ME THE MOST...
© 2004 PAWS, INC. All Rights Reserved.
IS THAT I DIDN'T FIND THAT AT ALL SURPRISING

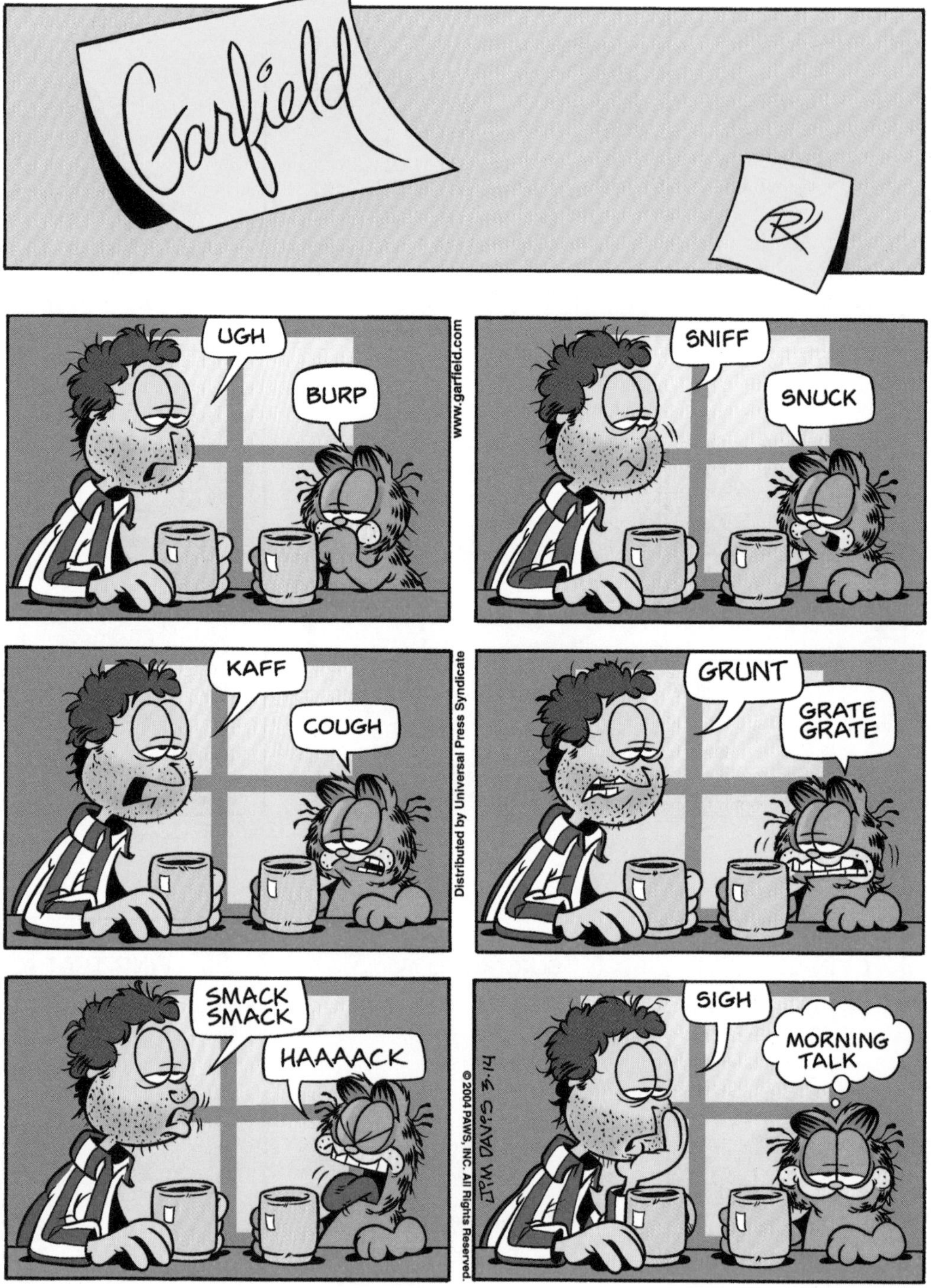
Garfield
UGH
BURP
SNIFF
SNUCK
KAFF
COUGH
GRUNT
GRATE GRATE
SMACK SMACK
HAAAACK
SIGH
MORNING TALK
www.garfield.com
Distributed by Universal Press Syndicate
© 2004 PAWS, INC. All Rights Reserved.
JIM DAVIS 3-14

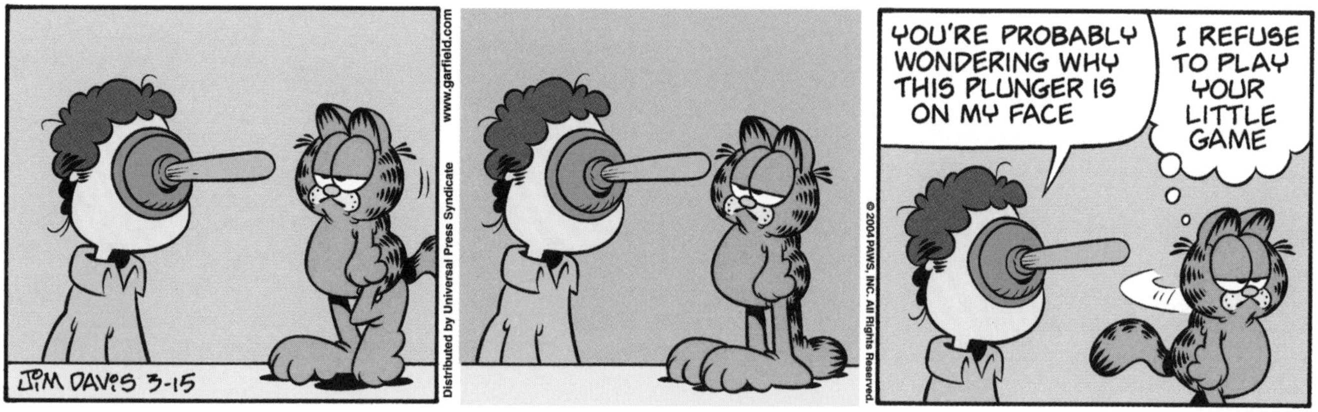
JIM DAVIS 3-15
www.garfield.com
Distributed by Universal Press Syndicate
© 2004 PAWS, INC. All Rights Reserved.
YOU'RE PROBABLY WONDERING WHY THIS PLUNGER IS ON MY FACE
I REFUSE TO PLAY YOUR LITTLE GAME

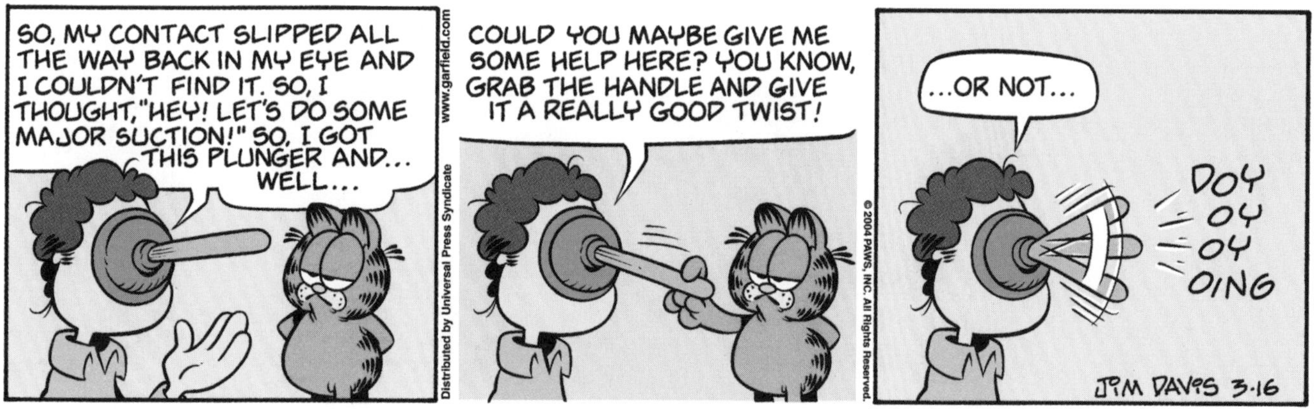
SO, MY CONTACT SLIPPED ALL THE WAY BACK IN MY EYE AND I COULDN'T FIND IT. SO, I THOUGHT, "HEY! LET'S DO SOME MAJOR SUCTION!" SO, I GOT THIS PLUNGER AND... WELL...
www.garfield.com
Distributed by Universal Press Syndicate
COULD YOU MAYBE GIVE ME SOME HELP HERE? YOU KNOW, GRAB THE HANDLE AND GIVE IT A REALLY GOOD TWIST!
© 2004 PAWS, INC. All Rights Reserved.
...OR NOT...
DOY
OY
OY
OING
JIM DAVIS 3-16

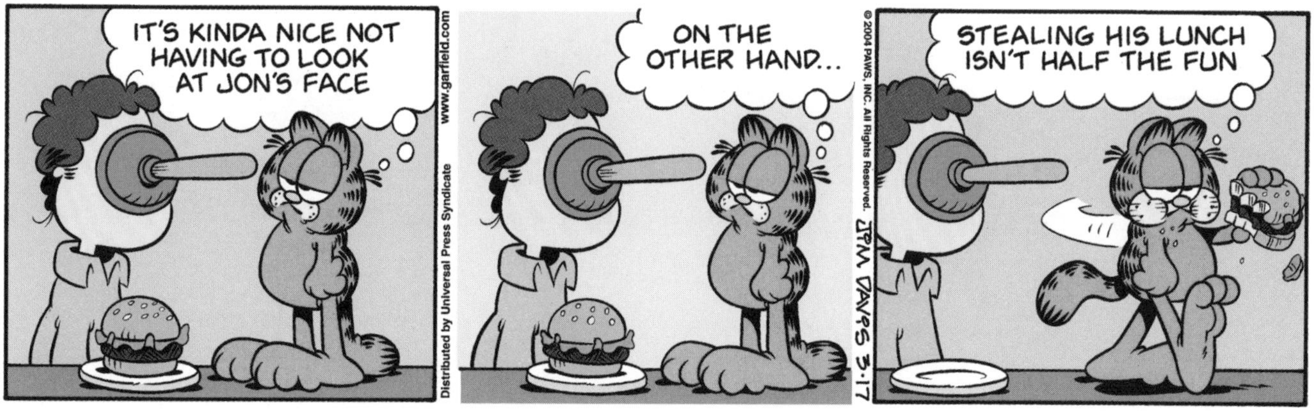
IT'S KINDA NICE NOT HAVING TO LOOK AT JON'S FACE
www.garfield.com
Distributed by Universal Press Syndicate
ON THE OTHER HAND...
© 2004 PAWS, INC. All Rights Reserved.
JIM DAVIS 3-17
STEALING HIS LUNCH ISN'T HALF THE FUN

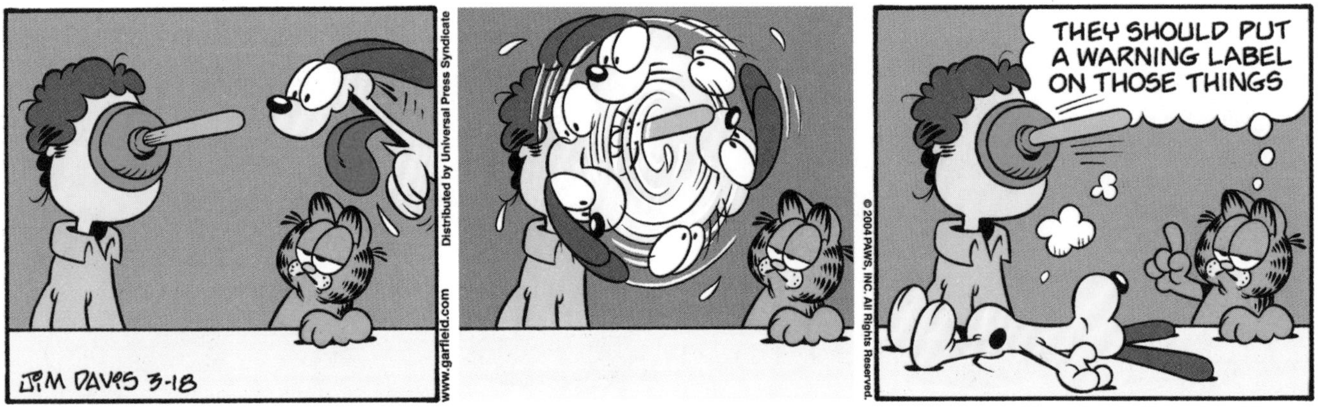
JIM DAVIS 3-18
www.garfield.com
Distributed by Universal Press Syndicate
© 2004 PAWS, INC. All Rights Reserved.
THEY SHOULD PUT A WARNING LABEL ON THOSE THINGS

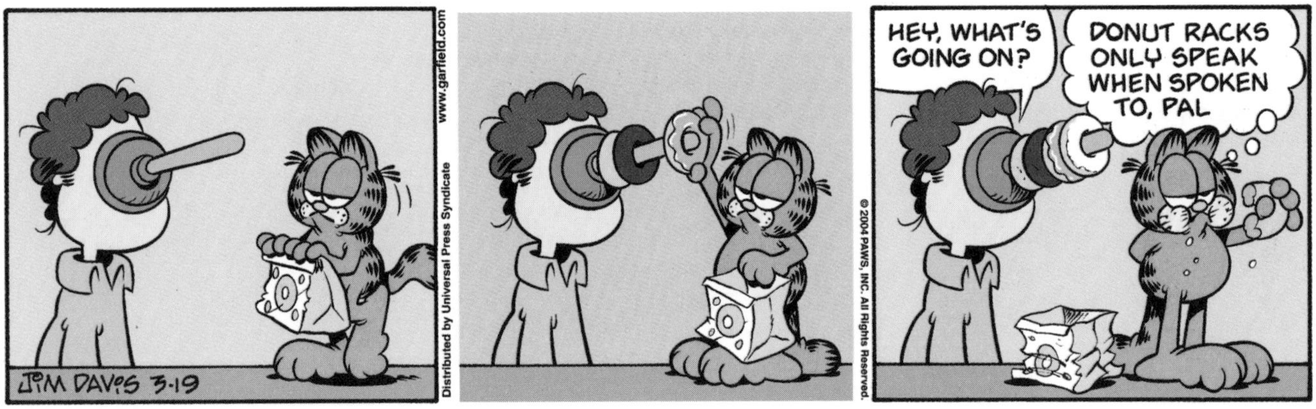
JIM DAVIS 3-19
www.garfield.com
Distributed by Universal Press Syndicate
© 2004 PAWS, INC. All Rights Reserved.
HEY, WHAT'S GOING ON?
DONUT RACKS ONLY SPEAK WHEN SPOKEN TO, PAL

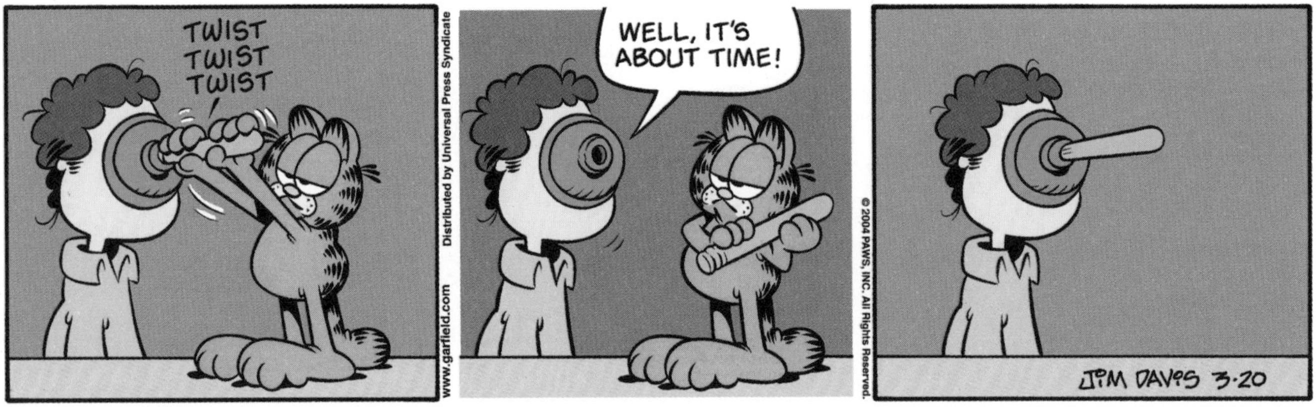
TWIST TWIST TWIST
Distributed by Universal Press Syndicate
www.garfield.com
WELL, IT'S ABOUT TIME!
© 2004 PAWS, INC. All Rights Reserved.
JIM DAVIS 3-20

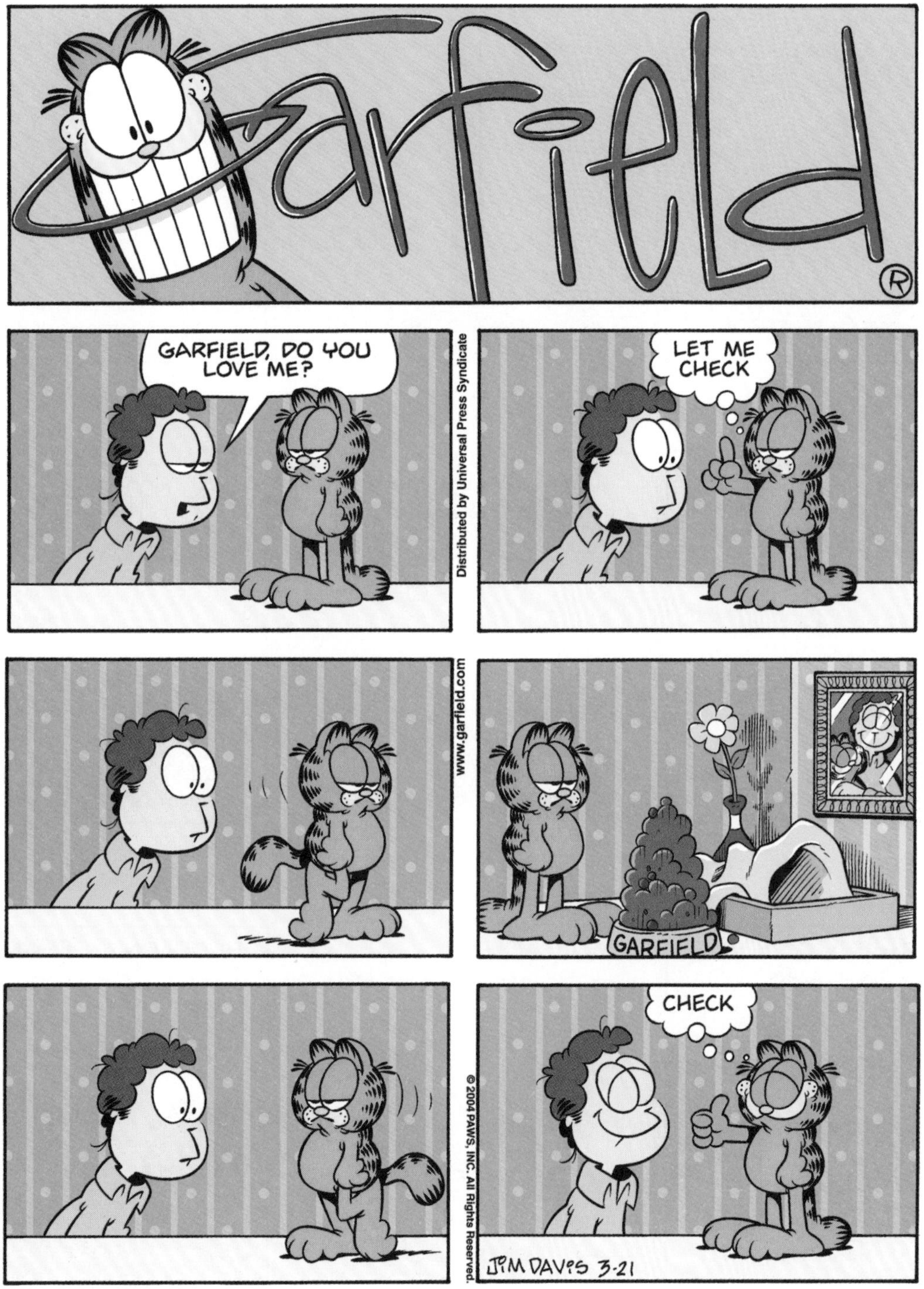
GARFIELD
GARFIELD, DO YOU LOVE ME?
LET ME CHECK
GARFIELD
CHECK
JIM DAVIS 3-21

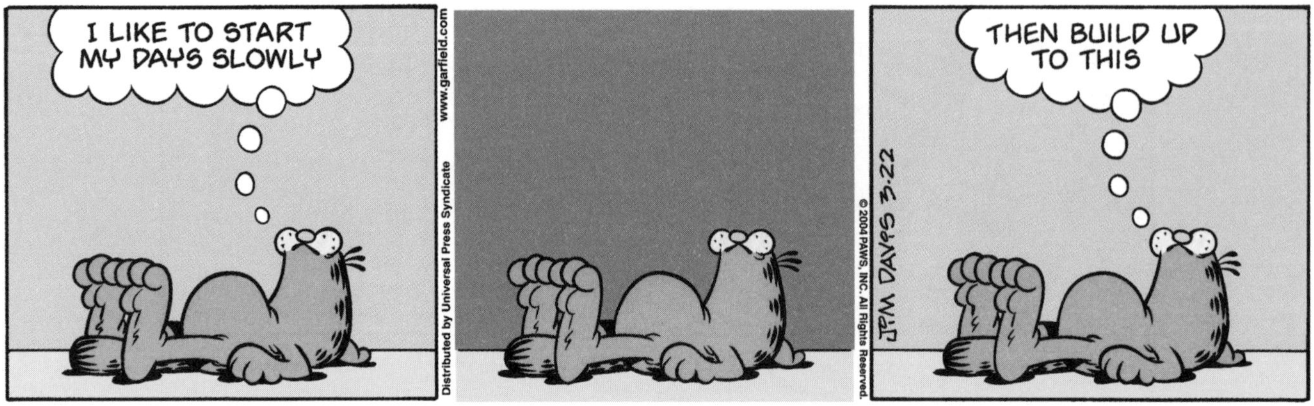
I LIKE TO START MY DAYS SLOWLY
www.garfield.com
Distributed by Universal Press Syndicate
THEN BUILD UP TO THIS
© 2004 PAWS, INC. All Rights Reserved.

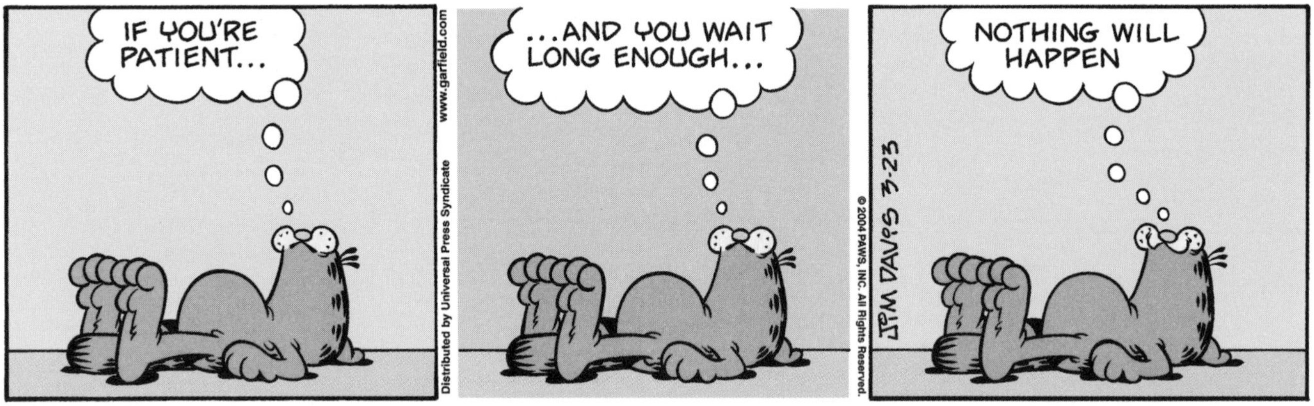
IF YOU'RE PATIENT...
www.garfield.com
Distributed by Universal Press Syndicate
...AND YOU WAIT LONG ENOUGH...
NOTHING WILL HAPPEN
© 2004 PAWS, INC. All Rights Reserved.

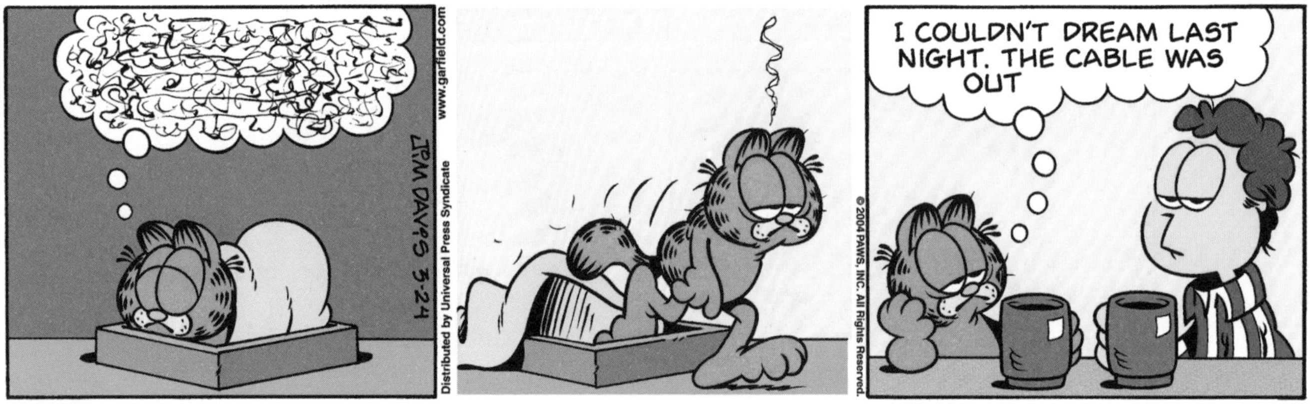
www.garfield.com
Distributed by Universal Press Syndicate
I COULDN'T DREAM LAST NIGHT. THE CABLE WAS OUT
© 2004 PAWS, INC. All Rights Reserved.

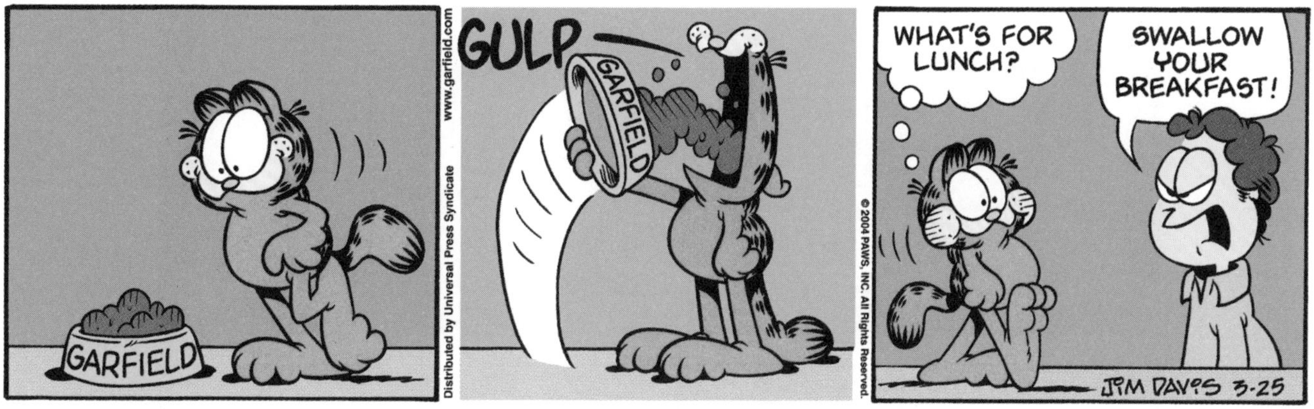
GULP
GARFIELD
WHAT'S FOR LUNCH?
SWALLOW YOUR BREAKFAST!
JIM DAVIS 3-25
www.garfield.com
Distributed by Universal Press Syndicate
© 2004 PAWS, INC. All Rights Reserved.

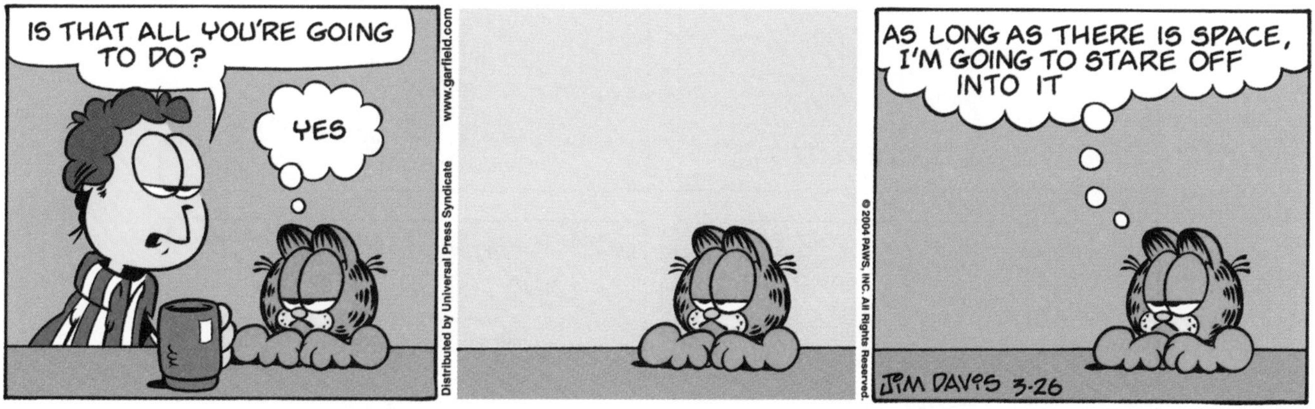
IS THAT ALL YOU'RE GOING TO DO?
YES
AS LONG AS THERE IS SPACE, I'M GOING TO STARE OFF INTO IT
JIM DAVIS 3-26
www.garfield.com
Distributed by Universal Press Syndicate
© 2004 PAWS, INC. All Rights Reserved.

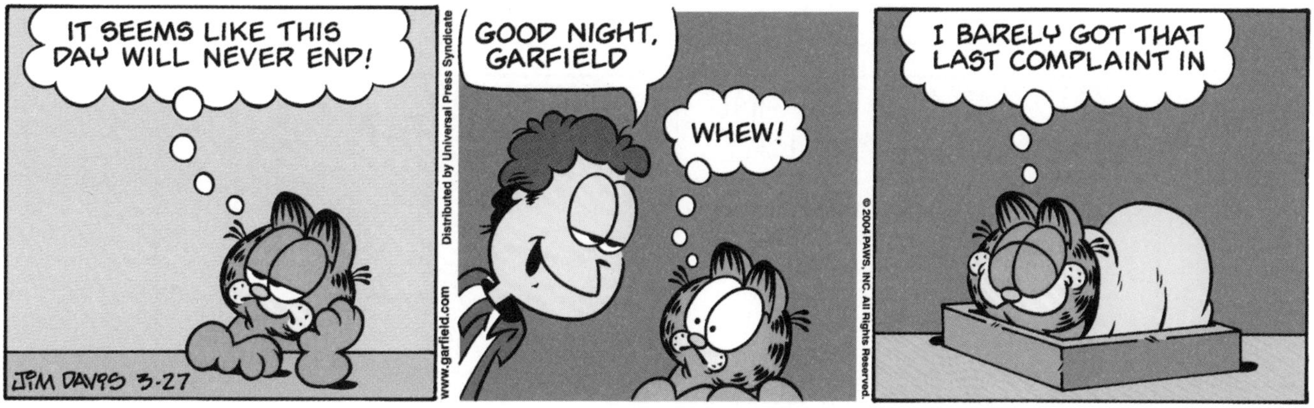
IT SEEMS LIKE THIS DAY WILL NEVER END!
JIM DAVIS 3-27
GOOD NIGHT, GARFIELD
WHEW!
I BARELY GOT THAT LAST COMPLAINT IN
Distributed by Universal Press Syndicate
www.garfield.com
© 2004 PAWS, INC. All Rights Reserved.

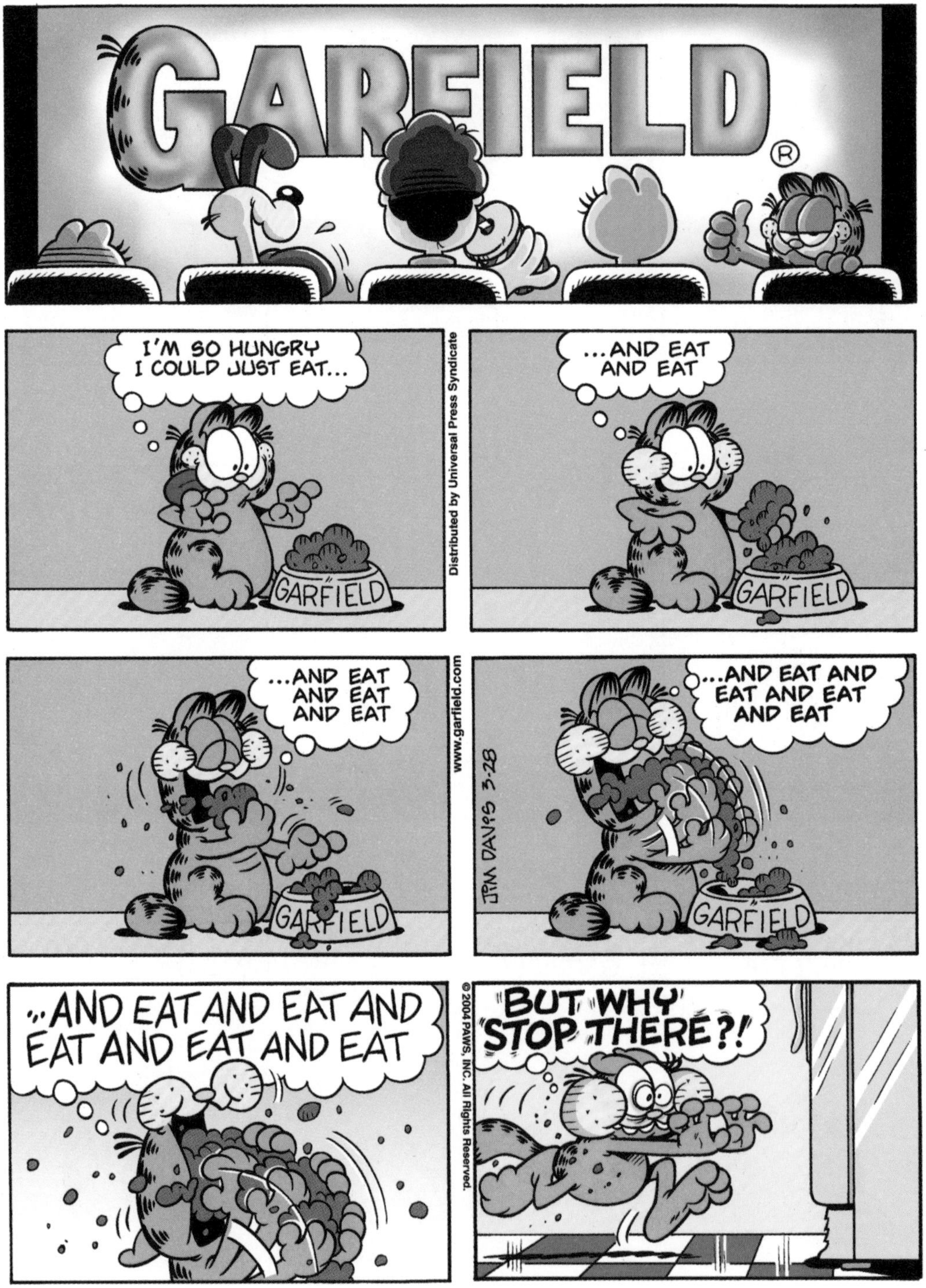
GARFIELD
I'M SO HUNGRY I COULD JUST EAT...
GARFIELD
...AND EAT AND EAT
GARFIELD
...AND EAT AND EAT AND EAT
GARFIELD
...AND EAT AND EAT AND EAT AND EAT
GARFIELD
...AND EAT AND EAT AND EAT AND EAT AND EAT AND EAT
BUT WHY STOP THERE?!
Distributed by Universal Press Syndicate
www.garfield.com
JIM DAVIS 3-28
© 2004 PAWS, INC. All Rights Reserved.

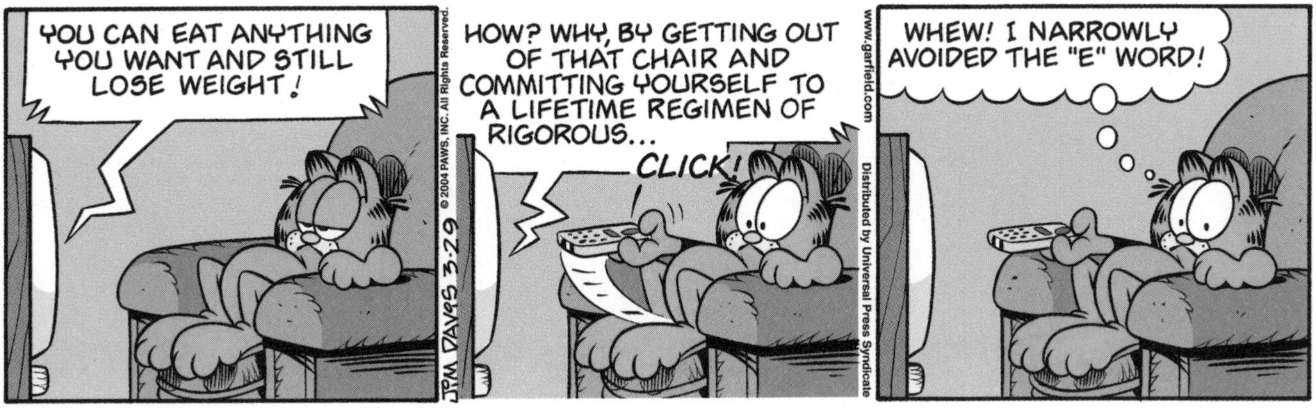
YOU CAN EAT ANYTHING YOU WANT AND STILL LOSE WEIGHT!
JIM DAVIS 3-29
© 2004 PAWS, INC. All Rights Reserved.
HOW? WHY, BY GETTING OUT OF THAT CHAIR AND COMMITTING YOURSELF TO A LIFETIME REGIMEN OF RIGOROUS...
CLICK!
www.garfield.com
Distributed by Universal Press Syndicate
WHEW! I NARROWLY AVOIDED THE "E" WORD!

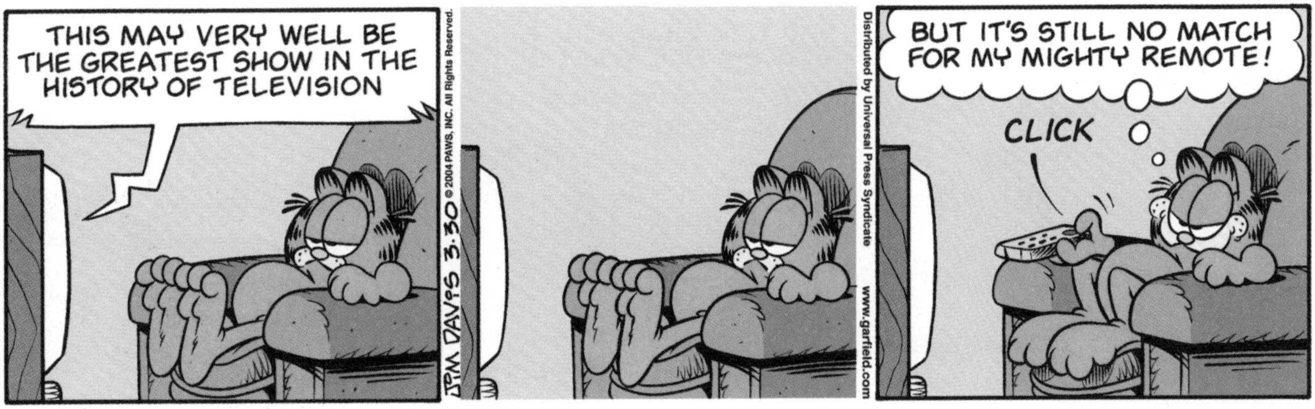
THIS MAY VERY WELL BE THE GREATEST SHOW IN THE HISTORY OF TELEVISION
JIM DAVIS 3-30
© 2004 PAWS, INC. All Rights Reserved.
Distributed by Universal Press Syndicate
www.garfield.com
BUT IT'S STILL NO MATCH FOR MY MIGHTY REMOTE!
CLICK

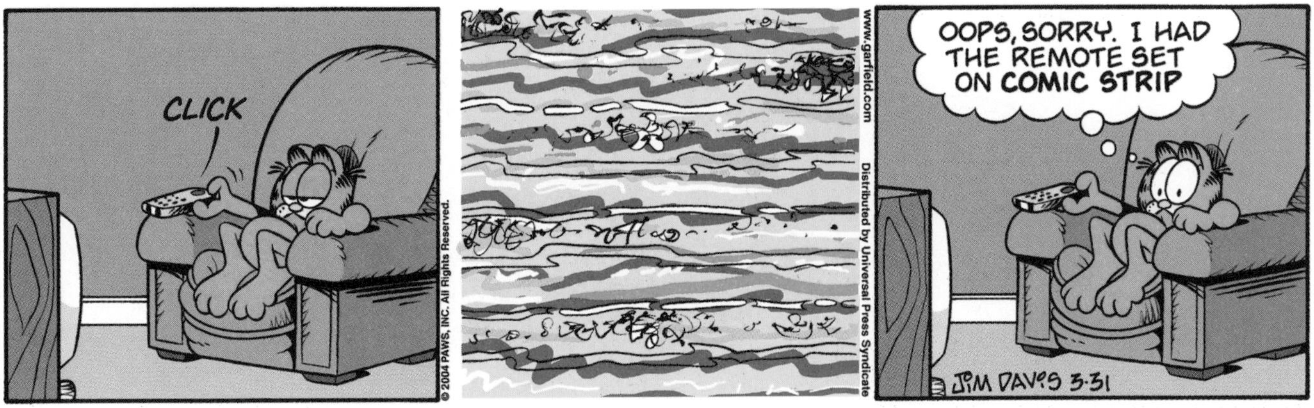
CLICK
© 2004 PAWS, INC. All Rights Reserved.
www.garfield.com
Distributed by Universal Press Syndicate
OOPS, SORRY. I HAD THE REMOTE SET ON COMIC STRIP
JIM DAVIS 3-31

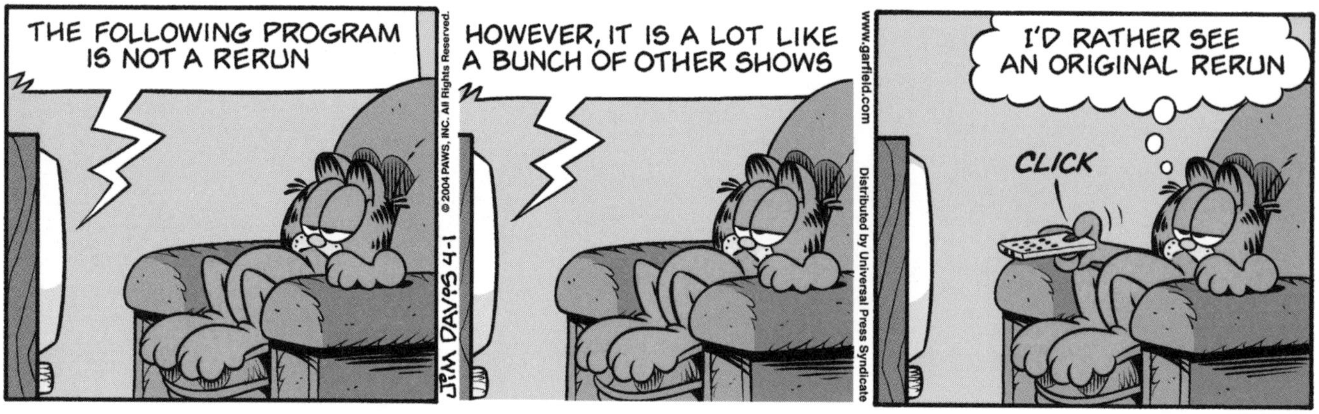
THE FOLLOWING PROGRAM IS NOT A RERUN
JIM DAVIS 4-1
© 2004 PAWS, INC. All Rights Reserved.
HOWEVER, IT IS A LOT LIKE A BUNCH OF OTHER SHOWS
www.garfield.com
Distributed by Universal Press Syndicate
I'D RATHER SEE AN ORIGINAL RERUN
CLICK

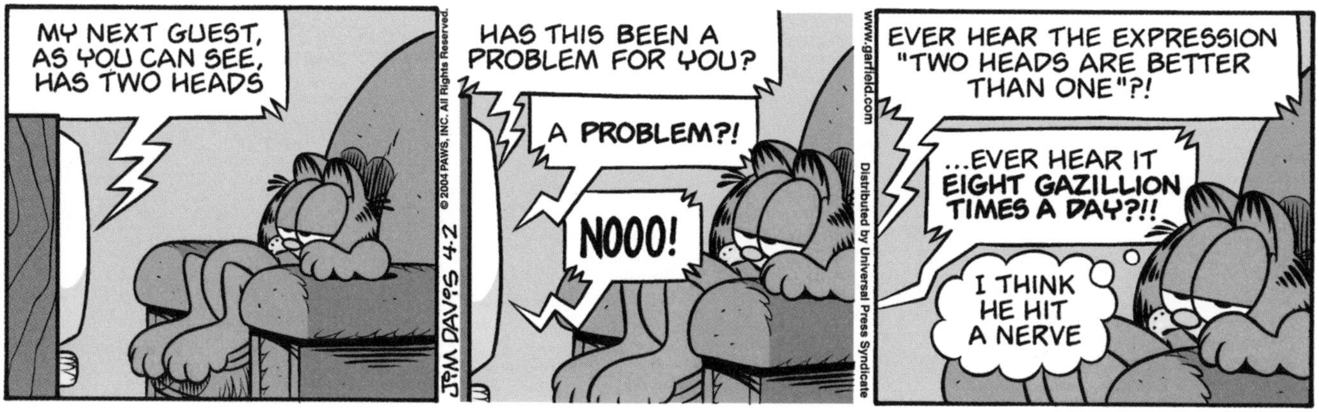
MY NEXT GUEST, AS YOU CAN SEE, HAS TWO HEADS
JIM DAVIS 4-2
© 2004 PAWS, INC. All Rights Reserved.
HAS THIS BEEN A PROBLEM FOR YOU?
A PROBLEM?!
NOOO!
www.garfield.com
Distributed by Universal Press Syndicate
EVER HEAR THE EXPRESSION "TWO HEADS ARE BETTER THAN ONE"?!
...EVER HEAR IT EIGHT GAZILLION TIMES A DAY?!!
I THINK HE HIT A NERVE

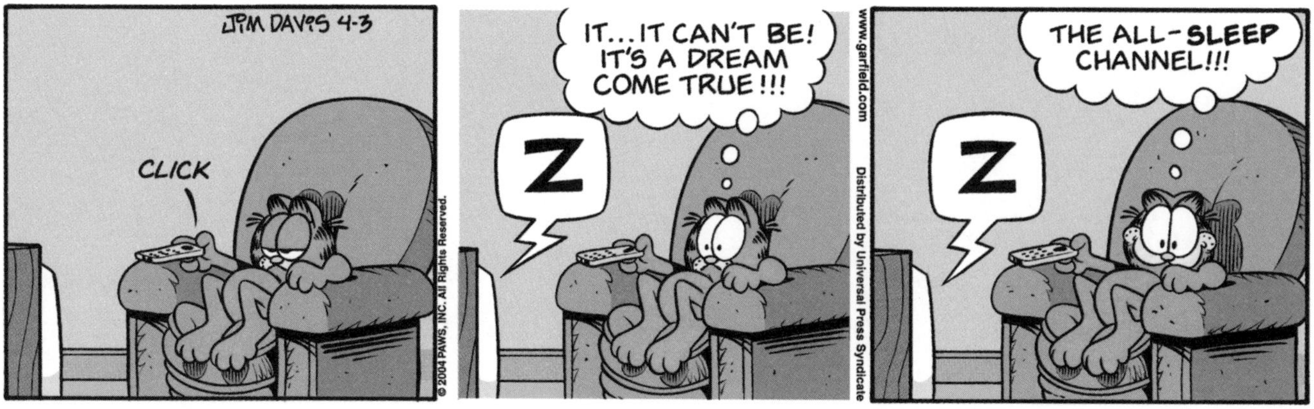
JIM DAVIS 4-3
CLICK
© 2004 PAWS, INC. All Rights Reserved.
Z
IT... IT CAN'T BE! IT'S A DREAM COME TRUE!!!
www.garfield.com
Distributed by Universal Press Syndicate
Z
THE ALL-SLEEP CHANNEL!!!

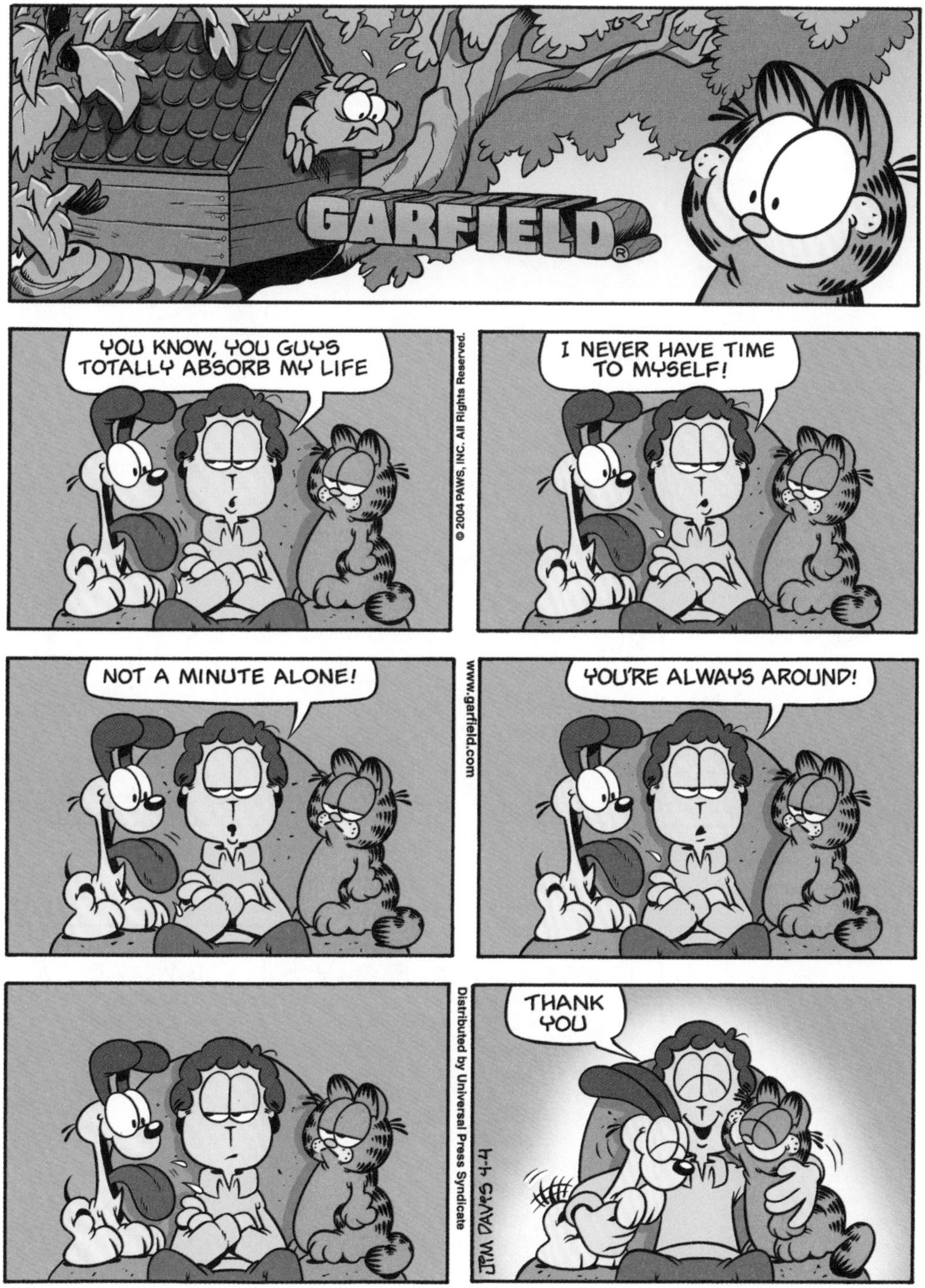
GARFIELD
YOU KNOW, YOU GUYS TOTALLY ABSORB MY LIFE
I NEVER HAVE TIME TO MYSELF!
NOT A MINUTE ALONE!
YOU'RE ALWAYS AROUND!
THANK YOU
JPM DAVIS 4-4

www.garfield.com
Distributed by Universal Press Syndicate

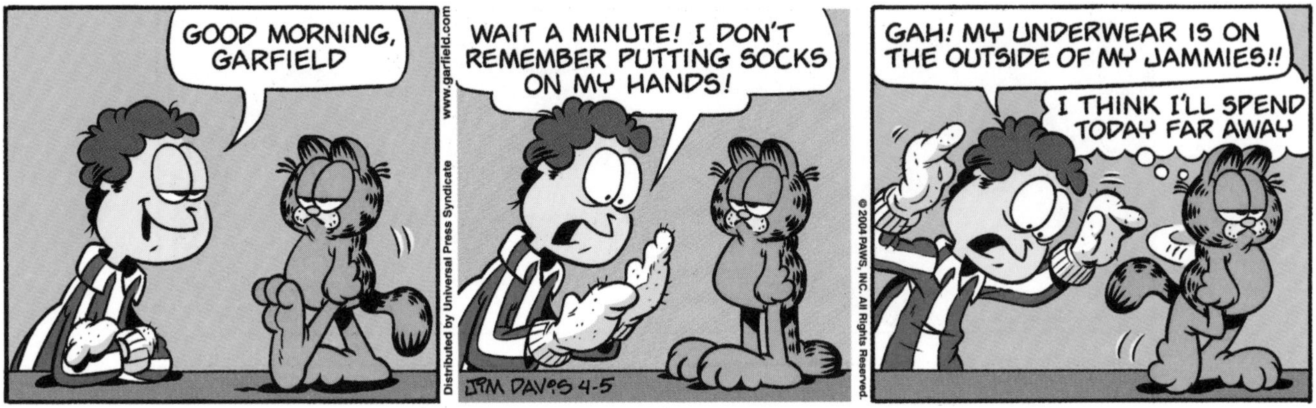
GOOD MORNING, GARFIELD
WAIT A MINUTE! I DON'T REMEMBER PUTTING SOCKS ON MY HANDS!
GAH! MY UNDERWEAR IS ON THE OUTSIDE OF MY JAMMIES!!
I THINK I'LL SPEND TODAY FAR AWAY
JIM DAVIS 4-5
www.garfield.com
Distributed by Universal Press Syndicate
© 2004 PAWS, INC. All Rights Reserved.

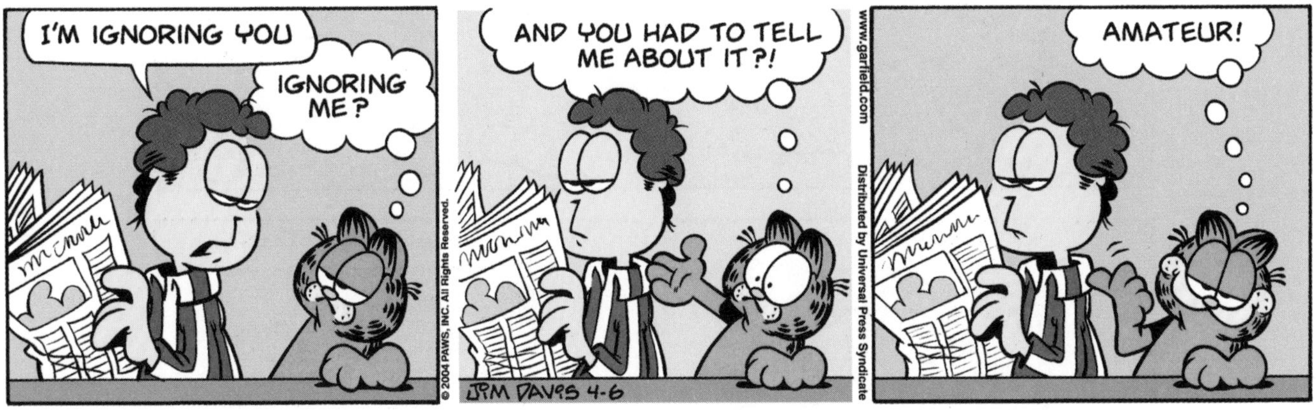
I'M IGNORING YOU
IGNORING ME?
AND YOU HAD TO TELL ME ABOUT IT?!
AMATEUR!
JIM DAVIS 4-6
© 2004 PAWS, INC. All Rights Reserved.
www.garfield.com
Distributed by Universal Press Syndicate

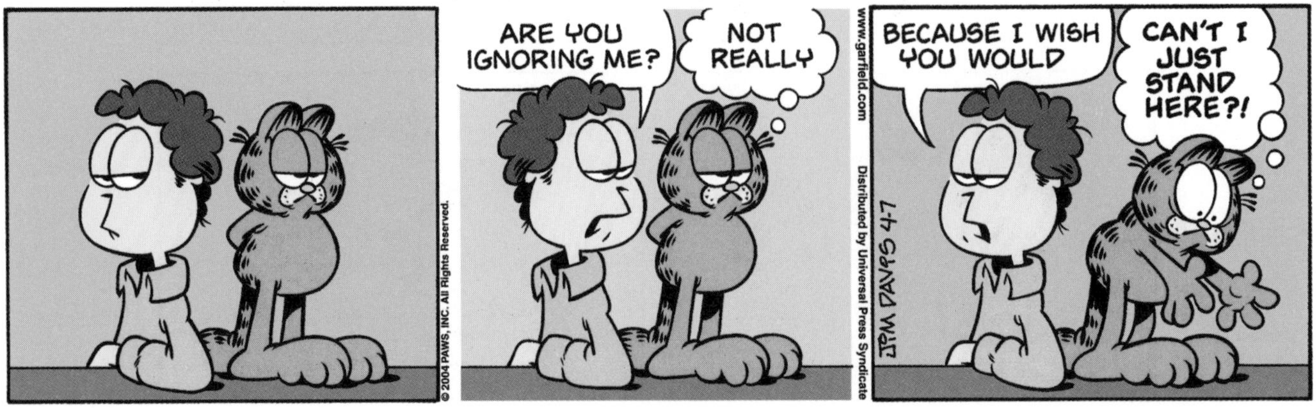
ARE YOU IGNORING ME?
NOT REALLY
BECAUSE I WISH YOU WOULD
CAN'T I JUST STAND HERE?!
JIM DAVIS 4-7
© 2004 PAWS, INC. All Rights Reserved.
www.garfield.com
Distributed by Universal Press Syndicate

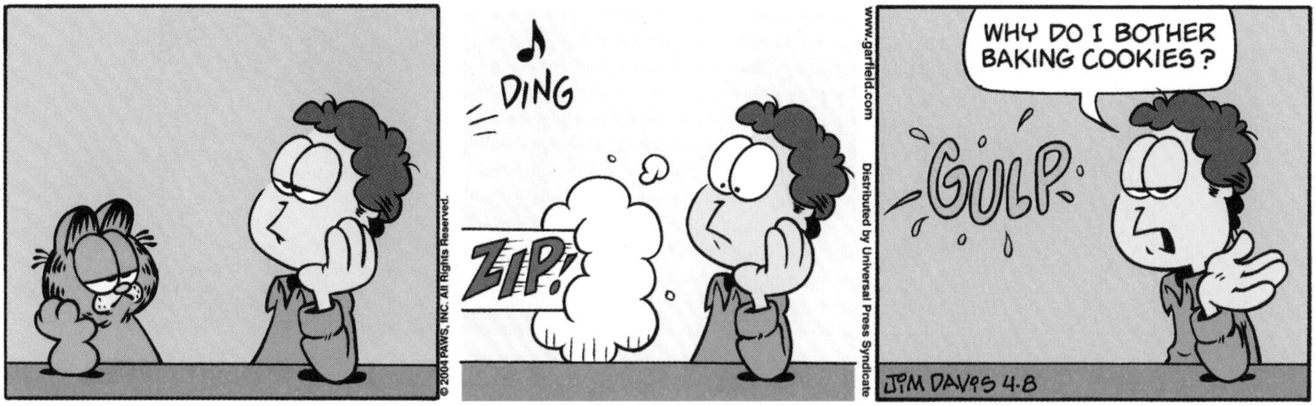
DING
ZIP!
GULP
WHY DO I BOTHER BAKING COOKIES?
JIM DAVIS 4-8
© 2004 PAWS, INC. All Rights Reserved.
www.garfield.com Distributed by Universal Press Syndicate

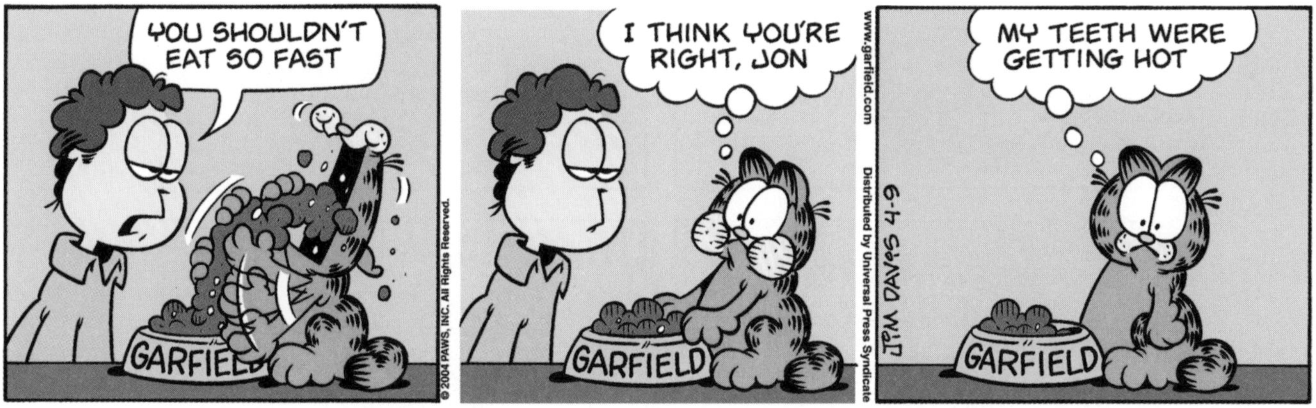
YOU SHOULDN'T EAT SO FAST
GARFIELD
I THINK YOU'RE RIGHT, JON
GARFIELD
MY TEETH WERE GETTING HOT
GARFIELD
JIM DAVIS 4-9
© 2004 PAWS, INC. All Rights Reserved.
www.garfield.com Distributed by Universal Press Syndicate

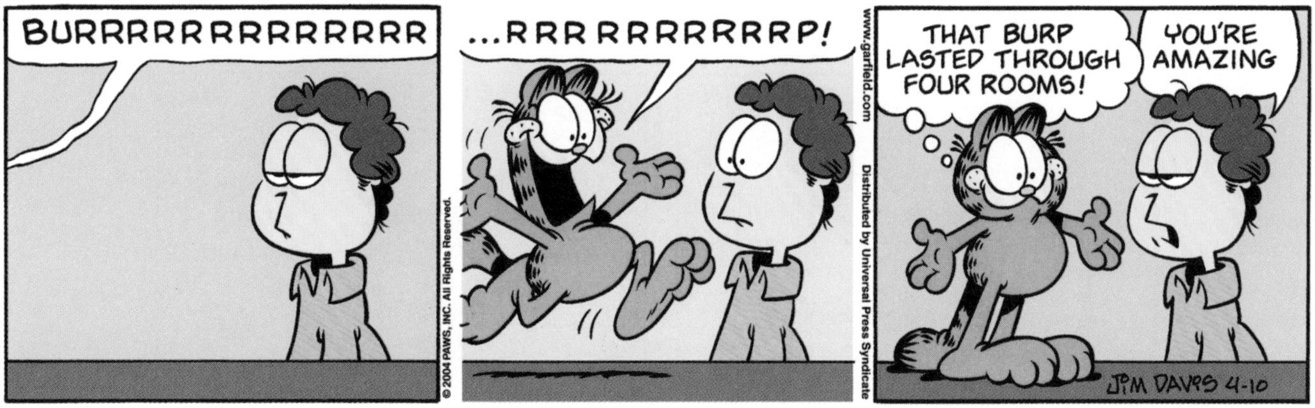
BURRRRRRRRRRRRRR
...RRRRRRRRRRRP!
THAT BURP LASTED THROUGH FOUR ROOMS!
YOU'RE AMAZING
JIM DAVIS 4-10
© 2004 PAWS, INC. All Rights Reserved.
www.garfield.com Distributed by Universal Press Syndicate

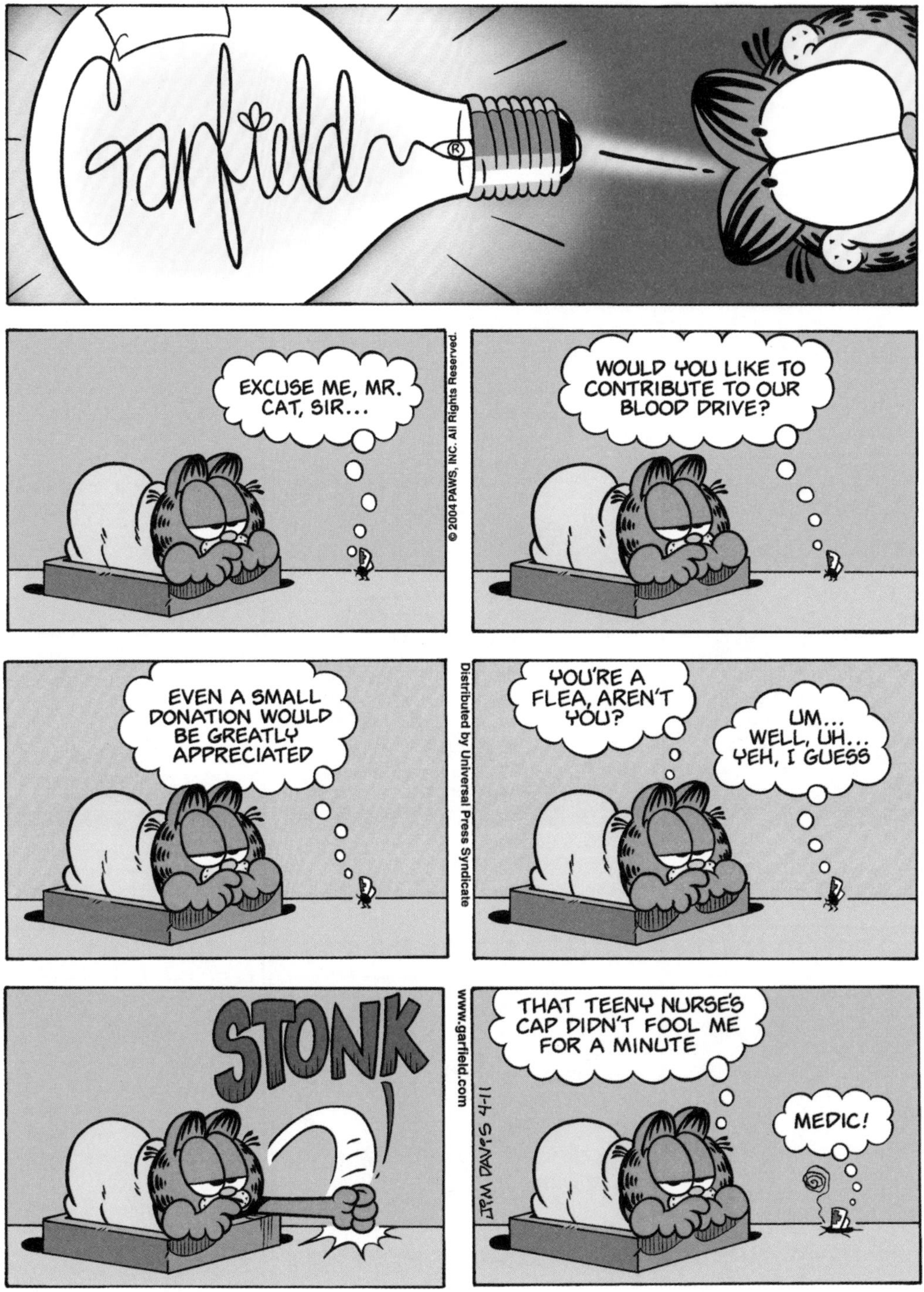
Garfield®
EXCUSE ME, MR. CAT, SIR...
WOULD YOU LIKE TO CONTRIBUTE TO OUR BLOOD DRIVE?
EVEN A SMALL DONATION WOULD BE GREATLY APPRECIATED
YOU'RE A FLEA, AREN'T YOU?
UM... WELL, UH... YEH, I GUESS
STONK
THAT TEENY NURSE'S CAP DIDN'T FOOL ME FOR A MINUTE
MEDIC!
© 2004 PAWS, INC. All Rights Reserved.
Distributed by Universal Press Syndicate
www.garfield.com
JPM DAVIS 4-11

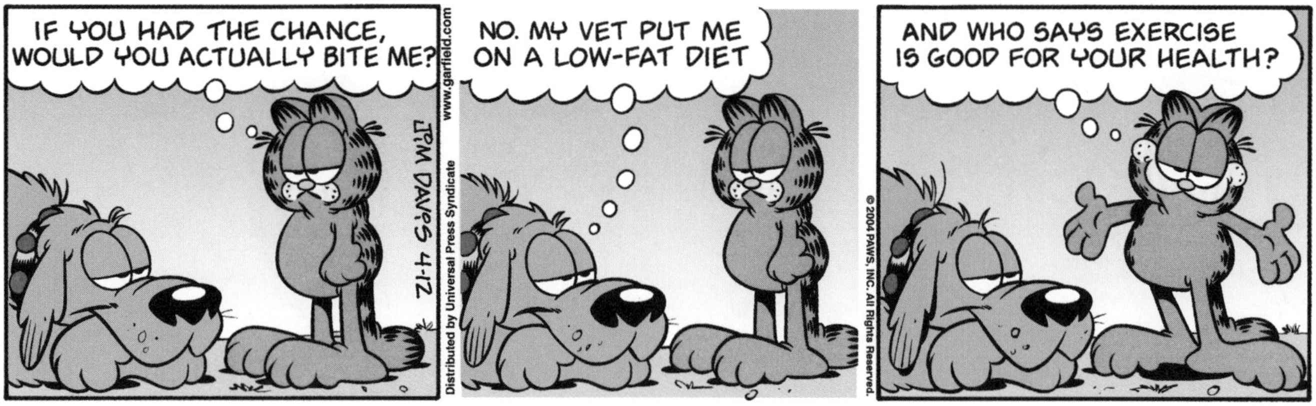
IF YOU HAD THE CHANCE, WOULD YOU ACTUALLY BITE ME?
JPM DAVIS 4-12
www.garfield.com
Distributed by Universal Press Syndicate
NO. MY VET PUT ME ON A LOW-FAT DIET
© 2004 PAWS, INC. All Rights Reserved.
AND WHO SAYS EXERCISE IS GOOD FOR YOUR HEALTH?

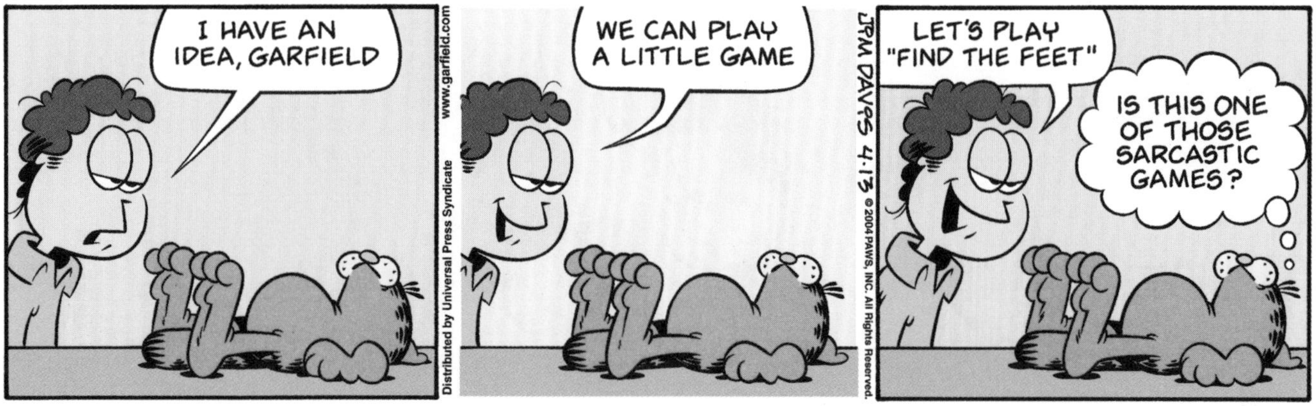
I HAVE AN IDEA, GARFIELD
www.garfield.com
Distributed by Universal Press Syndicate
WE CAN PLAY A LITTLE GAME
JPM DAVIS 4-13
© 2004 PAWS, INC. All Rights Reserved.
LET'S PLAY "FIND THE FEET"
IS THIS ONE OF THOSE SARCASTIC GAMES?

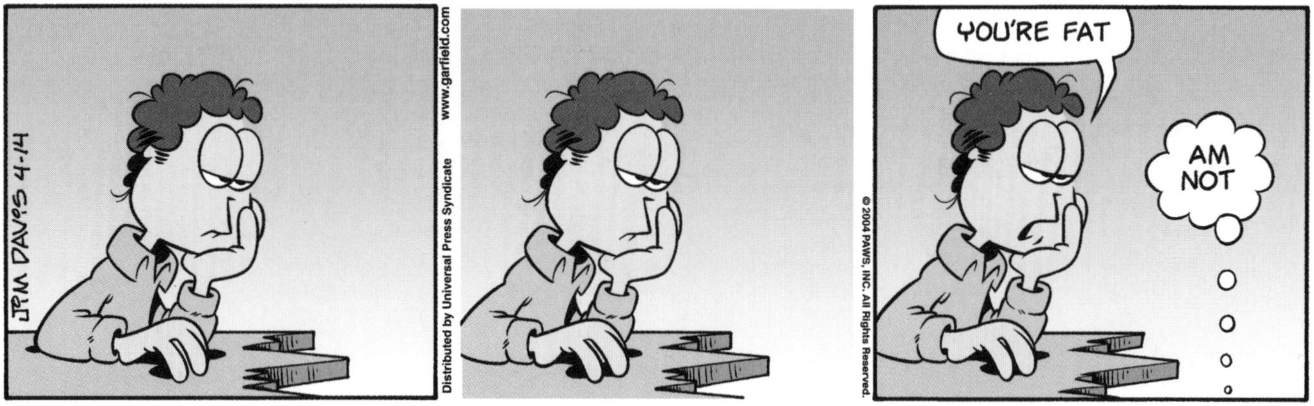
JPM DAVIS 4-14
www.garfield.com
Distributed by Universal Press Syndicate
© 2004 PAWS, INC. All Rights Reserved.
YOU'RE FAT
AM NOT

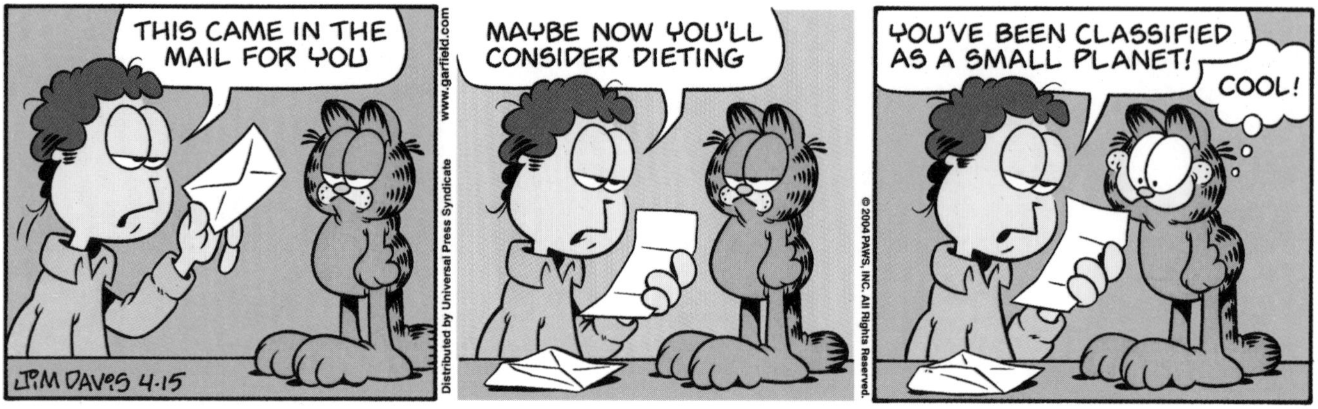
THIS CAME IN THE MAIL FOR YOU
JIM DAVIS 4-15
Distributed by Universal Press Syndicate www.garfield.com
MAYBE NOW YOU'LL CONSIDER DIETING
© 2004 PAWS, INC. All Rights Reserved.
YOU'VE BEEN CLASSIFIED AS A SMALL PLANET!
COOL!

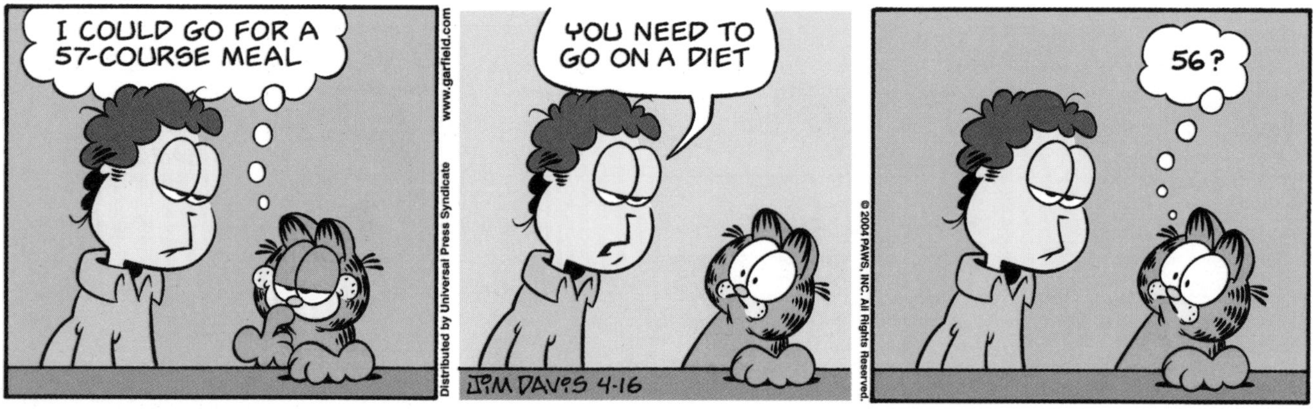
I COULD GO FOR A 57-COURSE MEAL
Distributed by Universal Press Syndicate www.garfield.com
YOU NEED TO GO ON A DIET
JIM DAVIS 4-16
© 2004 PAWS, INC. All Rights Reserved.
56?

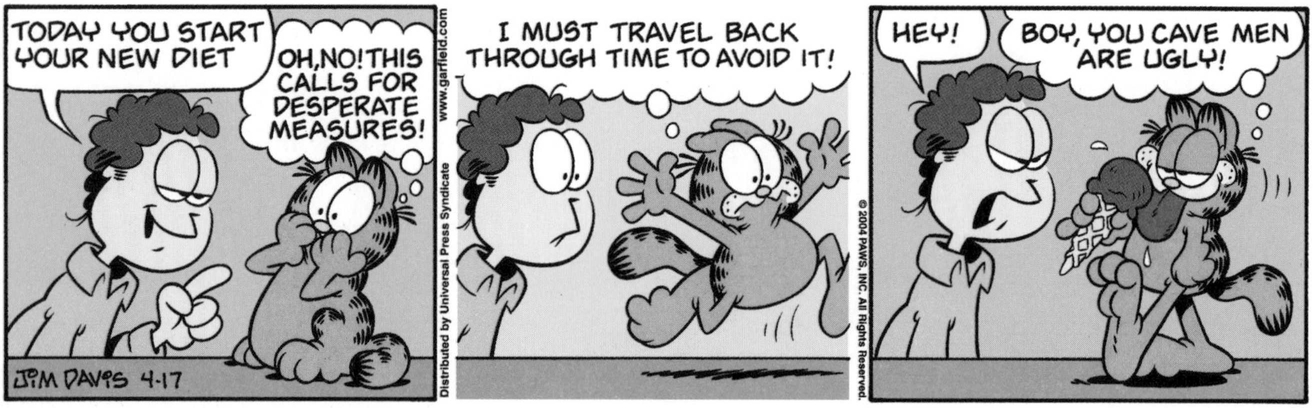
TODAY YOU START YOUR NEW DIET
OH, NO! THIS CALLS FOR DESPERATE MEASURES!
JIM DAVIS 4-17
Distributed by Universal Press Syndicate www.garfield.com
I MUST TRAVEL BACK THROUGH TIME TO AVOID IT!
© 2004 PAWS, INC. All Rights Reserved.
HEY!
BOY, YOU CAVE MEN ARE UGLY!

Cats Rule Dogs Drool

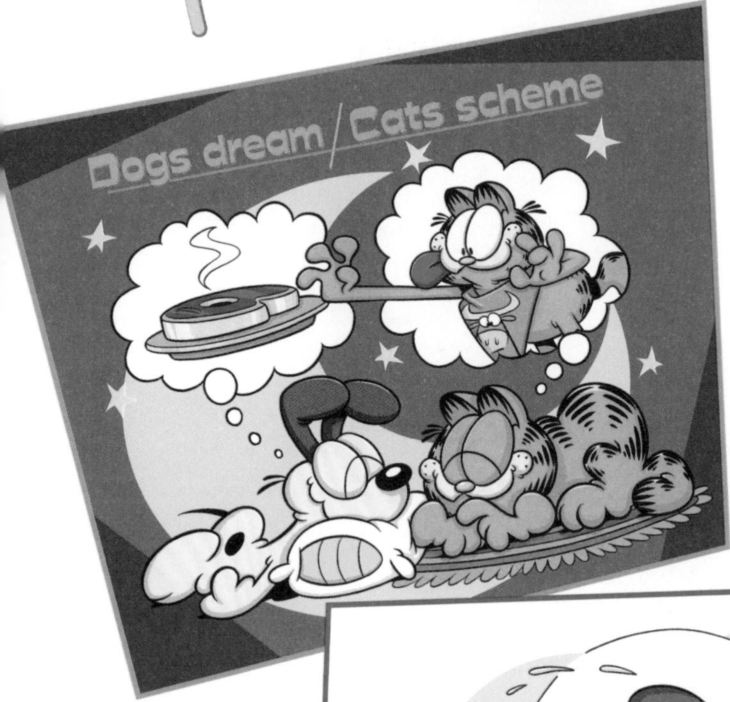
Dogs dream
Cats scheme

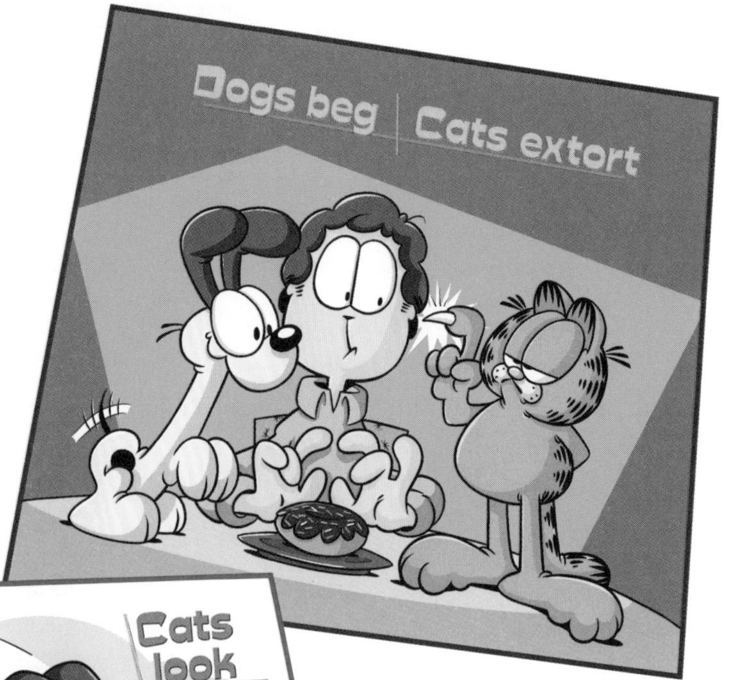
Dogs beg
Cats extort

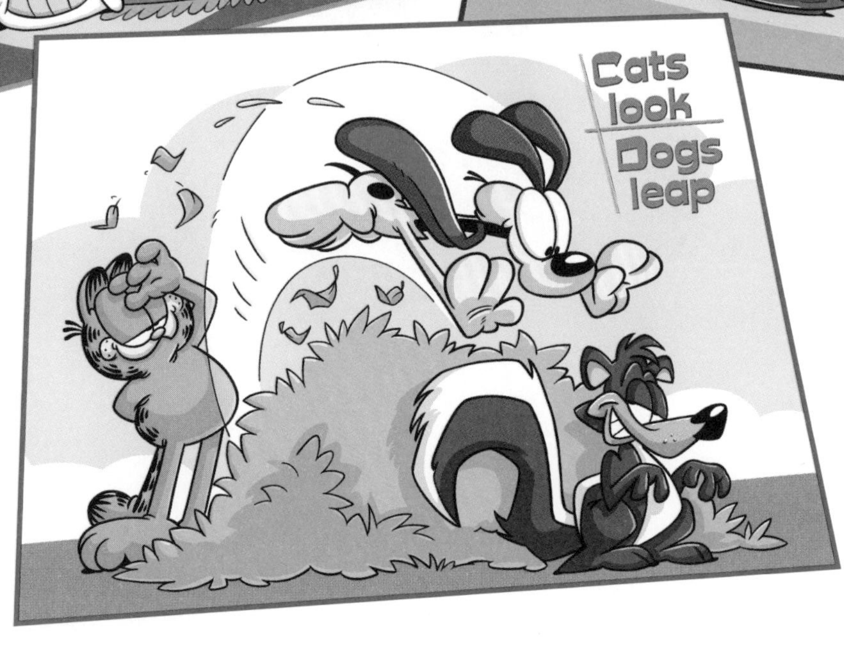
Cats look
Dogs leap

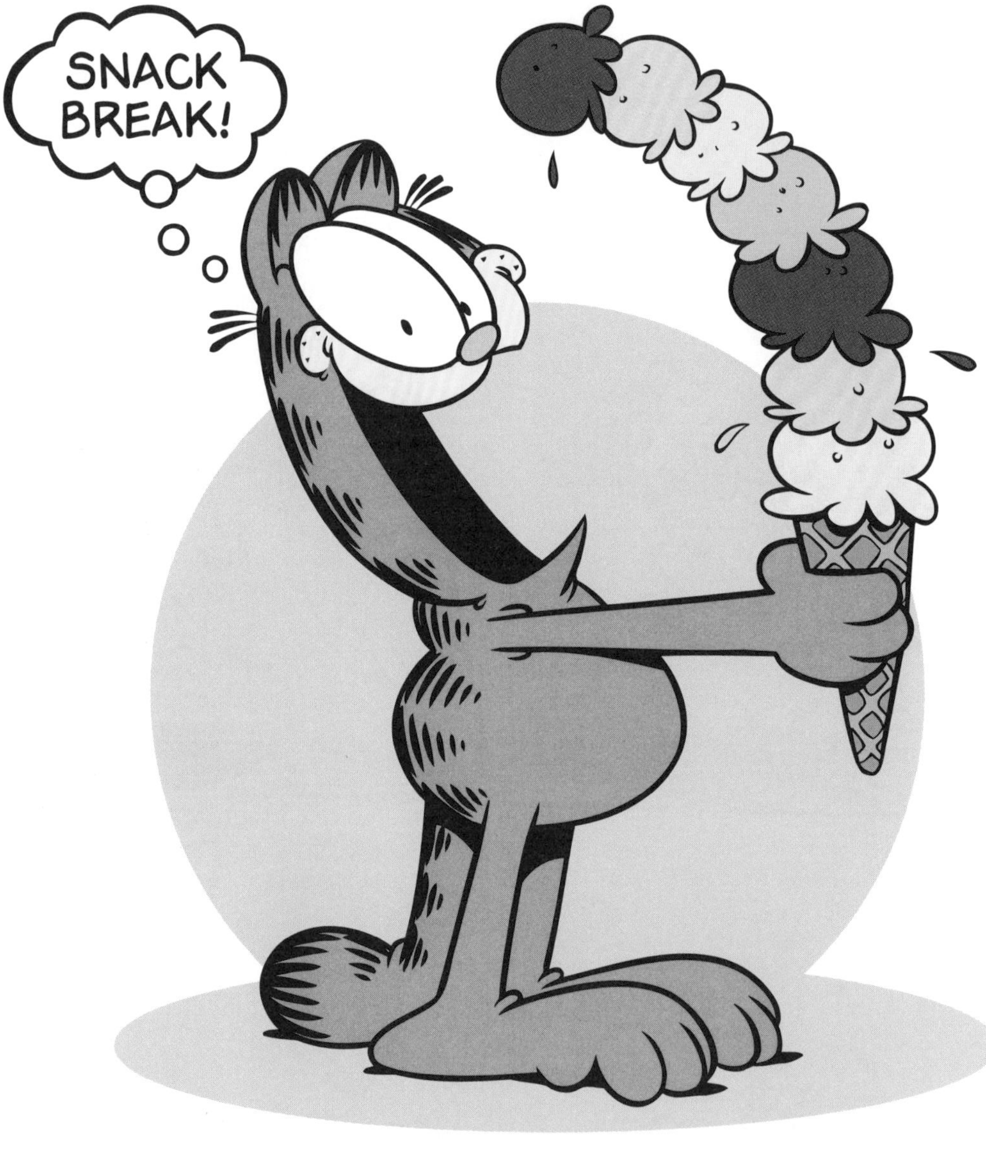
SNACK BREAK!

Garfield
Large & in Charge

BY JIM DAVIS

Ballantine Books ● **New York**

Garfield Goes to the Dogs

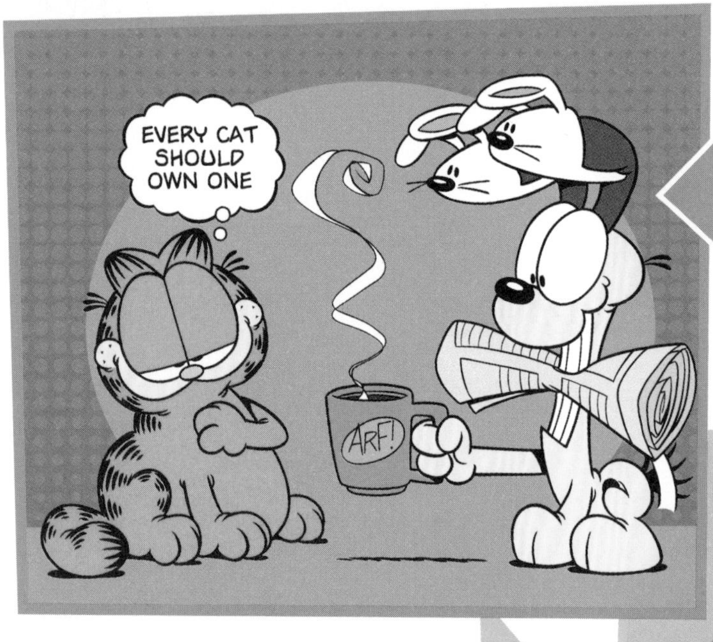
EVERY CAT SHOULD OWN ONE
ARF!

DOGS MAKE GOOD PETS.

DOGS TURN AROUND THREE TIMES BEFORE LYING DOWN.

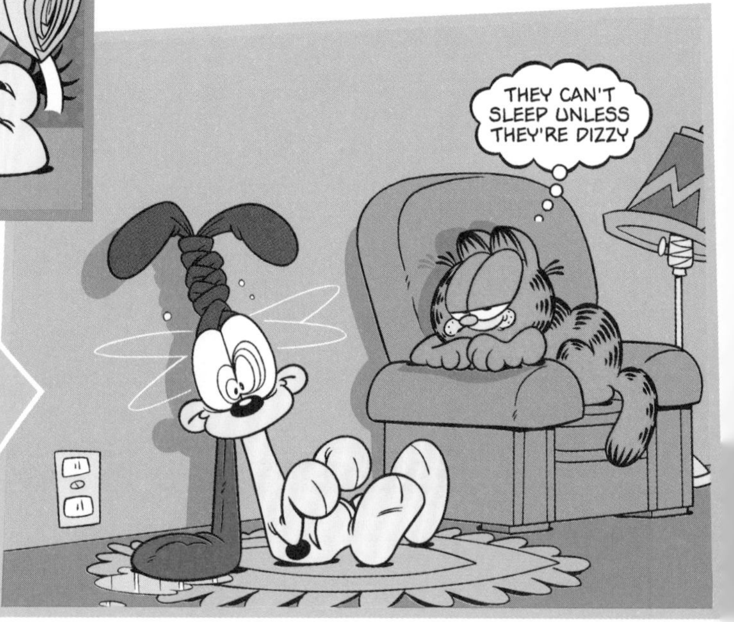
THEY CAN'T SLEEP UNLESS THEY'RE DIZZY

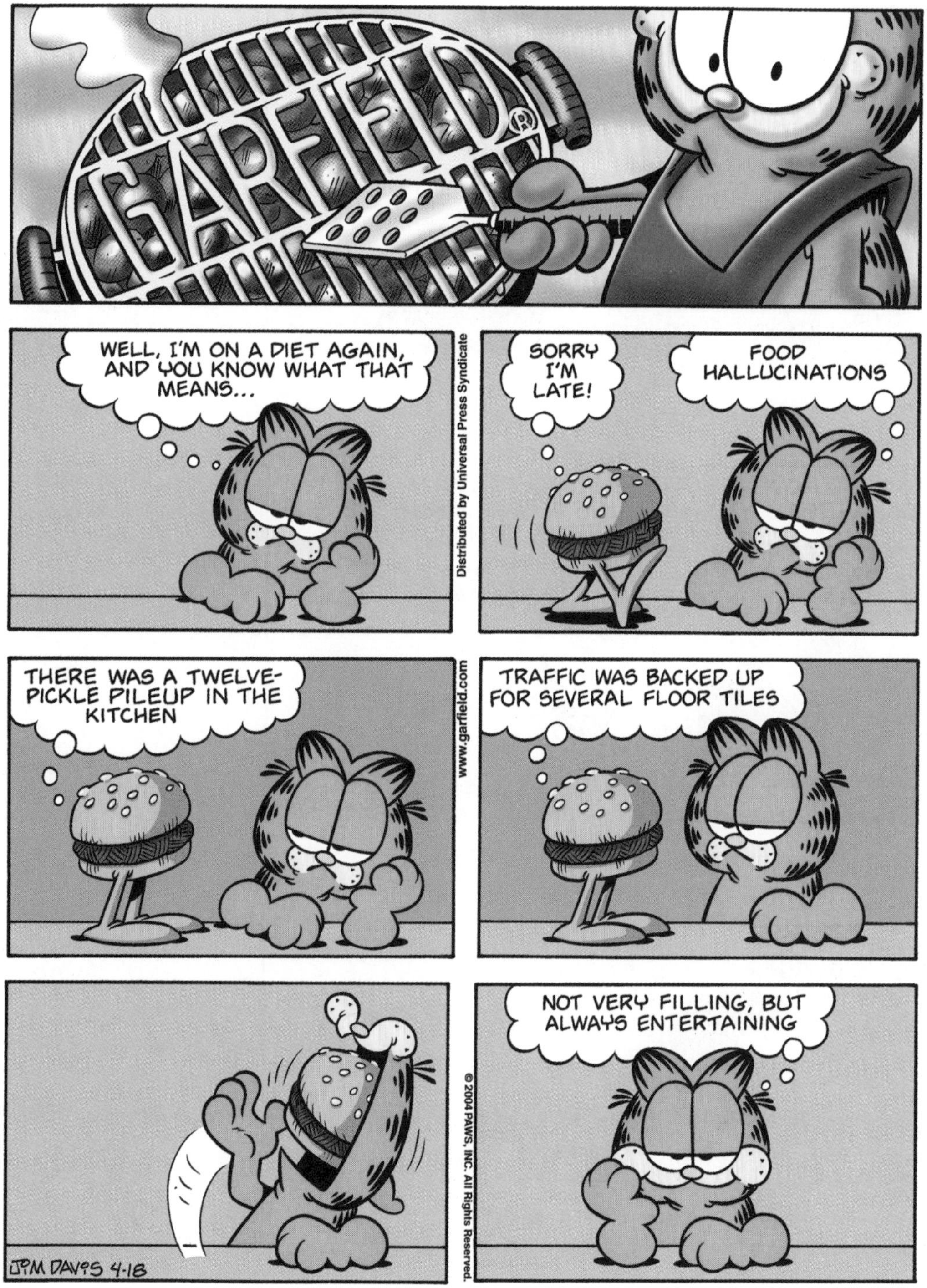
GARFIELD®
WELL, I'M ON A DIET AGAIN, AND YOU KNOW WHAT THAT MEANS...
SORRY I'M LATE!
FOOD HALLUCINATIONS
THERE WAS A TWELVE-PICKLE PILEUP IN THE KITCHEN
TRAFFIC WAS BACKED UP FOR SEVERAL FLOOR TILES
NOT VERY FILLING, BUT ALWAYS ENTERTAINING
JIM DAVIS 4-18
Distributed by Universal Press Syndicate
www.garfield.com
© 2004 PAWS, INC. All Rights Reserved.

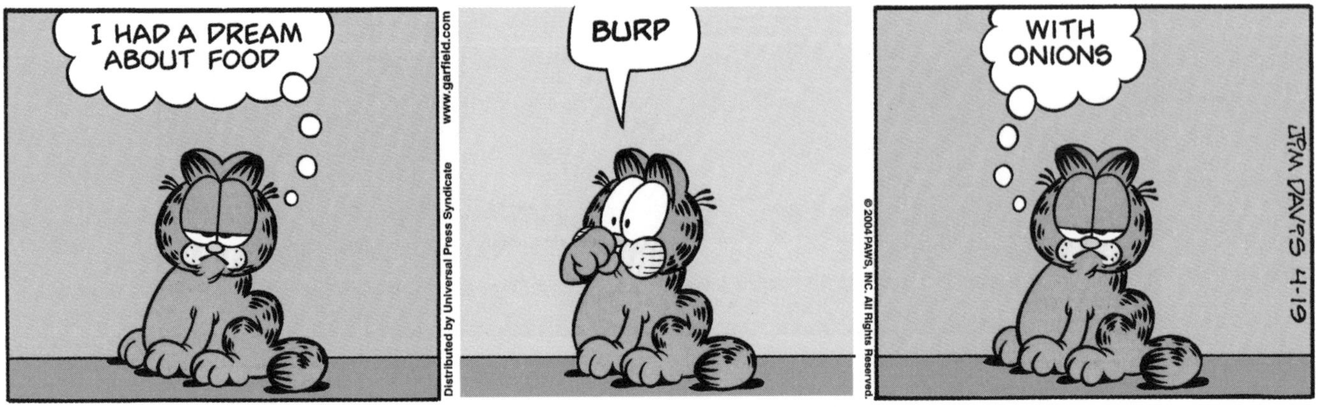
I HAD A DREAM ABOUT FOOD
BURP
WITH ONIONS
JIM DAVIS 4-19
Distributed by Universal Press Syndicate www.garfield.com
© 2004 PAWS, INC. All Rights Reserved.

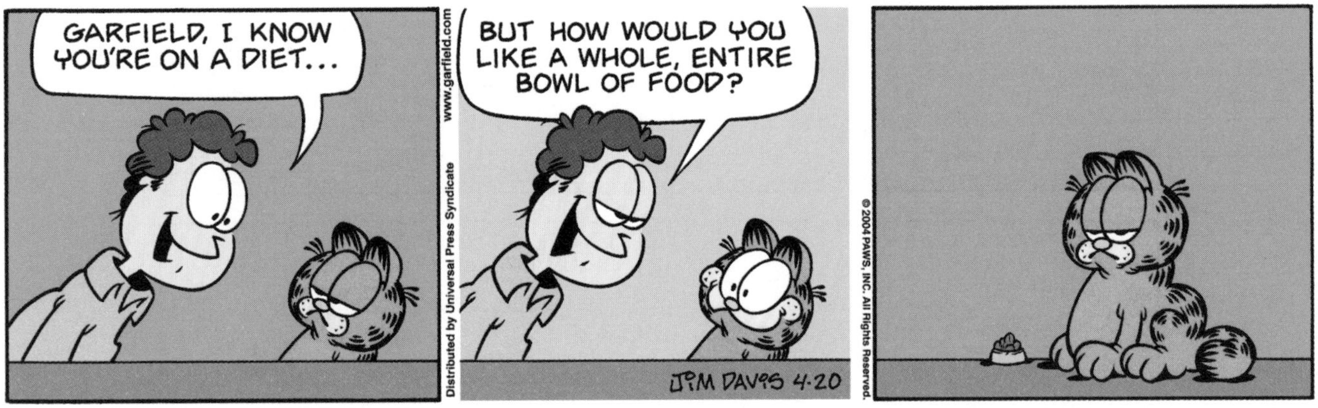
GARFIELD, I KNOW YOU'RE ON A DIET...
BUT HOW WOULD YOU LIKE A WHOLE, ENTIRE BOWL OF FOOD?
JIM DAVIS 4-20
Distributed by Universal Press Syndicate www.garfield.com
© 2004 PAWS, INC. All Rights Reserved.

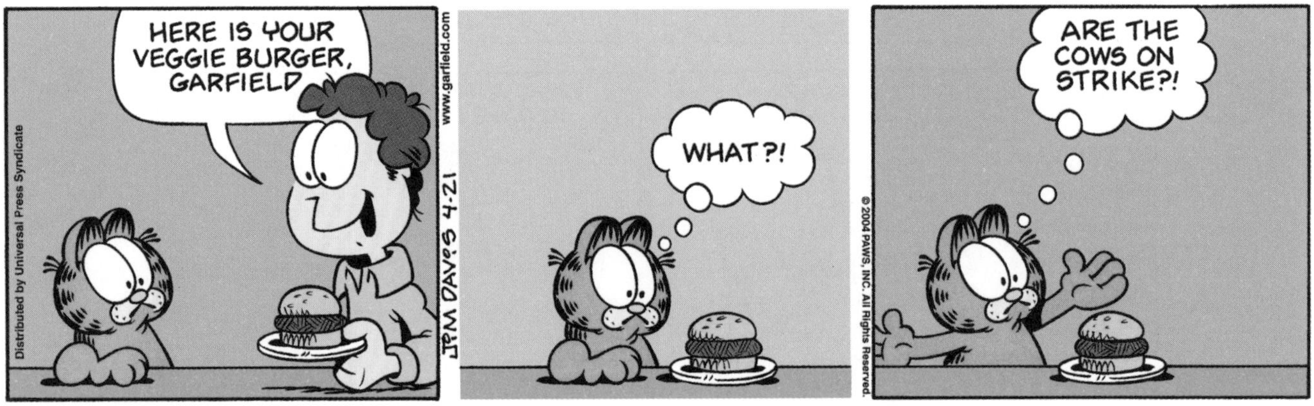
HERE IS YOUR VEGGIE BURGER, GARFIELD
WHAT?!
ARE THE COWS ON STRIKE?!
JIM DAVIS 4-21
Distributed by Universal Press Syndicate www.garfield.com
© 2004 PAWS, INC. All Rights Reserved.

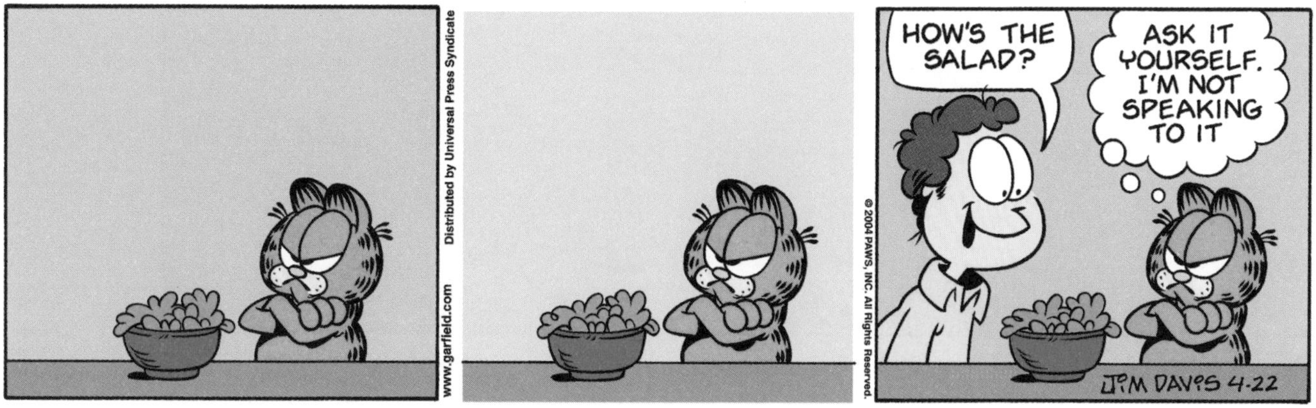
Distributed by Universal Press Syndicate
www.garfield.com
HOW'S THE SALAD?
ASK IT YOURSELF. I'M NOT SPEAKING TO IT
© 2004 PAWS, INC. All Rights Reserved.
JIM DAVIS 4-22

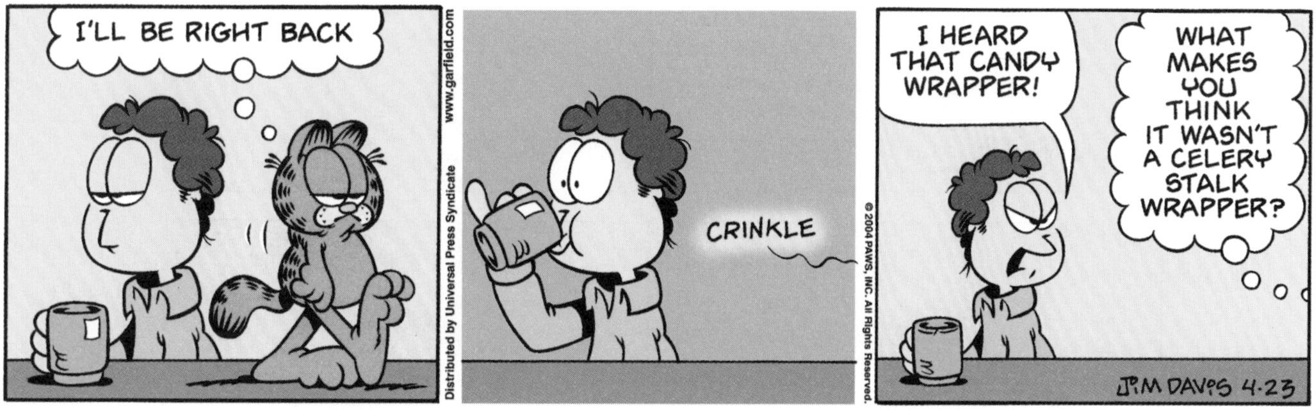
I'LL BE RIGHT BACK
www.garfield.com
Distributed by Universal Press Syndicate
CRINKLE
© 2004 PAWS, INC. All Rights Reserved.
I HEARD THAT CANDY WRAPPER!
WHAT MAKES YOU THINK IT WASN'T A CELERY STALK WRAPPER?
JIM DAVIS 4-23

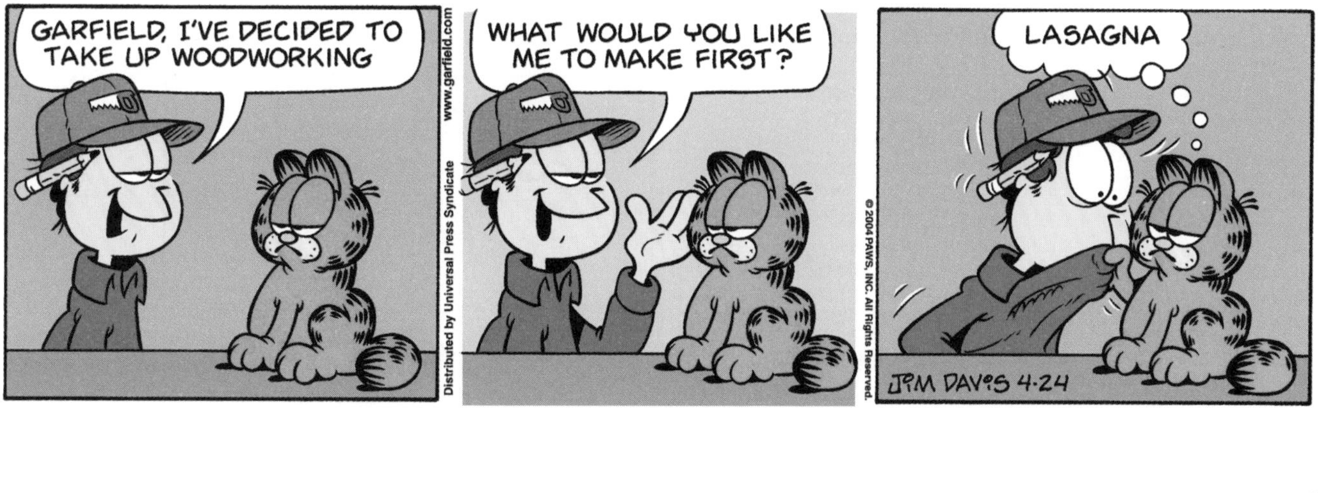
GARFIELD, I'VE DECIDED TO TAKE UP WOODWORKING
www.garfield.com
Distributed by Universal Press Syndicate
WHAT WOULD YOU LIKE ME TO MAKE FIRST?
© 2004 PAWS, INC. All Rights Reserved.
LASAGNA
JIM DAVIS 4-24

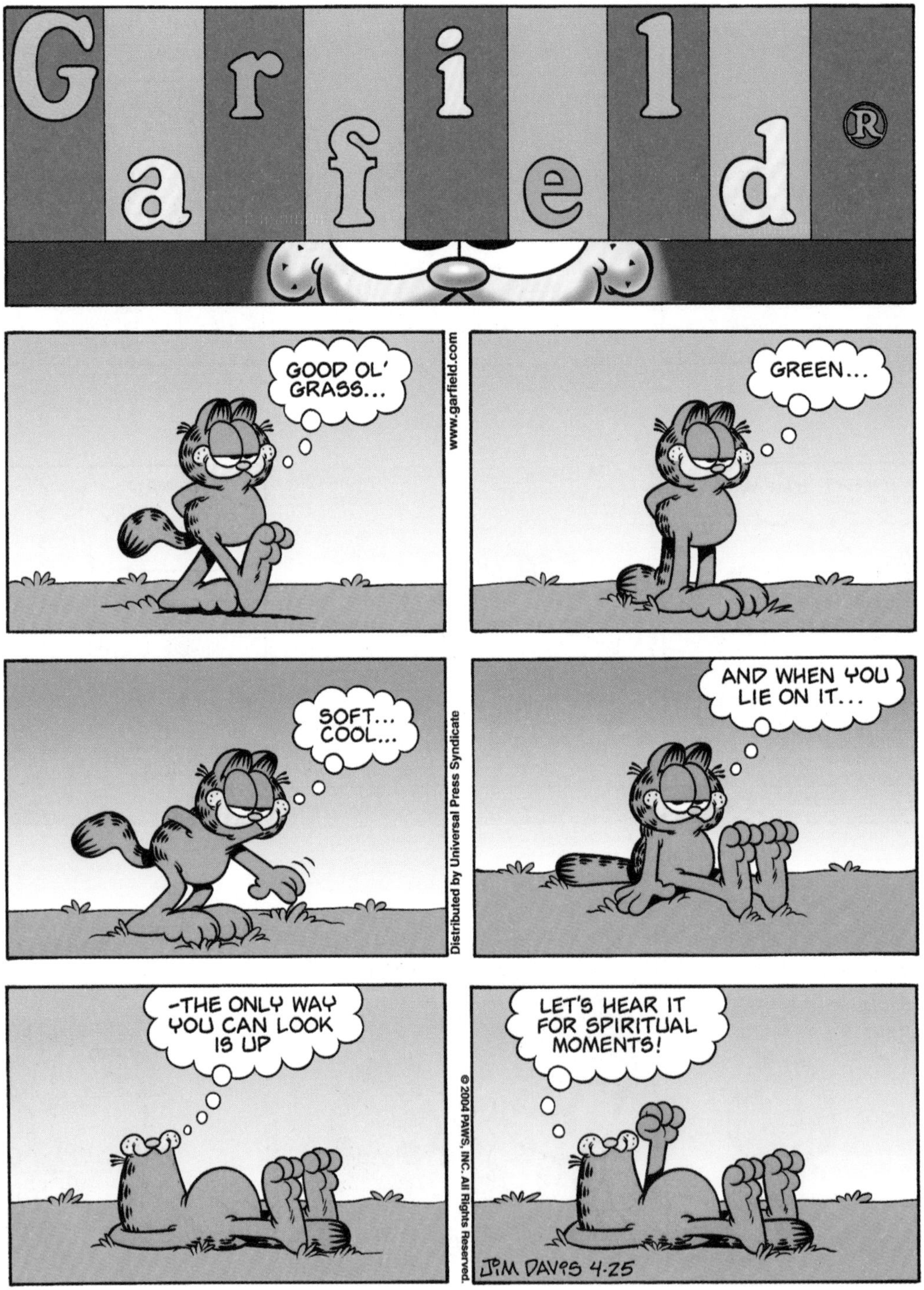
Garfield®
GOOD OL' GRASS...
GREEN...
SOFT... COOL...
AND WHEN YOU LIE ON IT...
-THE ONLY WAY YOU CAN LOOK IS UP
LET'S HEAR IT FOR SPIRITUAL MOMENTS!
JIM DAVIS 4-25
www.garfield.com
Distributed by Universal Press Syndicate
© 2004 PAWS, INC. All Rights Reserved.

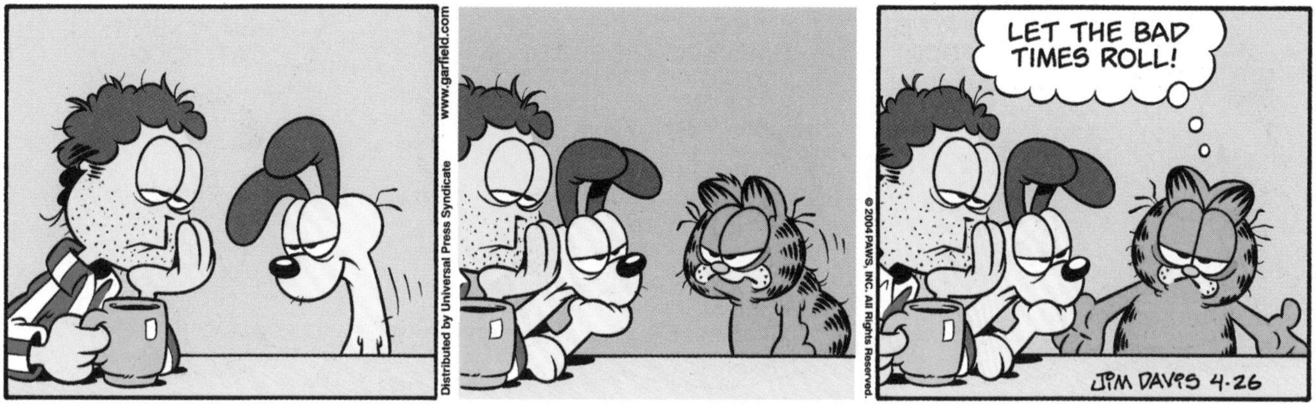
Distributed by Universal Press Syndicate www.garfield.com
© 2004 PAWS, INC. All Rights Reserved.
LET THE BAD TIMES ROLL!
JIM DAVIS 4-26

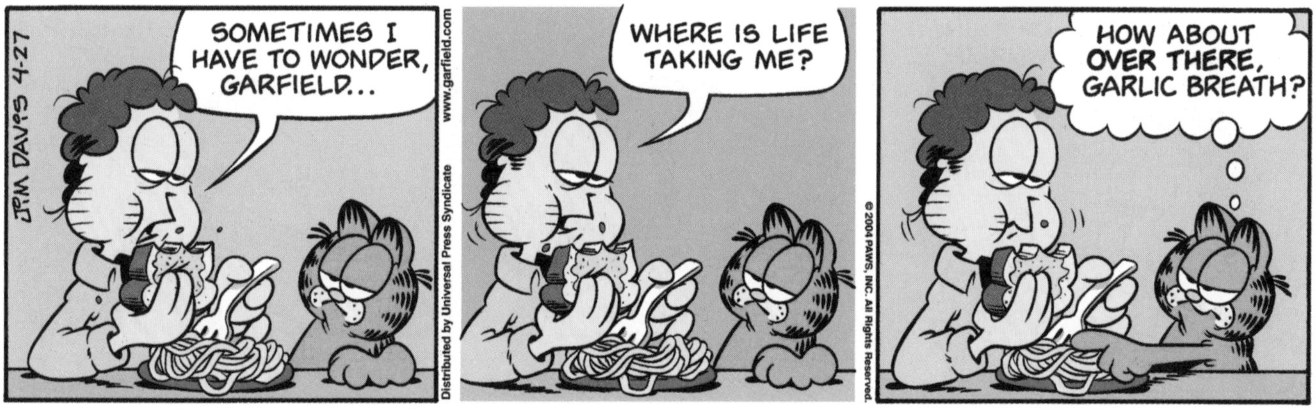
JIM DAVIS 4-27
SOMETIMES I HAVE TO WONDER, GARFIELD...
Distributed by Universal Press Syndicate www.garfield.com
WHERE IS LIFE TAKING ME?
© 2004 PAWS, INC. All Rights Reserved.
HOW ABOUT **OVER THERE**, GARLIC BREATH?

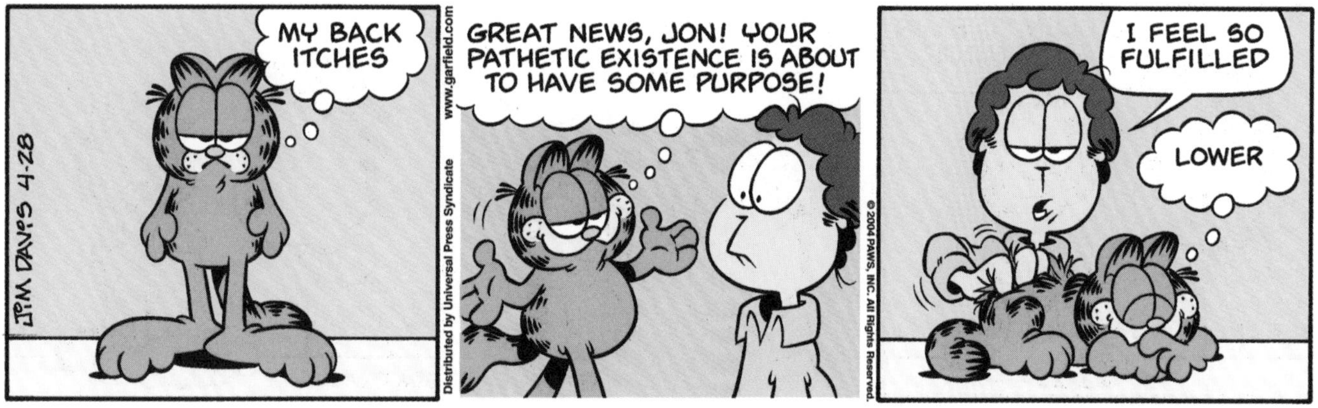
JIM DAVIS 4-28
MY BACK ITCHES
Distributed by Universal Press Syndicate www.garfield.com
GREAT NEWS, JON! YOUR PATHETIC EXISTENCE IS ABOUT TO HAVE SOME PURPOSE!
© 2004 PAWS, INC. All Rights Reserved.
I FEEL SO FULFILLED
LOWER

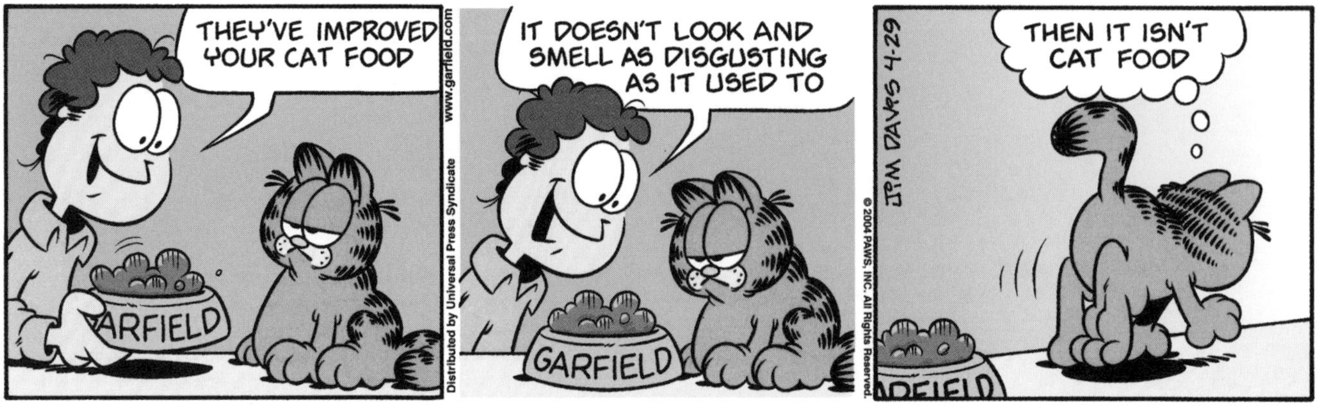
THEY'VE IMPROVED YOUR CAT FOOD
GARFIELD
IT DOESN'T LOOK AND SMELL AS DISGUSTING AS IT USED TO
GARFIELD
THEN IT ISN'T CAT FOOD
Distributed by Universal Press Syndicate www.garfield.com
JPM DAVPS 4-29
© 2004 PAWS, INC. All Rights Reserved.

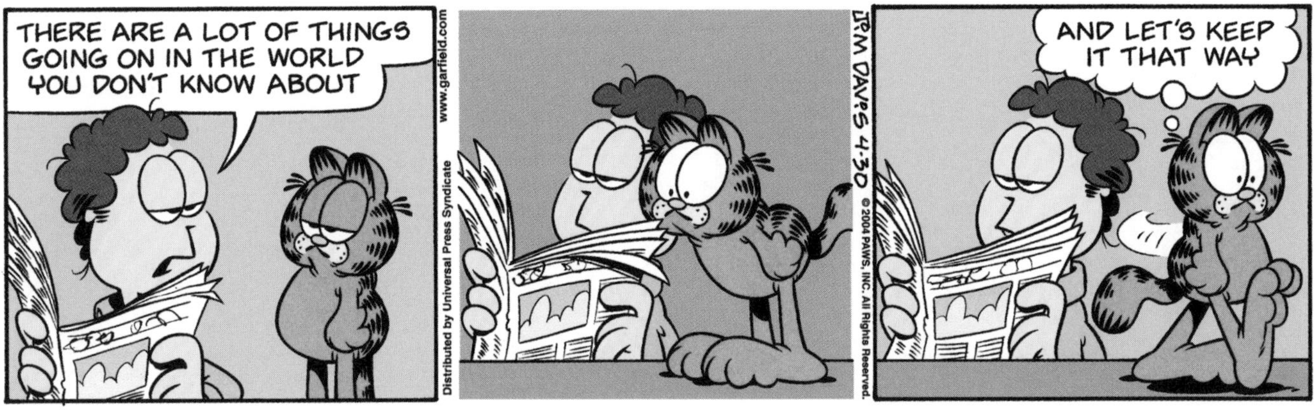
THERE ARE A LOT OF THINGS GOING ON IN THE WORLD YOU DON'T KNOW ABOUT
AND LET'S KEEP IT THAT WAY
Distributed by Universal Press Syndicate www.garfield.com
JPM DAVPS 4-30
© 2004 PAWS, INC. All Rights Reserved.

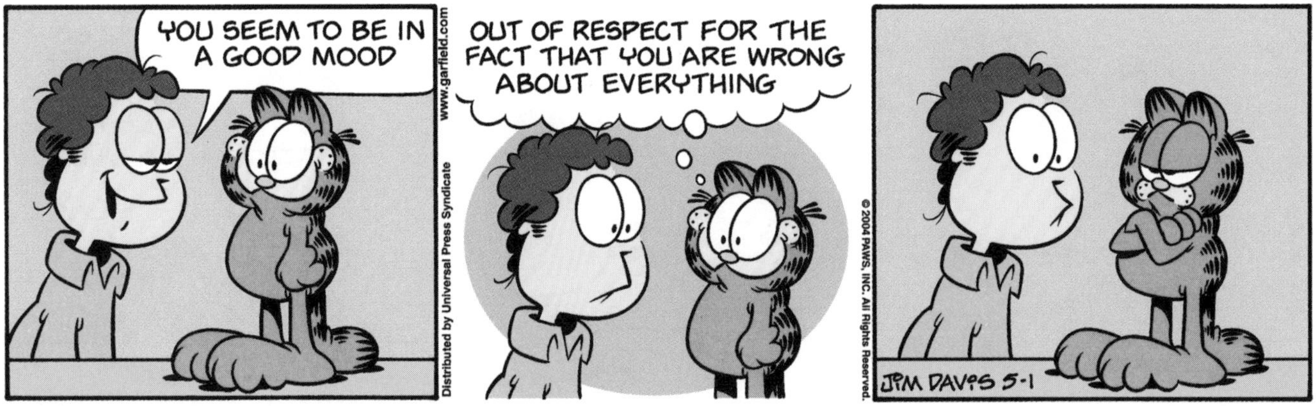
YOU SEEM TO BE IN A GOOD MOOD
OUT OF RESPECT FOR THE FACT THAT YOU ARE WRONG ABOUT EVERYTHING
Distributed by Universal Press Syndicate www.garfield.com
JPM DAVPS 5-1
© 2004 PAWS, INC. All Rights Reserved.

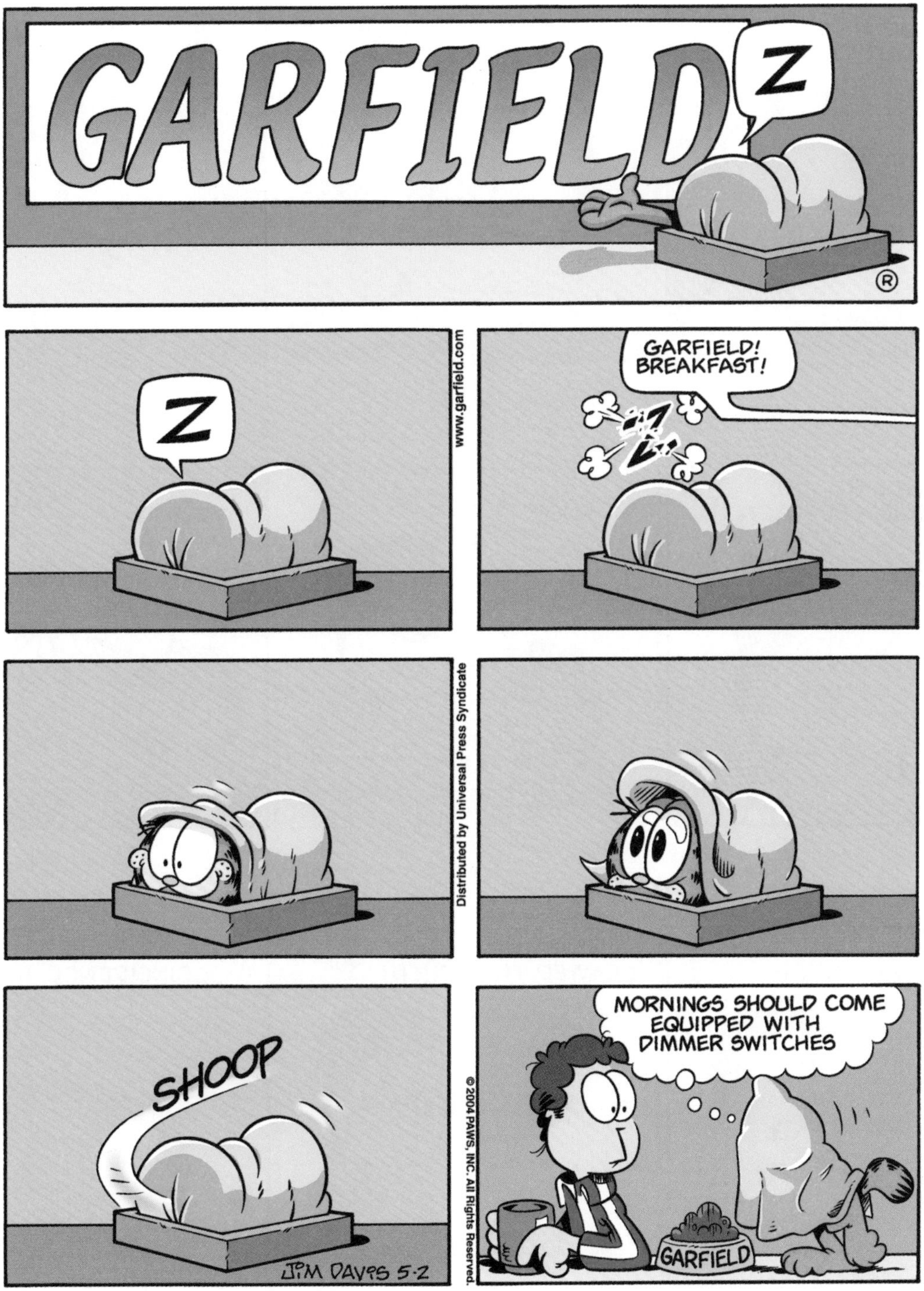
GARFIELD
Z
Z
GARFIELD! BREAKFAST!
Z
SHOOP
JIM DAVIS 5-2
MORNINGS SHOULD COME EQUIPPED WITH DIMMER SWITCHES
GARFIELD
www.garfield.com
Distributed by Universal Press Syndicate
© 2004 PAWS, INC. All Rights Reserved.

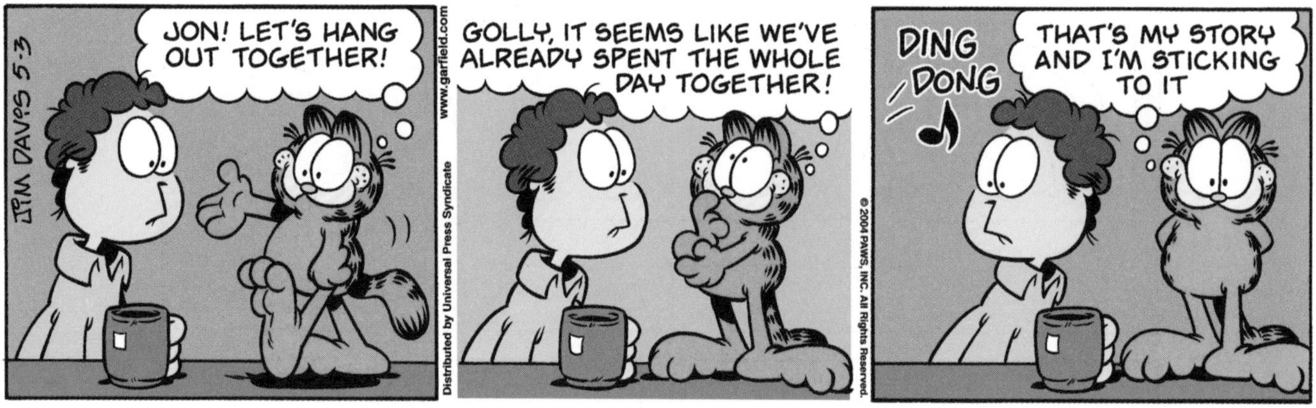
JIM DAVIS 5-3
JON! LET'S HANG OUT TOGETHER!
www.garfield.com
Distributed by Universal Press Syndicate
GOLLY, IT SEEMS LIKE WE'VE ALREADY SPENT THE WHOLE DAY TOGETHER!
© 2004 PAWS, INC. All Rights Reserved.
DING DONG
THAT'S MY STORY AND I'M STICKING TO IT

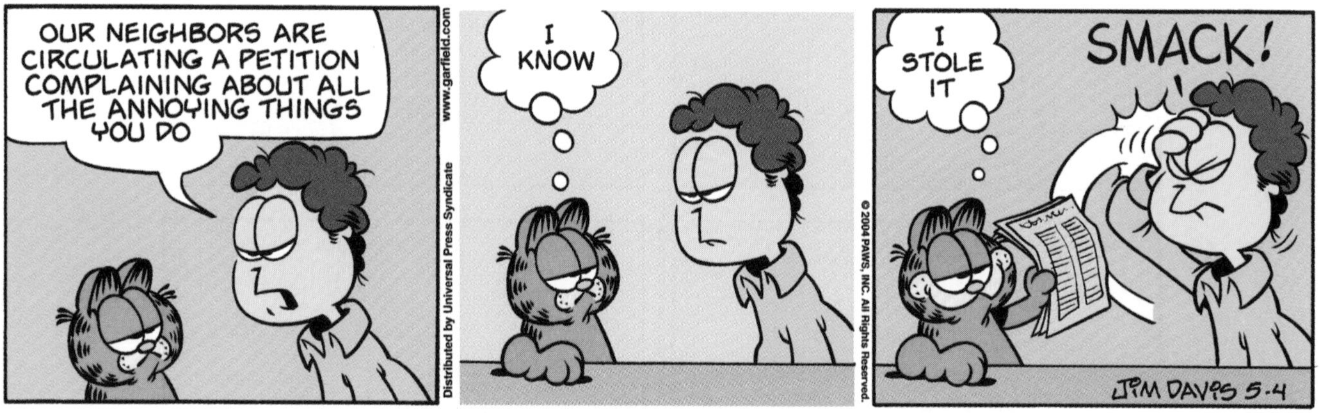
OUR NEIGHBORS ARE CIRCULATING A PETITION COMPLAINING ABOUT ALL THE ANNOYING THINGS YOU DO
www.garfield.com
Distributed by Universal Press Syndicate
I KNOW
© 2004 PAWS, INC. All Rights Reserved.
I STOLE IT
SMACK!
JIM DAVIS 5-4

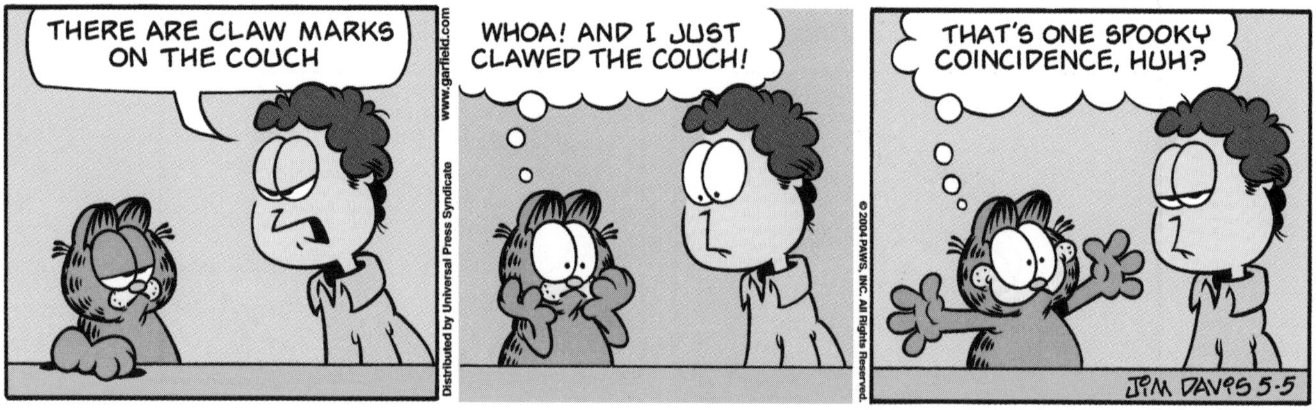
THERE ARE CLAW MARKS ON THE COUCH
www.garfield.com
Distributed by Universal Press Syndicate
WHOA! AND I JUST CLAWED THE COUCH!
© 2004 PAWS, INC. All Rights Reserved.
THAT'S ONE SPOOKY COINCIDENCE, HUH?
JIM DAVIS 5-5

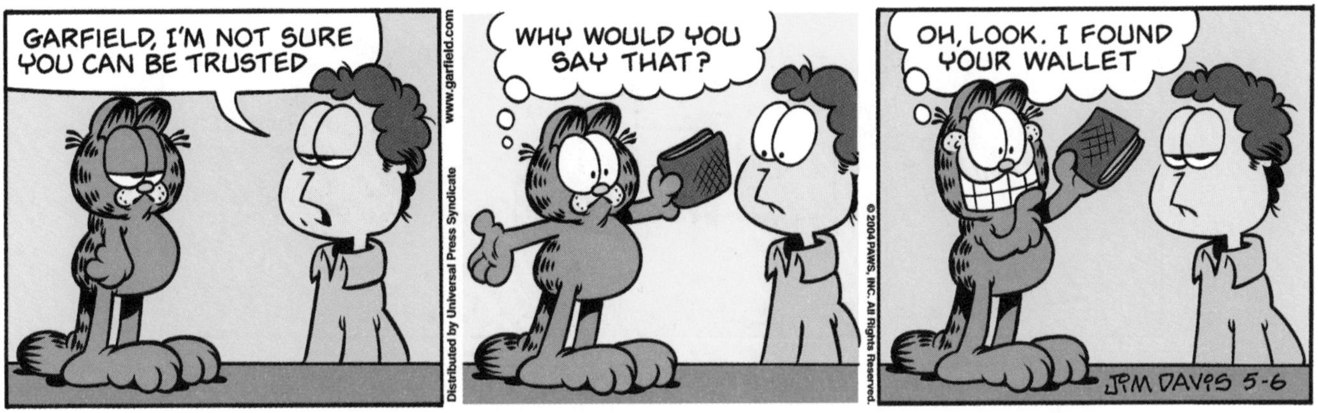
GARFIELD, I'M NOT SURE YOU CAN BE TRUSTED
WHY WOULD YOU SAY THAT?
OH, LOOK. I FOUND YOUR WALLET
JIM DAVIS 5-6
www.garfield.com
Distributed by Universal Press Syndicate
© 2004 PAWS, INC. All Rights Reserved.

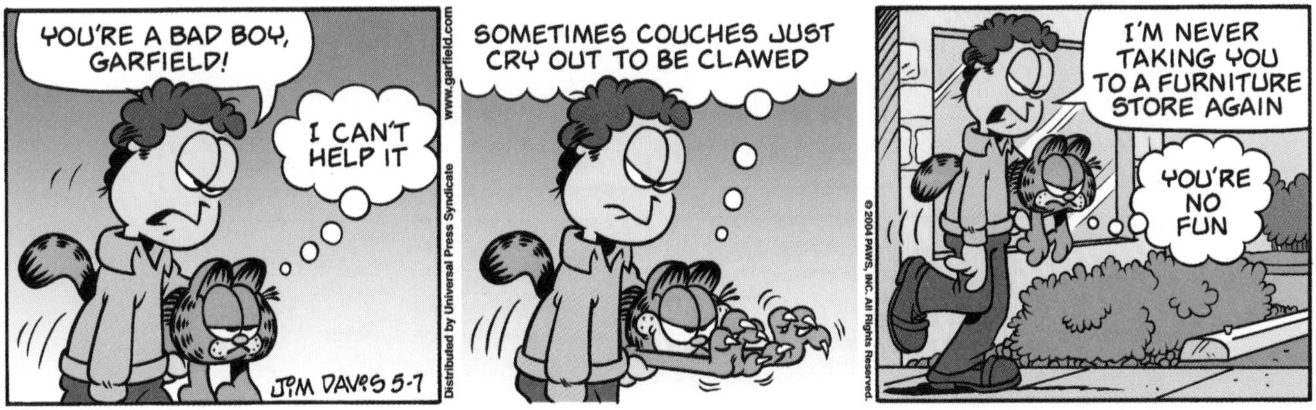
YOU'RE A BAD BOY, GARFIELD!
I CAN'T HELP IT
JIM DAVIS 5-7
SOMETIMES COUCHES JUST CRY OUT TO BE CLAWED
I'M NEVER TAKING YOU TO A FURNITURE STORE AGAIN
YOU'RE NO FUN
www.garfield.com
Distributed by Universal Press Syndicate
© 2004 PAWS, INC. All Rights Reserved.

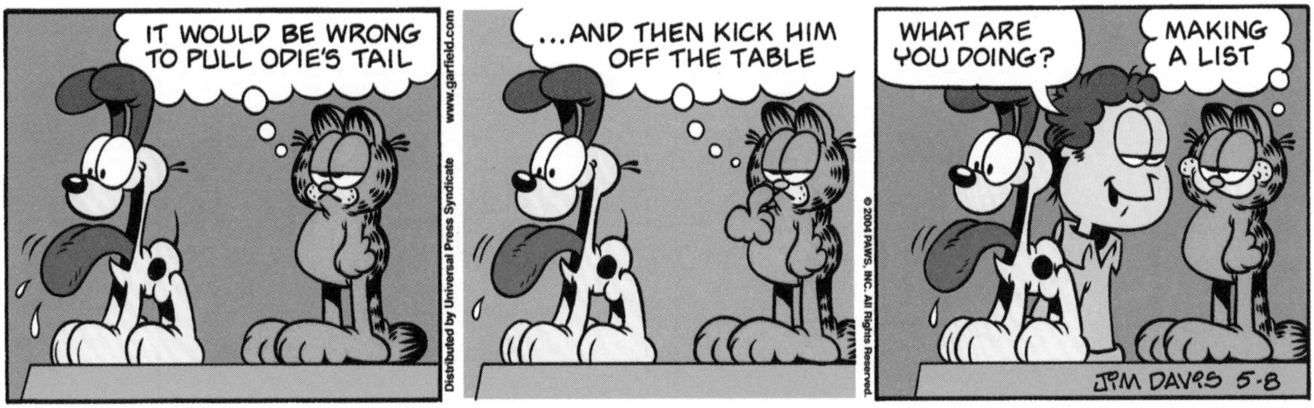
IT WOULD BE WRONG TO PULL ODIE'S TAIL
...AND THEN KICK HIM OFF THE TABLE
WHAT ARE YOU DOING?
MAKING A LIST
JIM DAVIS 5-8
www.garfield.com
Distributed by Universal Press Syndicate
© 2004 PAWS, INC. All Rights Reserved.

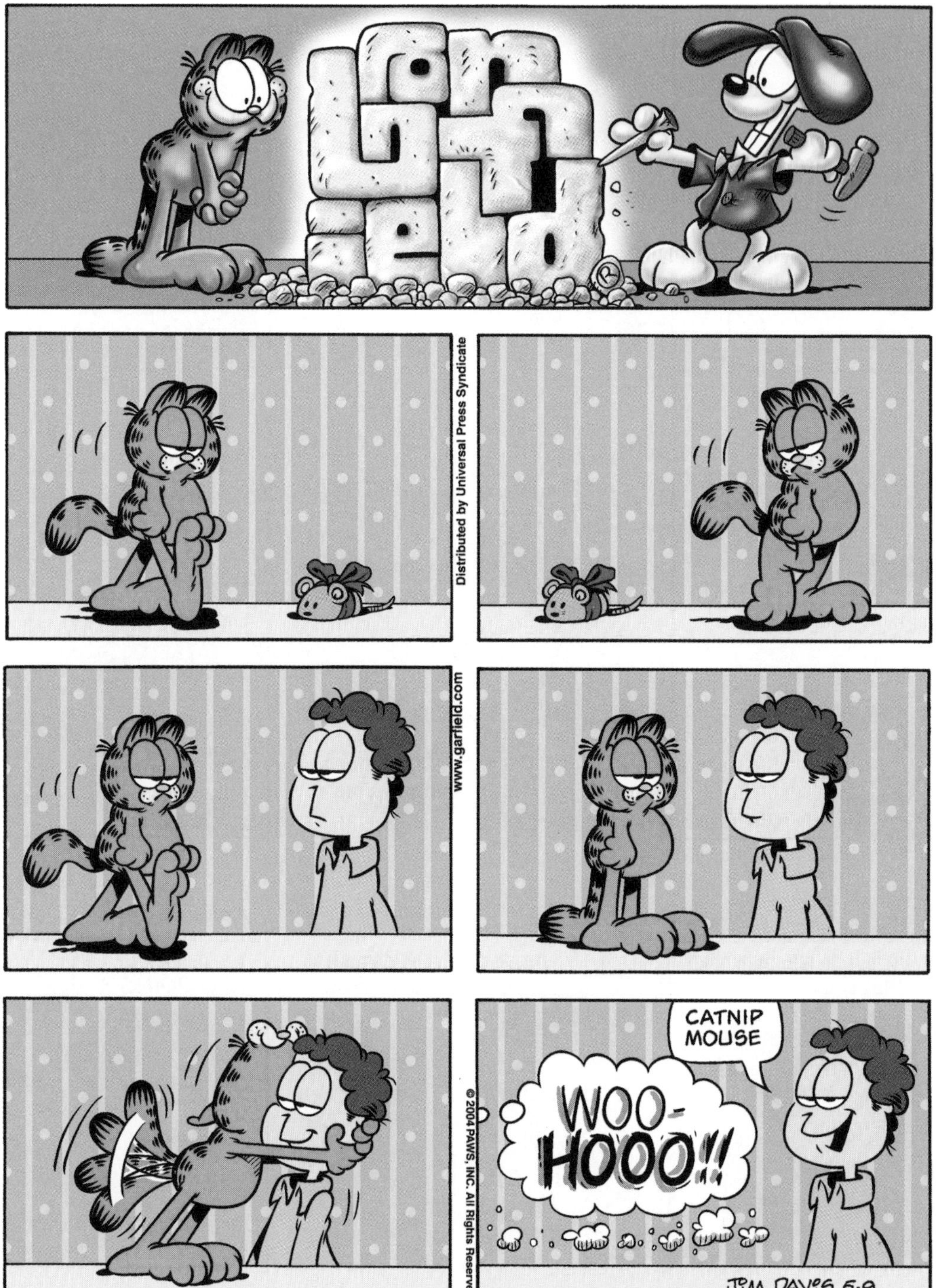
Distributed by Universal Press Syndicate
www.garfield.com
© 2004 PAWS, INC. All Rights Reserved.
CATNIP MOUSE
WOO-HOOO!!
JIM DAVIS 5-9

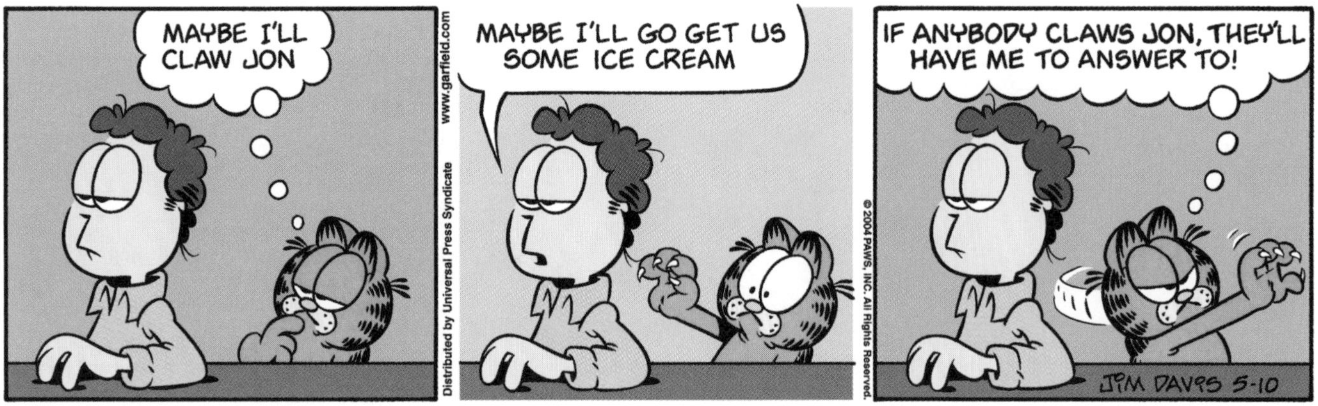
MAYBE I'LL CLAW JON
www.garfield.com
Distributed by Universal Press Syndicate
MAYBE I'LL GO GET US SOME ICE CREAM
© 2004 PAWS, INC. All Rights Reserved.
IF ANYBODY CLAWS JON, THEY'LL HAVE ME TO ANSWER TO!
JIM DAVIS 5-10

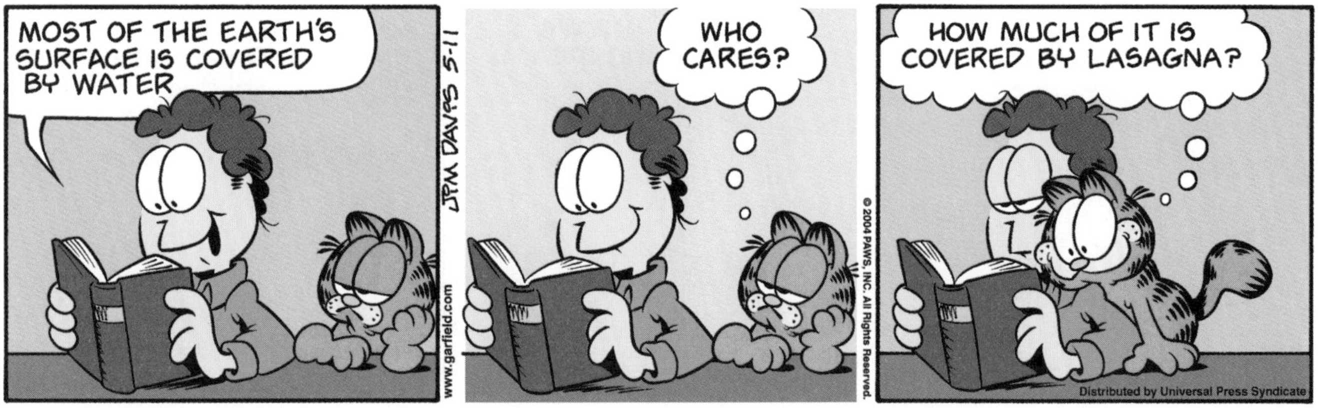
MOST OF THE EARTH'S SURFACE IS COVERED BY WATER
JIM DAVIS 5-11
www.garfield.com
WHO CARES?
© 2004 PAWS, INC. All Rights Reserved.
HOW MUCH OF IT IS COVERED BY LASAGNA?
Distributed by Universal Press Syndicate

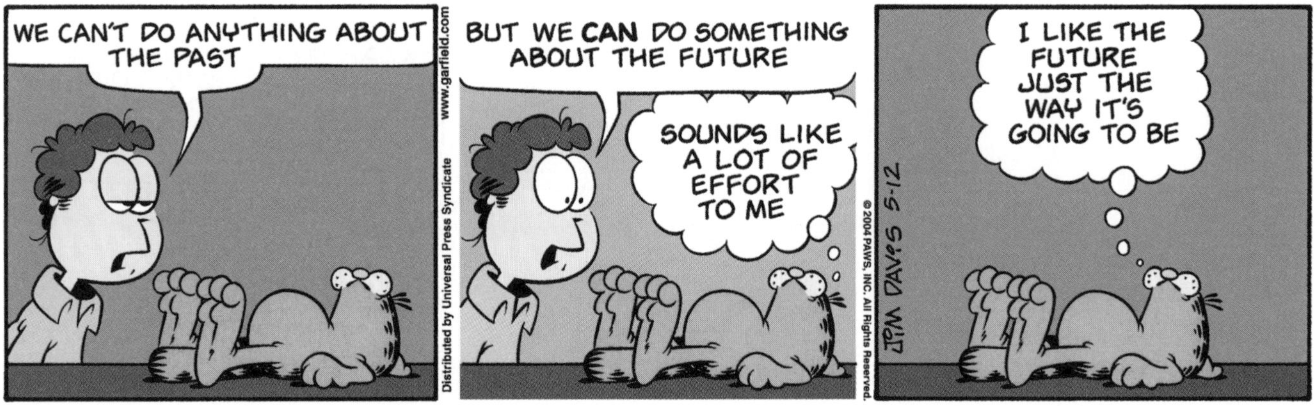
WE CAN'T DO ANYTHING ABOUT THE PAST
www.garfield.com
Distributed by Universal Press Syndicate
BUT WE CAN DO SOMETHING ABOUT THE FUTURE
SOUNDS LIKE A LOT OF EFFORT TO ME
© 2004 PAWS, INC. All Rights Reserved.
JIM DAVIS 5-12
I LIKE THE FUTURE JUST THE WAY IT'S GOING TO BE

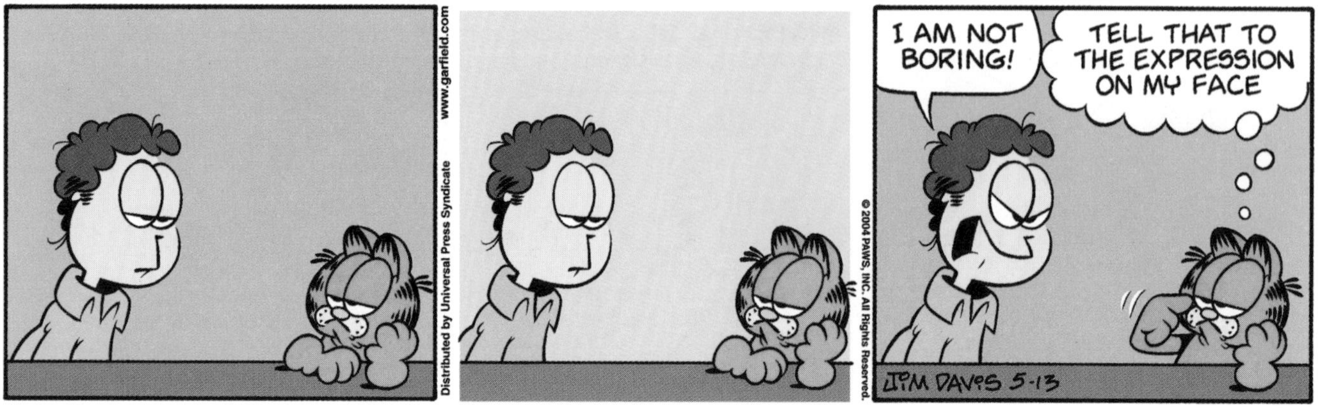
www.garfield.com
Distributed by Universal Press Syndicate
© 2004 PAWS, INC. All Rights Reserved.
I AM NOT BORING!
TELL THAT TO THE EXPRESSION ON MY FACE
JIM DAVIS 5-13

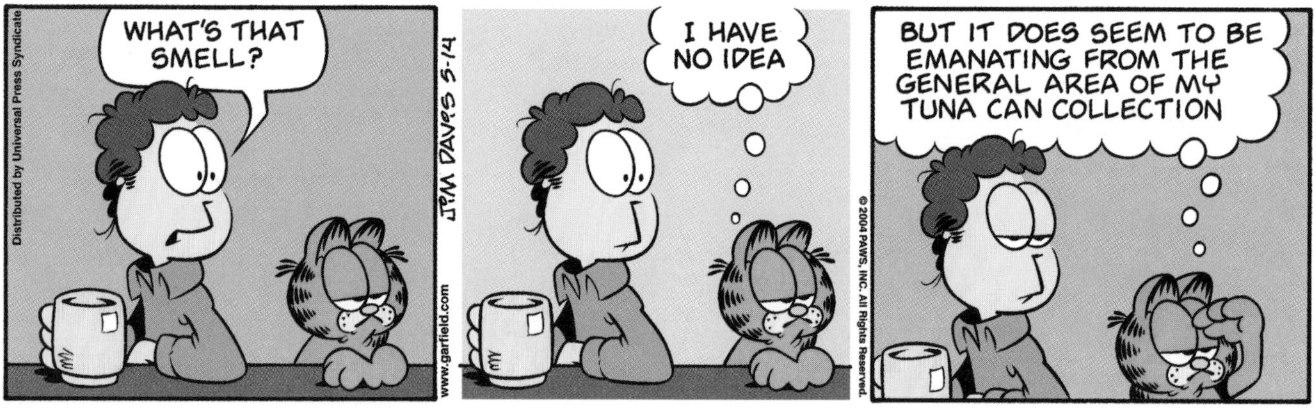
Distributed by Universal Press Syndicate
WHAT'S THAT SMELL?
JIM DAVIS 5-14
www.garfield.com
I HAVE NO IDEA
© 2004 PAWS, INC. All Rights Reserved.
BUT IT DOES SEEM TO BE EMANATING FROM THE GENERAL AREA OF MY TUNA CAN COLLECTION

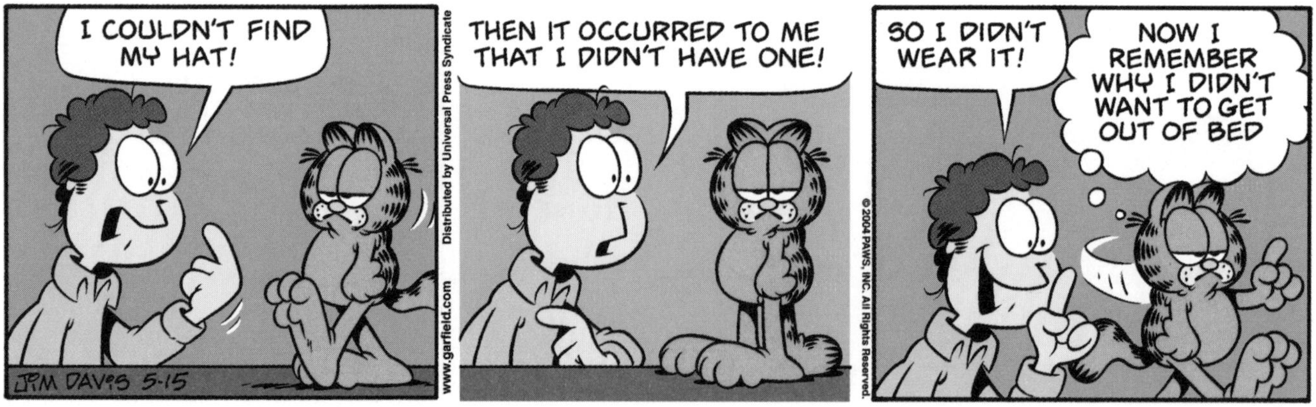
I COULDN'T FIND MY HAT!
JIM DAVIS 5-15
Distributed by Universal Press Syndicate
www.garfield.com
THEN IT OCCURRED TO ME THAT I DIDN'T HAVE ONE!
© 2004 PAWS, INC. All Rights Reserved.
SO I DIDN'T WEAR IT!
NOW I REMEMBER WHY I DIDN'T WANT TO GET OUT OF BED

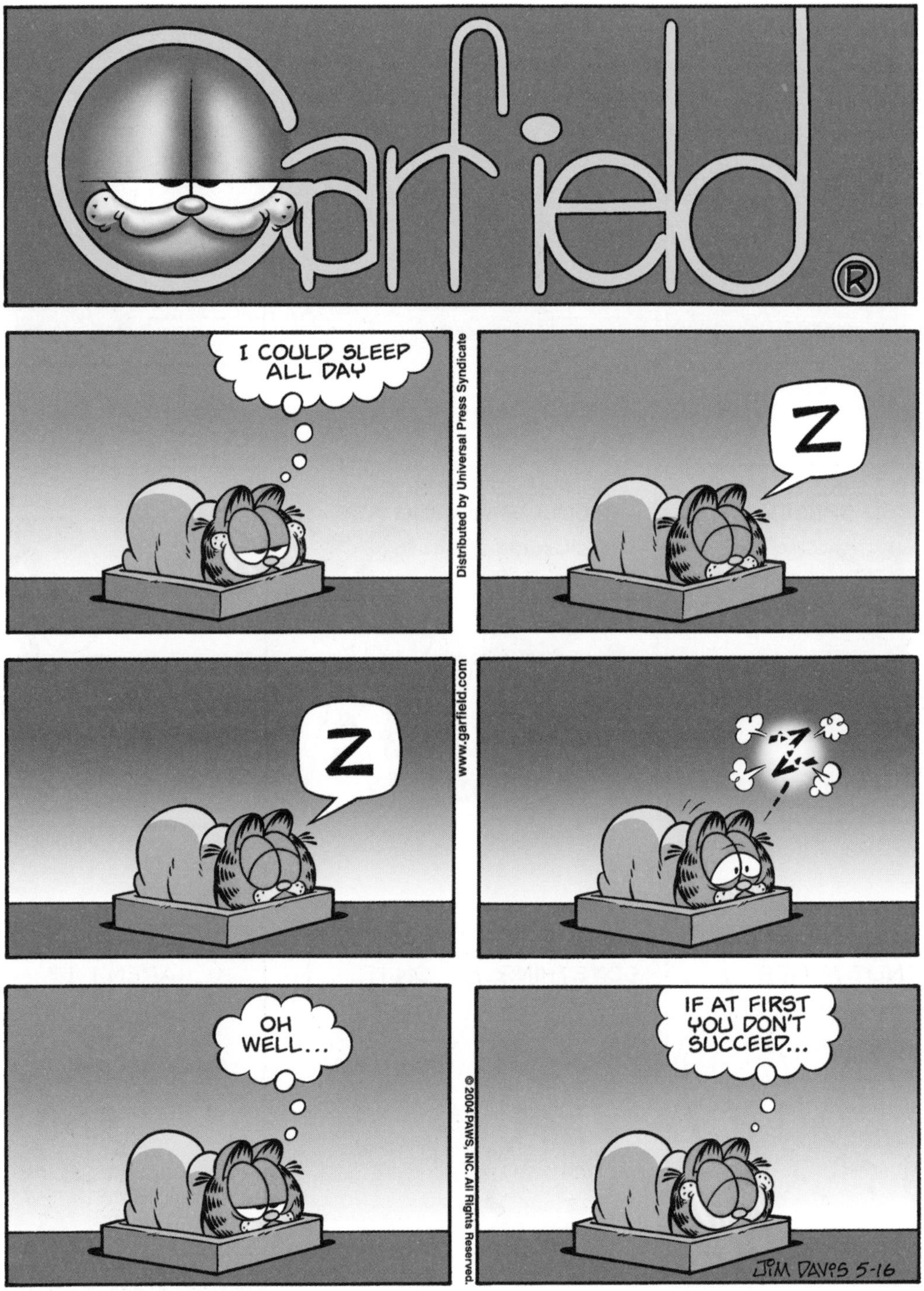
Garfield®
I COULD SLEEP ALL DAY
Z
Z
OH WELL...
IF AT FIRST YOU DON'T SUCCEED...
JIM DAVIS 5-16
Distributed by Universal Press Syndicate
www.garfield.com
© 2004 PAWS, INC. All Rights Reserved.

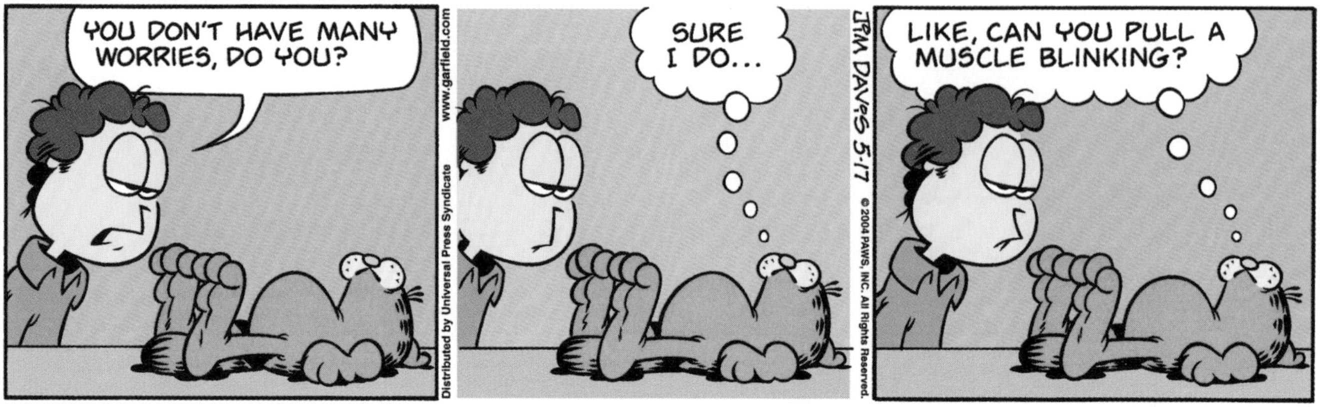
YOU DON'T HAVE MANY WORRIES, DO YOU?
SURE I DO...
LIKE, CAN YOU PULL A MUSCLE BLINKING?
JIM DAVIS 5-17
www.garfield.com
Distributed by Universal Press Syndicate
© 2004 PAWS, INC. All Rights Reserved.

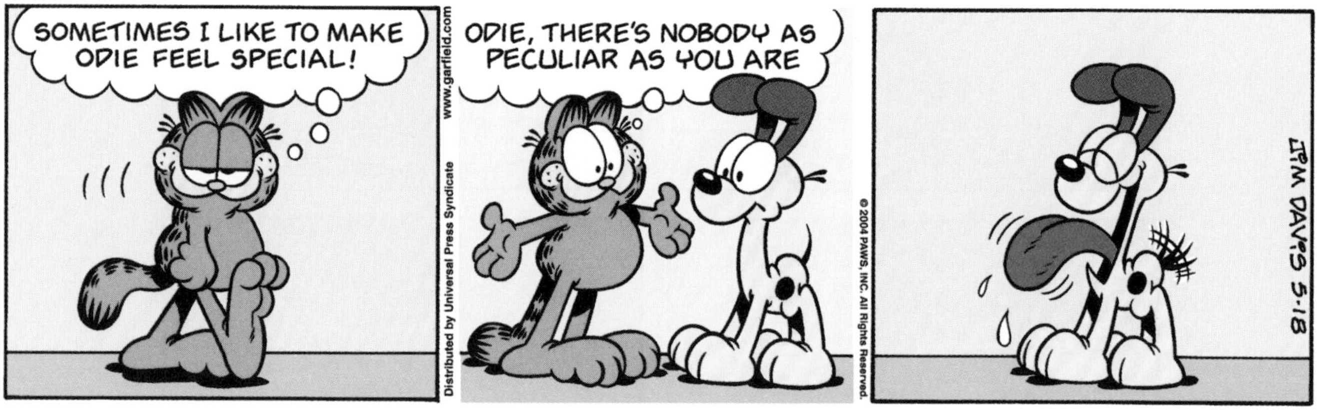
SOMETIMES I LIKE TO MAKE ODIE FEEL SPECIAL!
ODIE, THERE'S NOBODY AS PECULIAR AS YOU ARE
JIM DAVIS 5-18
www.garfield.com
Distributed by Universal Press Syndicate
© 2004 PAWS, INC. All Rights Reserved.

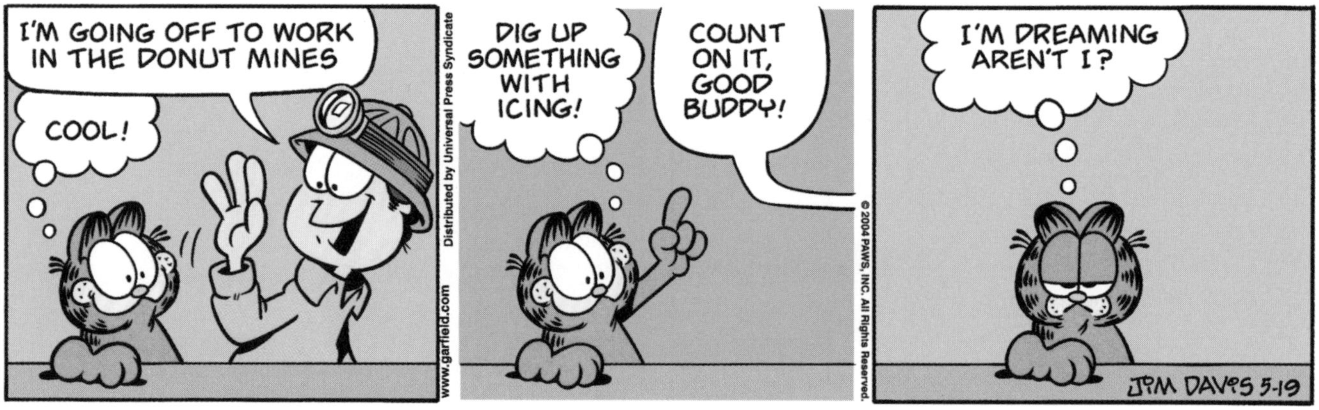
I'M GOING OFF TO WORK IN THE DONUT MINES
COOL!
DIG UP SOMETHING WITH ICING!
COUNT ON IT, GOOD BUDDY!
I'M DREAMING AREN'T I?
JIM DAVIS 5-19
www.garfield.com
Distributed by Universal Press Syndicate
© 2004 PAWS, INC. All Rights Reserved.

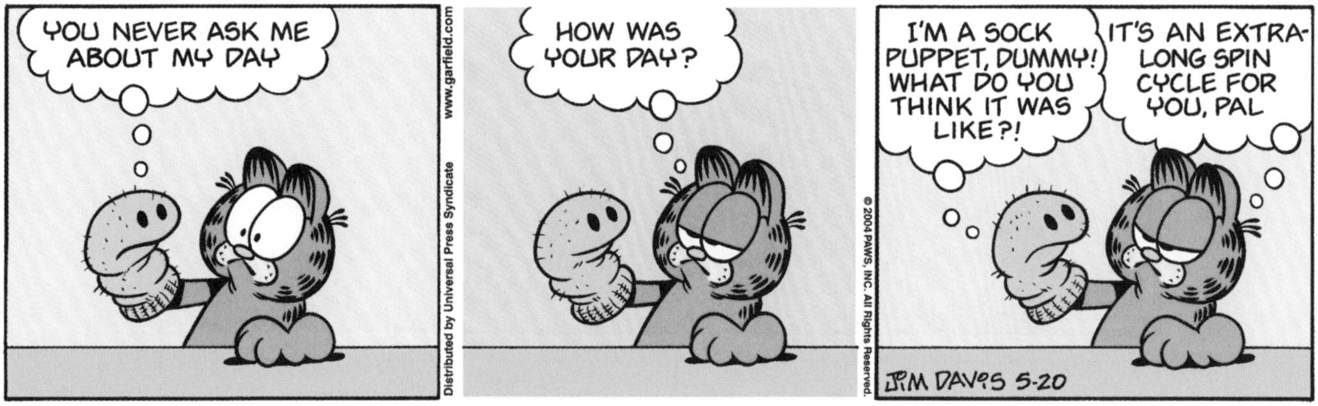
YOU NEVER ASK ME ABOUT MY DAY
HOW WAS YOUR DAY?
I'M A SOCK PUPPET, DUMMY! WHAT DO YOU THINK IT WAS LIKE?!
IT'S AN EXTRA-LONG SPIN CYCLE FOR YOU, PAL
JIM DAVIS 5-20
www.garfield.com Distributed by Universal Press Syndicate
© 2004 PAWS, INC. All Rights Reserved.

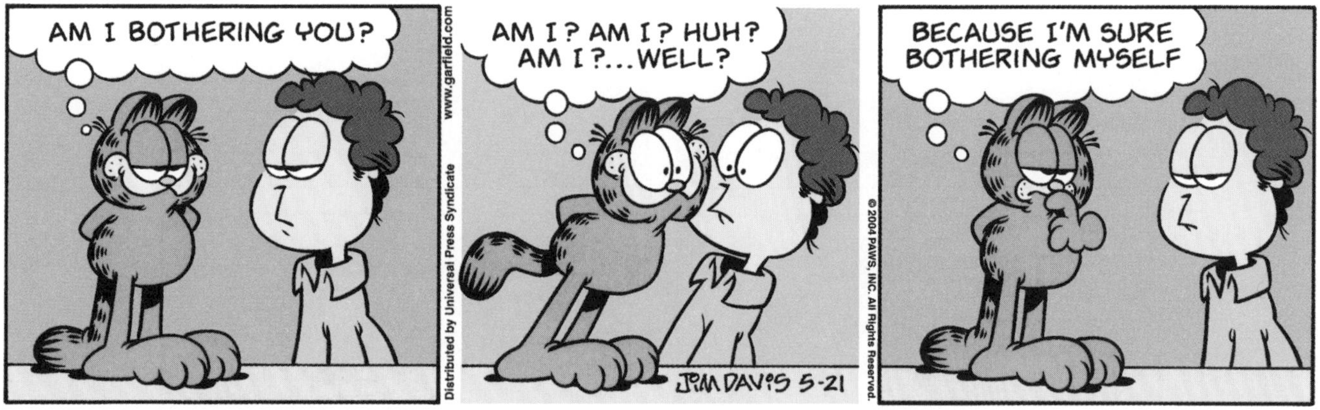
AM I BOTHERING YOU?
AM I? AM I? HUH? AM I?...WELL?
BECAUSE I'M SURE BOTHERING MYSELF
JIM DAVIS 5-21
www.garfield.com Distributed by Universal Press Syndicate
© 2004 PAWS, INC. All Rights Reserved.

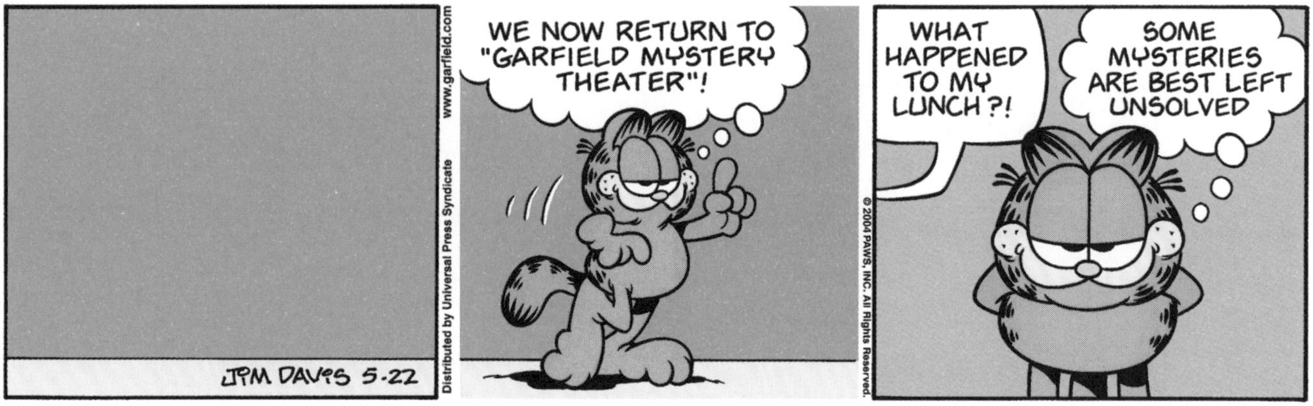
JIM DAVIS 5-22
WE NOW RETURN TO "GARFIELD MYSTERY THEATER"!
WHAT HAPPENED TO MY LUNCH?!
SOME MYSTERIES ARE BEST LEFT UNSOLVED
www.garfield.com Distributed by Universal Press Syndicate
© 2004 PAWS, INC. All Rights Reserved.

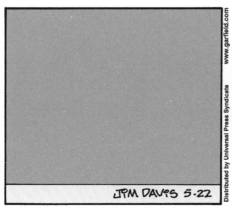

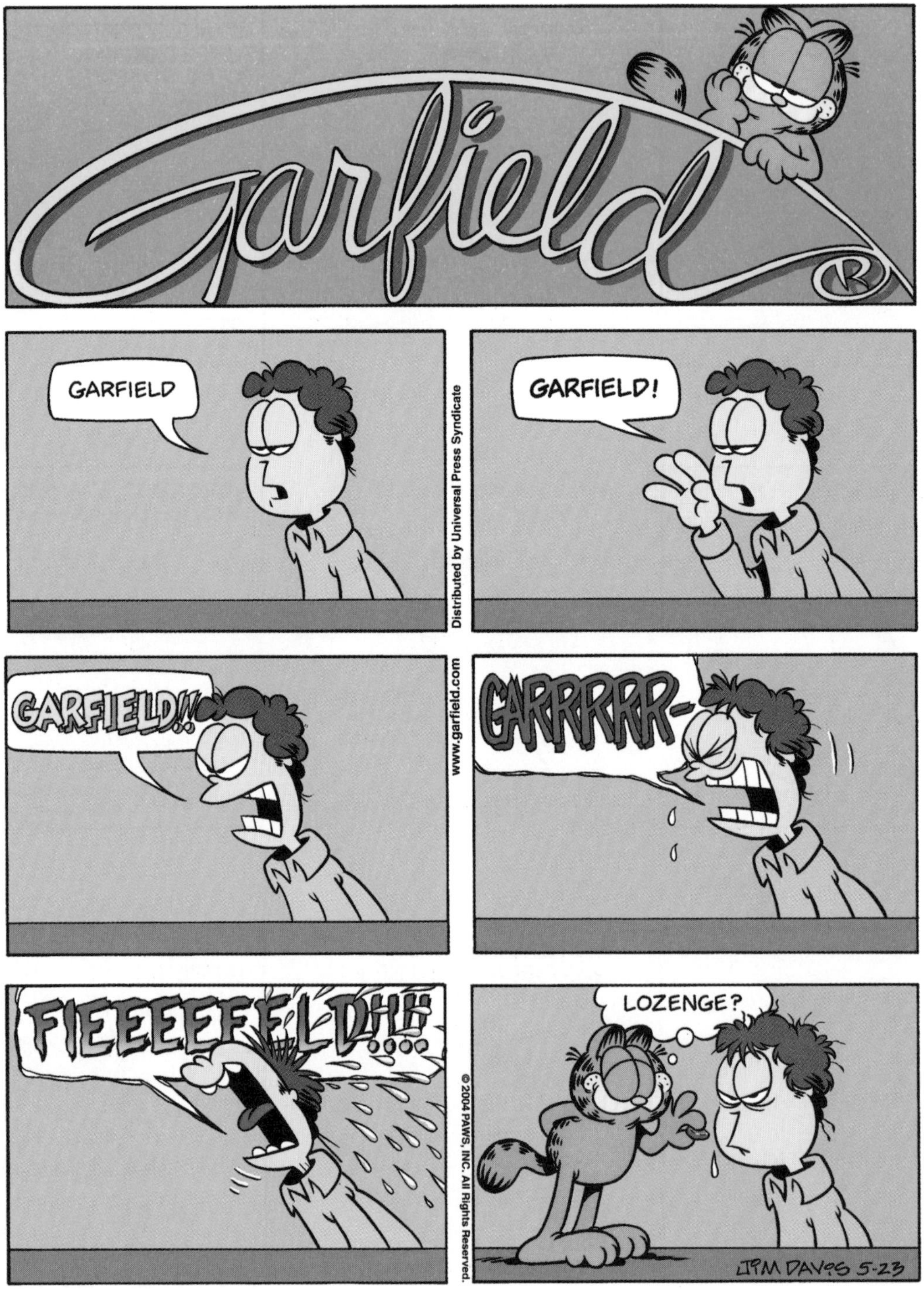
Garfield
GARFIELD
GARFIELD!
GARFIELD!!
GARRRRRR-
FIEEEEEELD!!!!
LOZENGE?
JIM DAVIS 5-23
Distributed by Universal Press Syndicate
www.garfield.com
© 2004 PAWS, INC. All Rights Reserved.

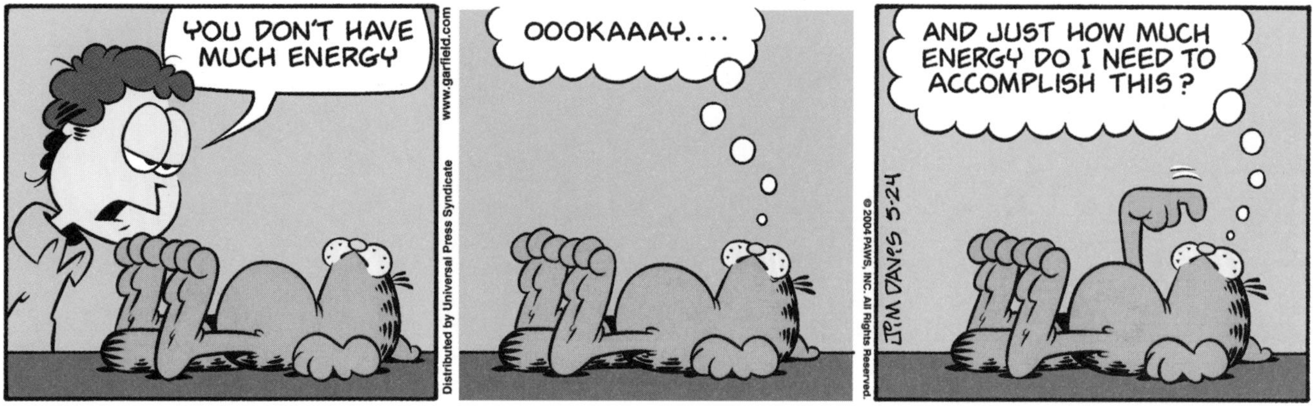
YOU DON'T HAVE MUCH ENERGY
OOOKAAAY....
AND JUST HOW MUCH ENERGY DO I NEED TO ACCOMPLISH THIS?
JIM DAVIS 5-24
www.garfield.com
Distributed by Universal Press Syndicate
© 2004 PAWS, INC. All Rights Reserved.

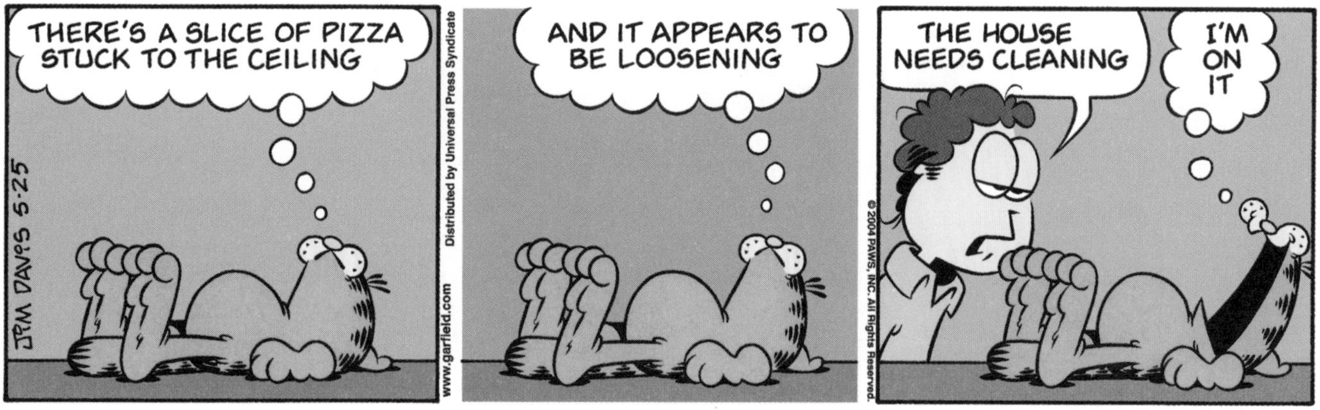
THERE'S A SLICE OF PIZZA STUCK TO THE CEILING
AND IT APPEARS TO BE LOOSENING
THE HOUSE NEEDS CLEANING
I'M ON IT
JIM DAVIS 5-25
www.garfield.com
Distributed by Universal Press Syndicate
© 2004 PAWS, INC. All Rights Reserved.

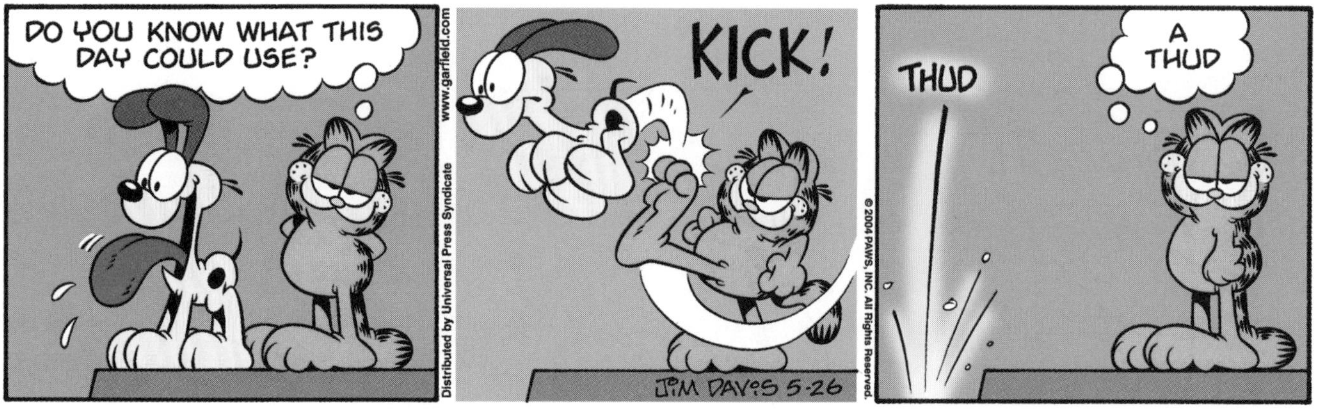
DO YOU KNOW WHAT THIS DAY COULD USE?
KICK!
THUD
A THUD
JIM DAVIS 5-26
www.garfield.com
Distributed by Universal Press Syndicate
© 2004 PAWS, INC. All Rights Reserved.

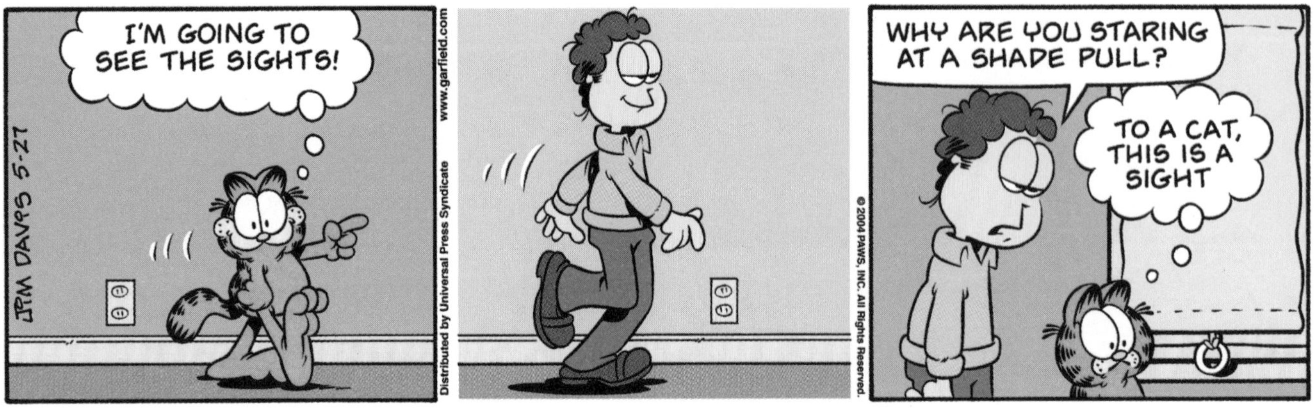
I'M GOING TO SEE THE SIGHTS!
JIM DAVIS 5-27
Distributed by Universal Press Syndicate www.garfield.com
WHY ARE YOU STARING AT A SHADE PULL?
TO A CAT, THIS IS A SIGHT
© 2004 PAWS, INC. All Rights Reserved.

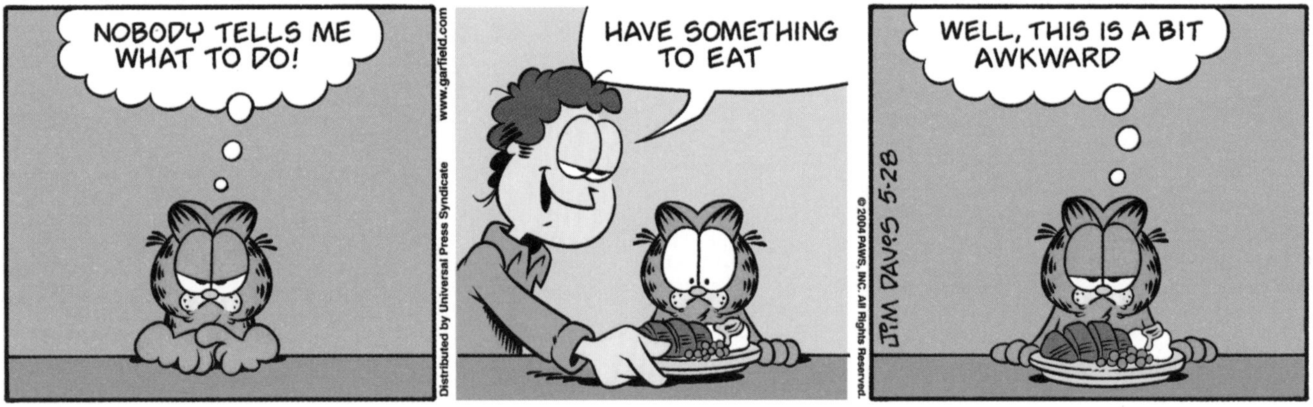
NOBODY TELLS ME WHAT TO DO!
Distributed by Universal Press Syndicate www.garfield.com
HAVE SOMETHING TO EAT
© 2004 PAWS, INC. All Rights Reserved.
WELL, THIS IS A BIT AWKWARD
JIM DAVIS 5-28

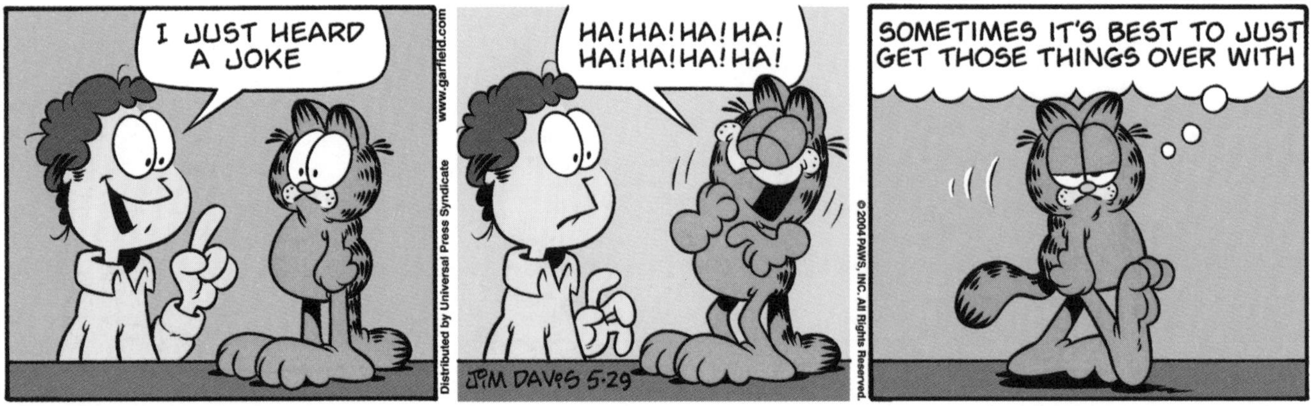
I JUST HEARD A JOKE
Distributed by Universal Press Syndicate www.garfield.com
HA! HA! HA! HA! HA! HA! HA! HA!
JIM DAVIS 5-29
© 2004 PAWS, INC. All Rights Reserved.
SOMETIMES IT'S BEST TO JUST GET THOSE THINGS OVER WITH

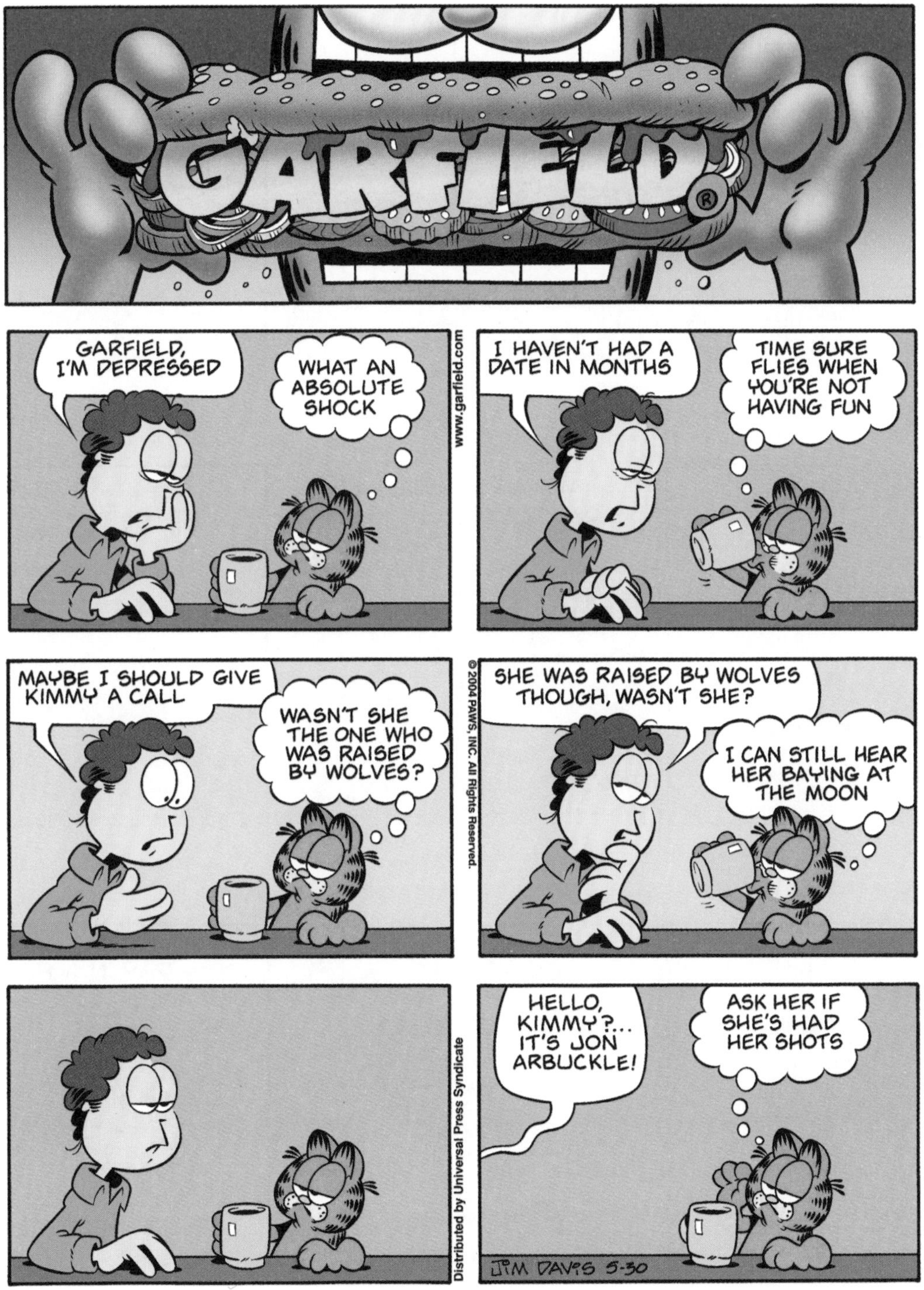
GARFIELD®
GARFIELD, I'M DEPRESSED
WHAT AN ABSOLUTE SHOCK
www.garfield.com
I HAVEN'T HAD A DATE IN MONTHS
TIME SURE FLIES WHEN YOU'RE NOT HAVING FUN
MAYBE I SHOULD GIVE KIMMY A CALL
WASN'T SHE THE ONE WHO WAS RAISED BY WOLVES?
© 2004 PAWS, INC. All Rights Reserved.
SHE WAS RAISED BY WOLVES THOUGH, WASN'T SHE?
I CAN STILL HEAR HER BAYING AT THE MOON
Distributed by Universal Press Syndicate
HELLO, KIMMY?... IT'S JON ARBUCKLE!
ASK HER IF SHE'S HAD HER SHOTS
JIM DAVIS 5-30

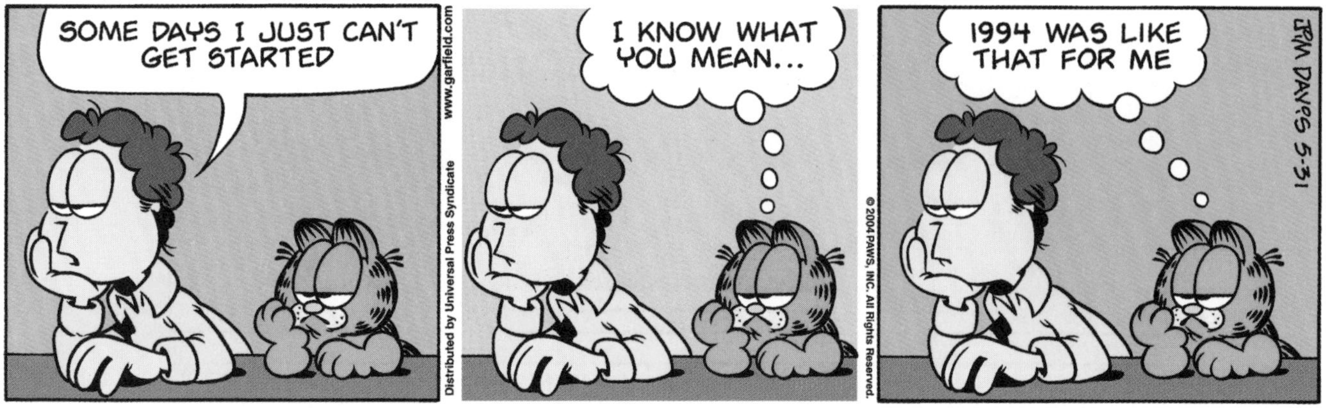
SOME DAYS I JUST CAN'T GET STARTED
www.garfield.com
Distributed by Universal Press Syndicate
I KNOW WHAT YOU MEAN...
© 2004 PAWS, INC. All Rights Reserved.
1994 WAS LIKE THAT FOR ME
JIM DAVIS 5-31

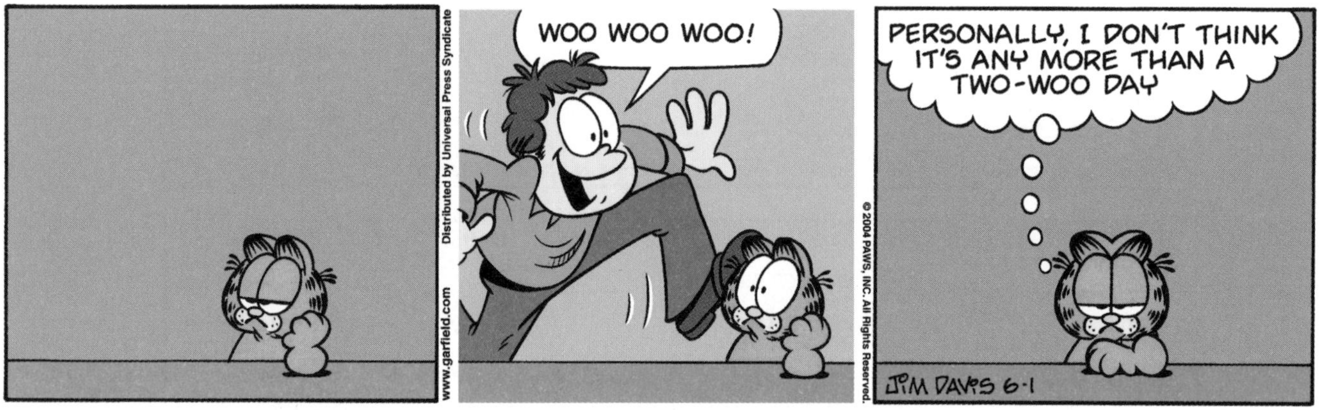
Distributed by Universal Press Syndicate
www.garfield.com
WOO WOO WOO!
© 2004 PAWS, INC. All Rights Reserved.
PERSONALLY, I DON'T THINK IT'S ANY MORE THAN A TWO-WOO DAY
JIM DAVIS 6-1

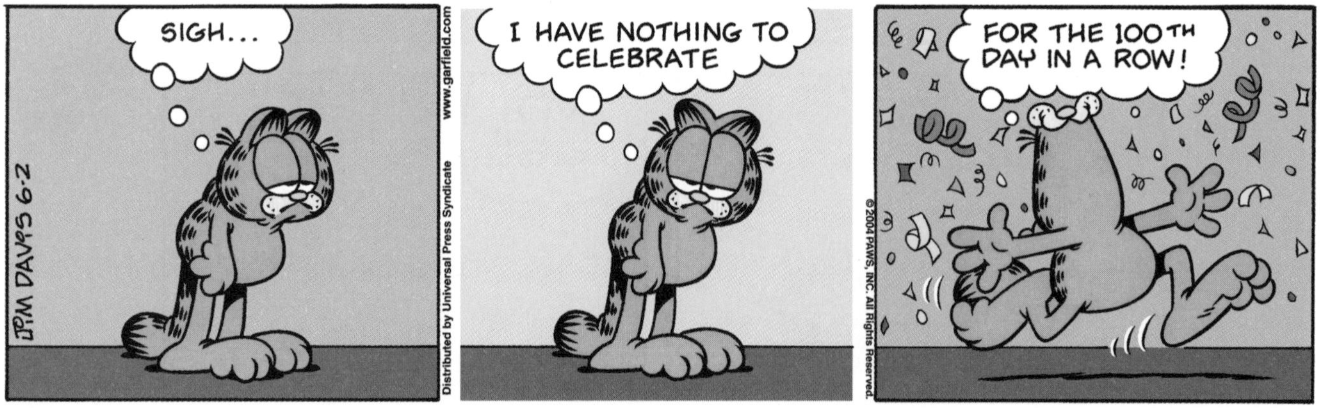
SIGH...
JIM DAVIS 6-2
www.garfield.com
Distributed by Universal Press Syndicate
I HAVE NOTHING TO CELEBRATE
© 2004 PAWS, INC. All Rights Reserved.
FOR THE 100TH DAY IN A ROW!

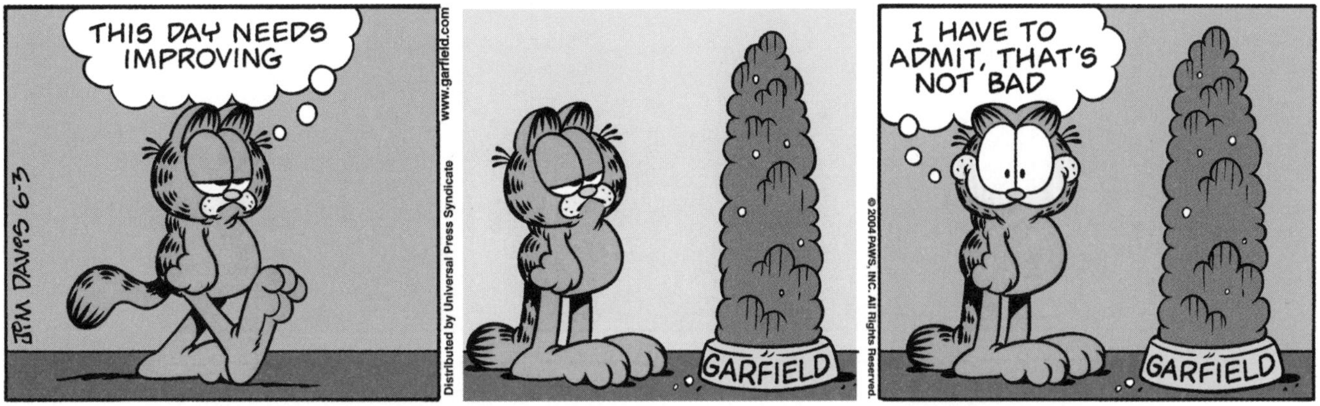
THIS DAY NEEDS IMPROVING
JIM DAVIS 6-3
Distributed by Universal Press Syndicate www.garfield.com
GARFIELD
I HAVE TO ADMIT, THAT'S NOT BAD
© 2004 PAWS, INC. All Rights Reserved.
GARFIELD

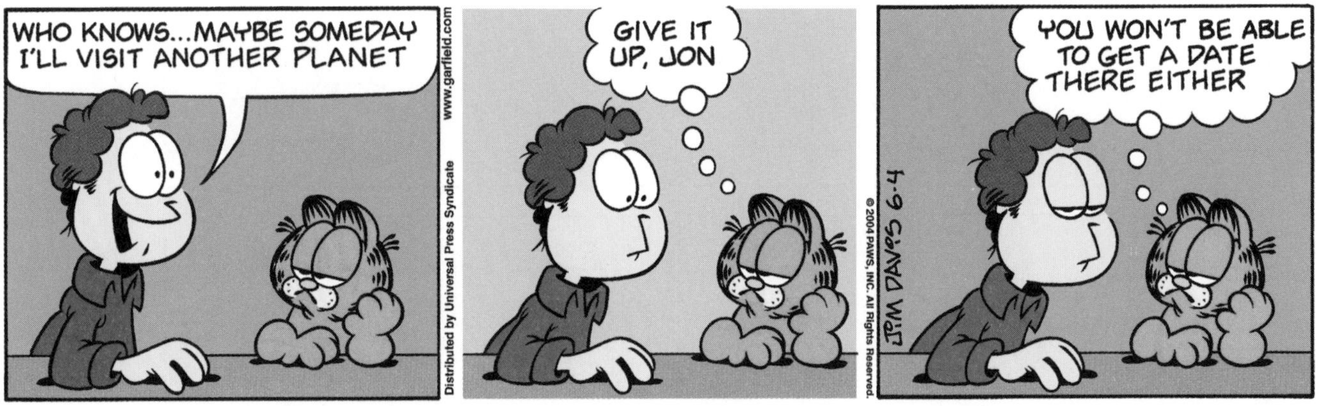
WHO KNOWS...MAYBE SOMEDAY I'LL VISIT ANOTHER PLANET
Distributed by Universal Press Syndicate www.garfield.com
GIVE IT UP, JON
© 2004 PAWS, INC. All Rights Reserved.
JIM DAVIS 6-4
YOU WON'T BE ABLE TO GET A DATE THERE EITHER

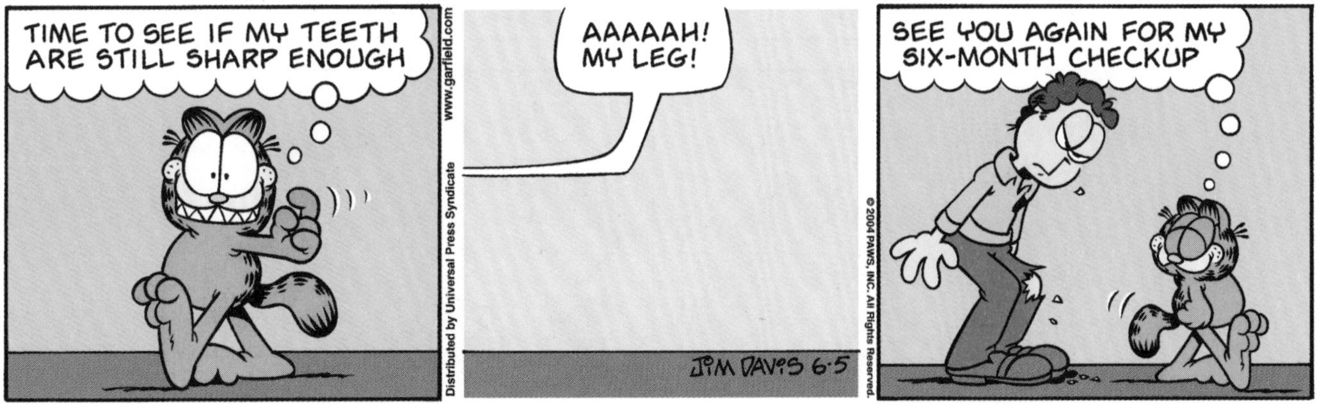
TIME TO SEE IF MY TEETH ARE STILL SHARP ENOUGH
Distributed by Universal Press Syndicate www.garfield.com
AAAAAH! MY LEG!
JIM DAVIS 6-5
© 2004 PAWS, INC. All Rights Reserved.
SEE YOU AGAIN FOR MY SIX-MONTH CHECKUP

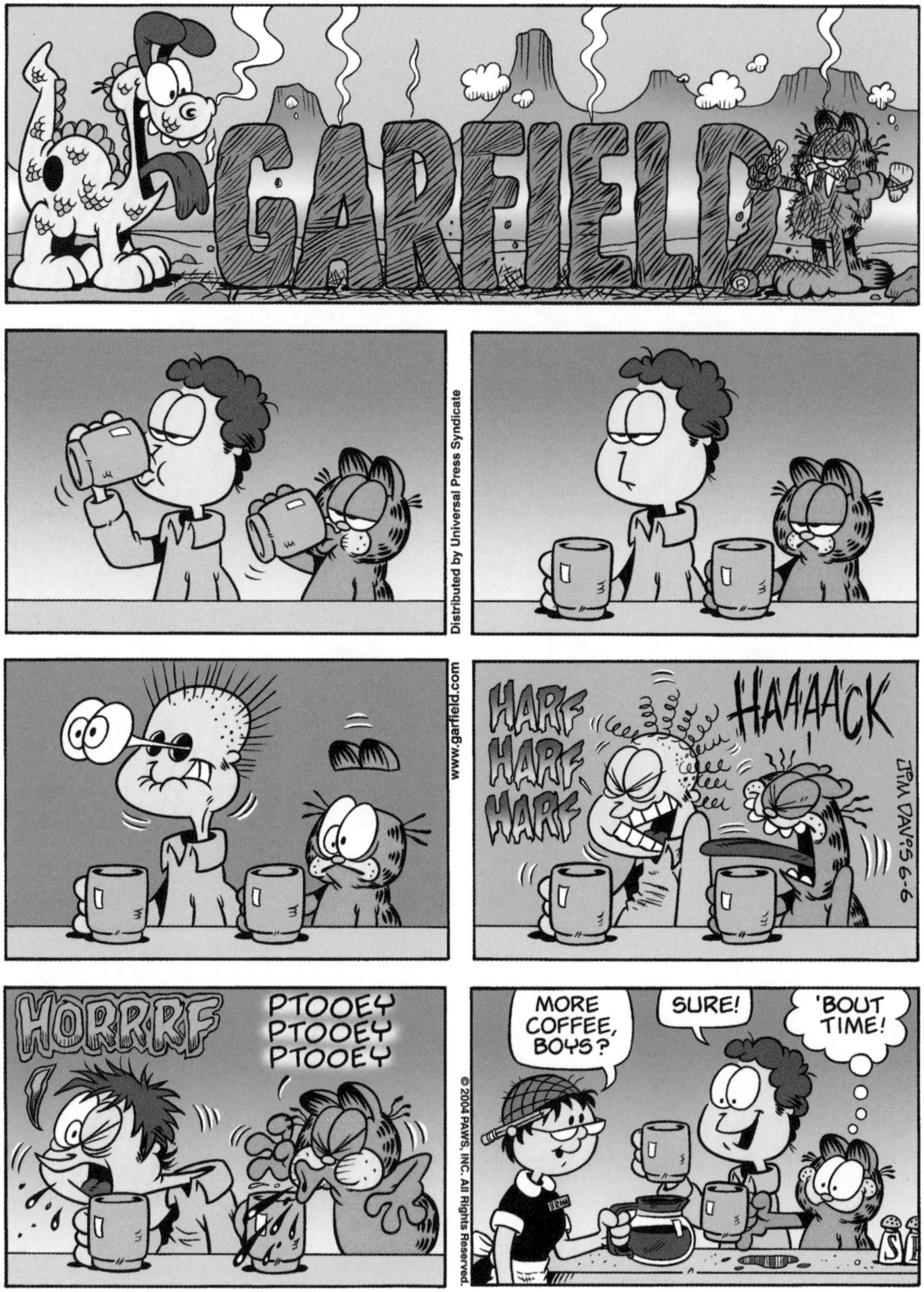
GARFIELD
Distributed by Universal Press Syndicate
www.garfield.com
HARF
HARF
HARF
HAAAACK
JIM DAVIS 6-6
HORRRF
PTOOEY
PTOOEY
PTOOEY
MORE COFFEE, BOYS?
SURE!
'BOUT TIME!
© 2004 PAWS, INC. All Rights Reserved.

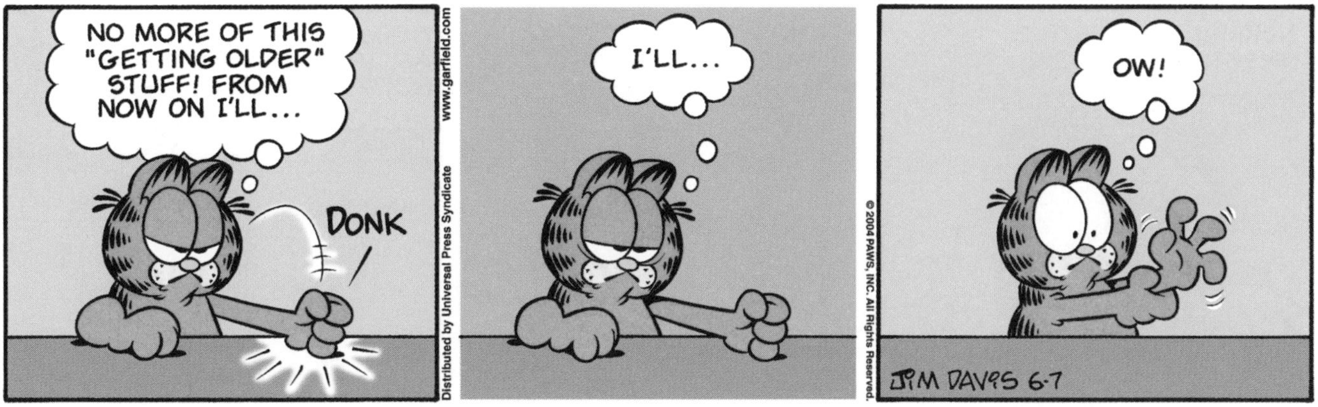
NO MORE OF THIS "GETTING OLDER" STUFF! FROM NOW ON I'LL...
DONK
I'LL...
OW!
JIM DAVIS 6-7
Distributed by Universal Press Syndicate www.garfield.com
© 2004 PAWS, INC. All Rights Reserved.

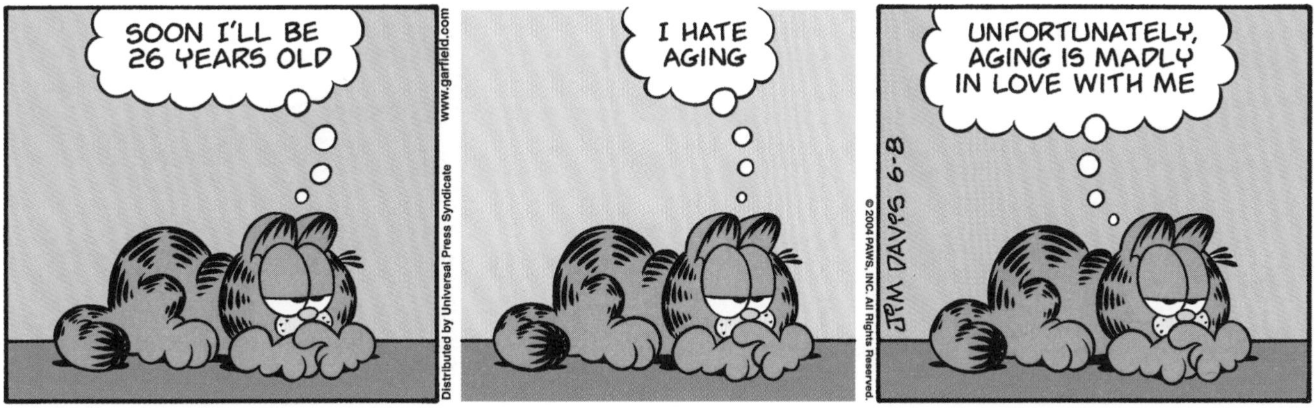
SOON I'LL BE 26 YEARS OLD
I HATE AGING
UNFORTUNATELY, AGING IS MADLY IN LOVE WITH ME
JIM DAVIS 6-8
Distributed by Universal Press Syndicate www.garfield.com
© 2004 PAWS, INC. All Rights Reserved.

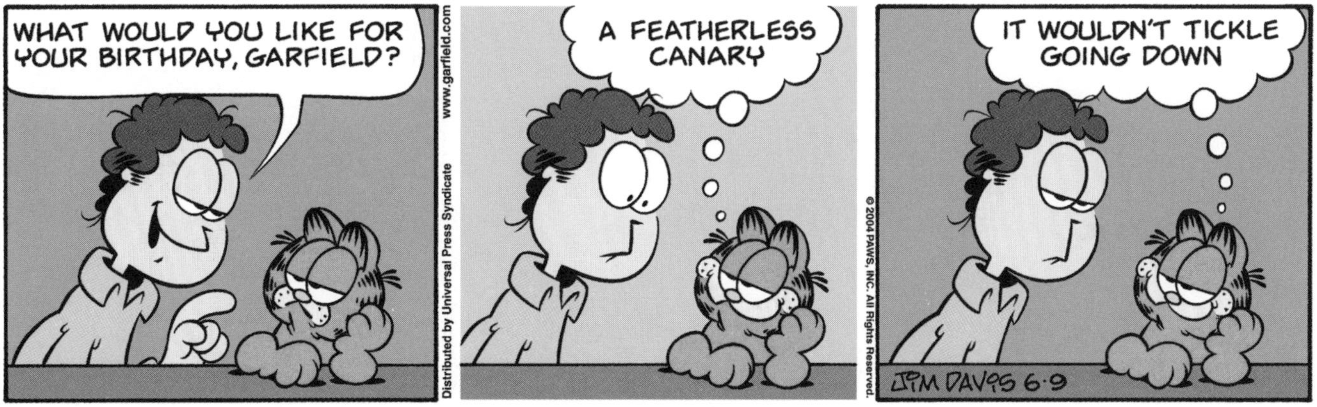
WHAT WOULD YOU LIKE FOR YOUR BIRTHDAY, GARFIELD?
A FEATHERLESS CANARY
IT WOULDN'T TICKLE GOING DOWN
JIM DAVIS 6-9
Distributed by Universal Press Syndicate www.garfield.com
© 2004 PAWS, INC. All Rights Reserved.

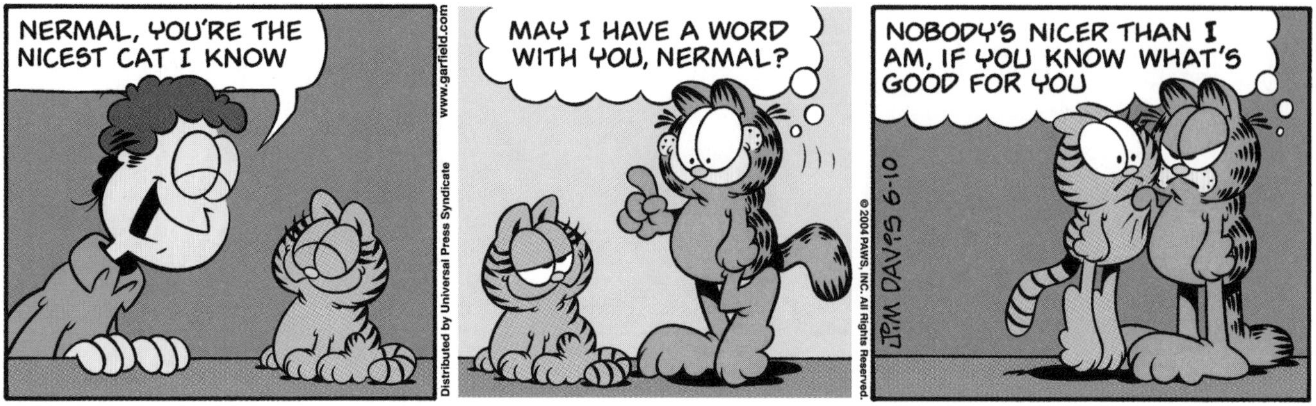
NERMAL, YOU'RE THE NICEST CAT I KNOW
Distributed by Universal Press Syndicate www.garfield.com
MAY I HAVE A WORD WITH YOU, NERMAL?
NOBODY'S NICER THAN **I** AM, IF YOU KNOW WHAT'S GOOD FOR YOU
JIM DAVIS 6-10
© 2004 PAWS, INC. All Rights Reserved.

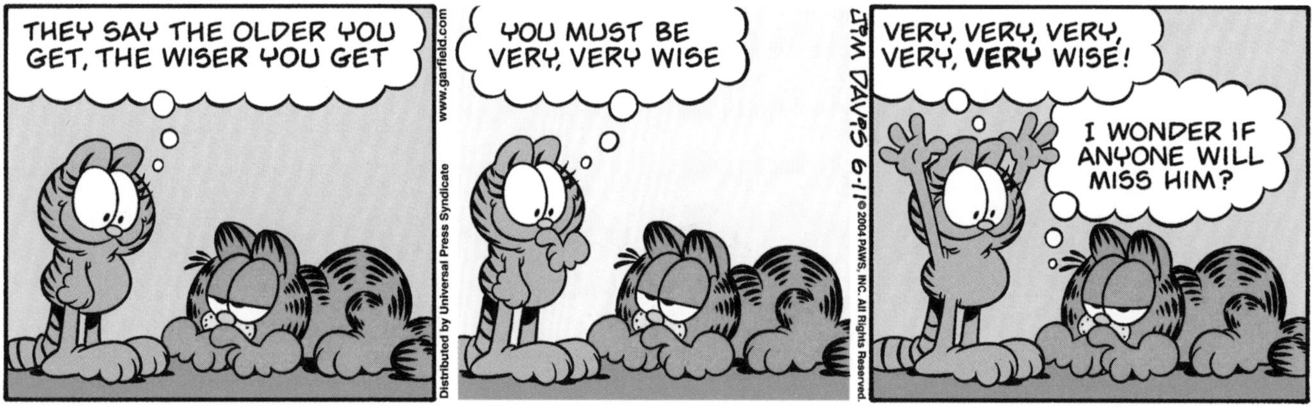
THEY SAY THE OLDER YOU GET, THE WISER YOU GET
Distributed by Universal Press Syndicate www.garfield.com
YOU MUST BE VERY, VERY WISE
JIM DAVIS 6-11
© 2004 PAWS, INC. All Rights Reserved.
VERY, VERY, VERY, VERY, **VERY** WISE!
I WONDER IF ANYONE WILL MISS HIM?

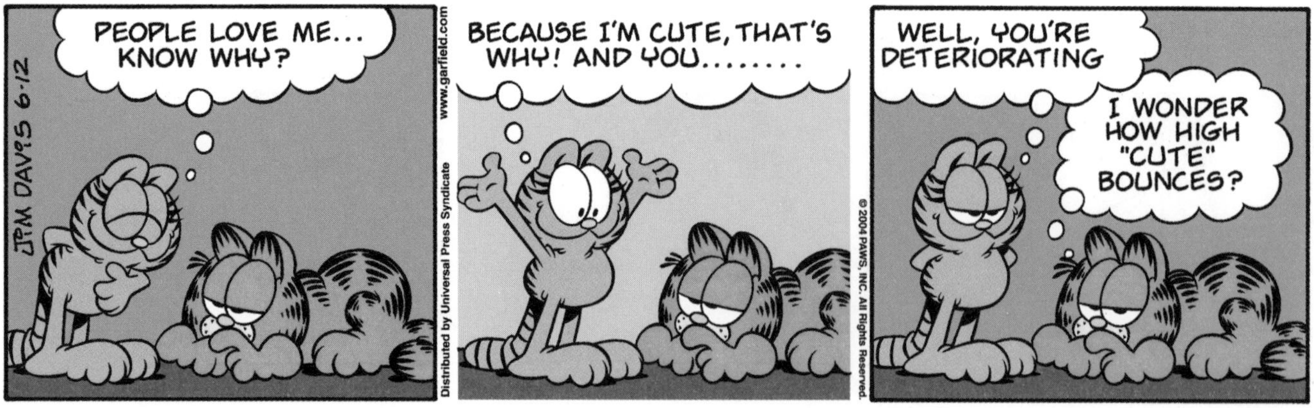
JIM DAVIS 6-12
PEOPLE LOVE ME... KNOW WHY?
Distributed by Universal Press Syndicate www.garfield.com
BECAUSE I'M CUTE, THAT'S WHY! AND YOU........
© 2004 PAWS, INC. All Rights Reserved.
WELL, YOU'RE DETERIORATING
I WONDER HOW HIGH "CUTE" BOUNCES?

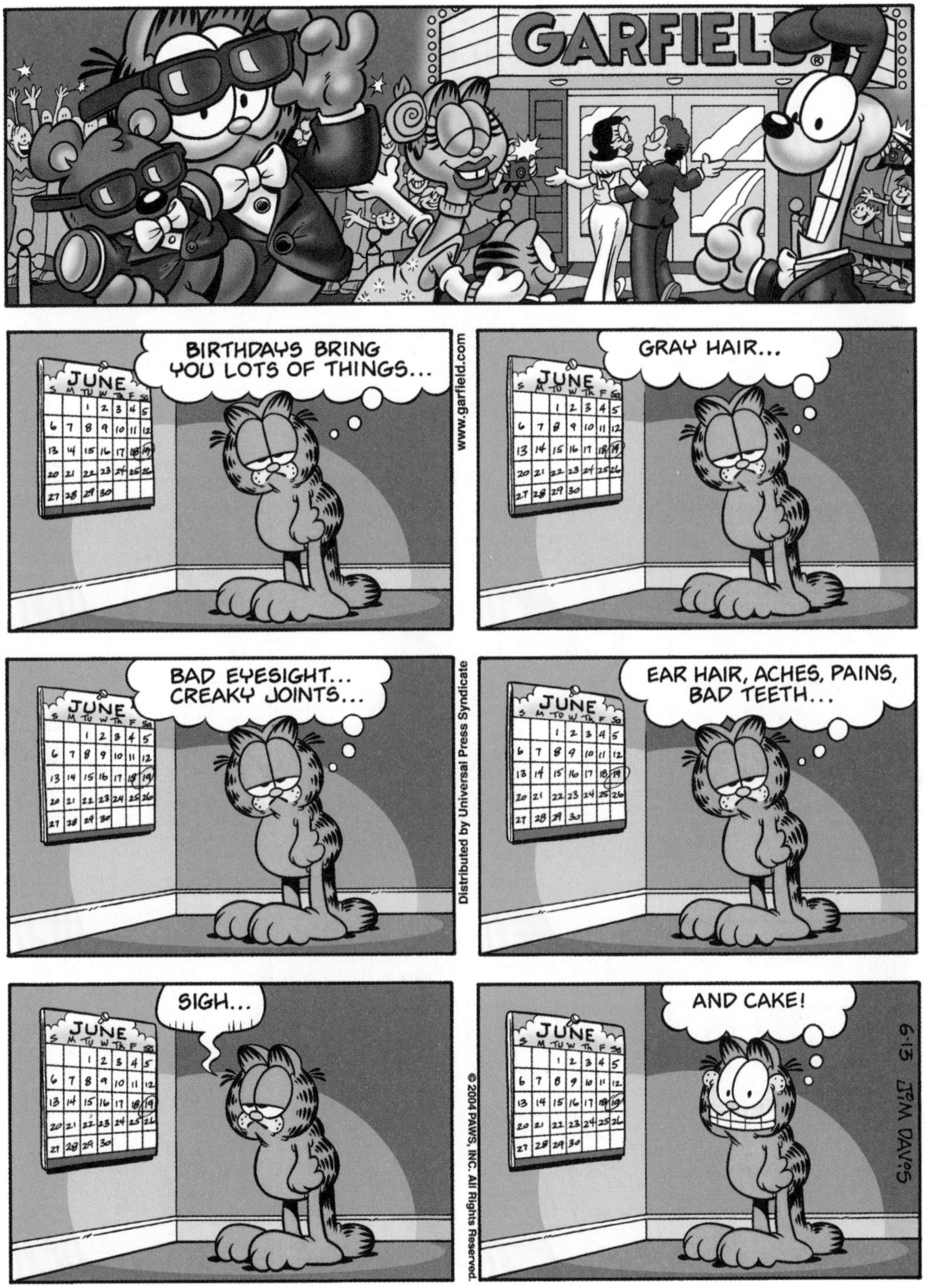

GARFIELD
BIRTHDAYS BRING YOU LOTS OF THINGS...
GRAY HAIR...
BAD EYESIGHT... CREAKY JOINTS...
EAR HAIR, ACHES, PAINS, BAD TEETH...
SIGH...
AND CAKE!
JUNE
www.garfield.com
Distributed by Universal Press Syndicate
© 2004 PAWS, INC. All Rights Reserved.
6-13 JIM DAVIS

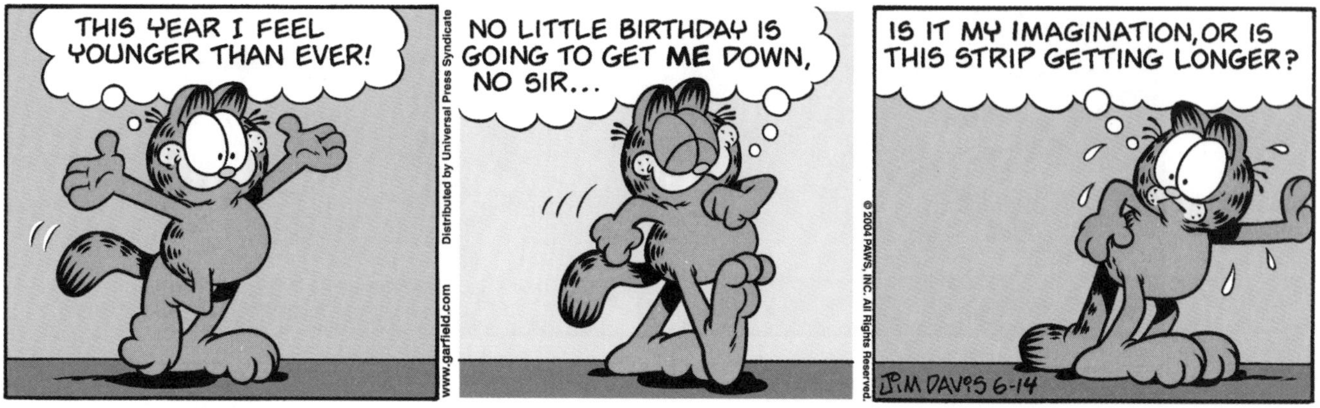
THIS YEAR I FEEL YOUNGER THAN EVER!
www.garfield.com
Distributed by Universal Press Syndicate
NO LITTLE BIRTHDAY IS GOING TO GET **ME** DOWN, NO SIR...
© 2004 PAWS, INC. All Rights Reserved.
IS IT MY IMAGINATION, OR IS THIS STRIP GETTING LONGER?
JIM DAVIS 6-14

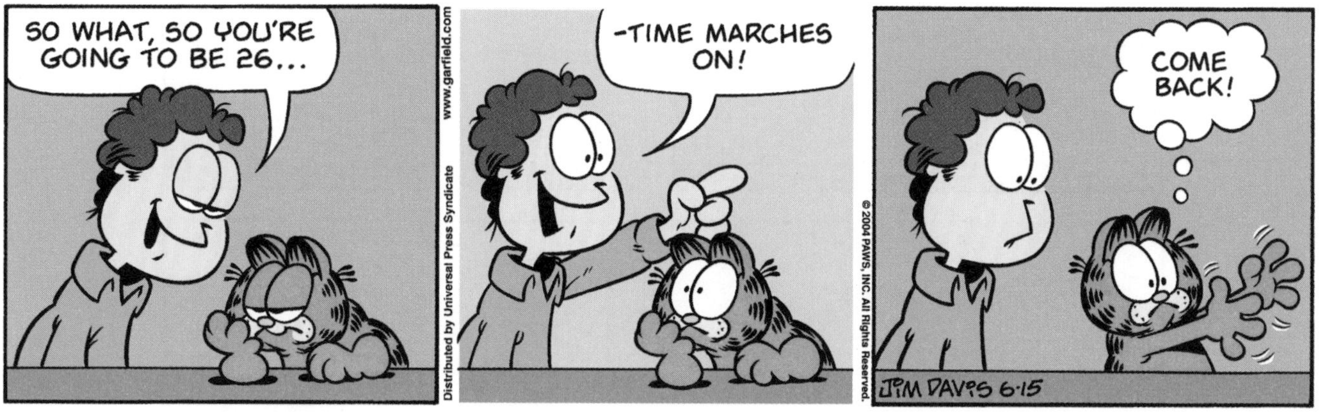
SO WHAT, SO YOU'RE GOING TO BE 26...
www.garfield.com
Distributed by Universal Press Syndicate
-TIME MARCHES ON!
© 2004 PAWS, INC. All Rights Reserved.
COME BACK!
JIM DAVIS 6-15

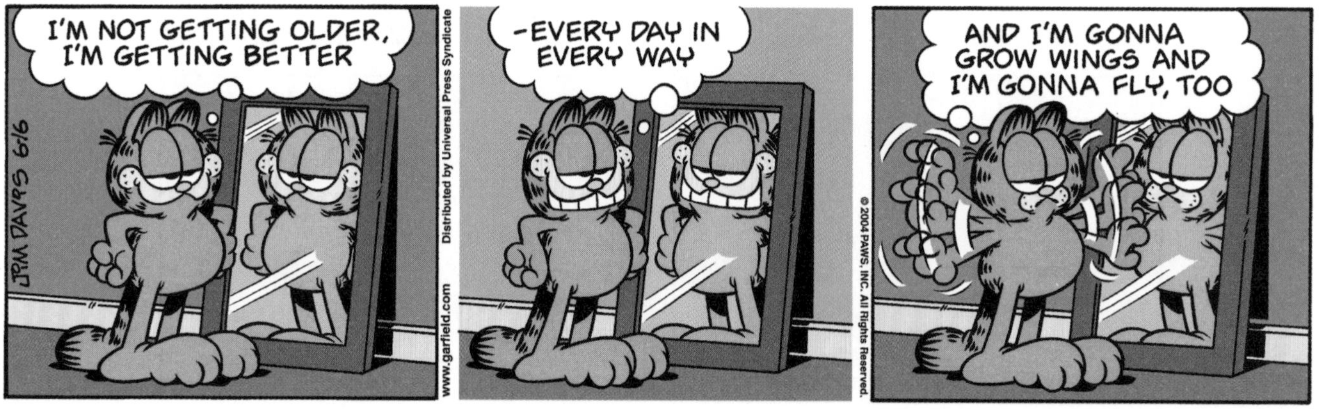
I'M NOT GETTING OLDER, I'M GETTING BETTER
JIM DAVIS 6-16
www.garfield.com
Distributed by Universal Press Syndicate
-EVERY DAY IN EVERY WAY
© 2004 PAWS, INC. All Rights Reserved.
AND I'M GONNA GROW WINGS AND I'M GONNA FLY, TOO

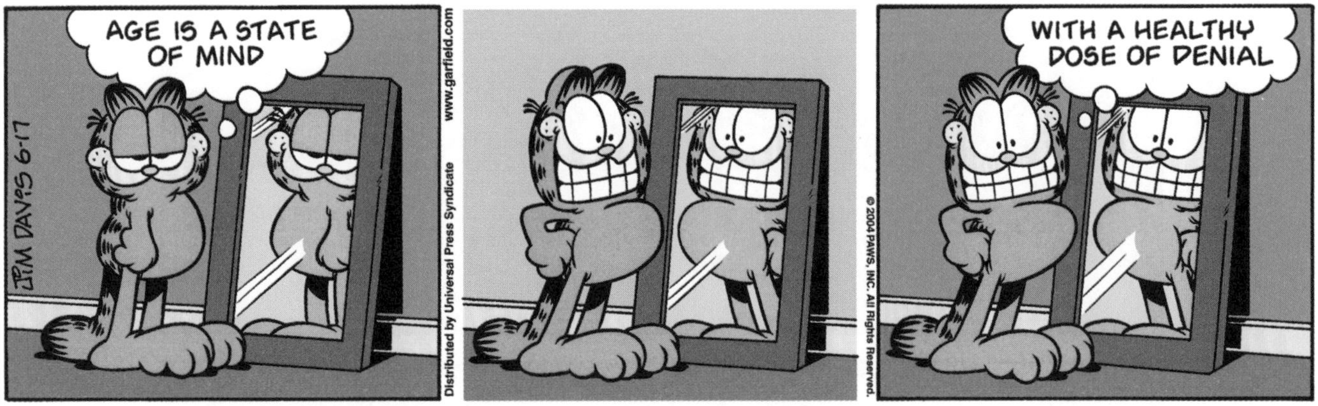
AGE IS A STATE OF MIND
JIM DAVIS 6-17
www.garfield.com
Distributed by Universal Press Syndicate
© 2004 PAWS, INC. All Rights Reserved.
WITH A HEALTHY DOSE OF DENIAL

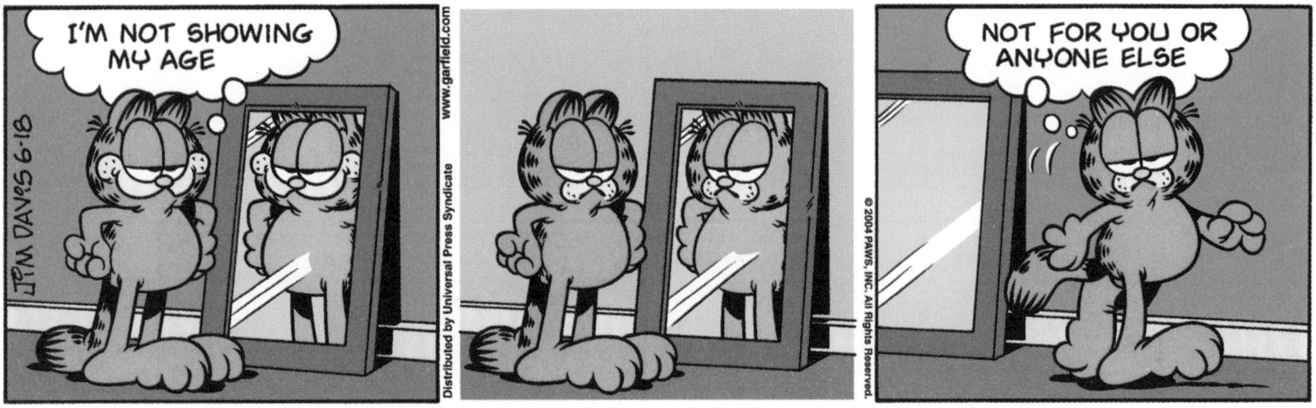
I'M NOT SHOWING MY AGE
JIM DAVIS 6-18
www.garfield.com
Distributed by Universal Press Syndicate
© 2004 PAWS, INC. All Rights Reserved.
NOT FOR YOU OR ANYONE ELSE

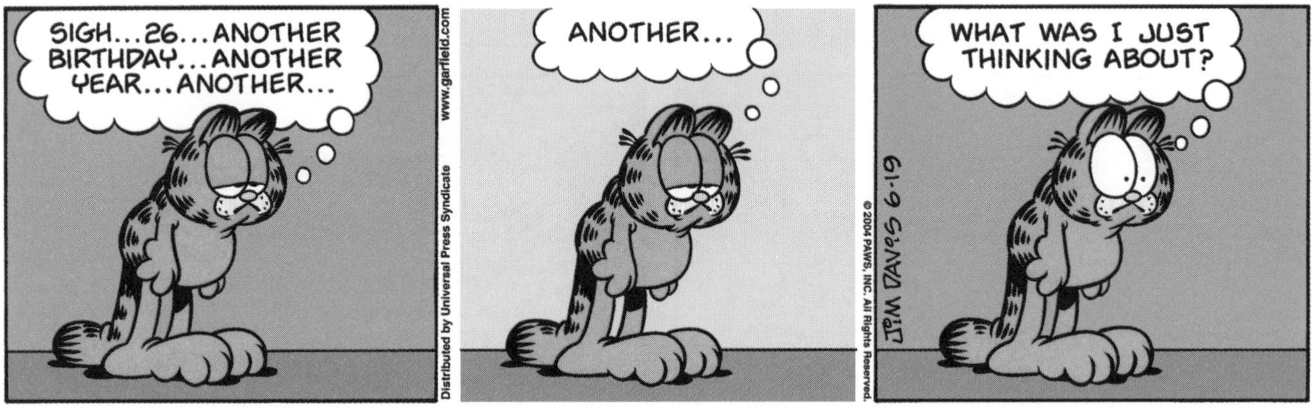
SIGH...26...ANOTHER BIRTHDAY...ANOTHER YEAR...ANOTHER...
www.garfield.com
Distributed by Universal Press Syndicate
ANOTHER...
© 2004 PAWS, INC. All Rights Reserved.
JIM DAVIS 6-19
WHAT WAS I JUST THINKING ABOUT?

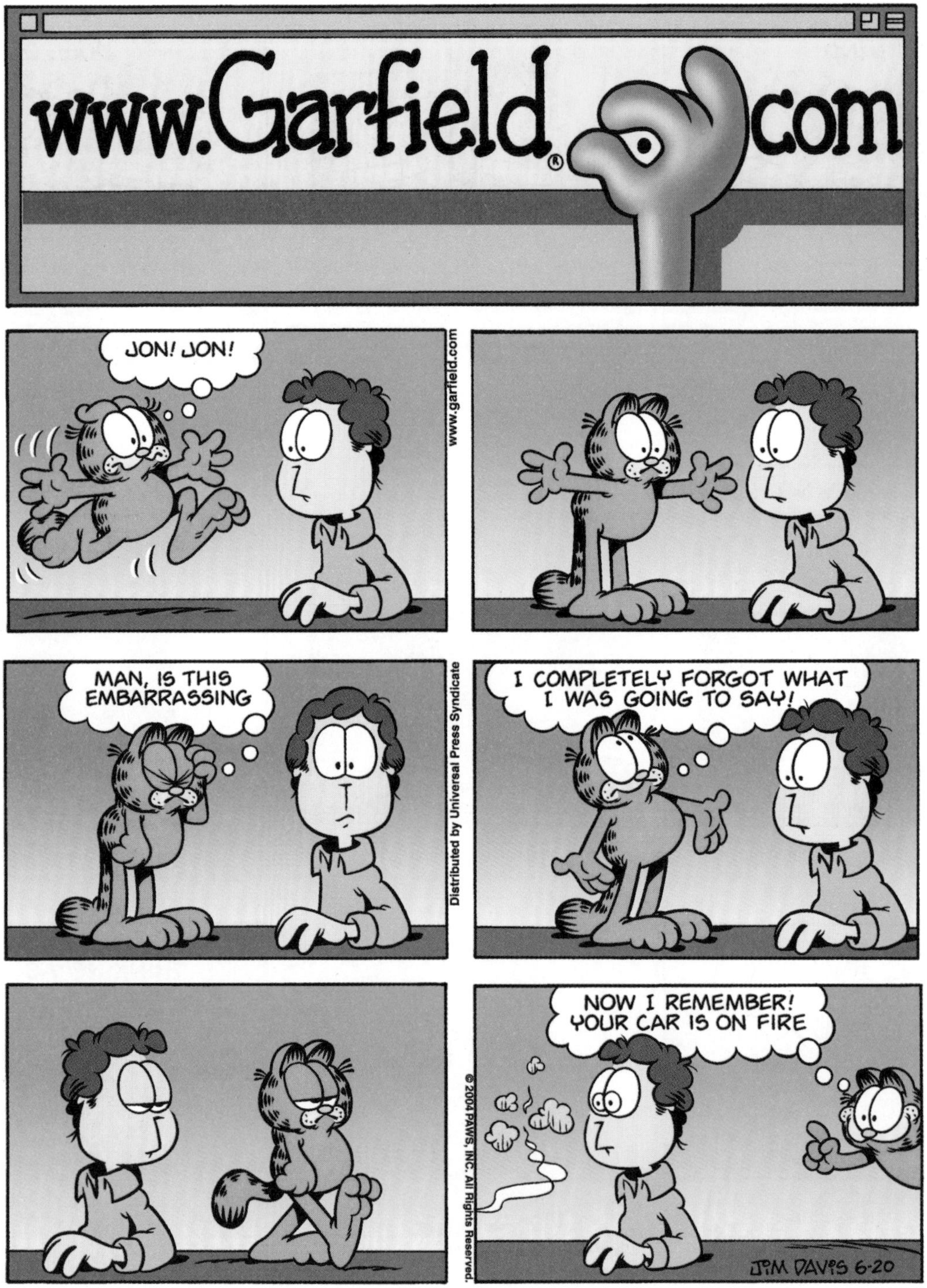
www.Garfield.com
JON! JON!
www.garfield.com
MAN, IS THIS EMBARRASSING
Distributed by Universal Press Syndicate
I COMPLETELY FORGOT WHAT I WAS GOING TO SAY!
© 2004 PAWS, INC. All Rights Reserved.
NOW I REMEMBER! YOUR CAR IS ON FIRE
JIM DAVIS 6-20

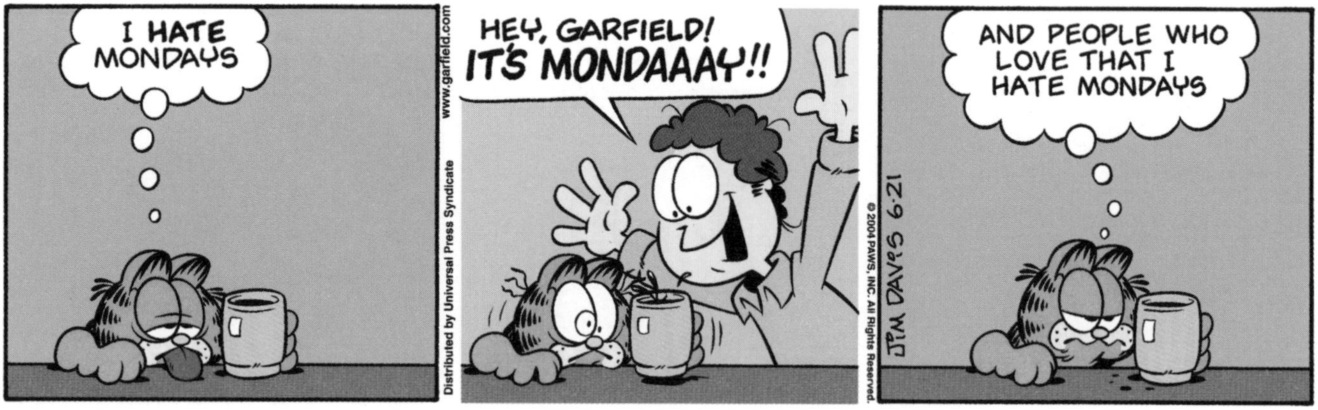
I HATE MONDAYS
HEY, GARFIELD! IT'S MONDAAAY!!
AND PEOPLE WHO LOVE THAT I HATE MONDAYS
JIM DAVIS 6-21
www.garfield.com
Distributed by Universal Press Syndicate
© 2004 PAWS, INC. All Rights Reserved.

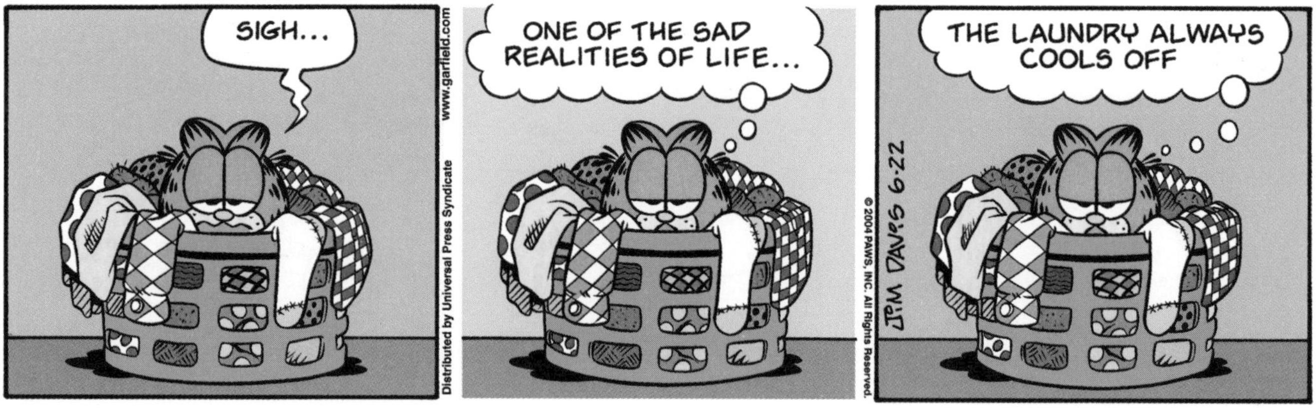
SIGH...
ONE OF THE SAD REALITIES OF LIFE...
THE LAUNDRY ALWAYS COOLS OFF
JIM DAVIS 6-22
www.garfield.com
Distributed by Universal Press Syndicate
© 2004 PAWS, INC. All Rights Reserved.

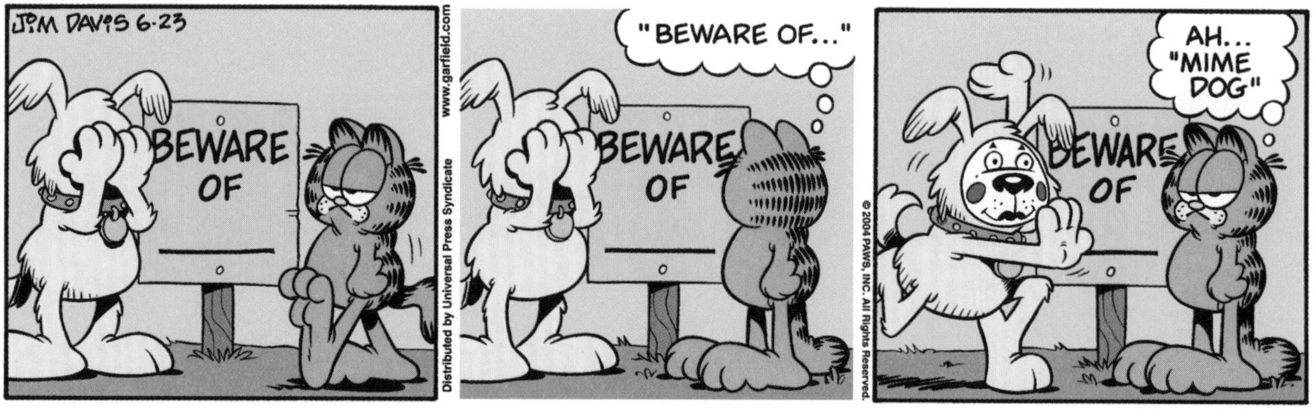
JIM DAVIS 6-23
BEWARE OF
"BEWARE OF..."
AH... "MIME DOG"
www.garfield.com
Distributed by Universal Press Syndicate
© 2004 PAWS, INC. All Rights Reserved.

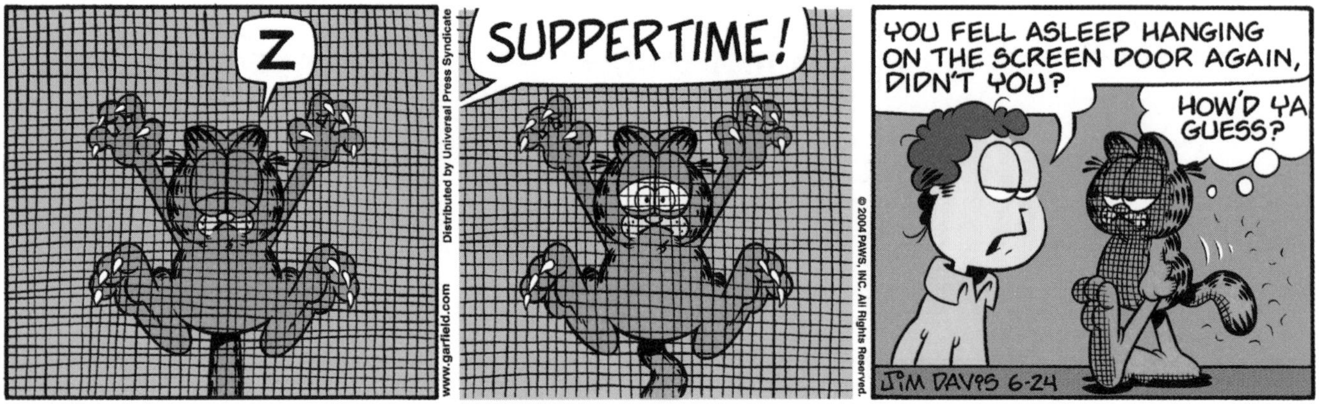
Z
SUPPERTIME!
YOU FELL ASLEEP HANGING ON THE SCREEN DOOR AGAIN, DIDN'T YOU?
HOW'D YA GUESS?
JIM DAVIS 6-24
www.garfield.com Distributed by Universal Press Syndicate
© 2004 PAWS, INC. All Rights Reserved.

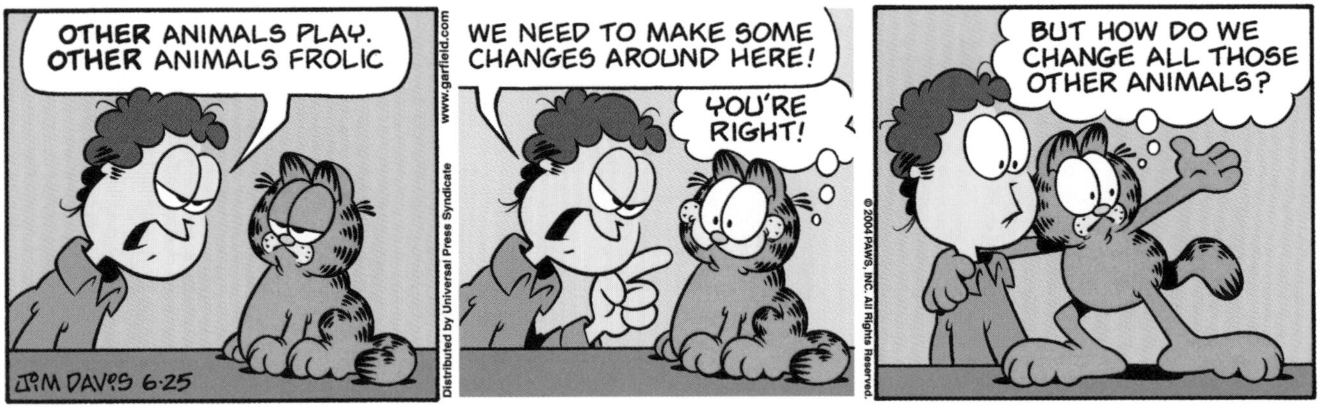
OTHER ANIMALS PLAY. OTHER ANIMALS FROLIC
WE NEED TO MAKE SOME CHANGES AROUND HERE!
YOU'RE RIGHT!
BUT HOW DO WE CHANGE ALL THOSE OTHER ANIMALS?
JIM DAVIS 6-25
Distributed by Universal Press Syndicate www.garfield.com
© 2004 PAWS, INC. All Rights Reserved.

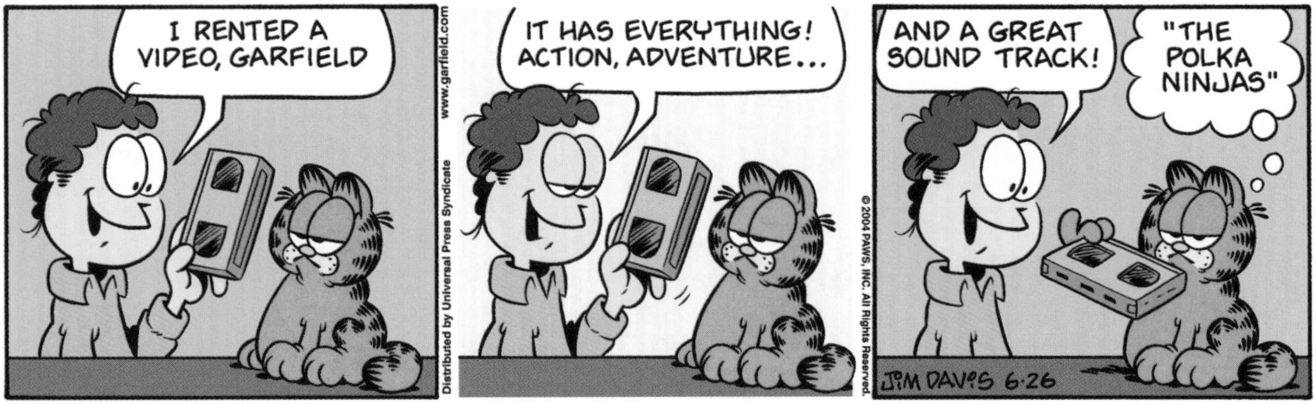
I RENTED A VIDEO, GARFIELD
IT HAS EVERYTHING! ACTION, ADVENTURE...
AND A GREAT SOUND TRACK!
"THE POLKA NINJAS"
JIM DAVIS 6-26
Distributed by Universal Press Syndicate www.garfield.com
© 2004 PAWS, INC. All Rights Reserved.

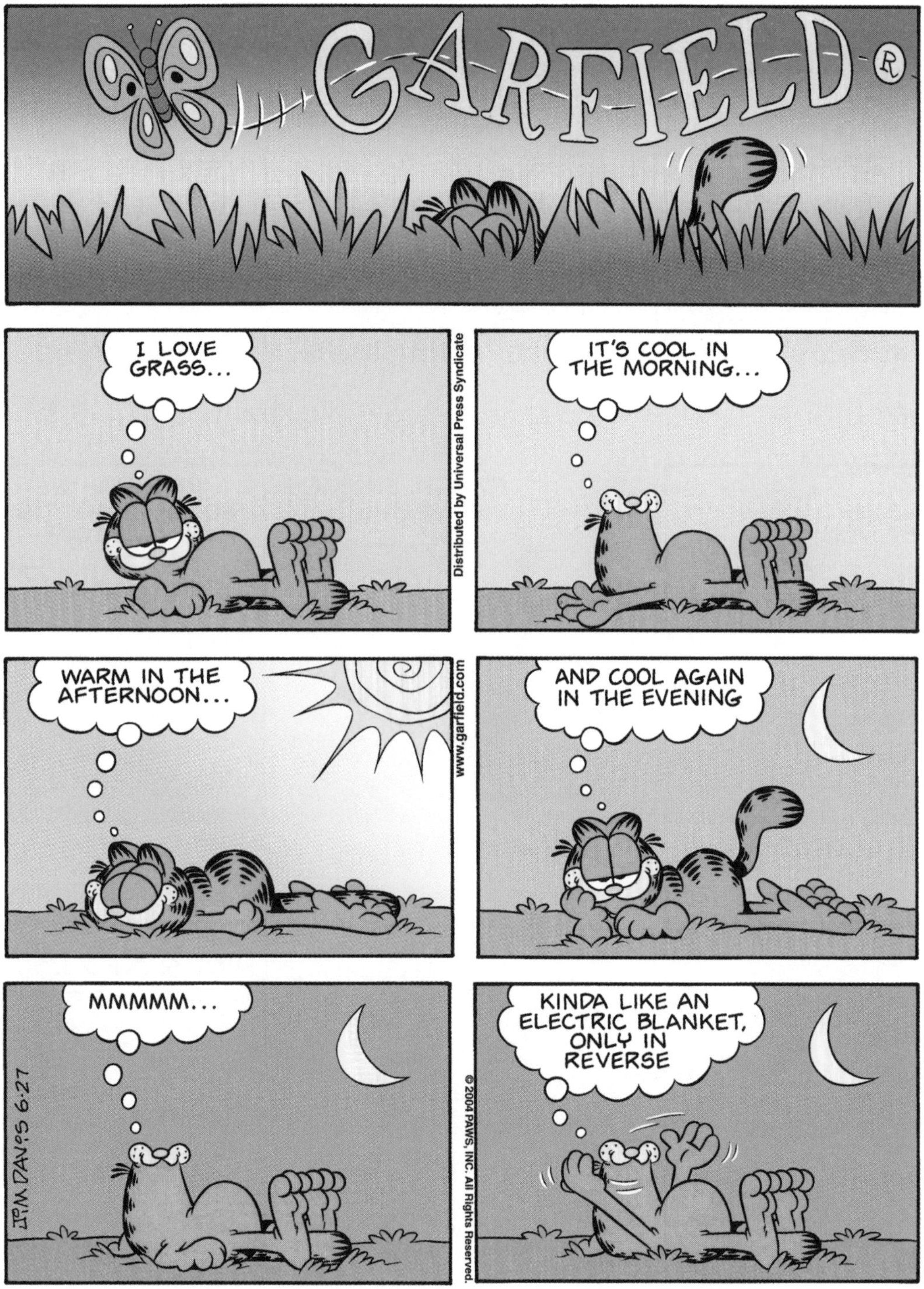
GARFIELD ®
I LOVE GRASS...
IT'S COOL IN THE MORNING...
WARM IN THE AFTERNOON...
AND COOL AGAIN IN THE EVENING
MMMMM...
KINDA LIKE AN ELECTRIC BLANKET, ONLY IN REVERSE
JPM DAVIS 6-27
Distributed by Universal Press Syndicate
www.garfield.com
© 2004 PAWS, INC. All Rights Reserved.

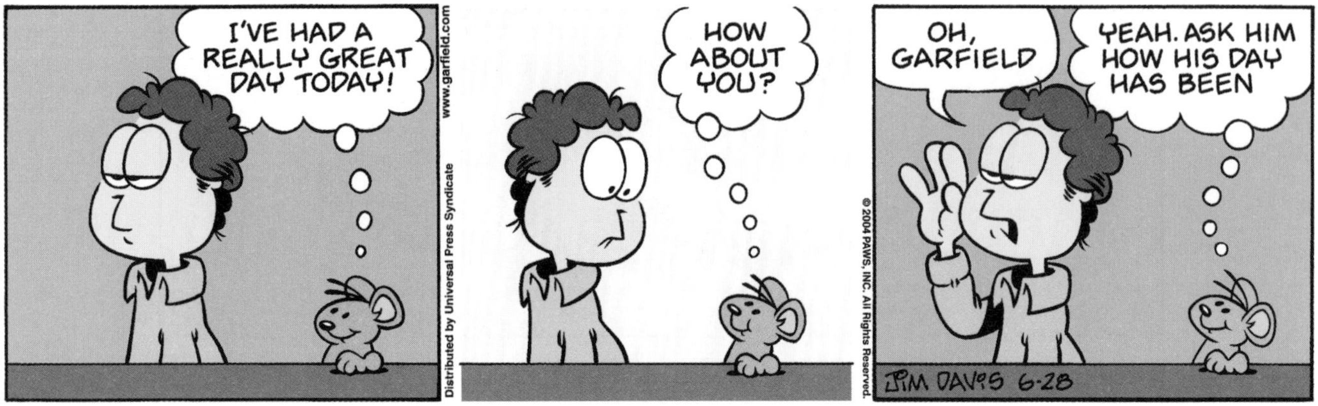
I'VE HAD A REALLY GREAT DAY TODAY!
www.garfield.com
Distributed by Universal Press Syndicate
HOW ABOUT YOU?
© 2004 PAWS, INC. All Rights Reserved.
OH, GARFIELD
YEAH. ASK HIM HOW HIS DAY HAS BEEN
JIM DAVIS 6-28

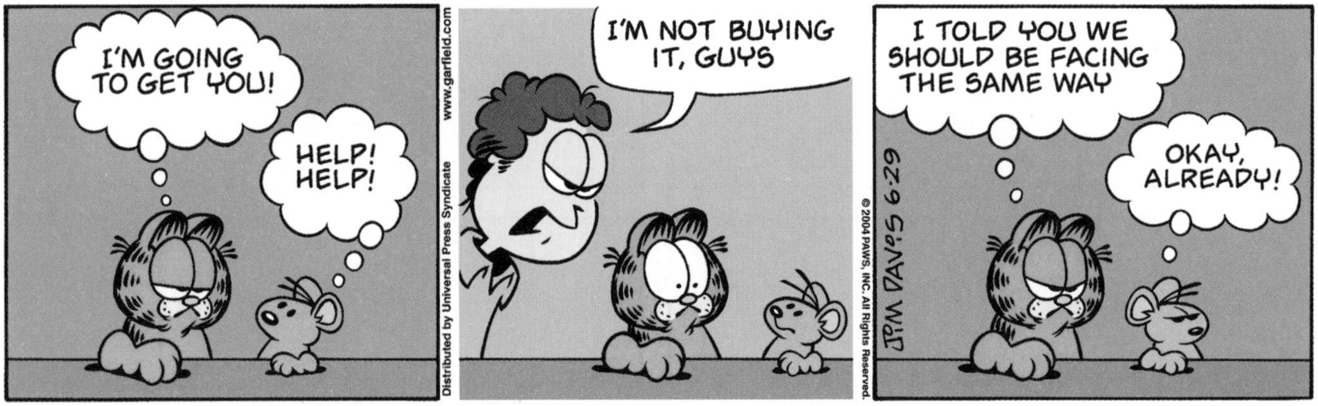
I'M GOING TO GET YOU!
HELP! HELP!
www.garfield.com
Distributed by Universal Press Syndicate
I'M NOT BUYING IT, GUYS
© 2004 PAWS, INC. All Rights Reserved.
JIM DAVIS 6-29
I TOLD YOU WE SHOULD BE FACING THE SAME WAY
OKAY, ALREADY!

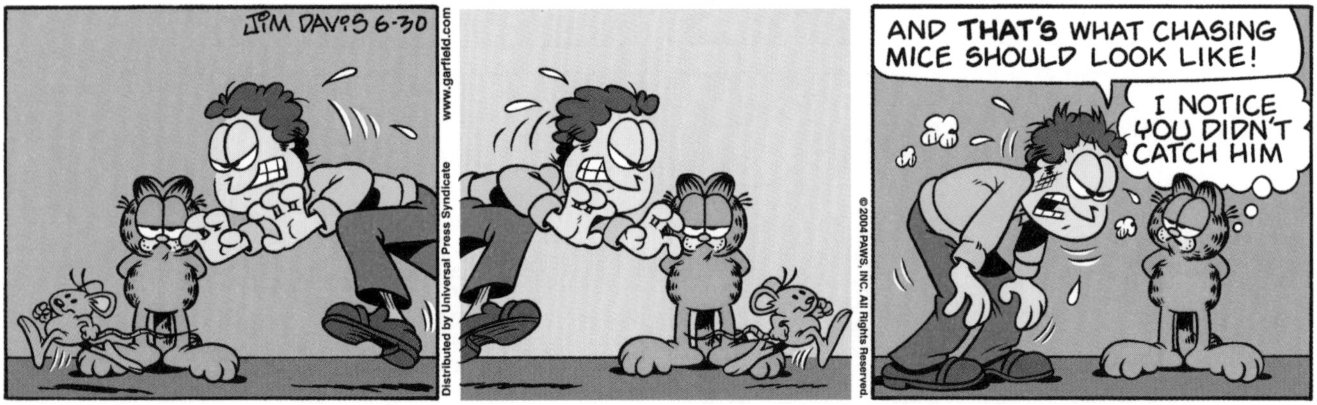
JIM DAVIS 6-30
www.garfield.com
Distributed by Universal Press Syndicate
© 2004 PAWS, INC. All Rights Reserved.
AND THAT'S WHAT CHASING MICE SHOULD LOOK LIKE!
I NOTICE YOU DIDN'T CATCH HIM

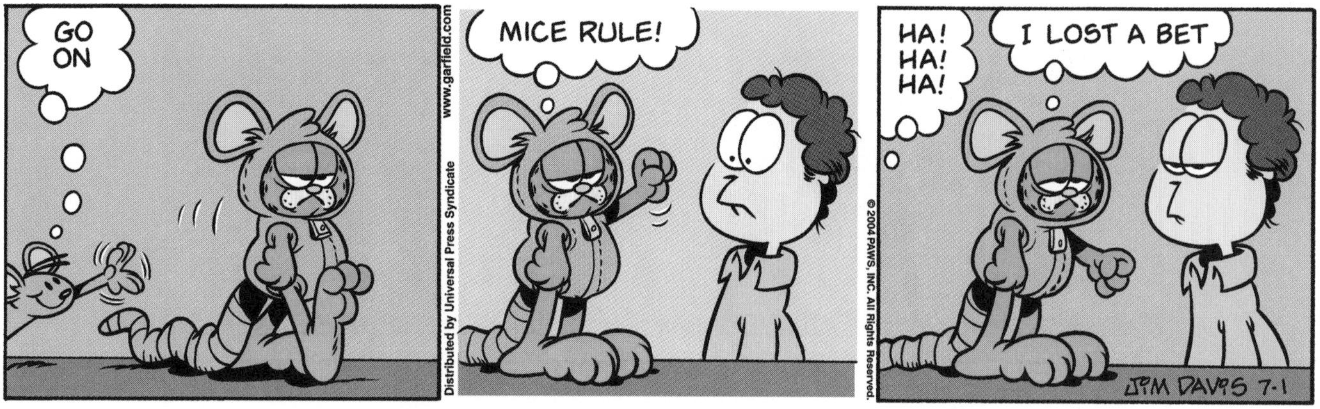
GO ON
MICE RULE!
HA! HA! HA!
I LOST A BET
JIM DAVIS 7-1
www.garfield.com
Distributed by Universal Press Syndicate
© 2004 PAWS, INC. All Rights Reserved.

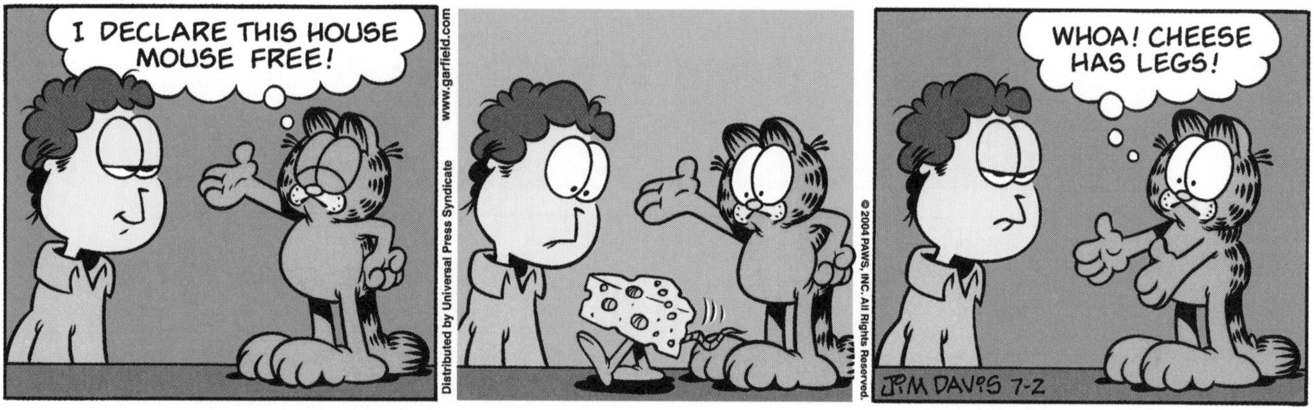
I DECLARE THIS HOUSE MOUSE FREE!
WHOA! CHEESE HAS LEGS!
JIM DAVIS 7-2
www.garfield.com
Distributed by Universal Press Syndicate
© 2004 PAWS, INC. All Rights Reserved.

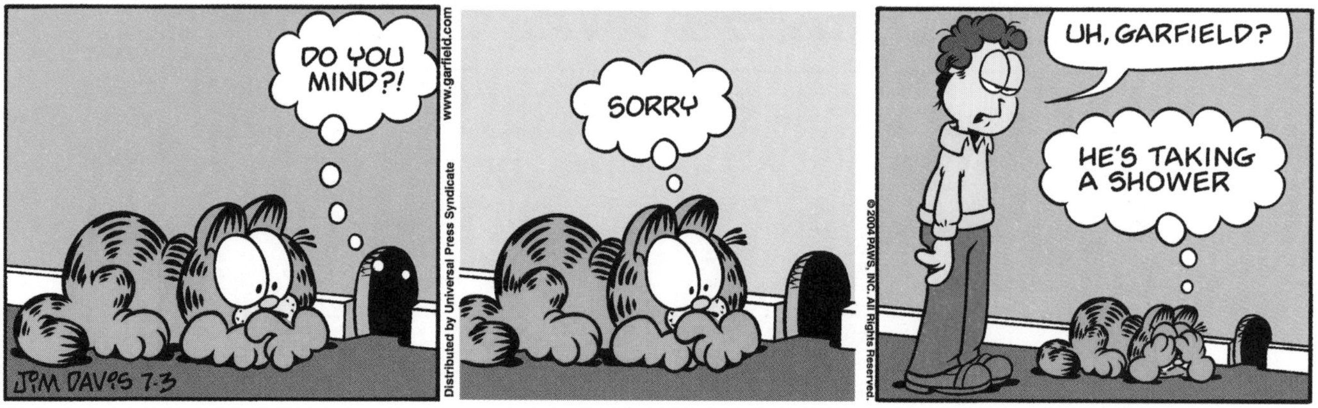
DO YOU MIND?!
SORRY
UH, GARFIELD?
HE'S TAKING A SHOWER
JIM DAVIS 7-3
www.garfield.com
Distributed by Universal Press Syndicate
© 2004 PAWS, INC. All Rights Reserved.

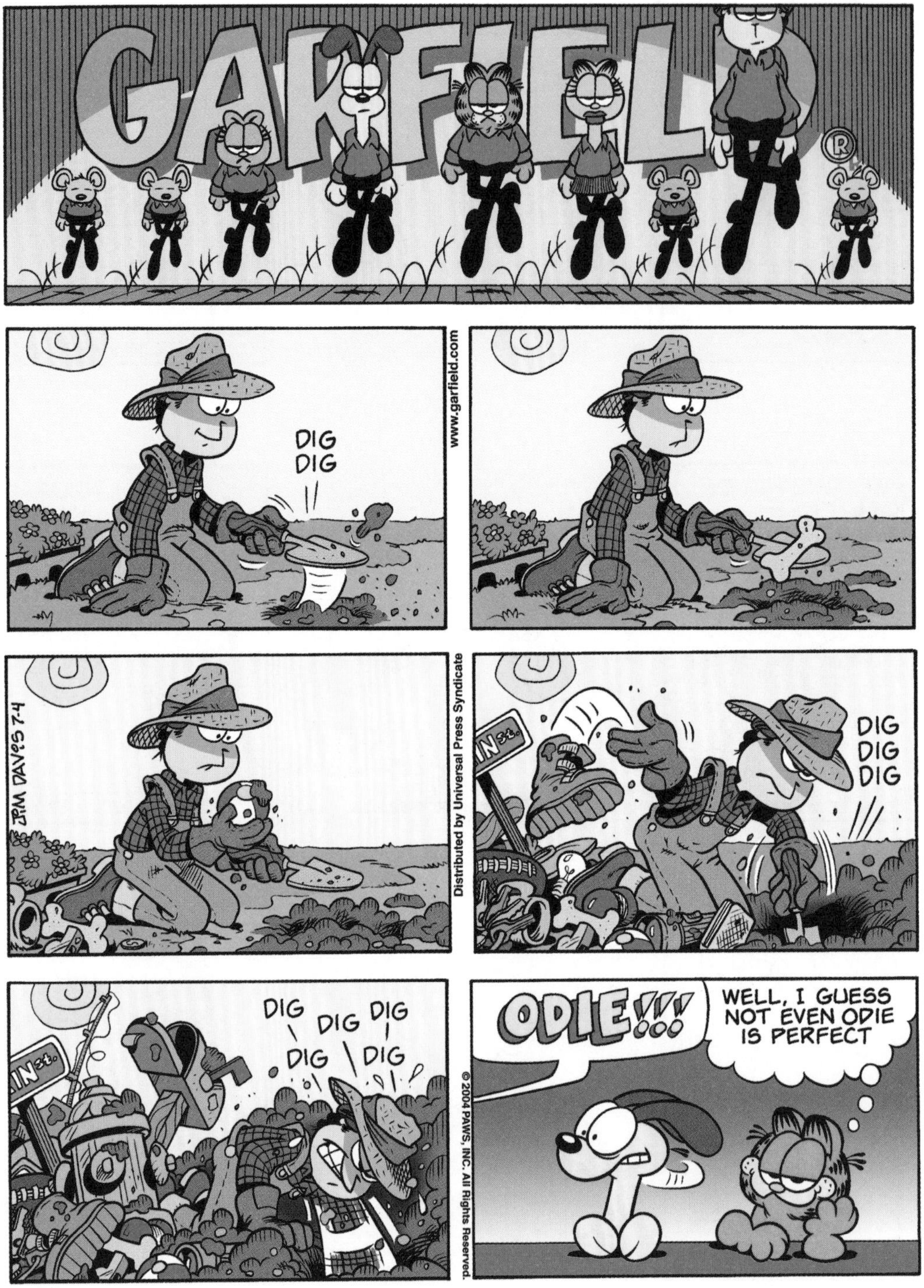
GARFIELD
DIG
DIG
www.garfield.com
JIM DAVIS 7-4
Distributed by Universal Press Syndicate
DIG
DIG
DIG
DIG
DIG
DIG
DIG
DIG
© 2004 PAWS, INC. All Rights Reserved.
ODIE!!!
WELL, I GUESS NOT EVEN ODIE IS PERFECT

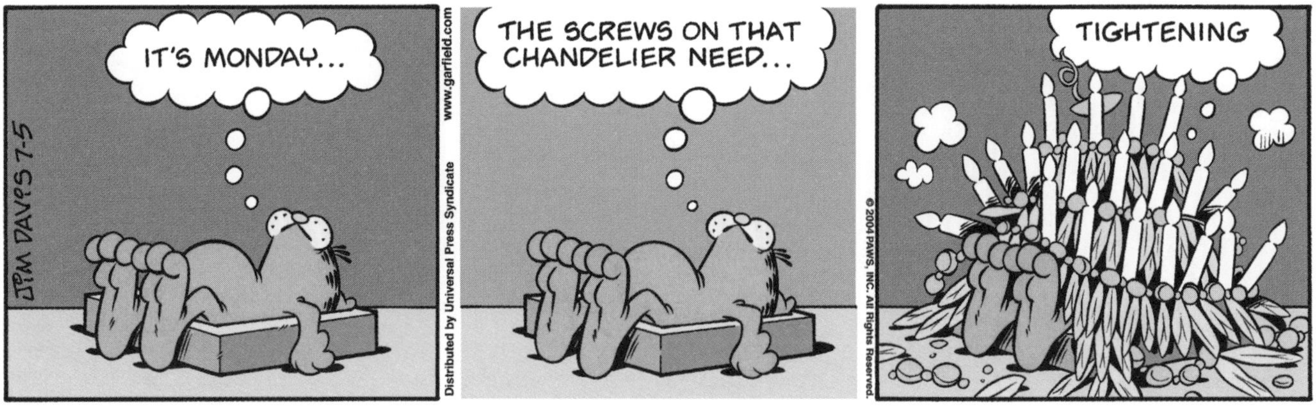
IT'S MONDAY...
THE SCREWS ON THAT CHANDELIER NEED...
TIGHTENING
JIM DAVIS 7-5
www.garfield.com
Distributed by Universal Press Syndicate
© 2004 PAWS, INC. All Rights Reserved.

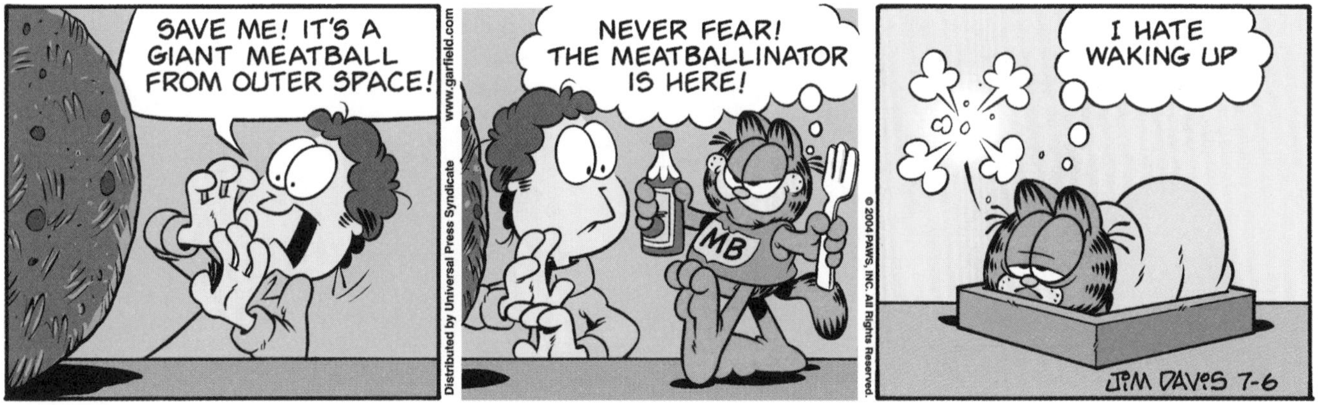
SAVE ME! IT'S A GIANT MEATBALL FROM OUTER SPACE!
NEVER FEAR! THE MEATBALLINATOR IS HERE!
MB
I HATE WAKING UP
JIM DAVIS 7-6
www.garfield.com
Distributed by Universal Press Syndicate
© 2004 PAWS, INC. All Rights Reserved.

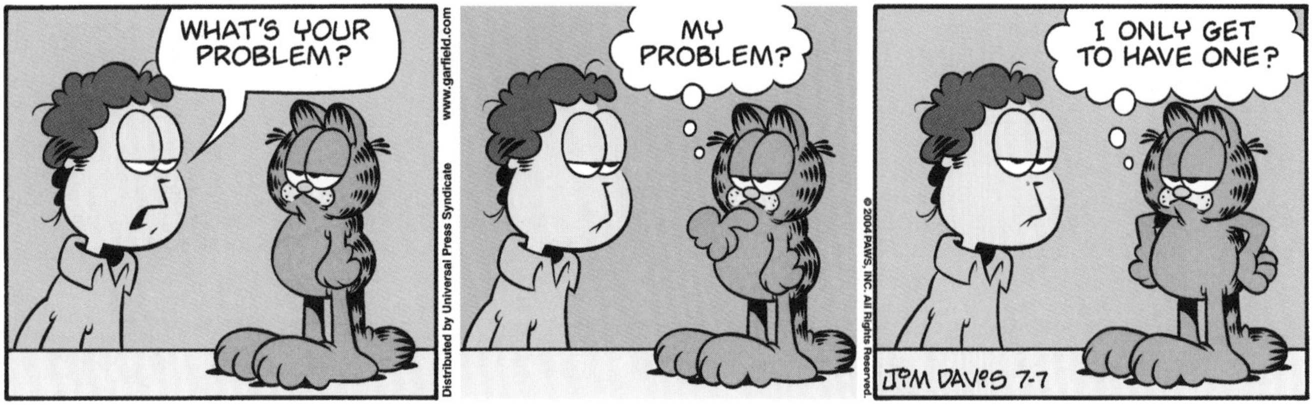
WHAT'S YOUR PROBLEM?
MY PROBLEM?
I ONLY GET TO HAVE ONE?
JIM DAVIS 7-7
www.garfield.com
Distributed by Universal Press Syndicate
© 2004 PAWS, INC. All Rights Reserved.

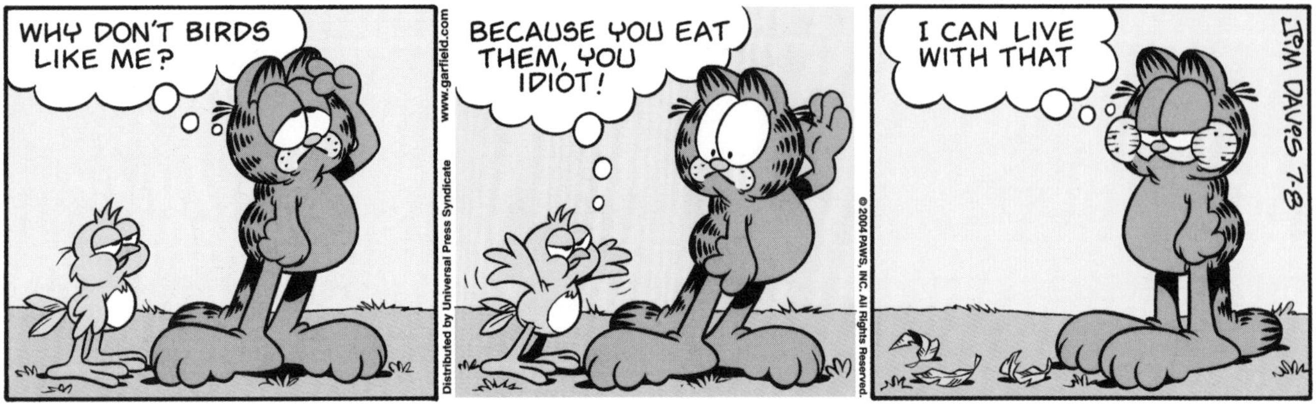
WHY DON'T BIRDS LIKE ME?
BECAUSE YOU EAT THEM, YOU IDIOT!
I CAN LIVE WITH THAT
www.garfield.com
Distributed by Universal Press Syndicate
© 2004 PAWS, INC. All Rights Reserved.

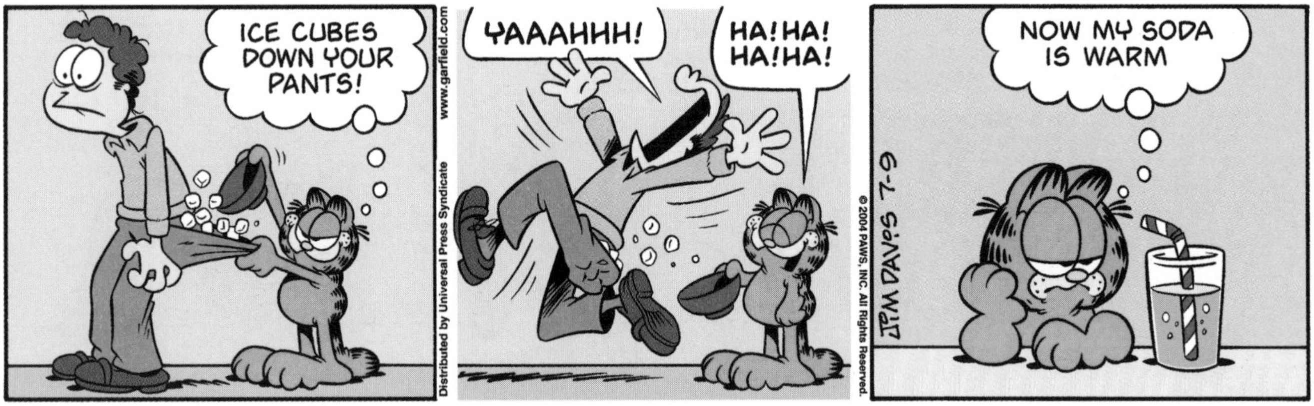
ICE CUBES DOWN YOUR PANTS!
YAAAHHH!
HA! HA! HA! HA!
NOW MY SODA IS WARM
www.garfield.com
Distributed by Universal Press Syndicate
© 2004 PAWS, INC. All Rights Reserved.

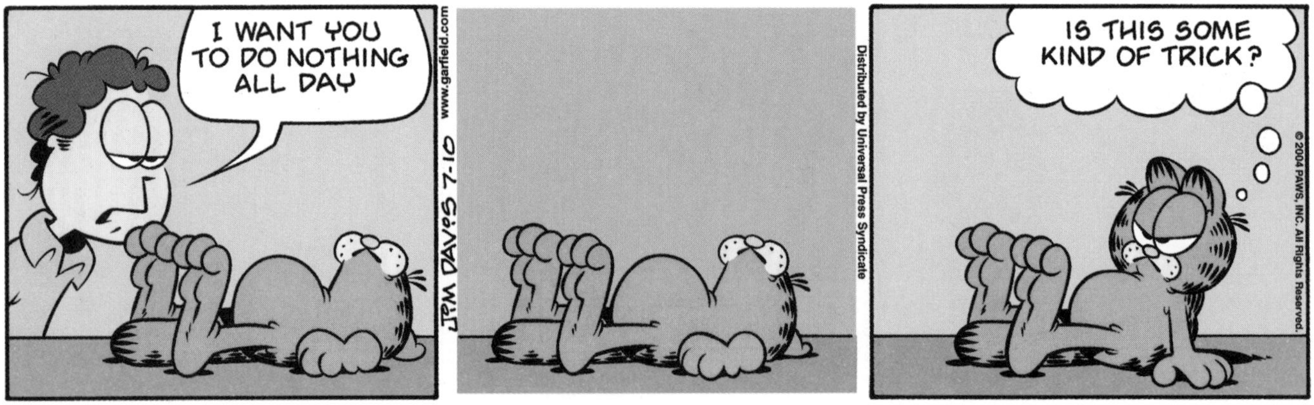
I WANT YOU TO DO NOTHING ALL DAY
IS THIS SOME KIND OF TRICK?
www.garfield.com
Distributed by Universal Press Syndicate
© 2004 PAWS, INC. All Rights Reserved.

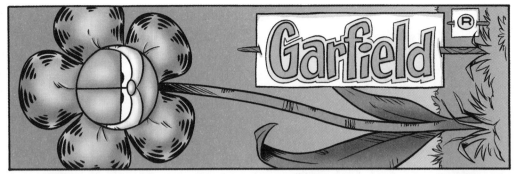

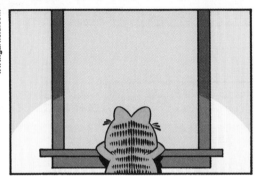

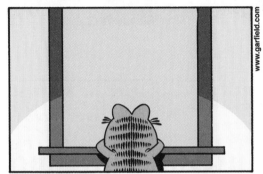

Garfield
www.garfield.com
THIS WINDOW IS FILTHY
Distributed by Universal Press Syndicate
I CAN'T SEE A THING
© 2004 PAWS, INC. All Rights Reserved.
JPM DAVPS 7-11
I KNEW THAT

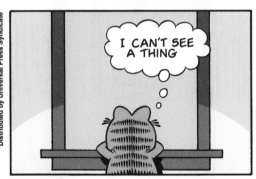

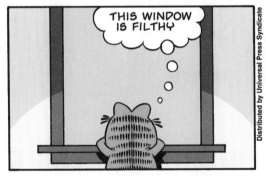

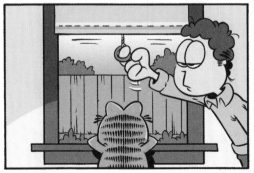

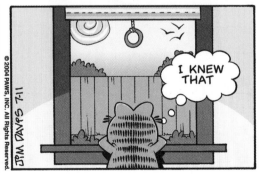

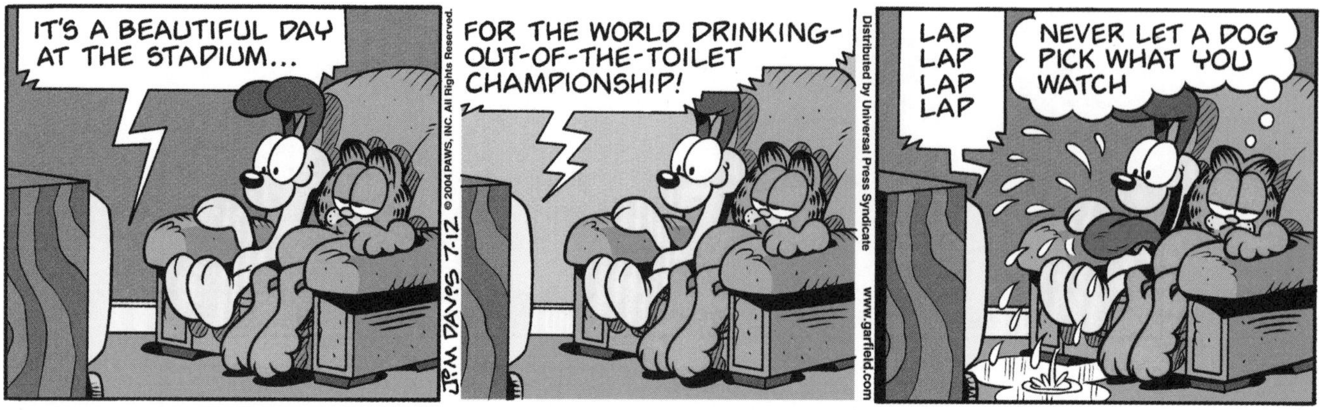
IT'S A BEAUTIFUL DAY AT THE STADIUM...
FOR THE WORLD DRINKING-OUT-OF-THE-TOILET CHAMPIONSHIP!
LAP LAP LAP LAP
NEVER LET A DOG PICK WHAT YOU WATCH
JPM DAVPS 7-12
© 2004 PAWS, INC. All Rights Reserved.
Distributed by Universal Press Syndicate
www.garfield.com

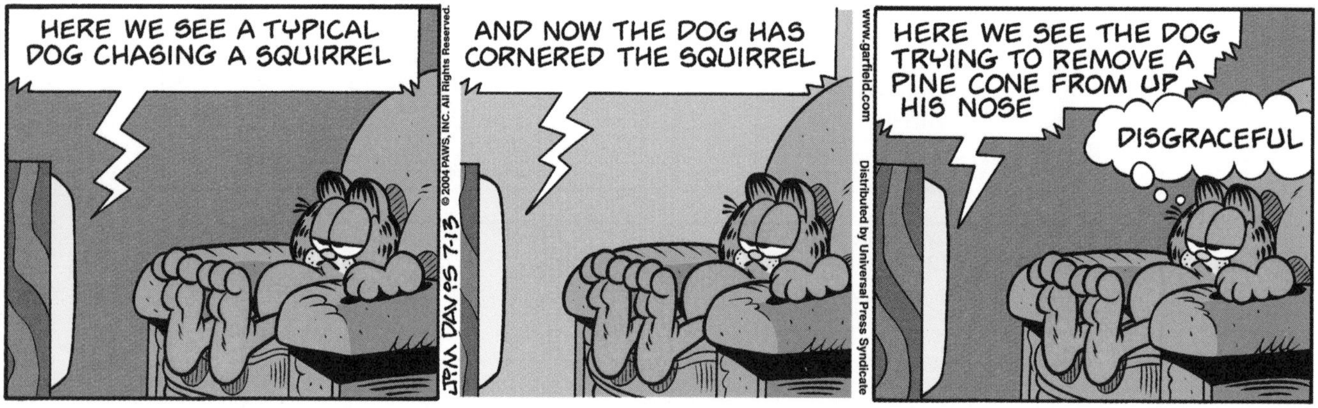
HERE WE SEE A TYPICAL DOG CHASING A SQUIRREL
AND NOW THE DOG HAS CORNERED THE SQUIRREL
HERE WE SEE THE DOG TRYING TO REMOVE A PINE CONE FROM UP HIS NOSE
DISGRACEFUL
JPM DAVPS 7-13
© 2004 PAWS, INC. All Rights Reserved.
www.garfield.com
Distributed by Universal Press Syndicate

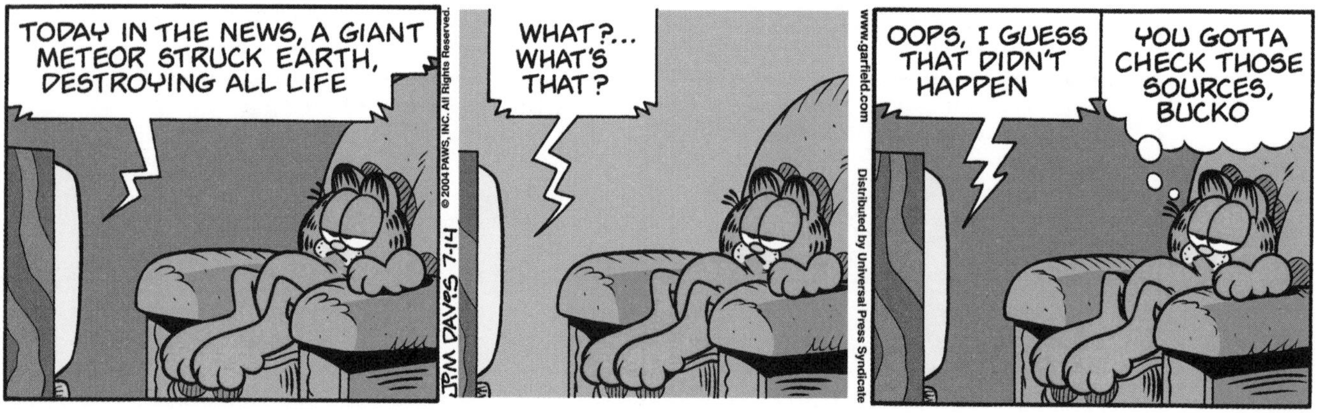
TODAY IN THE NEWS, A GIANT METEOR STRUCK EARTH, DESTROYING ALL LIFE
WHAT?... WHAT'S THAT?
OOPS, I GUESS THAT DIDN'T HAPPEN
YOU GOTTA CHECK THOSE SOURCES, BUCKO
JPM DAVPS 7-14
© 2004 PAWS, INC. All Rights Reserved.
www.garfield.com
Distributed by Universal Press Syndicate

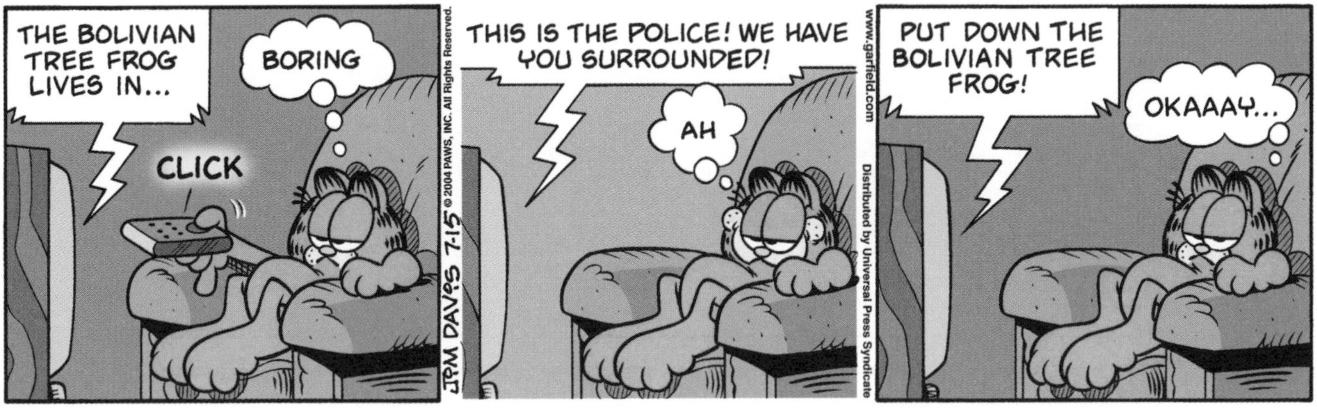
THE BOLIVIAN TREE FROG LIVES IN...
BORING
CLICK
JPM DAVPS 7-15
© 2004 PAWS, INC. All Rights Reserved.
THIS IS THE POLICE! WE HAVE YOU SURROUNDED!
AH
www.garfield.com
Distributed by Universal Press Syndicate
PUT DOWN THE BOLIVIAN TREE FROG!
OKAAAY...

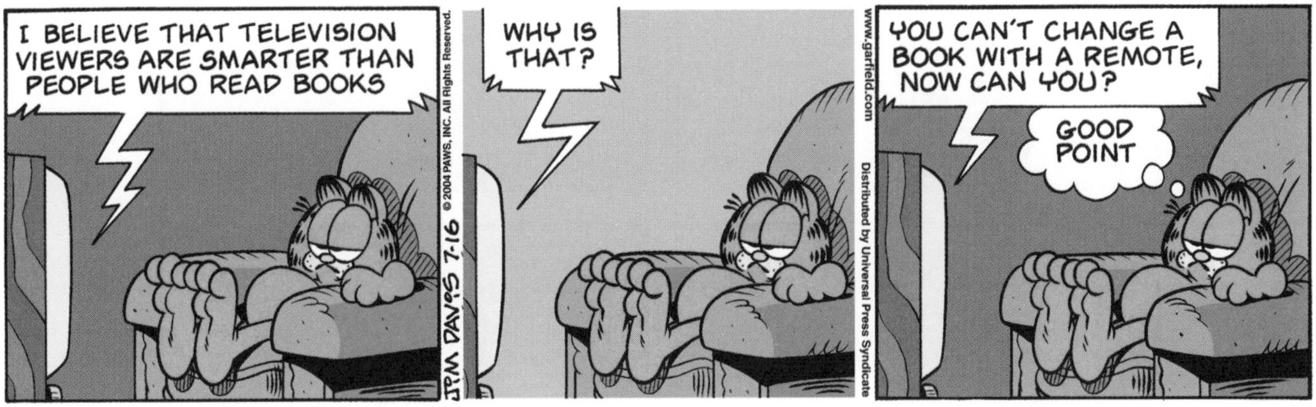
I BELIEVE THAT TELEVISION VIEWERS ARE SMARTER THAN PEOPLE WHO READ BOOKS
JPM DAVPS 7-16
© 2004 PAWS, INC. All Rights Reserved.
WHY IS THAT?
www.garfield.com
Distributed by Universal Press Syndicate
YOU CAN'T CHANGE A BOOK WITH A REMOTE, NOW CAN YOU?
GOOD POINT

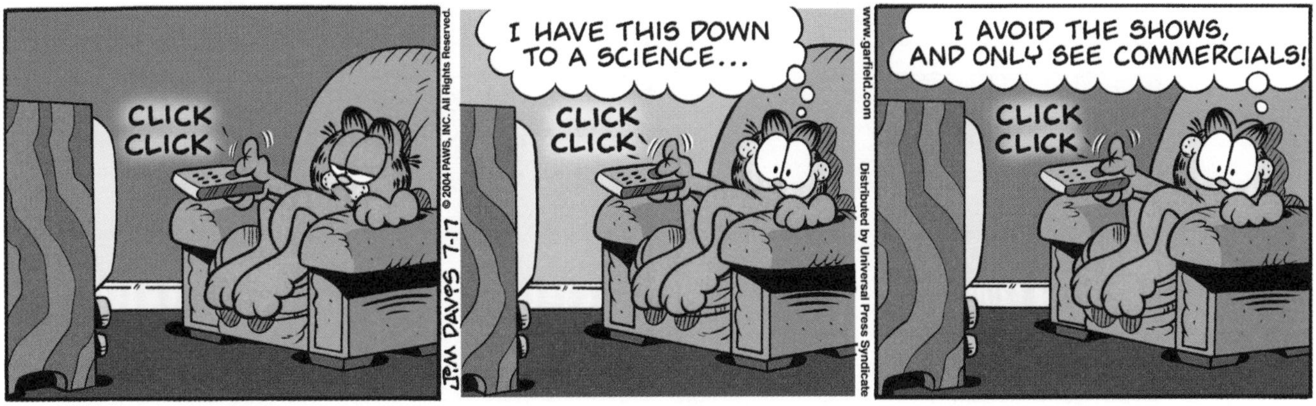
CLICK CLICK
JPM DAVPS 7-17
© 2004 PAWS, INC. All Rights Reserved.
I HAVE THIS DOWN TO A SCIENCE...
CLICK CLICK
www.garfield.com
Distributed by Universal Press Syndicate
I AVOID THE SHOWS, AND ONLY SEE COMMERCIALS!
CLICK CLICK

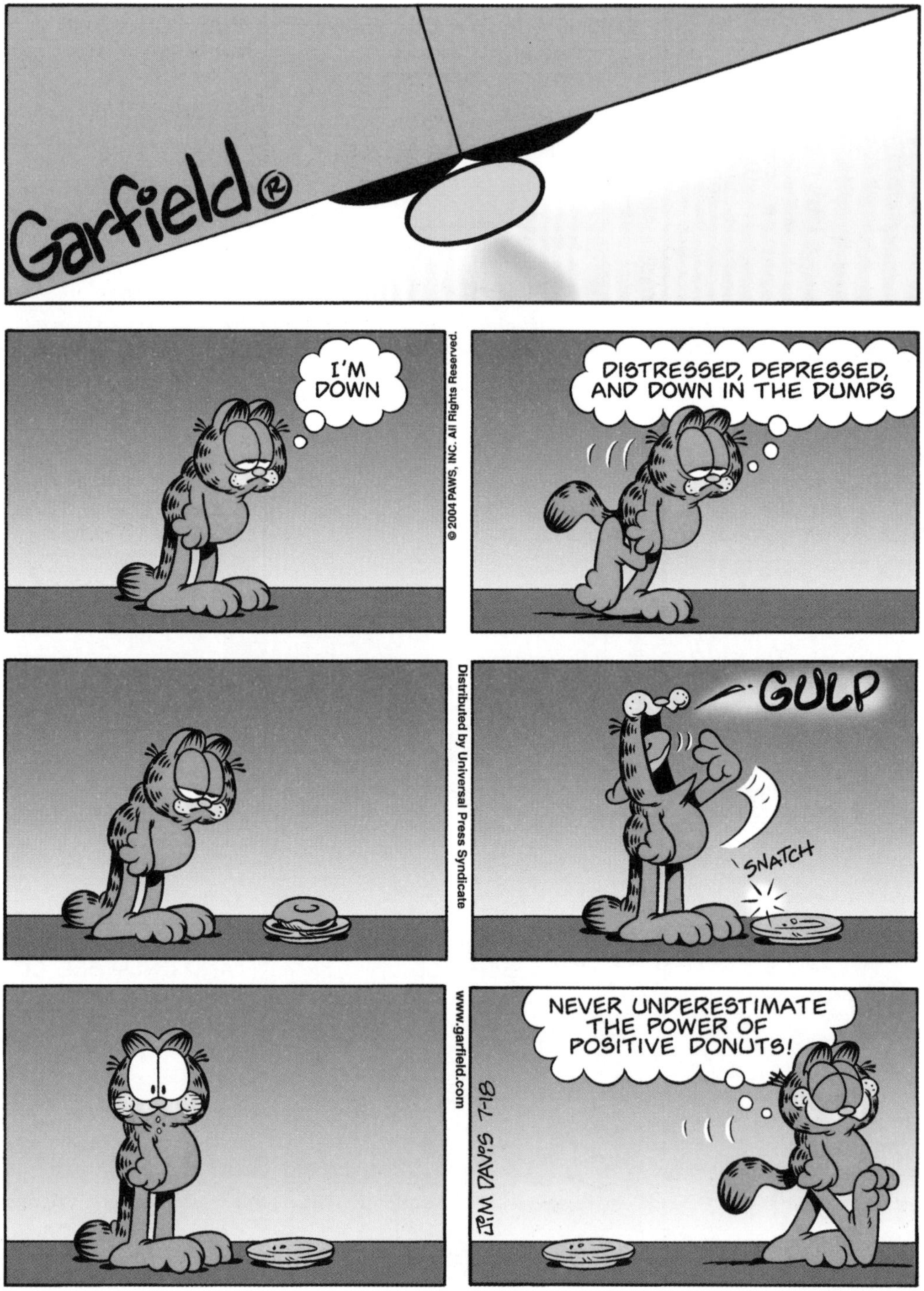
Garfield®
I'M DOWN
DISTRESSED, DEPRESSED, AND DOWN IN THE DUMPS
GULP
SNATCH
NEVER UNDERESTIMATE THE POWER OF POSITIVE DONUTS!
JIM DAVIS 7-18
© 2004 PAWS, INC. All Rights Reserved.
Distributed by Universal Press Syndicate
www.garfield.com

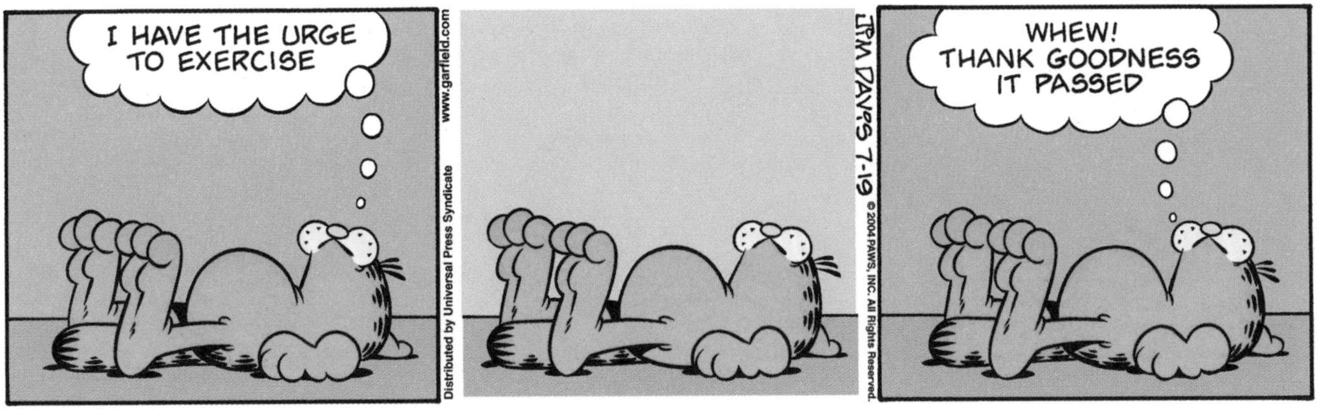
I HAVE THE URGE TO EXERCISE
WHEW! THANK GOODNESS IT PASSED
JIM DAVIS 7-19
Distributed by Universal Press Syndicate www.garfield.com
© 2004 PAWS, INC. All Rights Reserved.

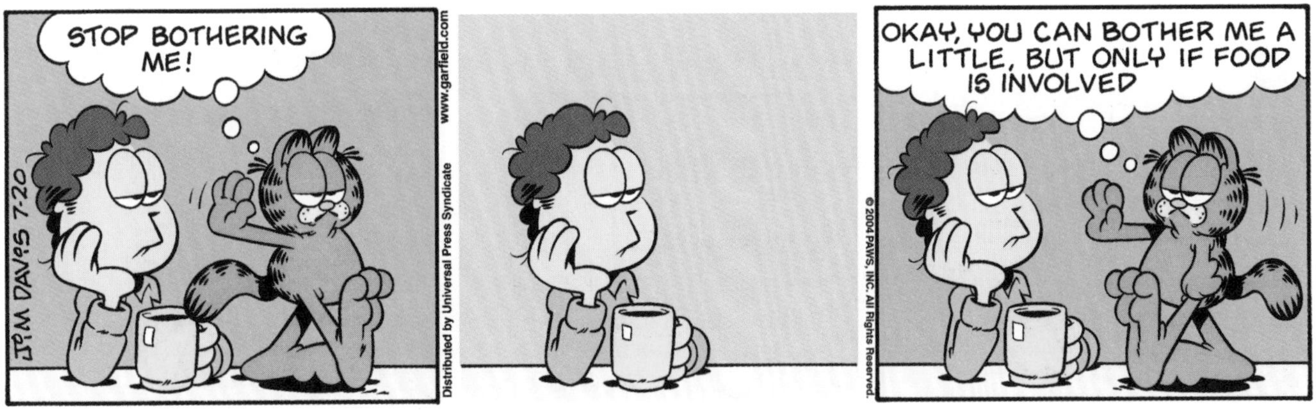
STOP BOTHERING ME!
OKAY, YOU CAN BOTHER ME A LITTLE, BUT ONLY IF FOOD IS INVOLVED
JIM DAVIS 7-20
Distributed by Universal Press Syndicate www.garfield.com
© 2004 PAWS, INC. All Rights Reserved.

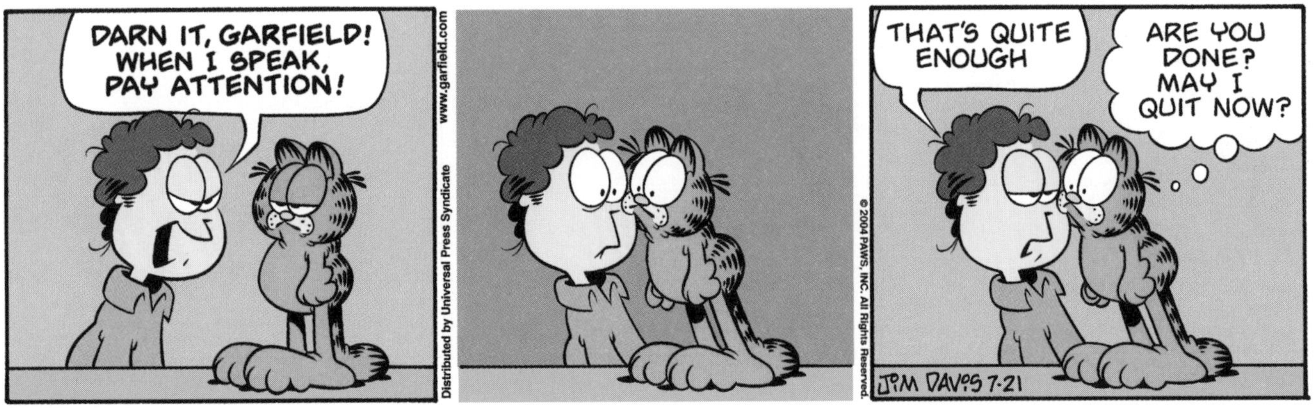
DARN IT, GARFIELD! WHEN I SPEAK, PAY ATTENTION!
THAT'S QUITE ENOUGH
ARE YOU DONE? MAY I QUIT NOW?
JIM DAVIS 7-21
Distributed by Universal Press Syndicate www.garfield.com
© 2004 PAWS, INC. All Rights Reserved.

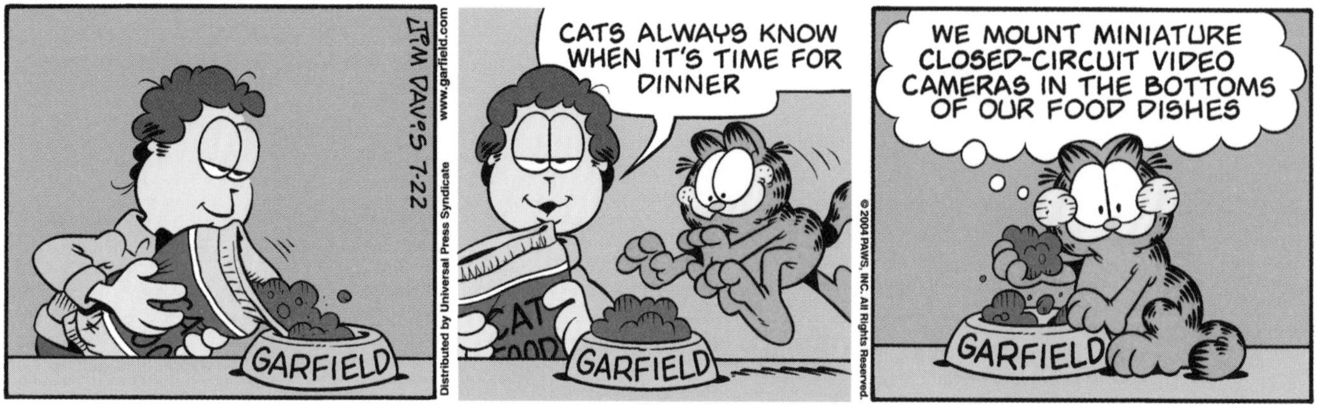
JIM DAVIS 7-22
Distributed by Universal Press Syndicate www.garfield.com
GARFIELD
CATS ALWAYS KNOW WHEN IT'S TIME FOR DINNER
CAT FOOD
GARFIELD
© 2004 PAWS, INC. All Rights Reserved.
WE MOUNT MINIATURE CLOSED-CIRCUIT VIDEO CAMERAS IN THE BOTTOMS OF OUR FOOD DISHES
GARFIELD

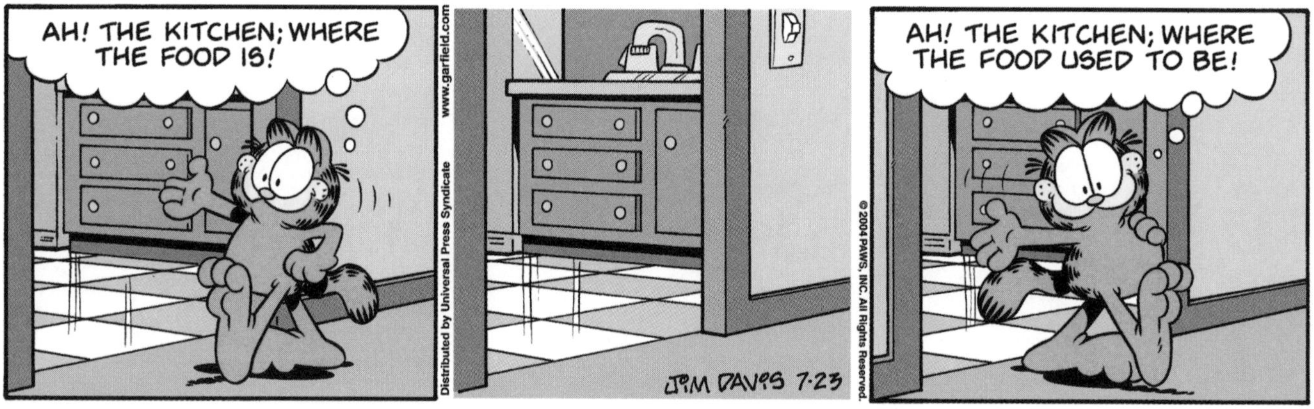
AH! THE KITCHEN; WHERE THE FOOD IS!
Distributed by Universal Press Syndicate www.garfield.com
JIM DAVIS 7-23
© 2004 PAWS, INC. All Rights Reserved.
AH! THE KITCHEN; WHERE THE FOOD USED TO BE!

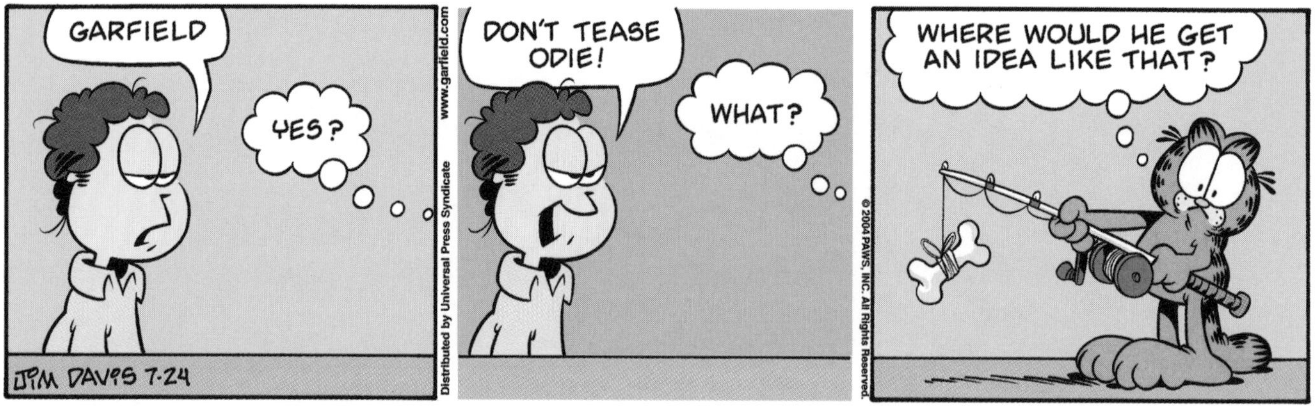
GARFIELD
YES?
JIM DAVIS 7-24
Distributed by Universal Press Syndicate www.garfield.com
DON'T TEASE ODIE!
WHAT?
© 2004 PAWS, INC. All Rights Reserved.
WHERE WOULD HE GET AN IDEA LIKE THAT?

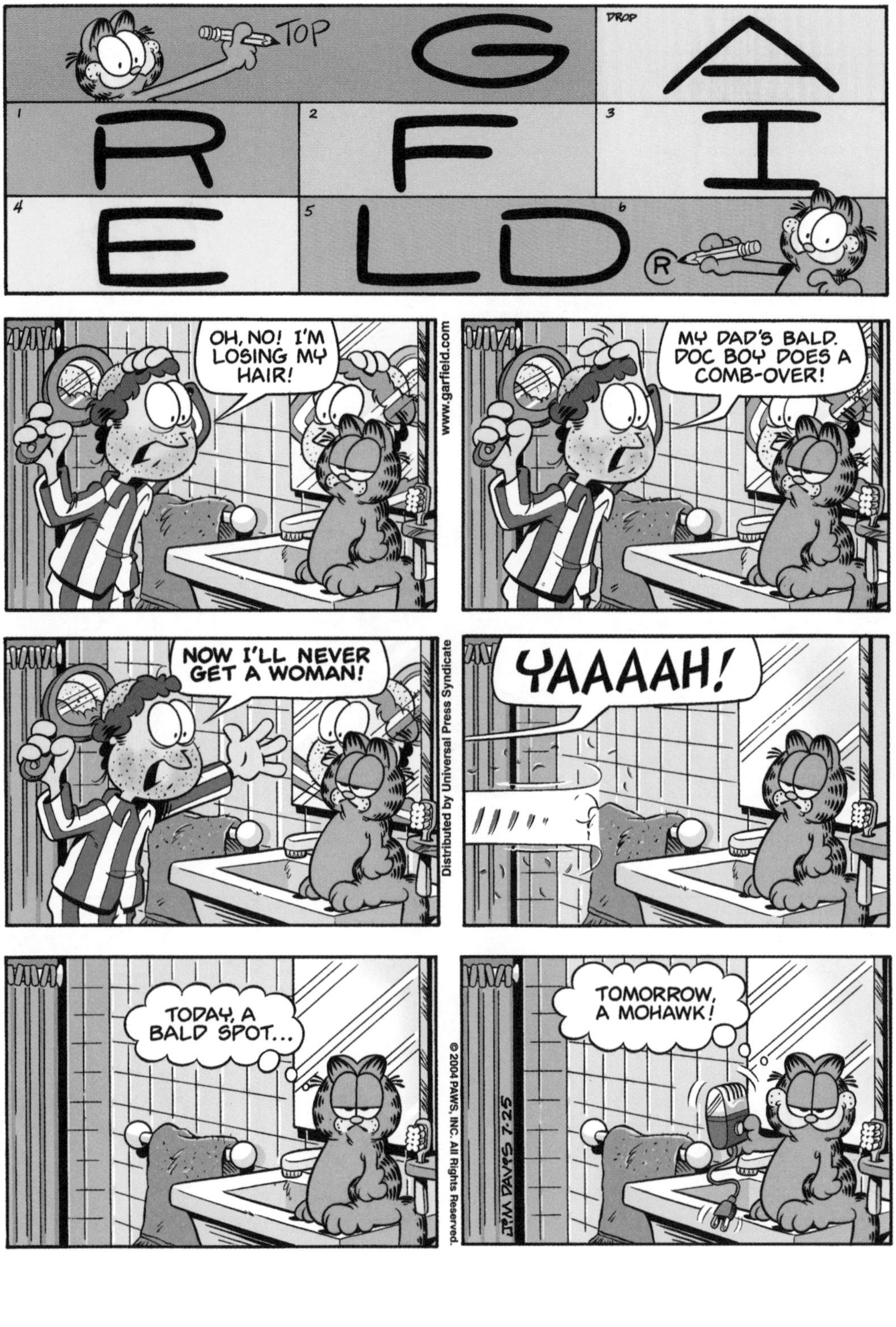
TOP
DROP
GARFIELD
OH, NO! I'M LOSING MY HAIR!
MY DAD'S BALD. DOC BOY DOES A COMB-OVER!
NOW I'LL NEVER GET A WOMAN!
YAAAAH!
TODAY, A BALD SPOT...
TOMORROW, A MOHAWK!
www.garfield.com
Distributed by Universal Press Syndicate
© 2004 PAWS, INC. All Rights Reserved.
JIM DAVIS 7-25

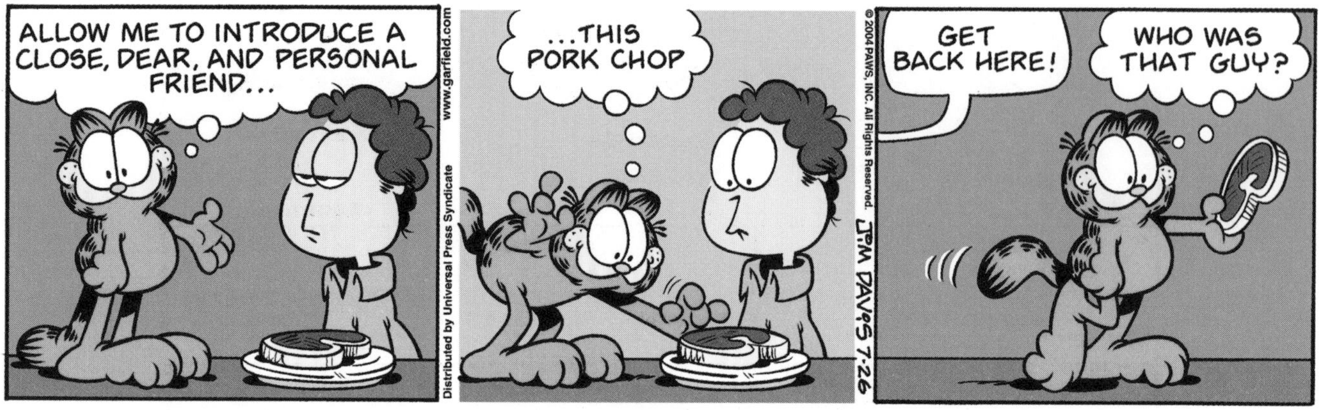
ALLOW ME TO INTRODUCE A CLOSE, DEAR, AND PERSONAL FRIEND...
www.garfield.com
Distributed by Universal Press Syndicate
...THIS PORK CHOP
JIM DAVIS 7-26
© 2004 PAWS, INC. All Rights Reserved.
GET BACK HERE!
WHO WAS THAT GUY?

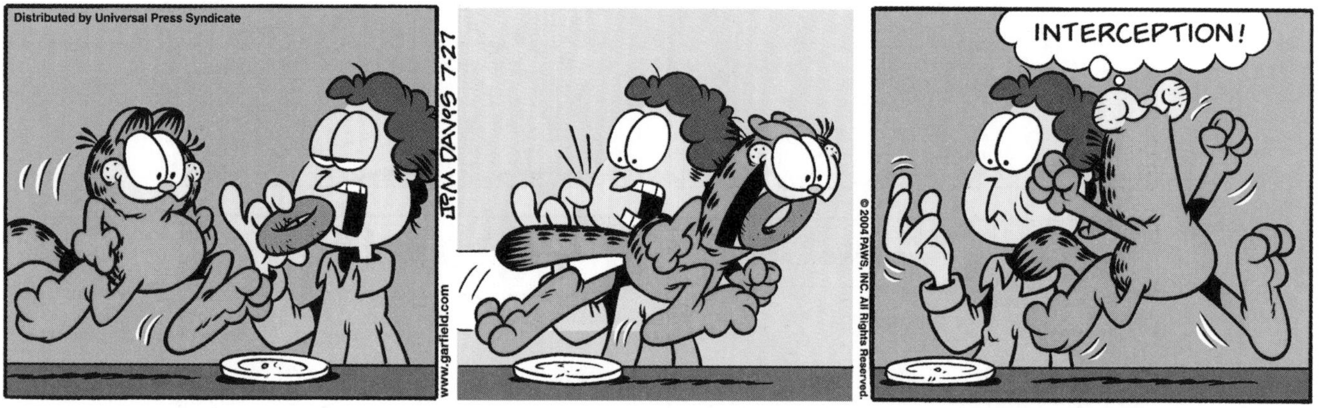
Distributed by Universal Press Syndicate
JIM DAVIS 7-27
www.garfield.com
© 2004 PAWS, INC. All Rights Reserved.
INTERCEPTION!

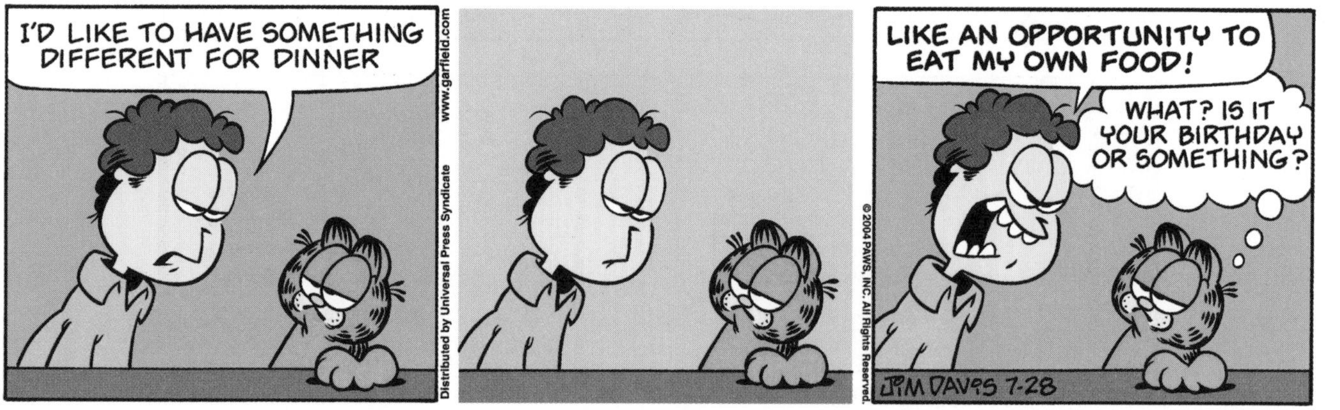
I'D LIKE TO HAVE SOMETHING DIFFERENT FOR DINNER
www.garfield.com
Distributed by Universal Press Syndicate
© 2004 PAWS, INC. All Rights Reserved.
LIKE AN OPPORTUNITY TO EAT MY OWN FOOD!
WHAT? IS IT YOUR BIRTHDAY OR SOMETHING?
JIM DAVIS 7-28

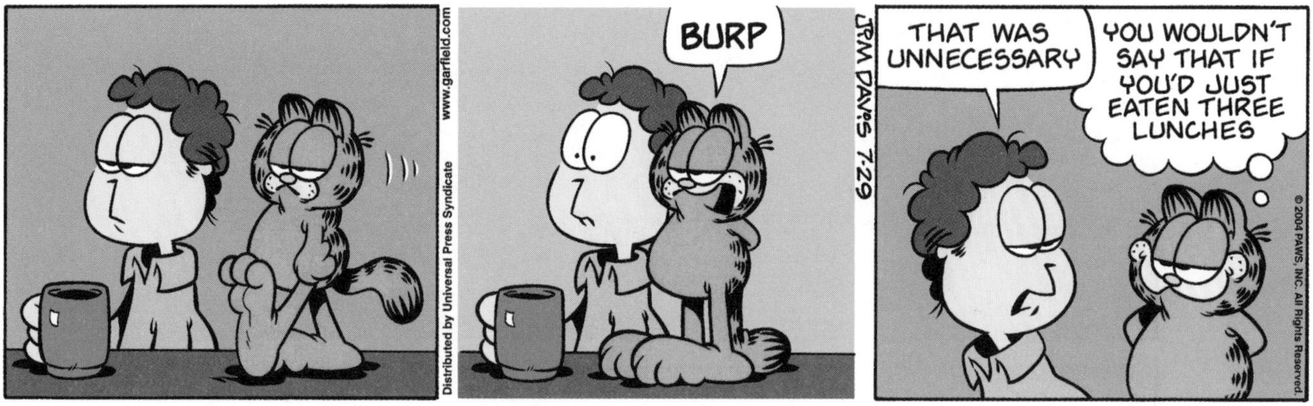
www.garfield.com
Distributed by Universal Press Syndicate
BURP
JIM DAVIS 7-29
THAT WAS UNNECESSARY
YOU WOULDN'T SAY THAT IF YOU'D JUST EATEN THREE LUNCHES
© 2004 PAWS, INC. All Rights Reserved.

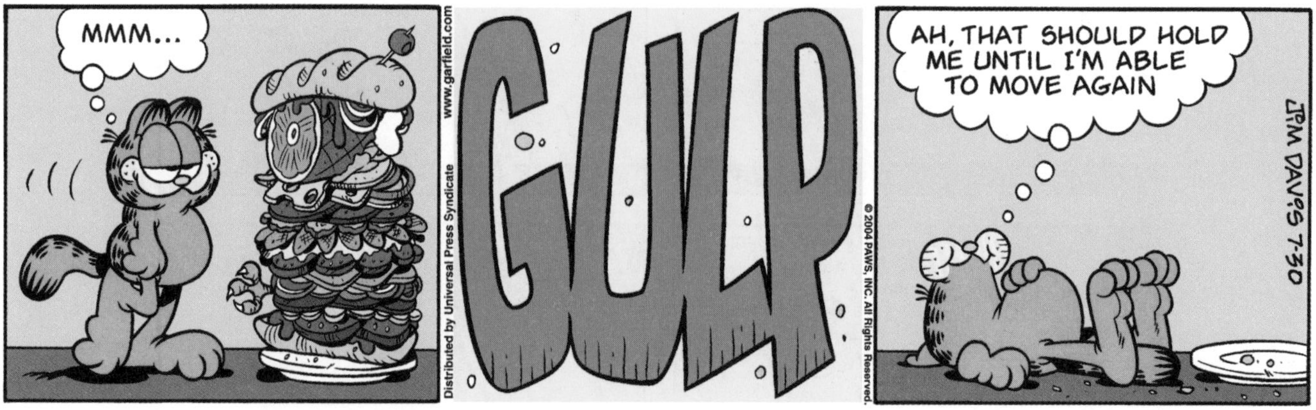
MMM...
www.garfield.com
Distributed by Universal Press Syndicate
GULP
© 2004 PAWS, INC. All Rights Reserved.
AH, THAT SHOULD HOLD ME UNTIL I'M ABLE TO MOVE AGAIN
JIM DAVIS 7-30

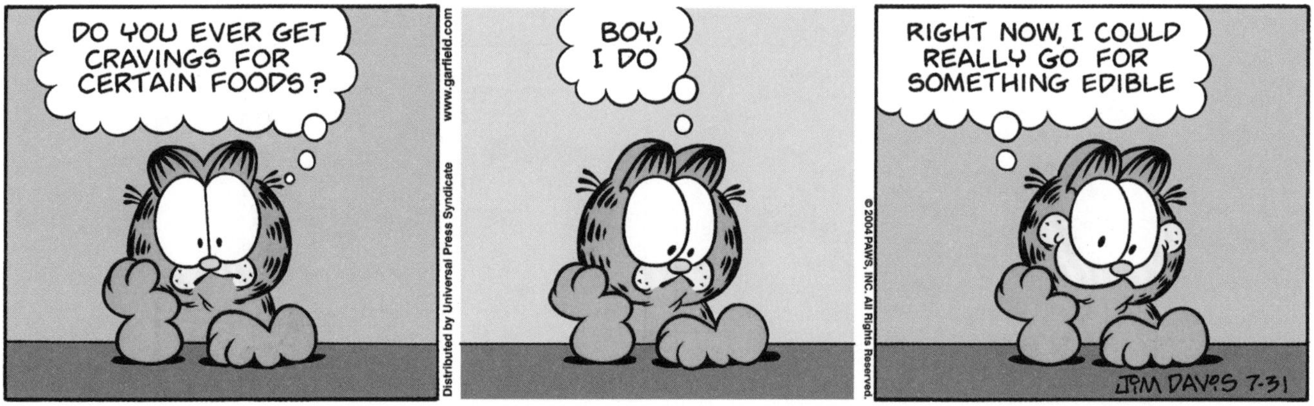
DO YOU EVER GET CRAVINGS FOR CERTAIN FOODS?
www.garfield.com
Distributed by Universal Press Syndicate
BOY, I DO
© 2004 PAWS, INC. All Rights Reserved.
RIGHT NOW, I COULD REALLY GO FOR SOMETHING EDIBLE
JIM DAVIS 7-31

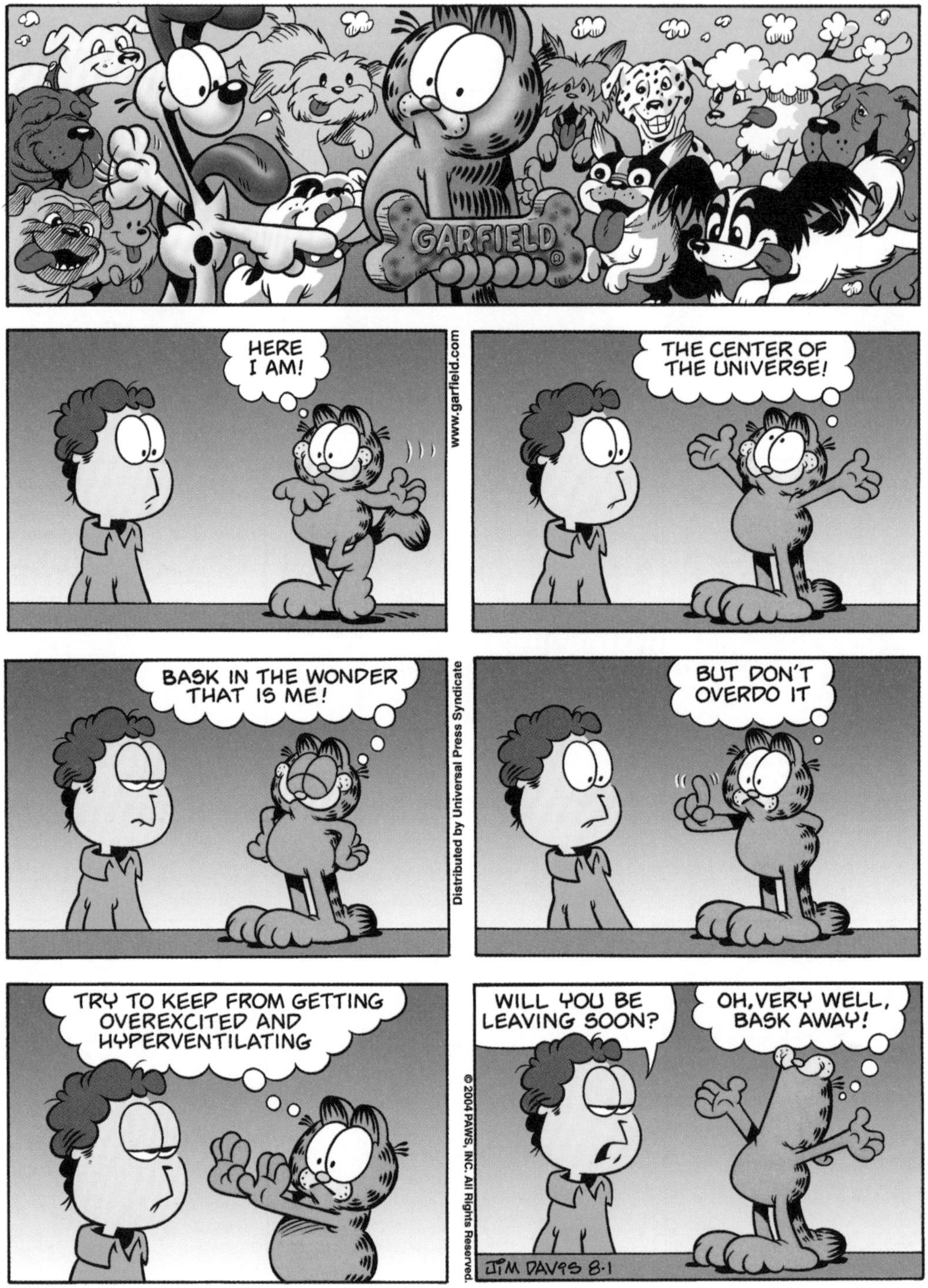
GARFIELD®
HERE I AM!
THE CENTER OF THE UNIVERSE!
BASK IN THE WONDER THAT IS ME!
BUT DON'T OVERDO IT
TRY TO KEEP FROM GETTING OVEREXCITED AND HYPERVENTILATING
WILL YOU BE LEAVING SOON?
OH, VERY WELL, BASK AWAY!
JIM DAVIS 8-1
www.garfield.com
Distributed by Universal Press Syndicate
© 2004 PAWS, INC. All Rights Reserved.

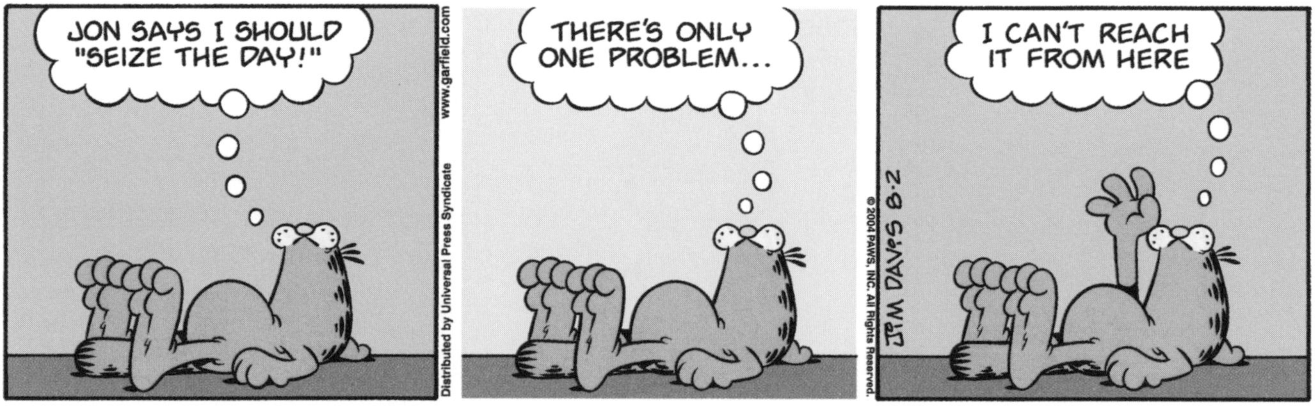
JON SAYS I SHOULD "SEIZE THE DAY!"
www.garfield.com
Distributed by Universal Press Syndicate
THERE'S ONLY ONE PROBLEM...
© 2004 PAWS, INC. All Rights Reserved.
JPM DAVPS 8-2
I CAN'T REACH IT FROM HERE

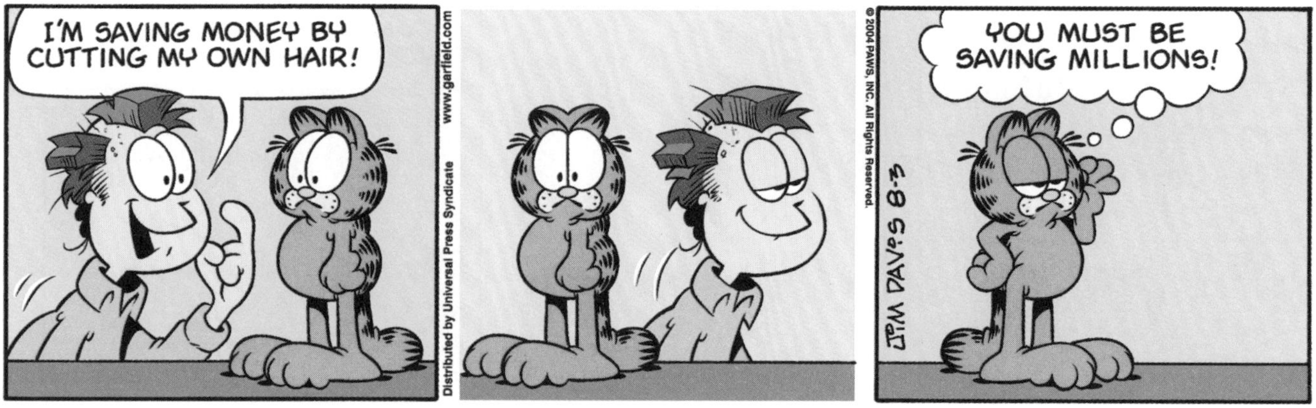
I'M SAVING MONEY BY CUTTING MY OWN HAIR!
www.garfield.com
Distributed by Universal Press Syndicate
© 2004 PAWS, INC. All Rights Reserved.
JPM DAVPS 8-3
YOU MUST BE SAVING MILLIONS!

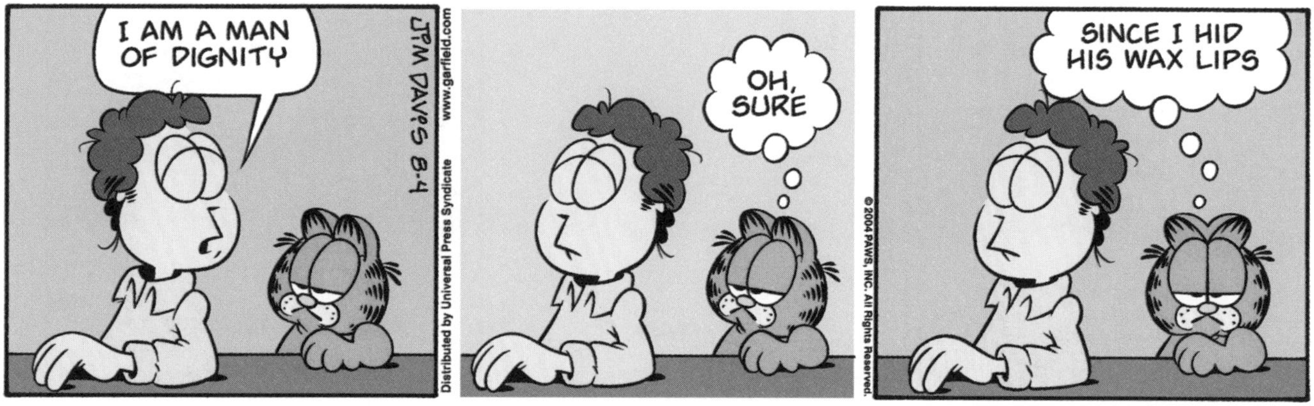
I AM A MAN OF DIGNITY
JPM DAVPS 8-4
www.garfield.com
Distributed by Universal Press Syndicate
OH, SURE
© 2004 PAWS, INC. All Rights Reserved.
SINCE I HID HIS WAX LIPS

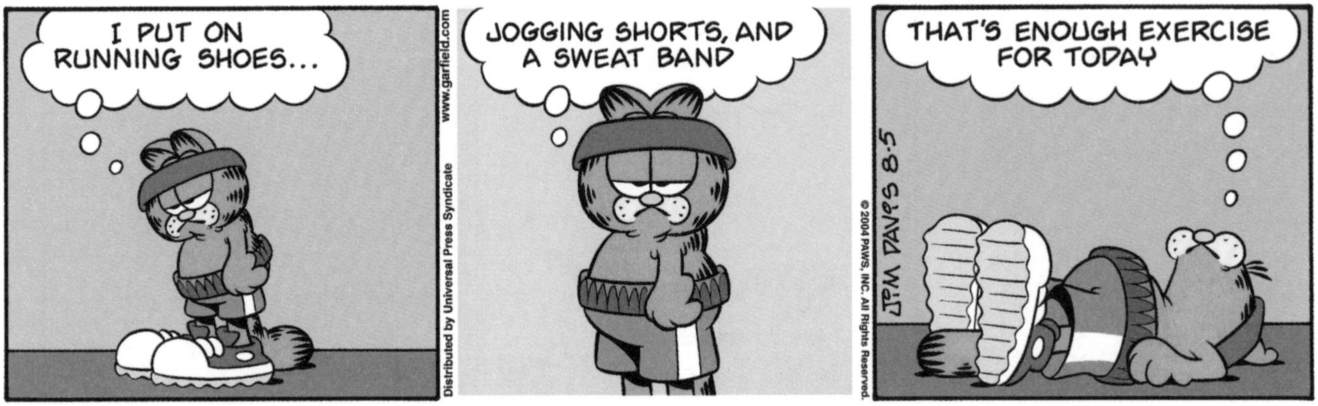
I PUT ON RUNNING SHOES...
www.garfield.com
Distributed by Universal Press Syndicate
JOGGING SHORTS, AND A SWEAT BAND
THAT'S ENOUGH EXERCISE FOR TODAY
JIM DAVIS 8-5
© 2004 PAWS, INC. All Rights Reserved.

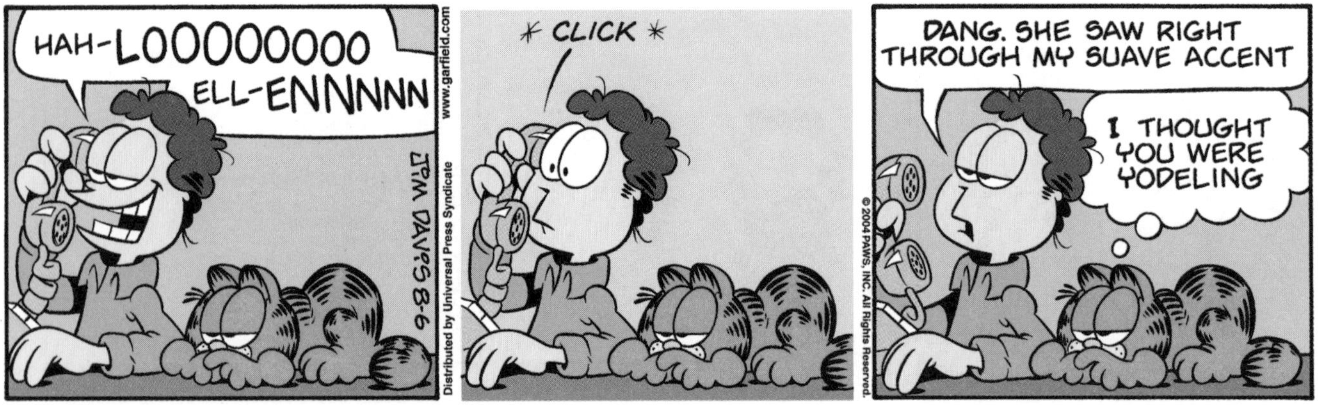
HAH-LOOOOOOOO ELL-ENNNNN
JIM DAVIS 8-6
www.garfield.com
Distributed by Universal Press Syndicate
* CLICK *
DANG. SHE SAW RIGHT THROUGH MY SUAVE ACCENT
I THOUGHT YOU WERE YODELING
© 2004 PAWS, INC. All Rights Reserved.

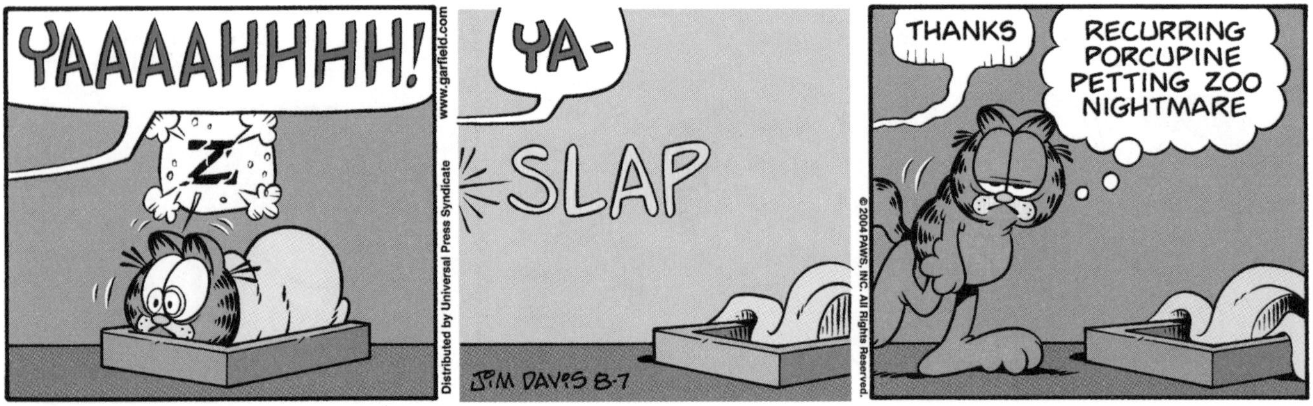
YAAAAHHHH!
Z
www.garfield.com
Distributed by Universal Press Syndicate
YA-
SLAP
JIM DAVIS 8-7
THANKS
RECURRING PORCUPINE PETTING ZOO NIGHTMARE
© 2004 PAWS, INC. All Rights Reserved.

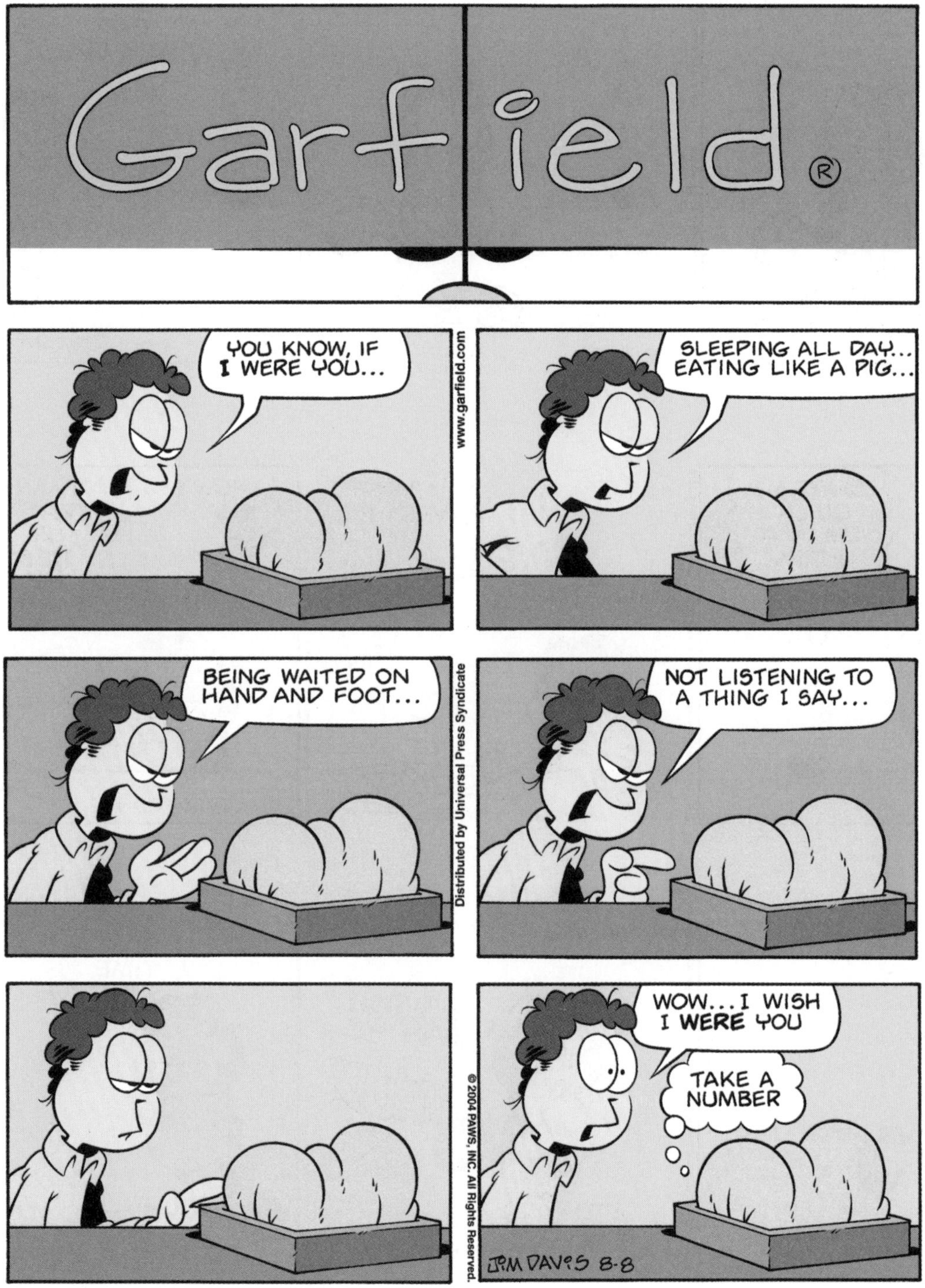
Garfield®
YOU KNOW, IF I WERE YOU...
SLEEPING ALL DAY... EATING LIKE A PIG...
BEING WAITED ON HAND AND FOOT...
NOT LISTENING TO A THING I SAY...
WOW... I WISH I WERE YOU
TAKE A NUMBER
JIM DAVIS 8-8
www.garfield.com
Distributed by Universal Press Syndicate
© 2004 PAWS, INC. All Rights Reserved.

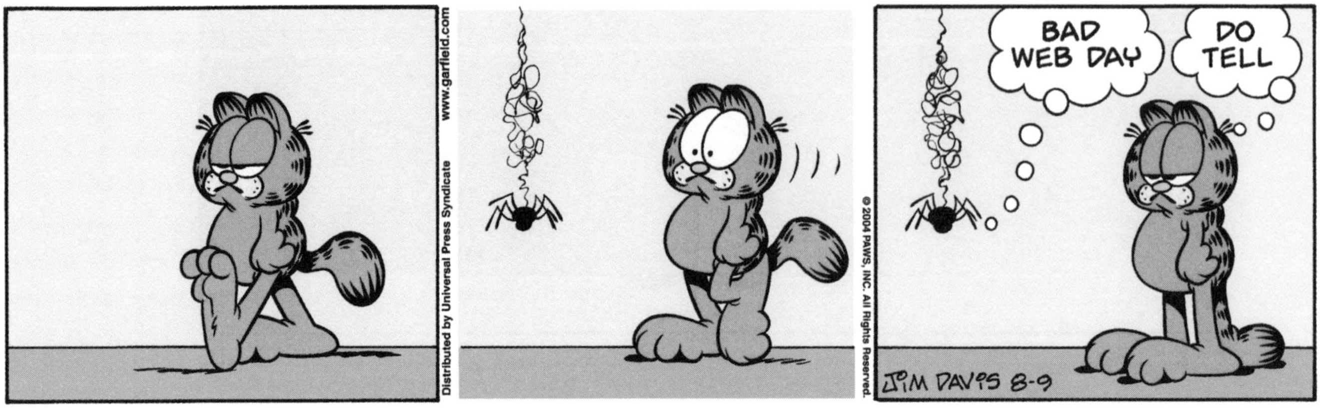
Distributed by Universal Press Syndicate www.garfield.com
© 2004 PAWS, INC. All Rights Reserved.
BAD WEB DAY
DO TELL
JIM DAVIS 8-9

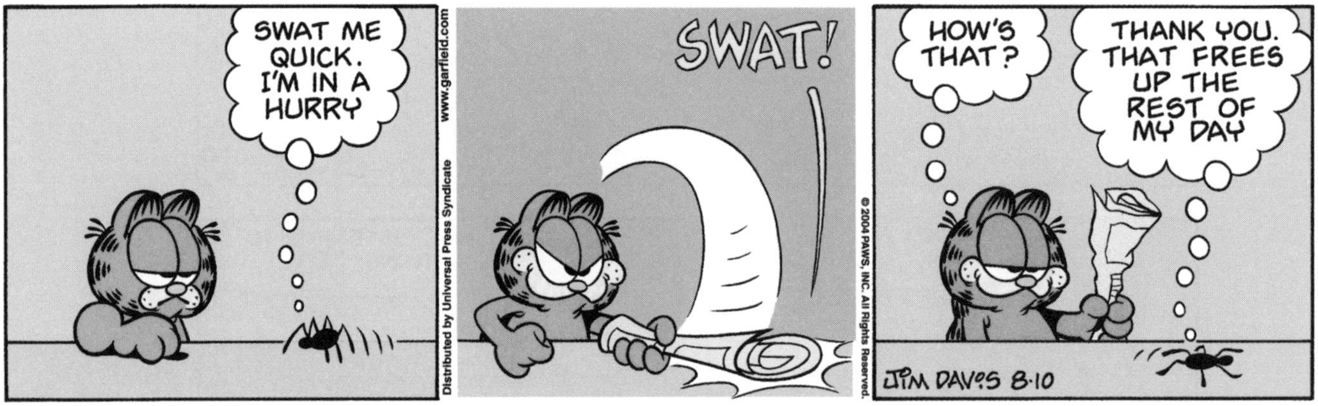
SWAT ME QUICK. I'M IN A HURRY
Distributed by Universal Press Syndicate www.garfield.com
SWAT!
© 2004 PAWS, INC. All Rights Reserved.
HOW'S THAT?
THANK YOU. THAT FREES UP THE REST OF MY DAY
JIM DAVIS 8-10

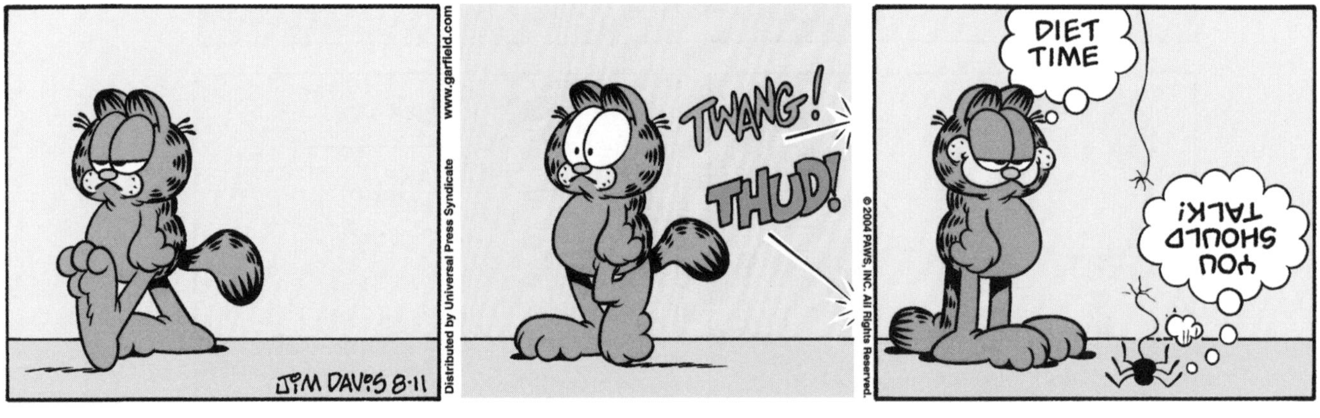
JIM DAVIS 8-11
Distributed by Universal Press Syndicate www.garfield.com
TWANG!
THUD!
© 2004 PAWS, INC. All Rights Reserved.
DIET TIME
YOU SHOULD TALK!

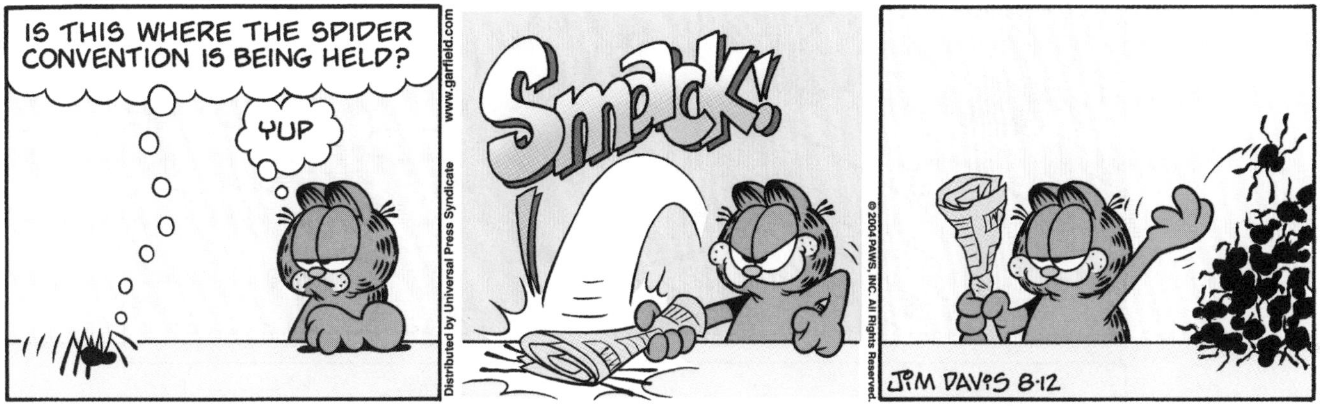
IS THIS WHERE THE SPIDER CONVENTION IS BEING HELD?
YUP
www.garfield.com
Distributed by Universal Press Syndicate
SMACK!
© 2004 PAWS, INC. All Rights Reserved.
JIM DAVIS 8-12

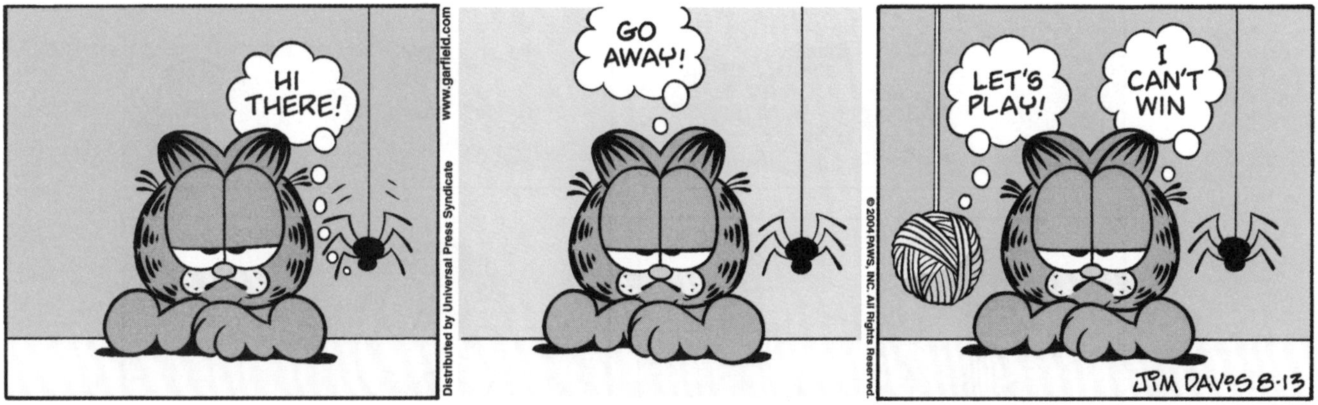
HI THERE!
www.garfield.com
Distributed by Universal Press Syndicate
GO AWAY!
© 2004 PAWS, INC. All Rights Reserved.
LET'S PLAY!
I CAN'T WIN
JIM DAVIS 8-13

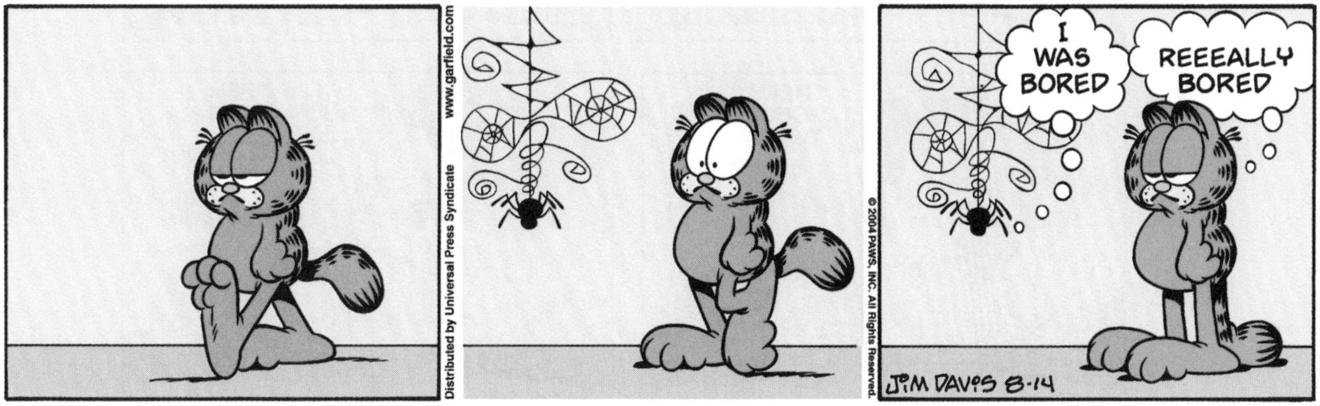
www.garfield.com
Distributed by Universal Press Syndicate
© 2004 PAWS, INC. All Rights Reserved.
I WAS BORED
REEEALLY BORED
JIM DAVIS 8-14

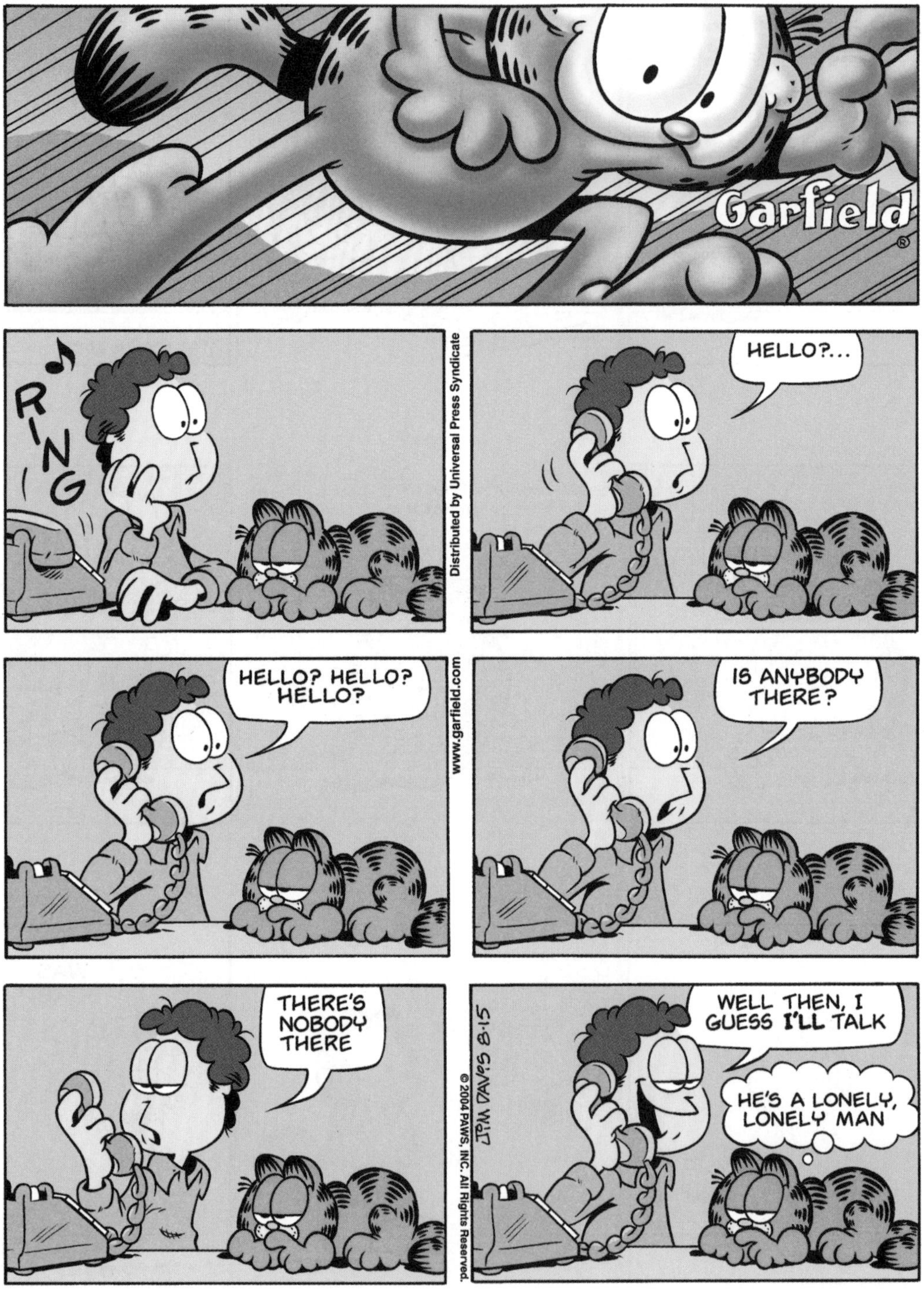
Garfield®
RING
HELLO?...
HELLO? HELLO? HELLO?
IS ANYBODY THERE?
THERE'S NOBODY THERE
WELL THEN, I GUESS I'LL TALK
HE'S A LONELY, LONELY MAN
JPM DAVIS 8-15

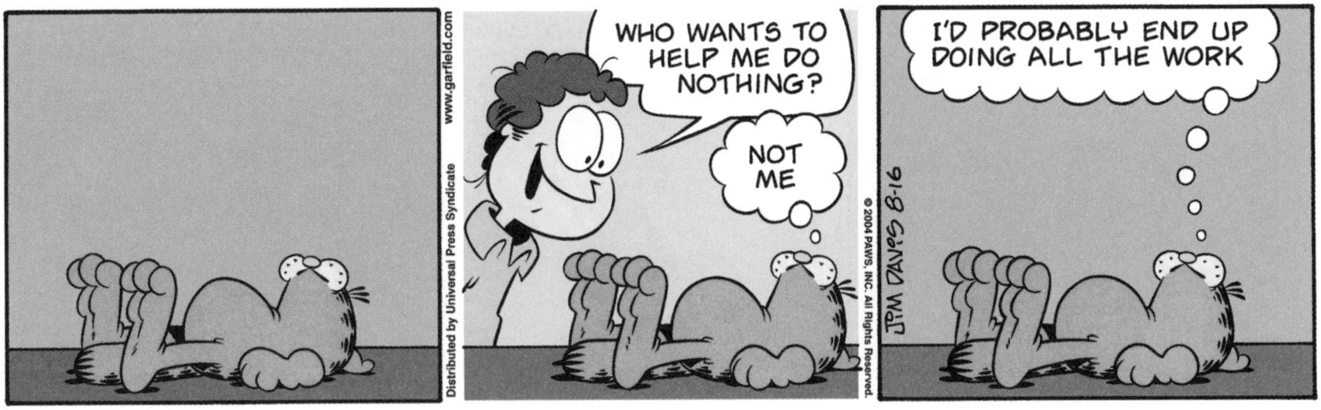
WHO WANTS TO HELP ME DO NOTHING?
NOT ME
I'D PROBABLY END UP DOING ALL THE WORK
www.garfield.com
Distributed by Universal Press Syndicate
© 2004 PAWS, INC. All Rights Reserved.
JIM DAVIS 8-16

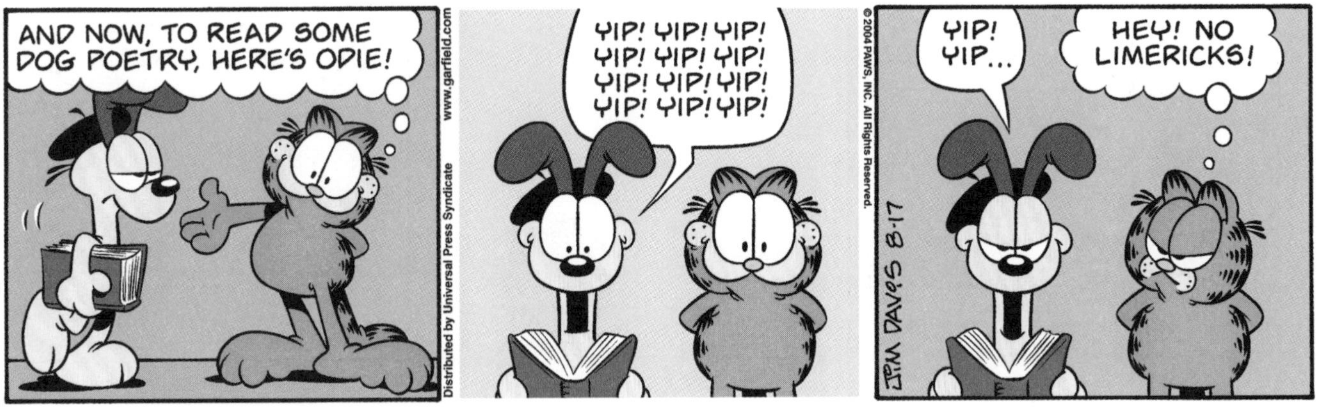
AND NOW, TO READ SOME DOG POETRY, HERE'S ODIE!
YIP! YIP! YIP! YIP! YIP! YIP! YIP! YIP! YIP! YIP! YIP! YIP!
YIP! YIP...
HEY! NO LIMERICKS!
www.garfield.com
Distributed by Universal Press Syndicate
© 2004 PAWS, INC. All Rights Reserved.
JIM DAVIS 8-17

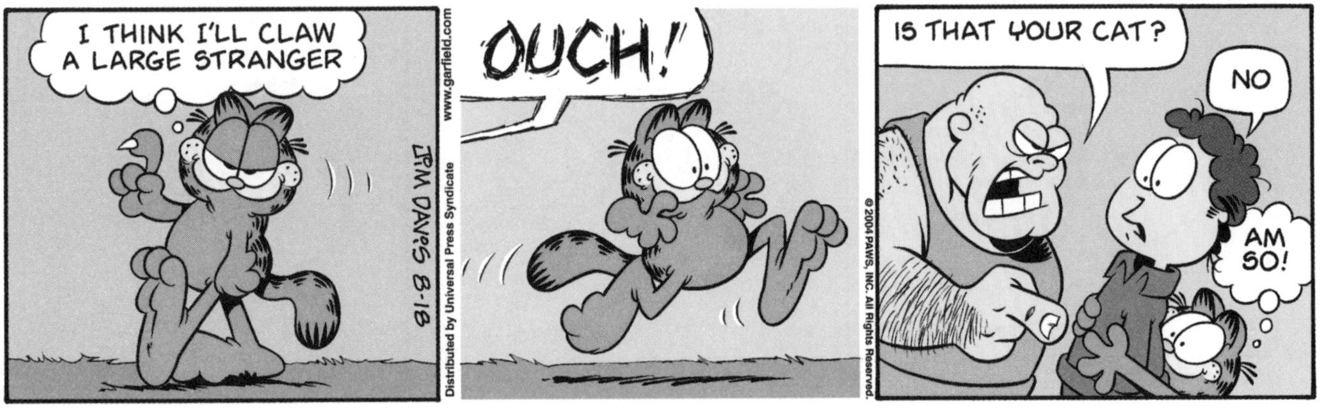
I THINK I'LL CLAW A LARGE STRANGER
OUCH!
IS THAT YOUR CAT?
NO
AM SO!
www.garfield.com
Distributed by Universal Press Syndicate
© 2004 PAWS, INC. All Rights Reserved.
JIM DAVIS 8-18

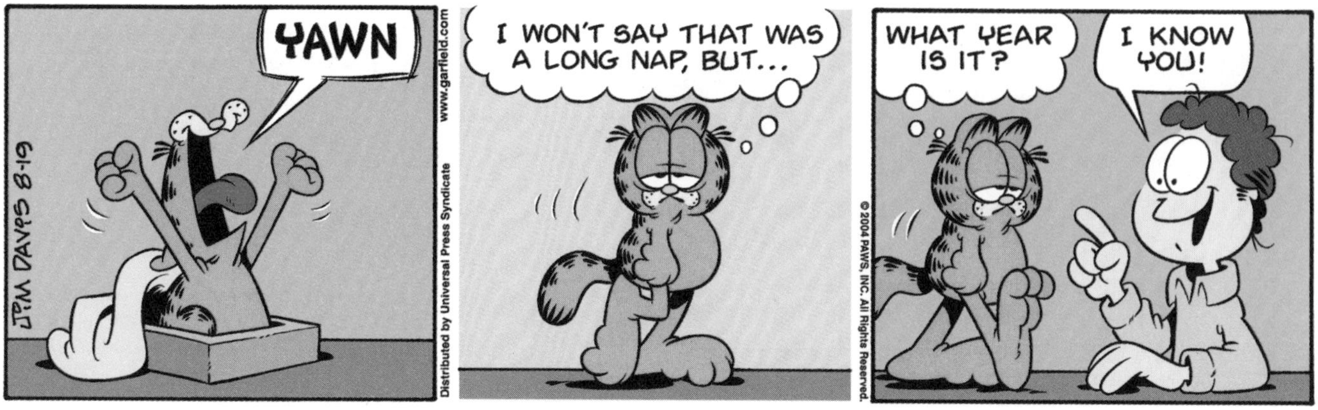
JIM DAVIS 8-19
YAWN
Distributed by Universal Press Syndicate www.garfield.com
I WON'T SAY THAT WAS A LONG NAP, BUT...
© 2004 PAWS, INC. All Rights Reserved.
WHAT YEAR IS IT?
I KNOW YOU!

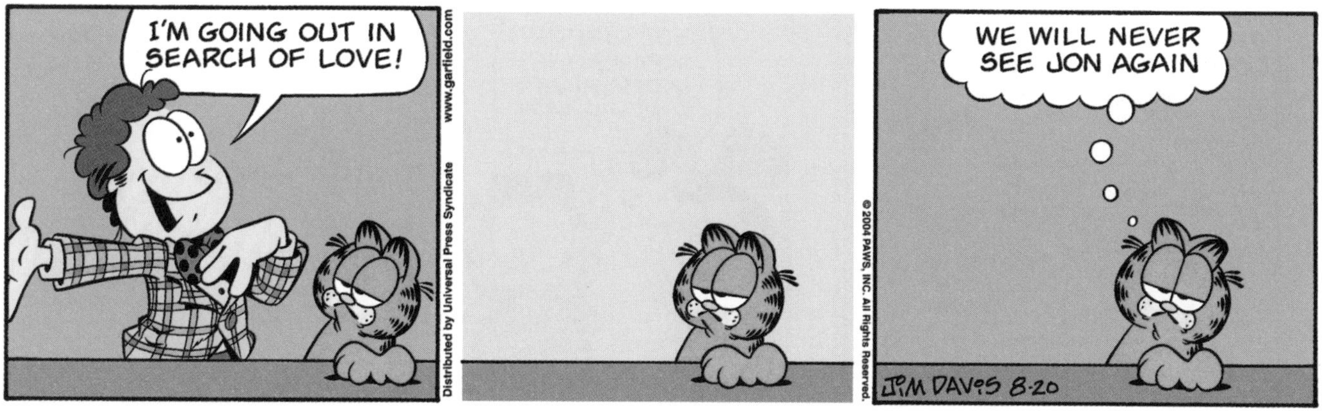
I'M GOING OUT IN SEARCH OF LOVE!
Distributed by Universal Press Syndicate www.garfield.com
© 2004 PAWS, INC. All Rights Reserved.
WE WILL NEVER SEE JON AGAIN
JIM DAVIS 8-20

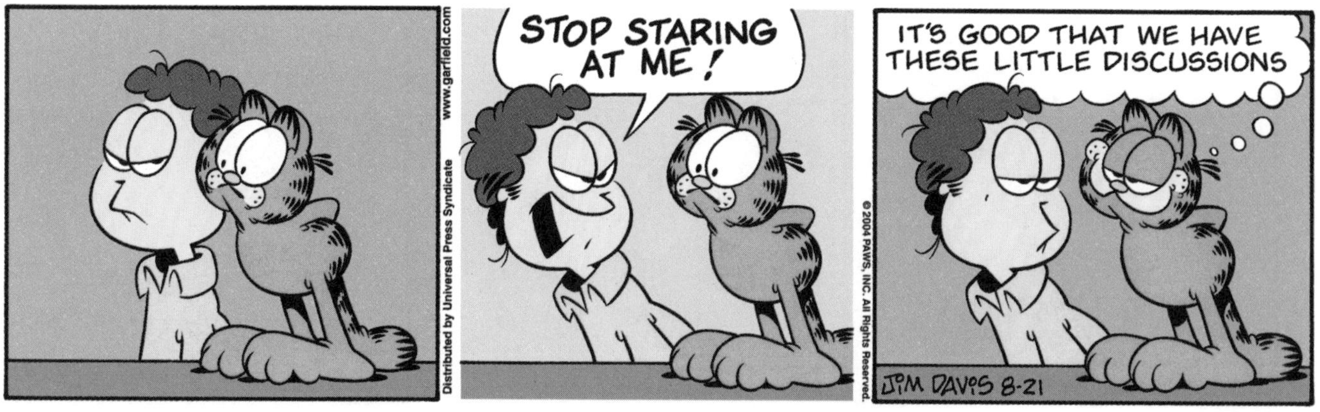
Distributed by Universal Press Syndicate www.garfield.com
STOP STARING AT ME!
© 2004 PAWS, INC. All Rights Reserved.
IT'S GOOD THAT WE HAVE THESE LITTLE DISCUSSIONS
JIM DAVIS 8-21

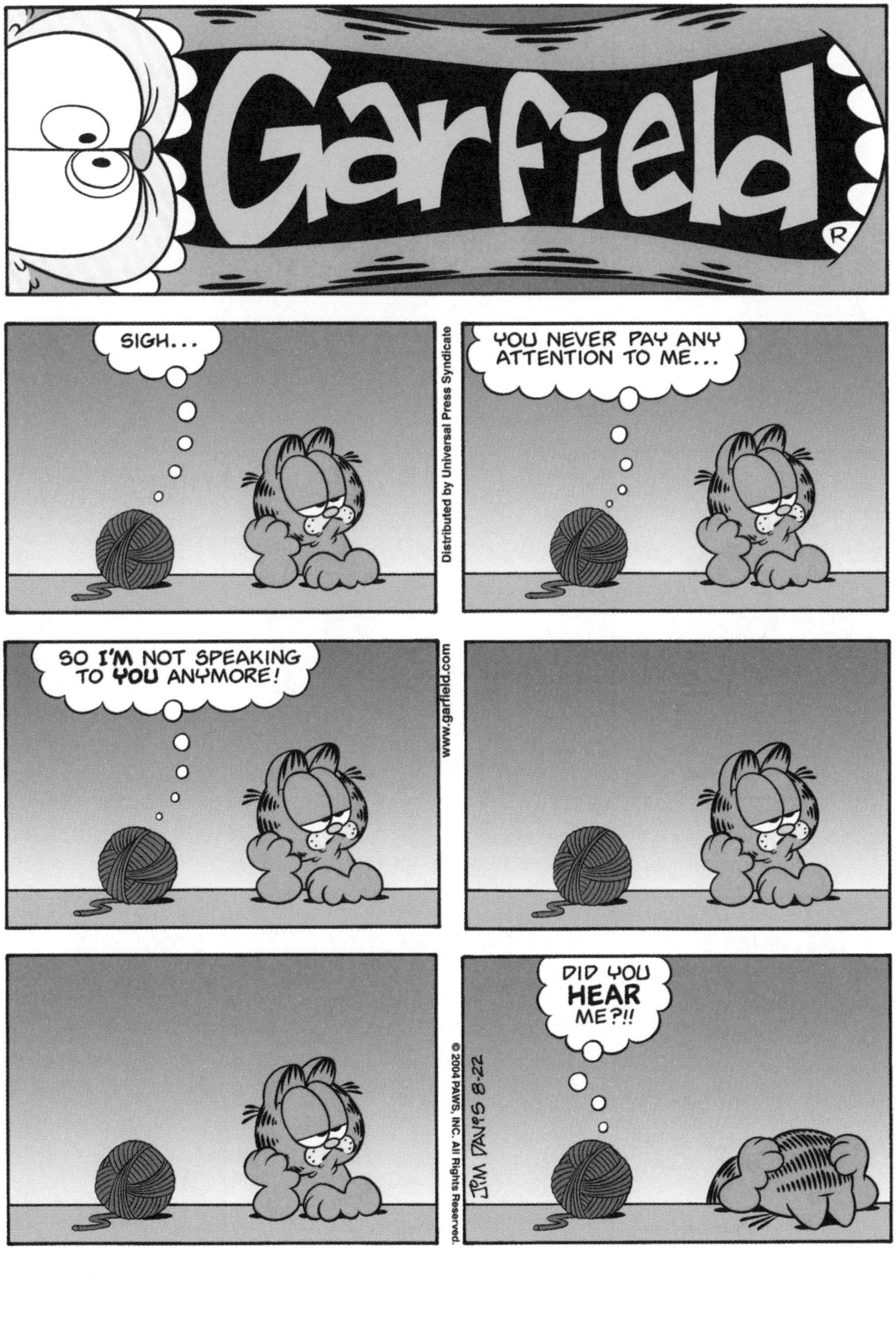

Garfield
SIGH...
YOU NEVER PAY ANY ATTENTION TO ME...
SO I'M NOT SPEAKING TO YOU ANYMORE!
DID YOU HEAR ME?!!
JPM DAVIS 8-22

Distributed by Universal Press Syndicate

www.garfield.com

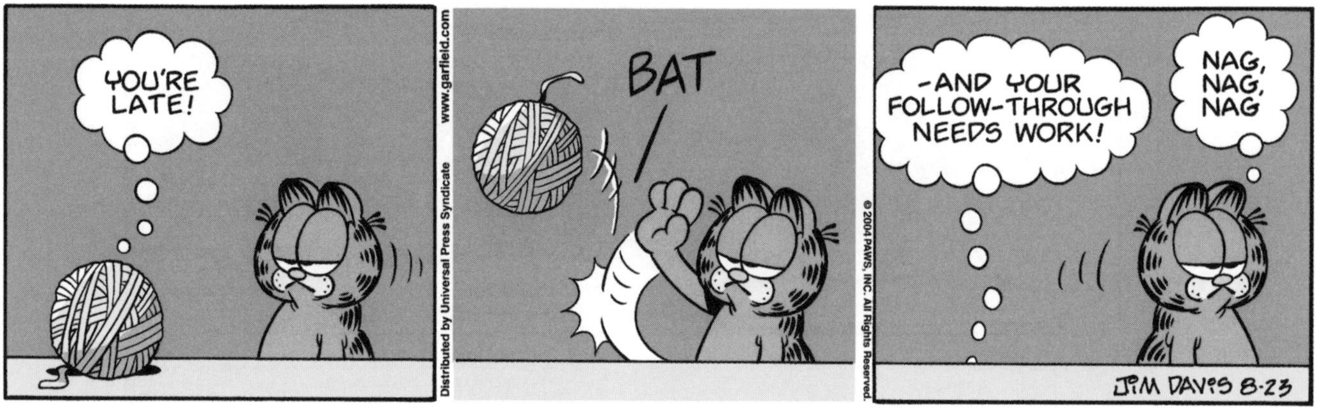
YOU'RE LATE!
BAT
-AND YOUR FOLLOW-THROUGH NEEDS WORK!
NAG, NAG, NAG
JIM DAVIS 8-23
Distributed by Universal Press Syndicate www.garfield.com
© 2004 PAWS, INC. All Rights Reserved.

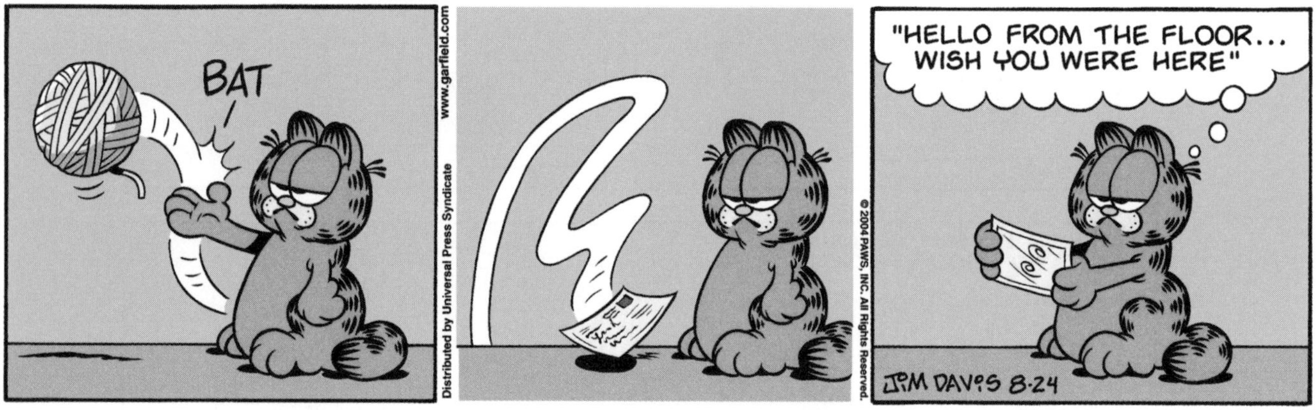
BAT
"HELLO FROM THE FLOOR... WISH YOU WERE HERE"
JIM DAVIS 8-24
Distributed by Universal Press Syndicate www.garfield.com
© 2004 PAWS, INC. All Rights Reserved.

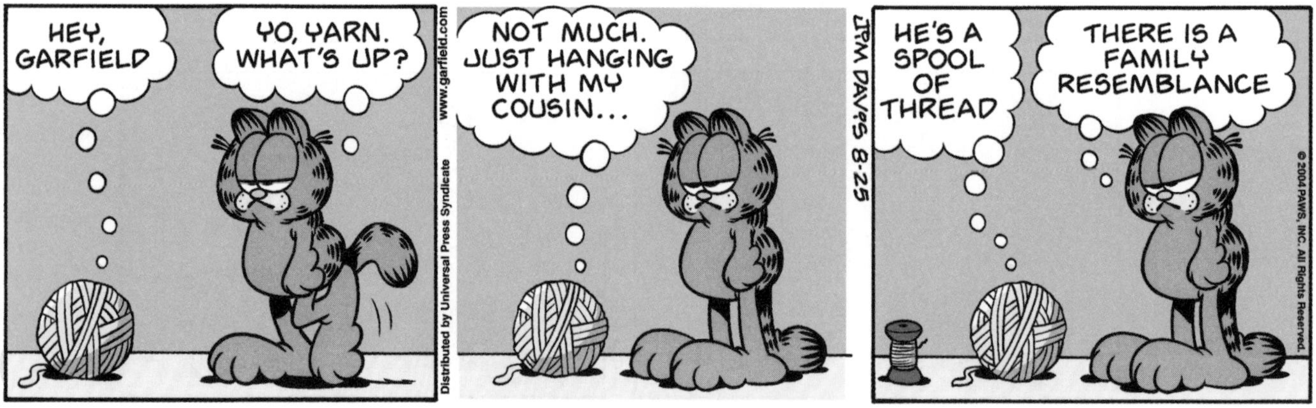
HEY, GARFIELD
YO, YARN. WHAT'S UP?
NOT MUCH. JUST HANGING WITH MY COUSIN...
HE'S A SPOOL OF THREAD
THERE IS A FAMILY RESEMBLANCE
JIM DAVIS 8-25
Distributed by Universal Press Syndicate www.garfield.com
© 2004 PAWS, INC. All Rights Reserved.

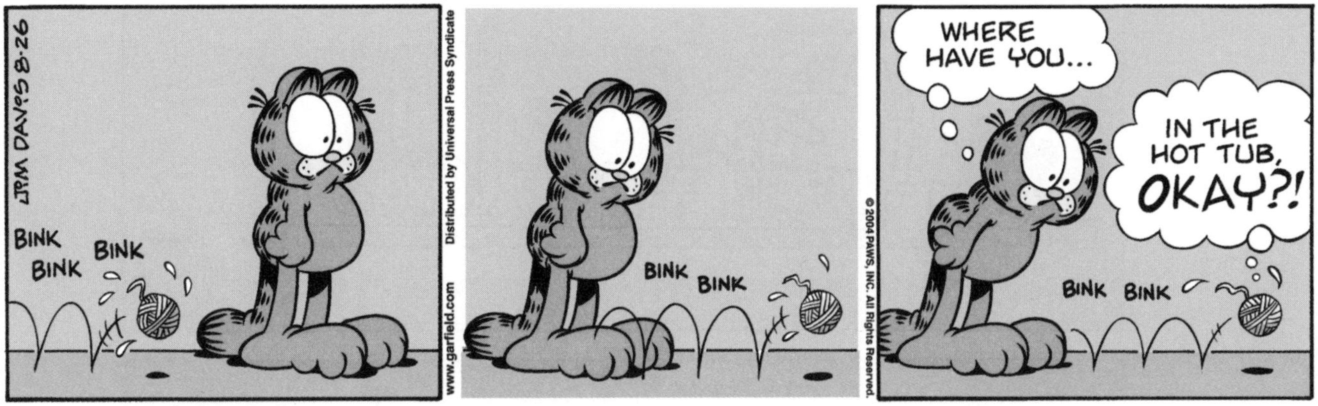
JIM DAVIS 8-26
BINK
BINK
BINK
Distributed by Universal Press Syndicate
www.garfield.com
BINK
BINK
© 2004 PAWS, INC. All Rights Reserved.
WHERE HAVE YOU...
IN THE HOT TUB, OKAY?!
BINK BINK

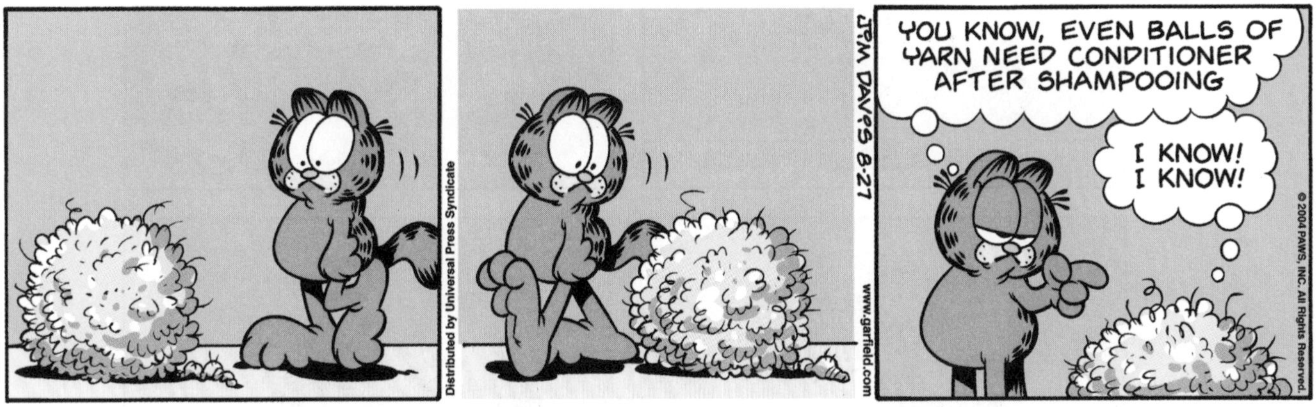
Distributed by Universal Press Syndicate
JIM DAVIS 8-27
www.garfield.com
YOU KNOW, EVEN BALLS OF YARN NEED CONDITIONER AFTER SHAMPOOING
I KNOW! I KNOW!
© 2004 PAWS, INC. All Rights Reserved.

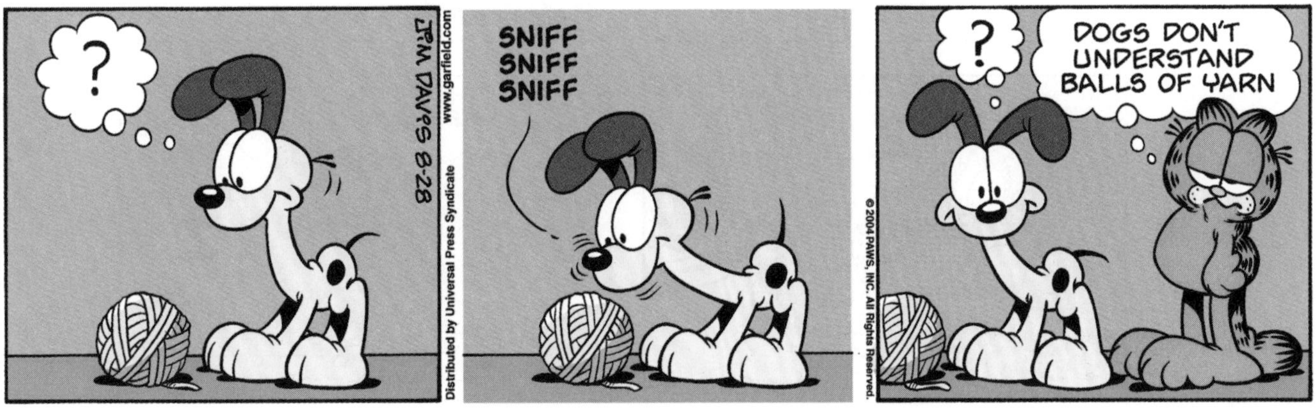
?
JIM DAVIS 8-28
www.garfield.com
Distributed by Universal Press Syndicate
SNIFF
SNIFF
SNIFF
© 2004 PAWS, INC. All Rights Reserved.
?
DOGS DON'T UNDERSTAND BALLS OF YARN

Garfield®
YAWN
www.garfield.com
Z
Distributed by Universal Press Syndicate
Z
Z
© 2004 PAWS, INC. All Rights Reserved.
THE GOOD SPOTS ARE ALWAYS TAKEN
Z
JIM DAVIS 8-29

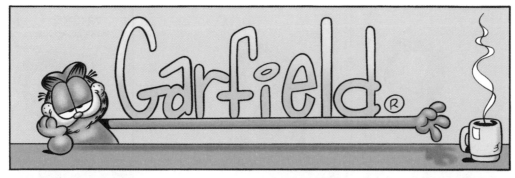

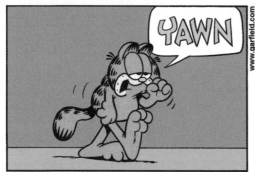

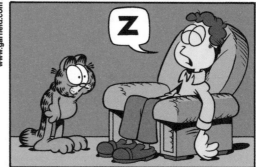

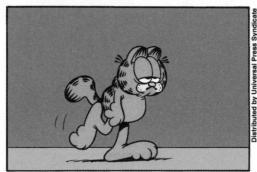

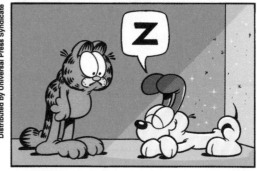

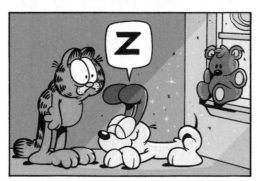

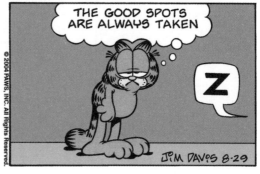

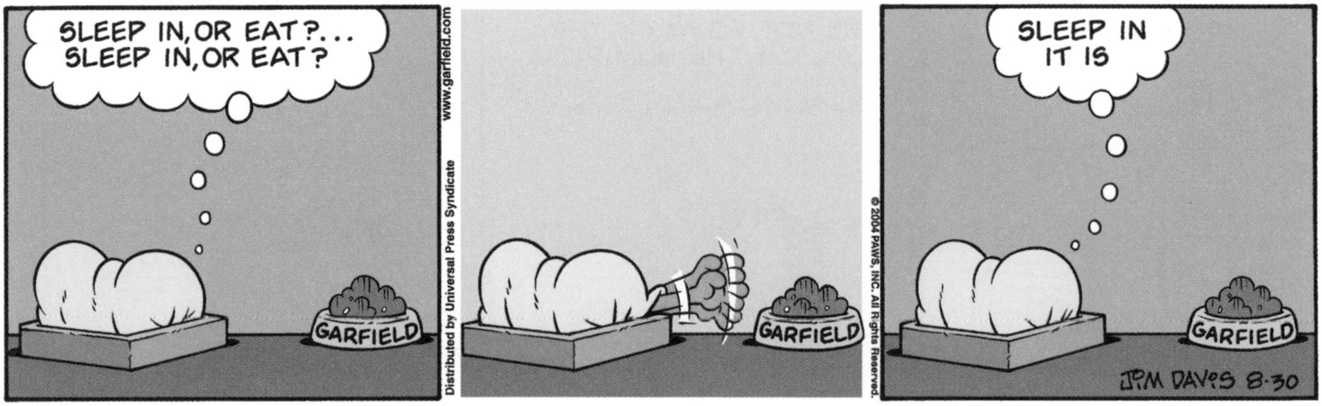
SLEEP IN, OR EAT?... SLEEP IN, OR EAT?
GARFIELD
GARFIELD
SLEEP IN IT IS
GARFIELD
JIM DAVIS 8-30
www.garfield.com
Distributed by Universal Press Syndicate
© 2004 PAWS, INC. All Rights Reserved.

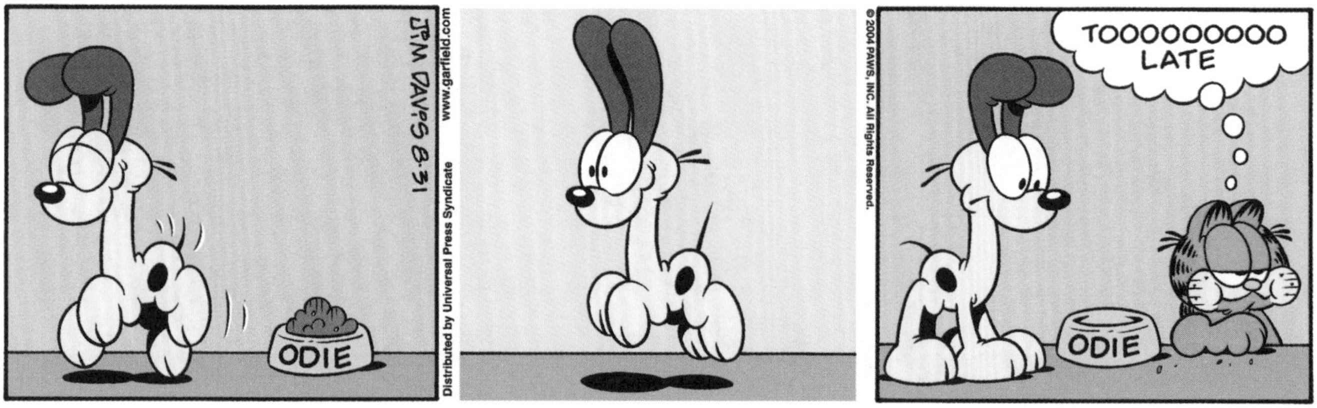
ODIE
JIM DAVIS 8-31
www.garfield.com
Distributed by Universal Press Syndicate
© 2004 PAWS, INC. All Rights Reserved.
TOOOOOOOOO LATE
ODIE

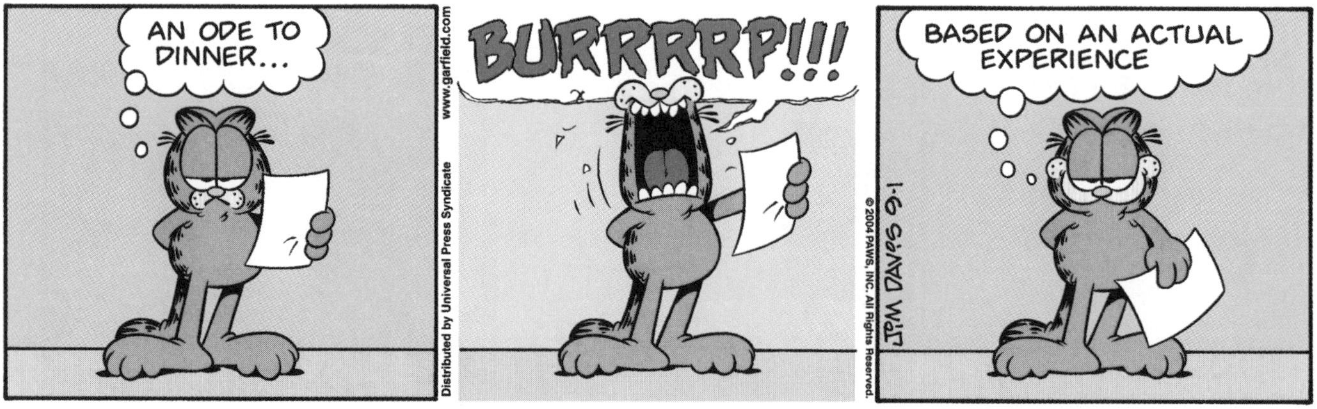
AN ODE TO DINNER...
www.garfield.com
Distributed by Universal Press Syndicate
BURRRRP!!!
© 2004 PAWS, INC. All Rights Reserved.
JIM DAVIS 9-1
BASED ON AN ACTUAL EXPERIENCE

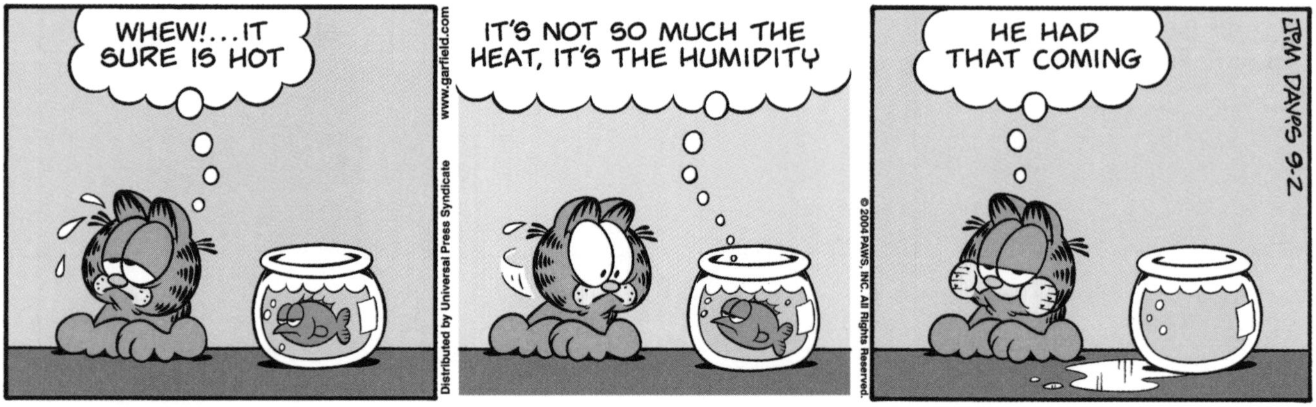
WHEW!...IT SURE IS HOT
IT'S NOT SO MUCH THE HEAT, IT'S THE HUMIDITY
HE HAD THAT COMING
JIM DAVIS 9-2
www.garfield.com
Distributed by Universal Press Syndicate
© 2004 PAWS, INC. All Rights Reserved.

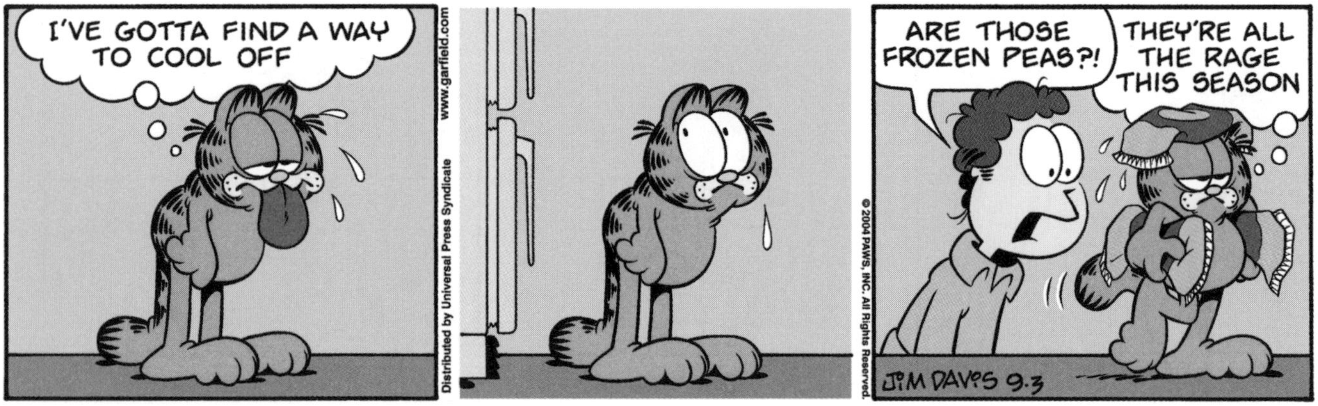
I'VE GOTTA FIND A WAY TO COOL OFF
ARE THOSE FROZEN PEAS?!
THEY'RE ALL THE RAGE THIS SEASON
JIM DAVIS 9-3
www.garfield.com
Distributed by Universal Press Syndicate
© 2004 PAWS, INC. All Rights Reserved.

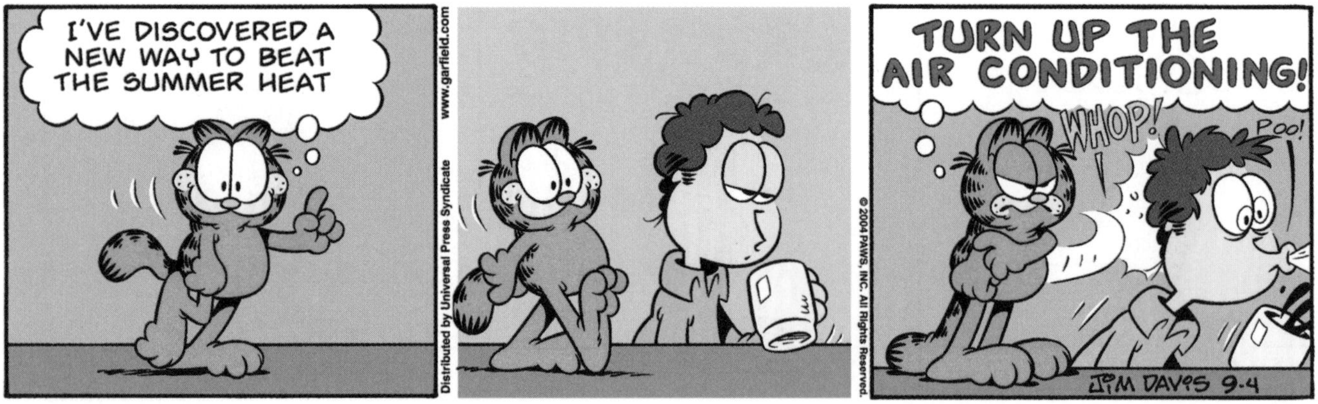
I'VE DISCOVERED A NEW WAY TO BEAT THE SUMMER HEAT
TURN UP THE AIR CONDITIONING!
WHOP!
POO!
JIM DAVIS 9-4
www.garfield.com
Distributed by Universal Press Syndicate
© 2004 PAWS, INC. All Rights Reserved.

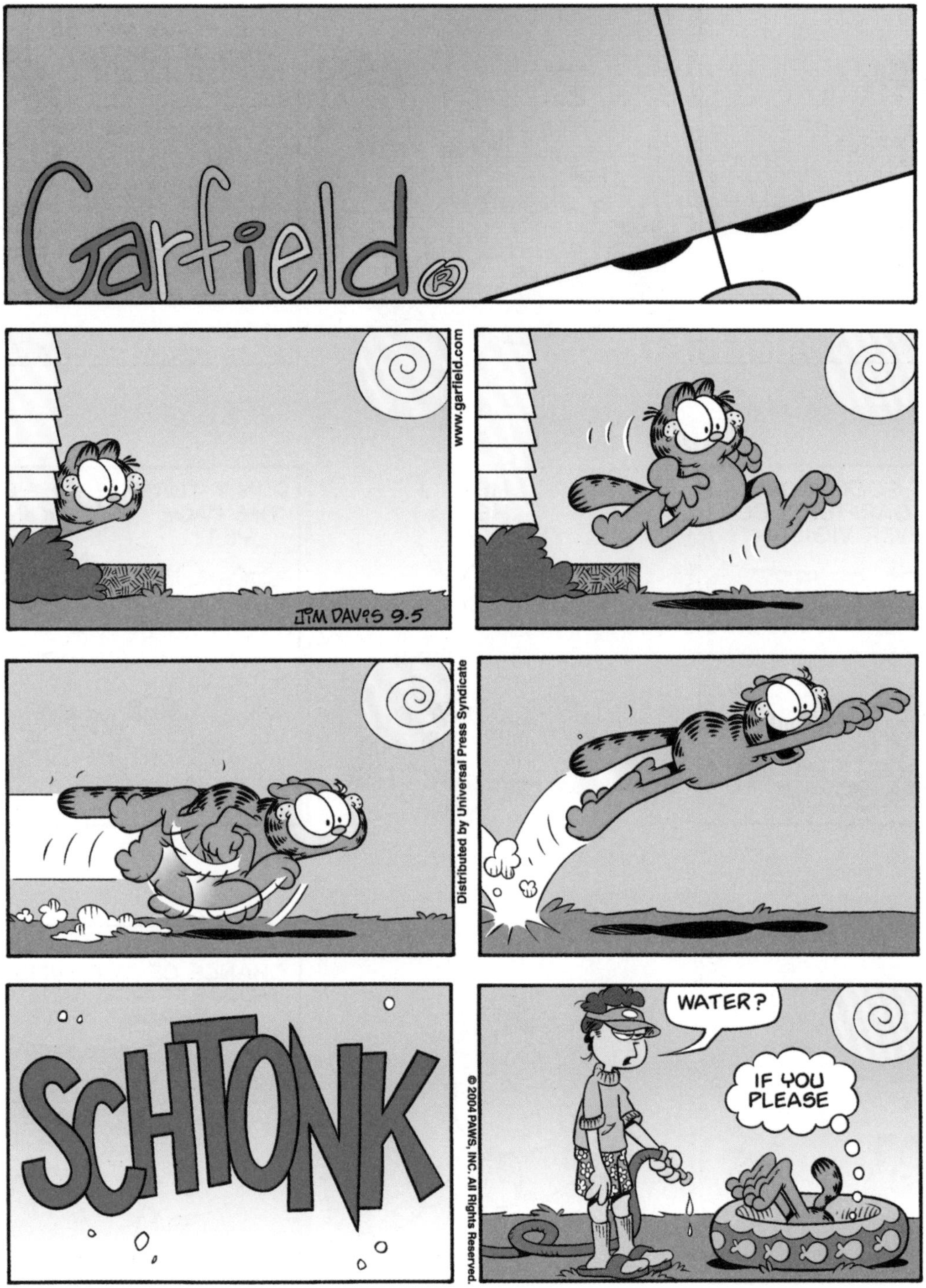
Garfield®
www.garfield.com
JIM DAVIS 9-5
Distributed by Universal Press Syndicate
SCHTONK
© 2004 PAWS, INC. All Rights Reserved.
WATER?
IF YOU PLEASE

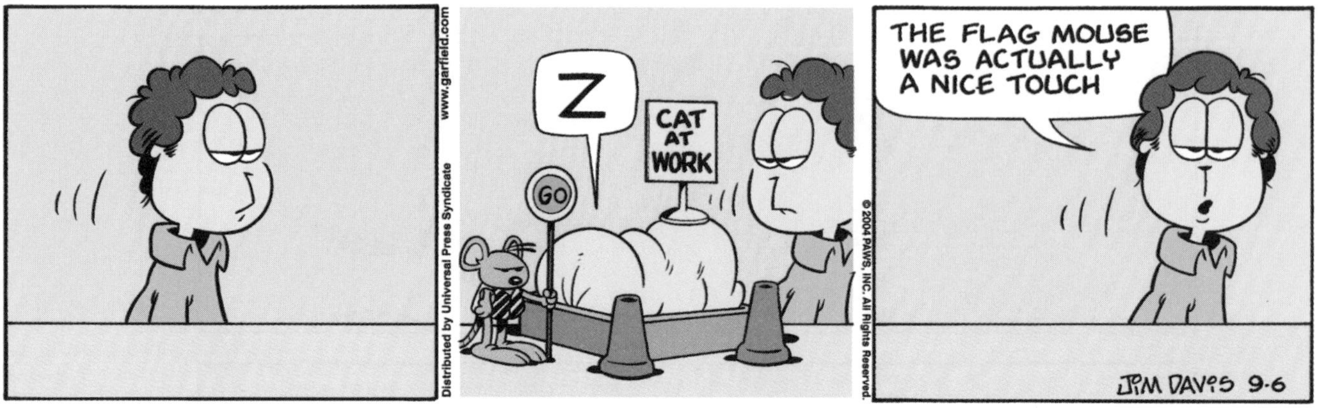
www.garfield.com
Distributed by Universal Press Syndicate
Z
GO
CAT AT WORK
© 2004 PAWS, INC. All Rights Reserved.
THE FLAG MOUSE WAS ACTUALLY A NICE TOUCH
JIM DAVIS 9-6

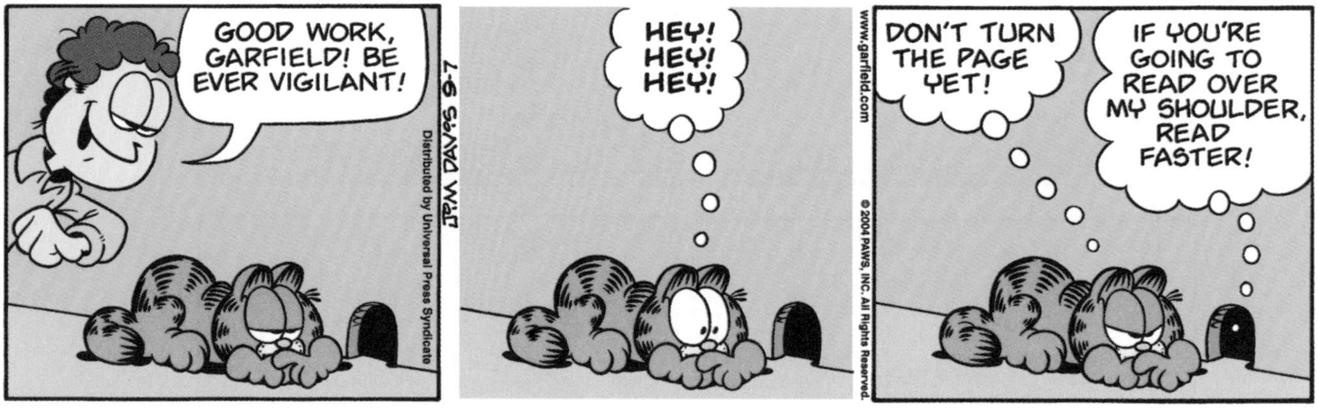
GOOD WORK, GARFIELD! BE EVER VIGILANT!
JIM DAVIS 9-7
Distributed by Universal Press Syndicate
HEY! HEY! HEY!
www.garfield.com
© 2004 PAWS, INC. All Rights Reserved.
DON'T TURN THE PAGE YET!
IF YOU'RE GOING TO READ OVER MY SHOULDER, READ FASTER!

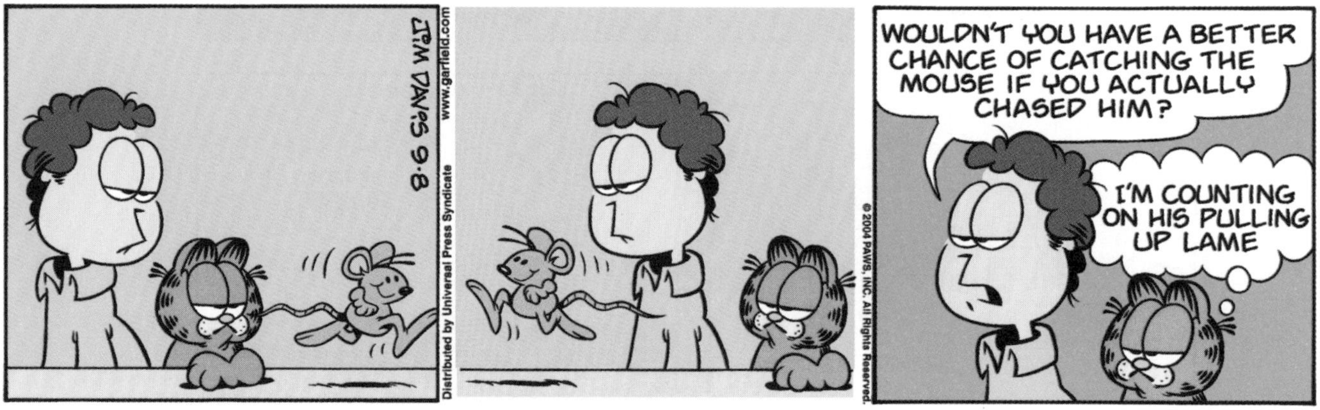
JIM DAVIS 9-8
www.garfield.com
Distributed by Universal Press Syndicate
© 2004 PAWS, INC. All Rights Reserved.
WOULDN'T YOU HAVE A BETTER CHANCE OF CATCHING THE MOUSE IF YOU ACTUALLY CHASED HIM?
I'M COUNTING ON HIS PULLING UP LAME

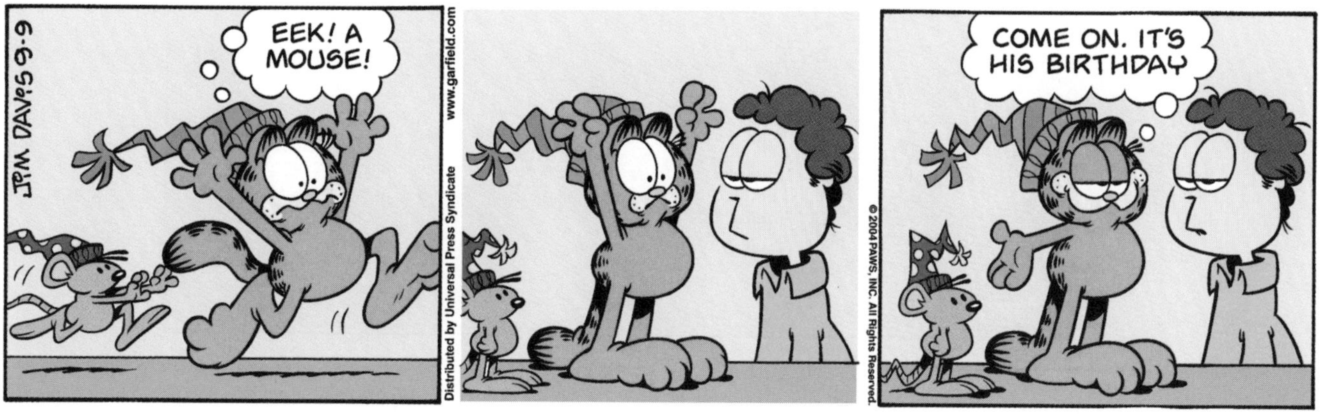
EEK! A MOUSE!
COME ON. IT'S HIS BIRTHDAY

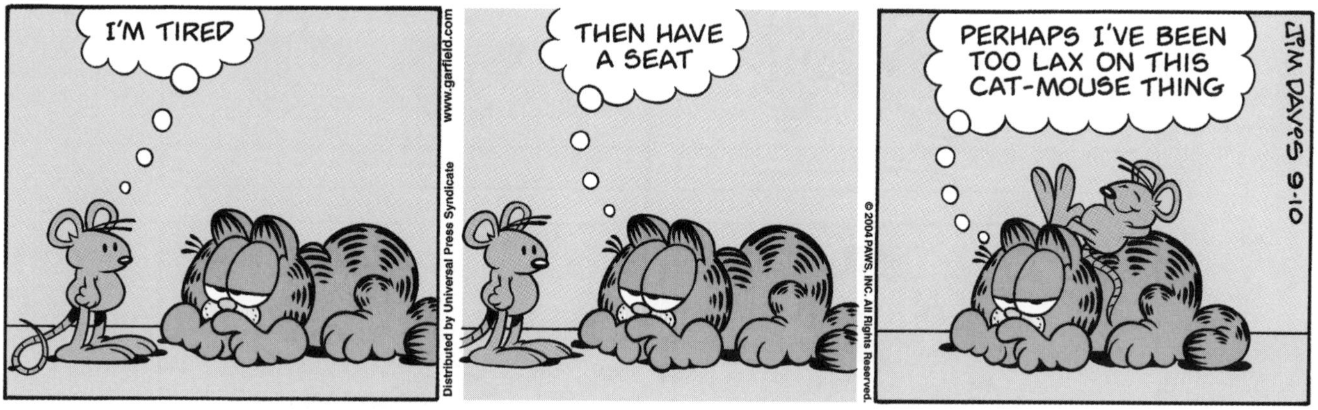
I'M TIRED
THEN HAVE A SEAT
PERHAPS I'VE BEEN TOO LAX ON THIS CAT-MOUSE THING

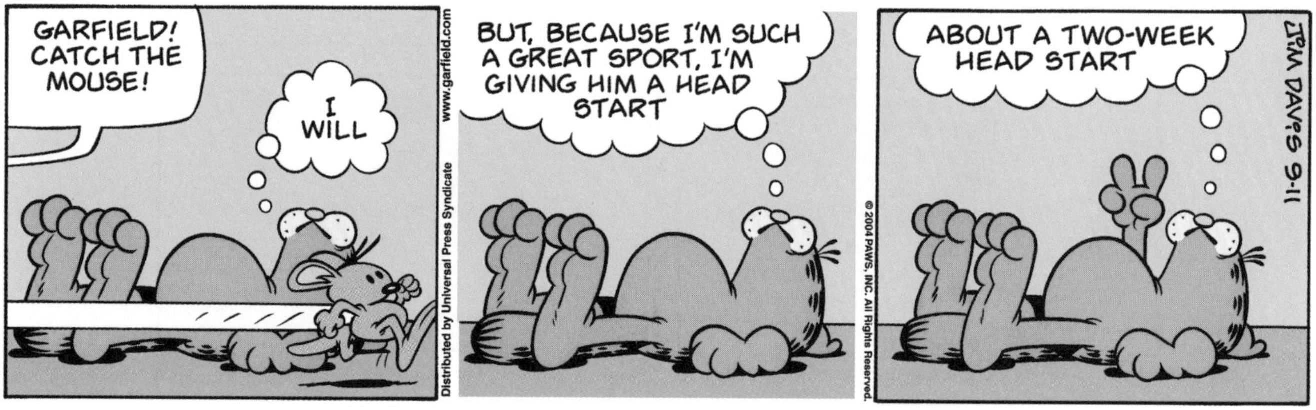
GARFIELD! CATCH THE MOUSE!
I WILL
BUT, BECAUSE I'M SUCH A GREAT SPORT, I'M GIVING HIM A HEAD START
ABOUT A TWO-WEEK HEAD START

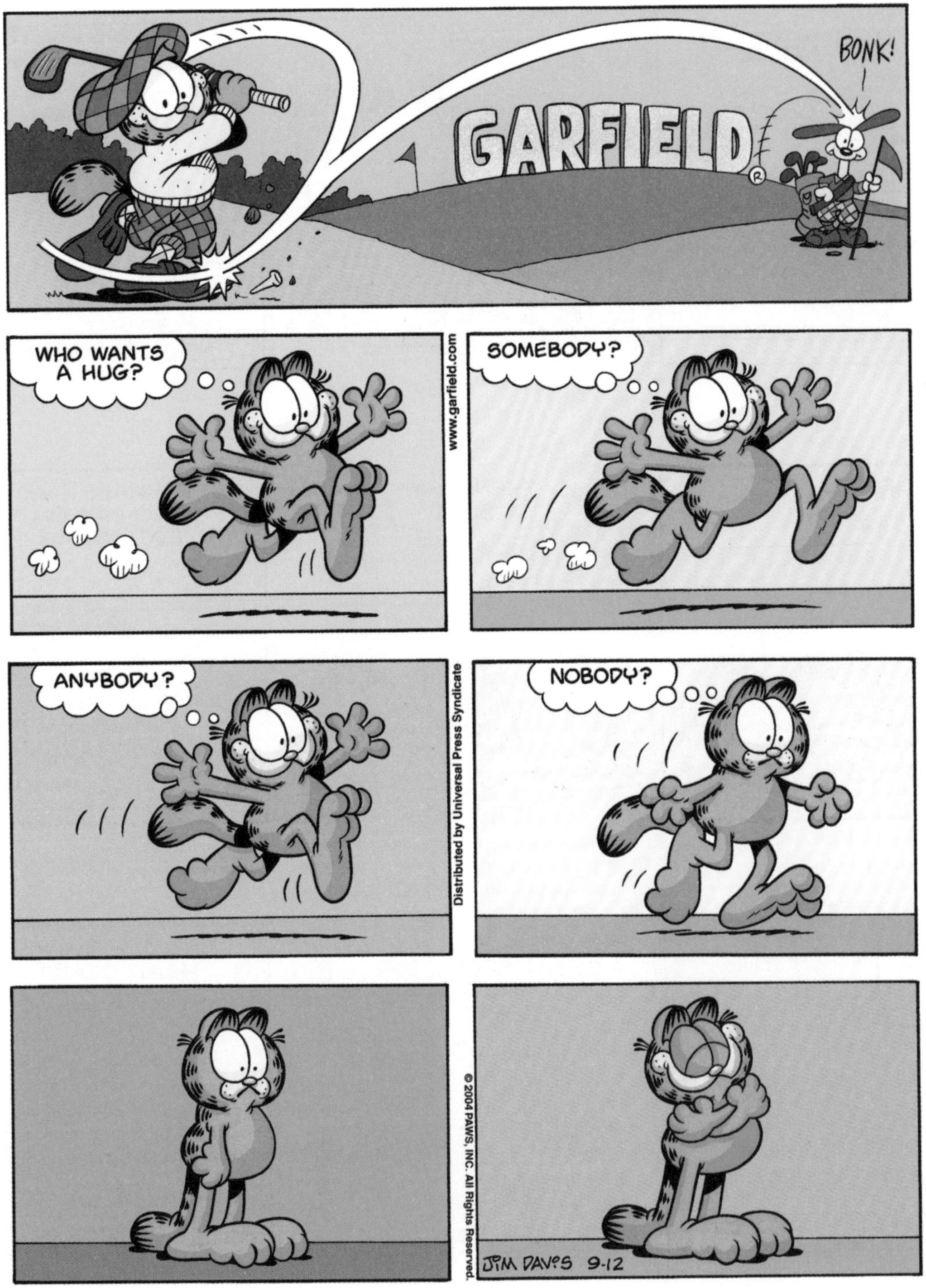
BONK!
GARFIELD
WHO WANTS A HUG?
SOMEBODY?
ANYBODY?
NOBODY?
JIM DAVIS 9-12

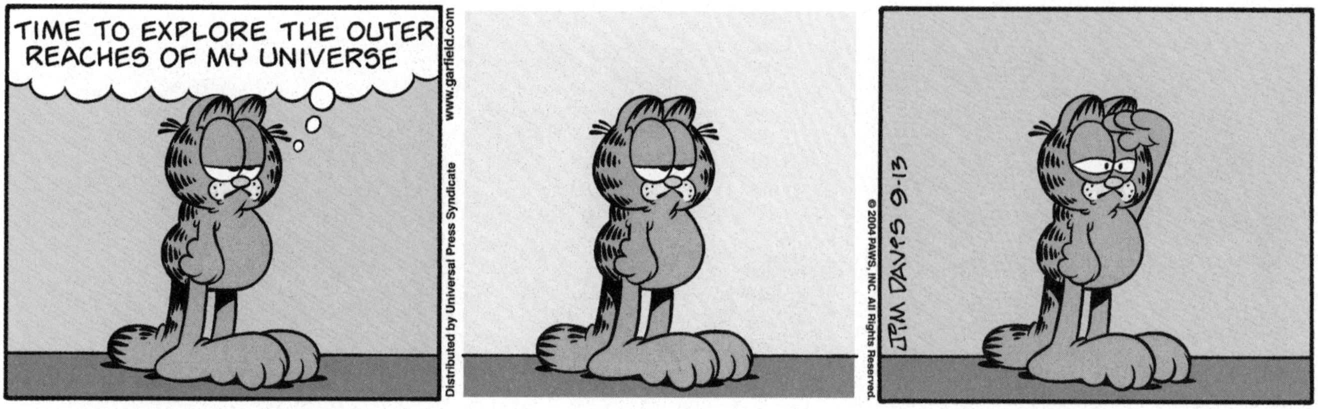
TIME TO EXPLORE THE OUTER REACHES OF MY UNIVERSE
Distributed by Universal Press Syndicate www.garfield.com
© 2004 PAWS, INC. All Rights Reserved.
JIM DAVIS 9-13

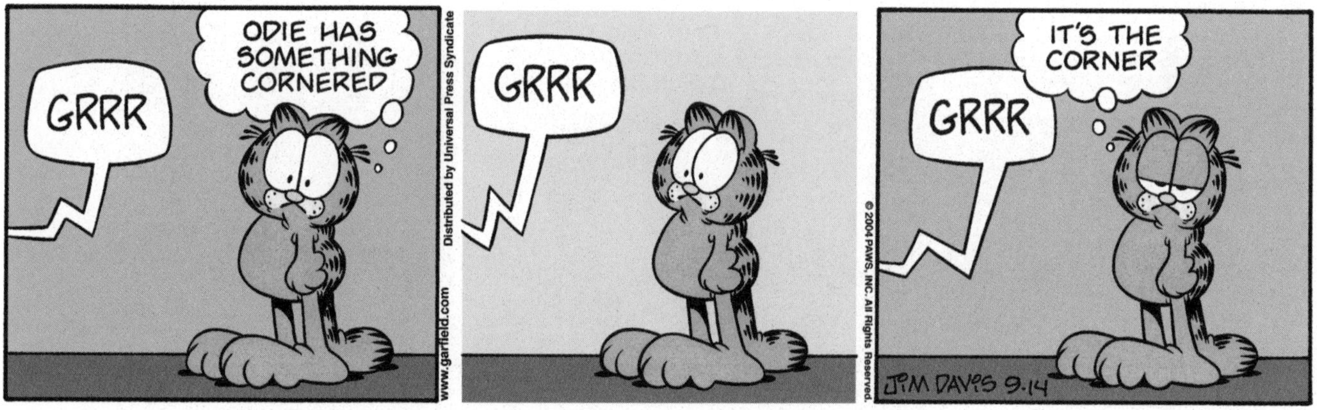
GRRR
ODIE HAS SOMETHING CORNERED
GRRR
GRRR
IT'S THE CORNER
www.garfield.com Distributed by Universal Press Syndicate
© 2004 PAWS, INC. All Rights Reserved.
JIM DAVIS 9.14

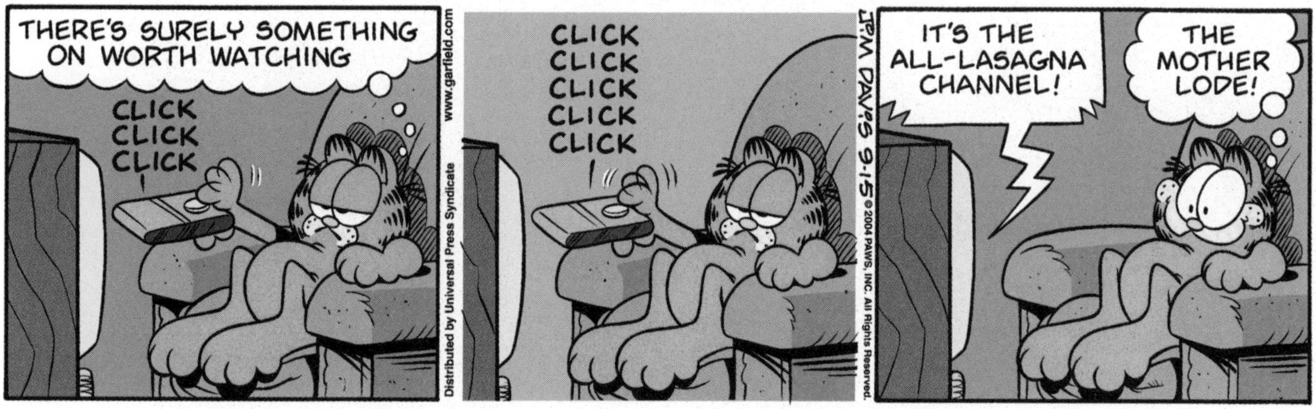
THERE'S SURELY SOMETHING ON WORTH WATCHING
CLICK CLICK CLICK
CLICK CLICK CLICK CLICK CLICK
IT'S THE ALL-LASAGNA CHANNEL!
THE MOTHER LODE!
Distributed by Universal Press Syndicate www.garfield.com
JIM DAVIS 9-15 © 2004 PAWS, INC. All Rights Reserved.

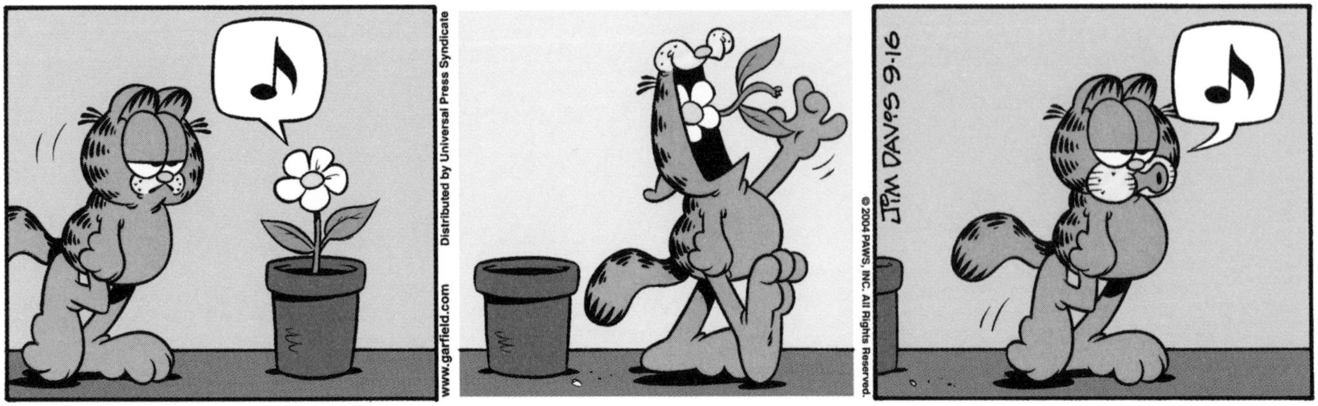
www.garfield.com
Distributed by Universal Press Syndicate
© 2004 PAWS, INC. All Rights Reserved.
JIM DAVIS 9-16

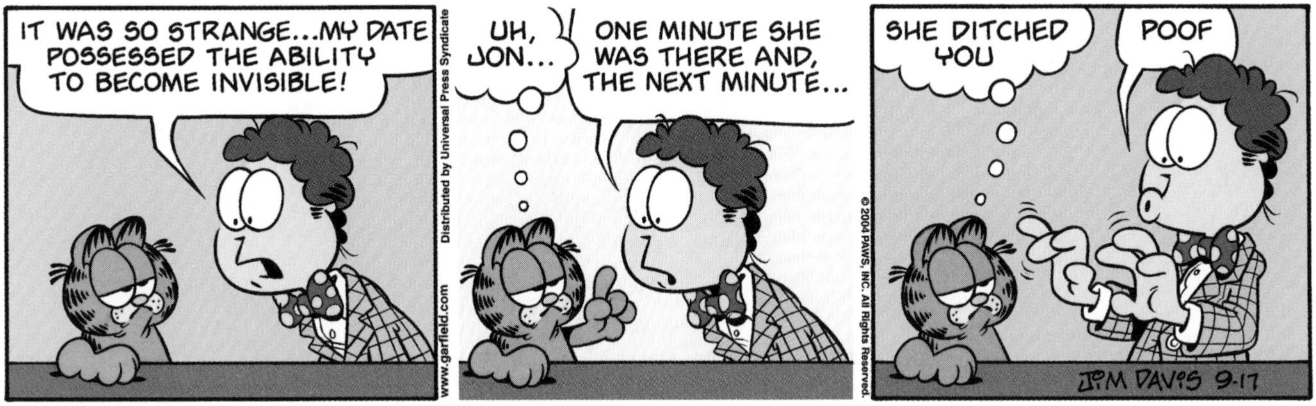
IT WAS SO STRANGE...MY DATE POSSESSED THE ABILITY TO BECOME INVISIBLE!
UH, JON...
ONE MINUTE SHE WAS THERE AND, THE NEXT MINUTE...
SHE DITCHED YOU
POOF
www.garfield.com
Distributed by Universal Press Syndicate
© 2004 PAWS, INC. All Rights Reserved.
JIM DAVIS 9-17

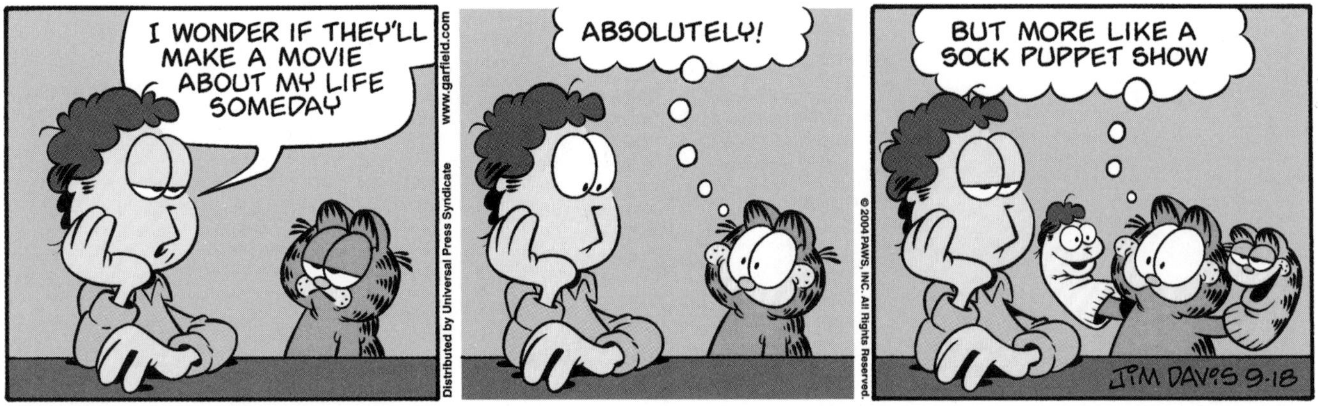
I WONDER IF THEY'LL MAKE A MOVIE ABOUT MY LIFE SOMEDAY
ABSOLUTELY!
BUT MORE LIKE A SOCK PUPPET SHOW
www.garfield.com
Distributed by Universal Press Syndicate
© 2004 PAWS, INC. All Rights Reserved.
JIM DAVIS 9-18

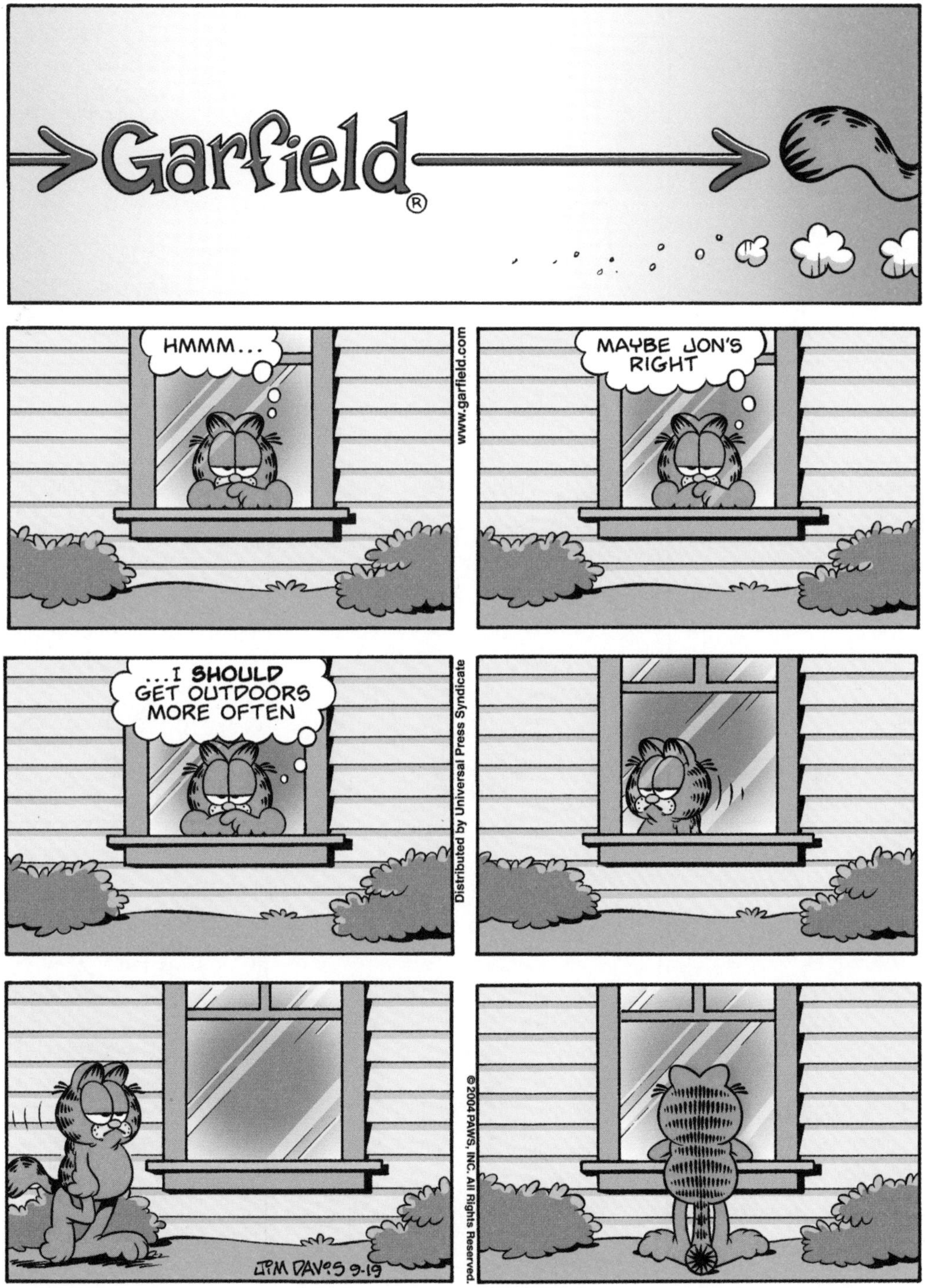
Garfield®
HMMM...
MAYBE JON'S RIGHT
...I **SHOULD** GET OUTDOORS MORE OFTEN
JIM DAVIS 9-19
www.garfield.com
Distributed by Universal Press Syndicate
© 2004 PAWS, INC. All Rights Reserved.

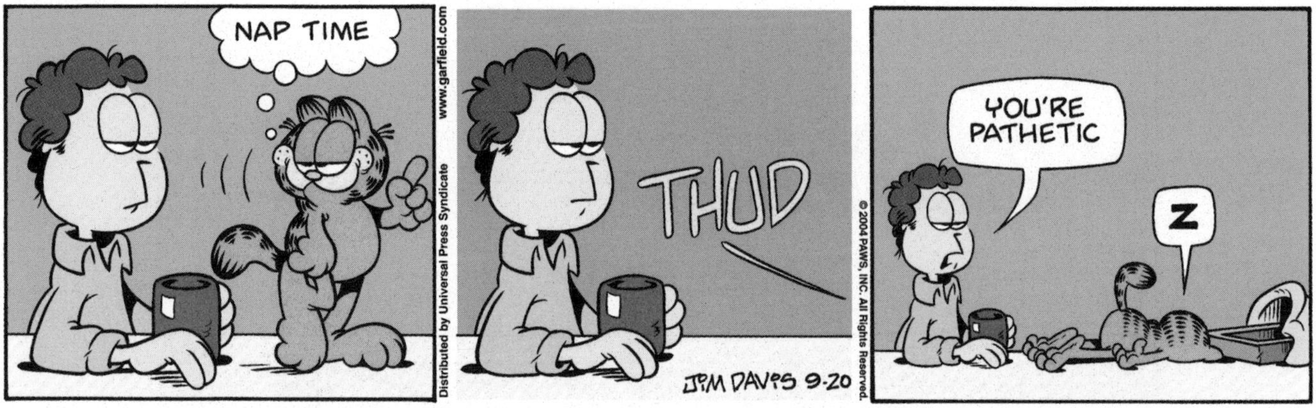
NAP TIME
THUD
JIM DAVIS 9-20
YOU'RE PATHETIC
Z
Distributed by Universal Press Syndicate
www.garfield.com
© 2004 PAWS, INC. All Rights Reserved.

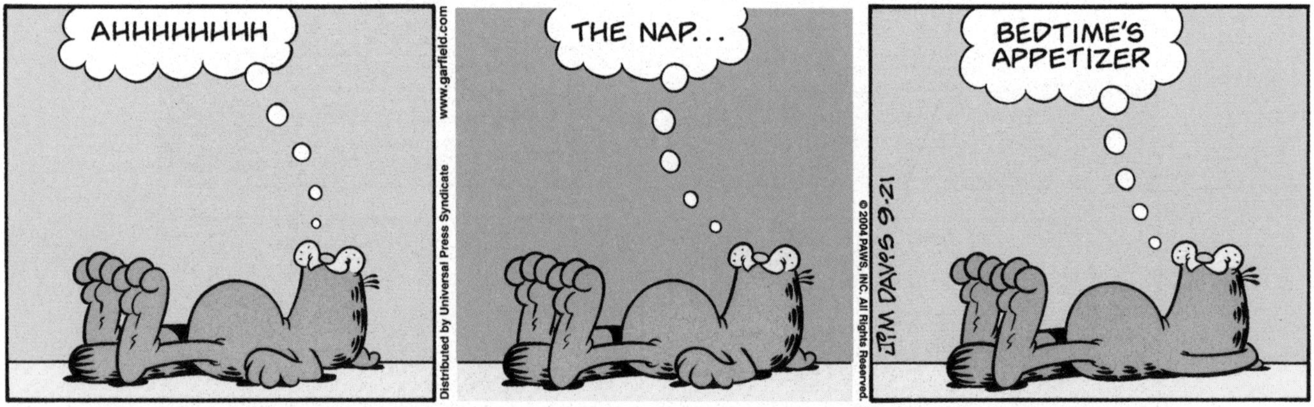
AHHHHHHHH
THE NAP...
BEDTIME'S APPETIZER
JIM DAVIS 9-21
Distributed by Universal Press Syndicate
www.garfield.com
© 2004 PAWS, INC. All Rights Reserved.

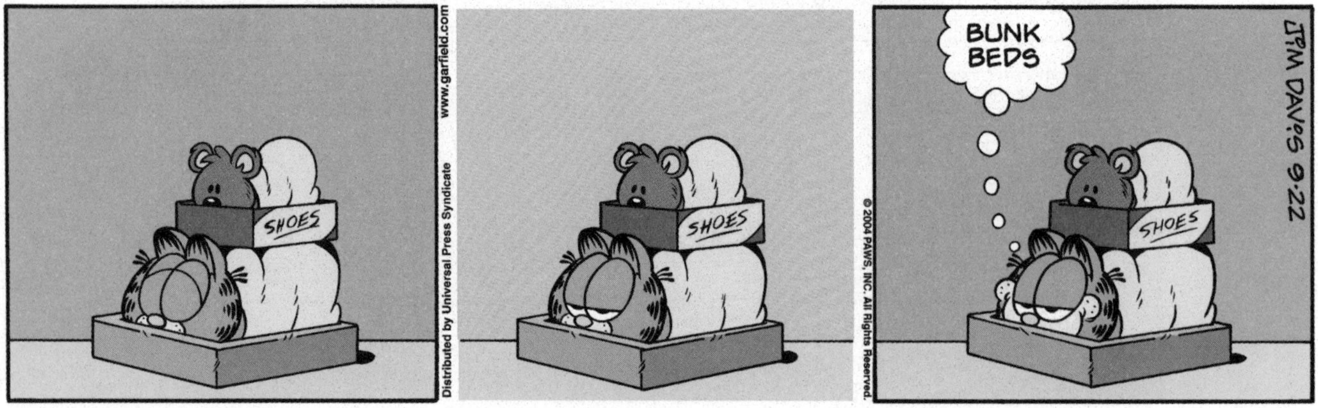
SHOES
SHOES
BUNK BEDS
SHOES
JIM DAVIS 9-22
Distributed by Universal Press Syndicate
www.garfield.com
© 2004 PAWS, INC. All Rights Reserved.

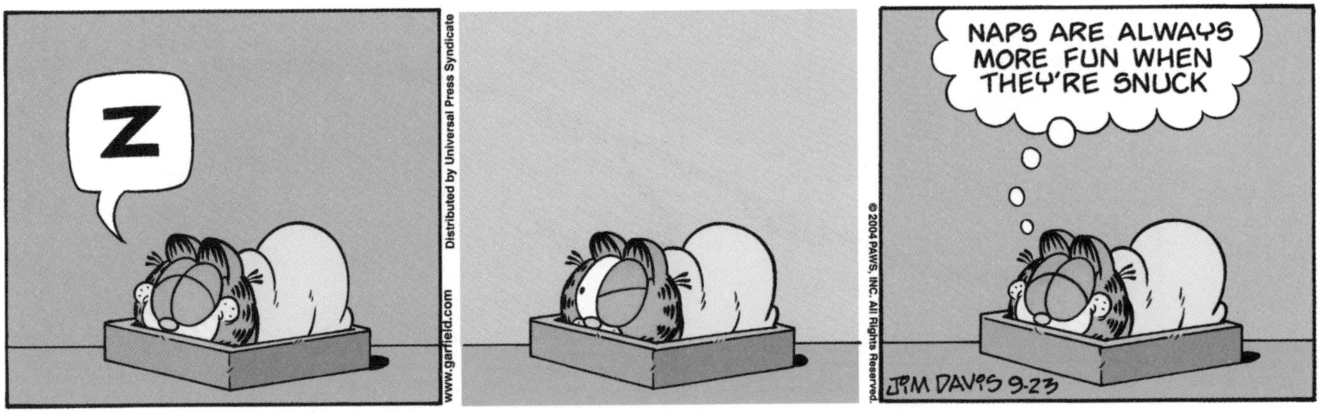
Z
NAPS ARE ALWAYS MORE FUN WHEN THEY'RE SNUCK
JIM DAVIS 9-23
www.garfield.com
Distributed by Universal Press Syndicate
© 2004 PAWS, INC. All Rights Reserved.

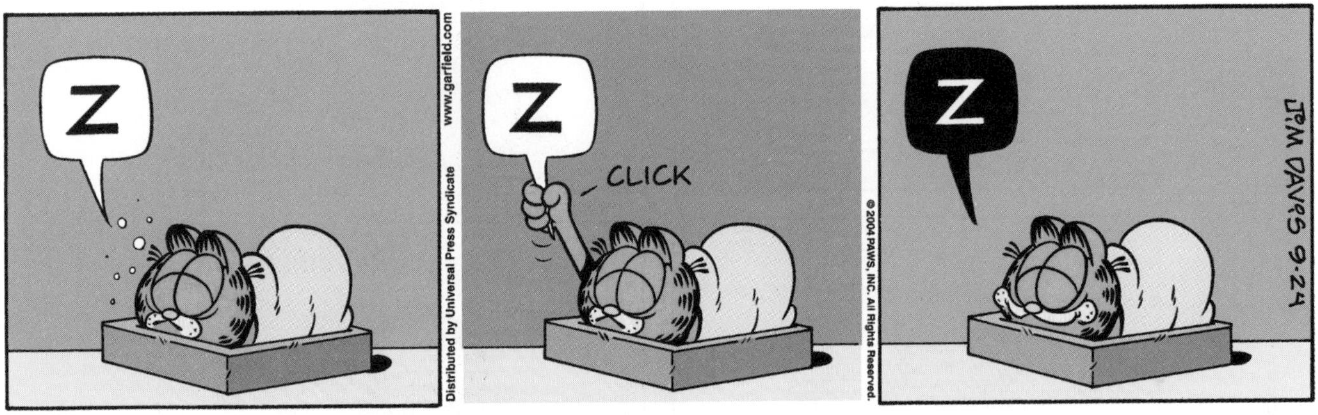
Z
Z
CLICK
Z
JIM DAVIS 9-24
www.garfield.com
Distributed by Universal Press Syndicate
© 2004 PAWS, INC. All Rights Reserved.

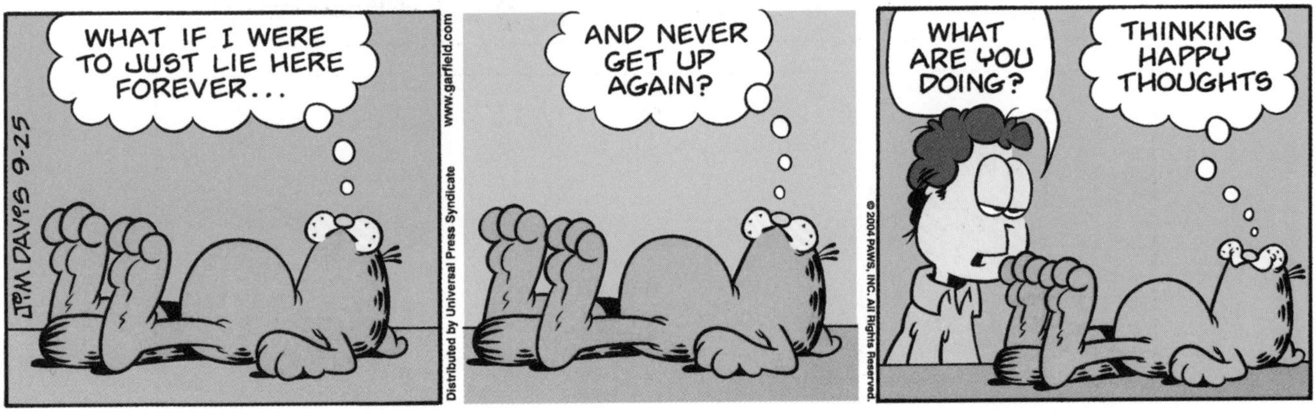
WHAT IF I WERE TO JUST LIE HERE FOREVER...
AND NEVER GET UP AGAIN?
WHAT ARE YOU DOING?
THINKING HAPPY THOUGHTS
JIM DAVIS 9-25
www.garfield.com
Distributed by Universal Press Syndicate
© 2004 PAWS, INC. All Rights Reserved.

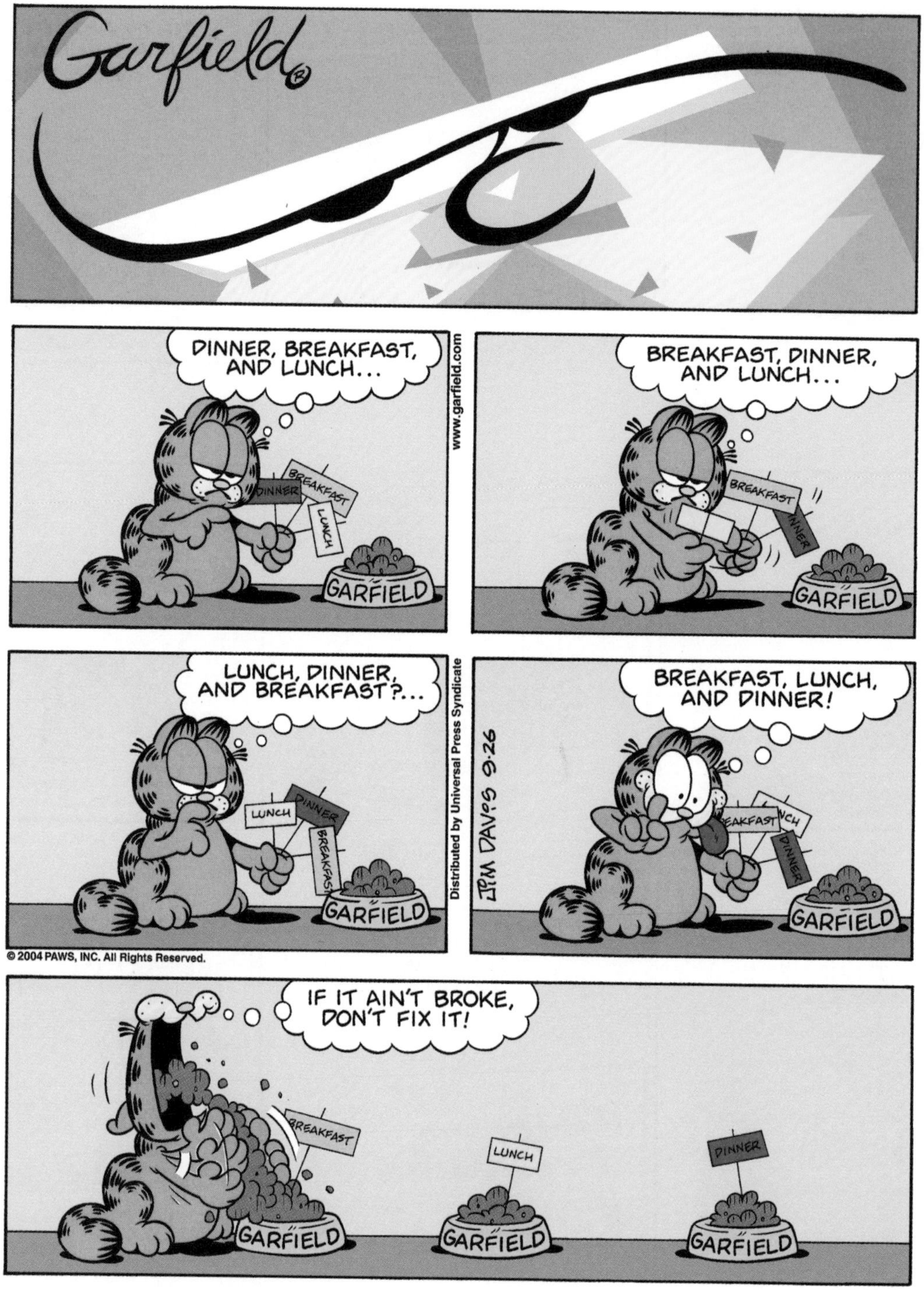
Garfield®
DINNER, BREAKFAST, AND LUNCH...
www.garfield.com
BREAKFAST, DINNER, AND LUNCH...
LUNCH, DINNER, AND BREAKFAST?...
Distributed by Universal Press Syndicate
JPM DAVIS 9·26
BREAKFAST, LUNCH, AND DINNER!
© 2004 PAWS, INC. All Rights Reserved.
IF IT AIN'T BROKE, DON'T FIX IT!
BREAKFAST
LUNCH
DINNER
GARFIELD

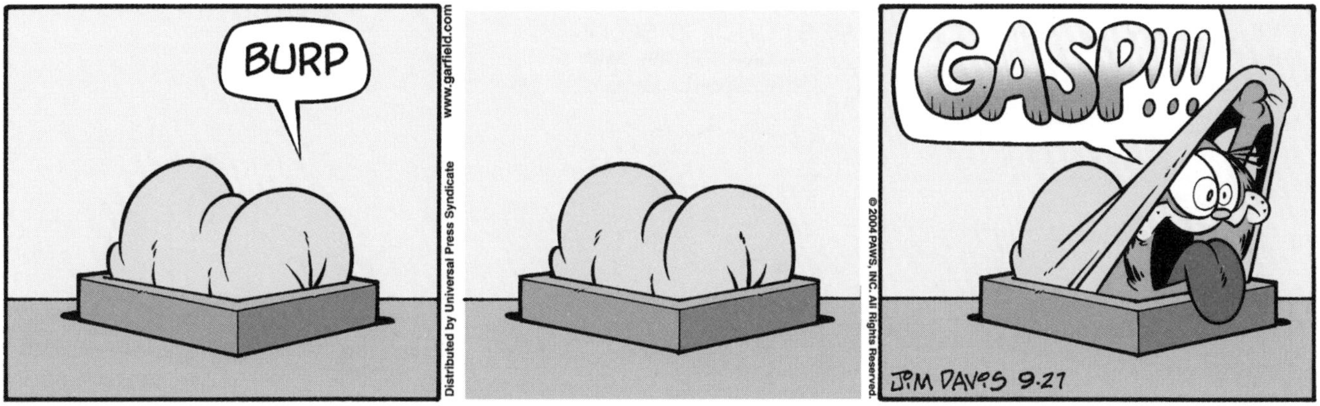
BURP
www.garfield.com
Distributed by Universal Press Syndicate
GASP!!!
© 2004 PAWS, INC. All Rights Reserved.
JIM DAVIS 9-27

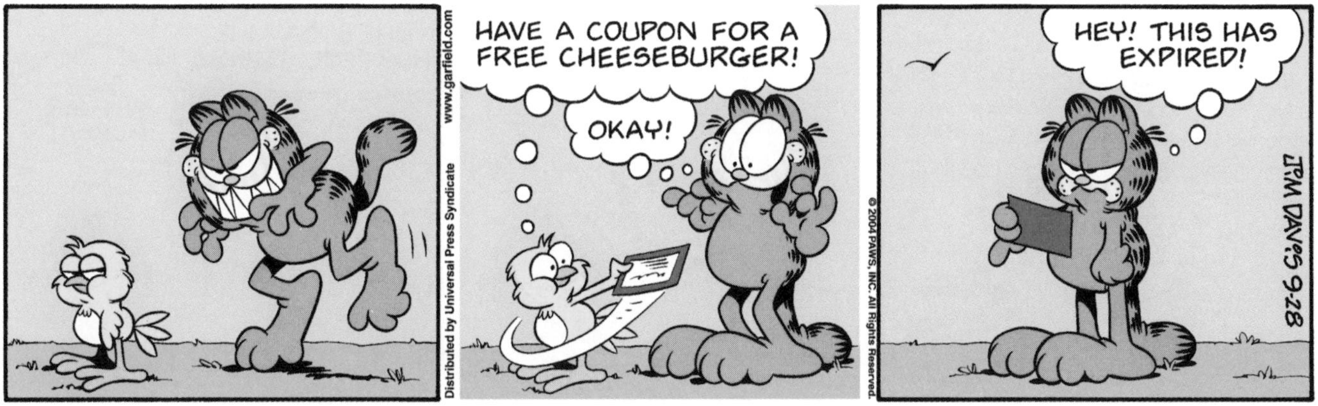
www.garfield.com
Distributed by Universal Press Syndicate
HAVE A COUPON FOR A FREE CHEESEBURGER!
OKAY!
© 2004 PAWS, INC. All Rights Reserved.
HEY! THIS HAS EXPIRED!
JIM DAVIS 9-28

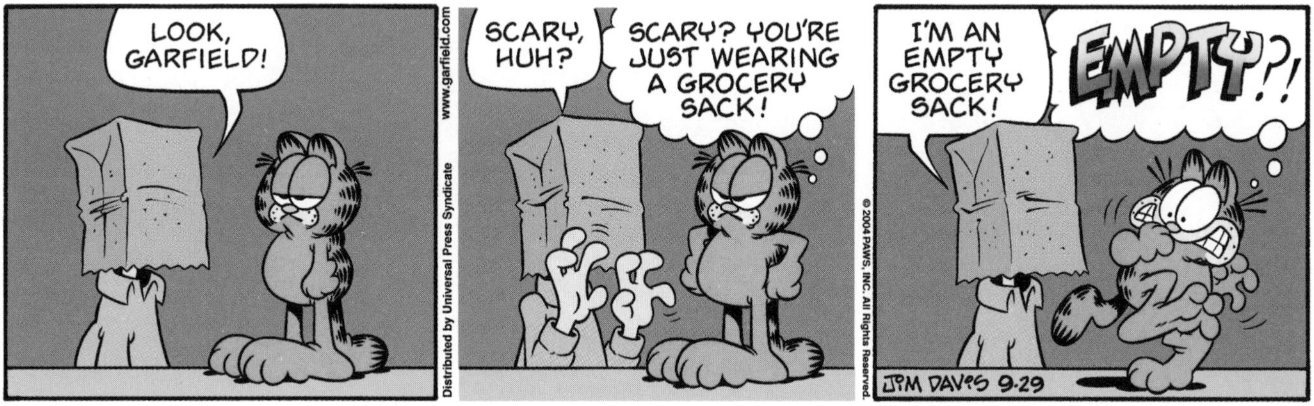
LOOK, GARFIELD!
www.garfield.com
Distributed by Universal Press Syndicate
SCARY, HUH?
SCARY? YOU'RE JUST WEARING A GROCERY SACK!
© 2004 PAWS, INC. All Rights Reserved.
I'M AN EMPTY GROCERY SACK!
EMPTY?!
JIM DAVIS 9-29

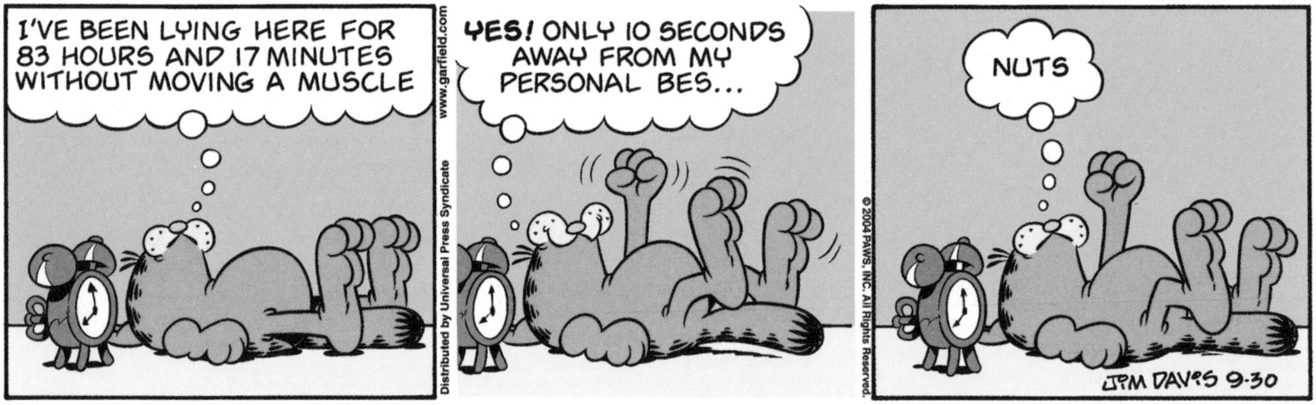
I'VE BEEN LYING HERE FOR 83 HOURS AND 17 MINUTES WITHOUT MOVING A MUSCLE
www.garfield.com
Distributed by Universal Press Syndicate
YES! ONLY 10 SECONDS AWAY FROM MY PERSONAL BES...
© 2004 PAWS, INC. All Rights Reserved.
NUTS
JIM DAVIS 9-30

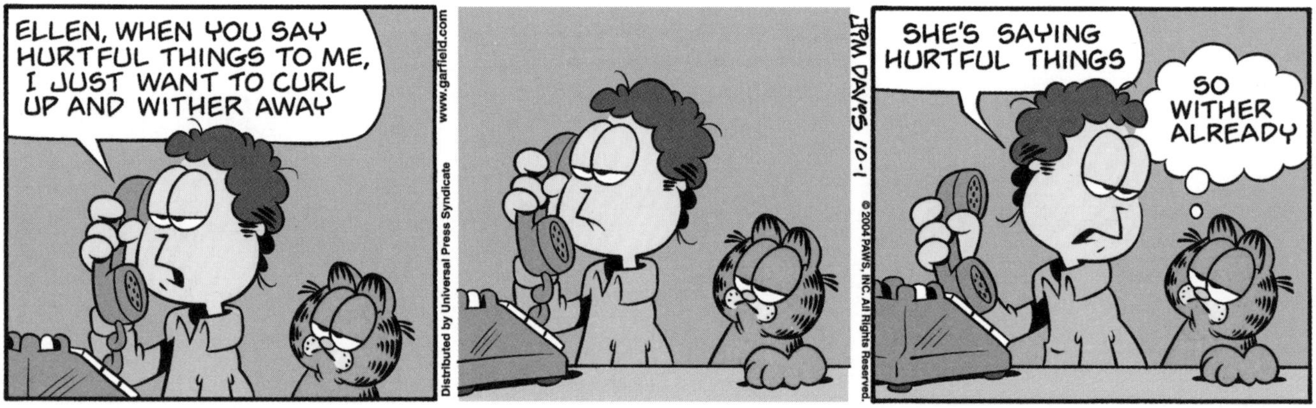
ELLEN, WHEN YOU SAY HURTFUL THINGS TO ME, I JUST WANT TO CURL UP AND WITHER AWAY
www.garfield.com
Distributed by Universal Press Syndicate
JIM DAVIS 10-1
© 2004 PAWS, INC. All Rights Reserved.
SHE'S SAYING HURTFUL THINGS
SO WITHER ALREADY

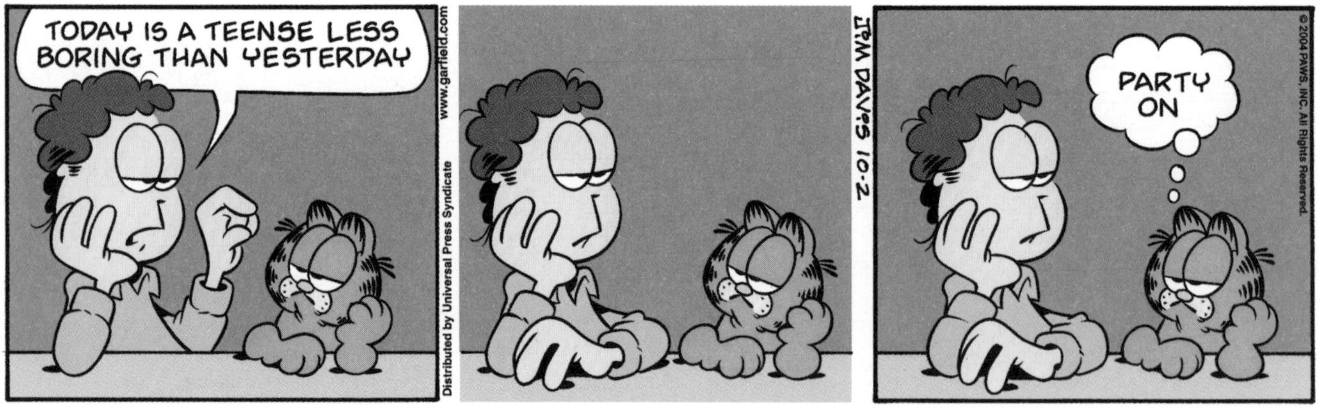
TODAY IS A TEENSE LESS BORING THAN YESTERDAY
www.garfield.com
Distributed by Universal Press Syndicate
JIM DAVIS 10-2
© 2004 PAWS, INC. All Rights Reserved.
PARTY ON

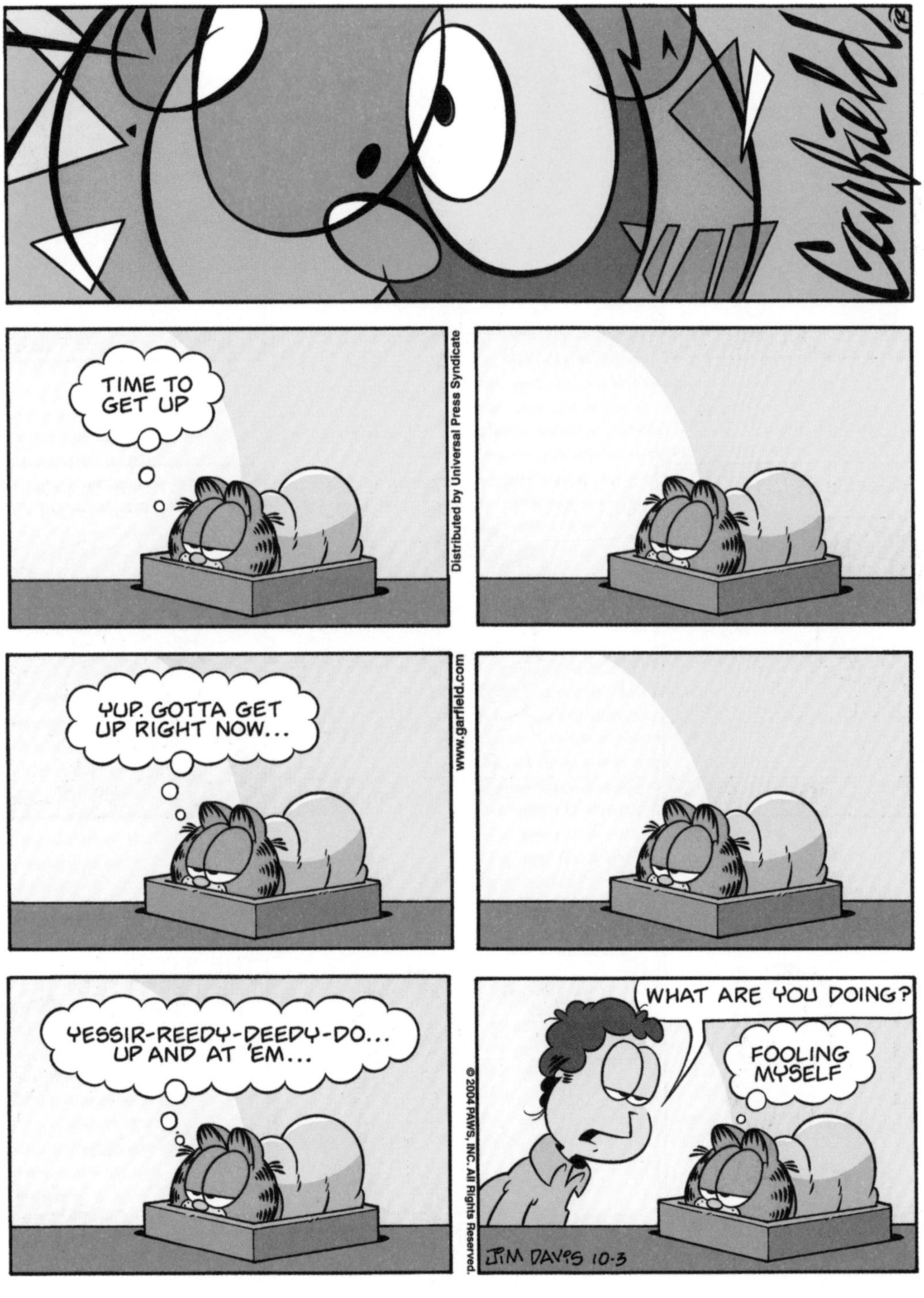
Garfield
TIME TO GET UP
Distributed by Universal Press Syndicate
YUP. GOTTA GET UP RIGHT NOW...
www.garfield.com
YESSIR-REEDY-DEEDY-DO... UP AND AT 'EM...
© 2004 PAWS, INC. All Rights Reserved.
WHAT ARE YOU DOING?
FOOLING MYSELF
JIM DAVIS 10-3

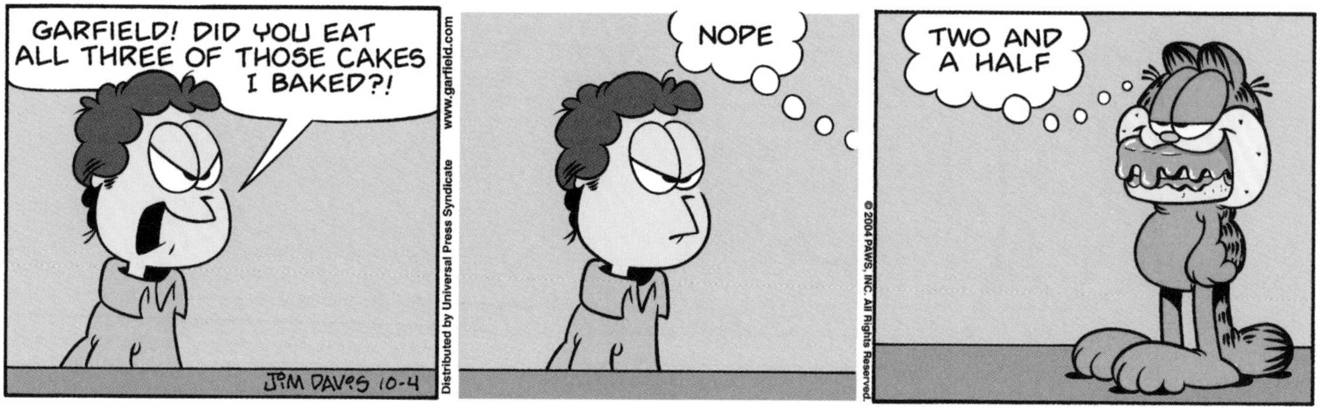
GARFIELD! DID YOU EAT ALL THREE OF THOSE CAKES I BAKED?!
JIM DAVIS 10-4
Distributed by Universal Press Syndicate www.garfield.com
NOPE
TWO AND A HALF
© 2004 PAWS, INC. All Rights Reserved.

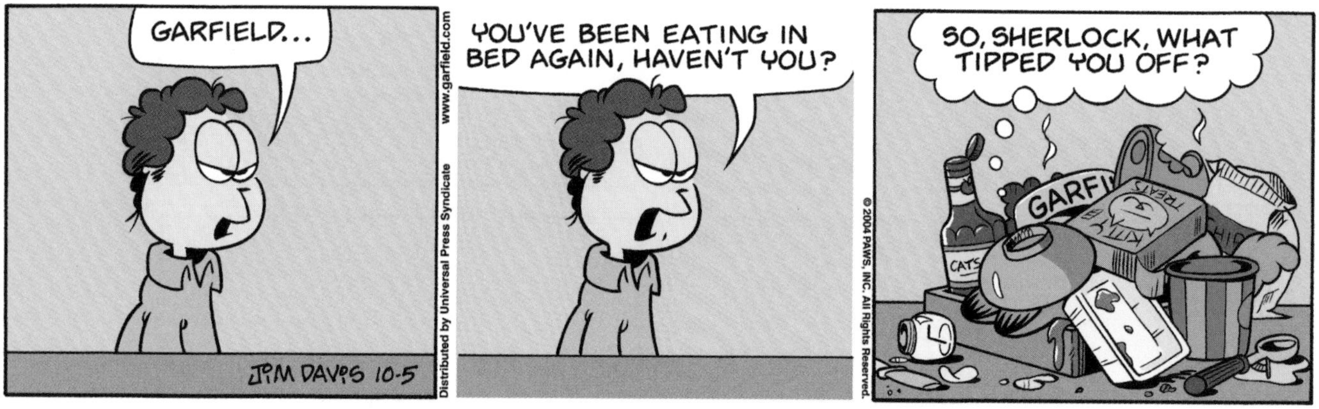
GARFIELD...
JIM DAVIS 10-5
Distributed by Universal Press Syndicate www.garfield.com
YOU'VE BEEN EATING IN BED AGAIN, HAVEN'T YOU?
SO, SHERLOCK, WHAT TIPPED YOU OFF?
GARFI
CATS
© 2004 PAWS, INC. All Rights Reserved.

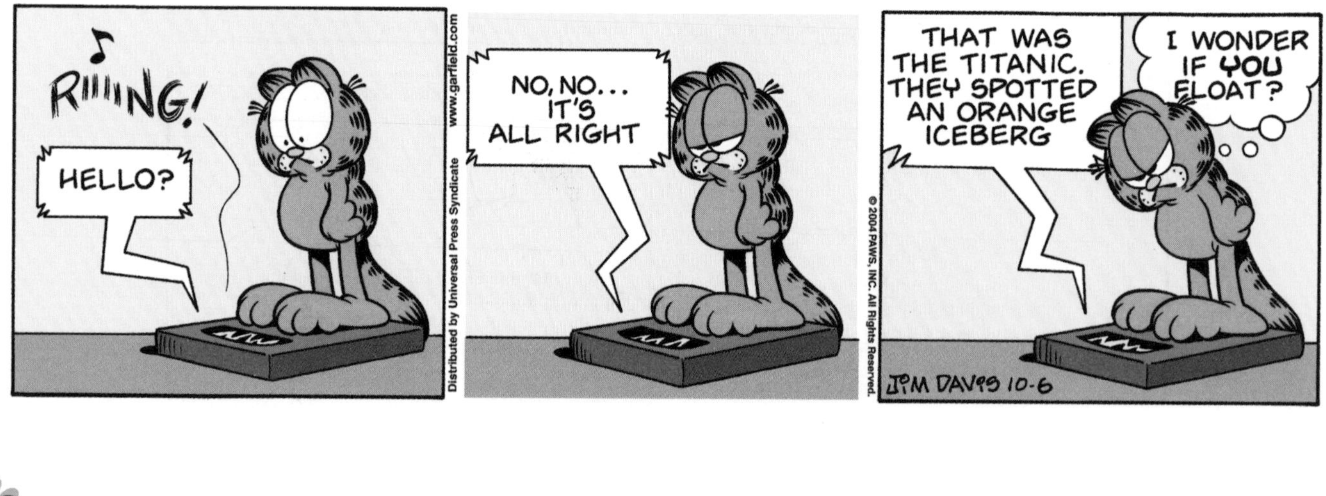
RIIING!
HELLO?
Distributed by Universal Press Syndicate www.garfield.com
NO, NO... IT'S ALL RIGHT
THAT WAS THE TITANIC. THEY SPOTTED AN ORANGE ICEBERG
I WONDER IF **YOU** FLOAT?
© 2004 PAWS, INC. All Rights Reserved.
JIM DAVIS 10-6

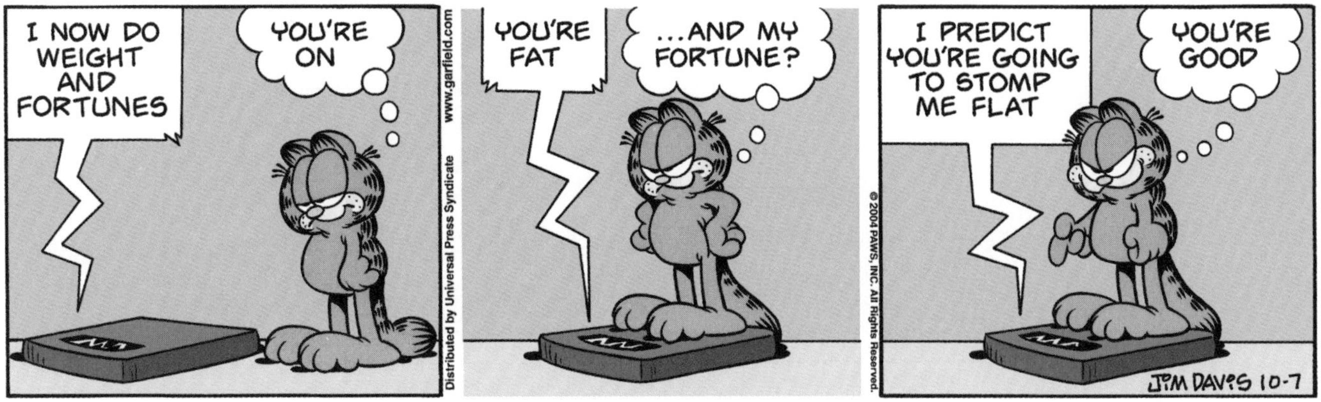
I NOW DO WEIGHT AND FORTUNES
YOU'RE ON
YOU'RE FAT
...AND MY FORTUNE?
I PREDICT YOU'RE GOING TO STOMP ME FLAT
YOU'RE GOOD
JIM DAVIS 10-7
Distributed by Universal Press Syndicate www.garfield.com
© 2004 PAWS, INC. All Rights Reserved.

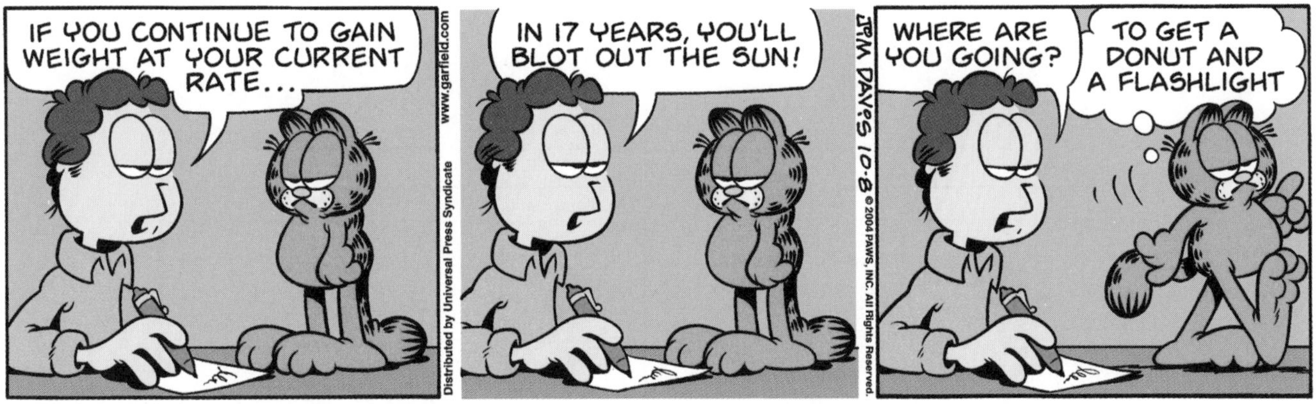
IF YOU CONTINUE TO GAIN WEIGHT AT YOUR CURRENT RATE...
IN 17 YEARS, YOU'LL BLOT OUT THE SUN!
WHERE ARE YOU GOING?
TO GET A DONUT AND A FLASHLIGHT
JIM DAVIS 10-8
Distributed by Universal Press Syndicate www.garfield.com
© 2004 PAWS, INC. All Rights Reserved.

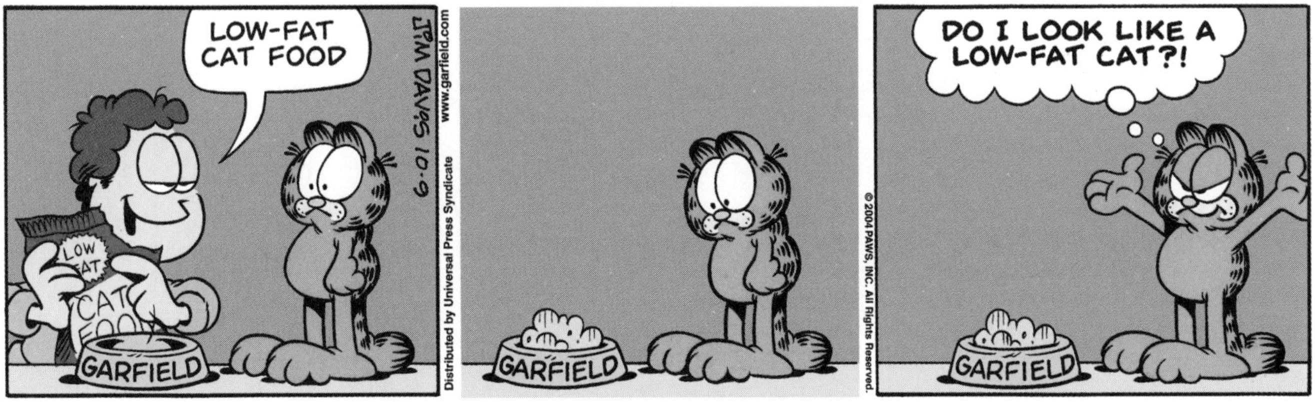
LOW-FAT CAT FOOD
LOW FAT
CAT FOOD
GARFIELD
GARFIELD
DO I LOOK LIKE A LOW-FAT CAT?!
GARFIELD
JIM DAVIS 10-9
Distributed by Universal Press Syndicate www.garfield.com
© 2004 PAWS, INC. All Rights Reserved.

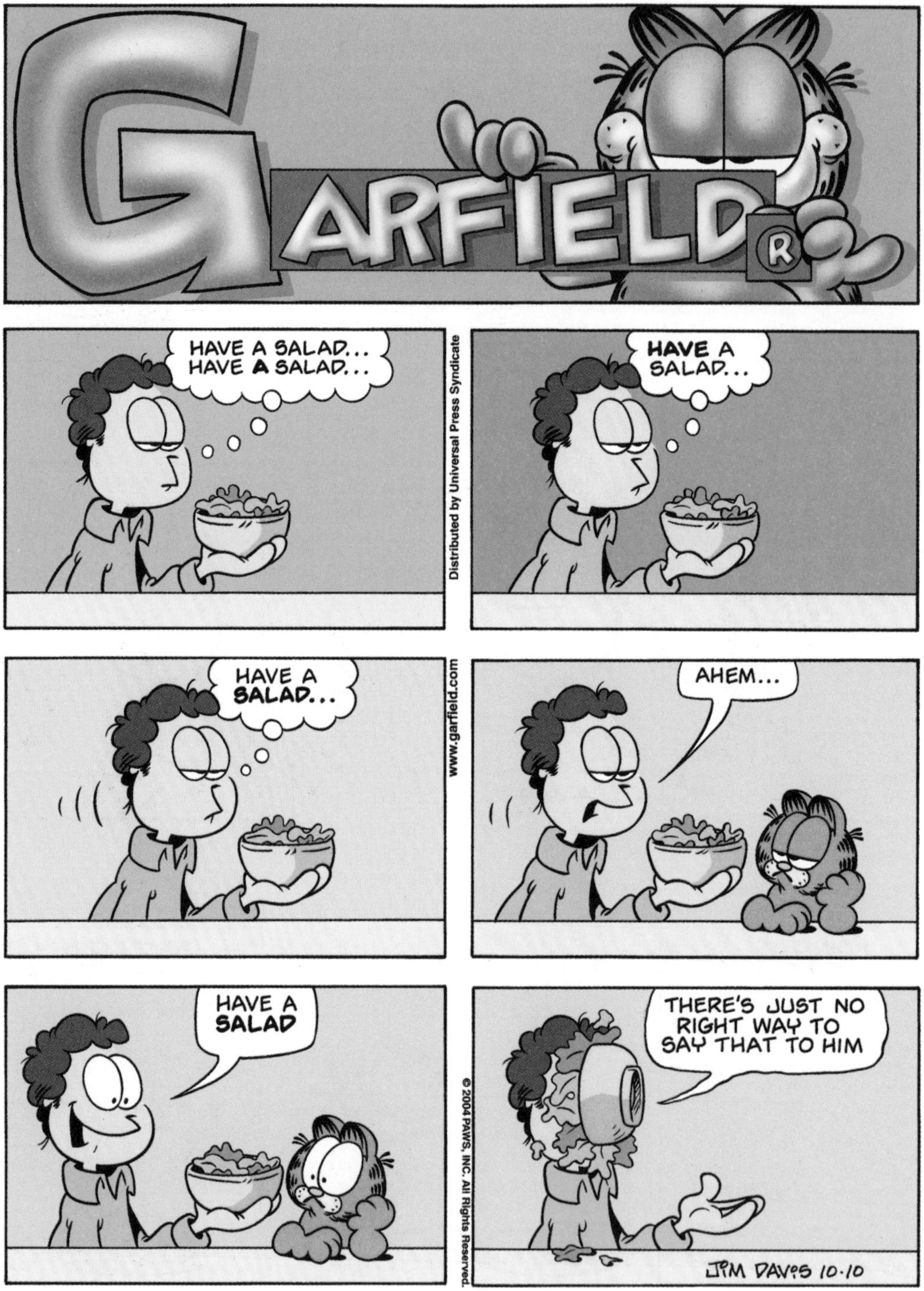
GARFIELD®
HAVE A SALAD... HAVE A SALAD...
HAVE A SALAD...
HAVE A SALAD...
AHEM...
HAVE A SALAD
THERE'S JUST NO RIGHT WAY TO SAY THAT TO HIM
JIM DAVIS 10-10
Distributed by Universal Press Syndicate
www.garfield.com
© 2004 PAWS, INC. All Rights Reserved.

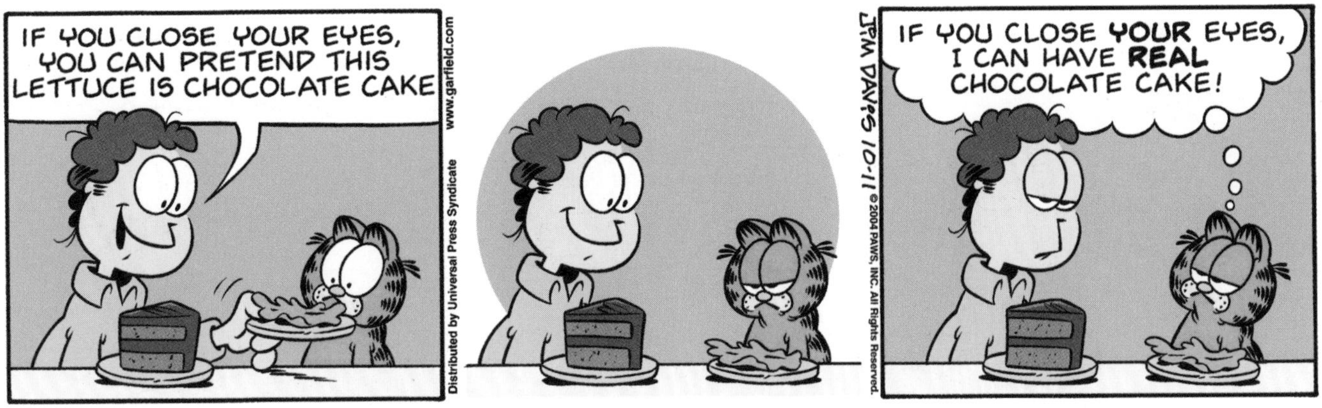
IF YOU CLOSE YOUR EYES, YOU CAN PRETEND THIS LETTUCE IS CHOCOLATE CAKE
www.garfield.com
Distributed by Universal Press Syndicate
JIM DAVIS 10-11
© 2004 PAWS, INC. All Rights Reserved.
IF YOU CLOSE **YOUR** EYES, I CAN HAVE **REAL** CHOCOLATE CAKE!

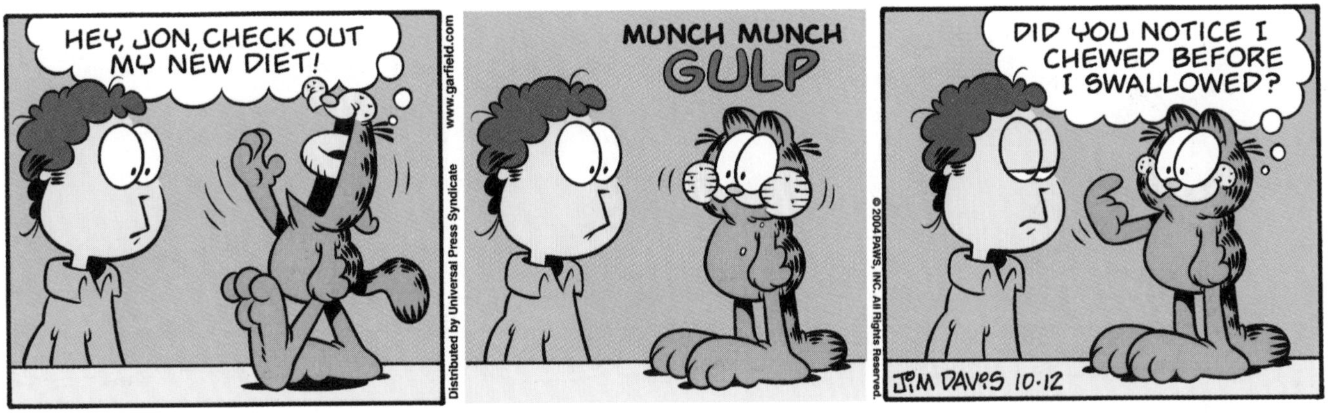
HEY, JON, CHECK OUT MY NEW DIET!
www.garfield.com
Distributed by Universal Press Syndicate
MUNCH MUNCH
GULP
© 2004 PAWS, INC. All Rights Reserved.
DID YOU NOTICE I CHEWED BEFORE I SWALLOWED?
JIM DAVIS 10-12

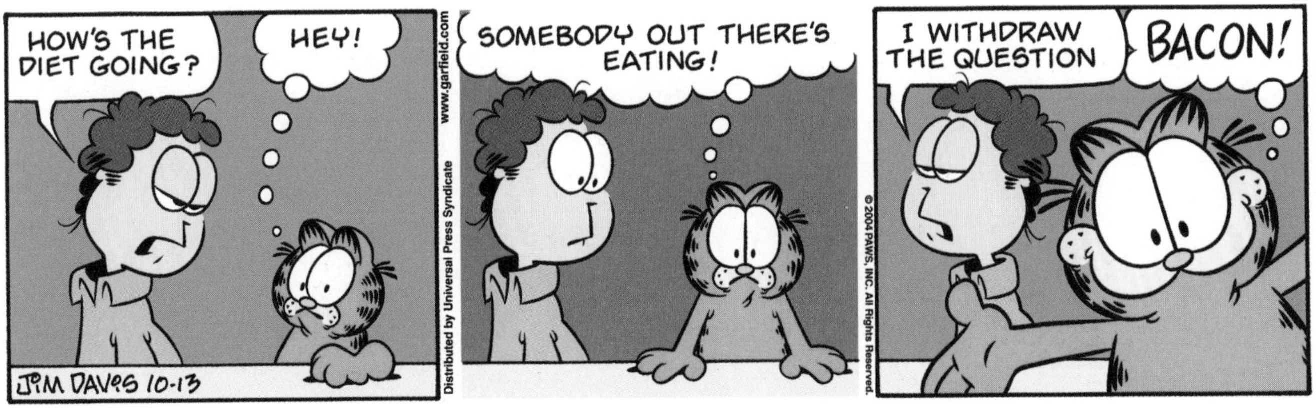
HOW'S THE DIET GOING?
HEY!
JIM DAVIS 10-13
www.garfield.com
Distributed by Universal Press Syndicate
SOMEBODY OUT THERE'S EATING!
© 2004 PAWS, INC. All Rights Reserved.
I WITHDRAW THE QUESTION
BACON!

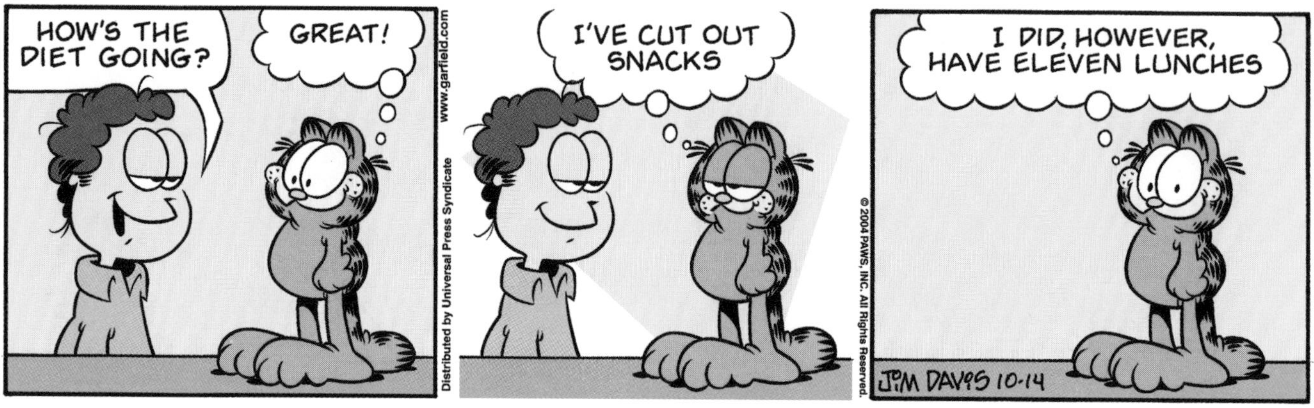
HOW'S THE DIET GOING?
GREAT!
www.garfield.com
Distributed by Universal Press Syndicate
I'VE CUT OUT SNACKS
© 2004 PAWS, INC. All Rights Reserved.
I DID, HOWEVER, HAVE ELEVEN LUNCHES
JIM DAVIS 10-14

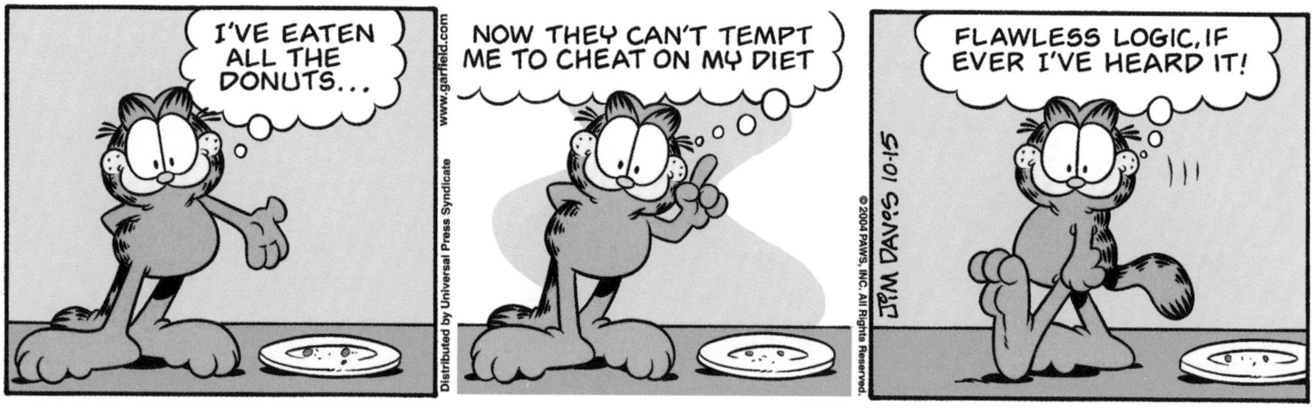
I'VE EATEN ALL THE DONUTS...
www.garfield.com
Distributed by Universal Press Syndicate
NOW THEY CAN'T TEMPT ME TO CHEAT ON MY DIET
© 2004 PAWS, INC. All Rights Reserved.
JIM DAVIS 10-15
FLAWLESS LOGIC, IF EVER I'VE HEARD IT!

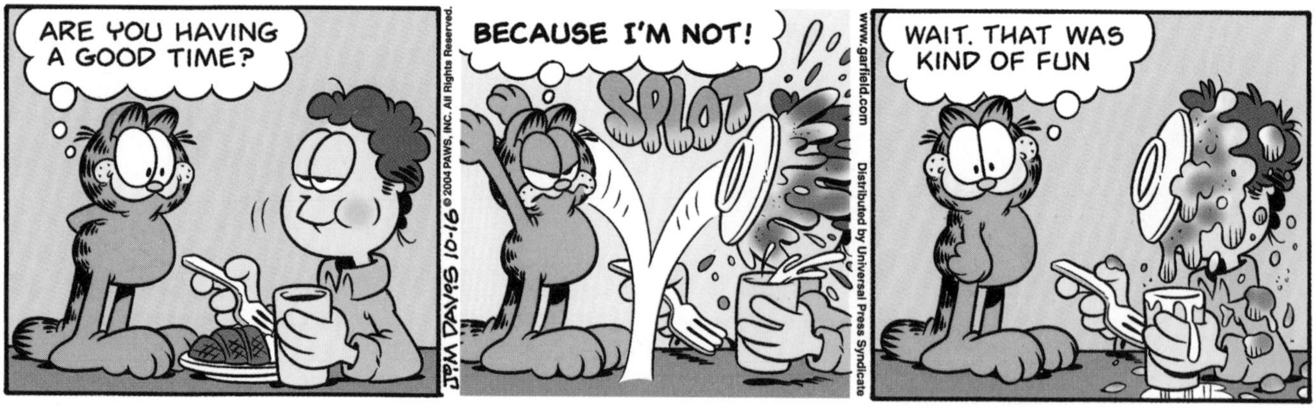
ARE YOU HAVING A GOOD TIME?
© 2004 PAWS, INC. All Rights Reserved.
JIM DAVIS 10-16
BECAUSE I'M NOT!
SPLOT
www.garfield.com
Distributed by Universal Press Syndicate
WAIT. THAT WAS KIND OF FUN

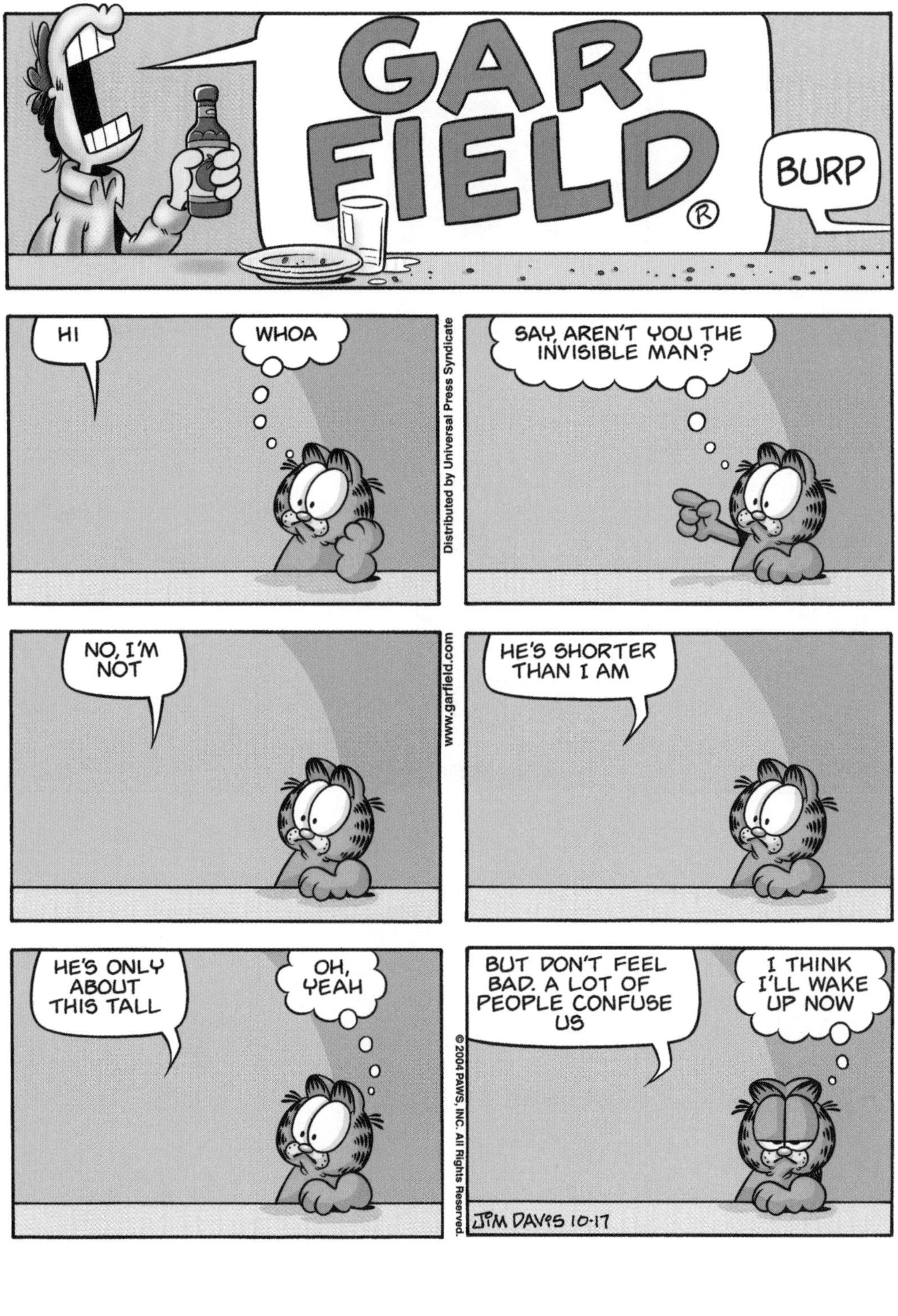
GAR-
FIELD
BURP
HI
WHOA
Distributed by Universal Press Syndicate
SAY, AREN'T YOU THE INVISIBLE MAN?
NO, I'M NOT
www.garfield.com
HE'S SHORTER THAN I AM
HE'S ONLY ABOUT THIS TALL
OH, YEAH
© 2004 PAWS, INC. All Rights Reserved.
BUT DON'T FEEL BAD. A LOT OF PEOPLE CONFUSE US
I THINK I'LL WAKE UP NOW
JIM DAVIS 10-17

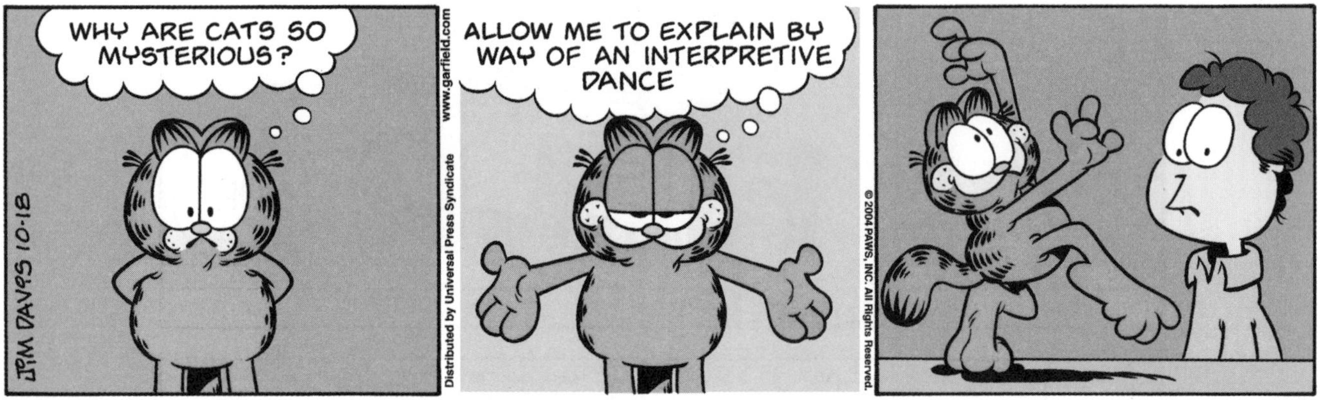
JIM DAVIS 10-18
WHY ARE CATS SO MYSTERIOUS?
ALLOW ME TO EXPLAIN BY WAY OF AN INTERPRETIVE DANCE
www.garfield.com Distributed by Universal Press Syndicate
© 2004 PAWS, INC. All Rights Reserved.

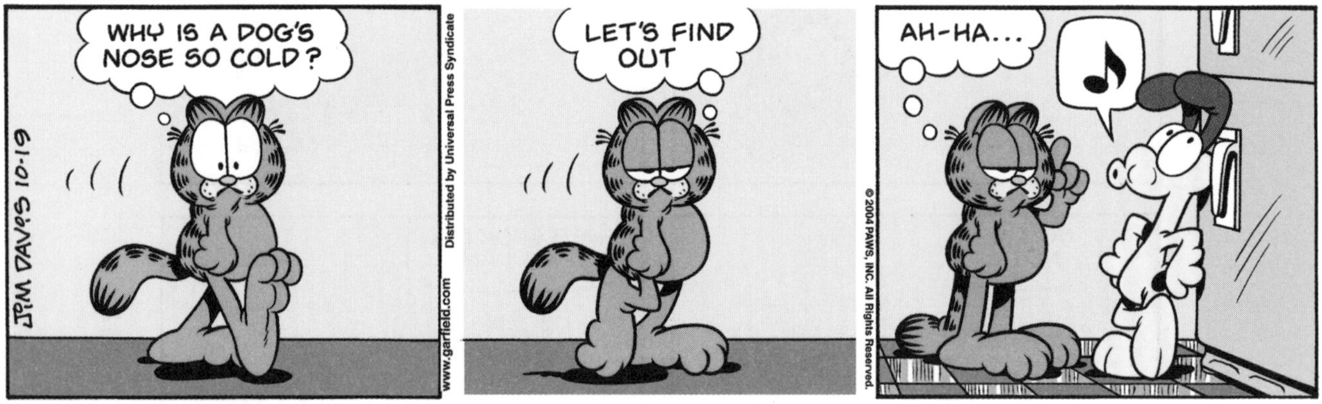
JIM DAVIS 10-19
WHY IS A DOG'S NOSE SO COLD?
LET'S FIND OUT
www.garfield.com Distributed by Universal Press Syndicate
AH-HA...
© 2004 PAWS, INC. All Rights Reserved.

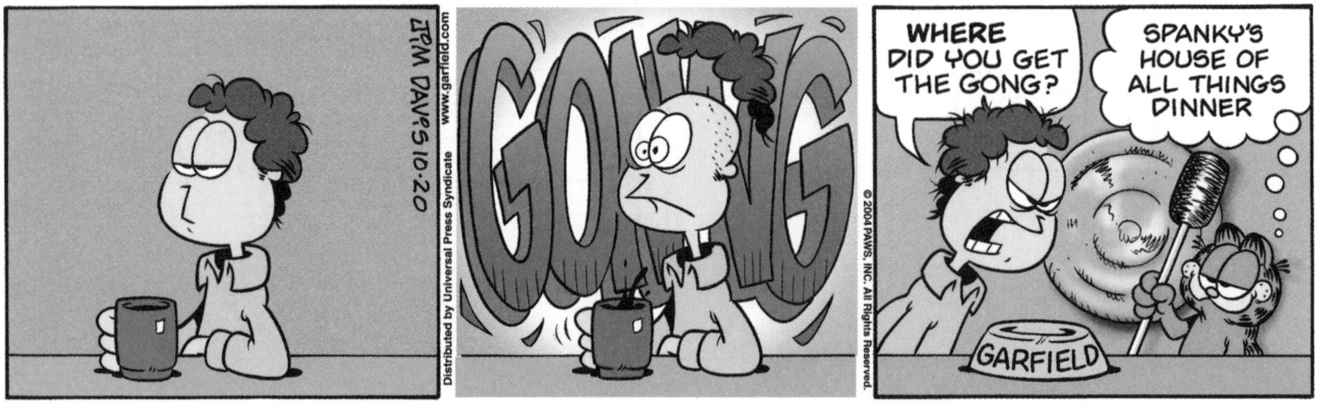
JIM DAVIS 10-20
www.garfield.com Distributed by Universal Press Syndicate
GONG
WHERE DID YOU GET THE GONG?
SPANKY'S HOUSE OF ALL THINGS DINNER
GARFIELD
© 2004 PAWS, INC. All Rights Reserved.

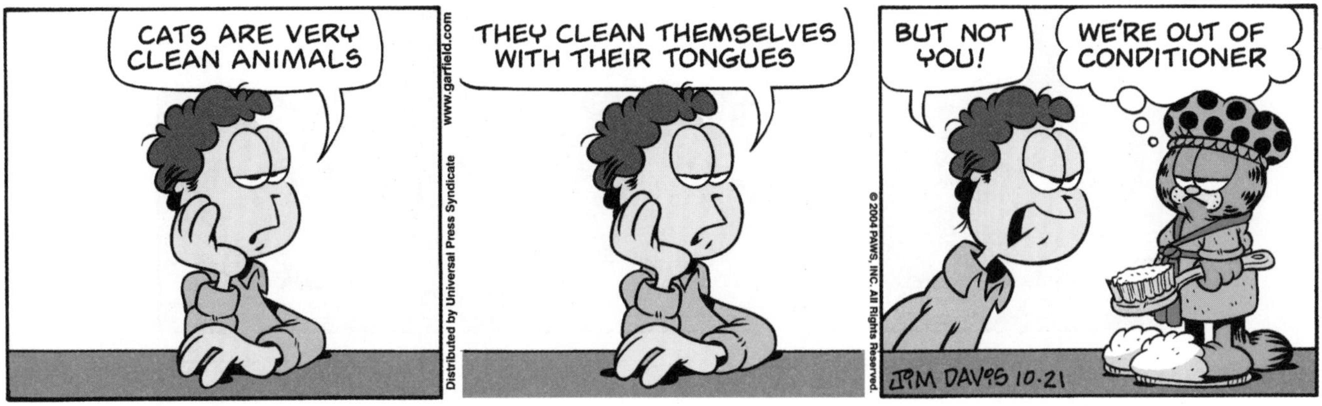
CATS ARE VERY CLEAN ANIMALS
www.garfield.com
Distributed by Universal Press Syndicate
THEY CLEAN THEMSELVES WITH THEIR TONGUES
© 2004 PAWS, INC. All Rights Reserved.
BUT NOT YOU!
WE'RE OUT OF CONDITIONER
JIM DAVIS 10.21

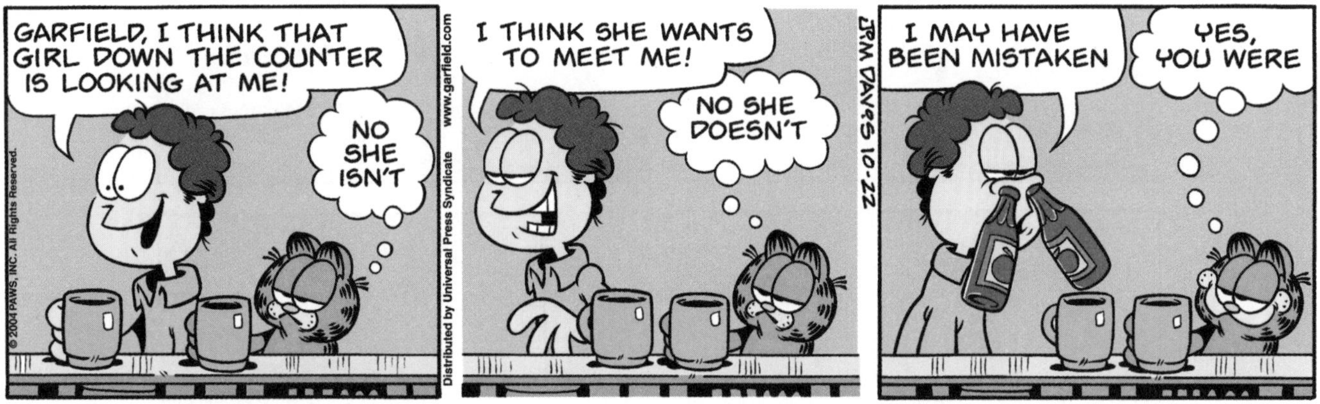
GARFIELD, I THINK THAT GIRL DOWN THE COUNTER IS LOOKING AT ME!
NO SHE ISN'T
© 2004 PAWS, INC. All Rights Reserved.
www.garfield.com
Distributed by Universal Press Syndicate
I THINK SHE WANTS TO MEET ME!
NO SHE DOESN'T
JIM DAVIS 10-22
I MAY HAVE BEEN MISTAKEN
YES, YOU WERE

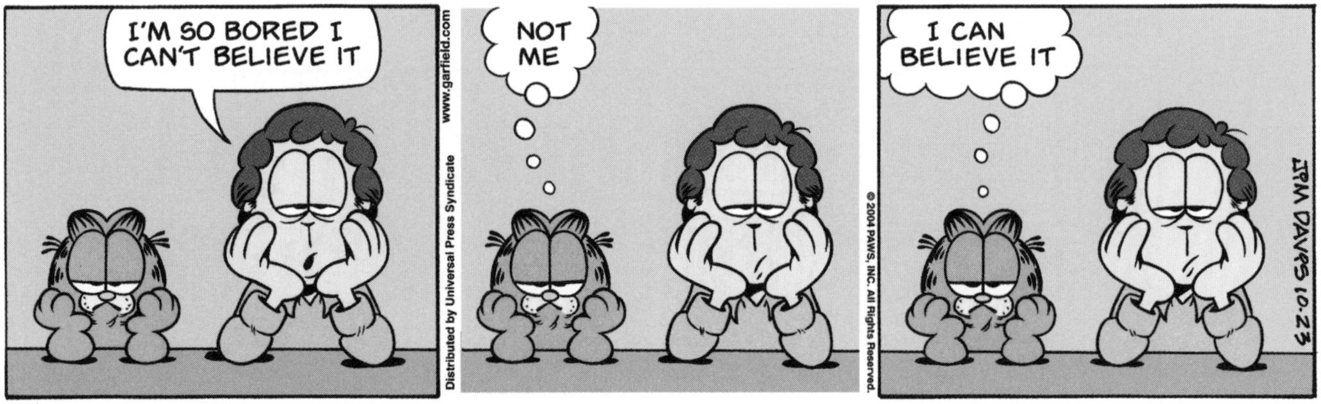
I'M SO BORED I CAN'T BELIEVE IT
www.garfield.com
Distributed by Universal Press Syndicate
NOT ME
© 2004 PAWS, INC. All Rights Reserved.
I CAN BELIEVE IT
JIM DAVIS 10-23

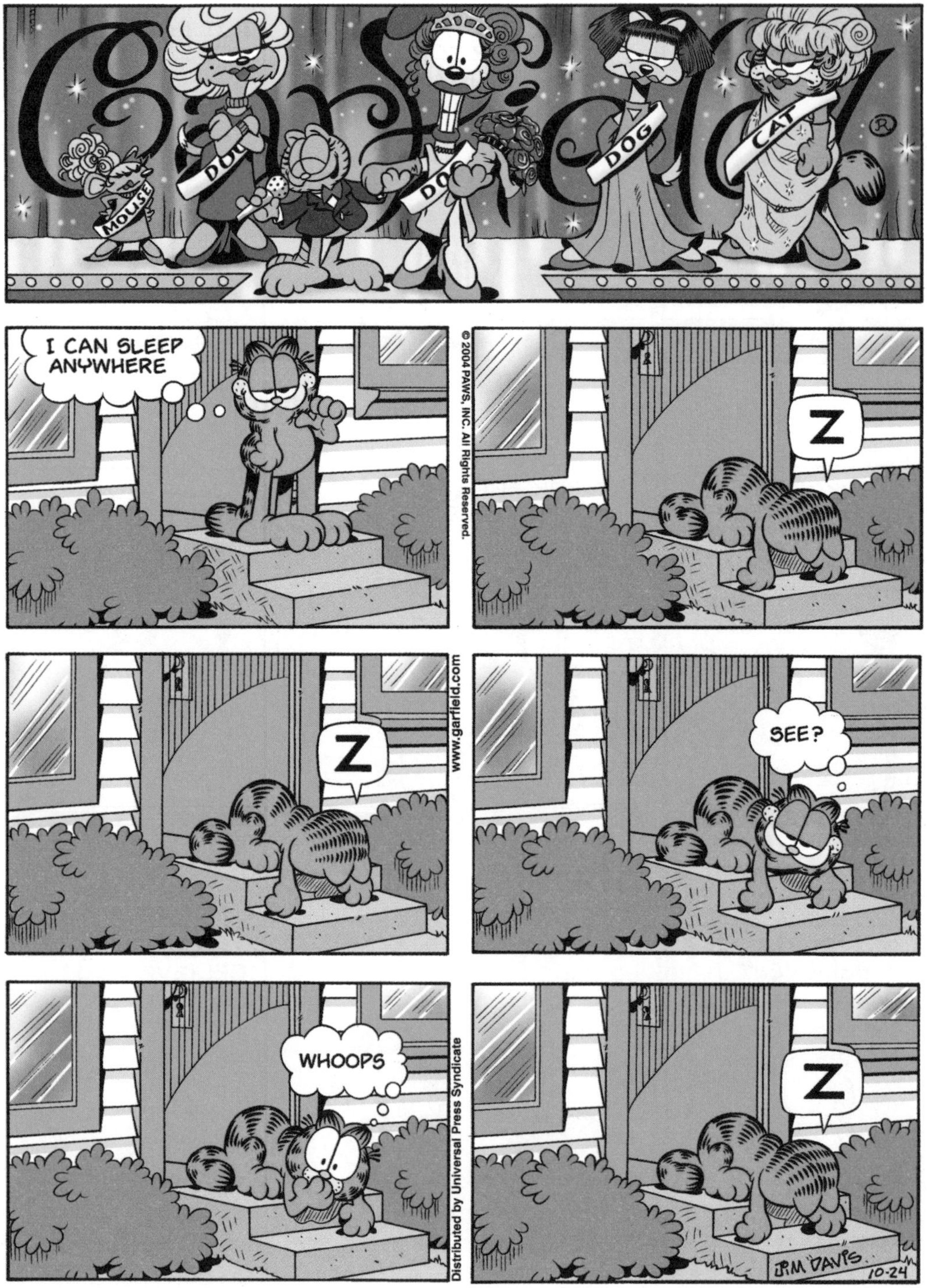
Garfield®
MOUSE
DOG
DOG
CAT
I CAN SLEEP ANYWHERE
© 2004 PAWS, INC. All Rights Reserved.
Z
www.garfield.com
Z
SEE?
WHOOPS
Distributed by Universal Press Syndicate
Z
JIM DAVIS 10-24

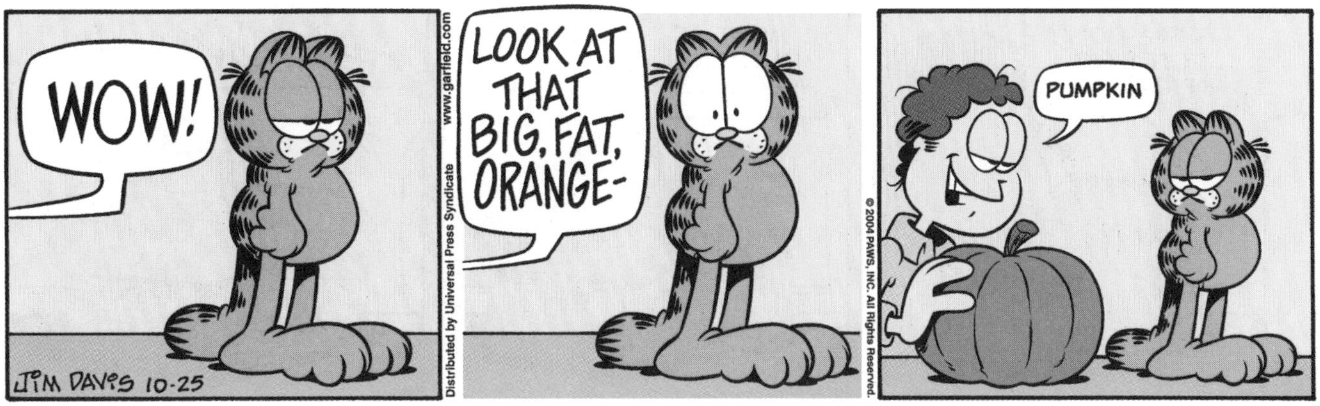
WOW!
JIM DAVIS 10-25
Distributed by Universal Press Syndicate www.garfield.com
LOOK AT THAT BIG, FAT, ORANGE-
© 2004 PAWS, INC. All Rights Reserved.
PUMPKIN

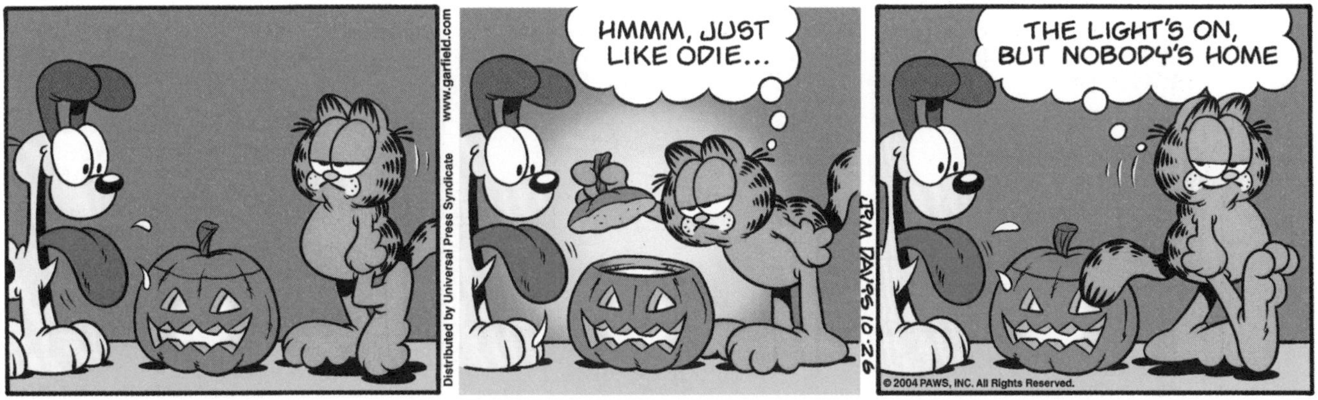
Distributed by Universal Press Syndicate www.garfield.com
HMMM, JUST LIKE ODIE...
JIM DAVIS 10-26
THE LIGHT'S ON, BUT NOBODY'S HOME
© 2004 PAWS, INC. All Rights Reserved.

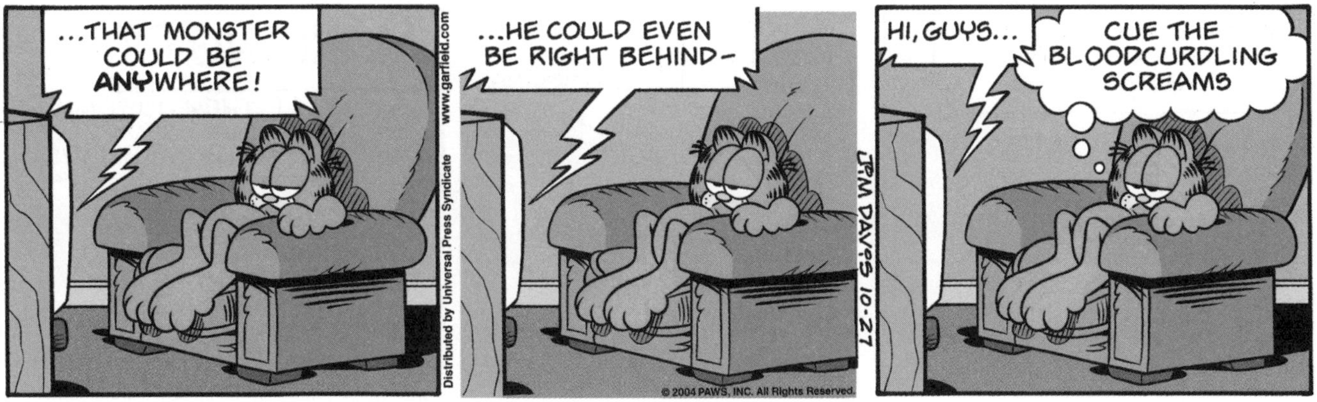
...THAT MONSTER COULD BE **ANY**WHERE!
Distributed by Universal Press Syndicate www.garfield.com
...HE COULD EVEN BE RIGHT BEHIND-
© 2004 PAWS, INC. All Rights Reserved.
JIM DAVIS 10-27
HI, GUYS...
CUE THE BLOODCURDLING SCREAMS

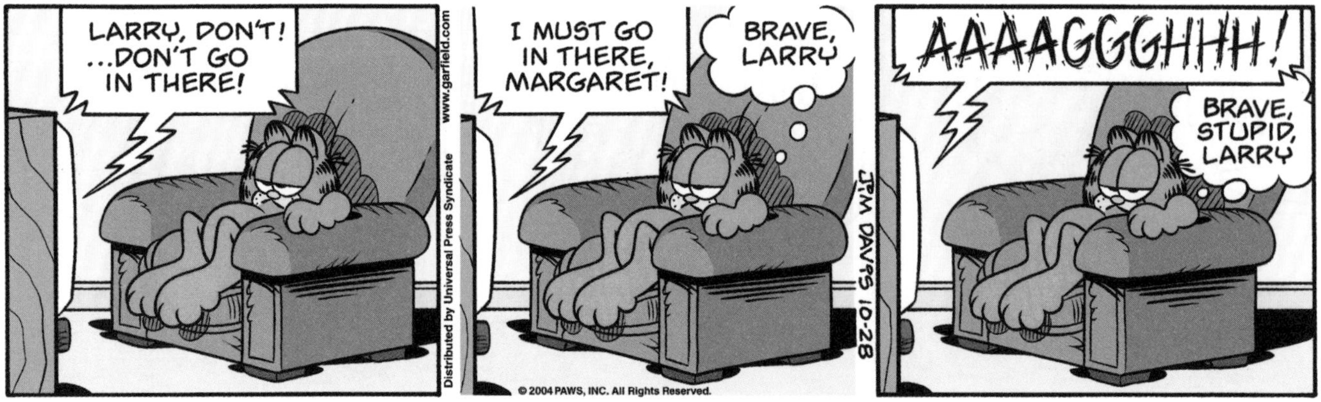
LARRY, DON'T! ...DON'T GO IN THERE!
I MUST GO IN THERE, MARGARET!
BRAVE, LARRY
AAAAGGGHHH!
BRAVE, STUPID, LARRY
www.garfield.com
Distributed by Universal Press Syndicate
JIM DAVIS 10-28
© 2004 PAWS, INC. All Rights Reserved.

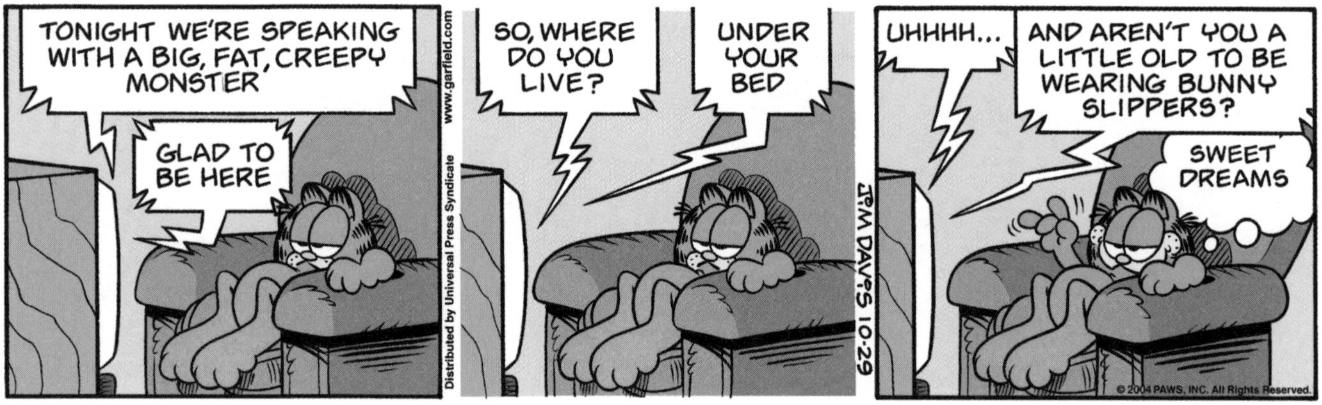
TONIGHT WE'RE SPEAKING WITH A BIG, FAT, CREEPY MONSTER
GLAD TO BE HERE
SO, WHERE DO YOU LIVE?
UNDER YOUR BED
UHHHH...
AND AREN'T YOU A LITTLE OLD TO BE WEARING BUNNY SLIPPERS?
SWEET DREAMS
www.garfield.com
Distributed by Universal Press Syndicate
JIM DAVIS 10-29
© 2004 PAWS, INC. All Rights Reserved.

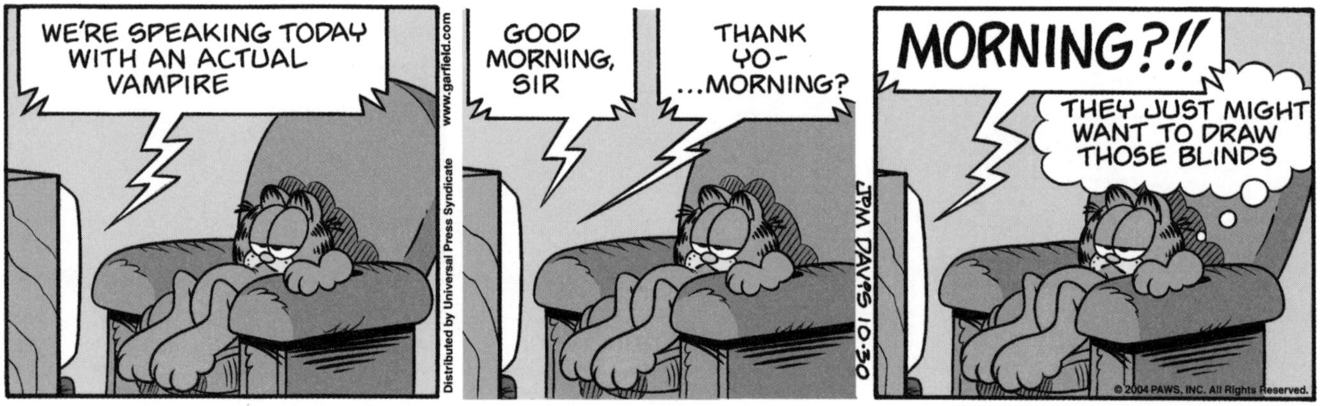
WE'RE SPEAKING TODAY WITH AN ACTUAL VAMPIRE
GOOD MORNING, SIR
THANK YO- ...MORNING?
MORNING?!!
THEY JUST MIGHT WANT TO DRAW THOSE BLINDS
www.garfield.com
Distributed by Universal Press Syndicate
JIM DAVIS 10-30
© 2004 PAWS, INC. All Rights Reserved.

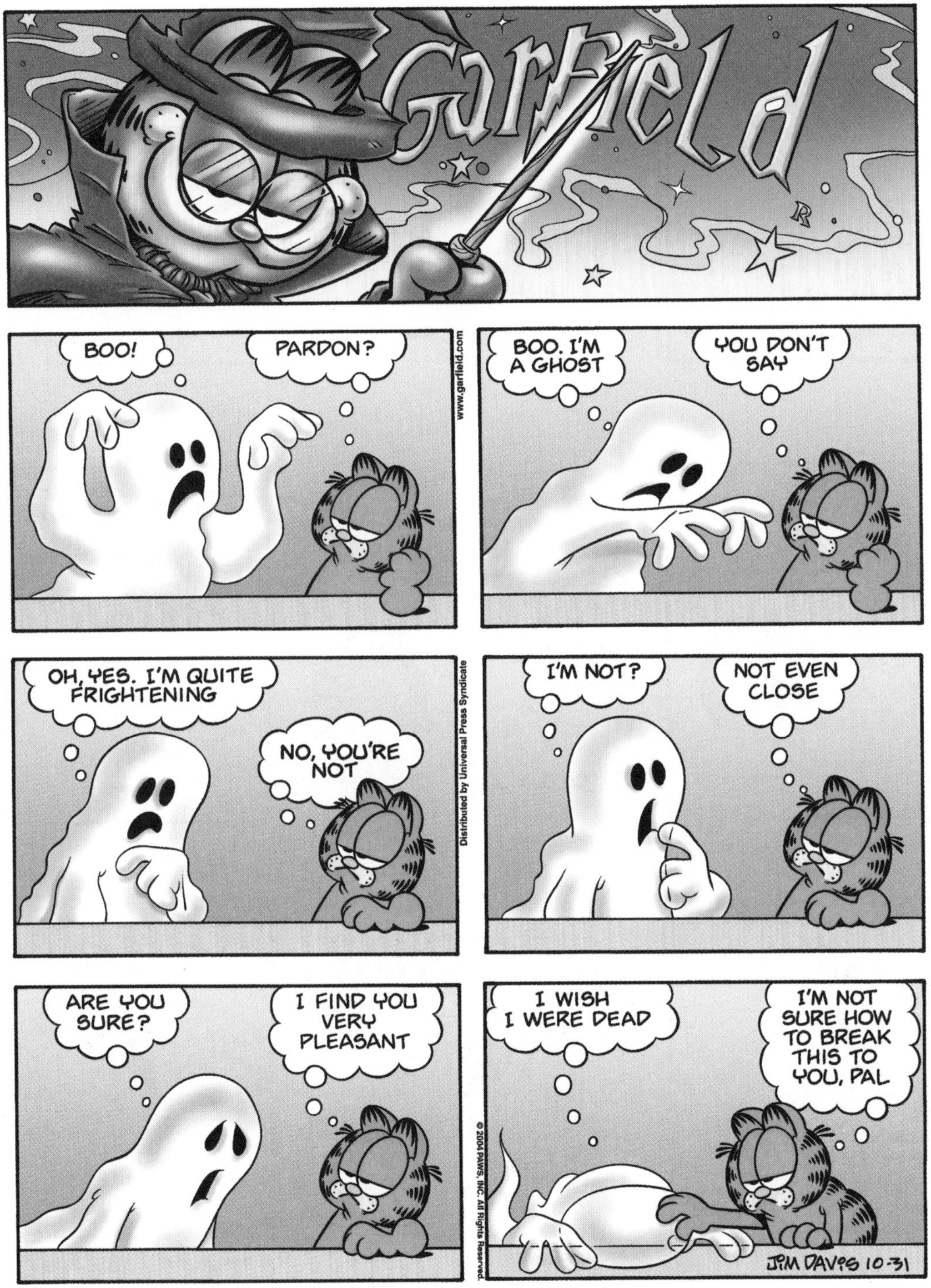

Garfield
BOO!
PARDON?
BOO. I'M A GHOST
YOU DON'T SAY
OH, YES. I'M QUITE FRIGHTENING
NO, YOU'RE NOT
I'M NOT?
NOT EVEN CLOSE
ARE YOU SURE?
I FIND YOU VERY PLEASANT
I WISH I WERE DEAD
I'M NOT SURE HOW TO BREAK THIS TO YOU, PAL
JIM DAVIS 10-31
www.garfield.com
Distributed by Universal Press Syndicate
© 2004 PAWS, INC. All Rights Reserved.

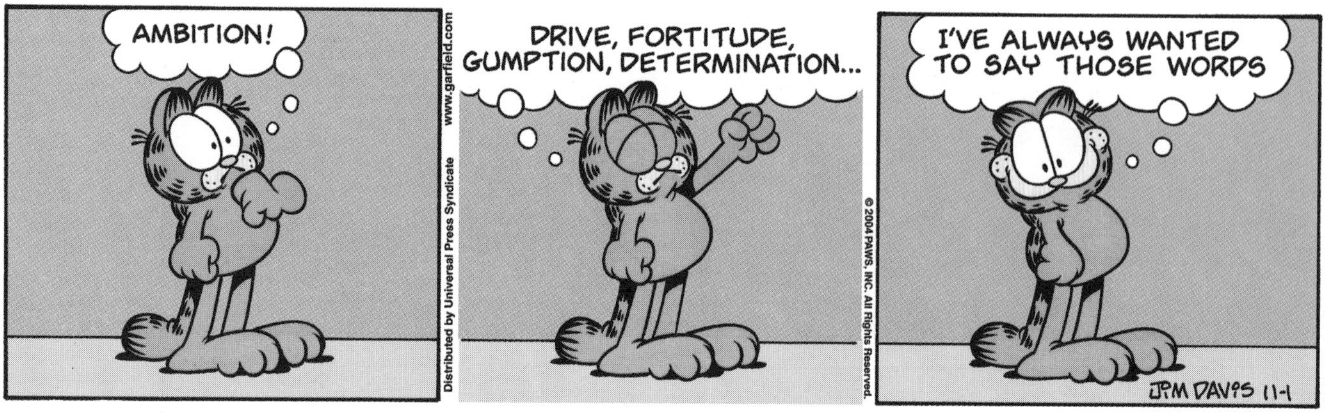
AMBITION!
DRIVE, FORTITUDE, GUMPTION, DETERMINATION...
I'VE ALWAYS WANTED TO SAY THOSE WORDS
JIM DAVIS 11-1
www.garfield.com Distributed by Universal Press Syndicate
© 2004 PAWS, INC. All Rights Reserved.

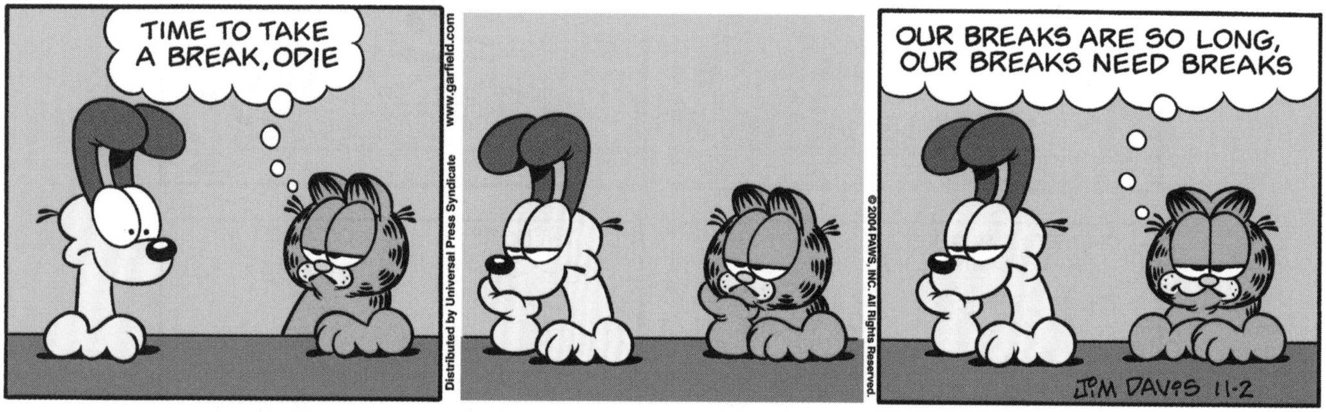
TIME TO TAKE A BREAK, ODIE
OUR BREAKS ARE SO LONG, OUR BREAKS NEED BREAKS
JIM DAVIS 11-2
www.garfield.com Distributed by Universal Press Syndicate
© 2004 PAWS, INC. All Rights Reserved.

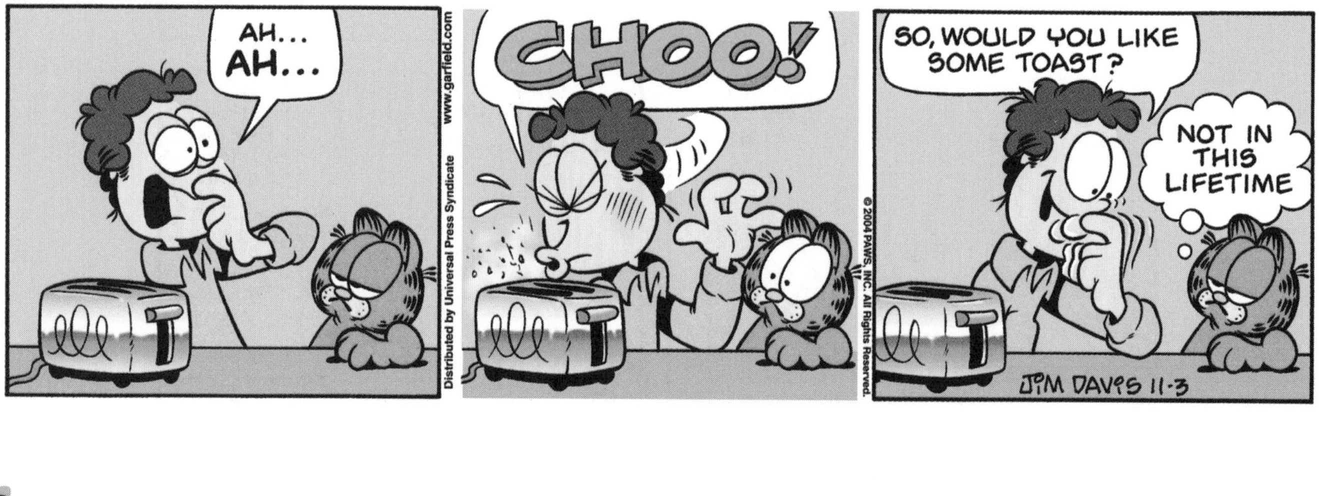
AH... AH...
CHOO!
SO, WOULD YOU LIKE SOME TOAST?
NOT IN THIS LIFETIME
JIM DAVIS 11-3
www.garfield.com Distributed by Universal Press Syndicate
© 2004 PAWS, INC. All Rights Reserved.

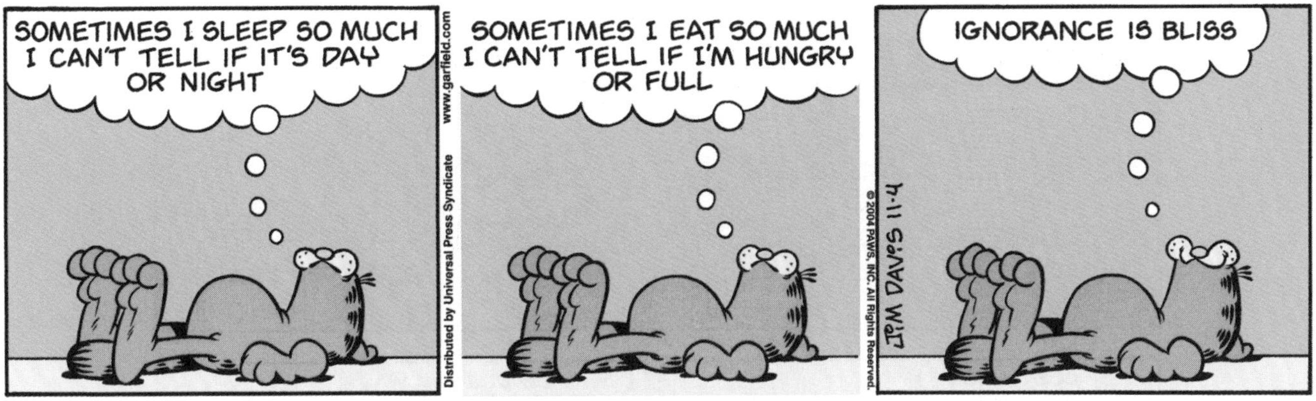
SOMETIMES I SLEEP SO MUCH I CAN'T TELL IF IT'S DAY OR NIGHT
SOMETIMES I EAT SO MUCH I CAN'T TELL IF I'M HUNGRY OR FULL
IGNORANCE IS BLISS
Distributed by Universal Press Syndicate www.garfield.com
© 2004 PAWS, INC. All Rights Reserved.
JPM DAVIS 11-4

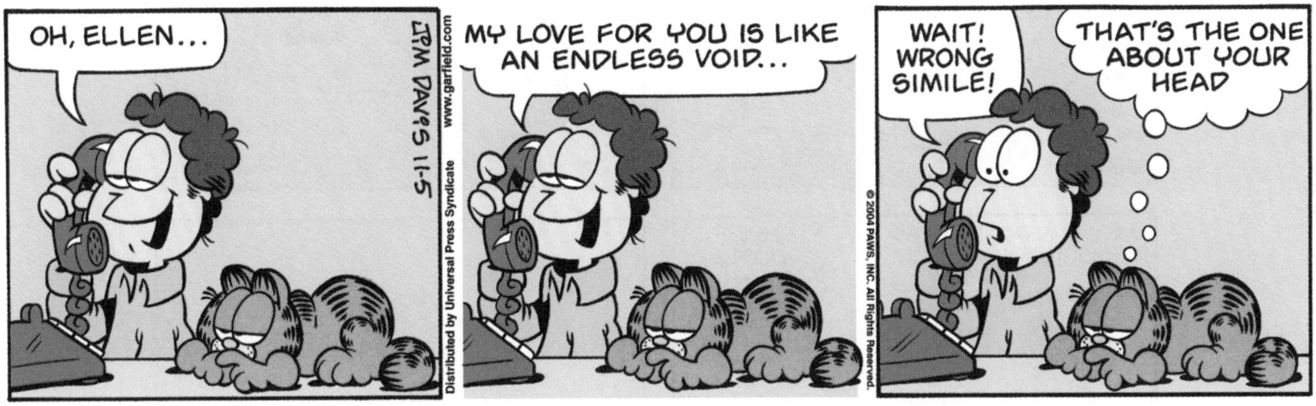
OH, ELLEN...
MY LOVE FOR YOU IS LIKE AN ENDLESS VOID...
WAIT! WRONG SIMILE!
THAT'S THE ONE ABOUT YOUR HEAD
JPM DAVIS 11-5
Distributed by Universal Press Syndicate www.garfield.com
© 2004 PAWS, INC. All Rights Reserved.

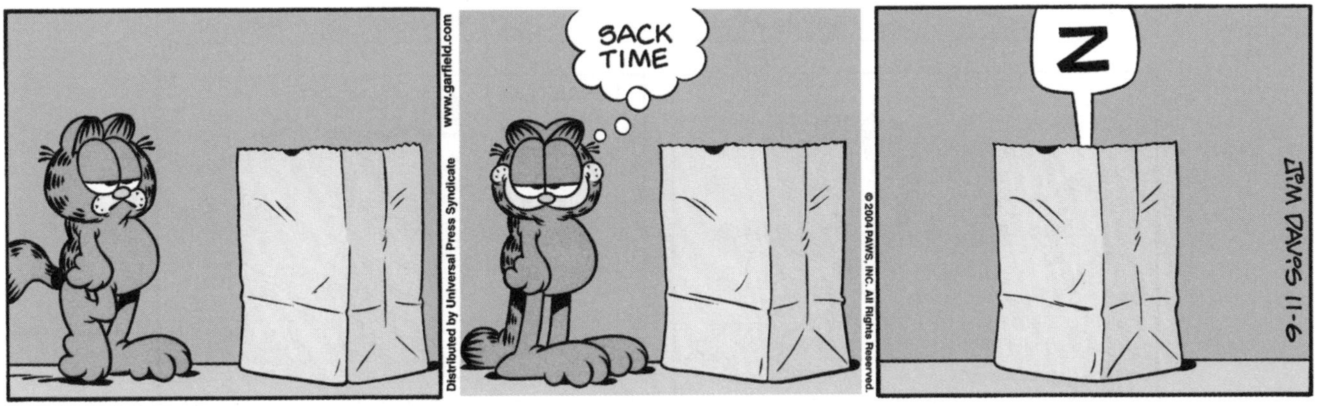
Distributed by Universal Press Syndicate www.garfield.com
SACK TIME
© 2004 PAWS, INC. All Rights Reserved.
Z
JPM DAVIS 11-6

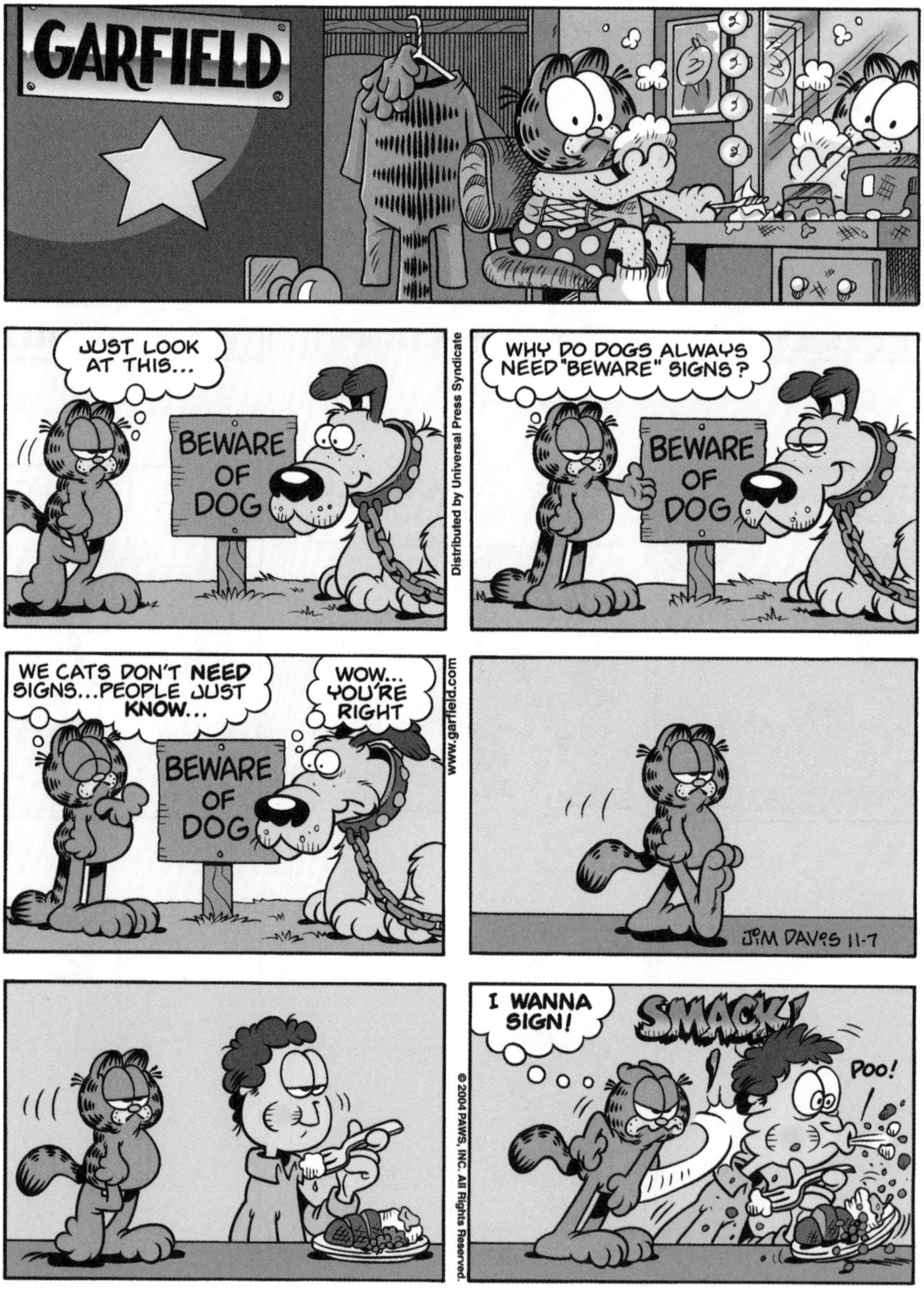
GARFIELD
JUST LOOK AT THIS...
BEWARE OF DOG
Distributed by Universal Press Syndicate
WHY DO DOGS ALWAYS NEED "BEWARE" SIGNS?
BEWARE OF DOG
WE CATS DON'T NEED SIGNS... PEOPLE JUST KNOW...
WOW... YOU'RE RIGHT
BEWARE OF DOG
www.garfield.com
JIM DAVIS 11-7
© 2004 PAWS, INC. All Rights Reserved.
I WANNA SIGN!
SMACK!
POO!

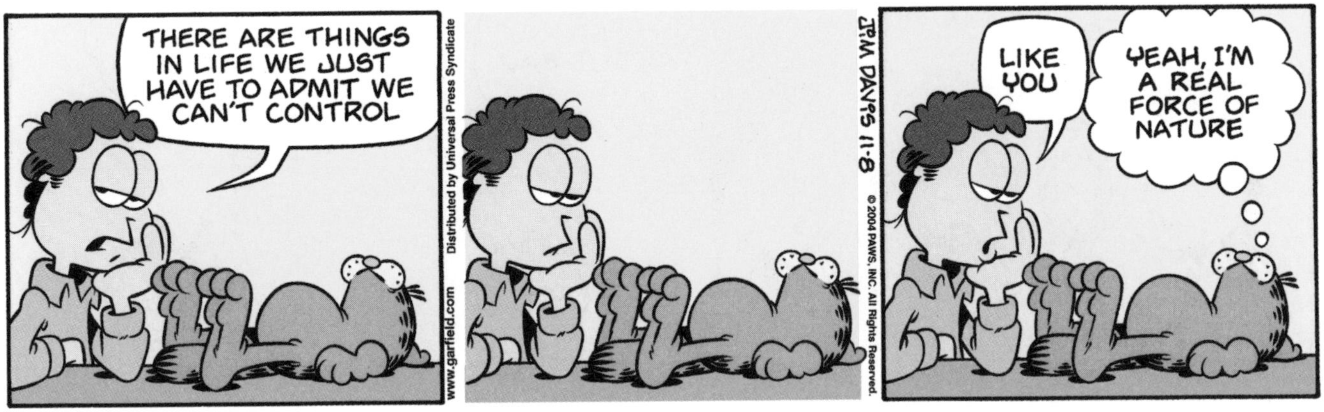
THERE ARE THINGS IN LIFE WE JUST HAVE TO ADMIT WE CAN'T CONTROL
LIKE YOU
YEAH, I'M A REAL FORCE OF NATURE
JIM DAVIS 11-8
Distributed by Universal Press Syndicate
www.garfield.com
© 2004 PAWS, INC. All Rights Reserved.

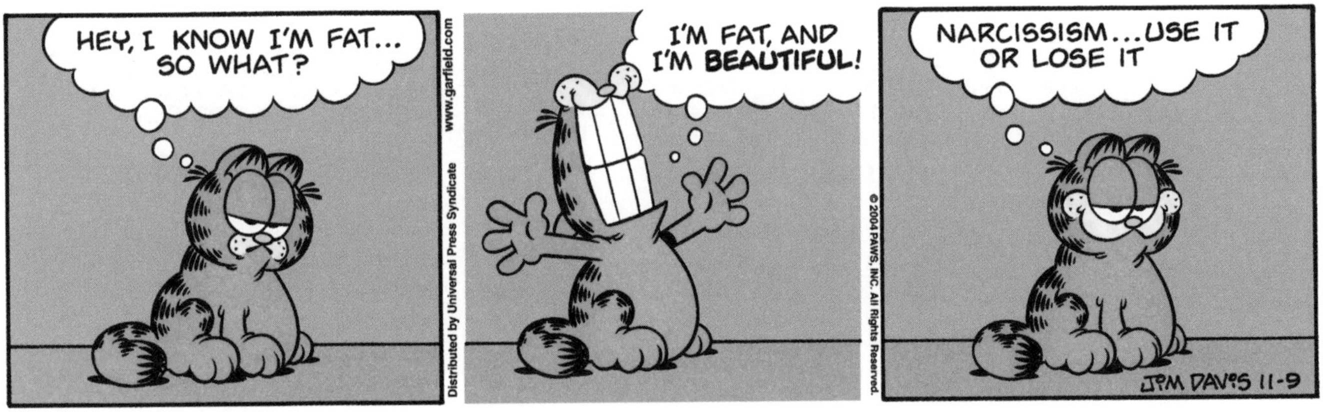
HEY, I KNOW I'M FAT... SO WHAT?
I'M FAT, AND I'M BEAUTIFUL!
NARCISSISM...USE IT OR LOSE IT
JIM DAVIS 11-9
Distributed by Universal Press Syndicate
www.garfield.com
© 2004 PAWS, INC. All Rights Reserved.

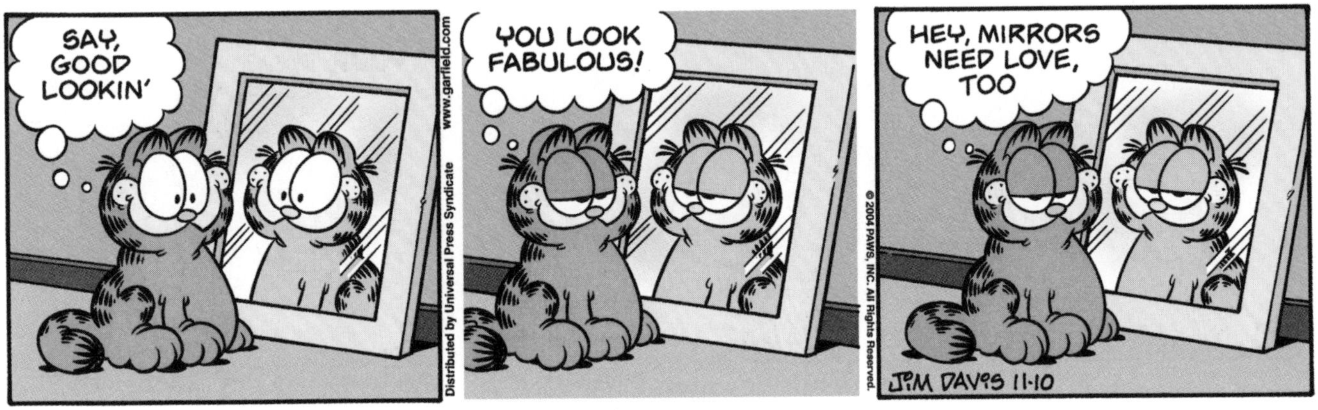
SAY, GOOD LOOKIN'
YOU LOOK FABULOUS!
HEY, MIRRORS NEED LOVE, TOO
JIM DAVIS 11-10
Distributed by Universal Press Syndicate
www.garfield.com
© 2004 PAWS, INC. All Rights Reserved.

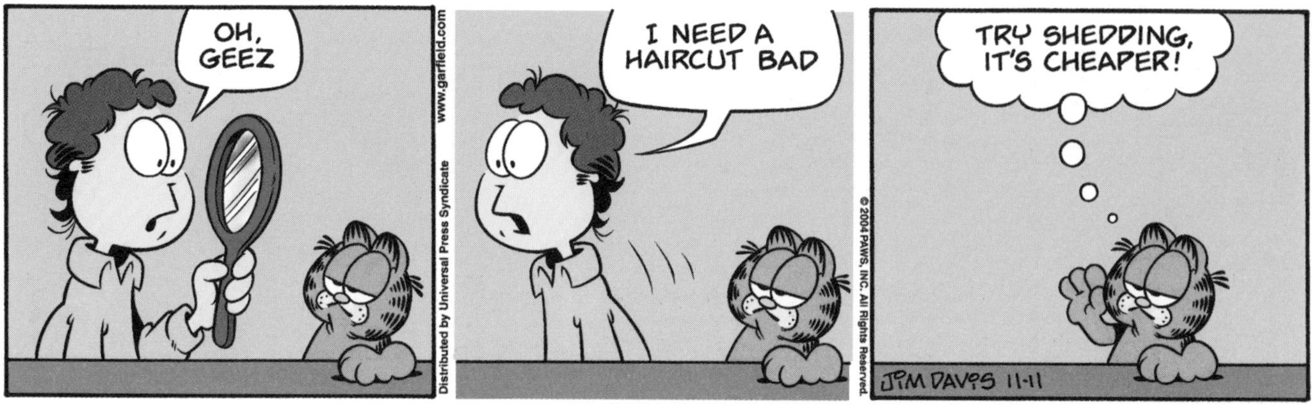
OH, GEEZ
I NEED A HAIRCUT BAD
TRY SHEDDING, IT'S CHEAPER!
JPM DAVPS 11-11
www.garfield.com
Distributed by Universal Press Syndicate
© 2004 PAWS, INC. All Rights Reserved.

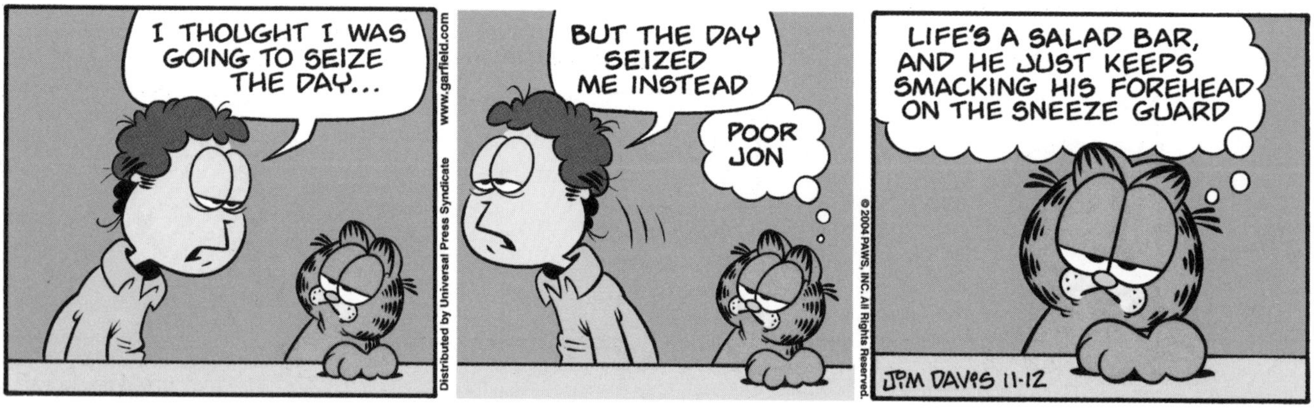
I THOUGHT I WAS GOING TO SEIZE THE DAY...
BUT THE DAY SEIZED ME INSTEAD
POOR JON
LIFE'S A SALAD BAR, AND HE JUST KEEPS SMACKING HIS FOREHEAD ON THE SNEEZE GUARD
JPM DAVPS 11-12
www.garfield.com
Distributed by Universal Press Syndicate
© 2004 PAWS, INC. All Rights Reserved.

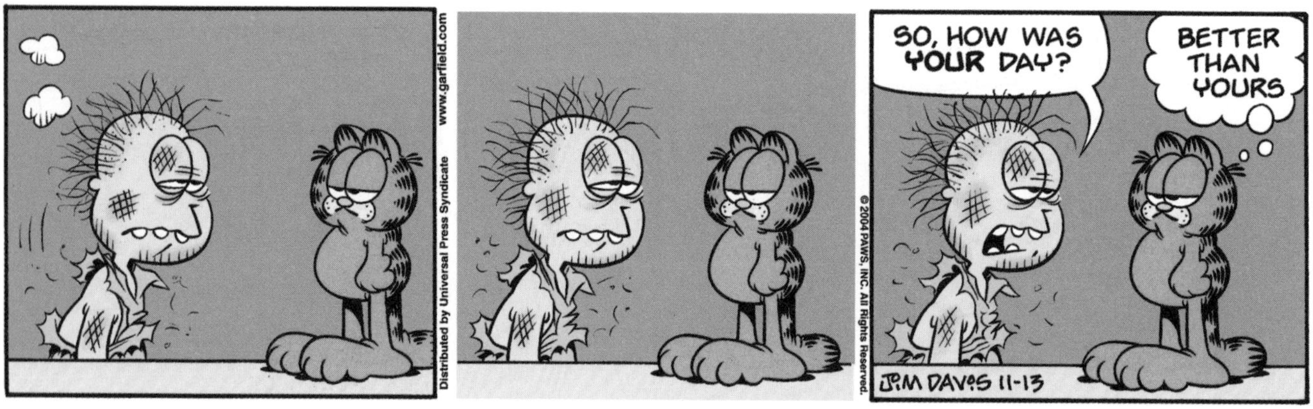
SO, HOW WAS **YOUR** DAY?
BETTER THAN YOURS
JPM DAVPS 11-13
www.garfield.com
Distributed by Universal Press Syndicate
© 2004 PAWS, INC. All Rights Reserved.

GaRFieLd GOes to thE DoGs

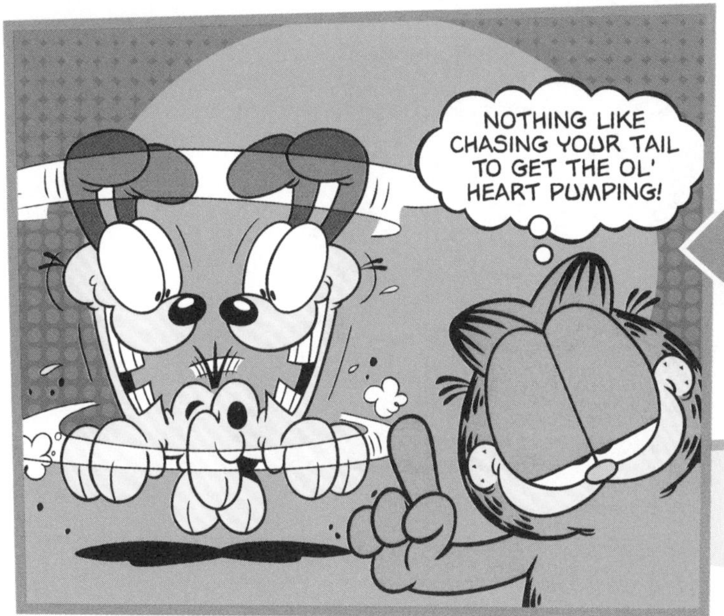
NOTHING LIKE CHASING YOUR TAIL TO GET THE OL' HEART PUMPING!

DOgS ENJOy eXeRCiSE.

A DOG's bARK iS WorsE ThAn hIS BITe.

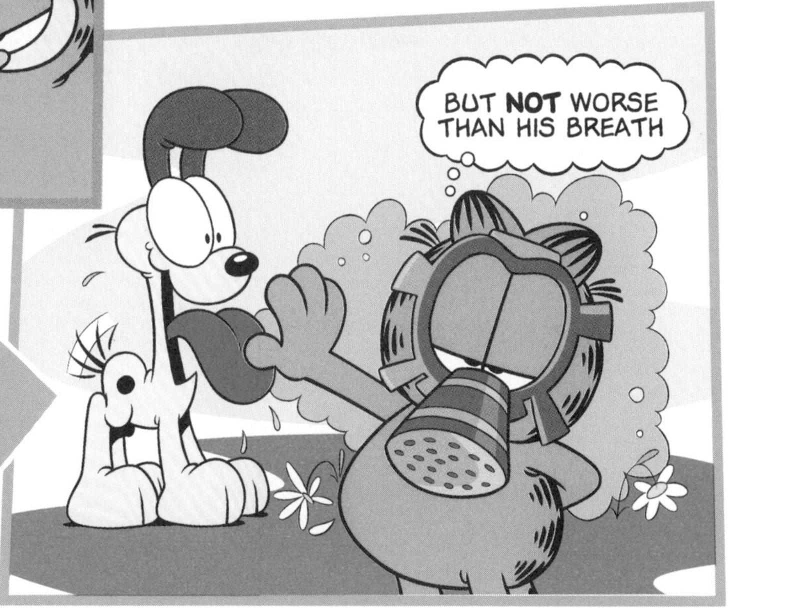
BUT **NOT** WORSE THAN HIS BREATH

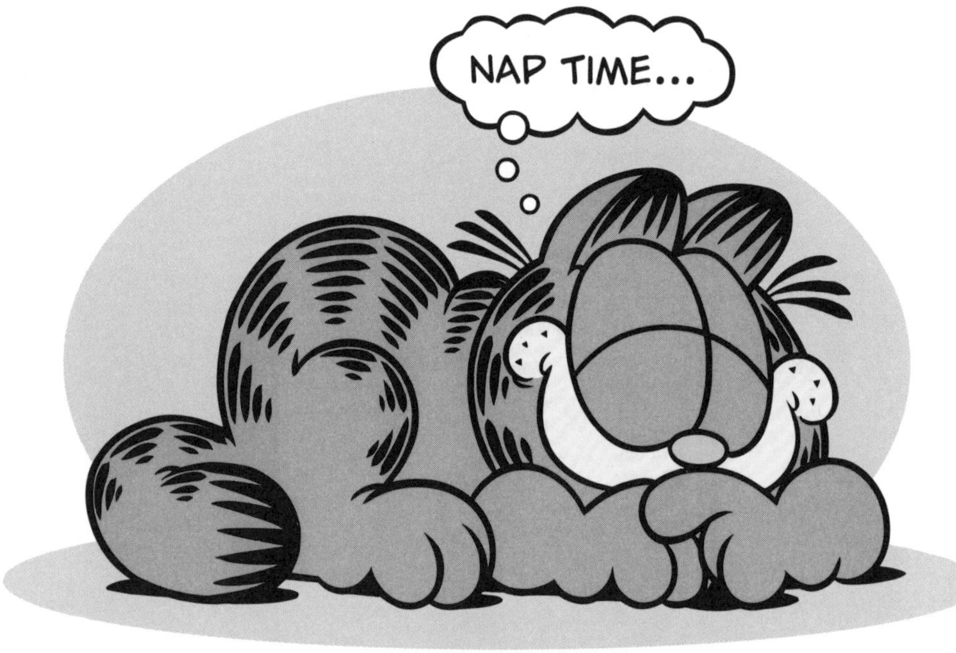
NAP TIME...